MVS Assembler Language

Mike Murach & Associates, Inc.

2560 West Shaw Lane, Suite 101
Fresno, California 93711-2765

MVS Assembler Language

CONCEPTS • PROFESSIONAL SUBSET • ADVANCED FUNCTIONS • DASD ACCESS METHODS • PROGRAM DEVELOPMENT TECHNIQUES

Kevin McQuillen
Anne Prince

Editorial team

Anne Prince
Mike Murach
Tim Schaldach

Production team

Steve Ehlers
Carl Kisling

Related Products

MVS JCL (Second Edition) by Doug Lowe
MVS TSO, Part 1: Concepts and ISPF by Doug Lowe
MVS TSO, Part 2: Commands and Procedures by Doug Lowe

20 19 18 17 16 15 14 13 12 11 10 9 8 7

Library of Congress Catalog Card Number: 86-63830

ISBN: 0-911625-34-8

Contents

Preface

This book is a long overdue revision of the second book we ever published back in 1975: *System/360-370 Assembler Language (OS)*. The first edition was used by more than 100 colleges and junior colleges for classroom instruction, and it was used in thousands of businesses for inhouse training. Nevertheless, we feel that this second edition is a major improvement over the first edition. It covers everything that the first edition did, but it does so in a more organized fashion. In addition, this book covers VSAM file handling and structured programming in assembler language, which the first edition didn't cover.

What this book does

When you develop a text for an assembler language course, one of the first jobs is deciding what the objectives of the course should be. Should you try to teach the student to write application programs in assembler language, to write special-purpose subprograms in assembler language, to do systems programming tasks in assembler language, or what? To complicate the problem, data processing is constantly changing so a reasonable objective of ten years ago isn't necessarily reasonable today. Furthermore, assembler language is far too extensive to cover completely in a single book, so you have to limit your objectives. As a result, we settled on three overall objectives for this book.

The first objective is to present an introduction to assembler language that will be useful to anyone who uses an MVS system, whether or not he or she ever writes programs in assembler language. If you've ever worked on an IBM mainframe, you know that all functions eventually get reduced to assembler language, so a knowledge of assembler language will help you use high-level languages and your MVS system more effectively. With this in mind, section 2 presents an introduction to assembler language that we feel is the least you should know about assembler language if you work on an IBM mainframe.

1

The second objective of this book is to teach you how to write special-purpose subprograms in assembler language that can be called by high-level languages like COBOL or PL/I. That's one reason why chapter 8 emphasizes subprogram linkage. Once you understand this linkage, you can write assembler language subprograms that do any of the functions presented in the other chapters of the book.

The third objective of this book is to prepare you to do systems programming tasks in assembler language: tasks like modifying a third-party application package, providing an exit routine for an operating system module, or writing an inhouse utility. Because this book doesn't begin to cover all of the capabilities of assembler language, I'm not saying that you'll be able to do all systems programming tasks once you complete it. But you should be able to do some systems programming tasks. More important, you should be able to research the related IBM manuals on your own so you'll be able to do whatever assembler language tasks you're assigned. To make this possible, section 4 shows you how to use the I/O macros for both the native access methods and for VSAM. This is a critical requirement that is missing in many competing texts.

Although it's not an objective, you should also be able to write application programs in assembler language when you complete this book. That was an objective for the first edition of this book, because in 1975 assembler language was second only to COBOL when it came to languages used for application programming. Today, however, few companies use assembler language for application programming. Although you may be asked to modify or rewrite an old application program, chances are slim that you'll be asked to write a new application program in assembler language.

Who this book is for

This book is for anyone who wants to learn assembler language as it is implemented on an MVS system. Since this book assumes that you have no data processing experience, the first three chapters present the hardware and software background you need for assembler language programming. As a result, if you've had experience with IBM mainframes, MVS, or programming, you may be able to skip some or all of these background chapters.

If you review the programming examples in this book, you'll see that most of them are simplifications of application programs. Remember, then, that their purpose is to illustrate the use of assembler language, not to teach application programming. We used application programs as examples because we felt they're easier to understand than systems programs. Once you learn assembler language by studying these examples, you can apply assembler language to whatever type of programmming problem you're assigned.

With that in mind, we feel that this book is suitable for independent study, an informal course, or a formal course in college or industry. It can be used in a data processing or a computer science curriculum. It can be used for a short course or a full-semester course. And, if it is supplemented by IBM manuals, it can be used as the basis for an in-depth, two-semester course.

Section	Chapters	Section title	Prerequisites	Design
1	1-3	Required background	None	Sequential
2	4-8	A professional subset of assembler language	Section 1	Sequential
3	9-12	Assembler language capabilities by function	Section 2	Random
4	13-16	Assembler language for DASD access methods	Section 2	Random after chapter 13
5	17-19	Program development techniques	Chapter 5 or Section 2	Sequential

Figure P-1   The basic organization of this book

How to use
this book

If you're reading this book as part of a course, your instructor should guide you through it. On the other hand, if you're reading this book on your own, you should realize that the chapters don't have to be read in sequence. Instead, they are grouped into five sections as indicated by the table in figure P-1. As the table shows, you can continue with any of the other sections in this book after you complete the first two sections.

This type of organization, which we call *modular organization*, gives you a number of options as you use this book. If, for example, you want to learn how to use the DASD access methods after you complete section 2, you can go directly to section 4. Similarly, if you're ready to assemble and test your programs after you complete section 2, you can go directly to section 5. In fact, you can read chapters 17 and 18 any time after you complete chapter 5 in section 2. However, you should complete all of section 2 before you read chapter 19.

Within each section, the chapters are designed in a sequential or random manner, as indicated by the table in figure P-1. If the chapters are sequential within a section, you have to read them in sequence. But if they are random, you can read them in whatever sequence you prefer and you can skip the chapters that don't pertain to your work. In section 3, for example, you may only be interested in chapter 11. If so, you can read it right after you complete section 2 and you can skip chapters 9, 10, and 12. If you check the design for section 4, you can see that it's random after you read chapter 13. This means that you can read chapters 14 through 16 in any order you prefer once you read chapter 13 in this section.

We used modular organization for this book for two reasons. First, it makes your learning more efficient because you learn a professional subset of assembler language in section 2. After that, you can easily add assembler language elements to this subset until you reach the level of expertise you desire. Second, the modular organization makes the book more useful to you as a reference after you've read the book for the first time because it groups the assembler language elements by function. Incidentally, modular organization is a unique feature of most of our books.

To help you learn from this book, each topic or chapter is followed by terminology lists and behavioral objectives. If you feel you understand the terms in each terminology list, it's a good indication that you've understood the content of the topic or chapter you've just read. In other words, we don't expect you to be able to define the terms in a list, but you should recognize and understand them. Similarly, if you feel that you can do what each objective requires, it's a good indication that you've learned what we wanted you to learn in each topic or chapter.

To give you a chance to apply your learning, appendix B presents a comprehensive case study. You can start working on this case study when you complete chapter 5. Then, as you complete each new chapter, the case study asks you to modify or enhance the program that you developed for chapter 5. Whether or not you have access to an MVS computer system so you can actually test your case study program, we recommend that you code the phases of the case study because that's a critical test of your learning progress. If you can code and test all phases of the case study so they work correctly, we feel that this book has accomplished its primary objectives.

Related products

Throughout this book, you'll learn the MVS JCL that you need for the assembler language functions that you'll be using. However, since this is an assembler language book, the JCL is presented at a low level. As a result, you may want to learn more about MVS JCL when you complete this book. If so, we recommend a new book by Doug Lowe called *MVS JCL*. If you use *MVS JCL* in conjunction with this book, you should end up knowing a great deal about your MVS system.

If you're an instructor in a school or a business, you will probably be interested in the *Instructor's Guide* that is available with this book. It presents complete solutions for the case study in appendix B. It gives you ideas and summary information for administering a course in assembler language. And it gives you masters for most of the figures in the text so you can make overhead transparencies for them.

Related reference manuals

Although you shouldn't have much need for IBM manuals when you use this book, you may want to refer to them occasionally. As a result, I've listed the related reference manuals in figure P-2. As you can see, except for the Principles of Operation manual and Reference Card, the titles don't specify a particular system. That is because MVS is essentially the same no matter which processor it runs on. So, in general, you can use the same

Order no.	Title
GA22-7000	System/370 Principles of Operation
GA22-7070	IBM 4300 Processors Principles of Operation
GA22-7085	System/370 Extended Architecture Principles of Operation
GC26-4013	MVS/Extended Architecture Data administration Guide
GC26-4014	MVS/Extended Architecture Data Administration: Macro Instruction Reference
GC26-4015	MVS/Extended Architecture VSAM administration Guide
GC26-4016	MVS/Extended Architecture VSAM Administration: Macro Instruction Reference
GC28-1154	MVS/Extended Architecture Supervisor Services and Macro Instructions
GC28-1376	MVS/Extended Architecture System Messages Volume 1
GC28-1377	MVS/Extended Architecture System Messages Volume 2
GC33-4010	OS/VS—DOS/VSE—VM/370 Assembler Language
GC33-4021	OS/VS—VM/370 Assembler Programmer's Guide
SC26-4036	Assembler H Version 2 Application Programming: Guide
GC26-4037	Assembler H Version 2 Application Programming: Language Reference
GX20-1850	System/370 Reference Card

Figure P-2   Related IBM reference manuals

manuals whether you're using a System/370, 4300, or any other system that supports MVS.

As you work your way through this book, you will probably want to refer frequently to two of the IBM manuals to see how they relate to this book. These manuals are the *Principles of Operation* manual for your system and the *OS/VS Assembler Language* manual. In addition, you'll be referred to some of the other manuals in various chapters of this book. If you want a quick reference for just the elements presented in this book, you can use the reference summary in appendix A.

Although this book is based upon OS/VS assembler language, you should realize that another assembler is available for MVS systems. It's an extended version of OS/VS assembler called assembler H. Any program written for OS/VS assembler will run using assembler H, but OS/VS assembler has some limitations that don't apply to assembler H. In any event, this book will prepare you for using either assembler.

Conclusion

Obviously, we believe that this book will help you learn MVS assembler language better than any competing product will. We're confident that this book will teach you a usable subset of assembler language and that it will let you learn as efficiently as possible.

If you have comments about this book, we welcome them. If you check the last few pages of this book, you'll find a postage-paid comment form. You'll also find a postage-paid order form in case you want to order any of our other products. We hope you find this book useful, and thanks for being our customer.

Mike Murach, Publisher
Fresno, California
January, 1987

Section 1

Required background

Before you can learn to develop programs in assembler language, you need some data processing background. The three chapters in this section present the minimum background that you need for this programming course. Chapter 1 introduces you to IBM mainframes because these are the machines that you use MVS assembler language on. Chapter 2 introduces you to the MVS operating system that you'll be using on an IBM main-frame. Chapter 3 presents a procedure for developing assembler language programs along with the job control language you'll need for translating and testing your programs.

Of course, if you already have programming experience or experience with an MVS system, you may already know much of the material in this section. If so, you can review the objectives and terminology lists at the end of each chapter or topic to see whether you need to study it.

Chapter 1

An introduction to IBM mainframes

 This chapter introduces you to the hardware components of an IBM mainframe system. Since you probably have had some previous exposure to data processing and programming, this chapter only presents those introductory concepts that are necessary for assembler language programming. If you're already familiar with IBM hardware, much of the material in this chapter will be review for you. If so, you can review the terminology and objectives at the end of the chapter to determine whether or not you need to read it.

For mainframe systems, IBM manufactures dozens of hardware devices. Moreover, most are available in different models and with a variety of features. As a result, this chapter won't try to teach you about all the devices that can be part of an IBM mainframe system. Instead, it describes three general types of components.

The first type is processors, the central components in mainframe systems. The second type includes all the peripheral devices that are used to transmit data to and receive data from the processor. The third type consists of intermediate devices, called channels, that manage the data transfer between peripheral devices and the processor.

PROCESSORS

The center of an IBM mainframe system is the *processor*; all the other devices that make up the system configuration attach to it in some way. For the purposes of this book, you can think of the processor as consisting of two main parts: the central processing unit and main storage. The *central processing unit* (or *CPU*) is a collection of circuits that execute program instructions for calculation and data manipulation. *Main storage* (or *main memory*) is the high-speed, general-purpose, electronic storage that contains both the data the CPU operates upon and the program instructions it executes.

To refer to the amount of main storage a system provides, the symbol *K* has traditionally been used. Because the word *kilo* refers to 1000, one K refers to approximately 1,000 storage positions. Thus, "a 128K system" means a computer system with approximately 128,000 storage positions in its main storage. I say "approximately" because one K is actually 1,024 storage positions.

Today, however, mainframe computers are sold with much larger memories than can be expressed conveniently in Ks. For instance, a small IBM mainframe will have at least one megabyte of storage (expressed as 1*M*, or 1 *MB*). The term *megabyte* refers to approximately 1,000,000 positions, or *bytes*, of storage. More precisely, a megabyte is 1,024K, or 1,024 times 1,024 bytes of storage. In chapter 4, you'll learn more precisely what a byte is.

Most IBM mainframes today run on processors that are members of the *System/360-370 family*. The System/360-370 family is a group of general-purpose processors that have developed over a 20-year span, beginning with the System/360 models of the mid-1960s and continuing with the System/370s and the 3030s of the 1970s. The 3080s, 4300s, and 3090s are the most commonly used processors today.

Of course, as IBM has developed new System/360-370 processors, it has used contemporary technologies to create better, faster, and cheaper machines. As a result, although the IBM mainframe processors of today are direct descendants of the System/360s, those older machines are all but obsolete.

For the purposes of this book, we assume that you are *not* using a System/360 processor since only a few are still in use. In addition, we want you to know that any reference we make to a System/370 means a System/370 or any of its successors in the System/360-370 family of computers. As far as assembler language goes, it works the same way on a 370 as it does on any of the successors.

INPUT/OUTPUT EQUIPMENT

The second group of mainframe devices consists of the peripheral devices connected to the processor. Collectively, these devices are called *input/output devices*, or just *I/O devices*. Input devices send data to the processor, and output devices receive data from it. Some machines can perform both functions.

If you have any data processing experience at all, you are probably familiar with printers, terminal devices, direct access storage devices, and

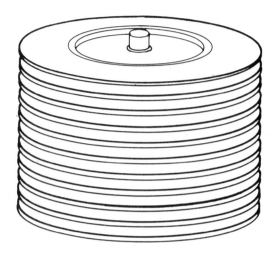

Figure 1-1   Conceptual illustration of a disk pack

tape devices. These are the most commonly used I/O devices today. In addition, you may be familiar with card devices. Although card devices were used extensively in the past, they are practically obsolete today. In any event, because so many devices can be part of an IBM mainframe, I'm not going to try to cover them all. Instead, because this book emphasizes the programming for direct access storage devices, I'm going to focus on some details you need to know about them.

Characteristics of direct access storage devices

A *direct access storage device (DASD)* makes it possible to access any record quickly. Because DASDs, regardless of their type, allow direct and rapid access to large quantities of data, they've become a key component of mainframe systems. They're used not only to store user programs and data, but also to store programs and data for operating system functions.

The most common type of DASD is the *disk drive*, a unit that reads and writes data on a *disk pack*. A disk pack, illustrated conceptually in figure 1-1, is a stack of metal platters that are coated with a metal oxide material. Data is recorded on both sides of the platters. A disk pack can be removable or it can be fixed in a permanent, sealed assembly inside the drive.

On each recording surface of a disk pack, data is stored in concentric circles called *tracks* as illustrated conceptually in figure 1-2. Although the number of tracks per recording surface varies by device type, the surface illustrated in figure 1-2 has 200 tracks, numbered from 000 to 199.

The data stored on a track is read by the DASD's *access mechanism*, which is an assembly that has one read/write head for each recording

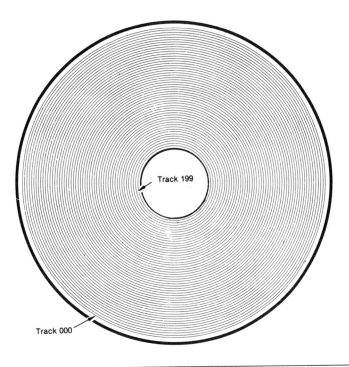

Track 199

Track 000

Figure 1-2   Conceptual illustration of the tracks on a disk surface

surface. This is illustrated conceptually in figure 1-3, which shows a side view of an access mechanism. As you can see, the access mechanism is positioned over the same track on all recording surfaces at the same time. As a result, all of these tracks can be operated upon, one after another, without moving the access mechanism.

The tracks that can be accessed by a single positioning of the access mechanism make up a *cylinder*. As a result, there are as many cylinders on a disk pack as there are tracks on a single recording surface. So if there are 200 tracks on each recording surface of a disk pack, the entire pack contains 200 cylinders.

In concept, one DASD's operation is about the same as another's, but DASDs vary in terms of speed and capacity. In practice, you don't have to know the technical distinctions between the IBM device types in order to write programs that use them. However, it's nice to know that IBM DASDs can be grouped into two broad categories: FBA devices and CKD devices.

Fixed-block architecture (FBA) devices are simpler in concept than CKD devices. On an FBA DASD, you can think of the entire disk area as a string of 512-byte blocks starting with block zero and extending up to the capacity of the unit. Then, the data on the device is accessed by block number. At present, no FBA devices are supported by MVS, so that's all I'm going to say about them in this book.

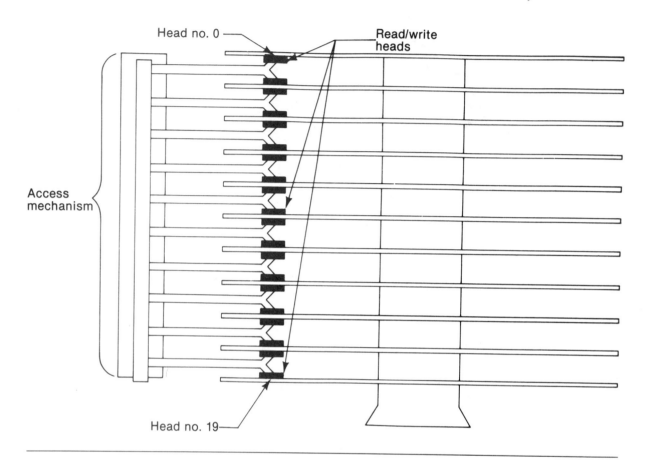

Figure 1-3   Conceptual illustration of a side view of an access mechanism

CKD devices

Count-key-data (CKD) devices make up the second category of DASDs on IBM mainframes. To understand what CKD refers to, you need to know the format of a track on a CKD device. This is illustrated in figure 1-4. In this format, each record on a track is preceded by a *count area* and a *key area*. Since the track in the illustration has four data areas, there are four count and four key areas on the track.

The count areas contain the disk addresses and lengths of the data areas following them. The key areas, which may be from 1 to 256 bytes in length, contain the control data that uniquely identifies the records in the file. For example, in a file of inventory master records, the part number is usually recorded in the key area. In a file of payroll master records, the employee number is usually recorded in the key area.

The difference between count and key, then, is that the count area contains a disk address that uniquely identifies a record location on the disk pack, and the key area contains a control field that uniquely identifies a record in a file. If the organization of a file doesn't require records with keys, the file can be defined without key areas, but all files require count areas. As you will see later, both count and key areas can be used to locate records that are being directly accessed.

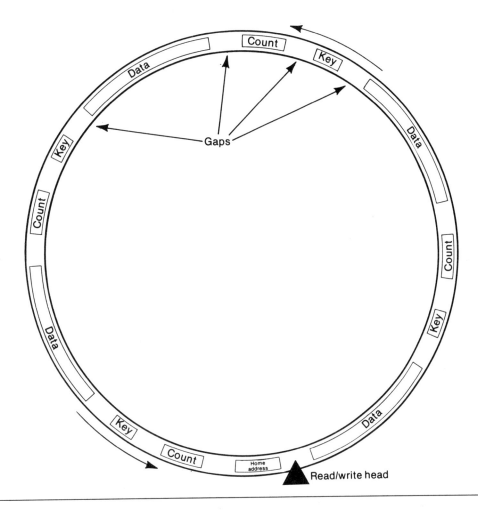

Figure 1-4   Count-key-data format on one track of a disk

In addition to count, key, and data areas, each track in the count-key-data format has a *home address*. The home address, which comes immediately before the first count area on a track, uniquely identifies each of the tracks on a disk pack. So, on a pack that contains 200 tracks and 20 recording surfaces, there are 4000 different home addresses.

Any programming references to data records on a CKD device are eventually reduced to cylinder number, head number, and either record number or key. The cylinders are numbered 0 through the number of tracks minus 1, the heads are numbered 0 through the number of recording surfaces minus 1, and record numbers start at 0 and go through the maximum number of records that can be stored on the track. Because record number 0 is used for control information, the first data record on a track is always record number 1. Thus, record number 1 on track 0 of cylinder 0 is actually the first data record on the first track of the first cylinder of a disk.

Blocked records

To make efficient use of DASD storage, the records in a file are often *blocked*. This means that more than one record is read or written by a single read or write command. To illustrate, suppose a block consists of five 120-byte records. That means there will be 600 bytes in the data area following each count area, and five records will be read by one read command.

Blocking is important because it reduces the time required to read or write a DASD file sequentially. To read or write a record or block of records sequentially, a program must first search for the record or block on the selected track. To do this, the disk drive waits for the next record or block in sequence to rotate to the access mechanism so it can be read. This waiting period is called *rotational delay*, and on the average it takes one-half the time required for the disk to make one complete rotation. With unblocked records, one rotational delay is required for each record to be read or written. But if the records are blocked, only one rotational delay is required for each block. By eliminating rotational delay, blocking can significantly reduce the time required to read the records in a file sequentially.

Blocking can also affect the storage capacity of a disk pack. On a 3350 pack, for example, one track can hold 30 456-byte records when they're unblocked. That means that 10,000 456-byte records take over 333 tracks, or over 11 cylinders. But if the records are blocked with ten records to a block, four blocks can be recorded on each track, or a total of 40 records per track. Then, the entire file requires only 250 tracks, or eight and one-third cylinders.

CHANNELS

When I said before that a particular device can be attached to the processor, I simplified the relationship between the processor and the I/O devices. Although it may seem like a peripheral device is attached directly to the processor, it's actually attached to an intermediate device called a *channel*. A channel is a small computer that executes I/O instructions called *channel commands*.

A channel on an IBM mainframe may be one of three types: (1) a selector, (2) a byte multiplexer, or (3) a block multiplexer. A *selector channel* is designed to operate with only one device at a time, and transfers data byte by byte until a complete record has been transferred. In contrast, *multiplexer channels* operate with more than one I/O device at a time by interleaving data items. A *byte multiplexer* is usually used to attach several low-speed I/O devices like card devices and printers to the processor. It transfers data one byte at a time. A *block multiplexer* is used to attach higher-speed devices like tape units and DASDs and transfers data in blocks rather than bytes.

Because the channel performs the I/O operations, it frees the processor to execute other instructions. As a result, processing and I/O operations can be overlapped, and overall system performance is improved. In chapter 4, you will learn more about overlap.

SYSTEM CONFIGURATIONS

With such variety in IBM mainframe processors and input/output devices, the number of possible *system configurations* is practically limitless. As a result, one IBM mainframe configuration is likely to be different from another. At this time, then, I'll present only one configuration to help you understand the system you're going to use.

Figure 1-5 represents a 4300 configuration. At the center of the system is a 4381 processor with 8M of main memory. Attached to the processor is a collection of devices you might find on a small MVS system.

For direct access storage, the configuration in figure 1-5 uses three groups of 3350s, each containing eight drives. As a result, the system has a total of 24 disk drives. Since each 3350 has a capacity of 317MB, the total DASD capacity of this system is about 7.6 billion bytes.

All 3350s are fixed-media DASDs; their disk packs can't be removed. To create backup copies of data on the 3350s, tape drives are used. The configuration in figure 1-5 contains four tape drives that can be used for that purpose.

The four 3279 operator consoles in figure 1-5 let system operators control the operation of the system. For instance, one of the consoles could be used for managing the tape drives, another for controlling the two 3211 line printers. In this system, the 3211 printers are the primary printing devices.

A local 3270 system, directly attached to the 4381 processor, provides 15 terminals and one printer. Its terminals are used by the programming staff, which is based in the same building that houses the computer. In contrast, the three modems connect to three remote 3270 systems via telephone lines. The terminals attached to the remote systems, which aren't shown in figure 1-5, are used by data-entry clerks and other end users.

In figure 1-5, I haven't included channels because they would make the drawing unnecessarily complicated. Remember, though, that each I/O device or group of I/O devices is connected to a channel that is connected to the processor.

DISCUSSION

This chapter certainly isn't meant to be a comprehensive treatment of the hardware components that might be on your system. Before you can develop assembler language programs, though, you need to know something about your system configuration. In particular, you need to know what I/O devices you're going to be using. Later on in this book, you'll see how you use this hardware knowledge during the development of a program.

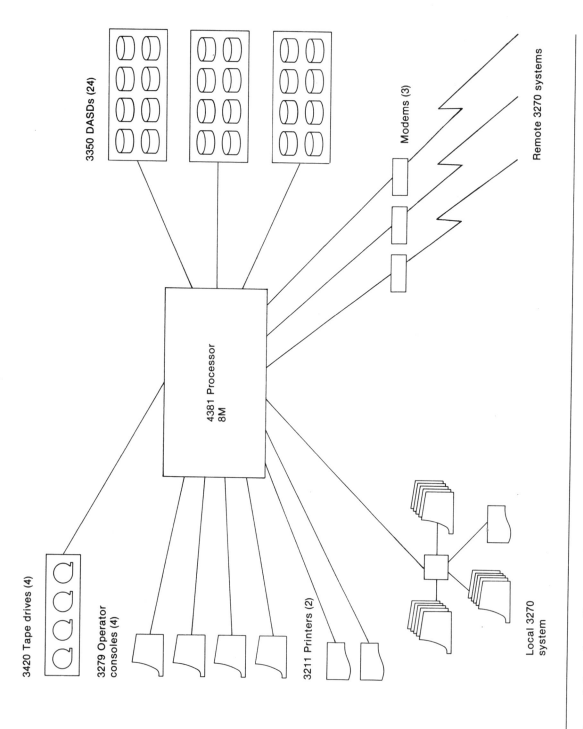

Figure 1-5   A small 4300 configuration

Terminology

processor
central processing unit
CPU
main storage
main memory
K
kilo
M
MB
megabyte
byte
System/360-370 family
input/output device
I/O device
direct access storage device
DASD
disk drive
disk pack
track
access mechanism
cylinder
fixed-block architecture device
FBA device
count-key-data device

CKD device
count area
key area
home address
blocked records
rotational delay
channel
channel command
selector channel
multiplexer channel
byte multiplexer
block multiplexer
system configuration

Objectives

1. Find out what I/O devices you will be using when you write assembler language programs.

2. Describe the format of count-key-data DASDs.

3. Explain what blocked records are.

Chapter 2

An introduction to MVS

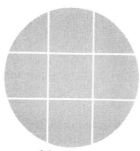 To write an assembler language program that will execute properly, you must know how to coordinate your program with your computer's operating system. An *operating system* is a collection of programs designed to improve the efficiency of a computer system. Today, on the mainframes in the System/370 family, the two most popular operating systems are called MVS and VSE. This book teaches you how to develop assembler language programs on an IBM mainframe that uses the MVS operating system; another one of our books teaches you assembler language for VSE systems.

From an historical point of view, MVS has evolved from a much earlier operating system for the System/360 called the full Operating System (or OS). During the last 20 years, OS has been used in versions called OS/MFT, OS/MVT, OS/VS1, and OS/VS2. In a sense, then, MVS is a more powerful version of these earlier operating systems. Similarly, VSE evolved from the Disk Operating System (or DOS), and it is a more powerful version of its predecessors.

MVS, which stands for Multiple Virtual Storage, is available in two forms called MVS/370 and MVS/XA (for Extended Architecture). MVS/XA provides for the use of extremely large mainframes that require 31 bits for storage addresses. In contrast, MVS/370 provides for storage addresses of 24 bits. From a practical point of view, the two operating systems work the same so we'll rarely distinguish between the two versions in this book. As a result, when I refer to MVS, I mean either MVS/370 or MVS/XA.

In this chapter, I'll introduce you to MVS and to some of the other programs that make up a typical MVS system. First, I'll describe how the system control programs manage processor storage. Then, I'll present some details on how MVS manages the data it stores; this emphasizes DASD storage. Finally, I'll describe the MVS library structure and introduce you to other components of a production system.

If you're already familiar with MVS, of course, this chapter will be review for you. If it is, you can review the terminology and objectives at the end of the chapter to decide whether or not you need to read it.

HOW MVS MANAGES PROCESSOR STORAGE

Although MVS performs a variety of functions, the most important one is probably processor storage management. So, I will begin your introduction to MVS by describing how it manages processor storage. First, I'll describe virtual storage; then, I'll describe multiprogramming.

Virtual storage

The idea of *virtual storage* is simple: a small CPU simulates a larger CPU. For example, a CPU with 8MB of virtual storage can be simulated on a CPU with only 2MB of *real storage*. To accomplish this simulation, MVS uses disk storage as an extension of CPU storage.

The advantage of virtual storage is that more programs can be operated upon at one time, as I'll explain in a moment. This increases the efficiency of the computer system. Although the operating system itself is less efficient because of the control functions it must perform, the productivity of the system as a whole increases. Fortunately, from the assembler language programmer's point of view, virtual storage appears to be real storage.

Multiprogramming

A common feature of mainframe computer systems is *multiprogramming*. When a system provides multiprogramming, it allows a single processor to execute more than one program at the same time. Actually, that's somewhat misleading, because only one program is executing at a given instant even though multiple programs are present in storage at the same time. Nevertheless, it looks like multiple programs are executing at one time.

Multiprogramming is important because it improves the overall productivity of a computing installation. Because internal processing speeds are far greater than input and output operation speeds and because most business applications do relatively little processing between I/O operations, a processor that executes only one program at a time is idle a large percentage of the time while the program waits for an I/O operation to finish. To make better use of this wasted time, multiprogramming allows additional programs to be in storage so their instructions can be executed while the first program waits for its I/O operation to be completed.

The *supervisor program*, or just *supervisor*, of MVS determines what program should be executing at any moment. A program that's executing is said to be in control of the system. When the program that's in control of the system must wait for an I/O operation to complete, it passes control back to the supervisor. The supervisor then passes control to another program.

To determine what program should execute next, the supervisor uses a scheme of priorities. A *priority* is a "rank" that determines a program's eligibility for receiving system services. If several programs are waiting to resume execution, the supervisor passes control to the one with the highest priority. This process of passing control among programs of different priorities is called *task selection*.

Under MVS, each program executes in an *address space*. You can think of an address space as a string of bytes as long as the amount of virtual storage on the system. For example, a 16 megabyte address space begins at byte 0 (numbering begins with 0, not 1) and extends to byte 16,777,215. Locations within the address space are identified by their displacement from its beginning. Under MVS, there is one address space for each program running on the system; in other words, there are Multiple Virtual Storages.

Figure 2-1 illustrates an address space under MVS/370. As you can see, the address space is divided into three areas: the system area, the private area, and the common area. The *system area* contains the nucleus, which consists of the most heavily used parts of the operating system, including the supervisor. It resides in the lowest portion of the address space.

After the system area comes the *private area*. The private area is the area of storage that is allocated for running a program. During multiprogramming, each program of the system has its own private area for program execution.

The highest portion of an address space is the *common area*, which contains additional components of the operating system. As its name implies, this area is common to all of the address spaces of the system. In addition to important system tables and data areas used by programs residing in the nucleus, the common area also contains program modules of the operating system. Some of these are I/O modules that are likely to be used by your assembler language programs.

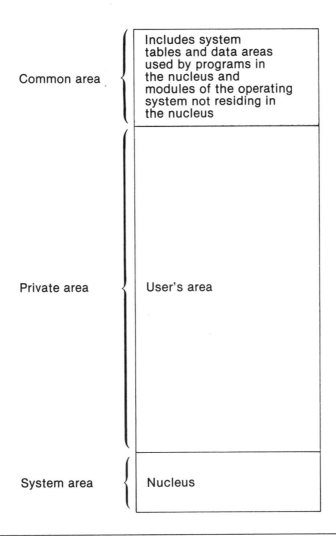

Common area — Includes system tables and data areas used by programs in the nucleus and modules of the operating system not residing in the nucleus

Private area — User's area

System area — Nucleus

Figure 2-1   An MVS address space

The organization of an address space under MVS/XA is more complicated than under MVS/370. That's because MVS/XA uses 31-bit addressing, but must also provide for the 24-bit addressing used by programs written for MVS/370. Since the actual layout isn't important for the purposes of this book, I won't present the details. In general, though, the three areas described for an address space under MVS/370 (system area, private area, and common area) have been extended under MVS/XA to provide for both 24- and 31-bit addressing.

HOW MVS MANAGES USER DATA

MVS provides a variety of facilities that let you manage data that resides on tape, DASD, and other I/O devices. To understand these facilities, you need a basic understanding of the concepts of MVS *data management*. In particular, you need to understand data set labelling, catalogs, data set organization, access methods, and control block generation. Using MVS terminology, a file is called a *data set*, so I'll use the terms "file" and "data set" interchangeably throughout the rest of this book.

Before I present these data management concepts, you need to be aware that two different data management environments coexist under MVS: *VSAM* and *non-VSAM*. VSAM, which stands for Virtual Storage Access Method, was announced in the early 1970's and was intended to replace the older non-VSAM data management functions. However, because VSAM wasn't able to meet all of a typical installation's data management needs, VSAM and non-VSAM data management facilities coexist on today's MVS systems. Because of this, I'll occasionally distinguish between VSAM and non-VSAM functions in this topic.

Data set labels

When data sets are stored on disk or tape, MVS identifies them with special records called *labels*. Later on, when your program processes a data set, you supply information in control statements that MVS compares with the label data to make sure that the correct data set is about to be processed.

To understand the basics of label processing, you need to understand the concepts of volumes and files. So, I'll present these concepts along with a description of labels. Then, in chapter 3, you will see how these labels relate to the JCL required to execute a program. Again, since this book emphasizes DASD storage, I will only cover label processing as it applies to disk files.

Volumes   A *volume* is a storage unit that can be mounted on an input/output device. For disk devices, a volume is a disk pack. As you learned in chapter 1, disk packs can be either fixed or removable.

A typical MVS shop has many volumes. As a result, they need to be labelled to insure that operators use the correct volumes at the correct times. Removable disk packs should have *external labels* so system operators can select the proper volumes for particular applications. External labels are often handwritten and attached to the outside of the disk pack.

Just as important as external labels are the *internal labels* that MVS writes on disks. Internal labels are data records stored on the disk, just like the records of a file. Then, when I/O operations are to be performed on the files of a particular volume, MVS can read the internal *volume label* to verify that the correct volume is mounted.

Each MVS disk pack *must* have a standard volume label. A *standard label* is one written in MVS format. A volume with standard labels has a

VOL1 label that contains all the information MVS needs to perform its label checking functions. A disk volume may also have from one to seven supplementary volume labels called VOL2 through VOL8. However, these are strictly for information since MVS doesn't use them when it checks volume labels.

Probably the most important data in the VOL1 label is the *volume serial number*, or *volser*. The volser is a six-character name that uniquely identifies the volume. When a disk pack or DASD with a non-removable pack is initialized, it should be assigned a volser that's unique in your installation.

Files   The user data recorded on a volume is organized in one or more *files*. A file is a collection of related records that are treated as a unit. For instance, an employee file usually contains one record for each of a firm's employees. Within a typical file, each record contains the same data elements as all the other records in the file.

The simplest case of a file-volume relationship is a single file on a single volume. Although it isn't common for a disk volume to contain only one file, it's not unheard of, particularly when a large file is stored on a DASD with removable packs. Logically, such a disk is called a *single-file volume*. It's much more likely, though, that a disk volume will hold several or many files. Then, it's called a *multi-file volume*.

Some files are too large to fit on a single volume. That doesn't mean that the file can't be stored, however, because it's possible for parts of a one file to be stored on different volumes in a *multi-volume file*. Large multi-volume files can reside on DASDs, but you're more likely to find them on tape because tape is an economical storage medium for large files.

All DASD files must have standard labels. These labels are called *Data Set Control Blocks*, or *DSCBs*. The DSCBs are stored in a special area on the disk volume called the *VTOC*, or *volume table of contents*. The VTOC contains one or more DSCBs for each file on the volume. The DSCBs identify the files and specify their locations on the pack.

For non-VSAM files, the file labels stored in the VTOC contain information that describes the files' characteristics, such as their organization and the sizes of their blocks and records. For VSAM files, however, the file labels play a less important role; they simply identify the DASD space occupied by VSAM files. The characteristics of those files are stored in catalog entries. I'll describe catalogs in a minute.

Figure 2-2 illustrates the concept of file labels for a DASD volume with six files. In this example, each file is contained in one contiguous area of storage, or *extent*, but that's not a requirement for DASD files. In addition, the volume contains three free extents. Notice that the DSCBs aren't adjacent to the files, but are stored together in the VTOC. Each DSCB contains the location information MVS uses to access the file. Notice, also, that the VTOC itself is a file; the records it contains are the DSCBs for the other files on the volume.

As you'd expect, figure 2-2 simplifies the organization of data on a DASD. First, a typical DASD volume contains more than six files.

Second, some files in a production environment may reside in more than just one extent. And third, although figure 2-2 suggests a sequential relationship between file positions on the volume and DSCBs in the VTOC, that's not necessarily the case.

Catalogs

MVS provides a comprehensive catalog facility that records the location of files so that you don't have to specify the volser of the volume that contains the file. There are two types of catalogs under MVS: *master catalogs* and *user catalogs*. Each MVS system has just one master catalog and an unlimited number of user catalogs. The master catalog contains entries that identify system data sets; that is, data sets that are required for the operating system to function. In contrast, the user catalogs contain entries that identify data sets that contain user data. In addition, each user catalog must be defined in the master catalog.

All files managed by VSAM must be cataloged. For VSAM files, the catalog contains not just information that locates the file, but information that specifies the file's characteristics as well. Since that information for non-VSAM files is stored in the data set labels in the VTOC, non-VSAM files don't have to be cataloged. Still, cataloging a non-VSAM file makes the file easier to locate later on because you don't have to remember the volser of the volume that contains the file.

Data set organizations

MVS also provides you with different ways to organize data sets on DASDs to meet different application requirements. *Data set organization*, or *file organization*, refers to the way an application views a file's structure. On a DASD, a file can have four organizations: (1) sequential organization, (2) indexed sequential organization, (3) direct organization, and (4) partitioned organization.

Sequential organization   In a file with *sequential organization*, records are stored one after another in consecutive order. Often, a data element within each record contains a key value that's used to sequence the records of the file in a particular order. To process the records in a sequential file, an application program normally reads or writes one record at a time in sequence. This is called *sequential processing*.

Indexed sequential organization   Using *indexed sequential organization*, it's possible to store records sequentially, but to access any one of them directly. To do this, an indexed sequential file contains two sections: a data section and an index section. Within the index section, each index entry contains a key field value and the location of the corresponding record within the data section of the file. Using this method of file organization, each key field must have a unique value. Then, if a record's key value is known, it's possible to access the record directly by retrieving its disk location from the index. On the other hand, it's possible to access the records sequentially without using the index because the records were

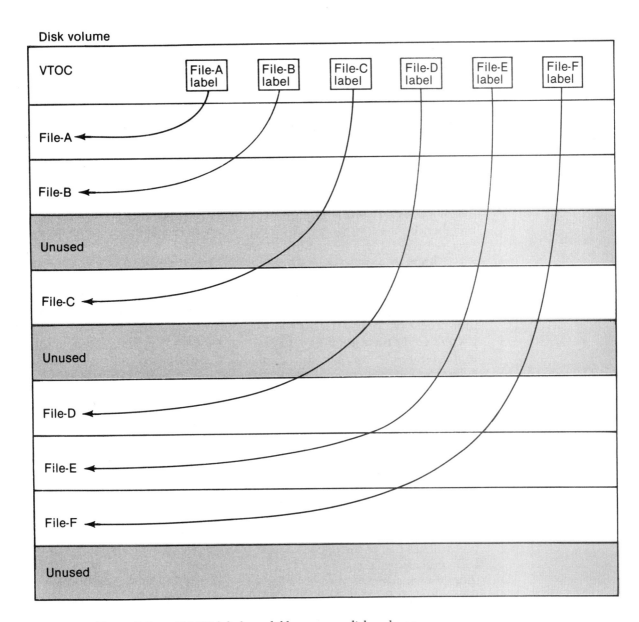

Figure 2-2   DASD labels and files on one disk volume

stored sequentially on the DASD in the first place. When you process records on a direct, rather than a sequential, basis, it is often referred to as *random processing*.

Direct organization   Like a record in a file with indexed sequential organization, a record in a file with *direct organization* can be accessed directly (randomly). Unlike a file with indexed sequential organization, though, a file with direct organization doesn't have an index. Instead, direct organization depends on a direct relationship between data in each record and a DASD address. The address is usually calculated using a formula that derives it from data in the record. This is called a *transformation algorithm*. When direct organization is used, access to the records is rapid, but in most cases the programming complexities involved don't warrant its use.

Partitioned organization   *Partitioned organization* can be thought of as one or more sequential files that can be accessed directly using indexes. In this case, each sequential file is a *member* of the partitioned data set. Then, a *directory* at the beginning of the data set provides an index to the members by their *member names*. Each entry in the directory points to the first record of a member in the data set.

Although partitioned data sets are rarely used for data files, they are heavily used for source programs, object programs, load modules, and procedures on DASD. To process these data sets, most installations use the utility programs that are supplied for this purpose. As a result, few user programs are written for processing partitioned data sets. That's why I won't cover the assembler language for processing partitioned data sets in this book, even though you can handle these data sets quite easily using assembler language macro instructions.

Access methods

To process files with these different types of organizations, an MVS system uses access methods. An *access method* serves as an interface between application programs and the physical operations of I/O devices. When you code an I/O instruction in an assembler language program, for example, you actually invoke an access method. Access methods relieve you of having to handle the complex details of using I/O devices.

The access methods available to you under MVS fall into three categories: basic, queued, and VSAM. For most input/output processing, you will use one of the *queued access methods* to take full advantage of its I/O processing assistance. The queued access methods are *QSAM* (*Queued Sequential Access Method*) and *QISAM* (*Queued Indexed Sequential Access Method*). You'll learn how to use these access methods in chapters 13 and 14.

In other cases, you will need to use the *basic access methods* that allow you to control your own I/O processing. The four basic access methods are *BSAM* (*Basic Sequential Access Method*), *BPAM* (*Basic Partitioned Access Method*), *BISAM* (*Basic Indexed Sequential Access Method*), and *BDAM* (*Basic Direct Access Method*). Since BSAM and BPAM are rarely used, I won't cover them in this book, but you'll learn how to use BISAM and BDAM in chapters 14 and 15.

The last category of access methods includes only one access method: *VSAM* (the *Virtual Storage Access Method*). Practically speaking, VSAM is now an integral part of MVS and is used for most DASD file processing. However, it's considered by IBM to be a separate software product.

Sequential processing

Organization	BSAM	QSAM	BISAM	QISAM	BDAM	VSAM
Sequential	Supported	Supported				Supported
Indexed sequential				Supported		Supported
Direct	Supported (Load only)					Supported

Random processing

Organization	BSAM	QSAM	BISAM	QISAM	BDAM	VSAM
Sequential						Supported
Indexed sequential			Supported			Supported
Direct					Supported	Supported

Figure 2-3   Access methods and file organizations for sequential and random processing

Unlike the basic and queued access methods, VSAM can support files with sequential, indexed sequential, or direct organization. In chapter 16, you'll learn how to use VSAM through assembler language.

At this point, you should realize that there is a difference between a file's organization and the access method that processes it. Organization is a logical concept related to the programs that use a file. Access methods are collections of program components that let you implement file organizations. Figure 2-3 shows the relationships between the organizations available under MVS (excluding partitioned organization) and the MVS access methods for both sequential and random processing.

Although VSAM supports all three of the file organizations presented in figure 2-3, you should realize that it implements them differently than they're implemented by either the basic or queued access methods. Therefore, a sequential file created using QSAM, for example, cannot be processed by VSAM, and vice versa.

Control block generation

Before a program can process a file it must establish a connection between the program, the data set, and an appropriate access method. For non-VSAM files, that connection is made through a special control block called a *Data Control Block*, or *DCB*, which is generated when a file is opened. For VSAM files, a control block called the *Access Method Control Block*, or *ACB*, has a similar function. A DCB or an ACB is simply a table in storage that contains vital information about the status of a data set as it's processed. You will see examples of how you define DCBs in assembler language programs throughout this book.

When a data set is opened, DCB or ACB information can come from three sources: the data set's label or catalog entry, the job control statements that define the file (which I'll describe in the next chapter), and the program itself. Any information supplied by the program overrides information supplied by job control statements, which overrides information taken from the data set's label or catalog entry. Since this book is intended to teach you assembler language, most of the information required to define the control blocks for the files used in the programs throughout this book are supplied by the program. However, in chapters 13 through 16, I will show you how you can supply some of this information through job control statements.

COMPONENTS OF A COMPLETE MVS SYSTEM

The material this chapter has presented so far has been related to basic MVS concepts. To really understand a production MVS system, though, you need to be familiar with a variety of files and software products and their interrelationships. At this time, then, I'm going to introduce you to some other files and software components you're likely to find on your MVS system. First, you'll learn about MVS libraries. Those are the specialized DASD files whose main purpose is to store programs in various forms. Then, I'll give you quick descriptions of some of the other software products that supplement MVS on a typical production system.

MVS libraries

The software components that make up a complete MVS system number in the hundreds, and they're all stored on DASD. As you can imagine, managing all of them as separate DASD files would be inefficient and could easily get out of control. So to help systems personnel keep track of them, MVS components are stored in special files called *libraries*. In addition, you can use libraries to store user-written programs.

The libraries of MVS are partitioned data sets as described earlier in this chapter. As you'll recall, they consist of a directory followed by a number of sequential files called members. For example, one library may contain the source code for a group of programs. Then, the source code for any one program is a member of that library.

When you're developing a program on an MVS system, you go through a standard series of steps before you can execute it. First, you code the program. Second, you compile (or assemble) it. Third, you link edit the program. And fourth, you code the control statements to invoke it. (You'll learn more about these steps in the next chapter.) As figure 2-4 shows, the four types of MVS libraries correspond to the outputs of each of these four steps.

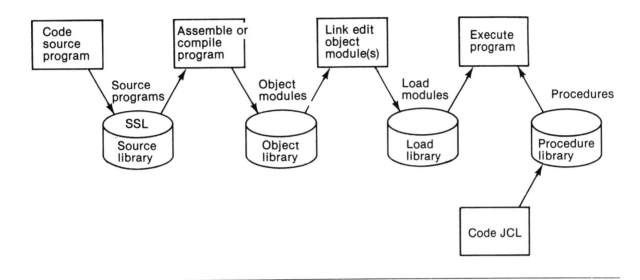

Figure 2-4   Program development and the MVS libraries

Source libraries   The output of the coding step is a *source program* in whatever language you use (such as COBOL, assembler, or PL/I). In a traditional OS environment, the source program was keypunched into a deck of cards. Today, it is much more common for programs to be entered using some type of interactive program development system. In any case, when a program is complete, it is added as a member to a *source library*.

Object libraries   The output of the compilation (or assembly) step is an *object module*. An object module is stored in an *object library*.

Load libraries   Before an object module can be executed, it has to be processed by the linkage editor program. The output of the linkage editor step is an executable module called a *load module*. Load modules are stored as members in *load libraries*. (As you'll learn in a moment, an object module can also be processed by the loader program before it is executed. In this case, however, the resulting load module is only temporary and can't be stored in a load library.)

Procedure libraries   When a program is complete, you use *job control statements* to assemble and execute it. Job control statements can be stored in a *procedure library*. A member in a procedure library is a *procedure*. Job control statements are also known as *job control language*, or *JCL*.

System libraries and user libraries   An MVS system usually has several different source, object, load, and procedure libraries. In a typical installation, for example, there are a number of *system libraries*. These are permanent libraries containing source statements, object modules, load modules, and procedures likely to be used only by the operating system. In addition, there may be one or more *user libraries* of each type. For instance, various application and system programming groups may each have one or more source, object, load, or procedure libraries. When you develop programs for this course, your procedures, source programs, object modules, and load modules will most likely be stored in user libraries.

MVS software components

A production MVS system uses a variety of related software products. Some of these are components of the operating system itself; others are separately licensed products. However, the practical distinction between programs in the two groups isn't clear. A fully functioning MVS system must use some separately licensed products and may not use all of the facilities of the basic operating system. As a result, in addition to being familiar with the critical components of MVS itself, you need to know about some of the other IBM software products that make up a complete system.

Job entry subsystem   To process the jobs entered on an MVS system, an important component of MVS called the *Job Entry Subsystem (JES)* is used. Simply put, the Job Entry Subsystem keeps track of jobs that enter the system, presents them to MVS for processing, and sends the job's spooled output to the correct destination, normally a printer. There are two versions of JES in use today: JES2 and JES3. Although you should know which of these versions your shop uses, it doesn't really matter in most cases, since both provide essentially the same services.

Jobs submitted to MVS for execution are placed in a system file on DASD called the *job queue*. Then, as I mentioned earlier, a scheme of priorities is used to determine when a job in the job queue will execute. When the job executes, its output, called *SYSOUT data*, is spooled to the appropriate device, depending on its *output class*. Because *spooling* is an important concept, you should understand how it works.

Spooling manages card devices and printers for application programs by intercepting program I/O requests for those devices and routing them to or from disk files instead. For example, if a processing program attempts to print a line on a printer, the line is spooled to a disk file. Because DASDs are faster than printers, spooling allows the processing program to resume execution more rapidly. Later, when the processing program has finished execution, the print lines temporarily stored on DASD are actually printed.

The benefits of spooling are twofold. First, programs can execute more rapidly because their I/O requests are satisfied at DASD rather than printer or card device speeds. Second, and probably more important, several programs that would otherwise require exclusive control of the same card devices and printers can execute at the same time. Without spooling, a program that writes to a printer has complete control of the device until it has finished executing, so other programs that need to do printer output have to wait.

Language translators and the linkage editor *Language translators* are the programs that convert source programs into object modules. One language translator, the OS/VS assembler, is supplied as a part of MVS. Other language translators like assembler H and the COBOL and FORTRAN IV compilers are separate products. The purpose of the language translators is to reduce the programming time required to prepare a working object program. You'll learn how to use the OS/VS assembler in chapter 3.

The loader program and the linkage editor When a program is compiled or assembled on an MVS system, the object program is in relocatable form. This means that the object program must be assigned to storage locations different than those given during the compilation before it can be loaded and executed. Under MVS, you can use either the loader program or the linkage editor program for this purpose.

The *loader program* converts the object program into a load module and executes it. It can also combine two or more object modules into a single load module and execute it. In either case, if you want to execute the same load module later, you have to run the loader program again. You'll learn how to use the loader program in chapter 3.

The *linkage editor program* creates a load module from the object program and places it in a library. Then, the load module can be executed again and again from that library. The linkage editor can also be used to combine two or more object modules into a single load module. You'll learn how to use the linkage editor in chapter 8.

Utility programs Certain routine processing functions are common to most computer installations, such as copying files and sorting and merging records from one or more files. As a result, most shops use a set of general-purpose *utility programs* (or *utilities*) to perform these functions. With utility programs, specialized programs don't have to be created to perform common functions. Instead, you can supply parameters to a general-purpose utility program to specify the exact processing it should do.

Library maintenance MVS also provides special utility programs to perform *library maintenance*. These programs can be used to add, modify, delete, and list the members of any system or user library.

DISCUSSION As you can tell by now, an MVS system is a complex collection of components. To use MVS effectively, you need to know how volumes, libraries, and files are organized. You also need to know what capabilities your system software provides. On the other hand, you don't really need to know the details of how virtual storage and multiprogramming operate. It's enough to have a conceptual view of their operation as presented in this chapter.

You should realize, of course, that this chapter only presents the minimum background you need for writing assembler language programs. To become a proficient user of an MVS system, you need to know much more about MVS and its job control language than this book presents. That's why we recommend *MVS JCL* by Doug Lowe for additional study.

Terminology

operating system
virtual storage
real storage
multiprogramming
supervisor program
supervisor
priority
task selection
address space
system area
private area
common area
data management
data set
VSAM data management
non-VSAM data management
label
volume
external label
internal label
volume label
standard label
VOL1 label
volume serial number
volser
file
single-file volume
multi-file volume
multi-volume file
Data Set Control Block
DSCB
VTOC
volume table of contents
extent
master catalog
user catalog
data set organization
file organization
sequential organization
sequential processing
indexed sequential organization

random processing
direct organization
transformation algorithm
partitioned organization
member
directory
member name
access method
queued access method
QSAM
Queued Sequential Access Method
QISAM
Queued Indexed Sequential
    Access Method
basic access method
BSAM
Basic Sequential Access Method
BPAM
Basic Partitioned Access Method
BISAM
Basic Indexed Sequential
    Access Method
BDAM
Basic Direct Access Method
VSAM
Virtual Storage Access Method
data control block
DCB
access method control block
ACB
library
source program
source library
object module
object library
load module
load library
job control statement
procedure library
procedure
job control language

JCL
system library
user library
Job Entry Subsystem
JES
job queue
SYSOUT data
output class
spooling
language translator
assembler
loader program
linkage editor program
utility program
utility
library maintenance

Objectives

1. Describe how MVS implements multiprogramming.

2. Explain the function of volume and file labels.

3. Describe the four file organizations available under MVS.

4. List the MVS access methods that can be used for each type of file organization supported by MVS, not including partitioned organization.

5. List the four types of MVS libraries (when classified by contents) and describe how they fit in the sequence of program development for a typical application.

6. Differentiate between a system library and a user library.

7. Describe the function of JES.

Chapter 3

An introduction to program development in assembler language

If you've already written programs for an MVS system in another language and if you already know how to use MVS JCL, you won't learn much from this chapter. I suggest, then, that you skim this chapter just trying to pick up any specific information related to assembler language and the assembly process. You can probably do this most easily by reviewing the figures in this chapter.

On the other hand, if you're new to programming and to MVS JCL, you should realize right now that there's more to writing a program in assembler language than just coding the program. To give you some idea of what's involved, topic 1 of this chapter describes the tasks of a student's procedure for developing assembler language programs. Then, topic 2 teaches you how to write the job control procedures that you will need when you compile and test your first assembler language programs on an MVS system. When you finish this chapter, you will be ready to learn assembler language itself.

TOPIC 1   A student's development procedure

When you write a program in assembler language, you should follow a standard development procedure. To some extent, this procedure will vary from one company or school to another. As a starting point, though, figure 3-1 lists the six tasks of a student's procedure for developing assembler language programs. In most training environments, you'll use a procedure like this when you develop case study programs like the one in appendix B.

Task 1: Get complete program specifications

As a programmer, it is your responsibility to make sure you know exactly what a program is supposed to do before you start to develop it. You must know not only what the inputs and outputs are, but also what processing is required to derive the desired output from the input. If you are assigned a programming problem that isn't adequately defined, be sure to question the person that assigned the program until you're confident that you know what the program is supposed to do.

Most companies have standards for what a complete program specification must include. In general, a complete program specification should include at least three items: (1) some sort of program overview, (2) record layouts for all files used by the program, and (3) print charts for all printed output prepared by the program. Other documents may be required for specific programs, but these are the most common ones.

The program overview   *Program overviews* can be prepared in many different forms. Most companies have their own standards. What's important is that a program overview must present a complete picture of what the program is supposed to do.

Figure 3-2 presents the kind of program overview we use in our shop. You will work with a program overview like this if you do the case study for this course. As you can see, the form is divided into three parts. The top section is for identification. It gives the name and number of the program as specified by the system documentation. The middle part of the form lists and describes all of the files that the program requires. In addition, it tells what the program will do with each of those files: use them only for input, use them only for output, or use them for update.

The last section of the form is for processing specifications. It's this section, of course, that is the most critical. Here, you must make sure that all of the information you need to develop the program has been provided. If it isn't all there, you must develop it yourself.

Analysis

1. Get complete program specifications.

Design

2. Design the program (chapters 3, 8, and 19).

Implementation

3. Code the program and enter it into the system (chapters 5 through 16).
4. Compile the program and correct diagnostics (chapter 17).
5. Test and debug the program (chapter 18).
6. Document the program.

Figure 3-1   A student's procedure for developing assembler language programs

Record layouts   For each file used by a program, your specification should include a *record layout*. Figure 3-3 shows a typical record-layout form. In general, a record layout shows what fields the record contains, what the format of each field is, and where each field is located in the record. In figure 3-3, for example, you can see that the item description is 20 characters long and that it occupies positions 6-25 of the inventory master record. In the characteristics portion of the form, CL20 means that the field contains character (C) data and that it has a length (L) of 20.

Print charts   A *print chart*, such as the one in figure 3-4, shows the layout of a printed report or other document. It indicates the print positions to be used for each item on the report. For example, on the print chart in figure 3-4, the heading INVESTMENT REPORT is to be printed in print positions 15-31 of the first line of the report; the column heading ITEM NUMBER is to be printed in print positions 2-7 of the second and third lines following the heading line; and so on. Similarly, the item-number field for each detail line (as opposed to a heading line) is to be printed in print positions 2-6 and the amount invested is to be printed in positions 38-46. At the end of the report, two lines are to be skipped and then a total of the amount invested is to be printed. This total is to be indicated by two asterisks printed in positions 48 and 50.

Task 2: Design the program

The traditional design document for an assembler language program has been the *program flowchart*. It shows the logic required to derive the intended output from the input, and it shows the sequence of the instructions to be used. As a result, it directly corresponds to the coding of the program.

Program: INVRPT PRODUCE INVESTMENT REPORT	Page: 1
Designer: Anne Prince	Date: 06-07-85

Input/output specifications

File	Description	Use
INVMAST	Inventory master file	Input
INVRPT	Investment report	Output

Process specifications

This program prepares an investment report from a file of inventory records. The records are in sequence by item number and the report should be printed in the same sequence. If a record is found to be out of sequence, the program should end and an appropriate message should be printed.

The basic processing requirements follow:

For each inventory record

1. Read the inventory record.
2. Calculate the investment amount.
    (Investment amount = on-hand balance x unit cost.)
3. Add the investment amount to the investment total.
4. Format and print a detail line.

After all records have been processed, prepare and print a total line.

Figure 3-2   A program overview

Field Name	Item number	Item description	Unit cost	Unit price	Reorder point	On hand	On order	
Characteristics	CL5	CL20	CL5	CL5	CL5	CL5	CL5	
Usage								
Position	1-5	6-25	26-30	31-35	36-40	41-45	46-50	

File name INVMAST   Record name Inventory Master Record   Date 6/7/85
Application
Comments

Figure 3-3   A record-layout form

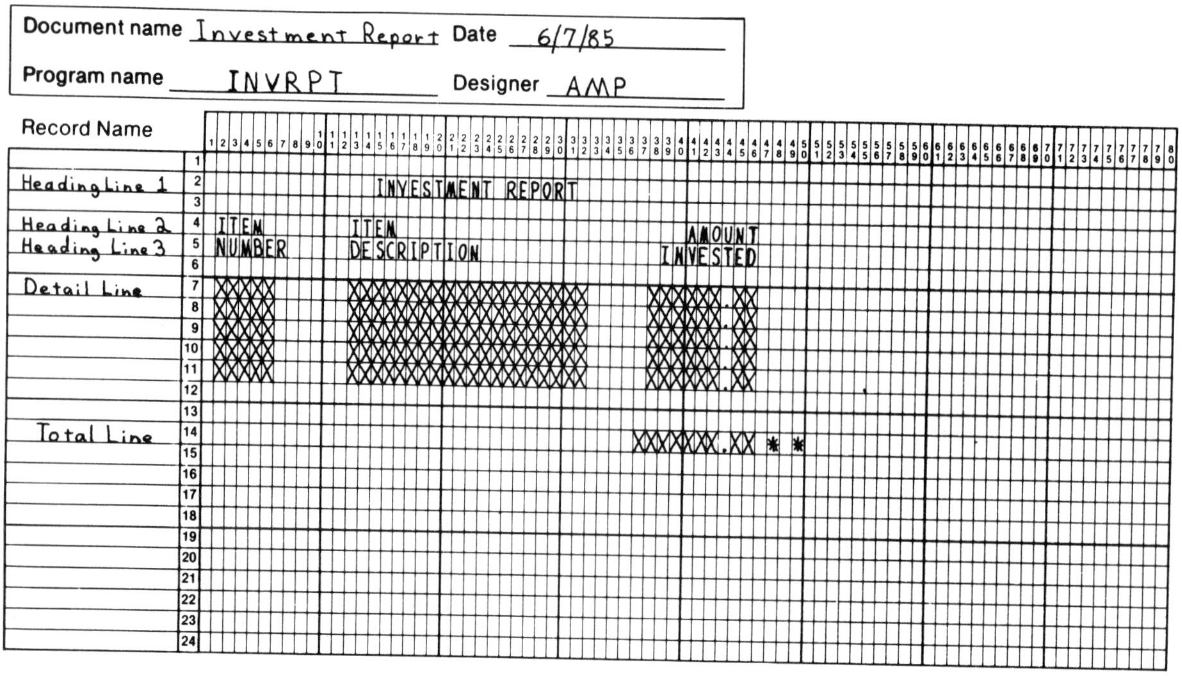

Document name Investment Report   Date 6/7/85

Program name   INVRPT   Designer AMP

Figure 3-4   A print chart

Figure 3-5, for example, is a program flowchart for an inventory program that prepares a report like the one specified by the print chart in figure 3-4 from a file of inventory records that have the format given in figure 3-3. Can you see how the flowchart corresponds to the process specifications given in the program overview in figure 3-2?

In case you're not familiar with flowcharting, figure 3-6 summarizes the five most commonly-used flowcharting symbols. These symbols conform to the flowcharting standards approved by the American National Standards Institute. The most important symbols are the I/O symbol, the process symbol, and the decision symbol.

To read a flowchart, you start at the top and read down and to the right, unless arrows indicate otherwise. When you come to a connector circle with a number in it, you continue at the connector circle with the same number in it. For example, after printing a detail line, the flowchart in figure 3-5 reaches a connector circle with a 1 in it. As a result, processing continues at the connector circle leading into the I/O symbol near the top of the flowchart.

In general, to draw a flowchart, you start at the top and try to show the main functions of the program in a continuous sequence of symbols, from top to bottom. You put functions that are done infrequently, like printing the total line and printing heading lines in figure 3-5, to the right of the mainline functions or on separate pages of the flowchart. Your main concern when drawing a flowchart is to show all of the major functions and all of the branching required by the program.

If the words you use on your flowcharts clearly indicate the functions to be done and the decisions to be made, they are acceptable. However, you may want to use words that correspond to assembler language coding so your flowchart will correspond more closely to the resulting program.

Frankly, we no longer believe that flowcharting is the best way to design a program. Flowcharting is time-consuming, error-prone, and the more complex a program is, the less useful flowcharting is. Nevertheless, because flowcharts are still used in many companies and because they are the traditional design document, we use them occasionally in this book to show the design of a program. Because the programs in this book are short, we think you'll find that our use of flowcharts is satisfactory.

In chapter 8, you'll be introduced to an improved method of flowcharting called *modular flowcharting*, or *modular program design*. It helps you divide a program into manageable modules so you can code and test your programs more efficiently.

Then, in chapter 19, we'll show you another way to design your programs. This design method is based on the theory of structured programming, and it is called *structured*, or *top-down*, *design*. When you develop programs of 200 lines or more, we think you'll find structured design far more effective than flowcharting. You can read chapter 19 any time after you finish the first eight chapters of this book, but we recommend that you read it sooner rather than later. You may even want to use structured design when you do the case studies for this course.

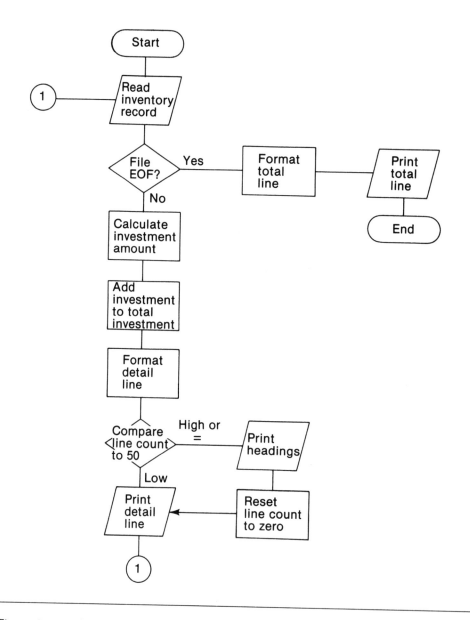

Figure 3-5 A program flowchart

Task 3: Code the program and enter it into the system

When you code a program in assembler language, you write the code that gets translated into an object program. Before this code can be translated, though, it must be entered into the computer system. Since the major purpose of this book is to teach you how to code in assembler language, I won't try to introduce coding at this time. However, I will give you some

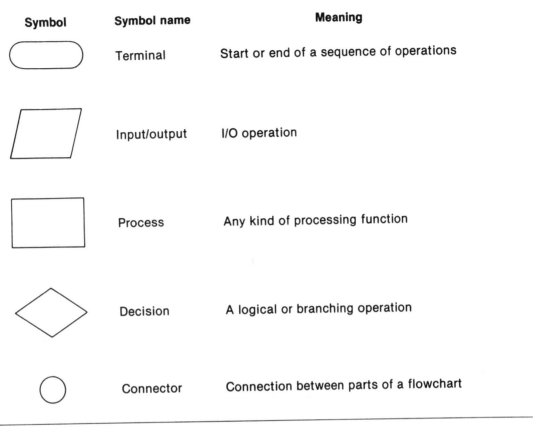

Symbol	Symbol name	Meaning
	Terminal	Start or end of a sequence of operations
	Input/output	I/O operation
	Process	Any kind of processing function
	Decision	A logical or branching operation
	Connector	Connection between parts of a flowchart

Figure 3-6   The most commonly-used ANSI symbols for program flowcharting

idea of how you will enter your code into the system. Then, chapters 5 through 16 will teach you how to code in assembler language.

In the past, when you coded an assembler language program, you coded it on a special coding form like the one in figure 3-7. Then, when you were finished, you keypunched one 80-column *source card* for each line on the coding form. After the cards were punched, they could be read into the computer system and stored in a source library.

Today, punched cards are nearly obsolete, so you will probably enter your source programs directly into the computer system on an interactive basis. In the system, the lines of code will be stored as 80-character records that you can think of as card images.

Although you may be asked to handcode your program on a coding form before you enter it into the system, this isn't really necessary. Instead, you can code your program as you enter it into the system using your flowchart or other design document as a guide for your entries. In fact, with a little practice, you'll find that you can enter your program directly into the system much faster than you can handcode your program and then enter it into the system.

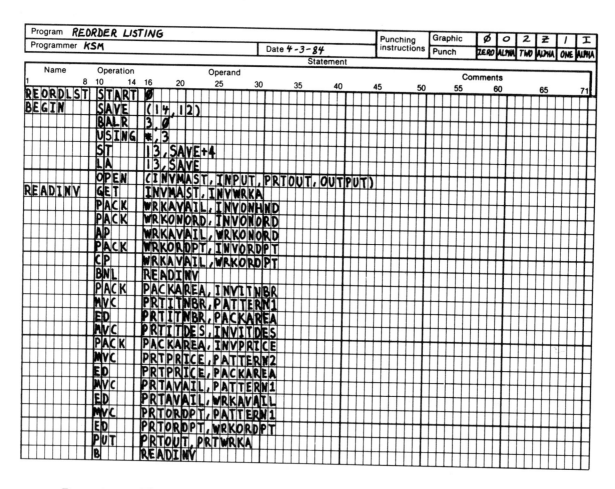

Program	REORDER LISTING											Punching instructions	Graphic	∅	O	2	Z	/	I
Programmer	KSM				Date 4-3-84								Punch	ZERO	ALPHA	TWO	ALPHA	ONE	ALPHA

Name	Operation	Operand	Comments
REORDLST	START	∅	
BEGIN	SAVE	(14,12)	
	BALR	3,∅	
	USING	*,3	
	ST	13,SAVE+4	
	LA	13,SAVE	
	OPEN	(INVMAST,INPUT,PRTOUT,OUTPUT)	
READINV	GET	INVMAST,INVWRKA	
	PACK	WRKAVAIL,INVONHND	
	PACK	WRKONORD,INVONORD	
	AP	WRKAVAIL,WRKONORD	
	PACK	WRKORDPT,INVORDPT	
	CP	WRKAVAIL,WRKORDPT	
	BNL	READINV	
	PACK	PACKAREA,INVITNBR	
	MVC	PRTITNBR,PATTERN1	
	ED	PRTITNBR,PACKAREA	
	MVC	PRTITDES,INVITDES	
	PACK	PACKAREA,INVPRICE	
	MVC	PRTPRICE,PATTERN2	
	ED	PRTPRICE,PACKAREA	
	MVC	PRTAVAIL,PATTERN1	
	ED	PRTAVAIL,WRKAVAIL	
	MVC	PRTORDPT,PATTERN1	
	ED	PRTORDPT,WRKORDPT	
	PUT	PRTOUT,PRTWRKA	
	B	READINV	

Figure 3-7   The start of an assembler language program coded on a coding form

When you enter a program into a system, you do it under the control of an interactive editor program. Although several different editors are available on an MVS system, chances are that you'll be using the editor that comes with SPF. In case you aren't familiar with SPF, I will briefly describe its editor at this time. Keep in mind, though, that this book doesn't attempt to teach you how to use SPF or any other program development system. That's beyond the scope of this book. The material that follows is designed only to introduce you to the idea of interactive program entry.

An introduction to SPF   *ISPF*, which stands for *Interactive System Productivity Facility*, is designed to increase your productivity in an MVS *Time-Sharing Option*, or *MVS/TSO*, environment. Commonly referred to as *SPF*, it lets you use most of the features of MVS in an interactive, menu-driven fashion. Under SPF, users at terminals can create, maintain,

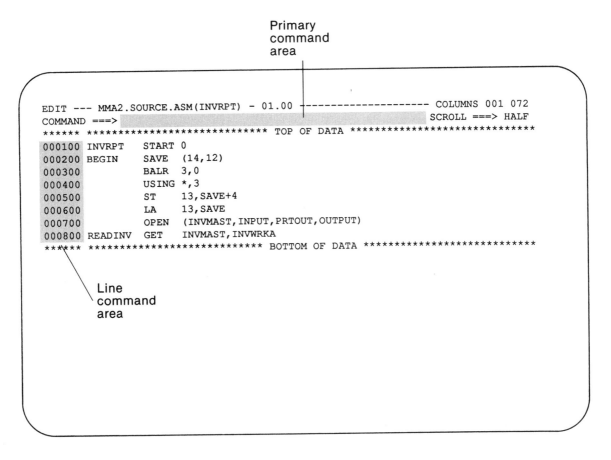

```
                                       Primary
                                       command
                                       area

   EDIT --- MMA2.SOURCE.ASM(INVRPT) - 01.00 +------------------ COLUMNS 001 072
   COMMAND ===>                                             SCROLL ===> HALF
   ****** ************************** TOP OF DATA ***************************
   000100 INVRPT     START 0
   000200 BEGIN      SAVE  (14,12)
   000300            BALR  3,0
   000400            USING *,3
   000500            ST    13,SAVE+4
   000600            LA    13,SAVE
   000700            OPEN  (INVMAST,INPUT,PRTOUT,OUTPUT)
   000800 READINV    GET   INVMAST,INVWRKA
   ****** ************************** BOTTOM OF DATA *************************

              Line
              command
              area
```

Figure 3-8   Command entry areas used by the SPF source file editor

and store card-image files that contain control statements, data, or source programs. SPF stores those card-image files on DASD.

When you use SPF to create source code, you invoke a program called the *source file editor*. The source file editor is a full-screen editor that lets you enter new source code and store it in a library member. In addition, it lets you retrieve source code from a library member and make changes to it.

Figure 3-8 presents the screen SPF displays when you invoke the source file editor to edit an existing file. The two areas shaded on the screen are command entry areas. You use the *primary command area* to enter editor commands that apply to the entire member. These commands perform functions like saving edited text, finding and changing character strings, and changing a file's profile settings. In contrast, you use the *line command area* to perform functions that affect individual lines. In addition to using these two command entry areas, you can edit within the screen window by simply typing over data or by using your terminal's editing keys (like insert, delete, and erase-EOF) for more complicated editing.

```
EDIT --- MMA2.SOURCE.ASM(INVRPT) - 01.00 -------------------- COLUMNS 001 072
COMMAND ===>                                               SCROLL ===> HALF
****** *************************** TOP OF DATA ****************************
000100 INVRPT    START 0
000200 BEGIN     SAVE  (14,12)
000300           BALR  3,0
000400           USING *,3
000500           ST    13,SAVE+4
000600           LA    13,SAVE
000700           OPEN  (INVMAST,INPUT,PRTOUT,OUTPUT)
000800 READINV   GET   INVMAST,INVWRKA
''''''
''''''
''''''
''''''
''''''
''''''
''''''
''''''
''''''
''''''
''''''
''''''
''''''
''''''
```

Figure 3-9   Entering new lines of code using the SPF source file editor (part 1 of 2)

To illustrate the use of the source file editor, suppose you want to add new lines to the end of the eight lines of source code that are shown in figure 3-8. First, you enter the INSERT (I) command in the line command area for line 800, and specify the number of lines you want to add to the file. Part 1 of figure 3-9 shows the result of this command if I specify that 15 lines are to be added. Then, you can enter source code on any of the 15 lines. When you press the enter key, any lines on which you entered code are added to the file; any lines you didn't use are deleted. Part 2 of figure 3-9 shows what happens when eight lines of code are added to the file.

Task 4: Assemble the program and correct the diagnostics

Assembling an assembler language source program means converting the source program into an object program. This translation of an assembler language *source program* into an *object program* is called an *assembly*. This is done by the computer under control of a translator program called the *assembler*.

In order to invoke the assembler, you must submit a *job control procedure* to the operating system. The statements within this procedure tell MVS to execute the assembler. They also tell MVS where to find the

```
EDIT --- MMA2.SOURCE.ASM(INVRPT) - 01.01 -------------------- COLUMNS 001 072
COMMAND ===>                                                  SCROLL ===> 20
****** *************************** TOP OF DATA ***************************
000100 INVRPT    START 0
000200 BEGIN     SAVE  (14,12)
000300           BALR  3,0
000400           USING *,3
000500           ST    13,SAVE+4
000600           LA    13,SAVE
000700           OPEN  (INVMAST,INPUT,PRTOUT,OUTPUT)
000800 READINV   GET   INVMAST,INVWRKA
000900           AP    COUNT=P'1'
001000           MVC   PRINTNBR,INVITNBR
001100           PACK  WRKITCST,INVITCST
001200           MVC   PRTITCST,PATTERN1
001300           ED    PRTITCST,WRKITCST
001400           PACK  WRKBOH,INVBOH
001500           MVC   PRTBOH,PATTERN2
001600           ED    PRTBOH,WRKBOH
****** *************************** BOTTOM OF DATA ***************************
```

Figure 3-9   Entering new lines of code using the SPF source file editor (part 2 of 2)

source program, where to store the object program, and what options should be in effect during the assembly. You will learn how to create some basic job control procedures in topic 2 of this chapter.

During the assembly, an *assembly listing* is printed by the computer. The assembly listing is a listing of the source program as well as a listing of various reference tables. If any errors are caught by the assembler during the assembly (as is usually the case the first time you assemble a program), one or more *diagnostic messages* (or *diagnostics*) are printed as part of the assembly listing and the object program isn't created. Each diagnostic calls attention to one error in the source code.

If there are diagnostics, you make the necessary corrections to the source code; then, you reassemble the program. You repeat this process until there are no more diagnostics in the assembly listing. At this point, the program is ready to be tested.

Chapter 17 will show you how to correct the diagnostics you encounter. It will also show you some of the optional output that can be part of the assembly listing. You can read chapter 17 any time after you've completed chapter 5. But you will certainly want to read this chapter when you complete your first assembly and receive your first diagnostic messages.

Task 5: Test and debug the program

Before you can test a program, the object module created during the assembly must be converted into an executable module called a *load module*. This can be done by the *loader program* or the *linkage editor program*. One of these programs is invoked by your job control procedure for assembly and testing as you'll learn in the next topic.

After creating the load module, your assemble-and-test procedure causes your program to be executed. The statements in the procedure tell MVS where to find the test files your program is going to process and where to put the files your program creates.

The test data in your test files should be designed to try all of the conditions that may occur when your program is used. After your program has been executed, you compare the actual output you got with the output you expected to get. If they agree, you can assume that the program does what you intended it to do.

More likely, however, the actual output and the intended output will not agree the first time the program is executed. If this is the case, you must *debug* the program. You must find the errors (*bugs*), make the necessary corrections to the source code using your interactive editor, reassemble the source program, and make another test run. This process is continued until the program executes as intended.

In some cases, your program may not even run to completion the first few times you test it. When a program terminates like this, it is referred to as an *abnormal termination*. An abnormal termination indicates that the program tried to do something invalid like trying to add two alphabetic fields. When an abnormal termination occurs, you use some special debugging techniques to find and correct the bug.

In actual practice, rather than making just one test run on a new program, you make a series of test runs using different sets of test data. The test data for the first test run is usually low in volume, perhaps only a half-dozen records, and may be designed to test only the main processing functions of the program. After you have debugged the program using this data, you may test it on data that tries the exceptional conditions that may come up during the execution of the program. Finally, you may test your program for conditions that depend upon larger volumes of data such as the page overflow condition when printing reports and other documents.

In chapter 18, you will learn how to test and debug your assembler language programs. You will learn how to debug programs that run to normal terminations as well as programs that terminate abnormally. You can read chapter 18 any time after you complete chapter 5 of this book. But you will certainly want to read this chapter when you get your first test run output or experience your first abnormal termination.

As you will see, chapter 18 doesn't try to teach you how to create the test data for your test runs. This book assumes, in fact, that you will be given the test files you need to test your case study programs. As a result, you won't need to create your own test data until you start writing production programs. At that time, you should find out what your shop's standards are for planning test runs and creating test data.

Task 6: Document the program

Documentation in data processing terminology refers to the collection of records that specifies what is being done and what is going to be done within a data processing system. For each program in an installation, there should be a collection of documents referred to as *program documentation*. As a programmer, one of your jobs is to provide this documentation for each program you write.

Program documentation is important because it is almost inevitable that changes will be made to a production program. Sometimes, the users of the program will discover that it doesn't work quite the way it was supposed to. Sometimes, the users will want the program to do more than they originally specified. Sometimes, a company will change the way it does some function, so the related programs have to be changed. No matter what the reason for the modifications, though, it is difficult indeed to modify or enhance a program that isn't adequately documented.

Fortunately, some of the most important components of program documentation are by-products of the program development process: the program overview, the record layouts, the print chart, and the design document. In addition, you should include the final assembly listing since it is the only document that shows the actual programming details. And, you may be asked to include your listings of test data and test run output.

For production programs, your shop standards should specify what's required for program documentation. For your case study programs, you should provide (1) your design document, (2) your final assembly listing, and (3) listings of your test run output, plus any other items your instructor may request.

Discussion

This topic is designed to give you a better idea of what you must do to develop an assembler language program in a training environment. If you follow the procedure shown in figure 3-1, you should be able to do your case study assignments with relative efficiency.

In contrast to the procedure in figure 3-1, figure 3-10 presents a typical procedure for developing assembler language programs in a production environment. Here, you can see that the programmer should get related source books and subprograms as a task in the analysis phase. You'll learn more about this in chapters 6 and 8. Then, task 3 in the design phase suggests the use of structured design and pseudocode as described in chapter 19. This is logical because production programs are generally longer and more complicated than case study programs so program design is more important. Finally, in the implementation phase, you can see that the procedure suggests that you plan the testing, code the procedures for the test runs, and create the test data for the test runs before any coding is done. Then, the program can be coded and tested, a few modules at a time, using a technique called top-down testing. These tasks show how important it is to test a program in a carefully-controlled manner.

Analysis

1. Get complete program specifications.
2. Get related source books and subprograms.

Design

3. Design the program using a structure chart for the entire program and pseudocode for the modules of the program.

Implementation

4. Plan the testing of the program by creating a test plan.
5. Code the job control procedures for the test runs.
6. If necessary, create the test data for the test runs.
7. Code and test the program using top-down testing.
8. Document the program.

Figure 3-10   A professional procedure for developing assembler language programs

Terminology

program overview
record layout
print chart
program flowchart
modular flowcharting
modular program design
structured design
top-down design
source card
ISPF
Interactive System Productivity Facility
Time-Sharing Option
MVS/TSO
SPF
source file editor
primary command area
line command area
source program
object program
assembly
assembler

job control procedure
assembly listing
diagnostic message
diagnostic
load module
loader program
link editing
linkage editor program
debugging
bug
abnormal termination
documentation
program documentation

Objective

List and describe the six tasks of the student's development procedure presented in this topic.

TOPIC 2 MVS JCL for assembling
and testing disk-to-printer programs

To assemble and test a program, you have to create the required job
control procedures. These job control procedures consist of *job control
statements* that are in a sense a language of their own. As a result, the code
used in job control statements is often referred to as *job control language*,
or *JCL*. A series of job control statements, possibly combined with some
data to be processed, is called a *job stream*.

In case you aren't familiar with JCL, this topic presents the JCL you'll
need to assemble and test disk-to-printer programs. If you are familiar
with JCL, you can go through this topic quickly just to pick up any JCL
considerations that apply to the assembly process. As you proceed
through this book, you will be shown more advanced job streams so you'll
always see how your assembler language program and its JCL are related.

HOW TO CODE JCL STATEMENTS

If you're not familiar with JCL at all, you first need to learn the general
format of JCL statements. Next, I'll show you how to code JCL statements
that require more than one line. Last, I'll show you how to code your
statements so they're easy to read and modify.

The format of JCL statements

MVS JCL statements are 80 characters long because they were originally in
the form of 80-column punched cards. Although columns 72 through 80
aren't used for the statements themselves, they can be used for sequence
numbers.

JCL statements can be divided into five different fields. However,
only the first two fields, identifier and name, have fixed positions. The
others are basically free-form. As I discuss these fields, please refer to the
sample JCL statement in figure 3-11.

The identifier field   The *identifier field* identifies a record as a JCL
statement. For most JCL statements, the identifier field occupies the first
two character positions of each record and must contain two slashes (//).
There are two exceptions, which you'll learn about later in this topic.

The name field   The *name field* comes immediately after the // with no
intervening spaces. The name can be from one to eight characters, which

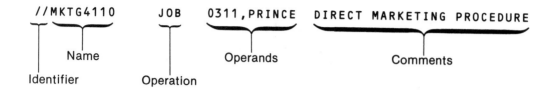

Figure 3-11   The format of an MVS job control statement

can be letters, numbers, or national characters (#, @, and $), but the first character must be a letter or national character. In figure 3-11, the name field is MKTG4110. As you will learn in a moment, the purpose of the name field varies from one type of JCL statement to another.

The operation field   The *operation field* begins at least one space after the name field. It specifies the statement's function. In figure 3-11, the operation code is JOB. As you will see, the most commonly used operation codes are JOB, EXEC, and DD.

The operands field   The *operands field* begins at least one space after the operation code and can continue through position 71. Within the operands field, you code one or more *operands*. Operands are also known as *parameters*, so I'll use the terms interchangeably throughout this book. Learning how to code JCL is largely a matter of learning how to code the operands for each of the JCL statements.

If a statement requires more than one operand, you separate them with commas. Since MVS assumes that the operands are complete when it encounters a blank, make sure that you don't put a blank between two operands by accident. If you need to include a space as a part of an operand value, you must enclose the value in apostrophes. In figure 3-11, the operands are 0311 and PRINCE.

The comments fields   The *comments field* begins at least one space after the operands field. The comments field ends in column 71. MVS ignores what you code here, so you can record any comments you wish. However, we recommend that you avoid coding comments. Usually, comments just state the obvious. In addition, if you do need to code a comment, we recommend that you use the comment statement, which I'll present in a minute.

How to continue JCL statements on subsequent lines

In some cases, it's necessary to continue the operands of a statement on subsequent lines. To do this, each line that's continued should end with the comma that follows an operand. Then, the continuation lines are indicated by coding // in the first two columns and starting the next operand in column 4 through 16, as in this example:

```
//INVMAST       DD  DSNAME=MMA.TEST.INVMAST,
//              DISP=SHR,
//              UNIT=SYSDA,
//              VOLUME=SER=MMA500
```

How to code your JCL statements to improve readability

When you code job streams, we recommend that you code them in a consistent, readable style. This makes them easier to modify when you have to change them. To do this, you can start by aligning operation and operand fields. In the job streams in this chapter, for example, all operation codes start in column 16, all operands start in column 22, and all operands in continuation lines start in column 15.

We also recommend that you code only one or two operands per line. This particularly applies to DD statements as you'll see in a moment. For these statements, we group related operands with a maximum of three operands per line. If you do this in addition to aligning the start of operation codes and operands, you'll keep your job streams manageable. These techniques are illustrated by the job streams in figures 3-16, 3-18, and 3-20.

JCL STATEMENTS

The primary JCL statements are the JOB, EXEC, and DD statements. In addition, you should know how to use the null, comment, and delimiter statements. The formats of all six of these statements are given in figure 3-12.

The JOB statement

A *job* is a unit of work on an MVS system. It consists of one or more *job steps*. Each job step consists of one program execution. The JOB statement tells MVS that a new job is being submitted to it for execution.

Because more than one job is usually running at the same time on an MVS system, it's useful to be able to refer to a job by job name. So, on the JOB statement, you code a *job name* in the name field. Then, when MVS issues messages about your job, it uses your job name. Also, listings produced by the job are labelled with your job name.

Because a typical MVS installation runs hundreds of jobs, their names need to be standardized. As a result, your shop or school probably has rules for creating job names. If so, you should find out what they are and use them.

There are 18 possible operands for the JOB statement, but only two are coded in most MVS installations. These are shown in figure 3-12: accounting information and programmer name.

Accounting information   The first operand, accounting information, is used as an identification code so the MVS system can keep a record of who uses the system and for how long. Sometimes, it's just an account number as shown in figure 3-11, but it may also include other information. If so, the subparameters should be coded within parentheses as in this example:

```
//MMA3100        JOB    (2009,2),MEADOWS
```

Here, the user has specified an account number of 2009 and a maximum time limit of 2 minutes in the accounting information operand. Since the format of the accounting-information operand is unique to each installation, you'll have to find out what's required by your system.

Programmer name   The second JOB statement operand is the programmer name, which can be up to 20 characters long. If it contains any characters other than letters, numbers, blanks, or periods, it must be enclosed in apostrophes, as in this example:

```
//MMA3200        JOB    0932,'MRM, JR.'
```

To be safe, we recommend that you always code your name within apostrophes.

The EXEC statement

The EXEC statement tells MVS to execute either a program or a procedure. A *procedure* is a set of frequently used job control statements that's cataloged in a procedure library so you don't have to reenter and resubmit the statements every time they're needed. A procedure tells MVS to execute one or more programs.

When you code a *procedure name* in an EXEC statement, it causes the JCL statements that make up the procedure to be retrieved from the procedure library. These statements are then inserted in place of the EXEC statement in your JCL. It's this combination of your job control statements and the inserted ones from the cataloged procedure that becomes the JCL that's actually submitted to the MVS job scheduler program. In a moment, I'll show you how to use cataloged procedures for assembling, link editing, and executing your assembler language programs.

Procedure name   All of the the EXEC statements in this book specify procedure names. For example, if you look ahead to figure 3-16, which is an assemble-only job, you'll see that a procedure named ASMFC is executed. This procedure contains an EXEC statement that executes the assembler. In addition, the procedure contains the job control statements necessary to define the files used by the assembler.

You can also code an EXEC statement for a procedure using the keyword PROC as in this example:

```
//              EXEC   PROC=ASMFC
```

The JOB statement

```
//jobname   JOB    accounting-information,
                   programmer-name
```

The EXEC statement

```
//         EXEC   procedure-name,
                  PARM[.stepname]='values'
```

The DD statement

```
//ddname   DD     DSNAME=data-set-name,
                  DISP=(status,normal-disposition,abnormal-disposition),
                  UNIT=group-name,
                  VOLUME=SER=serial-number
```

The null statement

```
//
```

The comment statement

```
//* comments
```

The delimiter statement

```
/*
```

Figure 3-12   The basic formats of six MVS JCL statements

If the word PROC is omitted, though, a procedure name is assumed. In this book, all EXEC statements are coded with just a procedure name.

To code an EXEC statement that executes a program, you have to use the keyword PGM as in this example:

```
//              EXEC   PGM=IFOX00
```

In fact, this is the EXEC statement that is used in a typical ASMFC procedure. In other words, the name of the assembler is IFOX00. Although we won't show you any job streams in this book that execute programs directly, you should realize that this is how it's done.

PARM   The PARM operand specifies parameter values that are passed to the program or procedure that's executed. In this course, you'll use the PARM operand most often to pass values to the assembler. These values control assembly options.

Output type	Option on	Option off	Option meaning
List	LIST	NOLIST	Print the assembly listing.
	ESD	NOESD	Print the external symbol dictionary.
	XREF(FULL) XREF(SHORT)	NOXREF	Print the cross-reference listing
	RLD	NORLD	Print the relocation dictionary.
	LINECOUNT(nn)		The number of lines to be printed on a page.
Object module	OBJECT or OBJ	NOOBJECT or NOOBJ	Create an object module on disk
	ALIGN	NOALIGN	Align all binary fields on the proper boundaries in the object module.

Figure 3-13   Common assembler options that control list and object module output

Figure 3-13 presents some of the most commonly used assembly options. As you can see, some of these options control list output and some of them control object module output. To turn an option on, you code the operand in the lefthand column of figure 3-13 like LIST or ESD. To turn an option off, you code the operand in the righthand column like NOLIST or NOESD. Figure 3-14 gives three examples of EXEC statements that use the PARM operand.

Before you turn any options on or off, though, you should realize that *default values* are in effect if you don't code a PARM operand. In most cases, the default options will be the ones you want when you assemble and execute your jobs. In general, then, you won't need to use the PARM operand for your assembly jobs. If you want to find out what the default options are, just run an assemble-only job like the one presented in figure 3-16. Near the end of your job output, you'll find a listing of the options in effect (the default options).

When you code the PARM operand, you should also realize that your parameter values replace any values that may already be coded for the specified job step within the procedure. So, to add or change a parameter value, you usually have to code all of the values you want to pass to the job step, not just the ones you're adding or changing.

When you code the PARM operand for an EXEC statement that executes a procedure, you should tell MVS which program in the procedure the PARM operand applies to. To do this, you *concatenate* the word PARM with the step name of the job step within the procedure that the parameter values are to be passed to. To concatenate two words, you

An EXEC statement that turns on the full cross-reference listing

```
//              EXEC   ASMFC,PARM.ASM='XREF(FULL)'
```

An EXEC statement that turns off the cross-reference listing and requests 56 lines per page on the assembly output

```
//              EXEC   ASMFC,PARM.ASM='NOXREF,LINECOUNT(56)'
```

An EXEC statement that turns off the cross-reference listing for the assembly and the CAL option for link editing

```
//              EXEC   ASMFCLG,
//              PARM.ASM='NOXREF',
//              PARM.LKED='NCAL'
```

Figure 3-14   EXEC statements that set options

code them together separated by one period. In figure 3-14, for example, the first PARM operand specifies the ASM job step by concatenating PARM and ASM:

```
PARM.ASM
```

Within a procedure that uses the assembler, the assembly step is usually named ASM.

You can also use the PARM operand to specify options for the linkage editor and loader programs. In general, these options are only used for special requirements so you won't need to code them often. Occasionally, though, you may need to turn off one of the options of the linkage editor by coding NCAL in the PARM operand for the linkage editor, as in this example:

```
PARM.LKED='NCAL'
```

Turning this option off lets the linkage editor link more than one object module to a main program.

If you need to specify more than one parameter in the PARM operand, they should be separated by commas and enclosed in apostrophes. In figure 3-14, for example, the second statement turns one option off and sets the line count to 56. If you need to set parameters for two different programs within a procedure, you can code two PARM operands. In figure 3-14, for example, the third statement turns one option off for the assembly and turns another option off for link editing.

The DD statement

The DD statement, which stands for Data Definition, names a file and defines its characteristics. This statement has many operands, but the four summarized in figure 3-12 are all that you need to know for defining disk files that are going to be read by your program. Later on, in chapter 13, I'll present a couple of other operands that you need to know if you're going to define output files or non-sequential files.

The name portion of the DD statement specifies a *ddname*. This must be the same as the ddname used in the program that processes the file. MVS uses this name to link the file information given in the program with the file information given in the operands of the DD statement.

DSNAME   This operand specifies the data set name for the file. In contrast to the ddname, the data set name gives the name in the file's internal label. This is how the ddname in the program gets associated with an actual file on disk.

DISP   The disposition operand (DISP) is composed of three subparameters: status, normal disposition, and abnormal disposition. The first subparameter, status, tells MVS whether the file is a new file being created in this job step (NEW), an existing file to which you want exclusive access (OLD), an existing file to which you do not need exclusive access (SHR for shared access), or an existing file you want to add records to (MOD for modify).

The second subparameter, normal disposition, tells MVS what to do with the file if the job step completes normally. Acceptable values are KEEP, CATLG (catalog), DELETE, and UNCATLG (uncatalog).

The third subparameter, abnormal disposition, tells MVS what to do with the file if the job step abnormally terminates. The values you may code are the same as those for normal disposition.

UNIT   The UNIT operand tells MVS what kind of hardware device the file is to be placed on or retrieved from. For this operand, you can specify a unit address, unit number, or group name. Since the first two options aren't commonly used, I won't present them in this book.

A *group name* includes all devices of a particular kind. Group names are given to categories of devices during system generation. The most common group name, and the only one I will use in this book, is SYSDA, which refers to direct access devices.

VOLUME   The VOLUME operand tells MVS the serial number of the volume the file is to be placed on or retrieved from. This operand isn't required for output files when you don't care what volume the file is placed on. In this case, the UNIT operand will identify the type, and MVS will choose the volume from that category. However, the VOLUME operand must be specified for an input file that's not cataloged.

The null statement	The *null statement* marks the end of a job. It consists of // in the first two positions and blanks in the rest of the statement. Although the null statement is optional, it's a good practice to end each job with one. If it's omitted, though, the next JOB statement tells MVS that the previous job has ended.
The comment statement	I mentioned earlier in this topic that you can use *comment statements* to place comments in your job. They can be used to clarify a confusing set of JCL statements or just to identify the purpose and operation of a job. Comment statements begin with two slashes and an asterisk starting in column 1, as in this example:

```
//* PAYROLL JOB DEFINED BY DFD 101 FOLLOWS
```

The entire comment statement is ignored, but it's printed along with the JCL listing. If you use comment statements, be sure to code them *after* the JOB statement since the JOB statement must always be the first JCL statement of the job.

The delimiter statement	The *delimiter statement* has a slash in column 1 and an asterisk in column 2. It is used to mark the end of data that is included in a job stream. I'll show you how it's used in just a moment.

HOW TO DEFINE FILES USING THE DD STATEMENT

Now that you know the operands of the DD statement, let me show you how to use them within a DD statement. To start, you need to know how to define four types of files: input disk files that are cataloged; input disk files that aren't cataloged; print files; and files within a job stream. Figure 3-15 shows DD statements that define a file of each type.

How to define a cataloged disk file   When a file has been cataloged, you only have to code two operands on its DD statement. The data set name coded in the DSNAME operand is all that MVS needs to find the file. Then, the DISP operand tells MVS the disposition of the file. For an input file that is going to be kept, you usually code the DISP operand as:

```
DISP=(SHR,KEEP)
```

or just

```
DISP=SHR
```

If the normal disposition for an old file isn't coded, the default is KEEP so both of these operands have the same effect. If you code OLD instead of SHR to access an old file, your program will have exclusive access to the input file, which usually isn't what you want unless the file is going to be updated.

How to define an uncataloged disk file   If a file hasn't been cataloged, you need to code the DSNAME, DISP, UNIT, and VOLUME operands. The UNIT and VOLUME operands identify the disk volume that is going to be used. Then, the DSNAME operand tells MVS the data set name of the file so MVS can find the file in the volume's VTOC. Finally, the DISP operand tells MVS the disposition of the file. For an input file that is going to be kept and is not going to be updated, the status is usually coded as SHR and the disposition for normal termination is coded as KEEP.

How to define a print file   To define a print file, you don't use the DD statement operands I summarized in figure 3-12. Instead, you simply code the SYSOUT operand like this:

```
//ddname        DD      SYSOUT=class
```

Here, class is a letter code that specifies the type of output that is to be printed. Most of the time, you code class A, which is standard printer output. Then, MVS spools your printed output to an appropriate print file on disk and prints it later on.

How to define a file within a job stream   In some jobs, you will want to code input within the job stream. This can be referred to as *instream data*. In other words, your input records will be coded within the JCL statements for the job. To do this, MVS has to know when the instream data starts and when it ends.

   To tell MVS that instream data will follow, you code the DD statement like this:

```
//ddname        DD      *
```

In other words, the asterisk (*) tells MVS that instream data will follow. After this, you code the data, followed by the delimiter statement to tell MVS that the instream data ends. As a result, the complete code for an instream file looks like this:

```
//ddname           DD      *
                   .
                   .  INSTREAM DATA
                   .
   /*
```

You'll see an example of instream data within a complete job in just a moment.

The DD statement for a cataloged file on disk

```
//INVMAST        DD      DSNAME=MMA.INVMAST,DISP=SHR
```

The DD statement for an uncataloged file on disk

```
//INVMAST        DD      DSNAME=MMA.INVMAST,DISP=SHR
//                       UNIT=SYSDA,VOLUME=SER=MMA800
```

The DD statement for a standard print file

```
//INVLIST        DD      SYSOUT=A
```

The DD statement for a file within the job stream

```
//INVTRANS       DD      *
                 .
                 .  INSTREAM DATA
                 .
/*
```

Figure 3-15   DD statements that define four different types of data sets

THREE PROCEDURES FOR ASSEMBLING AND TESTING PROGRAMS

When you develop assembler language programs, you normally use standard procedures for assembling and testing them. One of the procedures just assembles a source program; it consists of one job step. Another procedure assembles and tests a source program; it consists of two job steps. The third procedure assembles, link edits, and tests a source program; it consists of three job steps.

How to use an assemble-only procedure

Sometimes, when you first test a new program, you will want to assemble it without link editing or executing it. The reason for this is that you will most likely have diagnostics the first couple of times you assemble a program. Figure 3-16 illustrates the job control statements you need to assemble your source program using an assemble-only procedure. It shows how you can use this procedure with an instream source program as well as with a source program stored in a source library.

The EXEC statement for this procedure specifies the name ASMFC. In most shops, this is the name used for this procedure. It is a one-step procedure, and that step is usually named ASM. When the procedure is executed, the assembler reads the source program and prints the assembly listing along with diagnostic messages and other assembly output.

The DD statement identifies the source file to be assembled. The ddname in this statement is a concatenation of the step name (ASM) and the ddname required by the assembler (SYSIN). In the first job stream in figure 3-16, the source program is coded within the job so it follows the DD statement for the file. In other words, the source program is instream data. As you can see, the asterisk in the DD statement indicates that instream data follows, and the delimiter statement marks the end of the source program.

In the second job stream in figure 3-16, the source program is stored in a source library named MMA.USER1.SOURCE. Its member name is INV3520 . Because most source libraries are cataloged, you don't have to code the UNIT and VOLUME operands on the DD statement for the source library. Note, however, that the DISP operand specifies SHR so other users can access the library while INV3520 is being read and processed.

Whether you code your programs as instream data or as members of a source library depends on your installation practices. In all of the other examples of JCL in this book, though, the source programs are shown as instream data. So please remember that it's likely that you will assemble your programs as source members in a source library, not as instream data.

When you use the assemble-only procedure, you normally don't need to change the options of the assembler. As a result, you won't need to code the PARM operand on the EXEC statement. Keep in mind, though, that you can code this operand if you need to.

How to use an assemble-load-and-go procedure

The assemble-load-and-go procedure is a two-step procedure that is flowcharted in figure 3-17. In this example, the application program reads one disk file and produces printed output. In the first step, the assembler is executed to assemble the source program and produce the assembler list output and the object module. If necessary, the assembler gets copy books from the macro library as described in chapter 6.

In the second step, the loader program is executed to load the object module and execute it. This is considered one job step because the loader program transfers control to the object program itself; it doesn't pass control back to MVS and let MVS transfer control to the object program. If necessary, the loader program links the object module for the source program with any other object modules it requires. During its execution, it also produces some printed output called loader list output. Then, when the application program is executed, it reads the input file from disk and produces the printed output.

Normally, the first few times you assemble and execute a program, you'll use an assemble-load-and-go job. This job is similar to an assemble-

A job that assembles an instream source program

```
//PRINCE        JOB   (MMA,PRINCE),'ANNE PRINCE'
//              EXEC  ASMFC
//ASM.SYSIN     DD    *
                      .
                      .   SOURCE PROGRAM
                      .
/*
//
```

A job that assembles a source program in a source library

```
//PRINCE        JOB   (MMA,PRINCE),'ANNE PRINCE'
//              EXEC  ASMFC
//ASM.SYSIN     DD    DSNAME=MMA.USER1.SOURCE(INV3520),DISP=SHR
//
```

Figure 3-16   An assemble-only job

link-and-go job except that it always creates a temporary load module. In contrast, the assemble-link-and-go procedure can create a permanent load module that can be stored in a load library.

Figure 3-18 presents a job that executes the assemble-load-and-go procedure. In most shops, this procedure is named ASMFCG, and its two steps are named ASM (for the assembly step) and GO (for the load-and-execute step). As you can see, this job stream is like the one for the assemble-only job in figure 3-16, until you reach the delimiter statement at the end of the instream source program.

The three DD statements after the delimiter statement are for a storage dump file (SYSUDUMP) in case the program reaches an abnormal termination, for a print file (PRTOUT), and for an input disk file (INVMAST) that hasn't been cataloged. SYSUDUMP is a standard name for storage dump files, but PRTOUT and INVMAST are ddnames specified in the source program that has just been assembled. To associate these names with the load-and-go step of the procedure, the names are concatenated with the step name (GO).

As you can see, both the storage dump file and the print file are to be standard printer output (class A). The input disk file is named MMA.TEST.INVMAST, which can be found on a direct access device with a volume serial number of MMA800.

How to use an assemble-link-and-go procedure

A job to assemble, link, and execute a program consists of the three job steps that are flowcharted in figure 3-19. In the first step, the assembler is executed, thus preparing the assembler list output and the object module.

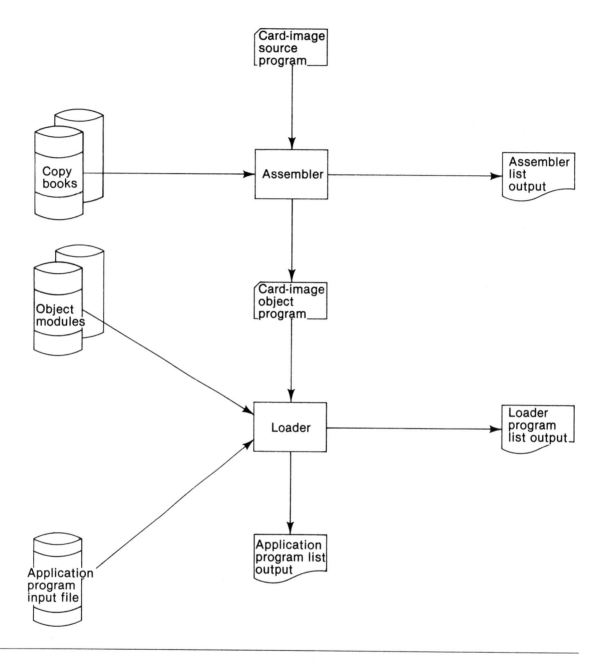

Figure 3-17 The steps in an assemble-load-and-go job for a disk-to-printer program

```
//PRINCE        JOB    (MMA,PRINCE),'ANNE PRINCE'
//              EXEC   ASMFCG
//ASM.SYSIN     DD     *
                .
                .  SOURCE PROGRAM
                .
/*
//GO.SYSUDUMP   DD     SYSOUT=A
//GO.PRTOUT     DD     SYSOUT=A
//GO.INVMAST    DD     DSN=MMA.TEST.INVMAST,DISP=SHR,
//                 UNIT=SYSDA,VOLUME=SER=MMA800,
//
```

Figure 3-18   An assemble-load-and-go job for a program that reads an uncataloged disk file and prepares printed output

During this step, the assembler may take some source code from copy books as you'll learn in chapter 6.

In the second step, the linkage editor is executed. During this step, the object module created in the first step is combined with any other object modules required by the program. The result is a load module. The linkage editor also produces list output that shows which object modules were combined.

In the third step, the load module that was created in the second step is executed. When executed, the operations you specified in your assembler language program are performed. As a result, the load module will read whatever old files you specified, create whatever new files you specified, and print whatever printed output you specified. In a simple disk-to-printer program, the load module will read the disk file or files and print the output you specified.

Figure 3-20 shows typical MVS job control statements for assembling, link editing, and executing an assembler language program. In most shops, the procedure name is ASMFCLG; the step names are ASM (for assembly), LKED (for link editing), and GO (for executing).

As you can see, the JCL for this job is similar to the JCL for the assemble-load-and-go procedure in figure 3-18, with three exceptions. First, the procedure name in the EXEC statement is ASMFCLG. Second, the program to be tested reads two input files with the ddnames INVMAST and INVEXT. Third, both of these files are cataloged so their DD statements don't include the UNIT and VOLUME operands.

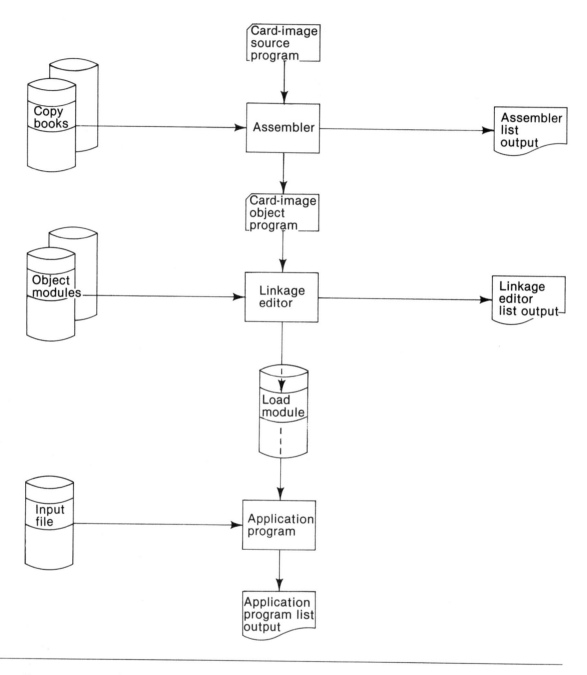

Figure 3-19   The steps in an assemble-link-and-go job for a disk-to-printer program

```
//PRINCE        JOB   (MMA,PRINCE),'ANNE PRINCE'
//              EXEC  ASMFCLG
//ASM.SYSIN     DD    *
                .
                .    SOURCE PROGRAM
                .
/*
//GO.SYSUDUMP   DD    SYSOUT=A
//GO.PRTOUT     DD    SYSOUT=A
//GO.INVMAST    DD    DSN=MMA.TEST.INVMAST,DISP=SHR
//GO.INVEXT     DD    DSN=MMA.TEST.INVEXT,DISP=SHR
//
```

Figure 3-20   An assemble-link-and-go job for a program that reads two cataloged disk files and prepares printed output

USING JCL ON AN INTERACTIVE BASIS

When you develop assembler language programs on an MVS system, you need to know job control language so you can assemble and test your programs. But how you use your job streams will depend on the program development software you're using.

Traditionally, a job stream like the one in figure 3-16 was punched in cards and submitted to the system by way of a card reader. Today, however, it's far more likely that you'll create your job streams interactively. Then, you can submit your jobs to a background partition using your system's facilities for program development.

To illustrate, suppose you're using SPF as introduced in topic 1 of this chapter to develop the program for the case study in appendix B. After you've created your source program and you're ready to assemble or test it, you add job statements before and after your source program as shown in figures 3-16, 3-18, and 3-20, using the SPF editor. Then, to submit the job for background processing, you enter the SUBMIT command in the primary command area. Once this command is executed, your job is placed in a queue of batch jobs and a message is returned to your screen indicating that the job was successfully submitted. As a result, you can continue with another SPF job. Meanwhile, your batch job will be executed by MVS when its turn comes up, and its printed output will be printed by one of the system's printers.

As I mentioned in topic 1, you may not use SPF in your shop. Also, SPF provides other ways in which you can assemble and test your programs. Since this book is about assembler language, not interactive program development, I only wanted to give you an idea of how you might use JCL in an interactive environment. It's your job to find out how you will actually use JCL in your shop.

DISCUSSION

When preparing assembler language programs, job streams like the ones in figures 3-16, 3-18, and 3-20 are all that you will need for sequential disk-to-printer programs. Normally, an assemble-only job stream is used until all diagnostics have been corrected. Then, an assemble-load-and-go job or an assemble-link-and-go job is used for a series of test runs. Each time an error is debugged, the source program is changed, and the program is reassembled and tested again.

In figures 3-16, 3-18, and 3-20 the shading indicates elements in the job streams that you may have to change to suit your circumstances. First, you will have to code job name, accounting information, and programmer name in the JOB statement in a way that conforms to the standards of your shop or school. Second, you will have to code the DD statements to reflect the proper specifications for the files your program requires. Third, you may have to code the PARM operand to reflect the requirements of your assembly.

You should be aware that there is another assembler procedure that I didn't present in this chapter. It is usually named ASMFCL. It assembles and link edits a program, but doesn't execute the load module. Since you won't need it for the case study in this book, that's all I'll tell you about it. But if you want to find out more about it, you can consult the *Programmer's Guide* for your system.

Needless to say, this topic is only the briefest of introductions to MVS JCL. So, I hope you realize that most of the statements I've shown have other operands and that MVS offers other JCL statements. Also, you should realize that you must know both assembler language and the related JCL if you want to become an effective programmer. As you go through this book, you'll be introduced to the JCL for using copy books, subprograms, and disk files. But if you want to become proficient at using MVS JCL, by all means get a copy of our *MVS JCL* book by Doug Lowe.

Terminology

job control statement
job control language
JCL
job stream
identifier field
name field
operation field
operands field
operand
parameter
comments field
job

job step
job name
procedure
procedure name
default value
concatenation
ddname
group name
null statement
comment statement
delimiter statement
instream data

Objective

Create job streams for assembling and for assembling and testing an assembler language program that requires disk input and printer output.

Section 2

A professional subset of assembler language

The five chapters in this section present a professional subset of assembler language. Once you have mastered it, you will be able to write assembler language programs and subprograms the way professional programmers write them.

Whether or not you ever write assembler language programs as a professional, we believe the material in this section will be useful to you if you work with an IBM mainframe under MVS. As you will see, a knowledge of assembler language helps you understand both IBM mainframes and MVS. That's why we think the material in this section is "the least you should know about assembler language."

Once you complete this section, the rest of the material in this book should be relatively easy for you to master. For instance, it should be easy for you to learn how to use the elements for table handling, the elements for writing macros, the elements for VSAM file access, and so on. As a result, you should be prepared to put more effort into this section than any of the other sections.

Chapter 4

CPU Concepts for IBM mainframes

To program in assembler language, you need considerable knowledge of the internal organization and operation of the System/370. This chapter is designed to provide that knowledge. First, it describes how data and instructions are stored in the System/370. Then, it explains how some commonly used instructions operate.

Throughout this chapter and the rest of this book, please keep in mind that a reference to the System/370 includes any of the other mainframes in the System/370 family of mainframes. Although these mainframes differ in terms of price and performance, their instructions all operate the same way from a conceptual point of view.

MAIN STORAGE

When a program is loaded into a computer, it is placed in the main storage of the CPU. In terms of MVS, it is placed in the private area of a user's address space. This area, consists of thousands of virtual *storage positions*, or *bytes*. For instance, a typical private area can be up to 8MB, or approximately 8 million bytes of virtual storage. When a program is loaded into a private area, though, the system allocates only as many bytes of virtual storage to the program as the program requires.

Associated with each of the storage positions of main memory is a number that identifies it; this number is called the *address* of the storage position. A computer with 1M of storage, for instance, has addresses ranging from 0 to 1,048,575. As a result, you can talk about the contents of the storage position at address 180, the contents of byte 4,482, and so on.

In a System/370, data can be stored in four different forms. In one form, one character is stored in each byte of storage. To illustrate this form, suppose the following boxes represent the twenty storage positions from 480 through 499:

Contents: | G | E | O | R | G | E | 3 | 4 | 3 | 9 | 9 | 8 | 2 | | * | 1 | 1 | 2 | 1 | 4 |

Addresses: 480   485   490   495

In this case, you can say that storage position 480 contains the letter G, storage position 487 contains the number 4, storage position 494 contains an asterisk, and position 493 contains a blank. Or you can say that there is a 2 at address 497 and the number 343 is stored in bytes 486 through 488. This is simply the way programmers talk about storage and its contents.

Several consecutive storage positions that contain one item of data such as item number or unit price are commonly referred to as a *field*. For example, bytes 486-490 (this is read as 486 through 490) might represent a balance-on-hand field, while positions 495-499 might represent an item-number field. To address a field, a System/370 instruction specifies the address of the leftmost storage position as well as the number of storage positions in the field. Thus, address 486 with a length of 5 would address the field in positions 486-490, while address 1024 with a length of 20 would address the field in positions 1024-1043.

Of course, a byte of storage isn't really a small box with a character of data in it. Instead, each storage position consists of electronic components that are called *binary components* because they can be switched to either of two conditions. These two conditions are commonly referred to as "on" and "off" and are represented by 0 and 1. In this case, 0 and 1 are called *binary digits*, or *bits*, and 0 represents an "off" bit while 1 represents an "on" bit.

In order to represent data, the bits at a storage position are turned on or off in selected combinations. Each combination represents a digit or digits, a letter, or a special character. On the System/370, for example, 11000010, 11110010, and 11111001 can be used to represent the characters B, 2, and 9. In other words, eight bits represent one storage position. You can also say that eight bits make up one byte of storage.

Although you rarely need to know it, each byte on the System/370 is actually made up of nine bits: eight data bits plus one *parity bit*. The parity bit is used as a check on operations that take place within the CPU. Each time a byte of data is moved into or out of storage during the execution of a program, the byte is *parity checked*. That is, the number of on-bits in the byte is checked to make sure that it is an odd number. If the number of on-bits is even, as in the code 011110011, an error is indicated.

Fortunately, parity errors on a modern computer system are extremely rare, and the parity checking that goes on is completely

Decimal	Binary	Hexadecimal
0	0000	0
1	0001	1
2	0010	2
3	0011	3
4	0100	4
5	0101	5
6	0110	6
7	0111	7
8	1000	8
9	1001	9
10	1010	A
11	1011	B
12	1100	C
13	1101	D
14	1110	E
15	1111	F
16	10000	10

Figure 4-1   Hexadecimal conversion chart

transparent to the programmer. As a result, the parity bit is usually ignored when discussing specific codes or storage forms, and the System/370 is usually said to have an eight-bit, rather than a nine-bit, byte. For this reason, no further mention of parity checking will be made. After all, parity checking is simply an electronic check on the accuracy of internal operations.

DATA STORAGE

Because it is awkward to work with binary codes, *hexadecimal* notation is commonly used to represent the contents of System/370 storage. The intent of hexadecimal notation is to provide a method of shorthand in which one group of four binary digits is replaced with one hexadecimal character. Figure 4-1 shows the relationship between binary, decimal, and hexadecimal notation. Thus, the binary 1111 is written as F in hexadecimal (or *hex*); the binary 1001 is a hex 9; and binary 0110 is a hex 6.

As I mentioned before, data can be stored in four forms in the System/370. Three of these are covered in this chapter. They are *EBCDIC*, *packed decimal*, and *fixed-point binary* (or just *binary*). The fourth form is called *floating-point binary*; it is presented in chapter 12.

EBCDIC

In *EBCDIC* code (pronounced ee'-bee-dick or ib'-si-dick), each byte of storage contains one character of data. Because eight bits can be arranged in 256 different combinations, EBCDIC can be used to represent the letters of the alphabet (both upper and lower case), the decimal digits, and many special characters. However, not all of the 256 combinations are used.

Figure 4-2 gives the EBCDIC codes for the more commonly used characters. It shows the binary code for each character as well as the hexadecimal code. As indicated in the figure, it is common to divide an EBCDIC code into two halves. The leftmost four bits represent the *zone bits*; the rightmost four bits represent the *digit bits*.

If you review the codes in figure 4-2, you can see that the zone bits for the letters A-I are 1100 (hex C); the zone bits for the letters J-R are 1101 (hex D); the zone bits for the letters S-Z are 1110 (hex E); and the zone bits for the digits 0-9 are 1111 (hex F). For special characters, other zone bit combinations are used. Thus, 01011011 is used for the dollar sign, 01001101 is used for the left parenthesis, and 01000000 is used for a blank (yes, a blank is considered to be a character). Although it is sometimes handy for a programmer to know the EBCDIC codes for numbers and letters, decoding special characters is usually unnecessary. If it is required, the codes can easily be looked up in reference tables.

To represent EBCDIC data in storage, hex can be used as in this example:

    E2 C1 D4 40 40 40 40 40 40 40

Here, the name SAM is stored in ten bytes (hex 40 represents a blank). Similarly, a six-byte numeric EBCDIC field containing 1234 can be shown as:

    F0 F0 F1 F2 F3 F4

This EBCDIC form of representing numbers is referred to as *zoned decimal*. You should notice from these two examples that an alphanumeric field is normally left-justified with blanks filling out the unused bytes to the right of the data. A numeric field is normally right-justified with zeros filling out the unused bytes in the left of the field.

To represent the sign of a zoned-decimal field, the zone portion of the rightmost byte of the field is used. If the zone portion is hex F or hex C, the number is positive; if the zone portion is hex D, the number is negative. Thus, a positive 1234 in four storage positions can be shown as:

    F1 F2 F3 C4

A negative 1234 can be shown as:

    F1 F2 F3 D4

Packed decimal

Packed decimal, in contrast to zoned decimal, is a more compact form of System/370 storage. Except for the rightmost byte of a packed-decimal field, two decimal digits are stored in each eight-bit byte. The rightmost byte of the field contains a decimal digit in its zone half and the sign of the field in its digit half. Using hex notation, the number +12345, stored in

Character	EBCDIC		Hexadecimal code
	Zone bits	Digit bits	
blank	0100	0000	40
.	0100	1011	4B
(	0100	1101	4D
+	0100	1110	4E
&	0101	0000	50
$	0101	1011	5B
*	0101	1100	5C
)	0101	1101	5D
;	0101	1110	5E
-	0110	0000	60
/	0110	0001	61
,	0110	1011	6B
%	0110	1100	6C
?	0110	1111	6F
#	0111	1011	7B
'	0111	1101	7D
=	0111	1110	7E
"	0111	1111	7F
A	1100	0001	C1
B	1100	0010	C2
C	1100	0011	C3
D	1100	0100	C4
E	1100	0101	C5
F	1100	0110	C6
G	1100	0111	C7
H	1100	1000	C8
I	1100	1001	C9
J	1101	0001	D1
K	1101	0010	D2
L	1101	0011	D3
M	1101	0100	D4
N	1101	0101	D5
O	1101	0110	D6
P	1101	0111	D7
Q	1101	1000	D8
R	1101	1001	D9
S	1110	0010	E2
T	1110	0011	E3
U	1110	0100	E4
V	1110	0101	E5
W	1110	0110	E6
X	1110	0111	E7
Y	1110	1000	E8
Z	1110	1001	E9
0	1111	0000	F0
1	1111	0001	F1
2	1111	0010	F2
3	1111	0011	F3
4	1111	0100	F4
5	1111	0101	F5
6	1111	0110	F6
7	1111	0111	F7
8	1111	1000	F8
9	1111	1001	F9

Figure 4-2   EBCDIC coding chart

three bytes, is shown as follows:

    12 34 5C

(Remember that either C or F is a valid sign for a positive field.) If the number -12345 is stored in four bytes, it can be shown as:

    00 12 34 5D

This illustrates that leading zeros must fill out the positions of a packed-decimal number if the number has fewer digits than the field allows.

Packed-decimal fields in hex are relatively easy to decode because the decimal digits 0 through 9 are also 0 through 9 in hex. The only problem, then, is determining the sign of the field by analyzing the digit portion of the rightmost byte of the field.

Binary

On the System/370, two or four consecutive bytes are used for a *binary* field. Thus, 16 or 32 bits are used to represent a binary number. A two-byte binary field is referred to as a *halfword* and a four-byte binary field as a *fullword*. For some conversion operations, an eight-byte field known as a *doubleword* is also used.

If a binary number is represented by binary digits, it can be converted by assigning a *place value* to each bit. The place values start at the rightmost bit position with a value of 1 and double for each position to the left. Thus, the place values for a 32-bit binary number are from right to left 1, 2, 4, 8, 16, 32, 64, and so on, until the next to the leftmost bit, the 31st bit, has a value of 1,073,741,824. The leftmost bit is used to indicate the sign of the number. If the leftmost bit is 0, the number is positive; if it is 1, the number is negative. In a 16-bit binary number, 15 bits are used for the number, while the leftmost bit indicates the sign.

To illustrate binary coding, consider the following binary number: 0010010000011011. Since the leftmost bit is 0, the number is positive. By adding the place values of the on-bits, you can determine that the decimal equivalent is 9243. The decoding process is illustrated in figure 4-3. The maximum value of a 16-bit binary number is a positive 32,767; the maximum value of a 32-bit number is a positive 2,147,483,647.

Using hex, the binary storage of decimal 9243 in a halfword can be shown as:

    24 1B

If 9243 is stored in a fullword, it can be shown as:

    00 00 24 1B

To convert the hex representation of a positive binary number to decimal, you can use a calculator that provides hex-to-decimal and decimal-to-hex conversion functions. If you don't have a calculator like

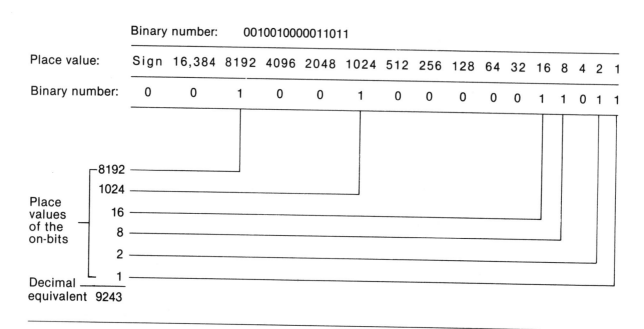

Figure 4-3   Converting a binary number to its decimal equivalent

this, you can use a chart such as the one in figure 4-4. By looking up the decimal value of each hex digit in the corresponding column in the chart and then adding the decimal values, the decimal number can be derived. Thus, hex A in the rightmost four bits of a binary number has a value of 10; hex 4 in the next four bits has a value of 64; and so on. When these decimal values are added, the decimal number 15,178 is derived from hex 3B4A. (Incidentally, the hex chart simply reflects the place values of a hex number. The rightmost hex digit has a place value of 1; the next hex digit to its left has a place value of 16; the hex digit to its left has a place value of 256; and so on.)

Because negative binary numbers are not simply binary numbers with a 1-bit preceding them, you will not be able to decode negative hex numbers by using this technique. Fortunately, though, you rarely (if ever) have to. For the most part, it is enough to know that any hex representation of a binary number in which the leftmost hex digit is 8 or greater is a negative number. More about negative binary numbers in chapter 7.

Data storage summary

With three different types of data representation, the number of storage positions required for a numeric field on the System/370 is determined by the number of digits in the field and the data format used. If, for example, a field is supposed to contain the number +205,597,474, it requires nine bytes of storage using zoned decimal, five bytes using packed decimal, and

FULLWORD															
HALFWORD								HALFWORD							
Byte 1				Byte 2				Byte 3				Byte 4			
Zone		Digit		Zone		Digit		Zone		Digit		Zone		Digit	
Hex	Decimal	Hex	Decimal	Hex	Decimal	Hex	Decimal	Hex	Decimal	Hex	Decimal	Hex	Decimal	Hex	Decimal
0	0	0	0	0	0	0	0	0	0	0	0	0	0	0	0
1	268,435,456	1	16,777,216	1	1,048,576	1	65,536	1	4,096	1	256	1	16	1	1
2	536,870,912	2	33,554,432	2	2,097,152	2	131,072	2	8,192	2	512	2	32	2	2
3	805,306,368	3	50,331,648	3	3,145,728	3	196,608	3	12,288	3	768	3	48	3	3
4	1,073,741,824	4	67,108,864	4	4,194,304	4	262,144	4	16,384	4	1,024	4	64	4	4
5	1,342,177,280	5	83,886,080	5	5,242,880	5	327,680	5	20,480	5	1,280	5	80	5	5
6	1,610,612,736	6	100,663,296	6	6,291,456	6	393,216	6	24,576	6	1,536	6	96	6	6
7	1,879,048,192	7	117,440,512	7	7,340,032	7	458,752	7	28,672	7	1,792	7	112	7	7
8	2,147,483,648	8	134,217,728	8	8,388,608	8	524,288	8	32,768	8	2,048	8	128	8	8
9	2,415,919,104	9	150,994,944	9	9,437,184	9	589,824	9	36,864	9	2,304	9	144	9	9
A	2,684,354,560	A	167,772,160	A	10,485,760	A	655,360	A	40,960	A	2,560	A	160	A	10
B	2,952,790,016	B	184,549,376	B	11,534,336	B	720,896	B	45,056	B	2,816	B	176	B	11
C	3,221,225,472	C	201,326,592	C	12,582,912	C	786,432	C	49,152	C	3,072	C	192	C	12
D	3,489,660,928	D	218,103,808	D	13,631,488	D	851,968	D	53,248	D	3,328	D	208	D	13
E	3,758,096,384	E	234,881,024	E	14,680,064	E	917,504	E	57,344	E	3,584	E	224	E	14
F	4,026,531,840	F	251,658,240	F	15,728,640	F	983,040	F	61,440	F	3,840	F	240	F	15
	8		7		6		5		4		3		2		1

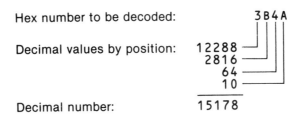

Hex number to be decoded:	3 B 4 A
Decimal values by position:	12288
	2816
	64
	10
Decimal number:	15178

Figure 4-4   Converting a hex number to its decimal equivalent

a fullword (four bytes) using binary. If a field consists of only one decimal digit such as the number +7, one byte is required using zoned decimal, one byte using packed decimal, and a halfword (two bytes) using binary. Figure 4-5 summarizes these examples.

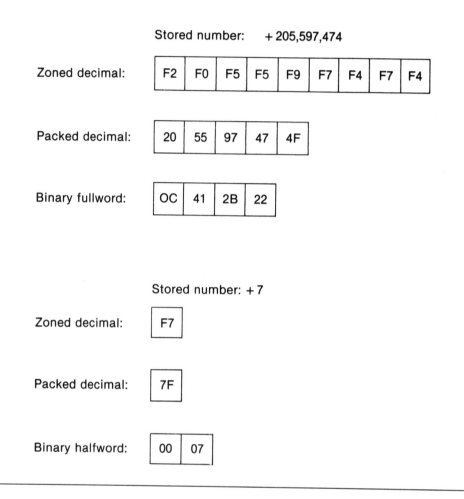

Stored number: + 205,597,474

Zoned decimal:

| F2 | F0 | F5 | F5 | F9 | F7 | F4 | F7 | F4 |

Packed decimal:

| 20 | 55 | 97 | 47 | 4F |

Binary fullword:

| OC | 41 | 2B | 22 |

Stored number: + 7

Zoned decimal:

| F7 |

Packed decimal:

| 7F |

Binary halfword:

| 00 | 07 |

Figure 4-5   Three forms of numerical representation on the System/370

INSTRUCTION FORMATS

While a program is being executed, both the instructions of the program and the data being processed are contained in storage. The instructions, in coded form, indicate both the operations that are to be performed and the addresses and lengths of the fields that are to be operated upon. In the System/370, instructions are two, four, or six storage positions in length, depending on the function of the instruction.

A six-byte instruction format

To illustrate the parts of a typical System/370 instruction, consider one of its basic move instructions called the *move characters instruction*. This instruction causes the data from one field in storage to be moved unchanged to another field. If, for example, a move characters instruction specifies that an EBCDIC field in bytes 1551-1555 should be moved to bytes 1701-1705, the execution of the instruction can be shown in hex notation as:

	Receiving field	Sending field
Before:	F0 F4 F3 F9 F9	F0 F0 F7 F0 F1
After:	F0 F0 F7 F0 F1	F0 F0 F7 F0 F1

The effect is that data in one field, called the *sending field*, is duplicated in the second field, called the *receiving field*. In this case, a zoned-decimal value of 701 replaces the previous contents of the receiving field.

The format of this move characters instruction is:

Op Code	Length Factor	Address-1	Address-2
0 7	8 15	16 31	32 47

The first byte (bits 0-7) of this six-byte instruction contains the *operation code*. There is a unique operation code for each of the System/370 instructions, and, in the case of the move characters instruction, the operation code is 11010010, or hex D2. The second byte of the instruction (bits 8-15) is a *length factor*, an eight-bit binary number from 0-255 that indicates how many storage positions should be moved. A length factor of 0 indicates one byte is to be moved; a length factor of 1 indicates two bytes are to be moved; and so on. In other words, length factor plus one is the number of bytes to be moved.

The last four bytes of the instruction represent two addresses that specify the starting locations of the fields involved in the instruction. If the length factor is a binary 9 (indicating that ten bytes should be moved), the ten bytes of data starting at the location specified as address-2 are moved to the ten bytes of storage starting at the location specified as address-1. In this instruction, as in most System/370 instructions, the address-2 field is the sending field, while the address-1 field is the receiving field.

An address in a System/370 instruction is actually made up of two parts: four bits that specify a *base register* and 12 bits that represent a *displacement factor*. The base register can be any one of the 16 *general purpose registers* that are components of the System/370's CPU. These general purpose registers consist of 32 bit positions, the equivalent of a fullword in storage. When a *register* is used as a base register, the rightmost 24 bit positions are used to represent a *base address*, which is always a positive number. To get the actual address, the base address is added to the displacement factor specified in the instruction. This is referred to as *base-plus-displacement addressing*.

To be more specific, then, the format of the move characters instruction is:

D2		L	B1	D1		B2	D2	
0	7	8	15 16 19	20	31	32 35	36	47

Here, D2 is the actual operation code in hex, L is the length factor, B1 and B2 are four-bit binary numbers that specify one of the 16 registers (numbered 0 through 15 or hex 0 through F), and D1 and D2 are 12-bit binary numbers that represent displacement factors.

With this as background, you should be able to understand that the instruction described above (moving bytes 1551-1555 to 1701-1705) might be represented in hex as:

    D20432A5320F

By breaking this down, you can determine that the operation code is D2; the number of bytes to be moved is 5 (hex 4+1); address-1 consists of a base address in register 3 plus a displacement of hex 2A5 (decimal 677); and address-2 consists of a base address in register 3 plus hex 20F (decimal 527). If register 3 contains hex 400 (decimal 1024) at the time the instruction is executed, bytes 1551-1555 will be moved to bytes 1701-1705. It is this type of decoding of the parts of an instruction that is done by the CPU at the time that an instruction is executed.

Two four-byte instruction formats

A second form of the move instruction, often called the *move immediate instruction*, illustrates a four-byte instruction format. When it is executed, one byte of data is moved from the instruction itself to a receiving field. This instruction's format is:

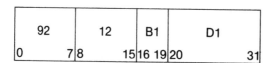

92		12	B1	D1	
0	7	8	15 16 19	20	31

Here, the operation code is hex 92. There is no length code since the move immediate always involves only one byte, and there is only one address since the data to be moved is stored in the second byte of the instruction (bits 8-15). Bits 16-31 give the base register and displacement of the receiving field.

Suppose, for example, that the move immediate instruction in hex is:

    92C1B100

This moves the letter A (hex C1) into the byte at the address computed by adding the contents of register 11 (hex B) to hex 100. If register 11 contains hex 1000, A is moved into the byte at address hex 1100, or decimal 4352. (By using the chart in figure 4-4, you can see that hex 1000 is 4096; hex 100 is 256; 4096 + 256 = 4352.)

Another four-byte instruction format is illustrated by the binary add instruction. This instruction adds the binary number in one fullword of storage to the contents of a general purpose register. If, for example, an instruction indicates that the fullword at address 8000 should be added to the contents of register 7, the instruction execution might be shown in hex as:

	Register 7	Fullword
Before:	00 00 00 10	00 00 00 0A
After:	00 00 00 1A	00 00 00 0A

Thus, the register is the receiving field because it receives the result (hex 1A), which is the sum of register 7's initial contents (hex 10) plus the fullword value (hex 0A).

The format of the fullword add instruction follows:

5A	R1	X2	B2	D2
0 7	8 11	12 15	16 19	20 31

Here, the operation code is 5A, the receiving register is specified in bits 8-11, and the address of the fullword is given in bits 16-31. No length factor is needed because this instruction always operates on a fullword.

Bits 12-15 in the format of the fullword add instruction can be used to specify an *index register*, signified by X2 in the format, which can be used for a function called *indexing*. When indexing is used, an address is derived by adding the base address, the displacement, and the contents of the index register. When bits 12-15 are zero, they are ignored.

A two-byte instruction format

A two-byte System/370 instruction is illustrated by the register-to-register add instruction. In this case, a binary number in one register is added to a binary number in another register as in this example:

	Register 1	Register 2
Before:	00 00 04 01	00 00 00 83
After:	00 00 04 84	00 00 00 83

Here, the contents of register 2 are added to the contents of register 1, and the result is stored in register 1.

The format of this register-to-register instruction is:

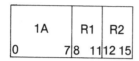

Quite simply, the register numbers of the two fields are given along with the operation code, hex 1A.

Instruction format summary   You have now seen examples of six-, four-, and two-byte instructions of the System/370. In order of presentation, they are often referred to as SS format (storage-to-storage), SI format (immediate-to-storage), RX format (storage-to-register), and RR format (register-to-register). These formats as well as RS format (another form of storage-to-register instructions) and a variation of SS format are presented in figure 4-6.

As you proceed through this book, you will learn how to use all of these types of instructions. By referring to the formats in figure 4-6, you will be able to understand how the assembler language code relates to the machine language. You will also be able to appreciate the value of assembler language when you see how the language frees the programmer from dealing with actual instruction formats.

INSTRUCTION SET   The term *instruction set* applies to the collection of machine instructions that a computer can execute. Of the 180 or more instructions in the System/370 instruction set, most assembler language programmers use only about 60 of them. The rest are used for specialized functions that are rarely needed for application programming.

In general, a computer's instruction set can be broken down into these functional groups:

1   Data movement instructions
2   Arithmetic instructions
3   Logical instructions
4   Input/output instructions

At this time, I'm going to present examples of System/370 instructions in each of these four groups. Because there is a close relationship between machine language instructions and assembler language instructions, this material will help you learn assembler language more easily later on.

Data movement instructions

Move characters (MVC)   You have already been introduced to *data movement instructions* in the form of the move characters instruction.

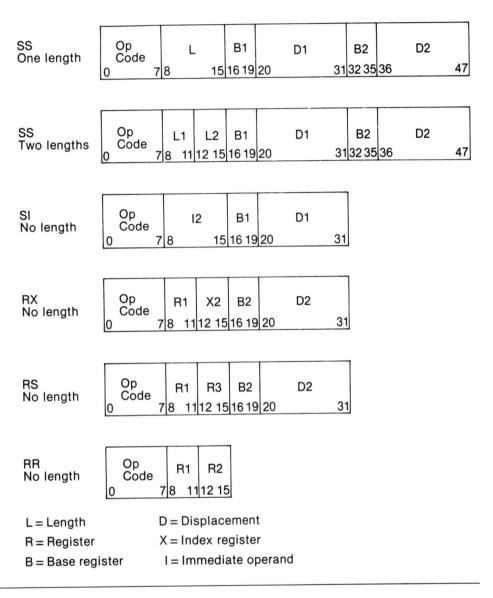

Figure 4-6   System/370 instruction formats

This instruction places the data from the second field specified (called the second *operand*) into the first field specified (called the first operand). The instruction moves one byte of data at a time, processing from left to right through each field.

MVC is the assembler language operation code for the move characters instruction. It is called a *mnemonic operation code* because the letters of the code are designed to aid memorization of the code, and the word *mnemonic* refers to memory. In the rest of this topic, the mnemonic operation codes are given along with the descriptions of the instruction. You will use these codes when you code assembler language programs later on.

Move immediate (MVI)   The move immediate instruction was introduced with the examples of instruction formats. It takes a byte from the instruction and places it into a byte of storage.

Edit (ED)   You use the edit instruction to refine (*edit*) the numeric data in a packed field prior to printing it. In its simplest form, for example, the edit instruction might change leading zeros in a packed field to blanks in an EBCDIC field as follows:

	Receiving field	Sending field
Before:	40 20 20 20 20 20	00 15 8C
After:	40 40 40 F1 F5 F8	00 15 8C

Here, the receiving field must be an *edit pattern* that determines the form in which the sending field is to be edited. To change lead zeros to blanks (called *zero suppression*), the pattern must consist of a lead blank (hex 40) followed by as many hex 20s as there are digits in the packed field. In this example, since there are five digits in the packed field, the sending field consists of five hex 20s preceded by a blank. When used in an edit pattern, hex 20 is called a *digit selector*. Incidentally, hex 20 is one of the 256 EBCDIC combinations that does not have a character to represent it.

You can use a more complex edit pattern with the edit instruction to insert a decimal point or commas into a number. For example, the packed decimal number 0512389 can be edited as follows:

	Receiving field	Sending field
Before:	40 20 20 6B 20 20 21 4B 20 20	05 12 38 9C
After:	40 40 F5 6B F1 F2 F3 4B F8 F9	05 12 38 9C

Because hex 6B is a comma and hex 4B is a decimal point, the receiving field after the editing operation would print as: 5,123.89.

Figure 4-7 gives several examples of the edit patterns required for suppressing lead zeros and inserting commas and decimal points into a number. In all cases, the leftmost character in the pattern, called the *fill character*, is a blank so that lead zeros are changed to blanks. Also, either a digit selector (hex 20) or a *significance starter* (hex 21) must be used wherever a digit from the sending field is to be placed. The significance starter is used for the same purpose as a digit selector except that it also indicates where lead zeros should start printing. In group 2, for example, the pattern 40 20 20 20 21 20 causes a packed-decimal field containing zero to be converted into a form that prints as 0. In other words, lead zeros aren't zero suppressed if they come to the right of the significance starter.

Group	Sending field	Receiving field pattern	Edited result field	Printed result field
1 Lead zero suppression	12345C	402020202020	40F1F2F3F4F5	12345
	00123F	402020202020	404040F1F2F3	123
	00000C	402020202020	4040404040	
2 Significance starting	00511F	402020202120	404040F5F1F1	511
	00001C	402020202120	4040404040F1	1
	00000C	402020202120	4040404040F0	0
3 Decimal point and comma insertion	123456789C	402020206B2020206B202120	40F1F2F36BF4F5F66BF7F8F9	123,456,789
	000123456C	402020206B2020206B202120	404040404040F1F2F36BF4F5F6	123,456
	000000123C	402020206B2020206B202120	40404040404040404040F1F2F3	123
	000000000C	402020206B2020206B202120	4040404040404040404040F0	0
	123456789C	40206B2020206B2020214B2020	40F16BF2F3F46BF5F6F74BF8F9	1,234,567.89
	000000123C	40206B2020206B2020214B2020	4040404040404040F14BF2F3	1.23
	000000005C	40206B2020206B2020214B2020	4040404040404040404BF0F5	.05
	1234567C	4020202020214B2020	40F1F2F3F4F54BF6F7	12345.67
	0000123F	4020202020214B2020	404040F14BF2F3	1.23
	0000005D	4020202020214B2020	40404BF0F5	.05
4 Minus sign message character for negative numbers	01234C	4020202020202060	4040F1F2F3F440	1234
	01234D	4020202020202060	4040F1F2F3F460	1234-
	00000C	4020202020202060	4040404040	
	1234567D	402020206B2020206B2020214B202060	40F1F26BF3F4F54BF6F760	12,345.67-
	0000123D	402020206B2020206B2020214B202060	4040404040404040F14BF2F360	1.23-
	0000005D	402020206B2020206B2020214B202060	404040404040404BF0F560	.05-

Figure 4-7 Some simple editing patterns

In group 3, commas and decimal points are used in edit patterns as *message characters*. As instruction execution proceeds from left to right through the sending and receiving fields, the message characters are unchanged if a *significant digit* (a non-zero digit) or the significance starter has been encountered. Thus, the commas and decimal points are inserted into the edited result. On the other hand, if significance hasn't been started by either a significant digit or the significance starter, a message character is changed to a blank (the fill character). Although message characters can be any hex code other than hex 20, 21, or 22, hex 6B (the comma) and hex 4B (the decimal point) are most commonly used.

In group 4, a minus sign (hex 60) is used as a message character to indicate that a field has a negative value. When a message character is coded to the right of all digit selectors, it is unchanged if the field that is edited is negative. However, the message character is replaced by the fill character if the field is zero or positive. As a result, the edited fields in figure 4-7 are followed by minus signs if they are negative; by blanks, if they aren't negative.

With these examples as guides, you should now be able to create a pattern that will do simple editing on any packed field. Then, in chapter 10, you will learn how to use more sophisticated edit patterns. The main point to remember now is that each pattern must consist of a leftmost fill character as well as one digit selector or significance starter for each digit in the packed decimal sending field. Logically, of course, there can only be one significance starter in an edit pattern.

Pack (PACK)   Since all System/370 arithmetic must be done on packed decimal or binary fields, EBCDIC fields must be converted to packed decimal or binary before they can be operated upon. The pack instruction, then, is one of the conversion instructions. It takes an EBC-DIC sending field and converts it into packed decimal in the receiving field as in this example:

	Receiving field	Sending field
Before:	99 99 99	F1 F2 F3 F4 F5
After:	12 34 5F	F1 F2 F3 F4 F5

As you can see, the zone and digit halves of the rightmost byte of the sending field are reversed in the rightmost byte of the receiving field. Thereafter, the digit portions of the bytes in the sending field are packed two digits per byte in the receiving field. Another view of the operation of the pack instruction is this:

Sending field: F1 F2 F3 F4 F5
Receiving field: 12 34 5F

The pack instruction, in contrast to the move or edit instruction, proceeds from right to left during execution. It uses the second form of the SS format shown in figure 4-6. This means that both sending and receiving fields have length factors. Therefore, it is possible to *pad* a field as in this example:

Sending field (length 4):   F2 F6 F4 F8
Receiving field (length 4):   00 02 64 8F

In other words, unfilled half-bytes are padded with zeros.
It is also possible to *truncate* a field as in this example:

Sending field (length 5):   F6 F3 F2 F0 F4
Receiving field (length 2):   20 4F

Because the receiving field is too small to receive all digits in the sending field, two significant digits are truncated.

Unpack (UNPK)   The unpack instruction converts a packed decimal field into an EBCDIC field as in this example:

Sending field: 56 43 7F
Receiving field: F5 F6 F4 F3 F7

As in the case of the pack instruction, both operands have length factors, so padding can take place:

Sending field (length 2):   03 4C
Receiving field (length 5): F0 F0 F0 F3 C4

And truncation can take place:

Sending field (length 3):   12 91 2D
Receiving field (length 2): F1 D2

In addition to pack and unpack, there are instructions that convert numbers from packed decimal to binary and vice versa. These data movement instructions are covered in chapter 7.

Arithmetic instruction

When arithmetic is done on packed decimal fields, it is referred to as *decimal arithmetic*. Because less conversion is required for decimal arithmetic than for binary arithmetic, decimal arithmetic is used for most of the arithmetic done in business programs. The five basic decimal instructions are add, subtract, multiply, divide, and zero-and-add.

Add decimal (AP)   When the add decimal instruction is executed, operand-2 is added to operand-1 and the result replaces operand-1. The second SS format is used for this instruction, so fields of different lengths (up to 16 bytes each) can be added as in this example:

	Operand-1	Operand-2
Before:	10 00 0F	01 0F
After:	10 01 0C	01 0F

Since 10 is added to 10000, the result is 10010. Either positive or negative fields can be added, and the sign of the result field is always hex C for positive or hex D for negative.

One thing to watch for when coding decimal operations is *arithmetic overflow*. This takes place when the receiving field is not large enough for the result. In the following example, arithmetic overflow occurs:

	Operand-1	Operand-2
Before:	87 11 0F	40 00 0F
After:	27 11 0C	40 00 0F

Since the actual result is 127110, the leftmost digit has been truncated due to the overflow. Because arithmetic overflow will cause inaccurate results, you should avoid overflow by making the receiving field large enough for any possible result.

Subtract decimal (SP)   The subtract decimal instruction operates in the same manner as the add instruction except that the operation is subtraction. Once again, the programmer should avoid overflow by making the receiving field large enough for any possible result.

Multiply decimal (MP)   When the multiply decimal instruction is executed, the first operand (the multiplicand) is multiplied by the second operand (the multiplier), and the result replaces the first operand. The multiplicand can be up to 16 bytes long and the multiplier can be up to 8 bytes long. To prevent overflow, the first operand should have at least as many leading bytes of hex zeros as the number of bytes in the second operand as in this example:

	Operand-1	Operand-2
Before:	00 00 8C	50 0F
After:	04 00 0C	50 0F

Here, operand-1 has two leading bytes of zeros and operand-2 is two bytes long, so overflow can't occur.

Divide decimal (DP)   The divide decimal instruction is similar to multiply decimal with one additional complication: the remainder. The first operand (the dividend) can be up to 16 bytes long, and the second operand (the divisor) can be up to 8 bytes long. When executed, the divisor is divided into the dividend, and the resulting quotient *and* the remainder replace the dividend. Here is an example:

	Operand-1	Operand-2
Before:	00 00 00 05 3C	00 7C
After:	00 00 7C 00 4C	00 7C

The remainder portion of the result is always the same number of bytes as the divisor, and it is located in the rightmost bytes of the operand-1 area. The quotient portion of the result, complete with valid sign, occupies the rest of the dividend area. Because of this, you must make sure that operand-1 has at least as many leading bytes filled with zeros as there are bytes in the divisor.

Zero-and-add (ZAP)   The zero-and-add instruction operates in the same manner as an add decimal instruction that adds a packed field to another packed field containing a value of zero. Here's an example of a zero-and-add instruction:

	Operand-1	Operand-2
Before:	12 45 9C	1C
After:	00 00 1C	1C

In other words, operand-1 is first changed to zero; then, operand-2 is added to it.

Logical instructions

The basic logical instruction and the basis of logic in the computer is the *branch instruction*. When a program is initially loaded into storage, the supervisor transfers control to its first instruction. Then, when the computer finishes executing one instruction, it continues with the next instruction in storage. After executing the instruction in bytes 1000-1005, for example, the computer executes the instruction starting at address 1006. The only exception to this involves the branch instruction. When the branch instruction is executed, it can cause the computer to break the sequence and continue with the instruction beginning at the address specified in the branch instruction.

When a branch instruction branches every time it is executed, it is called an *unconditional branch*. If, for example, an unconditional branch instruction in positions 4032-4035 specifies a branch to address 801, the computer will continue with the instruction starting in storage position 801.

Conditional branch instructions cause branching only when specified conditions are met. For example, a conditional branch instruction might branch only if the result of an arithmetic instruction is negative. To illustrate, suppose a branch instruction occupies storage positions 2044-2047 and specifies that the computer should branch to address 1000 if the result of the preceding arithmetic instruction is negative. Then, if the result is zero or positive, the computer continues with the instruction starting at address 2048, the next instruction in sequence. But if the result is negative, the computer continues with the instruction starting at address 1000.

One of the most useful conditions to be branched upon is based on the results of a comparison between two fields in storage. This branch instruction is used in conjunction with the other type of logical instruction, the *compare instruction*. The System/370 has compare instructions that compare EBCDIC, packed decimal, and binary fields. In the instruction descriptions that follow, the compare decimal instruction is presented followed by two of the System/370 branch instructions. Other compare and branch instructions are presented in other chapters of this book.

Compare decimal (CP)   The compare decimal instruction specifies that two packed decimal fields are to be compared. When it is executed, the computer determines the relationship between the fields: Are they equal? Is the first field greater in value than the second? Is the first field less in value than the second? Based on this comparison, a *condition code* is set that can be used by subsequent branch instructions.

The condition code can be thought of as four bits that are located in the CPU and that can be tested by a branch instruction. For the compare decimal instruction, if the leftmost bit of the condition code is turned on (bit 0), it indicates that operand-1 and operand-2 are equal. If bit 1 is turned on, it indicates that operand-1 is less than operand-2. If bit 2 is turned on, it indicates that operand-1 is greater than operand-2. The rightmost condition code bit (bit 3) isn't used by the compare decimal instruction.

Branch-on-condition (BC)   The most widely used branch instruction, called the branch-on-condition instruction, has this RX format:

47	M1	X2	B2	D2
0 7	8 11	12 15	16 19	20 31

When this instruction is executed, it compares the *mask* bits (bits 8-11) with the condition code. If the on-bit in the condition code has a corresponding on-bit in the instruction mask, the program branches to the address specified in bits 12-31 of the instruction (base register plus displacement plus the contents of an index register if bits 12-15 specify a

Condition code bit setting	0	1	2	3
Add decimal	Zero	Minus	Plus	Overflow
Compare decimal (A:B)	Equal	A low	A high	_____
Edit	Zero	Minus	Plus	_____
Subtract decimal	Zero	Minus	Plus	Overflow
Zero-and-add	Zero	Minus	Plus	Overflow

Figure 4-8   Condition code settings for the instructions presented so far

register number other than zero). If the on-bit in the condition code does not have a corresponding 1-bit in the mask, the program continues with the next instruction in sequence.

To illustrate, suppose that the condition code is 0100 after a compare decimal instruction has been executed. Then, if the mask in the branch-on-condition instruction is 0100 or 0110, the branch takes place. On the other hand, if the mask is 1011 or 0001, the branch will not take place.

The mask bits in an instruction can be used in any of the 16 combinations that are possible with four bits. This makes it possible for a branch-on-condition instruction to branch on multiple conditions. If, for example, the mask is 1010 following a compare decimal instruction, a branch will take place when the operands are equal (condition code is 1000) or when operand-1 is greater than operand-2 (condition code is 0010). If all four mask bits are on, the branch is unconditional (it will take place every time); if all four bits are off, it will never branch.

Figure 4-8 summarizes the condition code settings for the instructions that have been presented thus far that affect the condition code. It shows which bits are set on for each possible result of an instruction. The branch-on-condition instruction can branch based on the results of any of these instructions. You should realize that many instructions, such as move characters or add binary, do not change the condition code in any way.

Branch-and-link-register (BALR)   The branch-and-link-register instruction is a two-byte instruction in RR format. When this instruction is executed, it places the address of the next instruction in storage in the first register specified. Then, it branches to the address that is given by the second register specified. However, if zero is specified for the second register, no branch takes place.

To illustrate the execution of this instruction, suppose it is stored in bytes 5000-5001 and specifies register 8 as operand-1, and register 9, which contains the binary equivalent of 2048, as operand-2. When the branch-and-link-register instruction is executed, address 5002 will be stored in register 8 after which the program will branch to address 2048. In contrast, if zero was specified for register 2, 5002 would be stored in register 8 and no branch would take place. You will see this no-branching use of the branch-and-link-register instruction in chapter 5.

I/O instructions

The System/370 *I/O instructions* are perhaps the most complex instructions in the instruction set. In fact, a computer user's program never executes I/O instructions. Instead, all I/O operations are started by the MVS supervisor program. Then, whenever a user's program requires an I/O operation, it branches to the supervisor which in turn causes the appropriate instructions to be executed by a channel.

The operation of I/O instructions   When an I/O instruction is executed, it either reads a record from an input device into main storage or it writes a record from main storage to an output device. For example, an input instruction like a read-disk instruction might specify that one record is to be read and that its data is to be stored in the storage positions starting at address 5501. Then, if the disk record is 100 bytes long, its data will be stored in positions 5501-5600. In this case, bytes 5501-5600 are called the *input area* of the read instruction.

An output instruction like a print instruction specifies the storage positions from which the output data is to be written. This area of main storage is called the *output area* of the write instruction. If a print instruction specifies that a line should be printed from bytes 6601-6732 of main storage, the content of byte 6601 is printed in print position 1 on the printer (on the far left of the form), the content of byte 6602 is printed in print position 2, and so on.

If the data in an output area is to print properly, it must be in EBCDIC form prior to printing. Furthermore, a numeric field that carries a hex C or D sign must be edited if it is to print properly. To illustrate, suppose a zoned decimal field contains a positive 00557 in this form:

    F0 F0 F5 F5 C7

If it is printed, it will print as 0055G since G is the EBCDIC equivalent of hex C7. However, by packing the field and using the edit instruction prior to printing, the lead zeros can be suppressed and the hex C sign changed to hex F.

A similar problem occurs when printing negative fields. For example, a negative 12 will print as 1K. However, if a negative field is packed and edited using the patterns presented thus far, it can be printed correctly with a minus sign to its right.

Overlap and the need for dual I/O areas   On a modern computer system, an application program *overlaps* CPU operations with I/O operations. It does this by executing the internal processing instructions of a program while channels execute the I/O instructions. If a program is preparing a report from a disk file, for example, it's likely that one channel

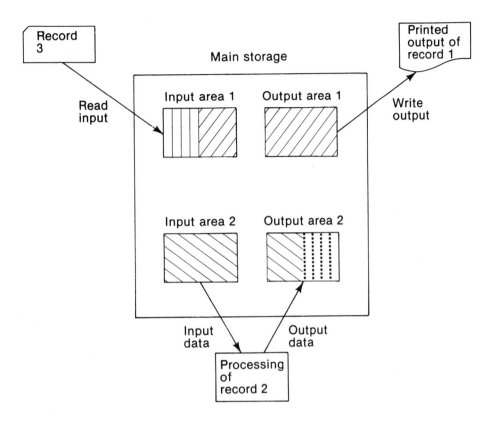

Note: Data is being moved into input area 1 and output area 2

Figure 4-9   A conceptual view of the need for dual I/O areas when CPU and I/O operations are overlapped

will be reading a record from a disk while another channel controls the printing of a record while the CPU executes data movement, arithmetic, or logical operations of the program...all at the same time. By overlapping I/O operations with processing, a program can be executed much more quickly than it can be without overlap.

For overlap to work, two I/O areas in storage must be used for each I/O operation. If, for example, only one output area were used for a print operation, the data for the second print record would be moved into the output area while the first record was being printed, thus causing errors in the printed data. As a result, for overlap to work, the data for the second record must be moved into a second output area while the first record is being printed from the first output area. Then, the third record can be moved into the first output area, while the second record is being printed from the second output area. And so on. This switching from one output area to the other, which is shown schematically in figure 4-9, must be continued throughout the execution of the program. Similarly, dual I/O areas must be used for all other I/O operations that are overlapped.

To relieve the programmer of the responsibility of switching I/O areas and coping with the other I/O complexities (such as writing channel commands), MVS supplies I/O modules that handle these functions. Although there is a complex relationship between the user's program, the I/O modules, and the supervisor, it is a complexity that the programmer need not be concerned with. As you will see in chapter 5, the programmer codes specifications for each of the files used by the program, and the rest is done by the assembler in combination with the MVS I/O modules and the supervisor.

DISCUSSION

The material you have just finished reading may seem to contain an overwhelming amount of detail. Nevertheless, this is the level of machine operation that you must understand if you are to be an effective assembler language programmer. As you will see in chapter 5, the knowledge you gain from this chapter will make your introduction to assembler language quite manageable.

If at this time you have a general understanding of the forms in which data and instructions are stored in a System/370 and if you have an appreciation for what happens when the 13 instructions presented in this chapter are executed, you should be able to continue with no problems. Later on, should you feel the need, you can refer back to the specific details presented in this chapter.

Terminology

storage position
byte
address
field
binary component
binary digit
bit
parity bit
parity checking
hexadecimal
hex
fixed-point binary
floating-point binary
EBCDIC
zone bits
digit bits
zoned decimal
packed decimal
binary
halfword
fullword
doubleword
place value

move characters instruction
sending field
receiving field
operation code
length factor
base register
displacement factor
general purpose register
register
base address
base-plus-displacement addressing
move immediate instruction
index register
indexing
instruction set
data movement instruction
operand
mnemonic operation code
mnemonic
editing
edit pattern
zero suppression
digit selector

fill character
significance starter
message character
significant digit
padding a field
truncating a field
arithmetic instruction
decimal arithmetic
arithmetic overflow
logical instruction
branch instruction
unconditional branch
conditional branch
compare instruction
condition code
mask
I/O instruction
input area
output area
overlap

Objectives

1. Given the hexadecimal code for an EBCDIC, packed decimal, or binary field, tell what data the field contains. (In the case of a negative binary field, simply indicate that it is negative.)

2. Given all related specifications, codes, and data for any of the 13 instructions described in this chapter, indicate what will happen when the instruction is executed. The 13 instructions described are: move characters, move immediate, edit, pack, unpack, add decimal, subtract decimal, multiply decimal, divide decimal, zero-and-add, compare decimal, branch-on-condition, and branch-and-link-register.

3. Explain what an input or output area is and how one relates to an I/O instruction.

4. Explain why two I/O areas are required for each input or output device if CPU processing and I/O operations are to be overlapped.

Chapter 5

An introductory
subset of assembler language

Officially, IBM's assembler language is known as *Basic Assembler Language*. As a result, you will sometimes see or hear assembler language referred to as *BAL*. In this book, though, we'll just refer to the language as assembler language.

This chapter presents an introductory *subset* of assembler language. In topic 1, you will be introduced to a complete assembler language program that illustrates some of the elements of this subset. Then, in topic 2, you will study an enhanced version of the first program that illustrates the assembler language elements that complete the introductory subset. When you complete this chapter, you should be able to code assembler language programs that require disk input, printer output, and decimal arithmetic. Since the remaining chapters in this book build upon this introductory subset, you should learn quite rapidly once you complete this chapter.

TOPIC 1   An introduction to assembler language

This topic introduces you to assembler language by presenting specifications for a program along with the complete assembler language program that satisfies the specifications. The idea is for you to see the complete picture right away. If you can do that, it should be relatively easy for you to learn the separate elements of assembler language. As a result, when you finish this topic, you shouldn't expect to be able to develop your own assembler language programs. But you should understand the relationships between the elements of an assembler language program.

THE REORDER-LISTING PROGRAM

Figure 5-1 presents the program specifications for a program that we call the reorder-listing program because it reads an inventory master file and prepares a listing of those items in inventory that need to be reordered. Figure 5-2 presents a program flowchart for this program, and figure 5-3 presents the assembler language code for this program.

Because you will be asked to refer to the program specifications, flowchart, and code for the reorder-listing program throughout this chapter, we suggest that you make photocopies of figures 5-1, 5-2, and 5-3 right now. Then, you can spread them out on your desk and study them as you read this topic. This will reduce the amount of page flipping you have to do, so it should improve your learning efficiency.

The program specifications

As you can see in the program overview in figure 5-1, one line should be printed on the reorder listing whenever an item's available stock (on-hand plus on-order) is less than its reorder point. If you check the record layout for the inventory master record, you can see that it is a 50-byte record that contains only seven fields. If you check the print chart for the reorder listing, you can see that neither heading lines nor total lines are required on the report. In other words, we've simplified this program as much as possible to make your introduction to assembler language as manageable as possible.

The program flowchart

Figure 5-2 is a program flowchart for this program. After doing some setup for the program (housekeeping), the program reads an inventory record, calculates the amount of available stock, and compares it with the reorder point. If the available stock is greater than or equal to the reorder point, the program branches back and reads another record. Otherwise, it

Program:	REORDLST PREPARE REORDER LISTING	Page: 1
Designer:	Anne Prince	Date: 06-07-85

Input/output specifications

File	Description	Use
INVMAST	Inventory master file	Input
PRTOUT	Print file: Reorder listing	Output

Process specifications

This program prepares a reorder listing from a sequential file of inventory records. The program reads the inventory records in sequence and prints one line on the reorder listing whenever the available stock for an inventory record is less than its reorder point. To simplify this introductory program, no headings or total lines are to be printed on the listing.

The basic processing requirements for each inventory record follow:

1. Read the inventory record.
2. Calculate the available amount.
   (Available = on hand + on order.)
3. If available is less than reorder point, format and print a detail line.

Figure 5-1   Specifications for a reorder-listing program (part 1 of 2)

Record layout for inventory master record

Field Name	Item number	Item description	Unit cost	Unit price	Reorder point	On hand	On order
Characteristics	CL5	CL20	CL5	CL5	CL5	CL5	CL5
Usage							
Position	1-5	6-25	26-30	31-35	36-40	41-45	46-50

Print chart

Figure 5-1   Specifications for a reorder-listing program (part 2 of 2)

constructs and prints the reorder line, then branches back to read another record. When the end-of-file (EOF) condition is reached, the program ends.

The program listing

Take time now to look at the program listing in figure 5-3. It is the complete program for printing a reorder listing from a sequential disk file of inventory records. As you will soon appreciate, any assembler language program can be divided into three types of statements: (1) instructions, (2) file definitions, and (3) data definitions. The file definitions give the characteristics of the input and output files; the data definitions define fields that are operated upon by the program; and the instructions use names defined by the file and data definitions to describe the sequence of operations required by the program. In figure 5-3, lines 100 through 3000 are instructions; lines 3100 through 3600 are file definitions; and lines 3700 through 6500 are data definitions.

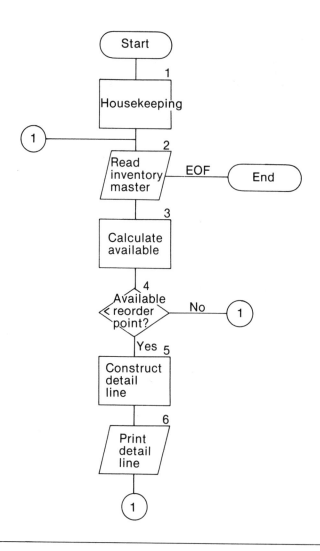

Figure 5-2   A flowchart for the reorder-listing program

To highlight various portions of this program, the programmer has used comment lines. A *comment line* has an asterisk in position 1 and a comment or note written by the programmer in the remaining positions. For example, lines 3100 and 3400 in figure 5-3 are comment lines. During assembly, the contents of the comment lines are printed, but otherwise they are ignored. As a result, they can be used by the programmer to make the program listing easier to follow, but they do not affect the resulting object code.

```
REORDLST START 0                               BLOCK 1:  HOUSEKEEPING          000100
BEGIN     SAVE  (14,12)                                                        000200
          BALR  3,0                                                            000300
          USING *,3                                                            000400
          ST    13,SAVE+4                                                      000500
          LA    13,SAVE                                                        000600
          OPEN  (INVMAST,INPUT,PRTOUT,OUTPUT)                                  000700
READINV   GET   INVMAST,INVWRKA               BLOCK 2:  READ RECORD           000800
          PACK  WRKAVAIL,INVONHND             BLOCK 3:  CALCULATE AVAILABLE   000900
          PACK  WRKONORD,INVONORD                                              001000
          AP    WRKAVAIL,WRKONORD                                              001100
          PACK  WRKORDPT,INVORDPT             BLOCK 4:  DECISION              001200
          CP    WRKAVAIL,WRKORDPT                                              001300
          BNL   READINV                                                        001400
          PACK  PACKAREA,INVITNBR             BLOCK 5:  CONSTRUCT DETAIL LINE 001500
          MVC   PRTITNBR,PATTERN1                                              001600
          ED    PRTITNBR,PACKAREA                                              001700
          MVC   PRTITDES,INVITDES                                             001800
          PACK  PACKAREA,INVPRICE                                             001900
          MVC   PRTPRICE,PATTERN2                                             002000
          ED    PRTPRICE,PACKAREA                                             002100
          MVC   PRTAVAIL,PATTERN1                                             002200
          ED    PRTAVAIL,WRKAVAIL                                             002300
          MVC   PRTORDPT,PATTERN1                                             002400
          ED    PRTORDPT,WRKORDPT                                             002500
          PUT   PRTOUT,PRTWRKA               BLOCK 6:  PRINT LINE            002600
          B     READINV                       UNCONDITIONAL BRANCH            002700
INVEOF    CLOSE (INVMAST,,PRTOUT)             END-OF-JOB ROUTINE             002800
          L     13,SAVE+4                                                      002900
          RETURN (14,12)                                                       003000
* THE INVENTORY FILE DEFINITION FOLLOWS                                       003100
INVMAST   DCB   DSORG=PS,RECFM=F,MACRF=GM,BLKSIZE=50,LRECL=50,           X   003200
                DDNAME=INVMAST,EODAD=INVEOF                                   003300
* THE PRINTER FILE DEFINITION FOLLOWS                                         003400
PRTOUT    DCB   DSORG=PS,RECFM=F,MACRF=PM,BLKSIZE=132,LRECL=132,         X   003500
                DDNAME=PRTOUT                                                 003600
*   THE DATA DEFINITIONS FOR THE INVENTORY FILE WORK AREA                     003700
INVWRKA   DS    0CL50                                                         003800
INVITNBR  DS    CL5                                                           003900
INVITDES  DS    CL20                                                          004000
          DS    CL5                                                           004100
INVPRICE  DS    CL5                                                           004200
INVORDPT  DS    CL5                                                           004300
INVONHND  DS    CL5                                                           004400
INVONORD  DS    CL5                                                           004500
*   THE DATA DEFINITIONS FOR THE PRINTER WORK AREA                            004600
PRTWRKA   DS    0CL132                                                        004700
PRTITNBR  DS    CL6                                                           004800
          DC    5C' '                                                         004900
PRTITDES  DS    CL20                                                          005000
          DC    4C' '                                                         005100
PRTPRICE  DS    CL7                                                           005200
          DC    4C' '                                                         005300
PRTAVAIL  DS    CL6                                                           005400
          DC    4C' '                                                         005500
PRTORDPT  DS    CL6                                                           005600
          DC    70C' '                                                        005700
*   THE DATA DEFINITIONS FOR OTHER REQUIRED WORK AREAS                        005800
SAVE      DS    18F                                                           005900
PATTERN1  DC    X'402020202020'                                               006000
PATTERN2  DC    X'4020202148 2020'                                            006100
WRKAVAIL  DS    PL3                                                           006200
WRKONORD  DS    PL3                                                           006300
WRKORDPT  DS    PL3                                                           006400
PACKAREA  DS    PL3                                                           006500
          END   BEGIN                                                         006600
```

Figure 5-3   The reorder-listing program

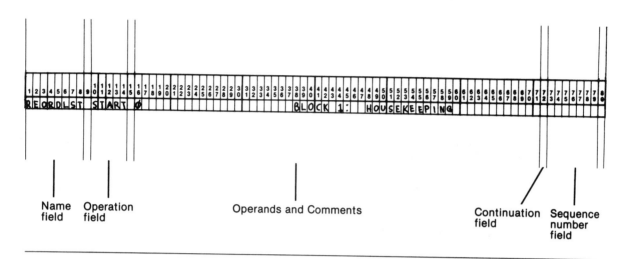

Figure 5-4   Format of an assembler language instruction

THE FORMAT OF AN ASSEMBLER LANGUAGE INSTRUCTION

Figure 5-4 presents the format of a typical line of code in assembler language. As you can see, each line of code can be broken down into six fields. Positions 1-8 contain the *label*, or *name*, field. This field can be used to give a symbolic name to a data field or an instruction. Thus, the instruction in the figure 5-4 has been given the name REORDLST.

Positions 10-14 contain the *operation* field. In this field, you code the mnemonic operation code of an instruction. In figure 5-4, the operation code is START.

Positions 16-71 contain the *operands* and *comments* fields. The operand or operands start in position 16. If there is more than one operand, they are separated by commas with no intervening blanks. In figure 5-4, the operand is 0.

After the operands, the programmer can code a comment in positions 16-71. However, the comment must be separated from the operands by one or more blanks. In figure 5-4, the comment is BLOCK 1: HOUSEKEEPING. Throughout the program in figure 5-3, comments are used to relate the assembler language code to the blocks in the flowchart in figure 5-2.

Column 72 of the coding line is used to indicate that an instruction is continued on the next line. Although most assembler language instructions must be written on one line, in a few cases it is necessary to use multiple lines. In figure 5-3, continuation codes are used in lines 3200 and 3500 to show that the instructions are continued on lines 3300 and 3600.

The last eight positions on a line, positions 73-80, can be used to identify and sequence the lines of the source program. Since most interactive program development systems provide automatic numbering capabilities, you don't usually have to sequence your own program. When the program is complete, you simply invoke the proper command and the program is numbered for you. In any case, positions 73-80 do not affect the resulting object program in any way.

FILE DEFINITIONS

For each file used by a program, there must be a *file definition*. These file definitions are referred to as *DCB (Data Control Block) statements*, or just *DCBs*. In the reorder-listing program, there is one DCB statement for the inventory master file, and one for the printer file. Although you may not be used to thinking of printer output as a file, you think of it that way in assembler language.

In the name portion of each DCB statement, you code a label that becomes the *filename* for the file. In the reorder-listing program, the inventory master file is named INVMAST; the printer file is named PRTOUT. When you code a filename, it must (1) start with a letter, (2) consist of only letters and numbers, and (3) be eight characters or less in length. As you will see later, this filename is used when coding I/O operations in the instruction portion of the program.

After the operation code are the operands that give the specific characteristics of a file. These are called *keyword operands*, because each operand consists of a *keyword* followed by an equals sign followed by programmer-supplied words.

The DCB operands

Figure 5-5 summarizes some of the most commonly used keywords of the DCB. If you compare the operands in these figures with those used in figure 5-3, I think you'll begin to understand what they specify.

DSORG   The DSORG operand indicates the organization of the data set being processed. For a sequential data set, you always code PS (Physical Sequential) no matter what device is used for the file.

RECFM   The RECFM operand tells what format the records in the file are in. They can be fixed-length (F), fixed-length blocked (FB), variable-length (V), and variable-length blocked (VB). For a printer file, you must also indicate whether you will be using ASA control characters for forms control (FA, FBA, VA, or VBA).

MACRF   The MACRF (macro form) operand indicates the form of the input or output instructions that will be coded for the file. For sequential files, you must specify whether the records will be read from the file using the GET instruction (G) and whether records will be written to the file using the PUT instruction (P). In this section of the book, all input files will be read using GET instructions and all output files will be written using PUT instructions, but you'll see other forms of I/O instructions in section 4.

Keyword	Programmer code	Remarks
DSORG	PS	Specifies the data set organization. PS for Physical Sequential is used for sequential disk files and for printer files.
RECFM	F, FA FB, FBA V, VBA	F is for fixed-length records; V for variable-length records. B indicates blocked records. A indicates that ASA control characters will be used for a print file. As a result, the most common code for a disk file is FB. The most common code for a print file is FA or FBA.
MACRF	GM, GL PM, PL	Specifies whether GET (G) or PUT (P) macros will be used for the file and whether the records will be processed in move (M) or locate (L) mode.
BLKSIZE	Block length	The block length for a file.
LRECL	Record length	The record length for a file. If fixed-length records aren't blocked, the record length will equal the block size.
DDNAME	DD name	This name must be the same as the ddname in the DD job control statement for the file.
EODAD	Instruction label	The label or address of the first instruction of the end-of-file (or end-of-data-set) routine.

Figure 5-5   DCB operand summary

When you code the MACRF operand, you must also indicate whether you will be using *move* (M) or *locate* (L) *mode* when you read and write the records. For example, for the inventory file in figure 5-3, I have coded GM to indicate that a GET instruction in move mode will be used for this file. For the printer file, I have coded PM to indicate that a PUT instruction in move mode will be used. In this chapter, you'll only learn how to use move mode. Then, in chapter 7, you'll learn how to use locate mode.

BLKSIZE   In chapter 1, you learned that records in a sequential file are usually blocked to increase program and storage efficiency. But, whether records are blocked or unblocked, the BLKSIZE operand specifies the length of each block of data. When a file contains unblocked records, the block size is equal to the length of a single record. Since the program in figure 5-3 processes an input file with unblocked records, the block size for the inventory file is 50.

LRECL   The LRECL operand specifies the length of a logical record. If the records in a file of fixed-length records are unblocked, the length is the same as the length coded in the BLKSIZE operand.

DDNAME   As you might guess, the entry here corresponds to the ddname used in the DD job control statement for the file. The ddname must consist of eight characters or less and start with a letter. Allowable characters are the letters, the digits, and the national characters (@, $, and #).

EODAD   The EODAD operand is required for an input file so a branch will take place when the end of the input file is reached. Then, when the end-of-file condition occurs during the execution of a GET instruction, the program branches to the label given in this operand. In figure 5-3, the program will branch to INVEOF when the end of the inventory file is reached.

DATA DEFINITIONS

Data definitions are used to give symbolic names to the fields in storage. The symbolic names can then be used as operands in the instructions of the program. In general, the programmer writes data definitions for the work areas required by the files and for any other areas or fields required by the program. These definitions are called *work areas* or *work fields*.

The disk file's work area

The data definitions for the disk file's work area in figure 5-3 (lines 3800-4500) follow:

```
INVWRKA  DS    0CL50
INVITNBR DS    CL5
INVITDES DS    CL20
         DS    CL5
INVPRICE DS    CL5
INVORDPT DS    CL5
INVONHND DS    CL5
INVONORD DS    CL5
```

For all of the coding lines, the operation code DS (Define Storage) is used. In positions 1-8 of the statements, names are given to the fields. These names must (1) start with a letter, (2) consist entirely of letters and numbers, and (3) be eight characters or less in length.

The first coding line assigns the name INVWRKA to the entire work area. Then, the next eight coding lines define fields within this 50-byte area. The name for this work area will be coded in the input instruction to cause the data in the record to be placed in this 50-byte area.

When creating names, you should try to make them as easy as possible to remember and use. Thus, I have given the name INVWRKA to the inventory (INV) work (WRK) area (A) and the name INVITNBR to the item-number field in the inventory record.

The operand for each DS statement has three parts: (1) a *duplication factor*, (2) a *type code*, and (3) a *length modifier*. In the statement

```
INVWRKA  DS    0CL50
```

the duplication factor is 0, the type code is C for EBCDIC (or character) data, and the length modifier is L50 indicating a length of 50 bytes.

A duplication factor of zero simply means that the fields that follow are within the area being defined. Since INVWRKA has a length of 50, the zero duplication factor means that the DS statements for the next 50 bytes are within the work area. Thus, INVITNBR, INVITDES, and so on, are within the work area.

When the duplication factor is omitted, it is assumed to be one. Thus,

```
INVITNBR DS        CL5
```

defines a field named INVITNBR that is five bytes long, should receive EBCDIC data, and is bytes 1-5 of the area named INVWRKA. Similarly, the remaining fields in the work area are defined so they correspond to the fields in the record layout for the input records. Since characters 26-30 of the record (the unit-cost field) aren't used by the program, bytes 26-30 of the work area aren't named.

The printer work area

The printer work area in the reorder-listing program is defined in lines 4700-5700 like this:

```
PRTWRKA   DS     0CL132
PRTITNBR  DS     CL6
          DC     5C' '
PRTITDES  DS     CL20
          DC     4C' '
PRTPRICE  DS     CL7
          DC     4C' '
PRTAVAIL  DS     CL6
          DC     4C' '
PRTORDPT  DS     CL6
          DC     70C' '
```

Here, the name given to the work area will be coded in the output instruction to cause the data to be written to the printer file. Since the duplication factor is 0 and the length modifier is L132, the next 132 character positions are within the print work area.

These definitions use the operation code DS as well as the operation code DC, which stands for Define Constant. The DC statement is coded in the same manner as a DS except that a value is also given to the field. This value is given between apostrophes (or single quotation marks) following the length modifier. This value is called the *nominal value*.

The first five bytes of the work area are defined as:

```
PRTITNBR DS     CL6
```

This field is given a length of 6 bytes rather than the 5 bytes indicated by the print chart because the edit pattern for item number requires 6 bytes. You'll see in a moment how this works.

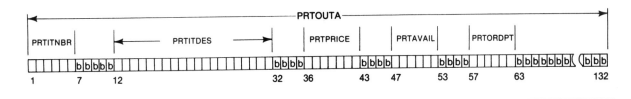

Figure 5-6   The printer work area

The five bytes following PRTITNBR are defined by this DC statement:

```
DC      5C' '
```

Here, no length modifier is given so the length is derived from the nominal value. Since one blank is coded between the apostrophes, the nominal value has a length of one and the length factor is assumed to be one. Since the duplication factor is five, this one-byte blank is duplicated five times. As a result, there will be five blanks between the item-number and item-description fields. This, of course, corresponds to the spacing indicated by the print chart in figure 5-1. An alternate way to code this operand is

```
DC      C'       '
```

which means a duplication factor of one and a length factor of five taken from the nominal value.

The remaining DS and DC statements in the printer work area are defined in a similar manner. Thus, PRTITDES is a 20-byte field followed by four blanks. Then, PRTPRICE is a 7-byte field followed by four blanks; and so on. The PRTPRICE, PRTAVAIL, and PRTORDPT fields are one byte longer than indicated by the print chart so the edit patterns for these fields will fit properly. The last DC for this area has an operand of 70C'b' (where b is one blank), so 70 blanks fill out the area. In figure 5-6, the names assigned to the work area are shown schematically.

Work fields

The last series of data definitions (lines 5900-6500) are for various work fields used by the program. They use the type codes F for fullword, X for hexadecimal, and P for packed decimal. For example,

```
SAVE    DS      18F
```

defines 18 fullwords of storage. Here, no length modifier is needed because a fullword is always four bytes.

Next, this code

```
PATTERN1 DC      X'402020202020'
```

defines a constant named PATTERN1 with a length of six containing the hex codes

```
40 20 20 20 20 20
```

When the type code X is used, two hex characters in the nominal value represent one byte of storage.

Similarly,

```
WRKAVAIL DS      PL3
```

defines a three-byte field named WRKAVAIL that should receive five digits of packed-decimal data. When a DC is used for a packed field, the nominal value is a decimal number with or without a leading plus or minus sign. The numeric value is then placed in the field in proper packed decimal format.

One type of code not shown that you may find useful is Z, which stands for zoned decimal. In a DC for a zoned decimal field, you code a decimal number, with or without a sign, as its nominal value. Then, the numeric value is stored in the field in proper zoned decimal format.

Although these examples should give you a good idea of how to code DS and DC statements, there are some other points you should become familiar with. First, you can give an implied length to a DS statement by using a nominal value just as you can with a DC statement. Thus,

```
INVITNBR DS      C'99999'
```

defines a five-byte field named INVITNBR. This is sometimes done deliberately to show how large a number a field can hold, but more often it happens when you code DS instead of DC by mistake. You must realize, then, that the DS statement is assembled, but no value is placed in the field.

Second, you can use a zero duplication factor to define subfields within fields as well as fields within areas. Thus,

```
DATE     DS      0CL6
MONTH    DS      CL2
DAY      DS      CL2
YEAR     DS      CL2
```

defines two-byte month, day, and year fields within a six-byte date field. The date field in turn can be part of a work area, so that as many levels of subdefinitions as are needed can be coded in assembler language. This is explained more fully in chapter 7.

Third, you should be aware that *padding* and *truncation* can occur when you code a DC statement. For zoned, packed, or hex fields, padding occurs to the left with zero values, as in these examples:

Source code			Resulting field in hex			
DC	Z'15'				F1	F5
DC	ZL4'15'		F0	F0	F1	F5
DC	P'15'				01	5C
DC	PL3'315'			00	31	5C
DC	XL3'0F'			00	00	0F

For character fields, padding occurs to the right with blanks, as in these examples:

Source code			Resulting field in hex				
DC	C'A'		C1				
DC	CL3'A'		C1	40	40		
DC	CL6'NAME'		D5	C1	D4	C5	40	40
DC	CL5' '		40	40	40	40	40

Similarly, truncation occurs on the left for zoned, packed, or hex fields, as in these examples:

Source code			Resulting field in hex			
DC	ZL2'-132'				F3	D2
DC	PL1'+12'					2C
DC	PL3'400382			00	38	2C
DC	XL2'140FB12C'				B1	2C

And, truncation occurs on the right for character fields, as in these examples:

Source code			Resulting field in hex		
DC	CL3'NAME'		D5	C1	D4
DC	CL1'YES'		E8		

Although padding is used intentionally by assembler language programmers, truncation usually results from a programming error. As a result, although you wouldn't intentionally code a DC statement for truncation, you should know what will happen if you do it by error.

Finally, you should know that you can't just code an apostrophe (') or an ampersand (&) in a DS or DC statement. To code a character constant containing one of these characters, you must code two ampersands or two apostrophes in the nominal value for each one you want. For instance,

```
DC    C'A''B'
```

defines a three-byte field containing the characters A'B. The DC statement

```
DC    CL5'S && R'
```

defines a five-byte field containing S & R.

INSTRUCTIONS   The instructions of this program are found in the first 30 lines. They correspond to the program flowchart in figure 5-2. In the comment field for the first instruction of a flowchart block, you'll find a comment that relates the code to the flowchart. When you use a flowchart as a design document, you use the flowchart as a guide for coding the instructions of the program.

The housekeeping routine

All assembler language programs start with some sort of *housekeeping routine* (or *initialization routine*). In the program in figure 5-3, the first seven instructions represent the housekeeping block of the flowchart. Not including the comments, these instructions are:

```
REORDLST  START  0
BEGIN     SAVE   (14,12)
          BALR   3,0
          USING  *,3
          ST     13,SAVE+4
          LA     13,SAVE
          OPEN   (INVMAST,INPUT,PRTOUT,OUTPUT)
```

Before I describe each of the individual instructions in detail, you should understand the three basic functions that must be performed in a standard MVS housekeeping routine. First, the housekeeping routine must provide *standard MVS program linkage*. This is done by the combination of the SAVE, ST, and LA instructions. Second, it must load and identify the base register for the program; the BALR and USING instructions perform this task. Third, it must make any preparations that are required by the main processing routine of the program. In the reorder-listing program, only the OPEN instruction is required for this function.

Standard program linkage   A basic feature of standard MVS program linkage is a *register save/restore technique*. It means that when one program passes control to another program, as when the MVS supervisor program passes control to the reorder-listing program, the contents of the 16 general purpose registers are stored, or *saved*. Then, when control is passed back to the supervisor at the end of the reorder-listing program's processing, the registers are reloaded, or *restored*, with the contents that were saved. This allows the supervisor to resume processing with undisturbed registers.

This standard save/restore technique is used in all MVS programs. Figure 5-7 illustrates how this standard linkage relates a program like the reorder-listing program to the MVS supervisor. Before the supervisor passes control to the reorder-listing program, it loads the address (LA) of its save area (SAVE) into register 13. Then, when the reorder-listing program gets control, the first operation it performs is to store the contents of the registers in the supervisor's save area. To do this, it uses the SAVE instruction. Next, the reorder-listing program stores the address of the supervisor's save area in register 13 in the second word of its own save

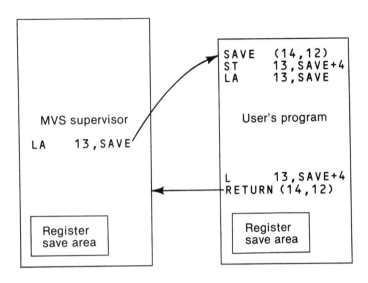

Figure 5-7   Standard program linkage under MVS

area (SAVE+4). Last, it loads the address of its own save area in register 13. Then, if the reorder-listing program calls a subprogram, the subprogram can use register 13 to save the contents of the registers in the reorder-listing program's save area.

The restore half of the technique is performed when a program returns control to the supervisor. Using the example in figure 5-7 again, before the reorder-listing program returns control to the MVS supervisor, it loads the contents of SAVE+4 into register 13. This means that register 13 contains the address of the supervisor's save area. Then, the reorder-listing program restores the registers from the supervisor's save area using the RETURN instruction. The RETURN instruction not only restores the registers, but it also returns control to the supervisor.

After you read the descriptions of the housekeeping and end-of-job routines in this topic, you should have a better idea of how standard program linkage works under MVS. However, you shouldn't expect to fully understand it until you finish chapter 8. In the meantime, you must code the required linkage just as it's described in this topic in each of your assembler language programs.

START   The first instruction of the housekeeping routine doesn't cause any object code to be assembled. It is one of several *assembler commands* that the programmer uses to control the assembly of his program. The START command signals the assembler that the source code is starting and tells the assembler the address at which the object code should start. Since the object program will be loaded into storage at a different address than the one specified in the START command, zero is the easiest value to use in the START command.

The name given for the START instruction becomes the *program name*. In this case, the program name is REORDLST. A name for the START instruction, or any other instruction, is formed by using the same rules as those used for field names: (1) a name must start with a letter; (2) it must use only letters and numbers; (3) it must be eight characters or less in length.

SAVE   The SAVE instruction is a *macro instruction* (or just *macro*) which means that more than one object instruction is assembled from it. Actually, the assembler first converts the macro into two or more source instructions; then, it converts the source instructions into object instructions. In contrast to macro instructions, only *one* object instruction is assembled from each machine instruction.

In the standard housekeeping sequence, the SAVE macro is always coded immediately following the START instruction. It generates a machine instruction that causes the contents of 15 of the 16 general purpose registers (all except register 13) to be stored in the register save area of the MVS supervisor program. The storage address of this save area has been placed in register 13 by the supervisor.

The operand of the SAVE macro specifies the range of registers to be stored. Although the operand can be coded for any range, you should code it as shown in figure 5-3 in all your housekeeping routines: (14,12). This means that fifteen registers, beginning with register 14 and proceeding with registers 15, 0, 1, 2, 3, and so on through register 12, will be stored in the save area whose address has been placed in register 13. (Notice that the register sequence automatically "wraps around" from 15 to 0.)

BALR   The branch-and-link-register instruction is the first *machine instruction* of the reorder-listing program. When it is assembled, one machine-language instruction will result from it.

The BALR instruction has two operands: 3 and 0. In chapter 4, you learned that the BALR instruction causes the address of the next instruction to be placed in operand-1 (in this case, register 3). Also, if the register specified by operand-2 is 0 (as in this case), no branching takes place and the program continues with the next instruction. If, for example, this program is loaded starting at address 5200, the BALR instruction will occupy bytes 5200-5201. Then, when the BALR instruction is executed, address 5202 will be stored in register 3, and the program will continue with the next instruction in sequence.

The purpose of this BALR instruction is to store a base address in a base register. Thus, register 3 will be used as the base register for this program. If a program is loaded into storage and a proper address is not loaded into the base register used by the program, the program will not execute as intended. As a result, a BALR instruction with zero for operand-2 is normally the first machine instruction of a program.

USING   A USING instruction is another assembler command. As a result, it generates no object code. Instead, it tells the assembler program which register is going to be used as the base register. The first operand (in this case, *) tells the assembler at which point in the program the base register should start being used. The second operand (in this case, 3) tells the assembler which register to use as the base register. Since * means "at this point" or "starting now," the USING statement of the reorder-listing program tells the assembler to use register 3 as the base register for all addresses following the USING statement. Since the preceding BALR instruction has already stored the address of the next instruction in register 3, the USING statement and BALR instruction are properly coordinated.

The BALR and USING instructions, coded as shown, are the standard method of loading and specifying the base register. Therefore, you will have similar instructions at the start of each of your programs. Since registers 0, 1, 2, 13, 14, and 15 are used by various programs of MVS, these registers are generally not used as base registers. Instead, registers 3 through 12 are used. More specifically, it is a common practice to use registers 3, 4, and 5 for base registers and registers 6 through 12 for other register operations. That's why we recommend that you use register 3 as the first base register of your programs.

A single base register can accommodate a program of up to 4096 bytes since the maximum displacement value is 4095 bytes. If a program is larger than this, additional base registers must be loaded and assigned. The coding required to load and specify multiple base registers is explained in the next chapter.

Store (ST)   This is the operation code for the store-register instruction. It is part of the standard program linkage and causes the contents of the register named as the first operand to be stored in the four-byte area addressed by the second operand. In this case, the contents of register 13 are to be stored in the area that is four bytes beyond the address assigned to the symbol SAVE; that is, SAVE+4. The effect of this instruction is to store the address of the supervisor's save area in bytes 5 through 8 of the reorder-listing program's own save area. Thus, the address of the supervisor's save area is stored for later use in restoring the contents of the registers before returning control to the supervisor.

Load address (LA)   The load-address instruction loads the storage address of the field named as the second operand into the register named as the first operand. In this case, the instruction loads the address of the reorder-listing program's own save area into register 13. Then, if the reorder-listing program branches to a subprogram, the subprogram can use this address to store the contents of registers 14 through 12. This instruction, always coded as shown, completes the standard linkage.

OPEN   The OPEN instruction is another macro instruction. An OPEN instruction must be executed before an input file can be read or an output file written. You can think of opening a file as checking to be sure the device is ready to operate. For an input file on disk, the OPEN instruction also checks to make sure the appropriate file is available to the program.

The operands of the OPEN macro must consist of paired entries for each file to be opened as follows:

```
OPEN (DCBname,option,DCBname,option,...)
```

The first entry in an operand pair must be the filename coded as the label of the DCB macro for the file. The second entry indicates how the file will be processed. In the reorder-listing program, INVMAST is opened as INPUT, and PRTOUT is opened as OUTPUT.

The mainline routine

The *mainline routine* is the part of a program that accomplishes the main processing of the program. It is usually a loop that includes input, processing, and output. In the flowchart in figure 5-2, blocks 2 through 6, including branching back to connector circle 1, make up the mainline routine.

Flowchart block 2   The first instruction of the mainline routine is:

```
READINV  GET    INVMAST,INVWRKA
```

The GET instruction is a macro instruction that causes a record to be read into storage. The first operand of the GET instruction names the DCB that describes the file to be read. The second operand, if present, names the work area in which the record is to be placed.

When an input command, such as a GET, is executed, a record or block of records is read into storage from the file and the data is placed in a *buffer area* supplied by the MVS supervisor program. A *buffer* is the MVS term for an input/output area. Then, depending on the mode of the input instruction, the next record to be processed is either moved to a program work area (move mode) or is left in the buffer with the address of the buffer placed in register 1 (locate mode).

As I mentioned earlier in this chapter, the mode of an input instruction is determined by the MACRF operand in the DCB. For the GET instruction, it can be coded MACRF=GM to indicate move mode or MACRF=GL to indicate locate mode. In the reorder-listing program, I coded MACRF=GM for the inventory file. As a result, when the GET instruction is executed, it moves the next record to be processed into the 50-byte work area named by the second operand of the GET instruction, INVWRKA.

Incidentally, MVS automatically provides dual buffer areas so I/O operations and CPU operations can be overlapped. I explained the concept of this in chapter 4. In other words, you don't have to provide any special code in your assembler language program to facilitate overlap. It's done for you by MVS.

The GET instruction corresponds to block 2 of the flowchart. Because the DCB for the inventory file specifies EODAD=INVEOF, the GET instruction will cause a branch to the instruction named INVEOF when the end-of-file condition is reached. The flowline out of block 2 in the flowchart represents this branching. As you can see in the listing in figure 5-3, INVEOF is the name given to the instruction coded in line 2800.

Flowchart block 3   The coding for block 3 of the flowchart indicates that the available inventory amount should be calculated. The program does this as follows:

```
PACK    WRKAVAIL,INVONHND
PACK    WRKONORD,INVONORD
AP      WRKAVAIL,WRKONORD
```

In other words, the input field named INVONHND is packed into the work field named WRKAVAIL; the input field named INVONORD is packed into the work field named WRKONORD; and WRKONORD is added to WRKAVAIL (which contains the value of the on-hand field). After the three instructions are executed, WRKAVAIL contains the available amount (on-hand plus on-order). You should realize that the names used as operands in these instructions must be identical to the names given in the data definitions.

Flowchart block 4   Block 4 of the flowchart is a decision block that tests whether the available amount is less than the reorder point. Its instructions are:

```
PACK    WRKORDPT,INVORDPT
CP      WRKAVAIL,WRKORDPT
BNL     READINV
```

Because the compare decimal (CP) instruction is used to compare available and reorder point, the reorder-point field (INVORDPT) must be packed before comparison. Then, WRKAVAIL and WRKORDPT are compared, and the condition code is set based on this comparison.

The third instruction of this decision block is a branch instruction. However, the instruction doesn't specify a mask for branching as described in chapter 4. Instead, it uses a mnemonic operation code that tells the assembler what the mask should be. These codes are summarized in figure 5-8. For instance, operation code B specifies an unconditional branch; operation code BE, following a compare instruction, specifies a branch when operand-1 equals operand-2; and BP, following an arithmetic operation, specifies a branch if the result is positive. You should realize that all of the operation codes in figure 5-8 cause one branch-on-condition instruction to be assembled, but the mask differs, depending on the operation code.

Type	Code	Meaning
Unconditional	B	Branch unconditionally
After compare instructions	BH	Branch on A high
	BL	Branch on A low
	BE	Branch on A equal B
	BNH	Branch on A not high
	BNL	Branch on A not low
	BNE	Branch on A not equal B
After arithmetic instructions	BO	Branch on overflow
	BP	Branch on plus
	BM	Branch on minus
	BZ	Branch on zero
	BNP	Branch on not plus
	BNM	Branch on not minus
	BNZ	Branch on not zero

Figure 5-8   Mnemonic codes for branch operations

In the reorder-listing program,

```
BNL    READINV
```

means that the program should branch to the instruction named READINV if WRKAVAIL is not less than WRKORDPT. If WRKAVAIL is less than WRKORDPT, the program continues with the next instruction in sequence.

This branching could also be coded this way:

```
BH     READINV
BE     READINV
```

In this case, if available is greater than reorder point, a branch to READINV takes place. If not, the second branch instruction is executed. Then, if available is equal to reorder point, the branch to READINV takes place. If not, the next instruction in sequence is executed.

Incidentally, the branch-on-condition instruction can also be coded by using a decimal number that represents the mask. For instance, this instruction

```
BC     15,READINV
```

gives a mask of decimal 15 (hex F, or binary 1111) so it is an unconditional branch to the instruction named READINV. Similarly, if operand-1 is an 8 (hex 8, or binary 1000), the branch only takes place if the first bit in the condition code is on. Following a compare decimal instruction,

```
BC     8,READINV
```

has the same effect as

```
BE      READINV
```

By using a decimal number from 0 through 15, any mask can be coded so the instruction can branch on any combination of condition codes. This form of coding is rarely used, however, since codes like BE, BH, and BNL are so much easier to use.

Flowchart block 5   Block 5 in the flowchart says "construct detail line." This means arrange the data in the printer work area in a form suitable for printing. This normally involves moving alphanumeric fields into the work area and editing numeric fields into the work area so that leading zeros are suppressed and commas and decimal points are inserted wherever needed.

Lines 1500-2500 represent this block of processing. For instance, the first three instructions following the branch instruction edit the item-number field into the printer work area:

```
PACK    PACKAREA,INVITNBR
MVC     PRTITNBR,PATTERN1
ED      PRTITNBR,PACKAREA
```

In the first instruction, the five-byte input field is packed into the three-byte work field named PACKAREA. Then, the hex pattern 402020202020 is moved into the first six bytes of the printer work area. Finally, the packed item number is edited into the pattern thus suppressing lead zeros.

The next instruction moves the item-description field, unchanged, into the printer work area. Then, the next seven instructions edit the unit price, available, and reorder point fields. Since available and reorder point are already in packed form, they do not need to be packed before editing. In all cases, an edit pattern is moved into the appropriate work field before the edit instruction is executed.

Flowchart block 6   Block 6 of the flowchart is an output block. It indicates that a line should be printed on the output listing. The instruction representing this block is:

```
PUT    PRTOUT,PRTWRKA
```

The PUT instruction is a macro instruction that causes output. Because the device is a printer, one line is printed each time the PUT is executed, and single spacing takes place.

As you might guess, the PUT instruction is much like the GET instruction. The first operand is the label of the DCB statement that describes the output file. The second operand, if present, names the work area from which the record is to be written.

Again, you can use either move mode or locate mode for a PUT instruction by specifying MACRF=PM or MACRF=PL in the DCB for the file. In the reorder-listing program, I specified MACRF=PM for the printer file. So, when a record is written to the printer, it is written from the work area named by the second operand of the PUT instruction, PRTWRKA.

As I explained in chapter 2, most print files are not written directly to the printer. Instead, they are spooled to disk files so they can be printed later on. In either case, MVS automatically provides for dual buffer areas and overlap. Whether or not spooling is used, you code the DCB and the PUT macros for a file just as I've done in figure 5-3. MVS will take care of everything else.

The connector circle   The final instruction of the mainline routine is:

```
B       READINV
```

This means an unconditional branch to the instruction named READINV is executed. It corresponds to the flowline leading to the connector circle on the flowchart. As a result, the program repeats the processing for the next record in the inventory file.

The end-of-job routine

An assembler language program normally ends with an *end-of-job routine,* or *EOJ routine.* At the least, this routine closes the files used by the program, restores the registers in the previous program's save area, and returns control of the system to the supervisor.

The end-of-job routine for the reorder-listing program is:

```
INVEOF  CLOSE (INVMAST,,PRTOUT)
        L     13,SAVE+4
        RETURN (14,12)
```

Since the name INVEOF is given for the keyword EODAD in the DCB for the input file, these instructions are executed when the end-of-file condition for the inventory master file is reached.

CLOSE   The CLOSE instruction parallels the OPEN instruction. It's a macro instruction that closes the files to further processing. The operands for the CLOSE macro are the same as for the OPEN macro:

```
CLOSE (DCBname,option,DCBname,option,...)
```

For most types of files, however, the option parameter doesn't have to be coded, but its absence must be indicated by coding two consecutive commas:

```
CLOSE (DCBname,,DCBname,,...)
```

The option parameter for the last DCB name in the list can be omitted entirely, though, including the commas.

Load (L) and RETURN   The last two statements of this end-of-job routine are related to the standard MVS program linkage at the beginning of the program. They form the restore half of the register save/restore technique that I discussed earlier. The load instruction reloads the address of the supervisor's save area into register 13 from where it was stored in the reorder-listing program's own register save area, at address SAVE+4. Then, the RETURN macro restores the contents of registers 14 through 12 from the area whose address is in register 13 and branches back to the supervisor. Since the address of the supervisor's save area was just placed in register 13, the effect of the RETURN macro is to reload the register contents that were stored by the SAVE macro in the initialization routine at the beginning of the program and to return control to the MVS supervisor.

As in the SAVE macro, the operand of the RETURN macro can specify any range of registers. It should, however, always specify the same registers as the SAVE macro with which it is paired. Notice that the RETURN macro has a six-character operation code, so you must start its operands in position 17, not 16, of the source statement.

The END instruction

The last instruction in an assembler language source program must always be the END instruction. It, like the START instruction, is an assembler command. It tells the assembler that there is no more source code and its operand tells the assembler where program execution should begin. In most cases, the operand is the name of the SAVE instruction that saves the general registers at the start of the program since this is the first executable instruction of the program.

In figure 5-3, the END instruction for the reorder-listing program specifies BEGIN as the operand since that's the first executable instruction of the program. However, it could also specify REORDLST. Since the START instruction generates no machine instructions, it has the same address as the SAVE instruction that follows it.

DISCUSSION

As you can see from this example, you actually write three types of instructions when you code an assembler language program: assembler commands, machine instructions, and macro instructions. In addition, you code file definitions and data definitions. As you code, you give names to all DCBs and to the data fields and instructions that are referred to by other instructions. These names are then used as operands in the instructions that refer to them.

In figure 5-3, the instructions are coded first followed by the file definitions followed by the data definitions. However, you don't have to put them in your program in that sequence because the assembler doesn't require any specific order. As a result, it is also common to code the file definitions first, the instructions second, and the data definitions last. If you don't code the instructions first, though, be sure your END instruction gives the label of the first executable instruction of the program. For the sake of efficiency, we recommend that you use the order shown in the reorder-listing program or the common variation I've just described.

By comparing assembler language code with the machine instructions presented in chapter 4, you can see how assembler language aids the programmer. First, by using symbolic names for files, data, and instructions, the programmer doesn't have to keep track of addresses and length codes. Second, by using mnemonic operation codes, the programmer doesn't have to remember hex operation codes. Third, by using macros, many machine instructions can be assembled from a single line of assembler language coding.

On the other hand, if you've used a higher-level language than assembler language, you can also see the limitations of assembler language. If, for example, you were to compare the program in figure 5-3 with a COBOL program for the same specifications, you would find the differences quite striking. First, operations that require only one statement in COBOL require two or more instructions in assembler language. Second, because you use English verbs like READ and ADD in your COBOL programs and because your data names can be up to 31 characters in length, COBOL is much easier to read than assembler language. Finally, it's obvious that the assembler language programmer has to know far more about the operations of a CPU than the COBOL programmer.

At this point, you should understand all of the code in the program in figure 5-3, except for the code related to standard MVS program linkage. Although you should have a basic understanding of how this linkage works, you won't understand it completely until you finish chapter 8. In the meantime, we recommend that you code this linkage mechanically, just as it's coded in figure 5-3.

Terminology

Basic Assembler Language
BAL
subset
comment line
label
name
operation
operand
comment
file definition
DCB statement
Data Control Block statement
DCB
filename
keyword operand
keyword
move mode
locate mode
data definition

work area
work field
duplication factor
type code
length modifier
nominal value
padding
truncation
housekeeping routine
initialization routine
standard MVS program linkage
register save/restore technique
save
restore
assembler command
program name
macro instruction
macro
machine instruction
mainline routine
buffer area
buffer
end-of-job routine
EOJ routine

Objectives

1. Given the program listing in figure 5-3 and samples of input data, describe the execution of any instruction or group of instructions in the program.

2. Given descriptions of storage areas or fields, code acceptable data definitions for them using C, Z, P, or X type codes.

TOPIC 2   Refining the reorder-listing program

The reorder-listing program in topic 1 presented the essential components of an assembler language program. In actual practice, though, even the simplest of programs would be much more complex than that reorder-listing program. As a result, this topic presents an enhanced version of the reorder-listing program. By the time you complete this topic, you will have learned an introductory subset of assembler language. You will then be able to develop simple programs of your own in assembler language.

Figure 5-9 shows an expanded print chart for the reorder-listing program. As you can see, a three-line heading is required at the top of each page of the reorder listing. Also, a count of the number of records in the input file is to be printed at the end of the listing. Otherwise, the specifications for this refined reorder-listing program are like those in figure 5-1.

A flowchart for this refined reorder-listing program is shown in figure 5-10. If you compare this with the flowchart in figure 5-2, you can see that the additional blocks on the enhanced flowchart provide for printing the heading lines and the count line. If more than 50 detail lines are printed on one page of the reorder listing, the form is skipped to the top of the next page and the headings are printed again.

Figure 5-11 shows the complete program for the refined reorder-listing program. This program not only provides for the enhanced printing requirements, but also for the use of blocked disk records. For efficiency, blocked disk records are normally used in production programs. If you review the program in figure 5-11, you can see that comments are used in many of the instructions to describe what the instructions do.

Coding one operand per line in your DCBs

Because it's difficult to read a DCB when several operands are coded in a single line, DCBs are often coded with one operand per line. This is illustrated by the DCBs in the program in figure 5-11. For example, the DCB for the inventory file is written like this:

```
INVMAST   DCB     DSORG=PS,                        X
                  RECFM=FB,                        X
                  MACRF=GM,                        X
                  BLKSIZE=500,                     X
                  LRECL=50,                        X
                  DDNAME=INVMAST,                  X
                  EODAD=INVEOF
```

When you code a DCB in this way, you must be sure that (1) the operands are separated only after commas, (2) a continuation character like X is coded in position 72 on every line preceding a continuation line, and (3) all continuation lines start in position 16.

Record Name			
	REORDER LISTING		
Heading-Line-1			
Heading-Line-2	ITEM	ITEM	UNIT	REORDER
Heading-Line-3	NO.	DESCRIPTION	PRICE AVAILABLE	POINT
Detail Line	XXXXX	XXXXXXXXXXXXXXXXXXXXX	XXX.XX XXXXXX	XXXXX
	XXXXX	XXXXXXXXXXXXXXXXXXXXX	XXX.XX XXXXXX	XXXXX
	XXXXX	XXXXXXXXXXXXXXXXXXXXX	XXX.XX XXXXXX	XXXXX
	XXXXX	XXXXXXXXXXXXXXXXXXXXX	XXX.XX XXXXXX	XXXXX
	XXXXX	XXXXXXXXXXXXXXXXXXXXX	XXX.XX XXXXXX	XXXXX
Count Line	XX,XXX RECORDS IN THE FILE		

Figure 5-9   The print chart for the refined reorder-listing program

When you code DCBs in this way, it's easier to modify the operands and the code is easier to read so this is a worthwhile coding practice. We also recommend that you code the operands in your DCBs in the same sequence every time since this too makes your code easier to read. In the rest of the programs in this book, we always code the operands in the same basic order with one operand per coding line.

Providing for blocked records

Look at the operands for the disk file's DCB in figure 5-11. The BLKSIZE operand specifies 500 bytes; the LRECL operand specifies 50 bytes; and the RECFM operand specifies fixed-length, blocked records (FB). This means that the 50-byte records are blocked with 10 records to a block.

This is the only coding that is required for processing blocked records under MVS. Then, whenever a GET instruction is executed for the disk file, the next record to be processed is moved from a buffer area into the work area specified in the instruction. As a result, you don't have to keep track of which record in which buffer is next to be processed. The assembler and its I/O modules take care of that for you. All you have to realize is that the next record is always available in the work area just as though the records weren't blocked.

Now, look at the operands for the printer's DCB in figure 5-11. The BLKSIZE operand specifies 1330 bytes; the LRECL operand specifies 133 bytes; and the RECFM operand specifies FBA. This means that the 133-byte records are blocked with a blocking factor of 10. Remember that print files are normally spooled to a disk file before printing, so these files are commonly blocked. Here again, though, MVS handles the blocking for you, so all you have to do is construct the next record to be printed in the work area of the print file before you issue the next PUT instruction for the file.

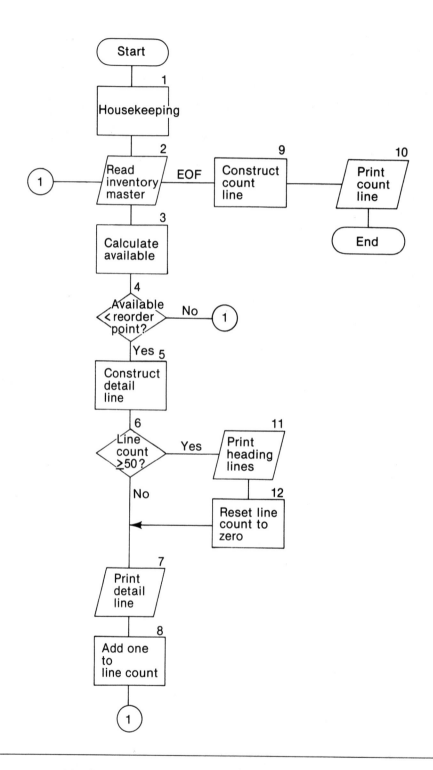

Figure 5-10   The flowchart for the refined reorder-listing program

```
REORDLST START 0                                                              000100
BEGIN     SAVE  (14,12)                  SAVE REGISTERS                       000200
          BALR  3,0                       LOAD BASE REGISTER                  000300
          USING *,3                                                           000400
          ST    13,SAVE+4                 STORE OLD SAVE AREA ADDRESS         000500
          LA    13,SAVE                   LOAD NEW SAVE AREA ADDRESS          000600
          OPEN  (INVMAST,INPUT,PRTOUT,OUTPUT)                                 000700
READINV   GET   INVMAST,INVWRKA           READ RECORD INTO WORK AREA         000800
          AP    COUNT,=P'1'               ADD ONE TO COUNT                   000900
          PACK  WRKAVAIL,INVONHND                                            001000
          PACK  WRKONORD,INVONORD                                            001100
          AP    WRKAVAIL,WRKONORD         ADD ON HAND AND ON ORDER           001200
          PACK  WRKORDPT,INVORDPT                                            001300
          CP    WRKAVAIL,WRKORDPT         COMPARE AVAILABLE, REORDER POINT   001400
          BNL   READINV                                                      001500
          PACK  PACKAREA,INVITNBR                                            001600
          MVC   PRTITNBR,PATTERN1                                            001700
          ED    PRTITNBR,PACKAREA         EDIT ITEM NUMBER FIELD             001800
          MVC   PRTITDES,INVITDES         MOVE ITEM DESCRIPTION              001900
          PACK  PACKAREA,INVPRICE                                            002000
          MVC   PRTPRICE,PATTERN2                                            002100
          ED    PRTPRICE,PACKAREA         EDIT UNIT PRICE                    002200
          MVC   PRTAVAIL,PATTERN1                                            002300
          ED    PRTAVAIL,WRKAVAIL         EDIT AVAILABLE                     002400
          MVC   PRTORDPT,PATTERN1                                            002500
          ED    PRTORDPT,WRKORDPT         EDIT ORDER POINT                   002600
          CP    LINECNT,=P'50'            COMPARE LINE COUNT TO 50           002700
          BL    PRTDET                    BRANCH ON LOW TO PRTDET            002800
          PUT   PRTOUT,HDGLINE1           PRINT FIRST HEADONG LINE           002900
          PUT   PRTOUT,HDGLINE2           PRINT SECOND HEADING LINE          003000
          PUT   PRTOUT,HDGLINE3           PRINT THIRD HEADING LINE           003100
          ZAP   LINECNT,=P'0'             RESET LINE COUNT TO ZERO           003200
          MVI   PRTDCTL,C'0'              MOVE ZERO TO ASA CONTROL BYTE      003300
PRTDET    PUT   PRTOUT,PRTDETL            PRINT DETAIL LINE                  003400
          AP    LINECNT,=P'1'             ADD ONE TO LINE COUNT              003500
          MVI   PRTDCTL,C' '              MOVE BLANK TO ASA CONTROL BYTE     003600
          B     READINV                                                      003700
INVEOF    ED    CNTPATRN,COUNT            EDIT COUNT                         003800
          PUT   PRTOUT,CNTLINE            PRINT COUNT LINE                   003900
          CLOSE (INVMAST,,PRTOUT)                                            004000
          L     13,SAVE+4                 LOAD OLD SAVE AREA ADDRESS         004100
          RETURN (14,12)                  RESTORE REGISTERS                  004200
*   THE INVENTORY FILE DEFINITION                                            004300
INVMAST   DCB   DSORG=PS,                                                  X 004400
                RECFM=FB,                                                  X 004500
                MACRF=GM,                                                  X 004600
                BLKSIZE=500,                                               X 004700
                LRECL=50,                                                  X 004800
                DDNAME=INVMST,                                             X 004900
                EODAD=INVEOF                                                 005000
*   THE PRINTER FILE DEFINITION                                              005100
PRTOUT    DCB   DSORG=PS,                                                  X 005200
                RECFM=FBA,                                                 X 005300
                MACRF=PM,                                                  X 005400
                BLKSIZE=1330,                                              X 005500
                LRECL=133,                                                 X 005600
                DDNAME=REPORT                                                005700
```

Figure 5-11   The refined reorder-listing program (part 1 of 2)

```
*  THE DATA DEFINITIONS FOR THE INVENTORY FILE WORK AREA       005800
INVWRKA  DS    OCL50                                           005900
INVITNBR DS    CL5                                             006000
INVITDES DS    CL20                                            006100
         DS    CL5                                             006200
INVPRICE DS    CL5                                             006300
INVORDPT DS    CL5                                             006400
INVONHND DS    CL5                                             006500
INVONORD DS    CL5                                             006600
         DS    CL30                                            006700
*  THE DATA DEFINITIONS FOR THE PRINTER HEADING LINES          006800
HDGLINE1 DS    OCL133                                          006900
         DC    C'1'                                            007000
         DC    24C' '                                          007100
         DC    C'REORDER LISTING'                              007200
         DC    93C' '                                          007300
HDGLINE2 DS    OCL133                                          007400
         DC    C'0'                                            007500
         DC    C'  ITEM              ITEM                 UNIT             X  007600
         REORDER'                                              007700
         DC    69C' '                                          007800
HDGLINE3 DS    OCL133                                          007900
         DC    C' '                                            008000
         DC    C'  NO.          DESCRIPTION          PRICE   AVAILABLEX  008100
         POINT'                                                008200
         DC    70C' '                                          008300
*  THE DATA DEFINITIONS FOR THE PRINTER DETAIL LINE            008400
PRTDETL  DS    OCL133                                          008500
PRTDCTL  DS    CL1                                             008600
PRTITNBR DS    CL6                                             008700
         DC    5C' '                                           008800
PRTITDES DS    CL20                                            008900
         DC    4C' '                                           009000
PRTPRICE DS    CL7                                             009100
         DC    4C' '                                           009200
PRTAVAIL DS    CL6                                             009300
         DC    4C' '                                           009400
PRTORDPT DS    CL6                                             009500
         DC    70C' '                                          009600
*  THE DATA DEFINITIONS FOR THE COUNT LINE                     009700
CNTLINE  DS    OCL133                                          009800
         DC    C'-'                                            009900
CNTPATRN DC    X'4020206B202020'                               010000
         DC    C' RECORDS IN THE INPUT FILE'                   010100
         DC    99C' '                                          010200
*  THE DATA DEFINITIONS FOR OTHER REQUIRED WORK AREAS          010300
SAVE     DS    18F                                             010400
PATTERN1 DC    X'402020202020'                                 010500
PATTERN2 DC    X'402020214B2020'                               010600
WRKAVAIL DS    PL3                                             010700
WRKONORD DS    PL3                                             010800
WRKORDPT DS    PL3                                             010900
PACKAREA DS    PL3                                             011000
COUNT    DC    PL3'0'                                          011100
LINECNT  DC    P'50'                                           011200
         END   BEGIN                                           011300
```

Figure 5-11   The refined reorder-listing program (part 2 of 2)

Although print files are commonly blocked, this is the only program in the book that treats the print file as blocked. All of the other programs specify FA in the RECFM operand for the print file. Nevertheless, you should find out what blocking factor to use for print files in your shop and code your DCBs for them accordingly.

Controlling printed forms

When a program prints a document, it normally has to control the skipping and spacing of the printed form. This is referred to as *forms control*. At the least, a program that prints a document must provide for *page overflow*. This means that the form should be skipped from the last printing line of one page to the first line of the next page so the printer doesn't print on the perforation between two forms. In general, you should provide for forms control by using control characters and line counting.

Control characters A *control character* is used as the first character in a print area to specify the spacing or skipping required before printing. When you use control characters, you must indicate it in the RECFM operand of the DCB for the printer file. In figure 5-11, then, the RECFM operand specifies FBA. This means that the records are fixed length and that the control characters recommended by the American National Standards Institute are going to be used. Since these characters are the most widely used characters today, they are the only ones we'll present in this book.

When control characters are used, one byte at the start of an output area indicates the skipping or spacing to be performed before the area is printed. That's why the BLKSIZE in the DCB for the printer file specifies 133; that is, one control byte followed by the 132 bytes corresponding to the 132 print positions of the printer. If you look at the data definitions for the printer work areas in figure 5-11, you'll see that this control byte is provided in each of these areas.

The four most commonly used ASA control characters are summarized in figure 5-12. If you check the code in figure 5-11, you can see that the work area for HDGLINE1 has a control character of 1. This means that the form will be advanced to the top of the next page before HDGLINE1 is printed. Similarly, the form will be advanced two lines before HDGLINE2 is printed, and one line before HDGLINE3 is printed. If you're interested, you can find the complete range of ASA control characters and their uses in Appendix E of IBM's *MVS Extended Architecture Data Administration: Macro Instruction Reference*, GC26-4014.

Line counting and literals The technique of *line counting* is used to determine when a page is full and the form should be advanced to the next page. If you look at the flowchart in figure 5-10, you can see that the logic for line counting is simple. The line-counting routine first checks to see whether 50 lines have been printed on a page. If yes, the program skips to the next page, prints headings, resets a field (called the line-count field) to zero, and continues. If no, the program prints a detail line, adds one to the line-count field, and continues.

To count the number of lines printed on a page, the program in figure 5-11 uses a field named LINECNT. It is defined in line 11200. This is a two-byte packed field with a starting value of 50. You'll see why it has this starting value in a moment. You'll also see that it is set to a value of zero each time the heading lines are printed for a page.

After a detail line is printed by the program, the value 1 is added to LINECNT using the AP instruction with a *literal* as an operand:

```
AP      LINECNT,=P'1'
```

A literal is identified by an equals sign. After the equals sign, the literal gives a value just as in a DC definition. In this case, the literal gives a value of one in packed decimal form. As a result, the AP instruction just shown is the equivalent of the instruction

```
AP      LINECNT,PCON1
```

and the data definition

```
PCON1    DC     P'1'
```

By using the literal, though, the amount of coding is reduced.

To code a literal operand, use an equals sign followed by a type code and a nominal value enclosed in single quotes. All of the DC type codes are valid, so any of the following are acceptable literals:

```
=P'-15'
=Z'+5000'
=X'40'
=C'ABC'
```

As you might guess, a literal can be used as the sending field in an instruction, but it cannot be used as the receiving field.

The line counting logic is given in lines 2700-3500 of the program in figure 5-11. The first two lines correspond to block 6 of the flowchart in figure 5-10:

```
CP      LINECNT,=P'50'
BL      PRTDET
```

First, LINECNT is compared to a packed value of 50. If LINECNT is less than 50, a branch to PRTDET takes place and a detail line is printed. But if LINECNT is equal to or greater than 50, no branch takes place. Since LINECNT has a starting value of 50, as defined in its DC, no branching takes place the first time through the program so the PUT instructions that follow are executed to print the heading lines of the reorder listing.

The instructions that follow the PUT instructions are these:

```
ZAP     LINECNT,=P'0'
MVI     PRTDCTL,C'0'
```

Character	Meaning
blank	Space one line before printing.
0	Space two lines before printing.
-	Space three lines before printing.
1	Skip to the top of the next page before printing.

Figure 5-12   ASA characters for forms control

The ZAP instruction first changes the value of LINECNT from 50 to 0; then, it adds the literal value zero to LINECNT. As a result, the ZAP instruction has the effect of resetting LINECNT to a value of zero.

The MVI instruction moves the control character 0 into the first byte of the work area for the detail print line. Note, however, that the second operand in this instruction isn't a literal because it doesn't start with an equals sign. Instead, the second operand of an immediate instruction (the SI format) is an *immediate operand*. It is specified using a type code and nominal value in the same manner as for a DC statement, but without the equals sign used in a literal operand.

The next three lines of code are:

```
PRTDET    PUT     PRTOUT,PRTDETL
          AP      LINECNT,=P'1'
          MVI     PRTDCTL,C' '
```

Since the control character in the PRTDETL area is set to zero after the heading lines are printed, the printer is spaced twice before printing the first detail line on a page. Then, after a detail line is printed, the AP instruction adds one to LINECNT and the MVI instruction changes the control character of the detail line back to blank for single spacing.

Printing headings

To print headings, work areas that contain the required heading data must be defined. Thus, the three heading lines needed for the reorder listing are defined in the work areas named HDGLINE1, HDGLINE2, and HDGLINE3 (lines 6900-8300 of figure 5-11). The data to be printed is defined using DCs, and continuation lines for the DCs are used whenever needed.

When a DC line is continued, the coding in the line continues through position 71. Next, a continuation character like X must be coded in position 72 of the line. Then, the instruction is continued starting in position 16 of the next coding line. Although you can code as many continuation lines as you need for macro instructions like DCBs, you can code a maximum of only two continuation lines for instructions like DCs.

Printing the
count line

In figure 5-11, right after the GET instruction for the inventory master file, an AP instruction is used to add one to a field named COUNT. As a result, COUNT, which was defined with a starting value of zero, keeps an accurate count of the number of records read by the program.

When the end-of-file condition is reached, the GET instruction causes a branch to INVEOF. The count is then printed using this code:

```
INVEOF   ED    CNTPATRN,COUNT
         PUT   PRTOUT,CNTLINE
```

Here, COUNT is first edited into an edit pattern that is part of the printer work area named CNTLINE. Then, the PUT macro causes the count line to be printed. Since the control character for CNTLINE is a minus sign, the form will be advanced three spaces before the line is printed.

Using
comments

Comments have been used extensively in the program in figure 5-11 with the hope that they will help you understand the program. In practice, however, it isn't usually necessary to go to this level of detail when coding comments. Instead, you'll want to use comment lines to document blocks of code as illustrated in the other programs of this book. When coding comments, be sure that they start one or more spaces after your operands and that they don't go beyond position 71 of your source lines.

Discussion

If you understand this refined reorder-listing program, you should be able to start coding programs of your own. Although I haven't illustrated the use of the SP, MP, and DP instructions yet, you should be able to use them because their coding is analogous to the coding for the AP instruction. Similarly, you should be able to code the UNPK instruction because it is the reverse of the PACK instruction. As you code your programs, though, you may want to refer back to chapter 4 to check the operational details of these instructions.

Terminology

forms control
page overflow
control character
line counting
literal
immediate operand

Objective

Given program specifications, code an assembler language program that meets the specifications. The specifications will require disk input, printer output, forms control, and decimal arithmetic.

Chapter 6

A basic subset of assembler language

In this chapter, you will be shown some instructions and techniques that will complete a basic subset of assembler language. Topic 1 is a collection of instructions and techniques that you need to know in order to clear work areas, round numeric results, and so on. Topic 2 presents some standard macros that let you access the current date and time of your system and that let you print the contents of storage when you encounter problems during program testing. Topic 3 presents some assembler commands that let you assign more than one base register to your program, copy source code from source libraries into your program, and control the way your assembly listing prints.

TOPIC 1   Other elements of the basic subset

Thus far, you have been introduced to the basic instructions and coding techniques of an assembler language program. In this topic, you will learn some additional techniques and instructions that complete a basic subset of assembler language. You will learn how to use relative addressing and explicit lengths, how to use overlapped operands, how to round your arithmetic results, and so on.

Relative addressing and explicit lengths

Figure 6-1 illustrates the use of relative addressing and explicit lengths. If the data definitions in this figure define a printer work area, the instructions set all the bytes of PRTDETL to blanks as follows:

```
MVI     PRTDETL,X'40'
MVC     PRTDETL+1(132),PRTDETL
```

Here, the MVI instruction moves one blank into the first byte of this area. Although PRTDETL has a length of 133 bytes, only one byte is affected because the MVI instruction has an implied length of only one byte. Since this first byte of the work area is the control character of the detail line, this instruction prepares the area for single spacing.

The second instruction, the MVC, uses a *relative address* and an *explicit length* for the first operand, PRTDETL+1(132). The relative address (PRTDETL+1) means that the address used in the instruction should be one greater than the address assigned to PRTDETL. The relative length in the instruction (132) means that the length used should be 132 rather than the 133 associated with the area named PRTDETL.

In other words, if address 8000 is assigned to PRTDETL when the program is executed, the first operand in the MVC instruction above refers to the 132 bytes beginning at address 8001. Since the second operand is PRTDETL and since the MVC instruction moves from left to right during execution, this means that blanks will be moved into the remaining 132-bytes of PRTDETL. First, the blank in byte 8000 will be moved to byte 8001; then, the blank in 8001 will be moved to byte 8002; and so on, until 132 blanks have been moved.

In many programs, this blanking technique is used to set a print area to blanks before moving data into the area. This sets any data left over from previous print lines to blanks. As a result, you don't have to define any of the fields in the work area with blank values. That's why all of the fields in figure 6-1 are defined with DS instructions. This contrasts the way in which PRTDETL is defined in the reorder-listing program in chapter 5.

```
PRTDETL   DS      0CL133
          DS      CL1
PRTITNBR  DS      CL6
          DS      CL5
PRTITDES  DS      CL20
          DS      CL4
PRTPRICE  DS      CL7
          DS      CL4
PRTAVAIL  DS      CL6
          DS      CL4
PRTORDPT  DS      CL6
          DS      CL70
              .
              .
              .
          MVI     PRTDETL,X'40'
          MVC     PRTDETL+1(132),PRTDETL
```

Figure 6-1   Using relative addressing, an explicit length, and overlapped operands to set a work area to blanks

To code a relative address, you use a plus or minus sign followed by a decimal number. Thus, PRTPRICE+11 has the same address as PRTAVAIL in figure 6-1. And PRTPRICE-24 addresses the first byte of the PRTITDES field.

An explicit length shows as a decimal number in parentheses following a data name or relative address. Thus, PRTPRICE(4) refers to the first four bytes of the 7-byte PRTPRICE field while PRTPRICE+5(2) refers to the last two bytes of the field. When you use relative addressing, you often code an explicit length. If you don't, the length is taken from the data definitions of the fields being operated upon. As a result, PRTPRICE+3 refers to seven bytes starting with the fourth byte of the PRTPRICE field. Since this would take three bytes from the field defined after PRTPRICE in figure 6-1, you would probably code an explicit length of four or less in a case like this. As a rule, you should code an explicit length whenever you require an operand length other than the one given in the data definition for the field. You'll see this illustrated more clearly in just a moment.

You can use an explicit length on any operand that has a length factor in its instruction format. If, for example, you refer to the formats given in figure 6-2, you can see that the MVC instruction can have an explicit length only on the first operand, but the AP instruction can have an explicit length on both operands as in this example:

```
AP      FIELDA+1(4),FIELDB+3(2)
```

Overlapped operands

The blanking technique in figure 6-1 also illustrates *overlapped operands.* This means that it is possible to have the same field specified in both operands for some of the data movement instructions. To blank the printer work area, for example, PRTDETL is given for both operands.

Then, when the operation is executed, the bytes of the area are operated upon in overlapped fashion.

Similarly, you can pack a field in its own area. Thus, this code is valid:

```
PACK   INVPRICE,INVPRICE
```

Then, if INVPRICE is a five-byte field, the instruction is executed as in this example:

INVPRICE

Before:	F0	F0	F4	F4	F0
After:	00	00	00	44	0F

In other words, when the instruction is executed, the five zoned decimal digits are packed into the rightmost three bytes of INVPRICE; the other two bytes are padded out with hex zeros.

Instructions for character comparisons

Thus far, you know how to compare packed decimal fields, but you don't know how to compare EBCDIC fields. To compare these fields, you use the CLC (compare logical characters) and the CLI (compare logical immediate) instructions. If the fields to be compared are over 256 bytes, you can also use the CLCL (compare logical long) instruction, but it isn't presented until the next chapter.

These instructions are called *logical* since they compare bit patterns rather than numeric values. Although the operands should normally be in EBCDIC format, a logical comparison will take place regardless of data format. In contrast to a logical comparison, the compare decimal instruction bases its comparison on the numeric values of the operands.

Compare logical characters (CLC)   The CLC instruction can be used to compare two areas of storage up to 256 bytes in length. Like the MVC instruction, the length code is taken from the first operand as in this example:

```
CLC    FIELDA,FIELDB
```

Here, FIELDA will be compared to a field of equal length beginning at the address represented by the label FIELDB. After a compare logical characters instruction, you normally code a branch instruction to test the result of the comparison.

Compare logical immediate (CLI)   The CLI instruction operates in the same manner as the CLC, except that only one byte of data is used in the

Instruction	Mnemonic operation	Implicit operand format
Compare logical characters	CLC	S1,S2 or S1(L),S2
Compare logical immediate	CLI	S1,I2
Edit	ED	S1,S2 or S1(L),S2
Move characters	MVC	S1,S2 or S1(L),S2
Move immediate	MVI	S1,I2
Move numerics	MVN	S1,S2 or S1(L),S2
Move with offset	MVO	S1,S2 or S1(L1),S2(L2)
Move zones	MVZ	S1,S2 or S1(L),S2
Pack	PACK	S1,S2 or S1(L1),S2(L2)
Unpack	UNPK	S1,S2 or S1(L1),S2(L2)
Branch and link register	BALR	R1,R2
Branch on condition	BC	M1,S2
Add decimal	AP	S1,S2 or S1(L1),S2(L2)
Compare decimal	CP	S1,S2 or S1(L1),S2(L2)
Divide decimal	DP	S1,S2 or S1(L1),S2(L2)
Multiply decimal	MP	S1,S2 or S1(L1),S2(L2)
Subtract decimal	SP	S1,S2 or S1(L1),S2(L2)
Zero and add decimal	ZAP	S1,S2 or S1(L1),S2(L2)
Shift and round decimal	SRP	S1,S2,I3 or S1(L1),S2(L2),I3

Figure 6-2   The implicit operand formats with explicit lengths for the instructions presented in chapters 1 through 6

comparison. The data in the field specified by the first operand is compared with the immediate operand given in the instruction. For example, when this instruction is executed,

```
CLI    FIELDZ,C'0'
```

the first byte of FIELDZ is compared to the character constant zero given in the instruction. If FIELDZ contained four bytes and you wanted to compare the rightmost byte with a hex F0, you could code it this way using a relative address:

```
CLI    FIELDZ+3,X'F0'
```

Remember that you code an immediate operand using type code X, Z, P, or C followed by a one-byte nominal value enclosed in single quotes. As a result, X'F0', C'0', and Z'0' are equivalent.

Collating sequence   When two fields are compared logically, they are considered equal if the bit patterns in both fields are identical. But what if they aren't? Is X-12-13 lower or higher than X12345? The answer depends on the binary values of the bytes being compared. In this case, since the CLC instruction operates from left to right, the leftmost bytes would be compared first and would be found to be equal. Then, the bit pattern for the hyphen (-) would be compared with the bit pattern for 1, or 01100000 would be compared with 11110001. Since 01100000 is less than 11110001 in terms of binary values, X-12-13 is considered less than X12345 by the System/370.

The sequence from lowest to highest of the characters within a coding system is called the *collating sequence*. The collating sequence of some commonly used EBCDIC characters from lowest to highest follows:

the blank

.

(

&

)

-

/

,

#

'

"

the letters A-Z
the numbers 0-9

Therefore, T/X is less than TOM, H&R is less than H-R, and T2S is less than T29.

Once you understand the notion of collating sequence, you can see why it is usually an error to compare logically two fields with different formats. For instance, if a CLC instruction compares an EBCDIC field containing 123 (hex F1F2F3) with a packed decimal field containing 58234 (hex 58234C), the EBCDIC field will be considered higher (the leftmost four bits are 1111 as compared with 0101). Data formats, then, are critical when using compare instructions, and the operands for a compare logical instruction should normally be in EBCDIC format.

Instructions for rounding packed-decimal fields

The System/370 decimal instructions operate only on whole numbers. For instance, a unit price of $4.49 is treated as 449 when arithmetic operations are performed on it. As a result, the programmer is responsible for keeping track of the location of decimal points and, if necessary, for rounding the results of calculations.

To code rounding operations, you often use relative addressing and explicit length codes along with two new move instructions, the move numerics (MVN) and the move-with-offset (MVO). After I show you how to round using these instructions, I'll show you an easier way using the shift-and-round-decimal (SRP) instruction. Since the SRP instruction is the easiest way to code rounding operations, you'll probably use it most of the time. Nevertheless, it's worth knowing how to use the MVN and MVO instructions too.

Move numerics (MVN)   The move numerics instruction operates in the same way as an MVC instruction, but only the digit (numeric) halves of the fields are moved. To illustrate, the instruction

```
MVN     RECEIVE,SEND
```

executes as in this example:

	Before				After			
SEND:	12	34	56	78	12	34	56	78
RECEIVE:	AA	BB	CC	DD	A2	B4	C6	D8

As you can see, the zone portions of the bytes in the receiving field are unchanged.

The MVN instruction is useful in rounding numbers as illustrated in figures 6-3 and 6-4. In figure 6-3, the problem is to multiply an amount field with two decimal positions by a percent field with two decimal positions and obtain a rounded result with two decimal positions. Two ways to do this are shown in figure 6-3.

Using the first technique, RESULT4 contains an unrounded result with four decimal positions after the multiply instruction has been executed. Then, 50 is added to this result by using a literal in the AP instruction. The effect of this is to increase the second decimal position by one if the third decimal position is 5 or over. In the example in figure 6-3, the third and fourth decimal positions contain 41 so when 50 is added to them the result is 91 and the second decimal position is unchanged. On the other hand, if the third and fourth positions had contained 71, the addition of 50 would have carried a one over to the second decimal position so the result would have been rounded up by one.

The next two instructions complete the rounding by dropping the rightmost two digits of RESULT4 as the result is moved to RNDRSLT2:

```
MVC     RNDRSLT2,RESULT4+1
MVN     RNDRSLT2+3(1),RESULT4+5
```

When the MVC instruction is executed, the second through fifth bytes of RESULT4 are moved into the four-byte RNDRSLT2 field. (Because the length is taken from operand-1 and RNDRSLT2 is defined as PL4, four bytes are moved; otherwise, explicit lengths could be used to move the appropriate number of bytes.) Then, when the MVN instruction is executed, the sign of RESULT4 is moved to RNDRSLT2 so RDNRSLT2 holds the rounded result field with two decimal positions.

The second technique in figure 6-3 is similar. After the literal 50 is added to the result field, the sign of RESULT4 is moved one byte to the left with this instruction:

```
MVN     RESULT4+4(1),RESULT4+5
```

Here, an explicit length is needed, so only one byte is operated upon. After the instruction is executed, the leftmost five bytes of RESULT4 have the rounded result value. These bytes are then moved to RNDRSLT2 by this ZAP instruction:

```
ZAP     RNDRSLT2,RESULT4(5)
```

Because the sending field has an explicit length of five, the rightmost byte of RESULT4 isn't added to RNDRSLT2. Because the receiving field is only four bytes long, the leftmost byte of RESULT4 is truncated. Thus, RNDRSLT2 holds the rounded result field with two decimal positions.

Move-with-offset (MVO)   The move-with-offset instruction has the unique attribute of offsetting the data one half-byte to the left during the move. As a result, this instruction

```
MVO     RECEIVE,SEND
```

executes as in this example:

	Before	After
SEND:	12 34 56	12 34 56
RECEIVE:	FF FF FF FF	01 23 45 6F

As you can see, the data from the sending field is placed in the receiving field, but it is offset one half-byte to the left. Meanwhile, the rightmost half-byte of the receiving field isn't changed. Also, the leftmost half-bytes that are not filled by the sending field are padded to hex zeros.

Truncation can also occur. For example, if the field RECEIVE is only three bytes, the leftmost half-byte is truncated as in this example:

	Before	After
SEND:	12 34 56	12 34 56
RECEIVE:	FF FF FF	23 45 6F

truncated

Source Code	AMOUNT2	PERCENT2	RESULT4	RNDRSLT2
		Field values after instruction execution		
Technique 1	12 34 56 7C	02 3F	00 00 12 34 56 7C 00 02 83 95 04 1C 00 02 83 95 09 1C	99 99 99 99 02 83 95 09 02 83 95 0C

```
ZAP   RESULT4,AMOUNT2
MP    RESULT4,PERCENT2
AP    RESULT4,=P'50'
MVC   RNDRSLT2+3(1),RESULT4+1
MVN   RNDRSLT2+3(1),RESULT4+5
```

Source Code	AMOUNT2	PERCENT2	RESULT4	RNDRSLT2
Technique 2	12 34 56 7C	02 3F	00 00 12 34 56 7C 00 02 83 95 04 1C 00 02 83 95 0C 1C	99 99 99 99 02 83 95 0C

```
ZAP   RESULT4,AMOUNT2
MP    RESULT4,PERCENT2
AP    RESULT4,=P'50'
MVN   RESULT4+4(1),RESULT4+5
ZAP   RNDRSLT2,RESULT4(5)
```

Problem

```
        12345.67
            23
        --------
     2839.5041

Rounded:  2839.50
```

Data definitions

```
AMOUNT2   DS   PL4
PERCENT   DS   PL2
RESULT4   DS   PL6
RNDRSLT2  DS   PL4
```

Figure 6-3   Rounding to an even number of decimal places using the MVN instruction

The operation of the MVO instruction, then, is similar to that of the packed decimal instructions, not to the operations of the other move instructions. The MVO instruction uses length factors on both operands, and execution moves from right to left. Padding with hex zeros and truncation can both occur.

The common use of the MVO instruction is in rounding packed-decimal numbers to an odd number of digits. In figure 6-4, the first technique illustrates a result with five decimal positions being rounded to two decimal positions. Since three positions must be dropped, the constant that is added to the result is 500 rather than 50 as in figure 6-3. In this example, the second decimal position is increased by one (from 6 to 7) when the AP instruction is executed.

Next, the MVO instruction moves the digits from the leftmost four bytes of RESULT5 to RNDRSLT2:

```
MVO    RNDRSLT2,RESULT5(4)
```

The explicit length of four is used so that three decimal positions are dropped during the move. Because the move is offset, the digit half of the rightmost byte of RNDRSLT2 is not changed by the move. Instead, this MVN instruction moves the sign from RESULT5 to RNDRSLT2:

```
MVN    RNDRSLT2+3(1),RESULT5+5
```

The second technique in figure 6-4 shows how overlapped fields can be used with the MVO instruction. When this MVO instruction is executed,

```
MVO    RESULT5,RESULT5(4)
```

it moves one byte at a time from right to left like this:

RESULT5

Before:	00	28	02	47	20	9C
After Byte 1:	00	28	02	47	24	7C
After Byte 2:	00	28	02	40	24	7C
After Byte 3:	00	28	02	80	24	7C
After Byte 4:	00	20	02	80	24	7C
Padding:	00	00	02	80	24	7C

Source Code	Field values after instruction execution			
	AMOUNT2	PERCENT3	RESULT5	RNDRSLT2

Technique 1
 	
`ZAP   RESULT5,AMOUNT2`
`MP    RESULT5,PERCENT3`
`AP    RESULT5,=P'500'`
`MVO   RNDRSLT2,RESULT5(4)`
`MVN   RNDRSLT2+3(1),RESULT5+5`
	12 34 56 7C	22 7C	00 00 12 34 56 7C
			00 28 02 46 70 9C
			00 28 02 47 20 9C
				99 99 99 99
				
				02 80 24 79
				02 80 24 7C

Technique 2
 	
`ZAP   RESULT5,AMOUNT2`
`MP    RESULT5,PERCENT3`
`AP    RESULT5,=P'500'`
`MVO   RESULT5,RESULT5(4)`
	12 34 56 7C	22 7C	00 00 12 34 56 7C
			00 28 02 46 70 9C
			00 28 02 47 20 9C
			00 00 02 80 24 7C	

Problem			12345.67 .227 2802.46709 Rounded: 2802.47	

Data definitions

```
AMOUNT2  DS   PL4
PERCENT  DS   PL2
RESULT5  DS   PL6
RNDRSLT2 DS   PL4
```

Figure 6-4 Rounding to an odd number of decimal places using the MVO and MVN instructions

| Instruction | ———————Values of FIELD——————— | |
	Before	After
SRP FIELD,2,0	00 12 34 56 7C	12 34 56 70 0C
SRP FIELD,5,0	00 12 34 56 7C	45 67 00 00 0C
SRP FIELD,63,5	00 12 34 56 7C	00 01 23 45 7C
SRP FIELD,62,5	00 12 34 56 7C	00 00 12 34 6C
SRP FIELD,59,5	00 12 34 56 7C	00 00 00 01 2C
SRP FIELD,63,0	00 12 34 56 7C	00 01 23 45 6C
SRP FIELD,62,0	00 12 34 56 7C	00 00 12 34 5C
SRP FIELD,59,0	00 12 34 56 7C	00 00 00 01 2C

Figure 6-5   Shifting and rounding fields using the SRP instruction

Of course, this technique for rounding can't be used if all the decimal positions in the field are needed in subsequent calculations. Obviously, when a result is rounded in its own field, the truncated decimal positions are not available for later processing.

Shift-and-round-decimal (SRP)   Shifting and rounding of packed decimal fields can also be accomplished by using the shift-and-round-decimal instruction. With it, you can shift the packed data in a field to the left or right any number of digit positions and round when required. Figure 6-5 gives some examples of how this instruction operates. In an instruction like

```
SRP     FIELD,3,0
```

the first operand specifies the packed-decimal field to be operated upon; the second operand indicates the shift direction and the number of digit positions to be shifted; and the third operand specifies the rounding factor.

Specifying the second operand can be the tricky part of using this instruction. This operand is actually interpreted as a 32-bit storage address. When the instruction is executed, bits 0 through 25 are ignored and bits 26 through 31 are treated as a 6-bit signed binary value. Positive values indicate left shifts and negative values indicate right shifts. Fortunately, though, you can code the second operand quite easily by using the values shown in figure 6-6. (In the next chapter, you will learn that these values for the second operand of the SRP instructions are actually explicit addresses, but you don't need to know that now.)

To shift a field 2 digit positions to the left, for example, you code:

```
SRP     FIELD,2,0
```

To round a field and shift it 3 digit positions to the right, you code:

```
SRP     FIELD,61,5
```

Operand-2 code	Number of shift-left positions
1	1
2	2
3	3
4	4
5	5

Operand-2 code	Number of shift-right positions
63	1
62	2
61	3
60	4
59	5

Figure 6-6   Operand-2 codes for the shift-and-round-decimal (SRP) instruction

This example illustrates the most common rounding factor, 5, which is added to the digit position to the right of the one being rounded to. The rounding factor is applied only to right shifts and must be in the range 0 through 9. When a field is shifted left, the rightmost digit positions are padded with zeros, so rounding doesn't apply. Note in figure 6-5 that no rounding takes place on a right shift when the rounding factor is zero.

Move zones (MVZ)

One other instruction that can be handy for manipulating numeric data is the move zones instruction. When it is executed, the zone halves of the bytes in the sending field are moved to the zone halves of the bytes in the receiving field. For example,

```
MVZ    FIELDA(3),=X'D0D0D0'
```

moves hex Ds into the zone portions of the first three bytes of FIELDA. You won't use this instruction for rounding packed decimal fields, but I wanted to cover it in this topic because it's so closely related to the MVN instruction.

Terminology

relative address
explicit length
overlapped operands
logical comparison
collating sequence

Objective

Apply the instructions and techniques of this topic to your programs.

TOPIC 2 Standard macros

There are several different kinds of standard macros that are provided with MVS. One kind you are already familiar with is *I/O macros* such as the DCB, OPEN, CLOSE, GET, and PUT macros. The two types of macros I'll present in this topic are supervisor communication macros and operator communication macros. Then, in chapter 8, you will learn how to use *program linkage macros* such as the SAVE and RETURN macros. In addition, MVS provides *system generation macros* and *multitasking macros*, but these are beyond the scope of this book.

Supervisor communication macros

One type of macro that almost all assembler language programmers use is the *supervisor communication macro*. This type allows you to get information from the supervisor, give information to it, or request a service from it. Some of the most widely used macros in this group are: TIME, ABEND, and SNAP.

TIME   Both the time of day and the current date are stored in a special area of the MVS supervisor program. To retrieve the current date and time from the supervisor, you use the TIME macro. When the TIME macro is executed, the time is stored in register zero and the date is stored in register 1.

The format of the time value stored in register zero is determined by the operand of the TIME macro. The three valid forms of the operand are:

```
TIME        DEC
TIME        BIN
TIME        TU
```

If the operand is omitted, DEC is assumed.

When DEC is coded or the operand is omitted, the time is returned as a modified packed-decimal number in the format HHMMSSTH where HH is hours, MM is minutes, SS is seconds, T is tenths of seconds, and H is hundredths of seconds. I say modified packed-decimal format because there is no valid sign in the rightmost half-byte. If, for example, the time is exactly 08:32:48, the four bytes of register 0 will contain hex 08324800.

Figure 6-7 illustrates a routine that gets the current time and edits it into a field named PTIME. In its edited form, the seconds are dropped so a time of 14:22:49 will be stored in PTIME as 14:22 with one leading blank.

```
          .
          .
          .
TIME      DEC
ST        0,TIMEWORK
MVN       TIMEWORK+3(1),=X'0F'
MVC       PTIME,PATTERN
ED        PTIME,TIMEWORK
          .
          .
TIMEWORK  DS    CL4
PATTERN   DC    X'4021207A2020'
PTIME     DS    CL6
```

Figure 6-7   A routine for storing the current time in a field named PTIME in the form HH:MM

After the TIME macro is executed, the ST instruction moves the time from register 0 to a four-byte field named TIMEWORK. In the next chapter, you'll learn how the ST instruction works in more detail, but for now it's enough to know that it stores the contents of a register in a four-byte field. Since registers are the equivalent of four bytes, this is logical enough.

After the time is stored in the work area, a move-numeric instruction is used to change the rightmost half-byte to the valid packed decimal sign, hex F. The value is now in normal packed-decimal format. Note, however, that the hundredth position of the seconds value is lost. Finally, after the MVC instruction moves an edit pattern into PTIME, the ED instruction edits TIMEWORK into PTIME. Since the pattern only provides for four decimal digits, the seconds are dropped when the time is edited. And, since hex 7A in the edit pattern is the code for a colon, PTIME ends up in the form HH:MM with one leading blank.

Although you'll normally use the DEC form of time, you may occasionally need one of the other forms. When BIN is coded as the operand, the time placed in register 0 is a binary number in units of 1/100 of a second. It represents the number of hundredths of a second that have elapsed since midnight. In other words, the value divided by 100 equals the number of seconds that have passed since the day started. The value TU also causes a binary value to be placed in register 1, but this value is in *timer units*. One timer unit is equal to 26.04 microseconds.

The date stored in register 1 by the TIME macro is always in the packed decimal format YYDDD where YY represents the last two digits of the year and DDD represents a number from 1 through 366 indicating the day of the year. This date is preceded by two hex zeros and is followed by a sign. In other words, February 27, 1987 (the 58th day of the year) will be stored in hex as 0087058C.

```
              .
              .
      TIME    DEC
      ST      1,DATEWORK
      MVC     PDATE,PATTERN
      ED      PDATE,DATEWORK+1
              .
              .
DATEWORK  DS  CL4
PATTERN   DC  X'40212061202020'
PDATE     DS  CL7
```

Figure 6-8   A routine for storing the current date in a field named PDATE in the form YY/DDD

Figure 6-8 illustrates a routine that gets the current date and edits it into a field named PDATE. After the TIME macro is executed, the ST instruction moves the date from register 1 to a four-byte field named DATEWORK. Again, you'll learn how the ST instruction works in the next chapter. Then, after the MVC instruction moves an edit pattern into PDATE, the ED instruction edits DATEWORK into PDATE. As you can see, relative addressing is used in the ED instruction so the leading zeros in the date are not edited into PDATE. Also notice that the edit pattern contains a hex 61, which is the code for a slash (/). As a result, PDATE ends up in the form YY/DDD with one leading blank.

In most cases, you'll want to convert the date from the form it's stored in by the TIME macro (called the Julian format) to the more useful format, MMDDYY (called the Gregorian format). To do that, however, you must provide your own conversion routine. Since this is a common need, most MVS installations have created their own subprogram to make the Julian-to-Gregorian conversion.

ABEND   As your programs become more complex and the number of possible error situations increases, you will find cases in which you'll want a storage dump to help you figure out what caused the problem. If you've already read chapter 18, you know that a *storage dump* is a printout of the contents of the general registers and storage in both hex and character formats. If you haven't read chapter 18, you'll learn more about storage dumps when you do. But right now, I want you to learn how to use the two standard macros that let you control storage dumps.

For the most catastrophic error conditions, you can code an ABEND macro, which causes the program to be cancelled. Its format is given in figure 6-9. As you can see, the macro has two required operands and one optional one. (There are three other optional operands, but they're beyond the scope of this book.)

The completion code operand is coded as a decimal value from zero through 4095. This value will appear as the "user code" in any console or printer messages that indicate the program terminated abnormally. Its

Format

```
ABEND completion-code,REASON=reason-code[,DUMP]
```

Explanation

completion-code   The completion code associated with the abnormal termination

reason-code   The reason code that will be passed to subsequent exit routines

---

Figure 6-9   The basic format of the ABEND macro

basic function is to provide an identification number so you'll be able to tell which ABEND macro caused the termination of the program.

The reason code operand is also coded as a decimal value. It's used to identify the specific cause of an abnormal termination. This code can then be passed to an exit routine and included in system messages.

The last operand is optional as indicated by the brackets. The DUMP operand causes a dump of main storage to occur if a SYSABEND or SYSUDUMP data set is defined in the job control statements for the program. The actual system areas included in the dump depends on what was specified for SYSABEND and SYSUDUMP when the system was generated. However, SYSABEND always includes the supervisor nucleus. Since this is usually a huge volume of output that is of little use to the assembler language programmer, SYSABEND is rarely used.

SNAP   For less critical errors, you may want to use the SNAP macro. The SNAP macro provides a dump of whatever portion of your program area you select. In addition, it allows your program to continue to execute.

The SNAP macro has nine possible operands that determine what will be contained in the snapshot dump. Since several of these refer to system control blocks and other control areas that are far beyond your needs at this point, I'll present only the four operands that are meaningful to you now. These four are summarized in figure 6-10. If, at a later time, you want to learn about the other operands, you can consult IBM's *MVS Supervisor Services and Macro Instructions* manual.

The first operand of the SNAP macro is the label of the DCB macro that defines the data set that will receive the snapshot dump. The standard operands for this DCB are given in figure 6-11. Since some of the options for these operands are different than what you've seen before, I'll discuss them briefly.

You're already familiar with the PS option of the DSORG operand; it specifies a physical sequential file. The record format option, RECFM, is coded as VBA. This means that the records are variable length (V), blocked (B), and will use ASA control characters (A). The MACRF operand is coded as W. This means that the WRITE macro will be used.

Format

```
label     SNAP    DCB=dcb-address,
                  ID=nnn,
                  PDATA=(codes),
                  STORAGE=(starting-address,ending-address,...)
```

Explanation

dcb-address	Label of the DCB macro that defines the file the dump is to be written to
nnn	Identification number indicating which SNAP macro caused the dump
codes	Areas of storage outside the program area that are to be included in the dump
starting-address	Program address at which the dump is to begin; usually coded as a label
ending-address	Program address at which the dump is to end; usually coded as a label

Figure 6-10   The basic format of the SNAP macro

The LRECL operand is coded as 125, which provides for a standard dump of 120 characters per line. The extra five characters are used for control data. The BLKSIZE operand should be coded as 882 or 1632. Finally, the option coded on the DDNAME operand must be the name specified in the DD job control statement for the file. Later on, you'll learn about variable length records and WRITE macros. For now, though, you should have no problem with data sets for snapshot dumps if you code their DCBs as shown in this topic.

The second SNAP operand is an identification number that can be any value from 0 to 255. It appears on the snapshot dump to indicate which SNAP macro caused the dump.

The remaining two operands, PDATA and STORAGE, determine which areas of storage appear on the output. The PDATA operand is used to select various areas outside your program area that may have a bearing on the problem. Again, there are several options, but only two of them are of real use to you. If the parameter REGS is coded, the snapshot dump will include the contents of the 16 general registers at the time the SNAP is issued. The other useful parameter is SA which causes a save area trace to be included in the dump. Either one or both can be coded, but you'll often want to include both of them like this:

```
PDATA=(REGS,SA)
```

The STORAGE operand determines what area or areas of storage will be dumped. It is coded with one or more pairs of parameters, each pair specifying a starting and ending address, and the whole group must be enclosed in parentheses. In most cases, these addresses are coded as labels

```
Label      DCB      DSORG=PS,
                    RECFM=VBA,
                    MACRF=W,
                    LRECL=125,
                    BLKSIZE=882,
                    DDNAME=ddname
```

Figure 6-11   Standard DCB operands for a SNAP file

and may include positive or negative adjustments. For example, if you want to dump a 2000-byte area starting with an instruction named BEGIN, you can code the STORAGE operand as:

```
STORAGE=(BEGIN,BEGIN+1999)
```

If you want to dump several 100-byte areas located in nonadjacent areas of storage, you can code something like this:

```
STORAGE=(AREA1,AREA1+99,AREA2,AREA2+99,...)
```

Figure 6-12 illustrates a SNAP macro as it might be coded in a job stream that includes the source program. In the source program, you can see the OPEN and CLOSE statements for the snapshot dump, the SNAP macro that causes the dump, and the DCB for the data set named SNAP-SHOT that receives the snapshot dump. In the job control statements after the source program, you can see the DD statement for the SNAPSHOT data set used in the GO step of the procedure.

In this case, the SNAP macro dumps the entire program area. Notice, too, that the data set is opened before the SNAP macro is issued and closed after it has been executed. If only one SNAP macro is present in a program and it will be executed only once, you should open the data set just before the SNAP macro and close it right after. However, if there are several SNAP macros or one that will be executed several times, it's better to open the file at the beginning of the program and close it at the end.

As you can imagine, the SNAP macro is a powerful debugging aid. For example, suppose you have an error in an arithmetic calculation but can't figure out where the error occurs just by examining the program output. In this case, you can put a SNAP macro in the calculation routine, at several points if necessary, to dump the storage area that contains the work fields involved in the calculation. You'll then have a "snapshot" dump of the values at various stages in the calculation, and you should be able to find the point at which the error is introduced.

You may also want to include SNAP macros as a permanent part of some error routines. This will allow you to get a snapshot dump of the troublesome data and then to continue to process the rest of the data. In chapter 8, you'll see how a SNAP function can be useful as an assembler language subprogram that is used by programs written in other languages.

```
//TEST32         JOB   . . .
//               EXEC ASMFCG
//ASM.SYSIN      DD    *
REORDLST START 0
BEGIN     SAVE  (14,12)
              .
              .
          OPEN  (SNAPSHOT,OUTPUT)
              .
              .
          SNAP  DCB=SNAPSHOT,                                      X
                ID=032,                                           X
                PDATA=(REGS,SA),                                  X
                STORAGE=(REORDLST,LAST+3)
              .
              .
          CLOSE SNAPSHOT
              .
              .
SNAPSHOT DCB   DSORG=PS,                                          X
               RECFM=VBA,                                         X
               MACRF=W,                                           X
               LRECL=125,                                         X
               BLKSIZE=882,                                       X
               DDNAME=SNAPDUMP
              .
              .
LAST     DS    CL4
         END   BEGIN
/*
              .
              .
//GO.SNAPDUMP  DD    SYSOUT=A
```

Figure 6-12   A SNAP macro in context

Operator communication macros

MVS also provides macros that allow communication with the operator
through system operator consoles and printers. The most commonly used
operator communication macro is WTO.

WTO   The WTO macro can be used to send messages to any number
of operator consoles. Its basic format is given in figure 6-13. The first
operand contains the message to be sent. It can be up to 125 characters in
length.

Format

```
label     WTO     'message',ROUTCDE=route-code,DESC=descriptor-code
```

Explanation

message	The message to be sent to the operator consoles (up to 125 characters)
route-code	A code that determines which operator consoles a message is to be sent to
descriptor-code	A code that determines the disposition of the message

Figure 6-13   The basic format of the WTO macro

The second operand, ROUTCDE, determines which consoles the message is to be sent to. When the system is generated, each console is assigned certain routing codes. Then, if a routing code specified in the WTO macro matches a routing code for a particular console, the message is sent to that console. Any number of routing codes can be specified.

The last operand, DESC, classifies the type of message being sent. For instance, descriptor code 1 indicates a system failure message; code 2 indicates a message that requires immediate action; and so on. This classification determines how the message is presented to the operator and what its final disposition is. For instance, some messages can be suppressed or queued for display, and others must be displayed immediately. Some messages are deleted at the end of the job step; some require operator response; and some are displayed indefinitely.

As an assembler language programmer, you probably won't use this macro very often. However, there are special situations when you may need to send a message to an operator. For example, if you write some special purpose utility program, you may need to inform an operator of its completion status. For instance, for a normal completion, you could code the WTO macro like this:

```
WTO    'FILE ANALYSIS PROGRAM-NO ERROR FOUND',ROUTCDE=2,DESC=7
```

Then, the message will be sent to any operator console with routing code 2. Descriptor code 7 means the message is from an application program and that the message should be deleted at the end of the job step.

Discussion

As I said at the start of this topic, MVS provides many macros. Now that you know how a few of them work, you can look up other macros in the appropriate reference manuals and they'll make more sense to you. Then, in chapter 11, I'll show you how to create macros of your own.

Terminology   I/O macro
                     program linkage macro
                     system generation macro
                     multitasking macro
                     supervisor communication macro
                     timer unit
                     storage dump
                     operator communication macro

Objective   Apply the macros in this topic to your programs.

Topic 3   Assembler commands

You are already familiar with a few assembler commands. For instance, START, USING, and END are all assembler commands. This topic will present several more assembler commands. First, this topic shows you how to code the USING command to specify more than one base register for a large program. Next, it shows you how to use the COPY command to copy source code into a program from a source library. Then, it presents two commands for controlling the assembly process: LTORG and EQU. Finally, it presents a few commands that control the appearance of the assembly listing.

How to specify more than one base register for a program with the USING command

In chapter 5, you learned that a single base register can serve a maximum program segment of 4096 bytes. This means that another base register must be assigned and loaded for each additional program segment of 4096 bytes. If, for example, a program requires three base registers, the base registers can be assigned and loaded as shown in figure 6-14.

In figure 6-14, after the BALR instruction loads the first base register as usual, the USING statement assigns register 3 as the first base register, but it also assigns registers 4 and 5 as succeeding base registers. As a result, the assembler will use register 3 as the base register until 4096 bytes have been defined. Then, for references to bytes 4097 to 8192, it will use register 4 as the base register. And, for references to bytes 8193 to 12288, it will use register 5.

To load the proper base addresses in registers 4 and 5, you can use the load multiple register (LM) instruction with *address constants* (or *adcons*). An address constant (type code A) causes the address or addresses of one or more locations in storage to be stored in one or more fullwords of storage. In figure 6-14, these address constants are used:

```
BASEADR   DC      A(START+4096)
          DC      A(START+8192)
```

Thus, the address of START+4096 is placed in the first fullword; the address of START+8192 is placed in the second fullword. You can get this same result by coding two addresses in one adcon like this:

```
BASEADR   DC      A(START+4096,START+8192)
```

```
PROGC614  START  0
BEGIN     SAVE   (14,12)
          BALR   3,0
          USING  *,3,4,5
START     LM     4,5,BASEADR
          B      EXEC
BASEADR   DC     A(START+4096)
          DC     A(START+8192)
EXEC      ST     13,SAVE+4
          LA     13,SAVE
                 .
                 .
                 .
```

Figure 6-14   Using more than one base register in a program

When the LM instruction in figure 6-14 is executed,

```
START     LM     4,5,BASEADR
```

the addresses in BASEADR are loaded into registers 4 and 5. When you code the LM instruction, operand-1 specifies the first register to be loaded, operand-2 specifies the last register in sequence to be loaded, and operand-3 specifies the storage location of the first address to be loaded. As a result, this instruction

```
START     LM     4,7,BASEADR
```

causes registers 4, 5, 6, and 7 to be loaded with the addresses that start at BASEADR. In this case, of course, you would have to make sure that BASEADR was the start of four valid addresses.

In figure 6-14, you should notice that the unconditional branch instruction branches over the address constants to the next instruction of the program. If it didn't, the program wouldn't run properly since an address constant isn't an instruction. Although the address constants can be defined anywhere within the first 4096-byte segment of the program, it is most common to find them in the housekeeping routine as shown in figure 6-14.

To determine the number of base registers required by your program, you can estimate the number of bytes that the program will require. To do this, use 100 bytes for each DCB statement and 5 bytes for each instruction. Then, add the DCB bytes, the instruction bytes, and the number of bytes for file work areas. This rough estimate should help you determine the number of registers needed. But if you assign too few, a diagnostic will call your attention to the error.

Copy member INVMAST in library USRSL1

```
INVMAST   DCB   DSORG=PS,                                         X
                RECFM=FB,                                         X
                BLKSIZE=500,                                      X
                LRECL=50,                                         X
                MACRF=PM,                                         X
                EODAD=INVEOF,                                     X
                DDNAME=INVMSTR
```

COPY command in source program

```
          COPY  INVMAST
```

EXEC statement in JCL for the assembly job

```
//        EXEC  ASMFC,MAC1='USRSL1'
```

Figure 6-15   Using the COPY command to insert a copy book into a source program

The COPY command

The COPY command is used to copy source code from a source statement library into your program. It is commonly used to copy code that is going to be used in one or more programs of a system, such as a file description or a standard report heading. By using the COPY command, you can save the time it would take to enter the code and you can be sure that the code will be free of errors.

Figure 6-15 shows how the source library, the COPY command, and the EXEC statement for assembling the program containing the COPY statement are related. To insert a copy book named INVMAST into a source program, you use this command:

```
          COPY  INVMAST
```

The code in the source book is then copied into your program right after the COPY command, just as if you had entered it yourself.

Since a system can have many different source libraries, you must make sure that MVS knows which library to use when it runs your assembly job. To do this, you can code the MAC1 operand with the name of the required source library on the EXEC statement for the assembly procedure. MAC1 is a *symbolic parameter* that's specified in the assembly procedure. In the example in figure 6-15, the library USRSL1 is specified, so any member in that library can be copied into the source program.

```
            .
            .
            .
            AP      QTYWORK,=P'1'
            .
            .
QTYWORK     DC      PL4'0'
            LTORG
PRTWK1      DS      CL133
INAREA1     DS      CL400
            END     BEGIN
```

Figure 6-16   Using LTORG

The LTORG
command

The assembler program normally places literal constants coded as instruction operands at the end of your program. By using the LTORG command, though, you can force placement of these literal constants at some other position in your program. You may want to do this as part of a debugging operation if your literals are being overlaid by data movement instructions that incorrectly address the fields before the literals.

In figure 6-16, for example, the LTORG instruction causes the literal constant =P'1' to be defined after the field QTYWORK and before the area named PRTWK1. If the LTORG command was omitted, the literal constant would have been defined after INAREA1. You can code any number of LTORG statements in a program. Each time the assembler encounters a LTORG instruction, it places all the literals defined in operands since the last LTORG statement immediately following the new LTORG.

The EQU
command

The EQU command lets you assign the attributes of one label to another label as:

```
FIELD1      DS      CL8
FIELD2      EQU     FIELD1
```

Here, the label FIELD2 is assigned the address and length attribute of FIELD1. Both labels then address the same 8-byte field.

One of the most common uses of the EQU command assigns labels to register numbers. Since labels are included in a cross-reference listing but registers aren't, using the EQU command allows you to get a trace of register usage that wouldn't normally be available. If, for example, the register numbers are equated with labels as shown in figure 6-17, you can substitute the equivalent labels whenever you require a register number as in these examples:

```
LM      R4,R5,BASEADR
BALR    R14,R15
```

Equating the numbers 0 through 15 to the labels R0 through R15

```
R0          EQU     0
R1          EQU     1
R2          EQU     2
              .
              .
              .
R14         EQU     14
R15         EQU     15
```

Instructions in the source program that use the equivalent labels

```
        LM      R4,R5,BASEADR
        BALR    R14,R15
```

Figure 6-17   Using the EQU command to assign labels to register numbers

Then, the statement numbers of the instructions that use the register equivalents will be included in the cross-reference listing that is prepared during assembly. This coding technique can be especially useful when you debug large programs.

Commands for controlling the assembly listing

You can use several different assembler commands to control the appearance of an assembly listing. These include PRINT, TITLE, EJECT, and SPACE.

The PRINT command   The PRINT command has three operands that can be in any order and in any combination. To start, you can code the ON or OFF operand as follows:

```
        PRINT ON
        PRINT OFF
```

This operand determines whether or not the listing will be printed at all. If you code ON or if you omit the operand, the listing is printed. If you code OFF, no assembly listing is printed. When you code OFF, the other operands and any other assembler commands that control the listing are ignored. The OFF operand is rarely used, but it can be used if you have made no changes to a source program since the last assembly and you need to assemble and test again.

A second operand controls the printing of the instructions generated by macros. If you code NOGEN, none of the generated instructions are

```
PROGC618  START  0
BEGIN     SAVE   (14,12)
          BALR   3,0
          USING  *,3
          ST     13,SAVE+4
          LA     13,SAVE
          B      PROCESS
          PRINT  NOGEN
DISKIN    DCB    DSORG=PS,...
PRTOUT    DCB    DSORG=PS,...
          PRINT  GEN
PROCESS   OPEN   (DISKIN,INPUT,PRTOUT,OUTPUT)
```

Figure 6-18   Using the NOGEN option of the PRINT command to suppress the printing of the instructions generated by the DTFs

printed. If you omit the operand or code GEN, all of the generated instructions are printed on the assembly listing and denoted with a plus sign to the right of the statement number.

Figure 6-18 illustrates a typical use of the PRINT instruction with the GEN/NOGEN operand. Here, the printing of macro-generated statements is turned off before the DCBs so the many statements generated by the DCBs will not be listed. After the DCBs, the printing of macro-generated statements is turned back on so the code generated by the other macros, such as the OPEN macro, will be printed on the listing.

The last PRINT operand controls the printing of the data generated by DC instructions and literals. If you code the operand DATA, each byte of generated data is printed in the object code column of the assembly listing, eight bytes per line. If you omit the operand or code NODATA, only the first eight bytes of the defined data appear on the listing.

You won't use the DATA operand often, because you generally don't need to see all of the data generated by DC instructions and literals. Sometimes, though, you'll want to use the DATA option so you can see the generated data. In figure 6-19, for example, you can see the use of the DATA option to print just the data in a table definition. The first PRINT instruction turns the option on so all the data in the table will print. The last PRINT instruction turns the option off again. You can then use the assembly listing to proofread the table definition. The listing can also serve as documentation for the contents of the table.

The TITLE command   The TITLE command causes a heading to be printed at the top of each page of an assembly listing as in this example:

```
TITLE 'PROG86 BILLING PROGRAM'
```

The TITLE instruction commonly appears as the first statement of a program, and the heading that prints is taken from its operand (the data enclosed in single quotation marks). The maximum length of the title is 100 characters.

```
                    .
                    .
                    .
            PRINT DATA
TABLE       DS    0CL176
            DC    18CL4'10AA'
            DC    C'11AB'
            DC    C'12AC'
            DC    4C'16DD'
            DC    20C'20XX'
            PRINT NODATA
                    .
                    .
                    .
```

Figure 6-19   Using the DATA option of the PRINT command to print table definitions

The EJECT command   The EJECT command causes the assembler to skip to the top of a new page before printing the next line of the assembly listing. EJECT has no operand, and its label is ignored.

The SPACE command   The SPACE command causes one or more lines to be skipped in the assembly listing. The operand must be a decimal number that specifies the number of lines to be skipped. If no value is coded, one line is skipped. If the number of lines to be skipped is more than the number of lines remaining on the page, the effect of SPACE is to EJECT.

Terminology

address constant
adcon
symbolic parameter

Objectives

1. Code the instructions and commands required when your program requires more than one base register. To do this, you will have to code the USING command, the LM instruction, and address constants.

2. Apply the commands presented in this topic to your programs.

Chapter   7

Register operations, binary arithmetic, and storage definition techniques

This chapter expands the assembler language subset presented in chapters 5 and 6 by presenting some instructions and techniques commonly used by professional programmers. Topic 1 presents instructions and techniques that involve the use of registers. Topic 2 shows you how to perform arithmetic operations using binary rather than packed decimal data. And topic 3 presents some advanced techniques for defining fields and areas in storage. When you complete this chapter, you should be able to code your programs more efficiently. Also, the material in this chapter will help you understand assembler language programs and subprograms written by professional programmers.

TOPIC 1   Register operations

On an IBM mainframe, there are more than 60 instructions that involve registers. This topic, though, presents only those that are most widely used by professional programmers. In addition, this topic shows you how to use explicit base registers and displacements to address fields and how to define the fields that are used by the register instructions.

EXPLICIT BASE REGISTERS AND DISPLACEMENTS

In chapter 6, you were introduced to explicit lengths; that is, the numbers in parentheses following labels or relative addresses that indicate the length of an operand. In addition, though, the assembler language programmer can code *explicit addresses* by coding *explicit base registers* and *explicit displacements*. This is illustrated by this instruction:

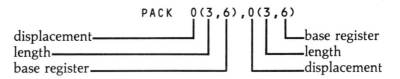

In other words, this PACK instruction uses overlapped operands to pack the three-byte field at the address in base register 6 to the three-byte field at the address in base register 6. In this example, the displacement values are zero.

Here's another instruction that illustrates explicit addressing:

```
AP      WKLYHRS,3(3,6)
```

This instruction adds the three-byte field that is explicitly addressed to the field labelled WKLYHRS. The address of operand-2 is calculated by adding the displacement 3 to the contents of base register 6.

Figure 7-1 gives the explicit instruction formats for all of the instructions presented in chapters 1 through 6 of this book, and figure 7-2 gives the explicit formats for the instructions presented in this chapter. The explicit formats for all of the instructions presented in this book are given in appendix A. In general, an operand in storage can be expressed as a displacement (D), length (L), and base register (B) in this form:

```
D(L,B)
```

That is, a number representing a displacement is followed by two numbers in parentheses: first, the number of bytes to be operated upon in decimal; second, the number of the base register in decimal.

Instruction	Mnemonic operation	Type	Explicit operand format
Compare logical characters	CLC	SS	D1(L,B1),D2(B2)
Compare logical immediate	CLI	SI	D1(B1),I2
Edit	ED	SS	D1(L,B1),D2(B2)
Move characters	MVC	SS	D1(L,B1),D2(B2)
Move immediate	MVI	SI	D1(B1),I2
Move numerics	MVN	SS	D1(L,B1),D2(B2)
Move with offset	MVO	SS	D1(L1,B1),D2(L2,B2)
Move zones	MVZ	SS	D1(L,B1),D2(B2)
Pack	PACK	SS	D1(L1,B1),D2(L2,B2)
Unpack	UNPK	SS	D1(L1,B1),D2(L2,B2)
Branch and link register	BALR	RR	R1,R2
Branch on condition	BC	RX	M1,D2(X2,B2)
Add decimal	AP	SS	D1(L1,B1),D2(L2,B2)
Compare decimal	CP	SS	D1(L1,B1),D2(L2,B2)
Divide decimal	DP	SS	D1(L1,B1),D2(L2,B2)
Multiply decimal	MP	SS	D1(L1,B1),D2(L2,B2)
Subtract decimal	SP	SS	D1(L1,B1),D2(L2,B2)
Zero and add decimal	ZAP	SS	D1(L1,B1),D2(L2,B2)
Shift and round decimal	SRP	SS	D1(L1,B1),D2(B2),I3

Figure 7-1 The explicit operand formats for the instructions presented in chapters 1 through 6

Other codes used in the explicit formats in figures 7-1 and 7-2 are I for an immediate operand, X for an index register, and M for a mask. In an instruction that provides for an index register, you will normally code a zero for the index register. Thus, an explicit address in the first add instruction in figure 7-2 can be coded in either of these two ways:

```
A       4,8(0,5)
A       4,8(,5)
```

Here, the second operand specifies the address calculated by adding the displacement 8 to the contents of register 5.

As an alternative, you can specify an index register instead of a base register when using this add instruction. Then, the add instruction can be written as:

```
A       4,8(5)
```

Instruction	Mnemonic operation	Type	Explicit operand format
Add	A	RX	R1,D2(X2,B2)
Add halfword	AH	RX	R1,D2(X2,B2)
Add register	AR	RR	R1,R2
Branch on count	BCT	RX	R1,D2(X2,B2)
Branch on count register	BCTR	RR	R1,R2
Compare	C	RX	R1,D2(X2,B2)
Compare halfword	CH	RX	R1,D2(X2,B2)
Compare register	CR	RR	R1,R2
Convert to binary	CVB	RX	R1,D2(X2,B2)
Convert to decimal	CVD	RX	R1,D2(X2,B2)
Divide	D	RX	R1,D2(X2,B2)
Divide register	DR	RR	R1,R2
Load	L	RX	R1,D2(X2,B2)
Load address	LA	RX	R1,D2(X2,B2)
Load halfword	LH	RX	R1,D2(X2,B2)
Load multiple	LM	RS	R1,R3,D2(B2)
Load register	LR	RR	R1,R2
Multiply	M	RX	R1,D2(X2,B2)
Multiply halfword	MH	RX	R1,D2(X2,B2)
Multiply register	MR	RR	R1,R2
Store	ST	RX	R1,D2(X2,B2)
Store halfword	STH	RX	R1,D2(X2,B2)
Store multiple	STM	RS	R1,R3,D2(B2)
Subtract	S	RX	R1,D2(X2,B2)
Subtract halfword	SH	RX	R1,D2(X2,B2)
Subtract register	SR	RR	R1,R2

Figure 7-2   The instructions for register operations that are presented in this chapter

Here, the second operand points to the address calculated by adding the displacement 8 to the contents of index register 5. Note that you don't have to code a comma after the index register when you omit the base register.

When coding explicit operands, you must remember that the formats for different instructions have different parts. For instance, the register instructions in figure 7-2 don't have lengths. Neither do the immediate instructions in figure 7-1, and the MVC instruction only has a length for operand-1. Because each explicit value is critical to the resulting object code, you must check the formats to be sure each explicit value means what you think it means.

INSTRUCTIONS THAT DEFINE HALFWORDS, FULLWORDS, DOUBLEWORDS, AND ADDRESS CONSTANTS

Most register instructions operate on fullwords. However, some operate on halfwords and doublewords of storage. As a result, you must know how to define these fields. In addition, you should know how to define address constants, because they are often useful when coding register operations.

Fullwords, halfwords, and doublewords

The type codes for fullwords, halfwords, and doublewords are F, H, and D as in these examples:

```
FWEX1      DC      F'1'
FWEX2      DS      4F
FWEX3      DC      F'-125'

HWEX1      DC      H'123'
HWEX2      DS      3H

DWEX1      DS      D
DWEX2      DS      3D
```

Because the length is always four bytes for a fullword, two for a halfword, and eight for a doubleword, no length factor is required. Duplication factors can be used as required, and the nominal value is a signed or unsigned decimal number. Thus, FWEX1 will have a starting binary value of +1; and FWEX3 will have a starting value of minus 125.

Note, however, that a nominal value cannot be used with type code D. If one is specified, it will cause a floating-point constant to be assembled. This will be explained in more detail in chapter 12.

Address constants

In the last chapter, you were introduced to *address constants*, or *adcons*. But I'll present them again here for completeness since they are often used in routines that involve registers. An address constant defines a fullword that gives the address of a label as in this example:

```
ADCON1     DC      A(START)
```

In this case, ADCON1 will be generated with a value equal to the address of the field or instruction named START. Because an adcon is a fullword, it can be loaded into a register. Then, the register can be used in an explicit address to refer to the field. You'll see this illustrated later on in this topic.

You can also define an address constant with a relative address as in this example:

```
DC      A(START+4096)
```

Here, the address that is stored in the constant is the sum of the address of START plus 4096. Beyond this, you can code more than one address constant in a single DC as in this example:

```
DC      A(START,START+4096,START+8192)
```

In this case, three consecutive fullwords of storage are defined, one word for each of the three addresses specified.

INSTRUCTIONS THAT USE REGISTERS

Figure 7-2 lists the instructions that are presented in this topic. In general, the first operand in one of these instructions is the number of a register. The second operand is either a label representing a fullword or halfword of storage or a register number. A few of the register instructions have three operands, in which case the second operand is a register number and the third operand is a label for a fullword of storage.

Instructions for loading registers

When you use registers, the first step is to get some data into one of them. Here are five instructions used for that purpose.

Load (L)   You can use the load instruction to load data from any fullword into any one of the 16 registers as in this example:

```
L       4,FWORD
```

This instruction places the contents of the fullword named FWORD into register 4. The first operand can be any register number from 0 through 15; the second operand can be the name of any fullword.

Load register (LR)   You can also load a register from another register as in this instruction:

```
LR      4,7
```

Here, the second operand is the number of one of the 16 registers. The effect of this instruction is to duplicate the contents of register 7 in register 4.

Load halfword (LH)   The load halfword instruction operates just like the load instruction (L). However, only two bytes of data are loaded into the register. All four bytes of the register, though, are set to the two-byte value that is loaded into it. For a positive value, that means that the first two bytes of the register will contain binary zeros.

Assembler language code

```
        LM      4,6,WORD1
        .
        .
        .
WORD1   DC      F'1'
WORD2   DC      F'2'
WORD3   DC      F'3'
```

Contents of registers 4, 5, and 6 in hex

	Before				After			
Register 4:	00	56	0A	71	00	00	00	01
Register 5:	00	00	0B	AA	00	00	00	02
Register 6:	34	B1	CC	00	00	00	00	03

Figure 7-3   The operation of the load multiple instruction

Load multiple (LM)   You can load two or more consecutive registers from an equal number of consecutive words of storage using the load multiple instruction. This is illustrated in figure 7-3. Here, registers 4, 5, and 6 are loaded with the data in the 12-byte area beginning with the byte referred to by the name WORD1. As a result, register 4 is loaded with bytes 1 through 4, register 5 with bytes 5 through 8, and register 6 with bytes 9 through 12.

In any instruction that refers to multiple registers, the *wrap-around concept* applies. Wrap-around means that the register numbers form an endless sequence with register 0 following register 15. As a result, a load multiple instruction can be coded like this:

```
        LM      14,1,FOURWORD
```

Then, register 14 will be loaded with the first fullword of storage beginning at FOURWORD, register 15 with the second word, register 0 with the third, and register 1 with the fourth.

Load address (LA)   The last of the five load instructions is the load address instruction. You can use it to load the address of a field into a register as in this example:

```
        LA      6,FIELDA
```

Here, register 6 is loaded with the address of FIELDA, not the data stored there. If, for example, FIELDA refers to a two-byte field containing hex C1C2 at location 004B60, 004B60 is loaded into register 6 when the instruction is executed.

Instructions for storing registers

After you code a program's register operations, you often code instructions to store the contents of the registers used. To do this, you use the store, store multiple, and store halfword instructions.

Store (ST)   The store instruction stores the contents of one register into a fullword of storage. In this and the other store instructions, the first operand is the sending operand and the second operand is the receiving operand. For instance, this store instruction places the contents of register 14 in the fullword named SAVE14:

```
ST     14,SAVE14
```

Store multiple (STM)   In a store multiple instruction, the contents of consecutive registers are stored in consecutive words as in this example:

```
STM    7,10,SAVE7
```

Here, the contents of registers 7, 8, 9, and 10 are stored in the four fullwords beginning at the byte addressed by the label SAVE7.

The wrap-around concept applies to the store multiple instruction just as it does to the load multiple. For instance, this instruction is commonly used to save all the general registers except register 13:

```
STM    14,12,SAVEAREA
```

In this case, 15 registers are stored in this sequence: 14, 15, 0, 1, 2, 3, 4, 5, 6, 7, 8, 9, 10, 11, 12.

Store halfword (STH)   The store halfword instruction stores the contents of the rightmost two-bytes of a register into a halfword of storage. Otherwise, it operates like the store (ST) instruction.

Instructions for register addition and subtraction

You can code add, subtract, multiply, and divide operations when using register instructions. In most cases, though, you only need addition and subtraction to manipulate explicit addresses. As a result, this topic only describes the add and subtract instructions. The multiply and divide instructions are covered in topic 2.

Add (A), add halfword (AH), and add register (AR)   The add and subtract instructions are available in the register-to-storage and the register-to-register forms. In each case, the first operand is a number that specifies the register that will receive the result. The second operand can be a fullword, a halfword, or another register.

Here are some examples of add instructions:

```
A     6,FW1
AH    7,HW1
AR    8,6
```

In the first instruction, the contents of the fullword named FW1 are added to the contents of register 6. In the second instruction, the contents of the halfword named HW1 are added to the contents of register 7. In the third instruction, the contents of register 6 are added to the contents of register 8. In each case, the result replaces the original contents of the register specified in the first operand.

Subtract (S), subtract halfword (SH), and subtract register (SR)   The subtract instructions are analagous to the add instructions only the operation is subtraction. Here are some examples of subtract instructions:

```
S     10,FW1
SH    11,HW1
SR    12,9
```

In the first instruction, a fullword is subtracted from register 10. In the second instruction, a halfword is subtracted from register 11. In the third instruction, the contents of register 9 are subtracted from the contents of register 12.

Instructions for comparison

Compare instructions allow you to compare the contents of a register with the contents of a fullword, halfword, or another register. Here, are some examples:

```
C     3,FW1
CH    4,HW1
CR    5,12
```

As in the case of the compare decimal or compare logical instructions, you would expect to find one of these compare instructions followed by a conditional branch instruction.

The branch-on-count instructions

Sometimes, you will want to use a register to count the number of times a routine is executed. Then, when the routine has been executed the right number of times, you will want your program to branch out of the loop. When you want to use registers in this way, you can take advantage of the branch-on-count instructions.

Field Name	Employee code	Hours worked day-1	Hours worked day-2	Hours worked day-3	Hours worked day-4	Hours worked day-5	Hours worked day-6	Hours worked day-7	
Characteristics	CL5	CL3	CL3	CL3	CL3	CL3	CL3	CL3	
Usage									
Position	1-5	6-8	9-11	12-14	15-17	18-20	21-23	24-26	

Figure 7-4   A record layout for a payroll transaction

The branch-on-count instructions are coded like this:

```
BCT   4,LOOP
BCTR  4,9
```

In the first example, the second operand is the label of an instruction. In the second example, the second operand is a register that should contain the address of an instruction.

Each time the branch-on-count instruction is executed, the value in the register specified as the first operand is reduced by one. Then, when the resulting value in this register becomes zero, control falls through to the next instruction in sequence. Otherwise, a branch is made to the address given by the second operand. You'll see this instruction illustrated in just a moment.

SOME EXAMPLES OF REGISTER OPERATIONS

To illustrate the use of register operations for repetitive processing, consider this problem. A payroll program reads an input record that has the record layout given in figure 7-4. To calculate the number of hours an employee worked during the week, one of the routines of the program must add the seven daily hours-worked fields. Although this routine could be coded using the basic subset of chapters 5 and 6, figures 7-5, 7-6, and 7-7 show routines that add these fields using register operations.

Example 1: The payroll routine using register operations

Figure 7-5 shows a routine that adds the seven fields using explicit addressing. For each input record, the first two instructions of the routine set up registers 4 and 6 for repetitive processing. The third instruction sets TOTHRS to zero. As you will see, TOTHRS is used to accumulate the total number of hours worked for each employee, register 6 is used as a temporary base register for the daily hours-worked fields, and register 4 is used to control the number of times the ADDLOOP routine is repeated.

The first instruction, the SR instruction, sets register 4 to zero by subtracting the contents of register 4 from itself. The second instruction, the LA instruction, places the address of the first daily hours-worked field in

```
                    .
                    .
                    .
                SR      4,4
                LA      6,PAYREC+5
                ZAP     TOTHRS,=P'0'
ADDLOOP         PACK    0(3,6),0(3,6)
                AP      TOTHRS,0(3,6)
                A       4,=F'1'
                A       6,=F'3'
                C       4,=F'7'
                BL      ADDLOOP
                    .
                    .
                    .
PAYREC          DS      CL26
TOTHRS          DS      PL3
```

Figure 7-5   A payroll routine using register operations

register 6; it uses a relative address: PAYREC+5. The third instruction, the ZAP instruction, sets TOTHRS to zero.

The next two instructions pack one hours-worked field and add it to TOTHRS. Both use an explicit address for the hours-worked field. These instructions will be repeated seven times, once for each hours-worked field in the input record. Because the instructions use explicit addresses, the same instructions will refer to all seven hours-worked fields. The explicit address consists of an explicit base register, 6, which is the one that has been loaded with the address of PAYREC+5. As a result, the explicit address refers to the first hours-worked field the first time through the loop.

The next four instructions cause the loop starting with ADDLOOP to be executed six more times:

```
                A       4,=F'1'
                A       6,=F'3'
                C       4,=F'7'
                BL      ADDLOOP
```

First, the binary constant 1 is added to the counter, which is register 4. Second, 3 is added to the base register, which is register 6. Third, register 4 is compared with a value of 7. Fourth, a branch to ADDLOOP takes place if the contents of register 4 are less than the value 7.

Since register 4 starts with a value of zero, the branch to ADDLOOP will take place six times for each input record. Since the contents of register 6 are increased by three each time through the loop, the PACK and AP instructions operate on successive hours-worked fields in the input record. If, for example, the base address is 6000 the first time the PACK instruction is executed, it will be 6003 the next time through.

```
             .
             .
             L      4,=F'7'
             LA     6,PAYREC+5
             ZAP    TOTHRS,=P'0'
ADDLOOP      PACK   0(3,6),0(3,6)
             AP     TOTHRS,0(3,6)
             A      6,=F'3'
             BCT    4,ADDLOOP
             .
             .
PAYREC       DS     CL26
TOTHRS       DS     PL3
```

Figure 7-6   The payroll routine with a branch-on-count refinement

Example 2: The payroll routine using the BCT instruction

Figure 7-6 shows the same payroll routine, but this time it uses the branch-on-count instruction to control the program flow. In effect, the BCT instruction takes the place of the add, compare, and branch-low instructions of the routine in figure 7-5. The first time through the loop, register 4 is decreased from its initial value of seven to six. Since the value is not yet zero, the branch to ADDLOOP takes place. On the seventh time through the loop, the BCT instruction will again reduce register 4 by one. But this time the result will be zero so the branch to ADDLOOP will not occur and control will pass to the next instruction in sequence.

Example 3: The payroll routine using a load-address refinement

Figure 7-7 shows how you can simplify the payroll routine one more step by using the load address instruction to load an initial value into register 4. This technique eliminates the need to use literals. For example, to load the initial value of seven into register 4, you can code this load address instruction:

```
         LA     4,7
```

This loads the value 7, as though it were an address, into register 4. If you check the explicit operand formats in figure 7-2, you will see that the 7 is treated as though it were the displacement for an operand with no index and no base register.

In figure 7-7, the load address instruction is also used to increase the value in a register by a positive value:

```
         LA     6,3(6)
```

```
                    .
                    .
          LA      4,7
          LA      6,PAYREC+5
          ZAP     TOTHRS,=P'0'
ADDLOOP   PACK    0(3,6),0(3,6)
          AP      TOTHRS,0(3,6)
          LA      6,3(6)
          BCT     4,ADDLOOP
                    .
                    .
                    .
PAYREC    DS      CL26
TOTHRS    DS      PL3
```

Figure 7-7   The payroll routine with a load-address refinement

If you look at the formats in figure 7-2 again, you will see that this instruction means that the address in index register 6 plus a displacement of 3 is to be placed in register 6. This has the effect of increasing the contents of register 6 by 3. You can increase the value in a register by any fixed amount with a load address instruction coded in this way.

SOME SYSTEM/370 INSTRUCTIONS

The MVC and CLC instructions that you learned about in chapters 5 and 6 operate on fields that are a maximum of 256 bytes long. But sometimes that can be a serious limitation. To remove these limitations, the System/370 designers put several instructions into its instruction set that weren't in the instruction set of the System/360 mainframes. Two of these instructions are the move long and the compare long instructions. Two others that you may find useful are the insert-characters-under-mask and the store-characters-under-mask instructions. These instructions are included in this topic because they all require the use of registers.

Move long
(MVCL)

The move long instruction is coded in register-to-register format as in this example:

```
     MVCL   6,10
```

Each operand, which must be an even-numbered register, represents an even-odd register pair. The even register of the first operand pair must contain the address of the first byte of the receiving field. The odd register of this pair, register 7 in the instruction above, must contain the length of the receiving field as a binary value.

Similarly, the even register of the second operand pair must contain the address of the sending field. The odd register of this pair must contain

```
      .
      .
      .
LA      8,RECVFLD
LA      9,800
LA      4,SENDFLD
LA      5,800
MVCL    8,4
      .
      .
      .
```

Figure 7-8   Moving one 800-byte field to another with the MVCL instruction

two values: (1) the length of the sending field in the second, third, and fourth bytes, and (2) a pad character which must be stored in the first, or leftmost, byte.

When the MVCL instruction is executed, the data from the sending field is moved to the receiving field, byte by byte from left to right. If the receiving field is shorter than or as long as the sending field, it executes just like the MVC instruction without the 256-byte limit. But, if the receiving field is longer than the sending field, the pad character is used to fill the extra bytes of the receiving field.

Figure 7-8 shows a typical use of the MVCL instruction. Here, the sending and receiving fields are the same length, and the load-address instruction is used to place the appropriate addresses and lengths into the four registers used by the instruction. The pad character in this case is hex 00 since it will be loaded into the leftmost byte of register 5 by the LA instruction. In this case, though, because both fields are the same length, the pad character won't be used.

Figure 7-9 shows how you can use the MVCL instruction to clear a storage area to blanks. In this case, the length of the sending field is intentionally set to zero and the pad character is set to blank (hex 40). As a result, pad characters fill in all 2000 bytes of the receiving field.

Compare long (CLCL)

The compare long instruction is coded in register-to-register format as in this example:

```
CLCL    4,8
```

Each operand, which must be an even-numbered register, represents an even-odd register pair. The even register of the first operand pair (register 4 in the example above) must contain the address of the first byte of the first field to be compared. The odd register of the pair (register 5 in the example) must contain the length of the first field as a binary value. Similarly, the even register of the second operand pair (register 8 above) must contain the address of the second field to be compared. The odd register must contain two values: (1) the length of the second field which must be stored in the second, third, and fourth bytes, and (2) a pad

```
            .
            .
            .
            LA      10,TABLE
            LA      11,2000
            LM      6,7,BLANK
            MVCL    10,6
            .
            .
BLANK       DC      X'00000000'
            DC      X'40000000'
            .
            .
```

Figure 7-9   Clearing a 2000-byte area to blanks with the MVCL instruction

character which must be stored in the first, or leftmost, byte. Then, the shorter of the two fields is considered to be extended with the pad character so that both fields are of equal length.

This instruction compares the bytes of the fields one at a time, from left to right, bumping the address registers by one and decrementing the length values by one as each byte is compared. If all the bytes are equal, the condition code is set to indicate an equal compare. But, if an unequal pair of bytes is found, the condition code is set to indicate whether operand A is low or high, and the contents of the address and length registers are left at their current settings. At that time, the address registers contain the addresses of the unequal bytes, and the length registers contain the number of bytes remaining to be compared. These addresses can then be used to locate the unequal bytes.

To illustrate, the routine in figure 7-10 uses CLCL to compare two 2000-byte records. If they are equal, a branch is made to NEXT so the next two records can be processed. But, if a mismatched pair of bytes is found, the unequal bytes are moved to fields named ERRBYTE1 and ERRBYTE2 using the addresses left in registers 4 and 8 by the compare instruction. Then, the BALR instruction branches to the routine that is addressed by the contents of register 12. After this routine returns to the next instruction in figure 7-10 (the one addressed by register 11), registers 4 and 8 are increased by one so they point to the first byte in each field that is after the unequal one. Also, the remaining length of each field is decreased by one. Then, the CLCL instruction is executed again so comparison of the two records continues.

If another unequal pair of bytes is found, they are stored in ERRBYTE1 and ERRBYTE2, the branch to the address in register 12 takes place, and, after the return to the next instruction, the addresses and lengths are adjusted and the CLCL is executed again. This procedure continues until all of the bytes of the two blocks have been compared and the branch to NEXT takes place.

```
              .
              .
              .
          LA    4,INREC1
          LA    5,2000
          LA    8,INREC2
          LA    9,2000
COMP      CLCL  4,8
          BE    NEXT
          MVC   ERRBYTE1(1),0(4)
          MVC   ERRBYTE2(2),0(8)
          BALR  11,12
          LA    4,1(4)
          LA    8,1(8)
          S     5,=F'1'
          S     9,=F'1'
          B     COMP
              .
              .
              .
```

Figure 7-10   Comparing two 2000-byte records with the CLCL instruction

If the lengths of the fields to be compared are not equal, the shorter of the two is considered to be extended with the pad character. The routine in figure 7-11 shows how this feature of CLCL can be used to find the first nonblank character in an area. Here, the odd register of the second operand pair (register 11) is loaded with the pad character and a zero length value. Each byte of the first operand is then compared with the pad character. When the first character that doesn't match the pad character is found, the instruction will stop and the address of the nonblank character will be left in the even register of the first operand pair, register 8.

Insert-characters-under-mask (ICM)

The insert-characters-under-mask instruction is a register instruction that operates much like a load instruction. However, it allows you to load data into selected bytes of the register instead of always filling all four bytes. Here's an example:

```
        ICM    6,12,SOURCE
```

When executed, bytes from the third operand are loaded into the register specified as the first operand. However, the second operand is treated as a four-bit mask that governs which of the register bytes are to be filled.

Figure 7-12 shows several examples of the insert-characters-under-mask instruction. When executed, each bit of the mask corresponds to a byte of the register: the first mask bit to the first byte of the register; the second mask bit to the second byte of the register; and so on. If a mask bit is on, the corresponding byte of the register is loaded. If a mask bit is off,

```
                    .
                    .
        NEWREC    LM     8,11,START
                  CLCL   8,10
                  BE     NODATA
                  ST     8,ADDR1
                    .
                    .
        ADDR1     DS     F
        START     DC     A(RECORD)
                  DC     A(80)
                  DC     A(0)
                  DC     X'40000000'
                    .
                    .
```

Figure 7-11   Searching for blanks with the CLCL instruction

Instruction		Mask	Register before	Storage	Register after
ICM	4,4,STOR	0100	00000000	FFFFFFFF	00FF0000
ICM	7,15,STOR	1111	00000000	804B36AD	804B36AD
ICM	10,10,STOR	1010	FFA33629	8000FFFF	80A30029
ICM	12,3,STOR	0011	00000000	F1F2F3F4	0000F1F2
ICM	11,8,PAD	1000	00007B36	40FFFFFF	40007B36

Figure 7-12   Some examples of the insert-characters-under-mask instruction

the corresponding byte is left unchanged. The selected register bytes are loaded from consecutive bytes of storage, beginning with the one addressed by operand three.

The last example in figure 7-12 shows how the instruction can be used to insert a pad character into the leftmost byte of a register. Since the move long and compare long instructions require a pad character in this byte of an odd register, the ICM and MVCL and CLCL instructions can be coded so they work together.

Store-characters-under-mask (STCM)

The store-characters-under-mask instruction is the converse of the insert-characters-under-mask instruction. That is, bytes selected from the register coded as the first operand are stored in consecutive bytes of storage beginning at the address of the third operand. The second operand in the instruction is the mask that determines which bytes are to be stored. Figure 7-13 shows three examples of this instruction.

Instruction		Mask	Register contents	Stored bytes
STCM	6,15,FLD	1111	00006A4C	00006A4C
STCM	12,4,FLD	0100	00367FA2	36
STCM	4,10,FLD	1010	80003D68	803D

Figure 7-13   Some examples of the store-characters-under-mask instruction

Terminology

explicit address
explicit base register
explicit displacement
address constant
adcon
wrap-around concept

Objective

Apply the register techniques and instructions presented in this topic to your programs.

TOPIC 2   Binary arithmetic

As I mentioned in chapter 4, there are two forms of binary data storage: fixed-point and floating-point. When arithmetic operations are performed using either binary form, the operations are faster than decimal arithmetic operations. Nevertheless, decimal instructions are used for most mathematical routines that are written in assembler language. You'll learn why by the time you complete this topic.

This topic shows you how to perform arithmetic operations using the fixed-point binary instructions. Then, in chapter 12, you'll learn how to use the floating-point instructions. Although there are times when you're likely to do arithmetic operations using the fixed-point instructions, you may never find the need for the floating-point instructions. In the remainder of this topic, whenever I refer to binary data or binary arithmetic instructions, please keep in mind that I'm referring to fixed-point binary, not floating-point binary.

In topic 1 of this chapter, you were introduced to many of the instructions that are used for binary arithmetic. There, you learned how to define halfwords, fullwords, and doublewords, how to load registers, how to code binary addition and subtraction instructions, how to compare binary operands, and how to store the contents of registers in storage fields. In this topic, then, all you need to learn is how to code the binary multiplication and division instructions and how to code the instructions for converting binary data to and from packed decimal format. In addition, you should learn more about the way negative numbers are stored in binary format.

Instructions for multiplication and division

Multiply (M), multiply halfword (MH), and multiply register (MR)   In a fullword instruction (M or MR), the multiplicand must be placed in the odd register of a pair of even-odd registers, such as registers 6 and 7 or registers 10 and 11, before the instruction is executed. The even register of the even-odd pair is specified as the first operand and the product (or result) is placed in the even-odd pair as a doubleword value. The sign of the product is developed according to the rules of algebra: like signs produce positive products, unlike signs produce negative products. To illustrate, figure 7-14 shows a routine that multiplies two fields, then stores the answer from registers 6 and 7 in a doubleword of storage.

Often, though, the range of values you deal with causes all significant bits in the product to be contained in the odd register of the even-odd pair. If this is the case, you can ignore the even register and just store the contents of the odd register as the product:

```
L     7,FIELDA
M     6,FIELDB
STM   6,7,DOUBLE
```

Figure 7-14   A binary multiplication routine

```
M     6,FIELDB
ST    7,FWORD
```

In the multiply halfword (MH) instruction, only one register is required and any register, odd or even, can be used. The product is a fullword value that replaces the contents of the register specified:

```
LH    9,FACTOR1
MH    9,FACTOR2
ST    9,FWORD
```

In any binary multiply instruction, arithmetic overflow isn't possible.

Divide (D) and divide register (DR)   The divide instruction also requires an even-odd pair of registers as the first operand. The dividend must occupy the pair as a doubleword value and the divisor must be a fullword or a register as in these examples:

```
D     6,FWORD1
DR    4,9
```

The quotient that results is stored as a fullword value in the odd register with its sign determined by the normal algebraic rules. The remainder is stored in the even register with its sign the same as the dividend's. If the values of the dividend and divisor are such that the quotient won't fit in the odd register, an abnormal program termination occurs due to a fixed-point divide exception.

Figure 7-15 illustrates a binary division routine that assumes that DIVIDEND will be a positive number since the SR register instruction will cause register 8 to contain a value of binary zero. As you'll see in a moment, binary zeros would *not* be an acceptable value for register 8 if DIVIDEND were a negative number.

Two's complement form for negative binary numbers

Using binary data format, a negative number is indicated by a binary 1 in the leftmost bit of the word. The rest of the word contains the binary number but in *two's complement form*. To get the two's complement of a binary number, you reverse the bits and add 1 to the rightmost bit as shown in figure 7-16. Here, the two's complement of decimal 93 is derived.

```
SR      8,8
L       9,DIVIDEND
D       8,DIVISOR
ST      9,QUOTNT
ST      8,REMNDER
```

Figure 7-15   A binary division routine

Negative value: 0000000001011101

1. Reverse the bits: 1111111110100010
2. Add 1:   + 1
                        _____
Two's complement: 1111111110100011

Figure 7-16   Deriving the two's complement of a number

Thus, negative 93 is stored in one fullword as this series of bits:

    1111   1111   1010   0011

Then, if you wanted to load this value as a dividend in registers 8 and 9, you would have to load this value in register 9 and hex FFFF in register 8.

Occasionally, when debugging, you may want to find the decimal value of a fixed-point field or register whose value is given in hex. If the value is positive as indicated by a hex value of seven or less in the leftmost half-byte of the word, you can convert to decimal as described in chapter 4. But, if the value is negative, you must determine the decimal value by using a technique like the one in figure 7-17.

Instructions for binary data conversion

The pack and unpack instructions let you convert numeric data from EBCDIC format to packed decimal format, and vice versa. Then, to convert from packed decimal to binary, and vice versa, you use the convert-to-binary and the convert-to-decimal instructions. Note that there isn't any instruction that directly converts data from EBCDIC to binary, and back again.

Convert to binary (CVB)   The convert-to-binary instruction converts a packed decimal value into a binary value. The packed decimal number must be stored in a doubleword area; the resulting binary value is stored

Fullword hex notation: FFE4

1. Convert to binary: 1111 1111 1110 0100
2. Subtract 1:   -1
                          _____
                          1111 1111 1110 0011
3. Reverse the bits: 0000 0000 0001 1100

4. Convert to decimal: -28

Figure 7-17   Converting a negative hex value to decimal

in a register. Here's an example:

```
CVB    12,DBLEPACK
```

When this instruction is executed, the packed decimal value stored in the doubleword named DBLEPACK is converted to binary and loaded into register 12.

As in all packed decimal instructions, the data in the doubleword must have a valid sign in the rightmost half-byte and decimal digits in all other half-bytes. Since packed decimal fields aren't normally defined as doubleword areas, you can use the zero-and-add (ZAP) instruction to insert your packed decimal value into a doubleword work area.

Convert to decimal (CVD)   The convert-to-decimal instruction is the opposite of the convert-to-binary. It converts a binary value in a register to packed decimal format and stores it in a doubleword area as in this example:

```
CVD    10,DBLEAREA
```

Here, the binary value in register 10 is packed into the doubleword named DBLEAREA.

A payroll routine that uses binary arithmetic

Just for illustration, figure 7-18 shows the payroll routine you last saw in figure 7-7 in another form. This time the arithmetic is done in binary. After each hours-worked field has been packed into the doubleword area, it is converted to binary in register 7 and then added to the weekly-hours total in register 5. When the hours for all seven days have been accumulated, control falls through the BCT instruction and the total hours in register 5 is converted back to packed decimal. The CVD instruction makes use of the same doubleword that had been used in the CVB instruction.

```
                    .
                    .
            SR      5,5
            LA      4,7
            LA      6,PAYREC+5
ADDLOOP     PACK    DBLEWRK,0(3,6)
            CVB     7,DBLEWRK
            AR      5,7
            LA      6,3(6)
            BCT     4,ADDLOOP
            CVD     5,DBLEWRK
            ZAP     TOTHRS,DBLEWRK
                    .
                    .
PAYREC      DS      CL26
DBLEWRK     DS      D
TOTHRS      DS      PL3
```

Figure 7-18   The payroll routine using binary arithmetic

Discussion

As the routine in figure 7-18 demonstrates, binary arithmetic requires some extra conversion instructions that aren't required when you use decimal arithmetic. That's why decimal arithmetic is normally used in business programs. On the other hand, the binary instructions execute more rapidly than the decimal instructions. As a result, binary arithmetic can be useful when arithmetic speed is critical and data conversions are minimal.

Terminology

two's complement form

Objective

Apply the binary arithmetic instructions to appropriate arithmetic routines in your programs.

TOPIC 3   Storage definition techniques

Chapters 5 and 6 presented the basic methods of defining work areas and work fields. You should realize, though, that you can use other elements and techniques to define and process storage areas. In particular, this chapter reviews the use of zero duplication factors and introduces you to the ORG instruction and to dummy sections.

How to use zero duplication factors to define fields within fields

Figure 7-19 shows you how zero duplication factors can be used to define a record area for an accounts receivable record. This illustrates that fields can be defined within fields within areas. In fact, any number of levels within levels can be defined.

Whenever a zero duplication factor is used, the assembler doesn't increase the value of its *location counter* during an assembly. The location counter keeps track of the next address to be used for an instruction or data element during an assembly. If its value isn't increased, two or more data elements can be assigned the same address.

In figure 7-19, for example, note that both ARBALFWD and ARDATE have a zero duplication factor. As a result, ARBALFWD refers to the 13 bytes that hold data from record positions 58-70; ARDATE refers to the 6 bytes that hold data from record positions 58-63; and ARMONTH refers to the 2 bytes that hold data for record positions 58 and 59. In other words, ARBALFWD, ARDATE, and ARMONTH all have the same address in the program. However, their lengths differ.

How to use the ORG instruction to redefine storage areas

Sometimes, a file will contain several types of records. For example, a transaction file for a billing program could contain a set of records for each shipment made. The first record of each set could contain the customer name and billing address and have a 1 in byte 1. The second record could specify the date of shipment and the shipping address and have a 2 in byte 1. And for each item of a shipment, there could be a third type of record that gives the identification number and quantity for one item of the shipment.

Rather than use three separate work areas for these records, though, you could use the ORG command to define all three formats in a single area. This is illustrated in figure 7-20. As you can see, three ORG commands are used to define all three record types in a single area. The ORG command is an assembler command that tells the assembler to change the value of its location counter.

Record layout

Field Name	Customer number	Customer name	Customer address				Balance forward			
			Street address	City	State	Zip code	Date			Amount
							Mo	Day	Yr	
Characteristics	CL5	CL15	CL15	CL15	CL2	CL5	CL2	CL2	CL2	ZL7
Usage										
Position	1-5	6-20	21-35	36-50	51-52	53-57	58-59	60-61	62-63	64-70

Record definition

```
            .
            .
ARREC     DS    0CL80
ARCUSTID  DS    0CL20
ARCUSTNO  DS    CL5
ARNAME    DS    CL15
ARADDR    DS    0CL37
ARSTREET  DS    CL15
ARCITY    DS    CL15
ARSTATE   DS    CL2
ARZIP     DS    CL5
ARBALFWD  DS    0CL13
ARDATE    DS    0CL6
ARMONTH   DS    CL2
ARDAY     DS    CL2
ARYEAR    DS    CL2
ARBALAMT  DS    ZL7
```

Figure 7-19   Using zero duplication factors to define fields within fields

When the ORG command is specified with an operand, it tells the assembler to set the location counter to the location of its operand. Thus, in figure 7-20, RECORD2 is given a location counter value that is the same as RECORD1's. As a result, the fields in RECORD2 are given location values that are in the RECORD1 area. Similarly, RECORD3 and its fields are given location values in the RECORD1 area. The final ORG command, without an operand, tells the assembler to set the location counter to the location value that represents the next available storage location. In figure 7-20, the next available location is the first byte following the 67-byte area defined and redefined as RECORD1, RECORD2, and RECORD3.

The operand for the ORG command can consist of names, decimal values, or the asterisk (which stands for the current location counter value) and can be combined in arithmetic expressions also. Thus, the first ORG command in figure 7-20 would have the same effect if coded as:

```
ORG    *-67
```

This means the current location counter value minus 67. Similarly, the second ORG command would have the same effect if coded as any one of

```
LOC CTR VALUE              STATEMENT

02A0            RECORD1    DS    0CL67
02A0            R1TYPE     DS    CL1
02A1            R1IDNUM    DS    CL4
02A5            R1NAME     DS    CL25
02BE            R1STRT     DS    CL15
02CD            R1CITY     DS    CL15
02DC            R1STATE    DS    CL2
02DE            R1ZIP      DS    CL5
02A0                       ORG   RECORD1
02A0            RECORD2    DS    0CL67
02A0            R2TYPE     DS    CL1
02A1            R2IDNUM    DS    CL4
02A5            R2DATE     DS    CL6
02AB                       DS    CL19
02BE            R2STRT     DS    CL15
02CD            R2CITY     DS    CL15
02DC            R2STATE    DS    CL2
02DE            R2ZIP      DS    CL5
02A0                       ORG   RECORD1
02A0            RECORD3    DS    0CL67
02A0            R3TYPE     DS    CL1
02A1            R3IDNUM    DS    CL4
02A5            R3DATE     DS    CL6
02AB            R3ITEM     DS    CL8
02B3            R3QTY      DS    CL6
02B9                       DS    CL42
02E3                       ORG
```

Figure 7-20   Using the ORG command to redefine a work area

the following:

```
ORG    RECORD2
ORG    *-67
ORG    R1TYPE
ORG    R2TYPE
ORG    R2DATE-5
```

Dummy sections   When you code an assembler language program or subprogram, it is a *control section*, or CSECT, in assembler language terms. For instance, the reorder-listing program of chapter 5 represented one control section. After assembly, a control section becomes a relocatable module that can be link edited and executed.

In contrast, a *dummy section*, or DSECT, doesn't become a relocatable module. When you use a dummy section, it's similar to using explicit addresses as discussed in topic 1. However, a dummy section lets you code labels instead of explicit addresses. This helps prevent coding errors and makes it easier for you to come back to a program later on and change it. As a result, DSECTs are commonly used by professional programmers.

```
INVPROG   START  0
BEGIN     SAVE   (14,12)
          BALR   3,0
          USING  *,3
          USING  INVLOC,8
          ST     13,SAVE+4
          LA     13,SAVE
          .
          .
          LA     8,INVSTOR
          LA     9,25
          ZAP    TOTQTY,=P'0'
ADDLOC    AP     TOTQTY,INVQTY
          LA     8,16(8)
          BCT    9,ADDLOC
          CP     INVONHND,TOTQTY
          BNE    ERROR
          .
          .
INVMSTR   DS     0CL430
INVITNBR  DS     CL10
INVITDES  DS     CL15
INVONHND  DS     PL5
INVSTOR   DS     CL400
INVLOC    DSECT
INVWHSE   DS     CL2
INVBIN    DS     CL3
INVQTY    DS     PL5
INVDATE   DS     0CL6
INVMONTH  DS     CL2
INVDAY    DS     CL2
INVYEAR   DS     CL2
INVPROG   CSECT
TOTQTY    DS     PL5
          .
          .
```

Figure 7-21   Using a DSECT to process 25 location segments

How to use a DSECT for repetitive processing   Figure 7-21 gives an example of the use of a DSECT to control the processing of 25 warehouse-location segments within an inventory master record. The inventory master record (INVMSTR in figure 7-21) is a 430-byte record that ends with a 400-byte area that contains 25 repetitions of a 16-byte warehouse-location segment. Each 16-byte segment contains the warehouse number, bin number, quantity stored in the bin, and date it was stored in this format:

Bytes	Field
1-2	Warehouse number
3-5	Bin number
6-10	Quantity stored
11-16	Date stored (MMDDYY)

In figure 7-21, a DSECT is used for each location segment so each of the 25 groups can be processed using the same labels. The DSECT is coded after the definitions for the 430-byte record area. When a DSECT is coded, no storage area is reserved for it (that's why it's called a dummy section). Instead, the location counter values for the fields within the DSECT are relative to the start of the DSECT. The CSECT instruction at the end of the dummy section restores the location counter value for the program so TOTQTY in figure 7-21 begins at the first location after the 430-byte area reserved for INVMSTR.

When you code a DSECT, you must also code a USING statement to tell the assembler what register to use as the base register for the DSECT fields. If you remember that the DSECT itself reserves no storage positions, you can see that the USING statement must relate the DSECT to some actual storage positions. In figure 7-21, this USING statement relates the DSECT to register 8:

```
USING INVLOC,8
```

Then, this instruction later on in the program puts the address of INVSTOR in register 8:

```
LA    8,INVSTOR
```

As a result, the first time the routine goes through the ADDLOC loop, the field names in the DSECT refer to the first of the 25 segments of the input record that are located in the 400-byte area named INVSTOR. After the first INVQTY is added to TOTQTY, this instruction increases the address in register 8 by 16:

```
LA    8,16(8)
```

So, the next time through the ADDLOC loop, INVQTY will refer to the second location segment in the 400-byte area. And so on. After the loop has been executed 25 times, the sum of the warehouse quantities is compared with the on-hand balance for the item. If they aren't equal, a branch to an error routine takes place.

The CSECT (Control Section) instruction at the end of the dummy section restores the original base register and location counter value for the continuation of the assembly. The label field of the CSECT instruction must be the program name taken from the label field of the START instruction for the control section. A DSECT should always end with either a CSECT or the DSECT of another dummy section.

```
REORDLST START  0
BEGIN    SAVE   (14,12)
         BALR   3,0
         USING  *,3
         USING  IMDSECT,4
         ST     13,SAVE+4
         LA     13,SAVE
           .
           .
           .
READINV  GET    INVMAST
         LR     4,1
         AP     COUNT,=P'1'
         PACK   WRKAVAIL,INVONHND
         PACK   WRKONORD,INVONORD
           .
           .
           .
INVMAST  DCB    DSORG=PS,                              X
                RECFM=FB,                              X
                MACRF=GL,                              X
                BLKSIZE=500,                           X
                LRECL=50,                              X
                EODAD=INVEOF,                          X
                DDNAME=INVMSTR
           .
           .
           .
IMDSECT  DSECT
INVITNBR DS     CL5
INVITDES DS     CL20
INVCOST  DS     CL5
INVPRICE DS     CL5
INVORDPT DS     CL5
INVONHND DS     CL5
INVONORD DS     CL5
REORDLST CSECT
           .
           .
           .
```

Figure 7-22   Using a DSECT to deblock records

How to use a DSECT for blocking and deblocking   When you use blocked records for a tape or DASD file, you can use a DSECT for blocking and deblocking records. If you do, you'll use locate mode instead of move mode, so you don't need to specify a work area for the file. When you use locate mode, the record or block of records remains in an MVS buffer area. Then, when a GET or PUT macro is executed, the address of the next record to be processed is placed in register 1. If, for example, the reorder-listing program of chapter 5 used a DSECT for deblocking the input records, it could be coded as shown in figure 7-22. Since blocking and deblocking are just forms of repetitive processing, this code is similar to the code in figure 7-21. As a result, I'll just point out the differences, which are shaded in figure 7-22.

First, note in figure 7-22 that the option GL is specified for the MACRF operand in the DCB for INVMAST. This option specifies that locate mode is to be used. As a result, you don't have to define a work area for the file. Instead, you define a DSECT for one record.

Second, notice that the USING statement for the dummy section does not specify register 1, even though that's where the address of the next record to be processed is placed by the GET macro. If register 1 were used to address the dummy section, the address of the current record would be lost if another operation was executed that used register 1. So, after each GET macro is executed, an LR instruction loads the value in register 1 into register 4. Then, register 4 is used to address the dummy section. As a result, register 1 can be used for other operations, such as another I/O operation.

Finally, remember that the address in register 1 is changed each time the GET macro is executed. As a result, it always addresses the next record to be processed, whether or not the records are blocked and whether or not two or more buffers are used for the file. In other words, MVS handles blocking and deblocking for you.

In section 4, you'll see other examples of DSECTs used for blocking and deblocking. For now, you should simply realize that you can provide for blocking and deblocking by using a work area. You can also provide for it by using a DSECT and locate mode.

Terminology	locate counter
	control sectin
	dummy section
Objective	Apply zero duplication factors, the ORG instruction, and dummy sections to your programs.

Chapter 8

How to use
subroutines and subprograms

This chapter is divided into three topics. The first shows you how to use subroutines; the second shows you how to use subprograms; the third shows you how to code the MVS JCL you will need when you use subprograms.

188

TOPIC 1   How to use subroutines

A *subroutine* is a group of instructions that is used within a larger routine or within a complete program. Subroutines are important for two main reasons.

First, subroutines can help you reduce coding duplication when the same routine is required in two or more portions of a program. By coding the routine as a subroutine, you only have to code it once. This can shorten the time you take to code a program, and it reduces the amount of storage required by the program.

Second, the use of subroutines lets you divide a program into smaller, more manageable modules. This in turn lets you develop a program one module (or subroutine) at a time, so both coding and testing become more manageable. Normally, though, when you develop a program as a series of subroutines, you must use a program design technique that is consistent with their use. So let's start this topic with some thoughts on program design.

Modular program design
Program flowcharts like the ones we've used so far in this book are okay...as long as the programs you're developing are short and simple. But as your programs increase in size and complexity, traditional flowcharts become less and less effective. In particular, these flowcharts don't encourage you to think of your programs as a collection of modules that fit together in an organized way. Instead, they treat a program, no matter how large, as a series of steps and logical branches.

In contrast, the idea behind *modular program design* is to divide a program into a number of separate modules: one mainline module and one or more subroutine modules. Then, each module can be designed so it will print on a single page or less of an assembly listing. And each page will have a limited amount of logic, or branching. This, in turn, makes it easier to code, test, and maintain the program.

When you use modular program design, you normally draw *modular flowcharts* to represent your design. To illustrate, figure 8-1 represents a modular flowchart for the mainline module of the refined reorder-listing program of chapter 5. If you compare figure 8-1 with the complete flowchart in figure 5-10, you can see that the modular flowchart for the mainline module is much simpler, with only four processing boxes and one decision symbol.

Each of the boxes in figure 8-1 that has a stripe across the top represents another module, or subroutine, of the program. Thus, the mainline module uses three subroutines named READREC, PROCESS, and PRTCOUNT. When one module uses a lower-level module, it is referred to as *calling a module*, or *calling a subroutine*. Then, the higher-level

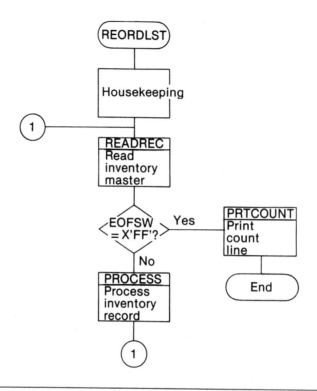

Figure 8-1   A modular flowchart for the mainline module of the refined reorder-listing program

subroutine is the *calling module*. And the lower-level subroutine is the *called module*, or *called subroutine*. In figure 8-1, three subroutines are called by the mainline module.

Figure 8-2 presents the modular flowcharts for the subroutines called by the module in figure 8-1. Here again, the striped boxes refer to lower-level modules. So, the PROCESS module calls the PRTDET module, and the PRTCOUNT module calls the PRINT module.

Figure 8-3 presents the modular flowcharts for the subroutines called by the modules in figure 8-2. Note, here, that PRTDET calls the PRINT module, which was also called by PRTCOUNT. In other words, the PRINT module is called from two modules, rather than one.

When you use modular program design, you'll often find that one module is called by two or more other modules. And this usually means that you have simplified your code by using modular program design. In contrast, using traditional flowcharting techniques, you may not even realize that you could use the same code in more than one place in your program.

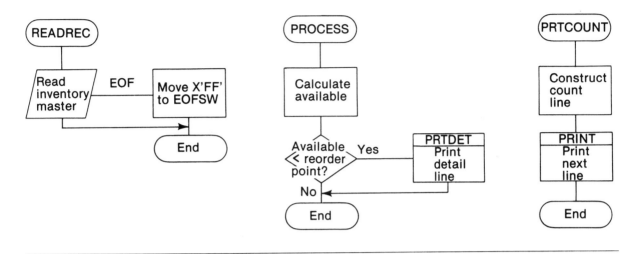

Figure 8-2   Modular flowcharts for the subroutine modules called by the mainline module in figure 8-1

Although the reorder-listing program is so simple that you can code it without designing it at all, I hope it serves to illustrate the value of modular flowcharting. When you use modular flowcharting, you can design your program so each module can easily be charted on a single page. This, in turn, means that you can code each module of the flowchart so it will print on a single page of the assembly listing. And that means your program will be easier to code, test, debug, and maintain. If you experiment with modular design, I think you'll discover how it can help you develop programs, even short programs. And the larger your programs are, the more modular design can help you.

How to code a modular program using subroutines

Figure 8-4 gives the coding for the program that is charted in figures 8-1, 8-2, and 8-3. However, this figure doesn't include the DCBs and data definitions that were used in the original version of the program shown in figure 5-11 since that coding is basically the same as in figure 5-11. Shading is used in figure 8-4 to show the statements that have been added to the program to provide for the linkage between the six modules of the program.

To understand this version of the program and to code one like it, you need to know how to code the instructions used for linkage (BAL and BR). You also need to know how to provide the extra coding required when nested subroutines are used. Finally, you should know how many entry and exit points you should allow for each subroutine.

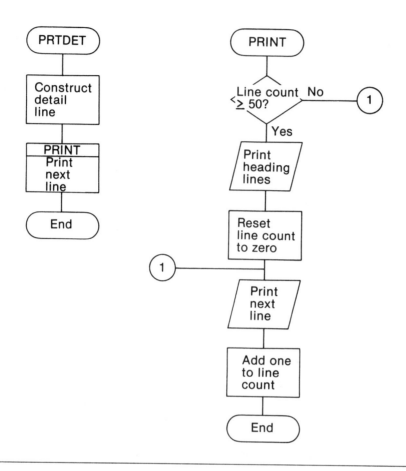

Figure 8-3   Modular flowcharts for the subroutine modules called by the subroutine modules in figure 8-2

The BAL and BALR instructions   To call a subroutine, the mainline module in figure 8-4 uses a branch-and-link (BAL) instruction like this one:

```
BAL    11,READREC
```

When this instruction is executed, the address of the first instruction after the BAL instruction is placed in the register specified as operand-1. Then, the BAL instruction causes a branch to the instruction named as operand-2. In the program in figure 8-4, this instruction causes the address of the CLI instruction to be placed in register 11; then, the program branches to READREC.

You could also code this call to READREC using a BALR instruction as follows:

```
LA     10,READREC
BALR   11,10
```

```
*
*          REORDLST:  THE MAINLINE MODULE
*
REORDLST START  0
BEGIN    SAVE   (14,12)
         BALR   3,0
         USING  *,3
         ST     13,SAVE+4
         LA     13,SAVE
         OPEN   (INVMAST,INPUT,PRTOUT,OUTPUT)
MAINLOOP BAL    11,READREC
         CLI    EOFSW,X'FF'
         BE     EOJRT
         BAL    11,PROCESS
         B      MAINLOOP
EOJRT    BAL    11,PRTCOUNT
         CLOSE  (INVMAST,,PRTOUT)
         L      13,SAVE+4
         RETURN (14,12)
*
*          READREC:  READ INVENTORY MASTER
*
READREC  GET    INVMAST,INVWRKA
         B      READEXIT
READEOF  MVI    EOFSW,X'FF'
READEXIT BR     11
*
*          PROCESS:  PROCESS INVENTORY RECORD
*
PROCESS  ST     11,PROCSAVE
         AP     COUNT,=P'1'
         PACK   WRKAVAIL,INVONHND
         PACK   WRKONORD,INVONORD
         AP     WRKAVAIL,WRKONORD
         PACK   WRKORDPT,INVORDPT
         CP     WRKAVAIL,WRKORDPT
         BNL    PROCEXIT
         BAL    11,PRTDET
PROCEXIT L      11,PROCSAVE
         BR     11
PROCSAVE DS     F
*
*          PRTCOUNT:  PRINT COUNT LINE
*
PRTCOUNT ST     11,PCNTSAVE
         ED     CNTPATRN,COUNT
         MVC    PRTNEXT,CNTLINE
         BAL    11,PRINT
         L      11,PCNTSAVE
         BR     11
PCNTSAVE DS     F
*
*          PRTDET:  PRINT DETAIL LINE
*
PRTDET   ST     11,PRTDSAVE
         PACK   PACKAREA,INVITNBR
         MVC    PRTITNBR,PATTERN1
```

Figure 8-4   Modular coding for the refined reorder-listing program (part 1 of 2)

```
           ED     PRTITNBR,PACKAREA
           MVC    PRTITDES,INVITDES
           PACK   PACKAREA,INVPRICE
           MVC    PRTPRICE,PATTERN2
           ED     PRTPRICE,PACKAREA
           MVC    PRTAVAIL,PATTERN1
           ED     PRTAVAIL,WRKAVAIL
           MVC    PRTORDPT,PATTERN1
           ED     PRTORDPT,WRKORDPT
           MVI    PRTDCTL,C' '
           MVC    PRTNEXT,PRTDETL
           BAL    11,PRINT
           L      11,PRTDSAVE
           BR     11
PRTDSAVE   DS     F
*
*          PRINT:  PRINT NEXT LINE
*
PRINT      CP     LINECNT,=P'50'
           BL     PRTNLINE
           PUT    PRTOUT,HDGLINE1
           PUT    PRTOUT,HDGLINE2
           PUT    PRTOUT,HDGLINE3
           ZAP    LINECNT,=P'0'
           MVI    PRTDCTL,C'0'
PRTNLINE   PUT    PRTOUT,PRTNEXT
           AP     LINECNT,=P'1'
           BR     11
```

Figure 8-4   Modular coding for the refined reorder-listing program (part 2 of 2)

Here, the BALR instruction first places the address of the next instruction in register 11; then, it branches to the address in register 10. Since register 10 has been loaded with the address of READREC, these instructions work the same as the one BAL instruction.

You can use any register for linking to a subroutine, but remember that most I/O operations use registers 14, 15, 0, and 1. As a result, if you were to use register 14 as a link register to a subroutine that does some input or output operation that uses register 14, the address in register 14 would be destroyed. However, you can use registers 14, 15, 0, and 1 if you save their contents as the first step of the subroutine and restore them just before exiting the subroutine. This save and restore technique is illustrated later in this topic.

The BR instruction   To return to a calling module from a subroutine, you code a branch register (BR) instruction like this:

```
           BR     11
```

This instruction branches unconditionally to the address given in the register specified. In the READREC module in figure 8-4, this instruction branches back to the CLI instruction in the REORDLST module since the address of the CLI instruction was loaded into register 11 before the branch to READREC took place. In figure 8-4, all subroutines are called using register 11 in a BAL instruction. So, all subroutines return to the calling module using register 11 in a BR instruction.

Nested subroutines   When a mainline module calls a subroutine that calls another subroutine, the subroutines can be referred to as *nested subroutines*. In figure 8-4, REORDLST calls PROCESS, which calls PRTDET, which calls PRINT, so these modules are nested four deep. Similarly, REORDLST calls PRTCOUNT, which calls PRINT, so these modules are nested three deep. When you design a modular program, it usually results in nested subroutines. And there's no limit to how deeply you can nest your modules.

When you code a subroutine in the middle of a nest, you must realize that you have to save the value of the register you're using for linkage or you can destroy the linkage chain. This is illustrated in figure 8-5, which shows just the coding of figure 8-4 that affects the *linkage* between REORDLST, PROCESS, PRTDET, and PRINT. Here, REORDLST is the top-level module in the nest of subroutines, PRINT is the lowest-level module, and PROCESS and PRTDET are in the middle of the linkage chain.

Note, then, that both PROCESS and PRTDET start by storing the contents of register 11 in a fullword save area. Then, they use register 11 as the linkage register in their calls to lower-level modules. After their subroutines return to them and they complete their processing, they load the contents of their save areas back into register 11 and use BR instructions to branch back to the module that called them.

Can you see why PROCESS and PRTDET must save the contents of register 11 before calling their subroutines? If they didn't, the *linkage chain* would be destroyed. If, for example, PROCESS didn't save register 11, the contents of register 11 would be replaced by the address of the instruction after its own BAL instruction when this BAL instruction is executed. Then, the BR instruction at the end of PROCESS would branch to one of its own instructions and an endless loop would be started. To keep the linkage chain intact, a subroutine in the middle of a nest must store and reload the address sent to it in the linkage register.

Incidentally, this saving and restoring of linkage registers can be useful during debugging. When a program terminates abnormally, the save area for the link register in each subroutine provides a trace back to the calling routine. As a result, you can recreate the series of links that took place before program termination by analyzing the storage dump.

Entry and exit points   When a BAL or BALR instruction is used to call a subroutine, the address in the operand-1 register is called the *return address*, and the operand-2 address is called the *entry point* of the subroutine. Similarly, the instruction of the subroutine that returns to the calling module is referred to as the subprogram's *exit point*.

```
*
*          REORDLST:   THE MAINLINE MODULE
*
REORDLST START 0
           .
           .
           BAL   11,PROCESS
           .
           .
*
*          PROCESS:   PROCESS INVENTORY RECORD
*
PROCESS   ST    11,PROCSAVE
           .
           .
           BAL   11,PRTDET
PROCEXIT L     11,PROCSAVE
          BR    11
PROCSAVE DS    F
           .
           .
*
*          PRTDET:  PRINT DETAIL LINE
*
PRTDET   ST    11,PRTDSAVE
           .
           .
           BAL   11,PRINT
           L     11,PRTDSAVE
           BR    11
PRTDSAVE DS    F
*
*          PRINT:  PRINT NEXT LINE
*
PRINT      .
           .
           .
           BR    11
```

Figure 8-5   The linkage for one set of nested subroutines in the reorder-listing program in figure 8-4

In figure 8-4, then, register 11 always contains the return address for the subroutine that is being executed. The first instruction of each subroutine is always the entry point of the subroutine. And the last instruction of each subroutine is its exit point. In other words, each subroutine has only one entry point and only one exit point. As you will learn in chapter 19, this is consistent with modern program development methods. So, when coding subroutines, we recommend that you follow the rule of only one entry and one exit point in each subroutine.

You should realize, though, that it is possible to code a subroutine with more than one entry or exit point. In fact, if you review the subroutines used in your shop, particularly, the older ones, you may find that many have multiple entry or exit points. For instance, completion of normal processing by a subroutine might have one exit point while some error routine within the subroutine might use a different exit point. Keep in mind, then, that modern programming practices dictate against this, and that it's always possible to code a subroutine so it has only one entry and one exit point.

How to code a generalized subroutine

Usually, when you write a subroutine, it will only be used in one program, your own. Sometimes, though, a *generalized subroutine* is valuable. A generalized subroutine is one that is written in a general way so it can be used in any program, not just one program. If, for example, the PRINT subroutine of figure 8-4 were generalized, it could be used in any program that requires page overflow and the printing of a three-line heading at the top of each printed page.

No matter how much you generalize a subroutine, though, the calling program has to know what the subroutine requires. For instance, to call a generalized version of the PRINT module, you must know what fields PRINT is going to operate on and how it's going to know where those fields are in your calling module.

To illustrate, figure 8-6 shows just a slightly generalized version of the PRINT module of figure 8-4 along with the linkage instructions in the two modules that call it. In this case, to use the PRINT subroutine, you must know that it expects the address of your print line in register 10 and it expects the return address in register 11. Also, PRTOUT must be the label of your printer DCB, the DCB must be coded with MACRF=PM, and the names of your heading line definitions must be HDGLINE1, HDGLINE2, and HDGLINE3.

The instructions in the PRINT subroutine that relate to its generalization are shaded in figure 8-6. In other words, register 10 is used as an explicit base address for the next line to be printed by the program. Also, the control character in the line addressed by register 10 is saved in PCTLSAVE when the heading lines are printed so the control character can be changed to provide for double spacing after the heading lines. Then, after the heading lines are printed, the control character in the line is restored to the value in PCTLSAVE so the subroutine won't affect the forms-control logic of the calling module.

Figure 8-7 presents a more generalized version of the PRINT subroutine. In this case, the calling module must place the address of an address list in register 9, the address of the next line to be printed in register 10, and the return address in register 11. The address list must contain three addresses that point to the heading lines to be printed at the top of each page. Then, the PRINT subroutine uses the three addresses in the address list and the one address in register 10 as it prints the next line of output. So the subroutine can store the three addresses in the list in registers 6, 7, and 8, the contents of these registers are stored at the start of

```
        LA     10,CNTLINE
        BAL    11,PRINT
        .
        .
        .
        LA     10,PRTDETL
        BAL    11,PRINT
        .
        .
        .
*
*      PRINT:   GENERALIZED ROUTINE TO PRINT NEXT LINE AND
*                        PROVIDE FOR PAGE OVERFLOW
*
*      ADDRESS OF NEXT LINE MUST BE IN REGISTER 10
*      RETURN ADDRESS MUST BE IN REGISTER 11
*      PRTOUT MUST BE LABEL OF PRINTER DCB
*      MACRF=PM MUST BE CODED FOR PRINTER DCB
*      HEADING LINES MUST BE NAMED HDGLINE1, HDGLINE2, & HDGLINE3
*
PRINT     CP     LINECNT,=P'50'
          BL     PRTNLINE
          PUT    PRTOUT,HDGLINE1
          PUT    PRTOUT,HDGLINE2
          PUT    PRTOUT,HDGLINE3
          ZAP    LINECNT,=P'0'
          MVC    PCTLSAVE,0(10)
          MVI    0(10),C'0'
PRTNLINE  PUT    PRTOUT,0(10)
          MVC    0(1,10),PCTLSAVE
          AP     LINECNT,=P'1'
          BR     11
LINECNT   DC     P'99'
PCTLSAVE  DS     CL1
```

Figure 8-6   A generalized PRINT subroutine

the subroutine and reloaded at the end of the routine. If you have any trouble understanding the coding in figure 8-7, you may want to review the material on register operations in topic 1 of chapter 7.

Whether a subroutine is only slightly generalized as in figure 8-6 or more heavily generalized as in figure 8-7, you still need to know what the subroutine expects before you can use it. As a result, there's a limit to how much effort you should put forth to generalize a subroutine. There's also a limit as to how useful a generalized subroutine can be. As a result, you may not use generalized subroutines in your shop at all.

Using COPY statements for generalized subroutines   If you do use generalized subroutines, you will probably get them into your source programs with COPY commands. If, for example, you're using the PRINT subroutine in figure 8-7, you can get it into your program using an instruction like this:

```
            LA      9,ADDRLIST
            LA      10,PRTDETL
            BAL     11,PRINT
            .
            .
ADDRLIST DC      A(HDGLINE1)
         DC      A(HDGLINE2)
         DC      A(HDGLINE3)
            .
            .
*
*           PRINT:  GENERALIZED ROUTINE TO PRINT NEXT LINE
*                   AND PROVIDE FOR PAGE OVERFLOW
*
*           ADDRESS OF ADDRESS LIST FOR 3 HEADING LINES MUST BE IN REG 9
*           ADDRESS OF NEXT DETAIL LINE MUST BE IN REGISTER 10
*           RETURN ADDRESS MUST BE IN REGISTER 11
*           PRTOUT MUST BE LABEL OF PRINTER DCB
*           MACRF=PM MUST BE CODED FOR PRINTER DCB
*
PRINT       STM     6,8,REGSAVE
            LM      6,8,0(9)
            CP      LINECNT,=P'50'
            BL      PRTNLINE
            PUT     PRTOUT,0(6)
            PUT     PRTOUT,0(7)
            PUT     PRTOUT,0(8)
            ZAP     LINECNT,=P'0'
            MVC     PCTLSAVE,0(10)
            MVI     0(10),C'0'
PRTNLINE    PUT     PRTOUT,0(10)
            MVC     0(1,10),PCTLSAVE
            AP      LINECNT,=P'1'
            LM      6,8,REGSAVE
            BR      11
REGSAVE  DS      3F
LINECNT  DC      P'99'
PCTLSAVE DS      CL1
```

Figure 8-7   A more generalized version of a PRINT subroutine

```
        COPY    PRINT
```

This assumes, of course, that PRINT is the name of the book that contains the PRINT subroutine in the source library. This also assumes that the library has been established in the EXEC statement for the job as described in chapter 6. Then, when the assembler encounters the COPY instruction, it will insert the book into your source program. This can reduce the amount of code you have to enter into the system for your program, so generalized subroutines like this do have their purpose.

Discussion

Subroutines are useful primarily because they provide a means of implementing a modular program design. However, subroutines are also useful when they help reduce the amount of coding required by a program. As a result, you may find a number of generalized subroutines in common use in your shop.

Since modular program design is a significant improvement over traditional flowcharting techniques, you may find it useful when you develop programs. However, you should realize that it's not the most current method of program design. Structured program design is. As a result, chapter 19 shows you how to develop structured programs in assembler language. When you read that chapter, you will see that structured programs require the use of subroutines in much the same way that modular programs do.

Terminology

subroutine
modular program design
modular flowchart
calling a module
calling a subroutine
calling module
called module
called subroutine
nested subroutines
linkage
linkage chain
return address
entry point
exit point
generalized subroutine

Objectives

1. Describe the benefits of modular program design.

2. Given a set of modular flowcharts, code the linkage between the program modules.

TOPIC 2   How to use subprograms

Like a subroutine, a *subprogram* represents one module of a program. Unlike a subroutine, though, a subprogram is assembled by itself. Then, it is combined with the other modules of the program by the linkage editor.

Subprograms are useful for two main reasons. First, some routines are repeated in many different types of programs. As a result, by treating them as subprograms, they only need to be coded and assembled once. This reduces coding duplication, and thus programming effort.

Second, some routines can be written more efficiently in one language than in another. For instance, some functions can't be coded at all in COBOL. In a case like this, a COBOL main program can call an assembler language subprogram to perform the function. Since all of a computer's functions can be coded in assembler language, writing special-purpose subprograms is one of the main uses of assembler language.

SUBPROGRAM LINKAGE

When a higher-level module transfers control to a subprogram, it is refer- red to as *calling the subprogram*. Then, the higher-level module is the *calling module* and the subprogram is the *called module*. The coding that provides for the transfer of control between calling and called module is referred to as the *subprogram linkage*. This terminology, of course, is like the terminology related to subroutines.

Similarly, the calling module provides a *return address* to the sub- program, and it enters the subprogram at its *entry point*. When the sub- program returns to the calling module, it leaves at its *exit point*.

Adcon resolution

When you use subprograms, the calling module and the called module are assembled separately. As a result, the assembler can't determine the address of the called module during the assembly. Instead, the program- mer uses assembler commands and adcons to tell the assembler that certain addresses can't be assembled correctly. Then, the linkage editor will resolve the addressing problems in a process called *adcon resolution* that is a part of linkage editing.

Figure 8-8 shows one way to provide for adcon resolution in the calling and called modules. This method uses EXTRN and ENTRY instruc- tions. Once you understand this method of providing for adcon resolu- tion, I'll show you three standard forms of subprogram linkage.

The EXTRN command in the calling module   Since the calling module doesn't know that RATESUB is the entry point of the subprogram, it can't be used as an operand in a BAL instruction that links to the subprogram. Instead, the name of the entry point in the subprogram must appear in an address constant like this:

```
ADDRSUB    DC      A(RATESUB)
```

Also, because RATESUB isn't defined in the calling module, this address constant must be preceded by an EXTRN command with RATESUB as the operand:

```
EXTRN RATESUB
```

The EXTRN command is a message to the assembler that the symbol appearing as an operand is external to this program. That is, it isn't defined within this program.

The EXTRN command causes the assembler to allow the address constant to be assembled as hex zeros (X'00000000'). It also causes the adcon to be put into a list for resolution by the linkage-editor program. Later on, the linkage editor will fill the adcon area with the proper address when it link edits the calling module and the subprogram.

An EXTRN command can have more than one operand. Also, you can code as many EXTRN commands as you need in a single program. For instance, a program that calls five subprograms might have these EXTRN statements:

```
EXTRN SUB1,SUB2,SUB3
EXTRN SUB4,SUB5
```

Since EXTRN statements don't generate any object code and therefore occupy no storage, they can be placed anywhere in a program. However, they must precede the use of the symbols that they define as external.

The ENTRY command in the subprogram   The ENTRY command in the subprogram in figure 8-8 tells the assembler to make the entry-point address available for resolution by the linkage editor. In other words, the ENTRY command is a counterpart to the EXTRN command. The ENTRY command also follows the same coding form as the EXTRN. You can use more than one operand in an ENTRY command and more than one command in a program.

In figure 8-8, an ENTRY command isn't actually needed because the subprogram only has one entry point. Instead, the subprogram could start with this instruction:

```
RATESUB   START  0
```

Since the address of the label on the START instruction is always available for adcon resolution, you don't have to code an ENTRY command if the entry point is the same as the address of the START instruction. In figure 8-8, both SUBPROG and RATESUB have the same address since the BALR instruction at RATESUB is the first machine instruction of the subprogram.

```
        Calling module                              Subprogram


                                        SUBPROG     START   0
          .                                         ENTRY   RATESUB
          .                             RATESUB     BALR    10,0
          L        12,ADDRSUB                       USING   *,10
          BALR     11,12
          .                                           .
          .                                           .
          .                                           .
          EXTRN    RATESUB                           BR      11
ADDRSUB   DC       A(RATESUB)                        END
```

Figure 8-8   Using EXTRN and ENTRY instructions to provide for adcon resolution

Multiple entry and exit points

In the last topic, I recommended that you write your subroutines with only one entry and one exit point. In general, that's true for subprograms also. Subprograms are easiest to manage when they have only one entry and one exit point. Since it's relatively easy to make sure each subprogram has only one exit point, there's usually no problem there. But sometimes, it makes sense to write a subprogram that has more than one entry point.

To illustrate, consider the PRINT subroutine in the last topic that printed one detail line and provided for headings and page overflow. Now, think what it would take to make that subroutine into a subprogram. So the subprogram can be assembled separately, the DCB statement for the print file has to be in the subprogram along with the definitions for the file's work area. No problem there, but remember that a print file has to be opened before it can print a record and it must be closed when a program ends. That means that the OPEN and CLOSE statements must also be in the subprogram.

If you're writing the subprogram, this leaves you with a design problem. Do you open and close the file each time the subprogram is called? That would be inefficient in terms of computer time. Or, do you provide three entry points for the subprogram: one for the opening of the file, one for the processing function of the subprogram, and one for the closing of the file? In many cases, this second alternative is the right solution for the problem.

If you code the subprogram with three entry points, the calling module must call the subprogram once at the start of the program using the first entry point to open the print file. It must call the subprogram repeatedly during the execution of the program to print the detail lines using the second entry point. And it must call the subprogram once at the end of the program using the third entry point to close the file. In a case like this, of course, the calling module must specify three entry points for adcon resolution. And the subprogram must specify three entry points too.

STANDARD LINKAGE

Figure 8-9 illustrates a form of subprogram linkage that is considered an informal standard within most IBM-supplied programs. As a result, it is often referred to as *standard linkage*.

Although figure 8-9 doesn't show the processing instructions of the subprogram, you should know that the subprogram finds an employee's pay rate (PAYRATE) when it is given the employee's pay class (PAYCLASS). In other words, the calling module sends the subprogram the PAYCLASS field and the subprogram returns the PAYRATE field. Both fields, however, are defined in the calling module. In this example, if the subprogram can't find the pay rate in the table, it returns a pay rate of 999.

The calling module

There are three important points to be noted in the calling module in figure 8-9. First, you should see how the PAYCLASS and PAYRATE fields are sent to the subprogram using an address list. Second, you should learn how to code a Vcon. Third, you should make sure you understand the use of the BALR instruction.

Loading the address of the address list in register 1   In figure 8-9, the calling module starts by loading an address into register 1:

```
        LA      1,ADDRLIST
```

Here, ADDRLIST is the starting address of two adcons that contain the addresses of PAYCLASS and PAYRATE, the two fields to be passed to the subprogram. In other words, these adcons make up the *address list* that is going to be passed to the subprogram. In standard linkage, the address of this address list must always be loaded into register 1.

The Vcon that identifies the subprogram's entry point   Near the bottom of the calling module, a V-type address constant is coded for the subprogram's entry point. The effect of a *Vcon* is equal to the combination of an A-type adcon and an EXTRN for the symbol. As a result, the last two lines in the calling module in figure 8-8 could be coded with the single Vcon in figure 8-9:

```
    ADDRSUB    DC      V(RATESUB)
```

This Vcon causes a four-byte address constant (initially filled with hex zeros) to be defined, and the adcon is placed in the external symbol list for adcon resolution by the linkage editor.

The BALR instruction that calls the subprogram   To transfer control to the subprogram, the calling module in figure 8-9 uses this code:

```
        L       15,ADDRSUB
        BALR    14,15
```

The first instruction loads the address constant for the subprogram into

Calling module

```
            .
            .
            .
            LA      1,ADDRLIST
            L       15,ADDRSUB
            BALR    14,15
            CP      PAYRATE,=P'999'
            BE      CLASSERR
            .
            .
            .
ADDRSUB     DC      V(RATESUB)
ADDRLIST    DC      A(PAYCLASS)
            DC      A(PAYRATE)
            .
            .
            .
```

Notes:

1. Register 1 points to an address list.

2. Register 15 contains the subprogram entry point.

3. Register 14 contains the return address.

4. The subprogram entry point is defined with a Vcon.

Subprogram

```
RATESUB     START   0
            USING   *,15
            STM     6,8,SAVE
            LM      6,7,0(1)
            .
            .
            .
            .
            .
RETURN      LM      6,8,SAVE
            BR      14
SAVE        DS      3F
            .
            .
            .
            END
```

Notes:

1. The entry point is the name given on the START command.

2. Register 15, loaded by the calling module, is used as the base register.

Figure 8-9   Standard subprogram linkage

register 15. Then, a BALR instruction puts the address of the next instruction in register 14, after which it branches to the address in register 15. In standard linkage, register 15 always contains the entry point of the subprogram that is being called, and register 14 always contains the return address.

The subprogram

The subprogram in figure 8-9 is, of course, coded to be compatible with the calling routine. Here, the ENTRY statement is omitted because the subprogram's only entry point, RATESUB, appears as the program name on the START instruction. There are several points to note in this subprogram related to the subprogram linkage so let's take them from the top.

The base register   Since subprograms are assembled separately, they are not addressed by the calling module's base register. As a result, in the subprogram in figure 8-8, register 10 is loaded and assigned as the base register with the standard BALR and USING technique. The previous contents of register 10 are thus destroyed.

In figure 8-9, though, the USING instruction says that register 15 should be used as the base register in the subprogram. This is a commonly-used technique when writing subprograms, because it avoids the possibility of destroying the contents of some other register that may be used by the calling module. Note that a BALR instruction to load register 15 isn't necessary because the calling routine has already loaded the subprogram's starting address into it.

Storing and reloading the registers used by the subprogram   In the subprogram in figure 8-9, the first machine instruction stores the contents of registers 6, 7, and 8:

```
STM    6,8,SAVE
```

It does this, because these are the registers that are going to be used by the subprogram. When the subprogram is ready to return to the calling module, it uses this instruction to reload the registers:

```
LM     6,8,SAVE
```

As a result, if the calling module is using registers 6, 7, or 8, the subprogram won't destroy the calling module's data.

Loading the address constants in the address list into registers   After the subprogram in figure 8-9 stores registers 6 through 8, it loads the addresses in the address list into registers 6 and 7 using this instruction:

```
LM     6,7,0(1)
```

Here, register 1 is used in an explicit address in the load multiple instruction. Remember that register 1 was loaded with the starting address of the address list by the calling module.

After this instruction is executed, register 6 addresses the PAYCLASS field in the calling module; and register 7 addresses the PAYRATE field in the calling module. Registers 6 and 7 can then be used in instructions with explicit addresses to operate upon the PAYCLASS and PAYRATE fields.

The BR instruction that returns to the calling module   Just as in a subroutine, the BR instruction is used in a subprogram to return to the calling module. In figure 8-9, this instruction is used:

```
BR      14
```

As I said, register 14 is always used for the return address when using standard linkage.

The END instruction   Note in the subprogram in figure 8-9 that the END instruction doesn't have an operand. That's because this module isn't going to be the first module in a phase that's assembled by the linkage editor. As a result, you should only specify an operand in your END statement when it won't be called by another module. You should never specify an operand in a subprogram.

STANDARD MVS PROGRAM LINKAGE WITHOUT MACROS

You'll remember from chapter 5 that every program should contain a standard set of instructions to save and restore the general registers. This is a part of *standard MVS program linkage*.

When you call a subprogram, this same type of linkage is required. Although you can use the standard subprogram linkage illustrated in figure 8-9, which only saves the registers actually used in the subprogram, it's more common to save all of the registers. That way, you're sure to save all of the registers that are used by the subprogram.

All of the programs in this book illustrate standard MVS program linkage using the SAVE and RETURN macros. However, you can also provide for standard program linkage without using macros. I'm going to illustrate this form of linkage first, because it will help you understand standard MVS macro linkage.

Figure 8-10 illustrates standard MVS linkage without macros. The linkage code in the calling module should look familiar since I've used it in every program in this book. However, I'll review it for you here so you can see how it applies to subprograms. Then, I'll explain the code used in the subprogram for saving and restoring the registers.

Calling module

```
            .
            .
       LA    13,SAVE
            .
            .
       LA    1,ADDRLIST
       L     15,ADDRSUB
       BALR  14,15
       CP    PAYRATE,=P'999'
       BE    CLASSERR
            .
            .
ADDRSUB   DC    V(RATESUB)
ADDRLIST  DC    A(PAYCLASS)
          DC    A(PAYRATE)
SAVE      DS    18F
            .
            .
            .
```

Notes:

1. Register 13 points to an 18-word save area.

2. Register 1 points to an address list.

3. Register 15 contains the subprogram entry point.

4. Register 14 contains the return address.

5. The subprogram entry point is defined with a Vcon.

Figure 8-10   Standard macro linkage (part 1 of 2)

The calling module

The first linkage instruction in the calling module in figure 8-10 is this:

```
       LA    13,SAVE
```

This loads register 13 with the address of an 18-word save area defined in the calling module. As you will see in a moment, this address is used by the subprogram to save the contents of all 16 registers. In other words, the register contents are saved in the calling module's area.

The subprogram

Storing the contents of the registers   The first instruction of the subprogram in figure 8-10 is this:

```
       STM   14,12,12(13)
```

Subprogram

```
RATESUB   START  0
          STM    14,12,12(13)
          BALR   3,0
          USING  *,3
          ST     13,SUBSAVE+4
          LA     13,SUBSAVE
          LM     6,7,0(1)
            .
            .
            .
RETURN    L      13,SUBSAVE+4
          LM     14,12,12(13)
          BR     14
SUBSAVE   DS     18F
            .
            .
            .
```

Notes:

1. The entry point is the name given on the START macro.

2. Registers 14 through 12 are stored in the calling module's save area.

3. Standard base register assignment is used.

4. Register 13 is stored in the second word of the subprogram save area.

5. Register 13 is loaded with the address of the subprogram save area.

6. Register 13 is reloaded with the address of the calling module's save area prior to return.

7. Registers 14 through 12 are reloaded from the calling module's save area.

8. The subprogram returns to the address in register 14.

Figure 8-10   Standard macro linkage (part 2 of 2)

Its function is to store the contents of the registers in the calling module's save area. To understand how this instruction works, you need to know the format of the save area. It's presented in figure 8-11.

As you can see, the fourth through eighteenth words of the save area are where the contents of the registers are stored. The important thing to notice is the sequence in which the registers are stored: register 14, register 15, register 0, register 1, and so on up to register 12. That's why the first two operands of the store-multiple instruction indicate that registers 14 through 12 are to be stored. The third operand specifies that these registers are to be stored beginning twelve bytes after the address specified in register 13. Since register 13 was loaded with the address of the save area in the calling module, the registers are stored in the appropriate locations in this save area.

Word	Displacement	Contents
1	0	Used by PL/I
2	4	Address of previous save area in calling program
3	8	Address of next save area
4	12	Contents of register 14
5	16	Contents of register 15
6	20	Contents of register 0
7	24	Contents of register 1
8	28	Contents of register 2
9	32	Contents of register 3
10	36	Contents of register 4
11	40	Contents of register 5
12	44	Contents of register 6
13	48	Contents of register 7
14	52	Contents of register 8
15	56	Contents of register 9
16	60	Contents of register 10
17	64	Contents of register 11
18	68	Contents of register 12

Figure 8-11   Assignments for a standard save area

Once the STM instruction has been executed, the subprogram can use any registers except 13 without disrupting the registers of the calling program. As a result, the subprogram in figure 8-10 uses a normal BALR/ USING combination to load and assign register 3 as the base register for the subprogram. Then, it can use any register except 3 or 13 for other register functions.

Loading the address of the subprogram's save area into register 13   The two instructions that follow the USING statement prepare this subprogram so it can call other subprograms if required:

```
ST      13,SUBSAVE+4
LA      13,SUBSAVE
```

First, the address of the calling program's save area in register 13 is stored in the second word of the subprogram's own 18-word save area, SUBSAVE+4. Second, register 13 is loaded with the address of its own 18-word save area, SUBSAVE. When this has been done, the subprogram can link to another subprogram using the standard linkage. I'll explain this "chaining" of save areas in more detail in a moment.

Restoring the contents of the registers   After the subprogram completes its lookup function, it can return to the calling module. But first, it must restore the original contents of the registers. To reload register 13, the subprogram uses this instruction:

```
L       13,SUBSAVE+4
```

This loads the contents of the second word of the subprogram's save area into register 13. Since the address of the calling module's save area was stored in SUBSAVE+4 at the start of the subprogram, register 13 addresses the calling module's save area after this instruction is executed.

To reload the rest of the registers, the subprogram uses this instruction:

```
LM      14,12,12(13)
```

Since register 13 contains the address of the calling module's save area, this instruction restores the contents of the registers that were stored there at the beginning of the program. After these registers have been restored, the subprogram branches back to the return address that has just been restored to register 14.

STANDARD MVS MACRO LINKAGE

Standard MVS macro linkage works the same way that the standard MVS linkage without macros works. However, the macro instructions make it easier for the programmer to facilitate the linkage. Standard macro linkage is illustrated in figure 8-12.

The calling module

When you use standard macro linkage, much of the code you use for standard linkage is done automatically. In particular, you don't need to define the entry point of the subprogram or the address list that's passed to it. And you don't have to load registers 1 and 15. This is all taken care of by the CALL macro.

The CALL macro   In figure 8-12, the calling module uses this CALL macro to link to the subprogram:

```
CALL   RATESUB,(PAYCLASS,PAYRATE)
```

Chapter 8

Calling module

```
          .
          .
          .
          LA      13,SAVE
          CALL    RATESUB,(PAYCLASS,PAYRATE)
          CP      PAYRATE,=P'999'
          BE      CLASSERR
          .
          .
SAVE      DS      18F
          .
          .
```

Notes:

1. Register 13 is loaded with the address of an
    18-word save area.

2. The CALL macro does four things:
    a. it contructs the adcon list and places
        the list address in register 1;
    b. it loads register 15 with a Vcon literal
        that contains the address of the
        subprogram entry point;
    c. it loads register 14 with the return
        address; and
    d. it generates a BALR to the subprogram.

Figure 8-12   Standard MVS macro linkage (part 1 of 2)

The first operand of the CALL macro is used in the definition of a V-type address constant; its address is loaded into register 15. The data names that appear in the second operand of the CALL macro (PAYCLASS and PAYRATE) are used to construct an address list; the address of this list is loaded into register 1. Finally, a BALR instruction is generated that uses register 14 for the return address and register 15 for the entry-point address. This causes the branch to the subprogram.

The subprogram   **The SAVE macro**   The first executable code in the subprogram in figure 8-12 is generated by this SAVE macro:

```
          SAVE    (14,12)
```

This macro generates a store multiple instruction, like the one in figure 8-10, that saves the contents of the register group specified within parentheses. It stores these registers in the 18-word save area addressed by register 13, having the format in figure 8-11.

Subprogram

```
RATESUB   START  0
          SAVE   (14,12)
          BALR   3,0
          USING  *,3
          ST     13,SUBSAVE+4
          LA     13,SUBSAVE
          LM     6,7,0(1)
          .
          .
          .
RETURN    L      13,SUBSAVE+4
          RETURN (14,12)
SUBSAVE   DS     18F
          .
          .
          END
```

Notes:

1. The SAVE macro stores registers 14 through 12 in the calling module's save area.

2. Standard base register assignment is used.

3. Register 13 is stored in the second word of the subprogram save area.

4. Register 13 is loaded with the address of the subprogram save area.

5. Register 13 is reloaded with the address of the calling module's save area prior to return.

6. The RETURN macro reloads registers 14 through 12 and returns to the calling module.

Figure 8-12   Standard MVS macro linkage (part 2 of 2)

Loading the address constants into registers   After the ST and LA instructions prepare the subprogram for calling another subprogram, an LM instruction loads the addresses of PAYCLASS and PAYRATE into registers 6 and 7:

```
          LM     6,7,0(1)
```

Because the CALL macro put the address of the address list in register 1, this LM instruction loads the registers starting with the word addressed by register 1. From this point on, the subprogram can operate upon the PAYCLASS and PAYRATE fields by referring to them using registers 6 and 7 as explicit base registers.

The RETURN macro   After the subprogram completes its lookup function and reloads register 13, this RETURN macro is executed:

```
                    RETURN (14,12)
```

You should remember from chapter 5 that this macro generates instructions that do two things. First, it generates a load-multiple instruction, like the one in figure 8-10, that reloads registers 14 through 12 from the calling module's save area, which is addressed by register 13. Second, it branches back to the calling program by using the return address in register 14.

NESTED SUBPROGRAMS   When one subprogram calls another subprogram, they are referred to as *nested subprograms*. And subprograms are frequently nested. In fact, you can think of MVS itself as a large nest of subprograms. A program of the operating system calls an application program that calls a subprogram and so on. That's why the chain that is provided by the standard MVS macro linkage can be so useful.

Figure 8-13 shows the linkage for three levels of nested subprograms. If you follow the flow from the CALL of the first module to the second, you can see that the coding in this subprogram is the same as that illustrated in figure 8-12. Note, however, that the save area in all three modules is named SAVE. This is okay because the modules are assembled separately. Because the relationship between the calling module and the called module is the same at any level, this nesting of subprograms can extend to any number of levels.

When you save and restore the registers using the SAVE and RETURN macros, you receive a special debugging benefit. Because the second word of each program's save area contains the address of the calling program's save area, a chain through each level of the structure exists. As a result, if the phase ends abnormally, the storage dump can be used to trace through each save area and figure out the path that was followed just before the abnormal termination.

LINKING A COBOL PROGRAM WITH AN ASSEMBLER LANGUAGE SUBPROGRAM

So far, I have only shown you the linkage from an assembler language calling module to an assembler language subprogram. But, as I've already mentioned, subprograms can be useful for performing tasks that are difficult or impossible to write in a higher-level language. At this time, then, I would like to present the linkage from a COBOL main program to an assembler language subprogram.

You will recall from topic 2 of chapter 6 that the SNAP macro provides a dump of the program area between two addresses that you supply as operands and, if you request it, a dump of the general registers and a trace of the save areas. Since you can't force a snapshot dump like this from a COBOL program, it is sometimes useful to call an assembler language subprogram for this function. Figure 8-14 shows the complete assembler language subprogram for this function along with the linkage for the COBOL program.

Main program

```
MAINPROG START  0
          SAVE   (14,12)
          .
          .
          ST     13,SAVE+4
          LA     13,SAVE
          .
          .
          .
          CALL   SUB1,(.....)
          .
          .
          .
          .
          .
          .
          .
          L      13,SAVE+4
          RETURN (14,12)
SAVE      DS     18F
```

Word 1: Not used

Word 2: Save address from MVS

Word 3: Not used

Word 4: Register 14, return address

Word 5: Register 15, SUB1 address

Words 6-18: Registers 0-12

First Subprogram

```
SUB1      START  0
          SAVE   (14,12)
          BALR   .....
          USING  .....
          ST     13,SAVE+4
          LA     13,SAVE
          .
          .
          CALL   SUB2,(.....)
          .
          .
          L      13,SAVE+4
          RETURN (14,12)
SAVE      DS     18F
          END
```

Word 1: Not used

Word 2: Save address in calling module

Word 3: Not used

Word 4: Register 14, return address

Word 5: Register 15, SUB2 address

Words 6-18: Registers 0-12

Second Subprogram

```
SUB2      START  0
          SAVE   (14,12)
          BALR   .....
          USING  .....
          ST     13,SAVE+4
          LA     13,SAVE
          .
          .
          .
          .
          .
          L      13,SAVE+4
          RETURN (14,12)
SAVE      DS     18F
          END
```

Word 1: Not used

Word 2: SAVE address in calling module

Words 3-18: Not used

Figure 8-13   Nested subprogram linkage using standard macros

COBOL calling program

```
 DATA DIVISION.
*
 FILE SECTION.
     .
     .
 01  WORK-FIELDS.
*
    05  SNAP-START          PIC X(10)      VALUE 'SNAP START'.
    05  WORK-FIELD-1        PIC S9(5).
    05  WORK-FIELD-2        PIC S9(7).
     .
     .
    05  SNAP-END            PIC X(8)       VALUE 'SNAP END'.
     .
     .
 PROCEDURE DIVISION.
*
     .
     .
    CALL 'SNAP' USING SNAP-START, SNAP-END.
     .
     .
```

Assembler language subprogram

```
SNAP        START 0
            SAVE  (14,12)
            BALR  3,0
            USING *,3
            ST    13,SAVE+4
            LA    13,SAVE
            LM    6,7,0(1)
            OPEN  SNAPSHOT
            SNAP  DCB=SNAPSHOT,                            X
                  ID=001,                                  X
                  PDATA=(REGS,SA),                         X
                  STORAGE=((6),(7))
            CLOSE SNAPSHOT
RETURN      L     13,SAVE+4
            RETURN (14,12)
SNAPSHOT DCB  DSORG=PS,                                    X
                  RECFM=VBA,                               X
                  MACRF=W,                                 X
                  BLKSIZE=882,                             X
                  LRECL=125,                               X
                  DDNAME=SNAPDUMP
SAVE        DS    18F
            END
```

Figure 8-14   An assembler language subprogram for a snapshot dump that is called by a COBOL program

As you can see, the COBOL main program provides the starting and ending addresses for the dump by referring to its own data names in its link to the subprogram. Like the CALL macro in assembler language, the CALL statement in COBOL does several things. First, it constructs an address list from the data names identified in the USING portion of the statement, and it places the address of this list in register 1. Then, it loads the address of the subprogram into register 15, and it executes a BALR that branches to the address in register 15 and uses register 14 as the return address.

In the assembler language subprogram in figure 8-14, standard MVS macro linkage is used, but standard MVS linkage without macros could be used as well. Notice that the linkage used is identical to the program linkage you've seen throughout this book. For that reason, you'll probably want to use standard macro linkage in most of the subprograms you write.

From this example, I think you can realize that it doesn't matter what language the calling program or subprogram are written in on an IBM mainframe. As long as you use one of the standard linkage techniques, you shouldn't have any linkage problems. Register 1 is always used as the address of the address list for the fields that are passed to the subprogram. Register 15 is always used for the address of the entry point in the subprogram. And register 14 is always used for the return address.

Terminology

subprogram
calling a subprogram
calling module
called module
subprogram linkage
return address
entry point
exit point
adcon resolution
standard linkage
address list
Vcon
standard MVS program linkage
standard MVS macro linkage
nested subprograms

Objectives

1. Given the description of a subprogram and its calling program, write the calling program in assembler language.

2. Given the description of a subprogram and its calling program, write the subprogram in assembler language.

TOPIC 3   MVS JCL for using subprograms

When you develop a program that calls one or more subprograms or when you develop a subprogram, you must provide JCL that assembles your program or subprogram, links the appropriate modules, and tests the resulting load module. When using subprograms, you're likely to encounter three combinations of calling modules and subprograms. In this topic, then, you'll learn how to code the job streams for these combinations.

MVS JCL for assembling and testing a program that calls one or more subprograms that are stored in an object library

Many of the assembler language programs you write will call one or more existing subprograms. After you code this type of program, you assemble it just as you do any other program. Then, once the program has assembled without errors, you link edit it with the called subprograms, and you test the resulting load module.

To assemble and test a program that calls subprograms, you normally use an assemble-link-and-go procedure like the one I presented in chapter 3. To review, this procedure consists of three steps. First, the main program is assembled (ASM). Then, the resulting object module is linked with the object modules for the subprograms (LKED). Finally, the resulting load module is executed (GO).

Figure 8-15 shows the JCL for executing a procedure like this, which is commonly named ASMFCLG. If all of the subprograms called by your program aren't in the object library identified by the procedure, you must specify any other libraries the subprogram modules are stored in. In figure 8-15, the DD statement for LKED.SYSLIB identifies that library. In this case, the subprogram modules are stored in a library named MMA.ASM.OBJECT. The linkage editor can figure out what modules it needs from the list of unresolved address constants created during the assembly process.

If you have to identify more than one object library to be used in the LKED job step, you can *concatenate* two or more data sets as in this example:

```
//LKED.SYSLIB   DD      DSNAME=MMA.USER1.OBJECT,DISP=SHR
//              DD      DSNAME=MMA.USER2.OBJECT,DISP=SHR
```

Because the second DD statement doesn't specify a ddname, MVS assumes that the second library is a continuation of the first.

```
//PRINCE        JOB    (MMA,PRINCE),'ANNE PRINCE'
//             EXEC   ASMFCLG
//ASM.SYSIN    DD     *
               .
               .  SOURCE CODE FOR MAIN PROGRAM
               .
/*
//LKED.SYSLIB  DD     DSNAME=MMA.ASM.OBJECT,DISP=SHR
//GO.SYSUDUMP  DD     SYSOUT=A
               .
               .  DD STATEMENTS FOR PROGRAM FILES
               .
//
```

Figure 8-15   MVS JCL for assembling a program, linking it with a subprogram that's in a object library, and testing the resulting load module

MVS JCL for assembling both calling program and subprogram, link editing them, and testing the resulting load module

Sometimes, you will develop both the calling program and the subprogram. In this case, you can assemble both modules at the same time, link edit them, and test them using a job like the one shown in figure 8-16. As you can see, this job requires two procedures: ASMFC (an assemble only procedure) and ASMFCLG (an assemble, link edit, and test procedure).

The first procedure assembles the main program. Since this procedure is typically used the first time a new program is assembled to get a diagnostics listing, an object module isn't normally created by this procedure. However, if the program is to be linked with another program later on, as is required by the job in figure 8-16, the procedure does have to create an object module.

To create an object module, you code the PARM operand on the EXEC statement as shown. Then, you code an ASM.SYSGO DD statement to tell the assembler where to store the object module. You should code the operands on this statement exactly as they are coded in the SYSGO DD statement in the ASMFCLG procedure. The coding should be something like that shown in figure 8-16, but you'll have to find out what is right for your system. The two ampersands (&&) that precede the data set name indicate that this is a temporary data set, one that will only last until the job is completed.

The second procedure in figure 8-16 is an assemble-link-and-go procedure. To understand why this will link the object module of the main program with the one for the subprogram, you need to know more about the ASMFCLG procedure.

```
//PRINCE        JOB    (MMA,PRINCE),'ANNE PRINCE'
//              EXEC   ASMFC,PARM.ASM=OBJ
//ASM.SYSGO     DD     DSNAME=&&OBJSET,DISP=(MOD,PASS),
             UNIT=SYSDA,SPACE=(80,(200,50))
//ASM.SYSIN     DD     *
                .
                .  SOURCE CODE FOR MAIN PROGRAM
                .
/*
//              EXEC   ASMFCLG
//ASM.SYSIN     DD     *
                .
                .  SOURCE CODE FOR SUBPROGRAM
                .
/*
//GO.SYSUDUMP   DD     SYSOUT=A
                .
                .  DD STATEMENTS FOR PROGRAM FILES
                .
//
```

Figure 8-16   MVS JCL for assembling a program and a subprogram, linking the modules into one load module, and testing the resulting load module

When the link portion of the ASMFCLG procedure is executed, it assumes that all of the object modules to be link edited are in the data set named &&OBJSET. You can be sure that the object module for the subprogram is there because that's where the ASMFCLG procedure puts it. In addition, though, you know that the object module for the main program is there because you coded a DD statement for it as part of the ASMFC procedure. Then, when the linkage editor is executed, the two modules are link edited together.

MVS JCL for assembling a subprogram, link editing it with a calling program that's in an object library, and testing the resulting load module

Occasionally, you have to test a subprogram that is called by a main program that's already tested and stored in an object library. Long after a subprogram has been put into production, for example, someone may discover a bug in it. Then, you have to modify the subprogram and test it to make sure that it works, even though the main program is assumed to work correctly.

Figure 8-17 shows the JCL you can use in this situation. This is like the code in figure 8-15 except for the input to the linkage editor. Since the linkage editor doesn't know what main program you want the subprogram linked to, you have to specify the correct object module for the main program. That's what the first DD statement labelled LKED.SYSLIN does. This data set then takes the place of the default data set named &&OBJSET that is specified in the ASMFCLG procedure. As a result,

```
//PRINCE          JOB    (MMA,PRINCE),'ANNE PRINCE'
//               EXEC   ASMFCLG
//ASM.SYSIN       DD     *
                   .
                   .  SOURCE CODE FOR SUBPROGRAM
                   .
/*
//LKED.SYSLIN     DD     DSNAME=MMA.ASM.OBJECT(MAINPROG),DISP=SHR
//               DD     DSNAME=&&OBJSET,DISP=(OLD,DELETE)
//GO.SYSUDUMP     DD     SYSOUT=A
                   .
                   .  DD STATEMENTS FOR PROGRAM FILES
                   .
//
```

Figure 8-17   MVS JCL for assembling a subprogram, linking it with a main program that's in an object library, and testing the resulting load module

your JCL must also specify the correct object module for the subprogram that has just been assembled. So that's what the next DD statement does. Because this statement has no ddname, the linkage editor knows that its data set is a concatenation of the SYSLIN data set. As a result, the linkage editor can find the object modules for both the main program and the subprogram.

Unless specified otherwise, the linkage editor assumes that the entry point to the load module is the entry point of the the first object module in the SYSLIN data set. That's why the JCL in figure 8-17 specifies the data set for the object module of the main program first, followed by the data set for the object module of the subprogram. In contrast, if you let the linkage editor default to &&OBJSET for the object module of the subprogram and then code another DD statement for the main program's object module, the entry point of the load module becomes the entry point of the subprogram, and that certainly isn't what you want.

Discussion

Although this topic shows you the JCL that you're likely to need when you use subprograms, there's obviously more to the JCL for link editing than what's shown here. As a professional programmer, for example, you need to know how to add modules to an object library and how to maintain the ones that are already in the library. To learn more about JCL, you can consult the *Programmer's Guide* for your system. In addition, let me recommend again our book by Doug Lowe called *MVS JCL*. In the meantime, though, I think the job streams in figures 8-15 through 8-17 will help you link edit and test most of your assembler language programs and subprograms.

Now that you know how to provide for the link editing of two or more object modules, you may want to consider what happens during link editing. Because base registers are used for addressing on an IBM mainframe, an object module can be loaded into any storage positions. Then, when the base registers are loaded during program execution, all operand addresses will address the appropriate fields or instructions. That, in fact, is one major reason for using base-plus-displacement addressing: the object modules can be easily relocated.

The only addresses that aren't base-plus-displacement addresses in an assembler language program are the address constants. During link editing, then, the linkage editor has to put the proper addresses in the adcons of a program in the process called adcon resolution. The editor does this after it assigns storage locations to each object module to be linked.

Terminology   None

Objective   Given a testing job in one of the three forms presented in this topic, code VSE job streams for assembling, link editing, and testing the specified-modules.

Section 3

Assembler language capabilities by function

Once you complete section 2, you can study any of the chapters in this section. In other words, you don't have to read chapters 9 through 12 in sequence. Each of the chapters in this section shows you how to use one or more of the assembler language functions such as table handling, bit manipulation, or macro writing.

Chapter 9

Table handling

Tables are used in many data processing applications. For example, a tax table may be used to look up the amount of income tax to be withheld from paychecks. To find the premium to be charged for an insurance policy, rating tables are often used. And in many statistical analyses, tables are printed to show how data breaks down into categories.

This chapter is divided into two topics. The first topic describes the coding and lookup techniques for simple tables, called single-level tables. The second topic describes the coding and techniques for more advanced tables, called multilevel tables.

TOPIC 1   Single-level tables

A *single-level table* is a table that tabulates data for one variable factor. For instance, the rate table in figure 9-1 is a single-level table in which the pay class is the variable. There are two standard methods for defining a table and looking up values in it. These two methods, called factor matching and positional lookup, are illustrated in this topic.

FACTOR MATCHING

Factor matching can be used for any table. In brief, the technique consists of searching through a table sequentially to find an entry that matches the variable factor you're looking for. But, before you can code the search routine, you must know how the table is defined.

How to define a table for factor matching

Suppose you want to store the rate table in figure 9-1 and use it to look up an employee's pay rate. Figure 9-2 shows two ways the table can be defined in assembler language. Both provide for the factor-matching method of lookup.

The first table consists of ten entries with each entry consisting of one pay class and one pay rate. Each pay class is two-bytes long in EBCDIC form. Each pay rate is two-bytes long in packed-decimal form.

The second table defines each entry in hex. In this case, the resulting object code for the entries is identical to that resulting from the first table definition. However, this second table ends with an entry containing hex FFFFFFFF. This entry will be used to indicate the end of the table in storage.

Although you can use either of the table definitions presented in figure 9-2, we recommend the second one. Since the second table ends with hex Fs, you don't have to know how many entries there are in the table so its processing routine can be more flexible than a routine using the first table definition. Since the second table definition uses only one line for each table entry, we think it is more readable than the first table definition.

In many cases, particularly if a table needs frequent changes, you won't define the values of the table in your program. Instead, you will read the table values into storage from a file at the start of the program using the register techniques described in chapter 7. Then, you only reserve the storage for the table in your program. If, for example, you were loading the first pay-rate table in figure 9-2 into your program from a table file, you could define the table area in your program like this:

```
PAYTABLE DS    10CL4
```

Pay Class	Pay Rate
1	4.21
2	4.39
3	4.58
4	4.77
5	4.97
6	5.17
7	5.38
8	5.60
9	5.81
10	6.03

Figure 9-1   A single-level table

When a table's values are loaded from a file, you can change the table values without changing the programs that use the table. Since that's an important benefit, the values for most tables are stored in table files. Then, any program that uses the table has to first read the file and load the table values. If you learn how to look up the rates in the tables defined in figure 9-2, you shouldn't have any trouble coding a routine that loads a table's values so I won't take the time to illustrate a loading routine.

How to use factor matching

When you use factor matching, you search a table sequentially. To show you how this is done, I will use the second table definition in figure 9-2. Starting at the first entry, you compare the input pay class with the pay-class value in the table. If the pay classes match, you use the corresponding pay rate to calculate the worker's pay. If the pay-class values don't match, you compare the input pay class with the next entry in the table. If you reach the end of the table without finding a match, you can assume that the input pay class is invalid.

This sequential search technique is illustrated by the routine in figure 9-3. This routine uses register 8 as a substitute base register so the search can be done in a loop. To start, register 8 is loaded with the address of the table by using the LA instruction. Then, the CLC instruction compares the pay-class field in the input record, EMPPAYCL, to the first two bytes of the first table entry. If they are equal, the BE instruction transfers control to the instruction named PAYFOUND, which is the first instruction of the routine that calculates the worker's pay. Since the pay rate to be used is two bytes beyond the address in register 8, the following instruction is the first one in the PAYFOUND routine:

```
PAYFOUND ZAP     PAYWORK,2(2,8)
```

It places the pay rate from the table (the two-byte field addressed by register 8 plus a displacement of 2) into the field named PAYWORK.

If EMPPAYCL and the pay class in the table don't match, control falls through the branch to the next instruction. Then, the CLI instruction

Method 1

```
PAYTABLE DS    0CL40
         DC    C'01'
         DC    PL2'421'
         DC    C'02'
         DC    PL2'439'
         DC    C'03'
         DC    PL2'458'
         DC    C'04'
         DC    PL2'477'
         DC    C'05'
         DC    PL2'497'
         DC    C'06'
         DC    PL2'517'
         DC    C'07'
         DC    PL2'538'
         DC    C'08'
         DC    PL2'560'
         DC    C'09'
         DC    PL2'581'
         DC    C'10'
         DC    PL2'603'
```

Method 2

```
PAYTABLE DS    0CL44
         DC    X'F0F1421C'
         DC    X'F0F2439C'
         .
         .
         .
         DC    X'F1F0603C'
         DC    X'FFFFFFFF'
```

Figure 9-2   Two table definitions for the factor-matching technique

checks to see if the end of the table has been reached. If the table entry is hex FF, indicating the end of the table, the BE instruction that follows will branch to an error routine named NOTFOUND. If neither a match nor end-of-table is found, the program must go through the loop again to examine the next table entry. To do this, the LA instruction increases register 8 by four so it contains the address of the next table entry, and the program branches to the beginning of the loop, CMPCLASS.

Factor matching can be used for many kinds of tables because the variable factors don't have to form a continuous sequence. If, for example, some old pay classes are deleted from the table and some new ones are added to it, the lookup routine in figure 9-3 will still work. Also, it doesn't matter what order the table entries are in. If the table entries are in reverse order or completely out of order, the proper pay rate will still be found by matching with the pay class.

The sequence of entries can, however, affect the efficiency of the lookup routine in terms of processing time. Since the table is always searched from the first to the last entry, the most-used entry should be the first one in the table and the least-used entry should be the last. If, for example, 65 of the 100 jobs in a factory are for pay class 4, why compare pay class to classes 1, 2, and 3 before getting to class 4? Instead, class 4 should be the first entry in the table. Similarly, the rest of the table should be sequenced according to frequency of use. You can imagine what a difference this could make for the pay-rate lookup if class 10 were the most frequently used class.

```
                    .
                    .
                    .
          LA      8,PAYTABLE
CMPCLASS  CLC     EMPPAYCL,0(8)
          BE      PAYFOUND
          CLI     0(8),X'FF'
          BE      NOTFOUND
          LA      8,4(8)
          B       CMPCLASS
                    .
                    .
                    .
PAYFOUND  ZAP     PAYWORK,2(2,8)
                    .
                    .
PAYTABLE  DS      0CL44
          DC      X'F0F1421C'
          DC      X'F0F2439C'
          DC      X'F0F3458C'
          DC      X'F0F4477C'
          DC      X'F0F5497C'
          DC      X'F0F6517C'
          DC      X'F0F7538C'
          DC      X'F0F8560C'
          DC      X'F0F9581C'
          DC      X'F1F0603C'
          DC      X'FFFFFFFF'
PAYWORK   DS      PL2
                    .
                    .
                    .
```

Figure 9-3   A table lookup routine that uses factor matching

POSITIONAL LOOKUP

When you use a *positional lookup* technique, you locate a table entry by its position in the table rather than by matching factors. To use this technique, the variable factors must form an unbroken sequence. Then, when you define the table, you don't have to include the variable factors.

How to define a table for positional lookup

To illustrate the table definition for a positional lookup, I will again use the rate table presented in figure 9-1. Since the variable factor in this table, pay class, forms an unbroken sequence, the positional lookup method can be used. Figure 9-4 shows a table definition that can be used with this method. Here, only the pay rates are defined in the table. The pay classes can be determined by the position of each entry in the table.

```
                    .
                    .
                    .
            PACK    PAYCLASS,EMPPAYCL
            CP      PAYCLASS,LOWLIMIT
            BL      CLASSERR
            CP      PAYCLASS,HILIMIT
            BH      CLASSERR
            LA      12,PAYTABLE
            ZAP     TABCOUNT,LOWLIMIT
COMPLOOP    CP      TABCOUNT,PAYCLASS
            BE      RATEFND
            AP      TABCOUNT,=P'1'
            LA      12,2(12)
            B       COMPLOOP
RATEFND     ZAP     WRATE,0(2,12)
                    .
                    .
                    .
TABCOUNT    DS      PL2
HILIMIT     DC      P'10'
LOWLIMIT    DC      P'1'
PAYCLASS    DS      PL2
WRATE       DS      PL2
PAYTABLE    DS      0CL20
            DC      PL2'421'
            DC      PL2'439'
            DC      PL2'458'
            DC      PL2'477'
            DC      PL2'497'
            DC      PL2'517'
            DC      PL2'538'
            DC      PL2'560'
            DC      PL2'581'
            DC      PL2'603'
```

Figure 9-4   A positional table lookup routine that uses the counting technique

How to use positional lookup

To look up a pay rate in this table, you must use the input pay class as some sort of index. There are two techniques for doing this. One is to start at the beginning of the table and count through the entries until the count is equal to the input pay class. The other is to convert the input pay class to a displacement value.

The counting technique   The first of these techniques, known as the *counting technique*, is illustrated in figure 9-4. The first five instructions of this routine check to see that the input pay class (EMPPAYCL) is a value from one through ten. If the value is less than one or more than ten, the program branches to a routine named CLASSERR and the lookup is *not* performed. If the pay class is a valid number, the address of the table is loaded into register 12 and a value of one is placed in the count field. The program then enters the table-lookup loop.

In the lookup loop, the counter field, TABCOUNT, is compared with the packed input pay-class field, PAYCLASS. If they are equal, register 12 points to the proper pay rate and the program branches to RATEFND. If they're not equal, TABCOUNT is increased by one, register 12 is increased by two so it points to the next pay-rate entry, and the program repeats the loop. Since the program has already checked to see that the input pay class is in the proper range, there should always be a match. In the RATEFND instruction (the first instruction of the pay-calculation routine), the table value addressed by register 12 is placed in the field named WRATE.

The direct-addressing technique   Figure 9-5 illustrates a second way to use the input pay class as an index to the positional pay-rate table. This is known as the *direct-addressing technique*. Here, the input pay class is converted to a displacement value. Then, by adding this displacement value to the starting address of the table, the proper pay rate can be addressed directly.

The first five instructions of this routine perform the range check of the input pay-class value. First, the pay class is packed into a doubleword work area so it will be ready to convert to binary. If the pay class is within the proper range (from one through ten), the lookup continues. If not, the routine branches to CLASSERR and the lookup isn't performed.

The next five instructions determine the address of the proper pay rate. First, the input pay class is converted to binary in register 7. Second, the value in register 7 is reduced by one. Third, the value in register 7 is multiplied by two. (Since the multiply instruction, described in chapter 7, requires an even-odd pair of registers as the first operand, the first operand is registers 6 and 7. When the multiply instruction is executed, the product is placed in both registers. In this case, since the product will be between zero and 18, all significant bits in the answer are in register 7.) Fourth, the address of the table is loaded into register 8. Fifth, the address in register 8 is added to the displacement in register 7 so register 7 contains the address of the appropriate table value. The next instruction,

```
ZAP    WRATE,0(2,7)
```

stores this rate in a work field named WRATE and the pay calculation begins.

Note that if a sequence of variable factors starts at a value other than one, this direct-addressing technique can still be used. In a case like this, you subtract an appropriate value from the variable factor at the start of the routine. If, for example, the pay classes started at 11, you would subtract 11 from pay class at the start of the routine. Similarly, the multiplication factor is determined by the length of the table entries. If the pay classes were four bytes long, the multiplication factor would be four.

```
                            .
                            .
                            .
                    PACK    DBLEWORK,EMPPAYCL
                    CP      DBLEWORK,LOWLIMIT
                    BL      CLASSERR
                    CP      DBLEWORK,HILIMIT
                    BH      CLASSERR
                    CVB     7,DBLEWORK
                    S       7,=F'1'
                    M       6,=F'2'
                    LA      8,PAYTABLE
                    AR      7,8
                    ZAP     WRATE,0(2,7)
                            .
                            .
                            .
DBLEWORK  DS        D
HILIMIT   DC        P'10'
LOWLIMIT  DC        P'1'
PAYTABLE  DS        0CL20
          DC        PL2'421'
          DC        PL2'439'
          DC        PL2'458'
          DC        PL2'477'
          DC        PL2'497'
          DC        PL2'517'
          DC        PL2'538'
          DC        PL2'560'
          DC        PL2'581'
          DC        PL2'603'
WRATE     DS        PL2
                            .
                            .
                            .
```

Figure 9-5   A positional table lookup routine that uses the direct-addressing technique

The direct-addressing technique, like the counting technique, works best if the variable factors form an unbroken sequence. If there are only a few "holes" in the sequence as in 1, 2, 3, 5, 6, 7, 9, 10, 11, and 12, you can fill them with dummy entries. However, if there are many holes in the table, the technique becomes inefficient.

Discussion

As you have seen, handling single-level tables in assembler language is quite easy once you know how to code register operations. In general, you search tables with simple loops by using explicit operands and manipulating the entry addresses in a substitute base register. Whenever you must design a table and the search routine that goes with it, your objectives should be (1) to cover all possible conditions and (2) to maximize processing efficiency.

Terminology

single-level table
factor matching
positional lookup
counting technique
direct-addressing technique

Objective

Given program specifications involving a single-level table, code the required assembler language routine.

TOPIC 2   Multilevel tables

For many table-lookup problems, single-level tables can't do the job. Then, *multilevel tables* must be used. Income tax withholding tables, for instance, vary based on two factors: amount of pay and number of dependents. Because two variables are involved, an income tax table can be referred to as a *two-level table*.

Three-level tables are also relatively common. Figure 9-6, for example, is a three-level insurance table. The three variable factors (age, sex, and job class) determine the premium to be charged for accident insurance.

How to define a multilevel table

A two- or three-level table can be designed as a factor-matching table, a positional table, or a combination of the two. For the table in figure 9-6, I would use factor matching for the age variable, and positional lookup for the sex and job class variables. I would choose factor matching for the age variable for two reasons: (1) because each table entry serves a range of ages, not just one age, and (2) because the size and range of the age brackets are likely to change. If the age factor were to be treated in positional terms, a change in the number of age brackets would cause a change in the table search routine. On the other hand, the number of sex and job class categories are fixed. These factors can therefore be handled most efficiently by using a positional lookup technique.

If the values in this table weren't ever going to change, I would define this three-level table as shown in figure 9-7. Here, there are six entries for each age bracket. The last entry has nines as the low and high age limit to indicate the end of the table.

In practice, though, the values in an insurance table like this are likely to change. As a result, the table values would probably be stored in a table file. Then, any program that uses the table has to first read the file and load the table values. If you learn how to look up the rates in the table defined in figure 9-7, though, you shouldn't have any trouble coding a routine that loads the table values so I won't take the time to illustrate one.

How to search a multilevel table

Figure 9-8 shows a lookup routine for the table defined in figure 9-7. This routine will find the proper insurance rate when age, sex code (M or F), and job-class code (1 or 2) are input fields. First, the address of the table is

	Men		Women	
Age	Class 1	Class 2	Class 1	Class 2
18-34	$23.50	$27.05	$24.75	$28.45
35-39	24.00	27.55	25.80	29.50
40-44	24.60	28.15	27.10	29.50
45-49	25.30	28.85	29.10	30.80
50-54	26.30	29.85	31.55	32.80
55-59	28.00	31.55	35.00	35.25
				38.70

Figure 9-6   A three-level insurance table

```
RATETAB   DS   0CL112
          DC   PL2'18'          Low age limit
          DC   PL2'34'          High age limit
Age       DC   PL3'2350'        Rate for men, class 1
Segment   DC   PL3'2705'        Rate for men, class 2
1         DC   PL3'2475'        Rate for women, class 1
          DC   PL3'2845'        Rate for women, class 2
                    .
                    .
                    .
          DC   PL2'55'          Low age limit
          DC   PL2'59'          High age limit
Age       DC   PL3'2800'        Rate for men, class 1
Segment   DC   PL3'3155'        Rate for men, class 2
6         DC   PL3'3500'        Rate for women, class 1
          DC   PL3'3870'        Rate for women, class 2
End of    DC   PL2'99'
Table     DC   PL2'99'
Entry     DC   4PL3'99999'
```

Figure 9-7   A three-level table definition

loaded into register 7, the input age (INPAGE) is packed, and its value is compared with the lower limit of the first age-bracket entry:

```
          CP     AGEWRK,0(2,7)
```

If the input age is lower than this lower limit of the table, a branch to AGEERR takes place and the table lookup isn't performed.

Next, the program enters a factor-matching loop for the proper age bracket. In this loop, a lower limit of 99 indicates that the end-of-table has been reached and a branch to AGEERR takes place. To find the proper bracket, the input age is compared with the higher limit of each age segment. If the age is lower than or equal to this higher limit, the proper

```
              .
              .
              .
          LA      7,RATETAB
          PACK    AGEWRK,INPAGE
          CP      AGEWRK,0(2,7)
          BL      AGEERR
AGELOOP   CP      0(2,7),=P'99'
          BE      AGEERR
          CP      AGEWRK,2(2,7)
          BNH     AGEFOUND
          LA      7,16(7)
          B       AGELOOP
AGEFOUND  LA      7,4(7)
          CLI     INPSEX,C'M'
          BE      MALE
          LA      7,6(7)
MALE      CLI     INPJOBCL,C'1'
          BE      RATEFND
          LA      7,3(7)
RATEFND   ZAP     RATEWRK,0(3,7)
              .
              .
              .
AGEWRK    DS      PL2
RATEWRK   DS      PL3
RATETAB   DS      0CL112
          DC      PL2'18'
          DC      PL2'34'
          DC      PL3'2350'
          DC      PL3'2705'
          DC      PL3'2475'
          DC      PL3'2845'
              .
              .
              .
          DC      PL2'55'
          DC      PL2'59'
          DC      PL3'2800'
          DC      PL3'3155'
          DC      PL3'3500'
          DC      PL3'3870'
          DC      PL2'99'
          DC      PL2'99'
          DC      4PL3'9999'
```

Figure 9-8   A three-level lookup routine that uses both factor matching and positional lookup techniques

bracket has been found. Otherwise, 16 is added to register 7 (the size of each age segment) and the loop is repeated.

When the age bracket is found, four is added to register 7. Then, the sex code is compared to M. If they are equal, the program goes to MALE and register 7 is left unchanged. If they are unequal, indicating a female, the program adds six to the address in register 7 so it points to the first of the women's rates instead of the men's.

Finally, a comparison of the input job class is made. If the job class is equal to one, the register is pointing at the proper rate-table entry. If it isn't one, the input pay class must be two. Then, three is added to the address in register 7 so it points to the rate that should be used.

As you should realize by now, this table-lookup routine is actually three single-level table lookups combined. The age-group lookup picks a table segment rather than an individual table entry. Then, within an age segment, the sex code picks a smaller segment composed of two individual rate entries. Finally, the job class is used to select one of the two rate entries.

This same type of table structure can be used for more than three levels. Then, each level of the structure corresponds to one input factor and you can use either factor-matching or positional lookup techniques for it. In practice, though, you will rarely come across tables that require more than three levels.

Discussion

Most tables are stored in files so they can be updated without making changes to the programs that use them. As a result, you must keep future changes in mind when you design multilevel tables and be sure to reserve space for these changes in your table definitions. You must also code your processing routines so they are adaptable to table changes. In figure 9-8, for example, you should note that the routine will work whether the number of age brackets is increased or decreased, whether the lower limit of the first age bracket is lowered, or whether any of the other age limits are changed.

Terminology

multilevel table
two-level table
three-level table

Objective

Given program specifications involving a multilevel table, code the required assembler language routine.

Chapter 10

Editing, bit manipulation, and translation

This chapter starts by presenting some new patterns that can be used with the edit instruction along with a new instruction, the edit-and-mark instruction. Next, it presents some instructions that let you manipulate the bits within bytes of data. Finally, it presents some instructions that let you translate data from one form to another or to manipulate the bytes within fields.

EDITING

In chapters 4 and 5 you were introduced to some simple editing patterns for the edit instruction. For completeness, figure 10-1 presents those patterns along with some new patterns. The patterns you already are familiar with are in groups 1 through 3.

In group 4, you can see patterns that use nonblank fill characters. If, for example, you use a dollar sign or an asterisk as the fill character, a string of those characters is made to precede the first significant digit in the edited result. This feature is commonly used when printing checks so the amount of the check cannot easily be tampered with.

In group 5, you can see how message characters can be used to indicate negative values. In the first three examples, you can see the minus sign used as the message charater. In the next three, the message characters are a blank followed by CR. When you use message characters to the right of the rightmost digit position in an edit pattern, the characters are left unchanged if the value being edited is negative. But, if the value is positive, these rightmost message characters are replaced by the fill character. As a result, you can print one or more message characters after a negative number. You can use any message characters to indicate a negative field, but the most common ones are CR, DB, and the minus sign.

In group 6, you can see date-field editing. Here, the message characters are inserted into a seven-digit date field. As the examples show, slashes, hyphens, or blanks are commonly used when editing a date.

Finally, in group 7, you can see patterns that cause an edit instruction to edit two or more fields. For this to work, the fields to be edited must be located in successive bytes of storage and the receiving field must have one or more *field separators* (hex 22s) between the individual edit patterns. As you can see in figure 10-1, you use only one fill character in the receiving field no matter how many fields are going to be edited by a single edit instruction. This fill character is used for all fields to be edited, and it replaces all field separators during editing.

Edit-and-mark (EDMK)

The edit-and-mark instruction is used primarily in programs that print money values. The EDMK instruction operates in exactly the same manner as the edit instruction except that it also stores the address of the first significant digit in register 1. You can then use this register 1 to place a dollar sign to the left of the first digit of the edited value. This is often referred to as using a *floating dollar sign*.

Figure 10-2 presents a routine that uses the edit-and-mark instruction. If the value is 1.23, the edited result will print as $1.23. If the value is .05, the edited result will print as $.05. Note that you must subtract one from register 1 to address the proper byte for the dollar sign in the edited result.

Did you notice this LA instruction at the start of the routine in figure 10-2?

```
LA      1,PRTVALUE+4
```

Group	Sending field	Receiving field pattern	Edited result field	Printed result field
1 Lead zero suppression	12345C 00123F 00000C	40202020202020 40202020202020 40202020202020	40F1F2F3F4F5 404040F1F2F3 40404040404040	12345 123
2 Significance starting	00511F 00001C 00000C	40202020202120 40202020202120 40202020202120	404040F5F1F1 4040404040F1 404040404040F0	511 1 0
	123456789C 000123456C 000000123C 000000000C	40202020206B2020206B202120 40202020206B2020206B202120 40202020206B2020206B202120 40202020206B2020206B202120	40F1F2F36BF4F5F66BF7F8F9 404040404040F1F2F36BF4F5F6 40404040404040404040F1F2F3 404040404040404040404040F0	123,456,789 123,456 123 0
3 Decimal point and comma insertion	123456789C 000000123C 000000005C 1234567C 0000123F 0000005D	40206B202020206B2020214B2020 40206B202020206B2020214B2020 40206B202020206B2020214B2020 402020202020214B2020 402020202020214B2020 402020202020214B2020	40F16BF2F3F46BF5F6F74BF8F9 404040404040404040F14BF2F3 4040404040404040404B F0F5 40F1F2F3F4F54BF6F7 404040404040F14BF2F3 40404040404040404BF0F5	1,234,567.89 1.23 .05 12345.67 1.23 .05
4 Non-blank fill character	12345C 00123F 00000C	5C202020202020 5C202020202020 5C202020202020	5CF1F2F3F4F5 5C5C5CF1F2F3 5C5C5C5C5C5C	*12345 **123 ******
	123456789C 000000123C 000000005C	5B206B202020206B2020214B2020 5B206B202020206B2020214B2020 5B206B202020206B2020214B2020	5BF16BF2F3F46BF5F6F74BF8F9 5B5B5B5B5B5B5BF14BF2F3 5B5B5B5B5B5B5B5B5B4BF0F5	$1,234,567.89 $$$$$$$1.23 $$$$$$$$$.05
5 Message characters for negative fields	01234C 01234D 00000C	40202020202060 40202020202060 40202020202060	4040F1F2F3F440 4040F1F2F3F460 40404040404040	1234 1234–
	00123C 00001D 00000C	402020214B202040C3D9 402020214B202040C3D9 402020214B202040C3D9	404040F14BF2F3404040 404040404BF0F140C3D9 404040404BF0F0404040	1.23 .01 CR .00
6 Date editing	0020485F 0121985F 0120285F	40202021612020612020 40202021602020602020 40202021402020402020	404040F261F0F461F8F5 4040F1F260F1F960F8F5 4040F1F240F0F240F8F5	2/04/85 12-19-85 12 02 85
7 Field separators	123C123C123F 100C000C001C	40202120222220212022222202120 40202120222220212022222202120	40F1F2F34040F1F2F34040F1F2F3 40F1F0F04040404040F04040404040F1	123 123 123 100 0 1
	123C12345C 001C000000C	40202120222222202020214B2020 40212120222222202020214B2020	40F1F2F34040040F1F2F34BF4F5 404040F14040404040404BF0F0	123 123.45 1 .00

Figure 10-1   Editing patterns

```
          LA     1,PRTVALUE+4
          MVC    PRTVALUE,PATTERN
          EDMK   PRTVALUE,VALUE
          S      1,=F'1'
          MVI    0(1),C'$'
          .
          .
          .
PRTVALUE  DS     CL7
VALUE     DS     PL3
PATTERN   DC     XL7'40202021482020'
```

Figure 10-2   A routine that uses the edit-and-mark instruction to place a floating dollar sign

This instruction loads the address that corresponds to the decimal point in the edited result field into register 1. This is required because the EDMK instruction doesn't load any value into register 1 if the sending field contains no significant digits until after the significance starter in the receiving field has been reached. As a result, a value like .05 doesn't cause a proper address to be loaded into register 1 by the EDMK instruction. If this routine didn't start with the LA instruction, the MVI instruction wouldn't put the floating dollar sign in the right place for a value like .05. But with the LA instruction, this routine works correctly whether significance is started by a significant digit or by a significance starter in the edit pattern.

BIT MANIPULATION

Bit manipulation instructions are often called "bit twiddlers" because you use them to test or change selected bits in an eight-bit byte. The three most important instructions in this group are the OR, the AND, and the test-under-mask instruction.

OR (OI, OC, O, OR)

When an OR instruction is executed, the bits in the sending field (operand-2) are used to modify the bits in the receiving field (operand-1) according to the table in figure 10-3. If, for example, the leftmost bit is 1 in the sending field and 0 in the receiving field, it is changed to 1 in the receiving field. You should be able to see from the table why this instruction is named OR. A bit in the receiving field is on after the execution of the OR instruction if the bit is on initially *or* if the associated bit in the sending field is on.

Figure 10-3 also illustrates the execution of an OR instruction on a one-byte field. As you can see, if both bits in a bit position are off, the result bit is off; otherwise, the result bit is on. By constructing a sending pattern of on-bits, you can force selected bits in the receiving field to be turned on, while leaving others unchanged. In this example, the zone bits are unchanged, while all of the digit bits are turned on.

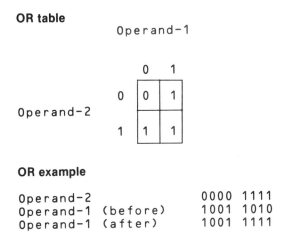

Figure 10-3   The execution of the OR instruction

The OR instruction is used in four forms. These are the immediate, storage-to-storage, register-to-storage, and register-to-register forms. They are illustrated in figure 10-4. The immediate and storage-to-storage forms are used most often.

How to use the immediate form of the OR instruction   The immediate form of the OR instruction offers an easy way to change the zone bits of a sign byte from hex C to hex F after unpacking a decimal field. This is illustrated in the first example in figure 10-4. Here, the type code B for binary is used in the immediate operand. Then, the binary digits 1 and 0 are used in the nominal value. This type code can also be used in DS and DC statements. Because any immediate operand with the same bit pattern, 11110000, can also be used, the following instructions have the same effect:

```
OI      PRTVALUE+4,X'F0'
OI      PRTVALUE+4,C'0'
```

The OR-immediate can also be used to turn bits on as program switches. For instance, the instruction

```
OI      PRGSWTCH,B'00000001'
```

sets the rightmost bit in the one-byte PRGSWTCH field to on. This bit might be used to indicate that the eighth field in an input record is invalid. The test-under-mask instruction can then be used to test this bit setting and set an appropriate condition code, as you'll learn in a minute.

The immediate form

```
        OI      PRTVALUE+4,B'11110000'
```

	Before	After
PRTVALUE	F0 F0 F6 F4 C3	F0 F0 F6 F4 F3

The storage-to-storage form

```
        OC      INPQTY,ORPATRN
        .
        .
        .
INPQTY  DS      CL4
ORPATRN DC      4X'F0'
```

	Before	After
INPQTY	40 40 C4 40	F0 F0 F4 F0

The register-to-storage form

```
        O       6,FULLWORD
        .
        .
        .
FULLWORD DC     F'1'
```

	Before	After
Register 6	00 00 03 02	00 00 03 03

The register-to-register form

```
        L       7,WORD1
        OR      6,7
        .
        .
        .
WORD1   DC      F'1'
```

	Before	After
Register 6	00 00 04 02	00 00 04 03

Figure 10-4   The four forms of the OR instruction

AND table

Operand-1

```
                    0   1
               ┌───┬───┐
            0  │ 0 │ 0 │
Operand-2      ├───┼───┤
            1  │ 0 │ 1 │
               └───┴───┘
```

AND example

```
Operand-2              1111  0000
Operand-1 (before)     1011  0101
Operand-1 (after)      1011  0000
```

Figure 10-5   The execution of the AND instruction

How to use the storage-to-storage form of the OR instruction   The storage-to-storage version of the OR instruction is often used to change blanks in numeric input fields to zeros as shown in the example in figure 10-4. This is done to prevent abnormal program terminations due to invalid numeric data (blanks). If the input field does contain numeric data, the OR doesn't change it at all because the digit bits in the second operand are all zeros. However, if a byte in the field contains a blank, it will be changed to hex F0.

Note in the example in figure 10-4 that an invalid character like the letter D will also be changed to a valid numeric value when this technique is used. If, for example, INPQTY contains a character D (hex C4) in its third byte, the byte will have a numeric value of 4 after the OR operation. Although it's sometimes okay to convert blanks to zeros in an editing routine, it usually isn't okay to convert letters and special characters to numbers. As a result, you must know what type of input data your program might encounter before you can code your editing routines properly.

AND
(NI, NC, N, NR)   The AND instructions are used to turn off selected bits in a receiving field. This is shown in figure 10-5. When an AND instruction is executed, the resulting bit is on only if both operands have an on-bit in the same position. You can see from the AND table why this instruction is named AND. A bit in the receiving field is on after the execution of an AND instruction only if the bit is on initially *and* if the related bit in the sending field is on.

```
NI       PRGSWTCH,B'11111110'
NC       FIELDA,ANDPATRN
N        6,FULLWORD
NR       9,3
```

Figure 10-6   The four forms of the AND instruction

The most widely used form of the AND instruction is the AND immediate, as illustrated in the first example in figure 10-6. In this case, the first seven bits of PRGSWTCH will be left unchanged. However, the eighth bit will be set to off no matter what its previous setting was.

When coding AND patterns, code a zero in all bit positions you want to set to off and a one in the positions you want to stay as they are. Although the storage-to-storage (NC), register-to-storage (N), and register-to-register (NR) forms of the AND instruction are available, they aren't commonly used.

Test-under-mask (TM)

The test-under-mask instruction allows you to check the status of one or more bits in a byte. This is an immediate instruction with the second operand used as a mask for selecting the bits to be tested. For example, the following test-under-mask instruction tests the condition of the one-byte field named PRGSWTCH:

```
TM       PRGSWTCH,B'00000001'
```

Since the mask only has a one-bit in the rightmost position, only that bit in PRGSWTCH will be tested. If you wanted to test both the seventh and eighth bits, you would code this instruction:

```
TM       PRGSWTCH,B'00000011'
```

When executed, the TM instruction sets a condition code based on the results it finds in the bit positions indicated by the mask. The resulting condition code can be used to alter the processing sequence of the program by using one of the mnemonic branch instructions in figure 10-7.

How to use the test-under-mask instruction to check program switches   The most common use of the test-under-mask instruction is to check the setting of program switches. To illustrate, suppose you are coding a portion of a program to check the validity of input data in four fields. If one of the four fields is invalid, the corresponding bit in a byte named ERRBYTE is turned on. Then, if one of these bits is on, your program must execute a routine that prints an error message. If they are all off, your program must continue with the processing of the input data.

Operation code	Meaning	Remarks
BO	Branch if ones	The branch is taken if all the tested bits are on.
BM	Branch if mixed	The branch is taken if some of the tested bits are on, some off.
BZ	Branch if zeros	The branch is taken if all the tested bits are off, or zero.
BNO	Branch if not ones	The branch is taken if one, some, or all of the tested bits are off.

Figure 10-7   The branch instructions used with the test-under-mask instruction

Bit meanings for ERRSWTCH

Bit 1:   Error in FIELD1
Bit 2:   Error in FIELD2
Bit 3:   Error in FIELD3
Bit 4:   Error in FIELD4

Code to test the error bits

```
        .
        .
        .
TM      ERRSWTCH,B'11110000'
BZ      PROCESS
        .
        .
        .
```

Figure 10-8   Code that uses the test-under-mask instruction to test the bits of an error switch

Figure 10-8 shows how you can check ERRBYTE using the test-under-mask instruction. After each of the data fields is examined and the appropriate bits are turned on in the program switch, the test-under-mask instruction is used to test the bits. If all of the bits tested are off, the program branches to the routine labeled PROCESS. Otherwise, control falls through the branch to the next instruction, which should be the first instruction of the error print routine.

TRANSLATION

Most high-level languages are limited when it comes to translating data from one code to another. They are also limited when it comes to handling free-form input data, the kind that is often used in teleprocessing applications. As a result, assembler language programs and subprograms are often used for functions like these. When you code these functions, you use the translate, the translate-and-test, and the execute instructions.

Translate (TR)

The translate instruction can translate the bit pattern of each byte in a field to any other bit pattern. This instruction works in conjunction with a table that gives the bit patterns of the replacement codes. Since there are 256 different patterns for an eight-bit byte, the maximum size of the translation table is 256 bytes, but, as you will see, it is sometimes possible to use a smaller table.

To code this instruction, you use the name of the field to be translated as the first operand and the name of the table as the second operand as in this instruction:

```
TR      FIELDA,TABLE
```

When the instruction is executed, the field is translated from left to right, one byte at a time. To find the appropriate code in the table, the code in the operand-1 field is treated as a binary value that is added to the address of the table. Then, the byte at the resulting address replaces the byte in the operand-1 field.

To illustrate, look at the translation routine in figure 10-9. Here, FIELDA is defined with a value of MOD14. Although it's unrealistic to define the value of a field to be translated with a DC, this routine is only intended to show you how the TR instruction works.

When the TR instruction is executed, the binary value of M (the first byte in the operand-1 field) is added to the address of TABLE. Since M is hex D4, or binary 11010100, it has a value of 212. As a result, the 213th byte in the table is substituted for the letter M. Since this byte contains hex 0E, the first byte of FIELDA will contain hex 0E after execution.

The TR instruction continues the translation with the remaining bytes in FIELDA on a left to right basis. Since the letter O has a binary value of 214, the 215th table value, hex 10, is substituted for it. Since the letter D has a binary value of 196, the 197th table value, hex 05, is substituted for it. Since the numbers 1 (hex F1) and 4 (hex F4) have binary values of 241 and 244, hex 00 is substituted for each of them. When the instruction finishes its execution, FIELDA contains this data:

```
0E  10  05  00  00
```

How to use the translate instruction to translate a specific range of characters   In practice, you can usually avoid defining a table of 256 bytes because the input data is normally restricted to a smaller range. For example, if you are translating the alphabetic characters of the EBCDIC

```
                TR      FIELDA,TABLE
                .
                .
                .
FIELDA          DC      CL5'MOD14'
TABLE           DS      0CL256
                DC      192X'00'
                DC      X'010203040506070809'
                DC      7X'00'
                DC      X'0A0B0C0D0E0F101112'
                DC      8X'00'
                DC      X'131415161718191A'
                DC      23X'00'
```

Figure 10-9   A translation routine that uses the translate instruction

code to some other bit patterns, the input range is from hex C1 (A) to hex E9 (Z). As a result, the translation table used to cover the range need be only 41 bytes long. (Hex C1 through hex E9 equals binary values 193 through 233.)

To refer to this table in the translate instruction, you adjust the beginning address of the second operand so the lowest binary value in the input range results in a displacement of zero. Since the low end of the range in this example is hex C1, the translate instruction should be coded as:

```
        TR      DATA,TABLE-193
```

The effect is that an input character A will be translated into the first byte of the table:

```
(TABLE-193) + X'C1' = (TABLE-193) + 193
                    = TABLE + 0
```

Note, however, that a bit pattern that isn't between hex C1 and hex E9 will not be translated properly.

How to use the translate instruction to translate from one data code to another   Though the need for it is rare, the translate instruction is ideal for translating a file from one data code to another. For instance, I once wrote a program to translate a group of magnetic tape files written by a Honeywell 200 computer to IBM System/360 format. The Honeywell tapes were written in *octal code*. Each character was made up of six bits treated as two groups of three. The program I wrote had to read the tape records into storage, allowing the System/360 hardware to add two high-order zero bits to each six-bit character. Then, my program had to translate the resulting bit patterns to EBCDIC.

```
                    .
                    .
                    .
            GET     TAPEFLE,TAPEREC
            TR      TAPEREC,TRANSTAB
                    .
                    .
                    .
TRANSTAB    DC      X'F0F1F2F3F4F5F6F7F8F9'
            DC      X'7D7E7A406E50F0'
            DC      X'C1C2C3C4C5C6C7C8C9'
            DC      X'5E4B5D4D5DF0'
            DC      X'D0D1D2D3D4D5D6D7D8D9'
            DC      X'7B5B5C7D5ED04C61'
            DC      X'E2E3E4E5E6E7E8E9'
            DC      X'7C6B4D605D4A'
TAPEREC     DS      CL200
                    .
                    .
```

Figure 10-10   A routine that translates octal code to hexadecimal code

This translation routine and table are illustrated in figure 10-10. Of course, I had to know what EBCDIC characters each of the six-bit octal codes represented so I could make up an appropriate translation table for the program. But once you create the table, the translate instruction does all the work.

In this example, the translation table didn't have to be 256 bytes long since each input byte had only six significant bits with two high-order zero bits added by the hardware. As a result, the maximum hex input value was B'00111111', or X'3F.' Since the range X'00' to X'3F' represents 64 combinations, my table only had to be 64 bytes long.

Translate-and-test (TRT)

The translate-and-test instruction operates somewhat like the translate instruction. That is, the data bytes of the first operand are used as displacements from the second operand address, which is the address of a table. Instead of replacing the data byte with the corresponding byte in the table, though, the TRT instruction only checks to see if the byte in the table is hex 00. If so, processing continues with the next byte in the first operand field. If not, execution of the translate-and-test instruction is halted, the address of the byte in the first operand is put in register 1, and the nonzero byte from the table is inserted into the rightmost byte of register 2.

One use of the translate-and-test instruction is to find certain characters in an input stream. For example, you might use this instruction to find the first blank in an input record as illustrated in figure 10-11. When the translate-and-test instruction is executed, each of the bytes in

```
                TRT     INPAREA,TRTTABLE
                .
                .
                .
INPAREA  DS     CL80
TRTTABLE DS     0CL256
         DC     64X'00'
         DC     X'40'
         DC     191X'00'
```

Figure 10-11   A routine to find the first blank in a record using the translate-and-test instruction

Condition code on-bit	Condition
Bit 0	All bytes in the input field have corresponding hex zeros in the table.
Bit 1	A nonzero table byte has been found.
Bit 2	The last byte in the input field has a corresponding nonzero byte in the table.

Figure 10-12   The conditions resulting from the translate- and-test instruction

the input area (processing from left to right) will be used as a displacement from the start of the table, TRTTABLE. Since all of the table bytes except the 65th byte (displacement of 64) are hex zeros, only a blank in the input field (hex 40) will cause the instruction to stop. Then, the address of the blank is put in register 1, and the nonzero table character, also a blank in this case, is put into the rightmost byte of register 2. If necessary, then, you can use the address in register 1 to calculate the length of the nonblank field in the input area.

When the translate-and-test instruction is executed, three conditions can result, as summarized in figure 10-12. Then, you can use the branch-on-condition instruction to alter the processing sequence based on the resulting condition code. For instance,

```
        BC      8,NOCHAR
```

will branch if only zero values are found for a field, while

```
        BC      2,LSTBYTE
```

will branch if a nonzero value has been found for the last byte in the operand-1 field.

Execute (EX)

The execute instruction is one of the more complex System/370 instructions. When it is executed, it does two things. First, it ORs the rightmost byte of the register that is specified as its first operand with the second byte (bits 8-15) of the instruction specified as the second operand. Second, it executes the operand-2 instruction using the results of the OR as the second byte of this instruction without actually changing the byte in the instruction. That is complicated, isn't it?

The execution instruction is often used in conjunction with the translate-and-test instruction. This is illustrated in figure 10-13. Once you understand this routine, you should understand more fully how the execute instruction works.

As you study figure 10-13, suppose that WRKAREA has this data in bytes 1-16:

```
THIS IS THE LAST
```

Suppose also that the address of WRKAREA is decimal 8000. Then, when the LA instruction at the start of the routine is executed, 8000 is loaded into register 4.

When the translate-and-test instruction that follows is executed, it will stop only when it encounters a blank in WRKAREA because TRT-TABLE is all hex zeros except for the 65th table entry. Since the first blank in WRKAREA is the fifth byte of the field, the TRT instruction will load address 8004 into register 1 and place hex 40 in the rightmost byte of register 2 when it stops. Then, the routine subtracts the contents of register 4 from register 1, leaving a value of 4, which is the length of the first word in the work area. Because the length stored in an instruction is one less than the number of bytes operated upon, the program next subtracts one from register 1 leaving a value of 3. At this point, register 1 contains a proper length factor for the MVC instruction labelled MOVEWORD, so it's time for this EX instruction:

```
EX    1,MOVEWORD
```

As I described before, the execute instruction does its work in two phases. In the first phase, it ORs the rightmost byte in register 1 with the second byte of the MVC instruction named MOVEWORD. You will remember from chapter 4 that the second byte of the MVC instruction is a length factor. So, since this move instruction specifies a length of zero, its second byte is hex 00, and the result of the OR operation is hex 03. Then, in the second phase, the execute instruction causes this MVC instruction to be executed using the length factor of hex 03. The result is that the word addressed by register 4 with a length factor of hex 3 (the input word THIS) is moved to the four bytes starting at the address given by register 5. Note, then, that the execute instruction wouldn't work as intended if the length specified in the MVC instruction wasn't hex zeros because the desired length wouldn't be ORed properly.

```
                    .
                    .
                    .
             LA     4,WRKAREA
             TRT    WRKAREA,TRTTABLE
             SR     1,4
             S      1,=F'1'
             EX     1,MOVEWORD
                    .
                    .
                    .
WRKAREA      DS     CL80
TRTTABLE     DS     0CL256
             DC     64X'00'
             DC     X'40'
             DC     191X'00'
MOVEWORD     MVC    0(0,5),0(4)
                    .
                    .
                    .
```

Figure 10-13   A routine that uses the TRT and EX instructions to locate the first words in an input area

A program that uses the execute instruction   Since the routine in figure 10-13 only gets the first word in the work area, I thought you might want to see a more complete routine. As a result, figure 10-14 illustrates an entire program that processes free-form input. Here, the input file contains address records with one complete address in each record. The output is a number of two-, three-, or four-line mailing labels.

The difficult part of the program is determining where the data for one address line ends and the next one begins, because a single slash is used to separate the address lines in an input record. Furthermore, the final address line in a record may or may not be ended by a slash. Before a label is printed, the program skips to the top of the next label using ASA control characters.

At the start of the program, the address of the work area for the input file is loaded into register 4; the length of the work area minus one (the length factor) is loaded into register 5; and a record is read. Then, this execute instruction is executed:

```
        EX    5,TRTINST
```

Since register 5 contains the length of the work area for the input file minus one, this instruction is executed with a length equivalent to 80:

```
TRTINST   TRT   0(0,4),TRTTABLE
```

Since this instruction uses register 4 as the base register, the field that is operated upon is the 80-byte work area for the address record.

```
LABELS    START  0                                                 000100
BEGIN     SAVE   (14,12)                                           000200
          BALR   3,0                                               000300
          USING  *,3                                               000400
          ST     13,SAVE+4                                         000500
          LA     13,SAVE                                           000600
          OPEN   (ADDREC,INPUT,PRINT,OUTPUT)                       000700
NEWREC    LA     4,ADDRWRK                                         000800
          LA     5,79                                              000900
          GET    ADDREC,ADDRWRK                                    001000
NXTFLD    EX     5,TRTINST                                         001100
          BC     8,LASTFLD                                         001200
          BC     2,LASTSLSH                                        001300
          SR     1,4                                               001400
          S      1,=F'1'                                           001500
          EX     1,MOVEFLD                                         001600
          AR     4,1                                               001700
          A      4,=F'2'                                           001800
          SR     5,1                                               001900
          S      5,=F'2'                                           002000
          PUT    PRINT,PRTWRK                                      002100
          MVI    PRTWRK,C' '                                       002200
          MVC    PRTWRK+1(132),PRTWRK                              002300
          B      NXTFLD                                            002400
LASTFLD   LA     1,ADDRWRK+79                                      002500
PRTLSTLN  SR     1,4                                               002600
          EX     1,MOVEFLD                                         002700
          PUT    PRINT,PRTWRK                                      002800
          MVC    PRTWRK+1(132),PRTWRK                              002900
          MVI    PRTWRK,C'1'                                       003000
          B      NEWREC                                            003100
LASTSLSH  LA     1,ADDRWRK+78                                      003200
          B      PRTLSTLN                                          003300
ADDREOF   CLOSE  (ADDREC,,PRINT)                                   003400
          L      13,SAVE+4                                         003500
          RETURN (14,12)                                           003600
ADDREC    DCB    DSORG=PS,                                    X    003700
                 RECFM=F,                                     X    003800
                 MACRF=GM,                                    X    003900
                 BLKSIZE=80,                                  X    004000
                 LRECL=80,                                    X    004100
                 DDNAME=ADDREC,                               X    004200
                 EODAD=ADDREOF                                     004300
PRINT     DCB    DSORG=PS,                                    X    004400
                 RECFM=FA,                                    X    004500
                 MACRF=PM,                                    X    004600
                 BLKSIZE=133,                                 X    004700
                 LRECL=133,                                   X    004800
                 DDNAME=PRINT                                      004900
SAVE      DS     18F                                               005000
ADDRWRK   DS     CL80                                              005100
PRTWRK    DC     CL133'1'                                          005200
TRTTABLE  DS     0CL256                                            005300
          DC     97X'00'                                           005400
          DC     X'61'                                             005500
          DC     158X'00'                                          005600
TRTINST   TRT    0(0,4),TRTTABLE                                   005700
MOVEFLD   MVC    PRTWRK+1(0),0(4)                                  005800
          END    BEGIN                                             005900
```

Figure 10-14   A program that prepares address labels from free-form input

The two BC instructions after the execute instruction branch if only zero values are found by the TRT instruction or if the nonzero value is for the last byte of the work area. Since either of these conditions indicates the end of the last address line in a record, the program branches to appropriate last-line routines.

Otherwise, the program continues with the next instructions:

```
SR    1,4
S     1,=F'1'
EX    1,MOVEFLD
```

First, the length of the address field minus one is calculated in register 1. Then, register 1 is used in the execute instruction to modify the length factor in the MVC instruction named MOVEFLD:

```
MOVEFLD  MVC   PRTIO+1(0),0(4)
```

When its execution is complete, one address line has been moved to the printer work area.

Next, register 4 is adjusted so it addresses the first byte of the next address field and register 5 is adjusted so it contains the length minus one of the remaining bytes in the input file's work area. Then, after the print line is printed by the PUT instruction, the print area including the control character is cleared to blanks. Since address lines of different lengths are being printed, data from a long line would overlap data from a shorter line and print again if the area were not cleared. Finally, the program branches back to the first execute instruction so the loop is repeated for the next address line.

If the last address field is indicated, an appropriate length is developed in register 1, and the MVC instruction is executed via the execute instruction. Next, a line is printed, the print area is cleared, and the line-control character is set to 1 to indicate a skip to the top of the next label before the next line is printed. The program then returns to NEWREC to set up registers 4 and 5 and read another record.

DISCUSSION

The elements presented in this chapter illustrate some of the power of assembler language. By using the bit manipulation, translation, and execute instructions, the assembler language programmer can code complex routines for input validation, translation, or free-form input manipulation. In contrast, routines like this can be difficult or impossible to code in a high-level language.

Terminology

field separator
floating dollar sign

Objective

Apply any of the instructions in this chapter to your programs.

Chapter 11

Writing macro definitions

The use of standard macros is a basic part of assembler language programming. For instance, GET and PUT macros, in combination with DCB macros, are used to perform most I/O operations. In addition, standard macros such as SAVE and RETURN for program linkage and TIME for supervisor communication provide special processing capabilities.

During assembly, each macro instruction is replaced by the instructions that are generated by the *macro definition*. This is referred to as *macro expansion*. For example, the GET macro in locate mode is expanded into two load instructions and a branch-and-link instruction that branches to an I/O module.

Usually, the macro definitions are stored in a source library. Then, each time the assembler finds a macro instruction in the source program, it looks up the macro definition in the source library. Based on the macro definition, the assembler generates instructions for the macro instruction and inserts them into the source program immediately following the macro instruction.

As an assembler language programmer, you can write macro definitions of your own. Why would you want to? For the same reason that the standard macros were written: to provide an easy way to code a frequently used series of assembler language instructions. Once your macro definition has been written and stored in the source library, you can use it just as you use any of the standard macros.

One reason some programmers don't write macro definitions is the difficulty involved in writing them. In truth, writing a macro like the DCB (which consists of more than 1200 coding lines) can be an extremely complex task. On the other hand, writing simple macro definitions is a manageable task, one that can improve the efficiency of a company's programming efforts.

This chapter is divided into two topics. Topic 1 presents the more straightforward forms of macro writing. These techniques are relevant to the needs of the typical assembler language programmer. Then, topic 2 presents advanced techniques for macro writing. These techniques are more relevant to the needs of the software specialist. Because of the complexity of the subject, you are probably better off if you study this chapter only after you have become quite proficient in assembler language coding.

TOPIC 1   Basic macro writing

Figure 11-1 presents a simple macro definition. This macro adds three binary fields to a register, subtracts one field from it, and adds the literal value 50 to it. The figure shows the macro definition, an example of its use in a macro instruction, and the expansion of the instruction.

THE MACRO DEFINITION

There are four parts in every macro definition. The *header statement* always has MACRO as the operation code; the *trailer statement* always has MEND as the operation code. Following the header statement is the *prototype statement* that gives the form in which the macro instruction must be written. After the prototype statement are the *model statements* that define the code that is to be inserted into the assembler language source program when the macro instruction is expanded.

The prototype statement

Depending on the function of the macro, the prototype statement can consist of just a macro operation code or it can consist of a macro operation code plus one or more *variable symbols*. The macro operation code can be from one to eight letters or numbers in length starting with a letter, but it cannot duplicate an assembler language operation code or another macro name. When variable symbols are used, they can be coded as positional operands or keyword operands, as you'll see in a moment.

How to use variable symbols in the prototype statement   A variable symbol consists of the & sign followed by from one to seven letters or numbers, the first of which must be a letter. Thus, in figure 11-1, &LABEL, &R1, and so on, are variable symbols.

The variable symbols in the prototype statement indicate the operands (or parameters) that can be used when coding the macro instruction. For instance, the SUMWDS macro in figure 11-1 has places for five operands. The SUMWDS macro also provides for a label, &LABEL, which isn't required, but can be used if the program must branch to the macro instruction. If you do code a label, the value assigned to it is the label of the macro instruction in the source program. You will see how this works in a minute.

How to code variable symbols as positional operands   When you code operands in the prototype statement as in figure 11-1, they are referred to as *positional operands*. This means that the position of each operand indicates its use in the macro expansion. If, for example, the SUMWDS macro were coded

```
SUMWDS WORDA,5,WORDB,WORDC,BCON
```

Macro definition

```
Header statement                    MACRO
Prototype statement    &LABEL       SUMWDS  &R1,&W1,&W2,&W3,&CON
Model statements       &LABEL       SR    &R1,&R1
                                    A     &R1,&W1
                                    A     &R1,&W2
                                    A     &R1,&W3
                                    S     &R1,&CON
                                    A     &R1,=F'50'
Trailer statement                   MEND
```

Macro instruction

```
            ROUT1       SUMWDS   5,WORDA,WORDB,WORDC,BCON
```

Macro expansion

```
            ROUT1       SR    5,5
                        A     5,WORDA
                        A     5,WORDB
                        A     5,WORDC
                        S     5,BCON
                        A     5,=F'50'
```

Figure 11-1   The SUMWDS macro definition with positional operands

WORDA would be substituted for &R1, which would result in faulty source code because &R1 is supposed to be a register number.

If you aren't going to use one of the positional operands when you code a macro, you omit it. If, for example, you wanted to omit operands 2 and 5 in the SUMWDS macro, you would code the macro instruction as:

```
            SUMWDS 5,,WORDB,WORDC
```

Because all of the SUMWDS operands are required, however, this statement would result in faulty code.

How to code variable symbols as keyword operands   The other way to specify operands is to use *keyword operands* in the prototype statement. These are the type of operands used in the DCB. If, for example, SUMWDS had been written using keyword operands, it would look like the macro definition in figure 11-2. Here, the parameters in the prototype statement, minus the leading & sign, are the keywords you must use in the macro instruction. Unlike positional operands, you can code keyword operands in any sequence.

Macro definition

```
        MACRO
&NAME   SUMWDS  &REG1=,&WORD1=,&WORD2=,&WORD3=,&CON=
&NAME   SR      &REG1,&REG1
        A       &REG1,&WORD1
        A       &REG1,&WORD2
        A       &REG1,&WORD3
        S       &REG1,&CON
        A       &REG1,=F'50'
        MEND
```

Macro instruction

```
        SUMWDS  WORD1=W1,WORD2=W2,WORD3=W3,REG1=7,CON=C1
```

Macro expansion

```
        SR      7,7
        A       7,W1
        A       7,W2
        A       7,W3
        S       7,C1
        A       7,=F'50'
```

Figure 11-2   The SUMWDS macro definition with keyword operands

If a keyword operand is to have a default value, the value is coded in the prototype statement after the equals sign. If, for example, you want the keyword &REG1 to have a default value of 5 in the SUMWDS macro, you code it as &REG1=5 in the prototype statement. Then, if this parameter is omitted when the macro is used, register 5 is assigned to it during the macro expansion. If a keyword is omitted that doesn't have a default value, no value is assigned to that parameter in the macro expansion.

How to code a combination of positional and keyword operands   It is legal, though rare, to define a combination of positional and keyword operands. When both are coded, they can appear in any order. In other words, the keyword operands can be intermixed with the positional operands. Here, then, is an example of a prototype statement that defines both positional and keyword operands:

```
&NAME       SMPLE &P1,&KEY1=,&P2,&KEY2=NO,&P3
```

When you code the SMPLE macro, the only restriction is that the positional operands appear in the same order as in the prototype statement.

For example,

```
SMPLE FIRST,SECOND,THIRD,KEY1=GO,KEY2=YES
```

and

```
SMPLE FIRST,KEY1=GO,SECOND,KEY2=YES,THIRD
```

would both result in the same macro expansion.

The model statements

The model statements represent the instructions to be used in the expansion of the macro. During expansion, the operands given in the macro instruction are substituted for the corresponding variable symbols in the prototype statement. In figure 11-1, for example, 5 is substituted for &R1 wherever &R1 appears in the model statements. Similarly, WORDC is substituted for &W3 wherever it appears in the model statements. The expanded instructions are then placed in the source program and the assembly continues.

How to use ordinary symbols in the model statements   Although the SUMWDS macro uses variable symbols in the model statements, you can also use *ordinary symbols* in the model statements. Ordinary symbols are those you normally code in a program. If, for example, you code this model statement

```
MVC     FLD1,FLD2
```

it will be generated unchanged whenever you use the macro instruction. You can define the ordinary symbols within the model statements or in the assembler language program itself.

Figure 11-3 gives an example of a macro that uses only ordinary symbols. It shows an easy way to code the record layout of an inventory master record that is used in several programs. To get the record definitions inserted into the program, you code:

```
ITMSTR
```

Of course, since the macro expansion defines fields, you can code the macro only once in a program. Otherwise, the fields will be defined more than once, which will result in diagnostics. Note that this use of a macro definition is similar to the use of a COPY statement.

How to combine ordinary and variable symbols   The symbols you use for labels and operands in model statements can also be combinations of ordinary and variable symbols. If, for example, an MVC instruction in a macro definition is coded like this

```
MVC     FLD&A,FLD&B
```

```
                 MACRO
                 ITMSTR
      ITMRCD     DS        OCL70        INV MSTR RCD LAYOUT
      IITEM      DS        CL6          ITEM NUMBER
      IDESC      DS        CL20         ITEM DESCRIPTION
      IUM        DS        CL4          UNIT OF MEASURE
      IOPOL      DS        CL2          ORDER POLICY CODE
      IOQTY      DS        PL4          ORDER QTY
      IOPNT      DS        PL4          ORDER POINT
      ISS        DS        PL4          SAFETY STOCK
      IBOH       DS        PL4          BALANCE ON HAND
      IOOQTY     DS        PL4          ON ORDER QTY
      IALLOC     DS        PL4          ALLOCATED QTY
                 DS        CL14         AVAIL FOR EXPANSION
                 MEND
```

Figure 11-3   An ITMSTR macro definition with ordinary symbols

the operands of the generated MVC instruction will be the characters FLD plus the values assigned to &A and &B. For instance, if &A equals 1 and &B equals 2, the generated instruction will be:

```
      MVC     FLD1,FLD2
```

You can also combine ordinary and variable symbols in reverse order. For example,

```
      MVC     &A.FLD,&B.FLD
```

will generate

```
      MVC     OUTFLD,INFLD
```

if &A equals OUT and &B equals IN. In this case, the period (.) in &A.FLD and &B.FLD is called a *concatenation character*. It is used to separate a variable symbol from an ordinary symbol so the assembler can tell which is which.

There are many ways in which you can combine variable and ordinary symbols in your model statements. Some of them are illustrated in figure 11-4. Note that a concatenation character is used whenever the assembler might be confused by two operand parts in succession.

Figure 11-5 is a version of the ITMSTR macro that uses symbol combinations. This time the prototype statement shows that a single operand is expected. The label of the macro instruction in the source program will be assigned to the first model statement through the variable symbol &LABEL, and the operand is used as a prefix for the field labels. Notice that the operand for the macro should start with a letter and be three characters or fewer, otherwise invalid labels for the fields will result. (In topic 2, you'll see how you can use conditional assembly instructions to check a macro instruction for valid operands during its expansion.)

Symbol coded in model statement	Values assigned to variable symbols	Generated symbol
&FLD.A	&FLD=SUM	SUMA
FIELD&A	&A=1	FIELD1
NAME.&Z	&Z=ZZZ	NAMEZZZ
&D1.X.&L1	&D1=B4	B4X32
	&L1=32	
&DISP.(&BASE)	&DISP=84	84(9)
	&BASE=9	
&F1+5*&F2	&F1=6	6+5*FACT
	&F2=FACT	

Figure 11-4   Some symbol combinations that can be used in model statements

TWO USEFUL MACROS

With this as background, you should be able to write some useful macros. But, to help you along, I'm going to present two additional macros that you should find useful. The first one is a macro to get the system date. The second one is a macro that uses a switch to provide for special processing the first time through a program.

A macro to get the system date

Since getting the date from the supervisor is a function that is done in many programs, the GETDATE macro in figure 11-6 is one that can be useful. This macro illustrates the use of a macro (TIME) within a macro definition. The TIME macro, which is described in chapter 6, places the address of the current date in register 1. Then, the GETDATE macro moves the date into the operand given in the macro instruction. As the comment in the macro definition indicates, the date field should be at least four bytes long since the date is in the packed-decimal form of 00YYDDDC.

Once this macro has been stored in the source library, you can store the date in a field named DATEFLD by coding this statement:

```
INITRT    GETDATE DATEFLD
```

Then, the macro expansion will generate these instructions:

```
INITRT    TIME
          MVC    DATEFLD(4),0(1)
```

When a macro is used within a macro, the inner macro doesn't appear as one of the generated instructions on the assembly listing. As a result, the TIME macro will not be shown on the assembly listing, but its generated instructions will be shown.

Macro definition

```
            MACRO
&LABEL      ITMSTR   &PF
&LABEL      DS       0CL70        INV MSTR RCD LAYOUT
&PF.ITEM    DS       CL6          ITEM NUMBER
&PF.DESC    DS       CL20         ITEM DESCRIPTION
&PF.UM      DS       CL4          UNIT OF MEASURE
&PF.OPOL    DS       CL2          ORDER POLICY CODE
&PF.OQTY    DS       PL4          ORDER QTY
&PF.OPNT    DS       PL4          ORDER POINT
&PF.SS      DS       PL4          SAFETY STOCK
&PF.BOH     DS       PL4          BALANCE ON HAND
&PF.OOQTY   DS       PL4          ON ORDER QTY
&PF.ALLOC   DS       PL4          ALLOCATED QTY
            DS       CL14         AVAIL FOR EXPANSION
            MEND
```

Macro instruction

```
MSTRWORK ITMSTR IM
```

Macro expansion

```
MSTRWORK  DS    0CL70        INV MSTR RCD LAYOUT
IMITEM    DS    CL6          ITEM NUMBER
IMDESC    DS    CL20         ITEM DESCRIPTION
IMUM      DS    CL4          UNIT OF MEASURE
IMOPOL    DS    CL2          ORDER POLICY CODE
IMOQTY    DS    PL4          ORDER QTY
IMOPNT    DS    PL4          ORDER POINT
IMSS      DS    PL4          SAFETY STOCK
IMBOH     DS    PL4          BALANCE ON HAND
IMOOQTY   DS    PL4          ON ORDER QTY
IMALLOC   DS    PL4          ALLOCATED QTY
          DS    CL14         AVAILABLE FOR EXPANSION
```

Figure 11-5   The ITMSTR macro with combined symbols

A first-time-switch macro

The purpose of a first-time-switch macro is to let a series of statements be executed the first time through a routine, but to branch around those statements on subsequent passes through the routine. Figure 11-7 shows one version of a first-time-switch macro definition.

To use this macro, you code the label of the instruction to be branched to after the first time through the program. For instance, you might code the routine in figure 11-8 in order to clear a print area the first time through a program and to leave it untouched on successive loops through the program. The generated instructions will then look like the second part of figure 11-8.

```
          MACRO
&LABEL    GETDATE &FLD
*  THE OPERAND FIELD SHOULD BE AT LEAST 4 BYTES
&LABEL    TIME
          MVC    &FLD.(4),0(1)
          MEND
```

Figure 11-6   A macro that gets the system date

```
          MACRO
&LABEL    FRSTSW  &BRCH
&LABEL    BC      0,&BRCH
          MVZ     *-3,=X'F0'
          MEND
```

Figure 11-7   A first-time-switch macro

Because the branch-on-condition (BC) instruction has a mask of zero, the branch to OTHER won't take place the first time through the program. (Remember from chapter 4 that a mask of hex zero means "never branch;" a mask of hex F means "always branch.") However, the MVZ instruction that follows the branch modifies the branch instruction's mask. Since the BC instruction is four bytes long, *-3 in the MVZ instruction refers to the second byte of the branch instruction. (Remember that * indicates the present location counter value.) Then, when the MVZ is executed, the mask in the BC instruction is changed from hex zero to hex F. As a result, the BC instruction will branch to OTHER on all subsequent passes through the routine.

MAKING THE MACRO DEFINITIONS AVAILABLE TO THE ASSEMBLER

Once you have defined a macro, you must make the definition available to your programs in order to test it. The normal way to do this is to put the macro definitions at the start of a source program that uses the macros. You can then use the macros in the program.

After you have successfully tested a macro definition, you normally catalog it in the system macro library or a source library. As a result, you should check your shop's standards to see which libraries you should use. Although this book doesn't show you how to add members to a source library, our MVS TSO book shows you how to do this in detail.

Source code

```
PRINT      FRSTSW  OTHER
           MVI     PRTAREA,X'40'
           MVC     PRTAREA+1(132),PRTAREA
OTHER      .
           .
           .
```

Source code with macro expansion

```
     PRINT     FRSTSW  OTHER
+    PRINT     BC      0,OTHER
+              MVZ     *-3,=X'F0'
               MVI     PRTAREA,X'40'
               MVC     PRTAREA+1(132),PRTAREA
     OTHER     .
               .
               .
```

Figure 11-8   A routine that uses the first-time-switch macro

Terminology

macro definition
macro expansion
header statement
trailer statement
prototype statement
model statement
variable symbol
positional operand
keyword operand
ordinary symbol
concatenation character

Objective

Given specifications for a macro, code its macro definition using the elements presented in this topic.

TOPIC 2   Advanced macro writing

The macros in topic 1 accomplish two types of macro expansion. The first, called *text insertion*, simply inserts the model statements into the source program. For example, the first ITMSTR macro and the standard TIME macro accomplish text insertion only.

The second level of macro expansion is called *text insertion with modification*. The macros with operands in topic 1 are examples at this level since they cause the model statements to be modified based on the operands given. Nevertheless, these macros still involve a fixed series of model statements that are to be inserted into the source program.

The highest level of macro writing involves *text manipulation*. This means that the operands of the macro determine which instructions are inserted into the source program as well as the form those instructions are to take. A GET macro, for example, can be coded with filename as its only operand (locate mode) or it can have a work-area name as its second operand (move mode). When the macro is expanded, the generated instructions vary depending on whether the work-area operand is present.

In order to write text manipulation macros, you need to know how to define and use *SET symbols*. These symbols can have their values changed during macro expansion. In addition, you need to know how to write *conditional assembly statements*. These statements can alter the sequence in which the assembler expands a macro. In fact, these instructions can direct the assembler to loop through the model statements in a macro definition, generating several source statements from a single model statement.

Quite frankly, writing macro definitions for text manipulation is a skill that cannot be mastered by all programmers. On the programming staff of a large company, for instance, perhaps only one programmer will be capable of writing a macro for a specialized I/O function. Nevertheless, the macro writing facilities of assembler language are important because they let you create a macro language within assembler language. That's why macro writing is of interest to computer scientists and software specialists.

Because SET symbols and conditional assembly statements work together, you must know something about both before you can understand text-manipulation macros. As a result, this topic presents the macro writing facilities in this sequence: (1) SET symbols, (2) symbol attributes, (3) assigning values to SET symbols, and (4) conditional assembly statements. After you become familiar with these elements, you'll be introduced to a few text-manipulation macros.

SET symbols   SET symbols are variable symbols that are defined in a macro definition. They can be defined as one of three types and in one of two ranges. First, I will discuss these types and ranges. Then, I will show you how these symbols are defined. You will see later how values are assigned to these symbols.

Types of SET symbols   The three types of SET symbols are arithmetic (A), binary (B), and character (C). An arithmetic SET symbol can be assigned any numeric value between -2^{31} and $+2^{31}-1$. This is the same range that a binary fullword has. In contrast, a binary SET symbol can be assigned only two values: 0 and 1. A character SET symbol can be assigned a string of up to eight characters.

Ranges of SET symbols   A SET symbol is either *local* or *global* depending on its range within a program. If the value assigned to a SET symbol is effective within only one macro expansion, it is called local. In this case, if the same SET symbol is defined in two different macros, it is two different symbols. In contrast, a global SET symbol that is defined in two different macros is treated as one symbol. In other words, a global SET symbol is common to an entire assembly and is available for use by other macros. Nevertheless, it must still be defined in each macro it is used in. In this book, you won't see examples of macro definitions that use global SET symbols.

How to define SET symbols   All SET symbols used in a macro definition must be defined (or declared). This is referred to as *symbol declaration*. In a statement that defines symbols, the label area must be blank.

The six operation codes for symbol declaration are shown in the examples of SET statements in figure 11-9. The operation code starts with either GBL (global) or LCL (local), which is followed by the type code of the SET symbols that are going to be defined by the statement. Since SET symbols are a type of variable symbol, the first character of each SET symbol name must be &. Notice that multiple SET symbols can be declared in one statement by separating the names with commas.

When a SET symbol is declared, it is assigned an initial value of zero for A and B types and null for C types. A null value means literally nothing: zero length and no data. To illustrate SET symbol declarations, figure 11-10 shows the prototype statement from the standard SAVE macro followed by its declarations. Here, &A, &B, and &C are assigned an initial value of zero when the macro is expanded and &E, &F, &G, and &H are assigned null values.

Symbol attributes   All symbols (ordinary, variable, and SET symbols) have attributes. Two attributes you are familiar with are *length* and *type*. For instance, an ordinary symbol defined as PL3 has a length attribute of 3 and a type code of P. In addition to the normal type codes used in DS and DC statements, though, there are others.

Figure 11-11 summarizes the common type codes for symbols. If, for example, a macro operand is omitted, its type attribute is O. If it is a number, its type attribute is N (a number is a self-defining value).

In addition to length and type, macro symbols also have number, count, scaling, and integer attributes. Since scaling and integer attributes are rarely used, they aren't covered in this book. But the number and count attributes can be important.

How to use the number attribute   The *number attribute* applies only to symbolic parameters that have *sublists*. The term sublist refers to the fact that one symbolic parameter can have several values. The parameter must then have a *subscript* added to identify an individual value in the sublist. The subscript is a number in parentheses following the symbol name. For instance, &P(2) refers to the second item in the sublist for the symbol &P; &P(5) refers to the fifth item in the sublist.

For an operand with a sublist, the prototype statement can indicate the maximum number of values within the sublist as illustrated in figure 11-12. Here, the prototype statement indicates that the symbolic parameter &P2 may have five sublist values. Although you don't have to indicate the maximum number of values for a sublist parameter in a prototype statement, it makes the macro definition easier to understand.

When a macro instruction with one or more sublist parameters is coded in a program, the sublist operands must be separated by commas and enclosed in parentheses as in this example:

```
SAMP   SUM,(X,Y,,AZ)
```

If the macro definition is the one shown in figure 11-12, parameter &P2 will have the values indicated assigned to it. Since the third and fifth names in the sublist are omitted, they are considered to be undefined.

The number attribute of a symbol is equal to the number of sublist positions coded in the macro instruction. More specifically, the number attribute is one more than the number of commas in the parentheses. For &P2 in the macro statement in figure 11-12, the number attribute is 4 because three commas are used. When the sublist operand is omitted, the number attribute is 0. For most parameters (those with no sublist), the number attribute is 1.

How to use the count attribute   The *count attribute* is equal to the number of characters in the operand of an instruction. To illustrate, suppose a prototype statement is coded as:

```
&LABEL   GSPLX &OP1,&OP2
```

Then, if the macro statement is coded as

```
PICT    GSPLX FIELD1,X
```

```
GBLA      &NBR1
GBLB      &B1,&B2,&SWITCH
GBLC      &STR,&X37
LCLA      &VAR1,&TIP
LCLB      &OFF
LCLC      &NAME,&FIELD
```

Figure 11-9   SET symbols that use the six valid operation codes

```
&NAME     SAVE    &REG,&CODE,&ID
          LCLA    &A,&B,&C
          LCLC    &E,&F,&G,&H
```

Figure 11-10   The prototype statement and symbol declarations of the SAVE macro

Type codes for symbols defined in DS and DC statements

A   A-type address constant
B   Binary
C   Character
D   Long floating-point
E   Short floating-point
F   Fullword fixed-point
H   Halfword fixed-point
P   Packed decimal
V   V-type address constant
Z   Zoned decimal

Type codes for symbols defined as instruction labels

I   Machine instruction
M   Macro instruction

Type codes for symbols defined as macro operands

N   A self-defining term (number)
O   An omitted term

Figure 11-11   Type codes for symbols

Prototype statement

```
&LABEL    SAMP   &P1,&P2(5)
```

Macro instruction

```
          SAMP   SUM,(X,Y,,AZ)
```

Values assigned to the parameters

Parameter   Value

```
&P1                SUM
&P2(1)             X
&P2(2)             Y
&P2(3)             Undefined
&P2(4)             AZ
&P2(5)             Undefined
```

Figure 11-12   Symbolic parameters including one with a sublist

the count attribute of &LABEL is 4. Similarly, the count attribute of &OP1 is 6 and of &OP2 is 1. As you can see, then, the count attributes of the operands may differ each time the macro instruction is coded.

Assigning values to SET symbols

You assign values to SET symbols during macro expansion by using the SETA (arithmetic), SETB (binary), and SETC (character) statements.

The SETA statement   The label of the SETA statement must be the variable symbol to which a value is to be assigned. The operand of the statement is an *arithmetic expression* that represents the value to be assigned. For instance, the following SETA statement assigns a value of 46 to the SET symbol named &A1:

```
&A1       SETA   46
```

In this case, the arithmetic expression is a *self-defining term*, the number 46.

The arithmetic expression can range from a self-defining term to a complex expression involving many variables and the *arithmetic operators*: + for plus, - for minus, * for multiply, and / for divide. Here's a more involved arithmetic expression used as the operand of a SETA statement:

```
&DELTA    SETA   &X1+10/&X2
```

Operator	Meaning
E Q	Equal to
N E	Not equal to
L T	Less than
L E	Less than or equal to
G T	Greater than
G E	Greater than or equal to

Figure 11-13   The logical operators that can be used in the operand of a SETB statement

In an expression like this, the evaluation proceeds from left to right with multiplication and division done first, followed by addition and subtraction. If, for example, &X1 has a value of 10 and &X2 has a value of 2, &DELTA will be assigned a value of 15.

If parentheses are used in an arithmetic expression, the expressions within the innermost sets of parentheses are evaluated first. If, for example, the statement above is coded as

```
&DELTA    SETA    (&X1+10)/&X2
```

&DELTA is assigned a value of 10 if &X1 equals 10 and &X2 equals 2. Within parentheses, evaluation proceeds as before, with multiplication and division first.

An attribute can also be assigned to a SET symbol by using the SETA statement, provided the attribute is numeric. For example, the following code assigns a value equal to the length attribute of &A1 to &LA1:

```
&LA1      SETA    L'&A1
```

In other words, if the length of the operand that is coded in the macro instruction for &A1 is 8, &LA1 is assigned a value of 8. To indicate an attribute, you use L' (for length), T' (for type), K' (for count), or N' (for number). Since L', N', and K' are numeric, they can be used in SETA expressions.

The SETB statement   The SETB statement can assign a value to a binary SET symbol in much the same way that a SETA statement assigns a value to an arithmetic SET symbol. This is illustrated by this statement:

```
&SW1      SETB    0
```

Here, a value of zero is assigned to &SW1.

The operand of a SETB statement can also be a *logical expression* that is evaluated by the assembler as true or false. If the expression is true, the SET symbol is assigned the value 1. If the expression is false, zero is assigned. Logical expressions are composed of two arithmetic expressions or two character expressions connected by one of the *logical operators* illustrated in figure 11-13.

True logical expressions

Statement			Variable values
&X3	SETB	(8 GT 3)	
&LIMIT	SETB	(&INDEX LE &HIGH)	&INDEX=19 &HIGH=20
&SWITCH	SETB	(&PARM1+5 NE &PARM2*3)	&PARM1=4 &PARM2=6
&DONE	SETB	(4 EQ L'&KEY2)	Length of &KEY2 is 4

False logical expressions

Statement			Variable values
&B1	SETB	(&NAME EQ 'FIRST')	&NAME='BRK'
&B2	SETB	(T'&P1 NE 'C')	Type code of &P1='C'
&SYMB	SETB	(&KEY4 EQ &END)	&KEY4='NXT' &END='END'

Figure 11-14   Some SETB statements with logical expressions as operands

The expressions that are compared by the logical operators can be self-defining terms, arithmetic expressions composed of arithmetic operators and variable names, or symbol attributes. In the first group of examples in figure 11-14, the logical expressions are all true, so the value assigned in each case is 1. In the second group of SETB statements in figure 11-14, each logical expression is false so the value assigned to the binary SET symbol is zero.

The SETC statement   Character SET symbols are assigned values with a SETC statement. The operand can be a self-defining character string, another variable symbol, or any combination or concatenation of the two. The operand can also be an attribute of a variable symbol. Except for an attribute operand, the operand must be enclosed in single quotes as in the examples in figure 11-15.

A duplication factor may also precede the operand of a SETC statement or any part of a concatenated operand, unless the operand is an attribute. For example, the fourth SETC statement in figure 11-15 indicates a duplication factor of three. When this statement is executed, the operand is evaluated first and is then duplicated the indicated number of times. When a duplication factor is coded, it must always be enclosed in parentheses.

Some SET statement examples   Figure 11-16 gives several examples of each type of SET statement and shows the resulting value assigned to the

Statement			Remark
&STRING	SETC	'KEY'	The operand is a self-defining string.
&NAME	SETC	'&KEY1'	The operand is a variable symbol.
&NAME	SETC	'MR &KEY1' or 'MR '.'&KEY1'	The operand is a string plus a variable symbol.
&DUP	SETC	(3)'KEY'	The operand is a self-defining string duplicated three times.
&TYPE	SETC	T'&PARM1	The operand is the type attribute.

Figure 11-15   Different types of operands allowed in the SETC statement

symbol. Note in the fourth SETC statement that two periods in a character string are required for one period to show in the resulting value because a period is the concatenation character. Similarly, two consecutive apostrophes are required for one apostrophe to show in the resulting value.

Conditional assembly statements

Normally, the assembler processes the instructions in a source program in sequence. When you use conditional assembly statements, though, you can control the sequence in which the source statements are processed. For instance, you can cause the assembler to skip some of the instructions and jump ahead in the source statement sequence. And, you can cause the assembler to branch backward in the sequence so some of the source code can be processed again, just as if it had been coded in the source program more than once.

The primary conditional assembly statements are the AGO and AIF statements. They are similar to an unconditional branch instruction and a conditional branch instruction, but they direct the assembly of the source program rather than the execution of the object program. Related to the use of the AGO and AIF statements are the MNOTE, MEXIT, and ANOP statements.

The AGO statement   To illustrate the AGO statement, let's consider the portion of the macro definition in figure 11-17. Here, the AGO statement causes the assembler to skip ahead to the last MVC instruction. As a result, the two LA instructions, the first MVC instruction, and any other instructions before .END aren't generated in the resulting source code.

Here, the label .END is called a *sequence symbol*. Sequence symbols are labels that can be referred to in conditional assembly statements in order to direct the assembly sequence, but they aren't generated with the rest of the statement that they label. A period is the first character of a sequence symbol.

Statement examples			Symbol values	Assigned value
&A72	SETA	72		72
&NBR	SETA	&INDEX+10	&INDEX=3	13
&LIMIT	SETA	&BASE*5-&ORG	&BASE=100,&ORG=37	463
&LGTH	SETA	L'&P1-1	Length of &P1=7	6
&SW1	SETB	0		0
&YES	SETB	(&PARM2 EQ 'YES')	&PARM2='NO'	0
&TOOLONG	SETB	(L'&FLD LE 256)	Length of &FLD=180	1
&STRING	SETC	'AB C'		'AB C'
&NAME	SETC	'&KEY1'	&KEY1=JONES	'JONES'
&NAME	SETC	'MR .&KEY1'	&KEY1=JONES	'MR JONES'
&PRT1	SETC	'MR.. &KEY1'	&KEY1=BOLTZ	'MR. BOLTZ'
&DUP1	SETC	(2)'ABC'		'ABCABC'
&DUP2	SETC	'A'.(2)'B'.(3)'C'		'ABBCCC'
&TNAME	SETC	T'&NAME	Type attribute of &NAME=C	'C'

Figure 11-16   Some additional SET statement examples

The AIF statement   The operand of the AIF statement must be a logical expression followed by a sequence symbol. A logical expression is formed just as it is in a SETB statement. If the expression is true, the assembler branches to the sequence symbol that follows the logical expression. If the expression is false, the assembler continues processing the statements sequentially.

In the example that follows, a variable symbol, &LGTH, is compared to a value of 256:

```
AIF  (LGTH LE 256).SHORT
```

If &LGTH is less than or equal to 256, the expression is true and the assembler branches to the statement starting with the sequence symbol .SHORT. If the expression is false, the assembler processes the statement after the AIF statement.

When you code a logical expression, you can use the operators OR, AND, and NOT in various combinations to form complex logical expressions. For example, the logical expression

```
(&A GT 14 AND &B LT 12)
```

is true only if both logical terms are true. In contrast,

```
(&A GT 14 OR &B LT 12)
```

is true if either one or both of the logical terms are true.

Sometimes, it's necessary to use multiple sets of parentheses to group the various logical expressions so they will be evaluated properly:

```
((&A GT 2 AND &A LT 13) OR
(&A GT &B AND NOT &A GT 15))
```

```
                    .
                    .
                    .
          AGO       .END
          LA        &R1,256(&R1)
          LA        &R2,256(&R2)
          MVC       0(256,&R2),0(&R1)
                    .
                    .
                    .
.END      MVC       0(&LGTH,&R2),0(&R1)
                    .
                    .
                    .
```

Figure 11-17   Part of a macro definition that shows the use of the AGO instruction

In this example, if either of the internal expressions is true, the overall expression is true. Since the internal expressions are made up of two expressions in AND relationships, both expressions in the AND relationships must be true to make an internal expression true. Although the AND, OR, and NOT operators can be used in logical expressions for both SETB and AIF statements, they are used most often in AIF statements.

The MNOTE statement   Macro definitions often include some checking or editing of the macro instruction in the source program. When they do, conditional assembly statements are used to check that all the necessary operands are present, that certain operands are numeric, and so on. If any improper conditions are found, the MNOTE statement can be used to print an error message on both the source listing and the diagnostic listing.

The format of the MNOTE statement is:

```
MNOTE severity-code,'message'
```

If the *severity code* is present, the message will be printed in the diagnostic listing at the end of the assembly listing as well as in the source listing immediately following the macro. If the severity-code operand is omitted, the MNOTE message is only printed in the source listing.

In many of the IBM-supplied macros, you'll find that the MNOTE statement isn't used. For example, even though the GET macro definition in figure 11-18 performs some error checking, the MNOTE statement isn't used. Instead, whenever an error occurs, another macro, called IHBERMAC, is executed. The purpose of this macro is to display error codes and messages for all different types of errors. You'll see this macro used in many of the IBM-supplied macros.

The MEXIT statement   The MEXIT statement causes the assembler to stop the macro expansion and go back to the source program. It is generally used when an uncorrectable error is detected, such as an invalid operand. An MEXIT can have a sequence symbol, but no operands. In the

GET macro definition in figure 11-18, you can see that three MEXIT statements have been used.

The ANOP statement   The ANOP statement is a no-operation statement. It is used to provide a statement on which to place a sequence symbol when the sequence symbol can't be coded directly on the model statement. In figure 11-18, the sequence symbols .NJES and .JES are coded on ANOP statements.

Some related ideas

When to use internal comments   An *internal comment* has .* in columns 1 and 2 and can have any characters in the remaining columns. Unlike a regular comment, though, an internal comment isn't printed on the source listing when the macro is expanded. It prints only when the macro definition itself is listed.

Internal comments can be used in any macro definition. However, you shouldn't use them unnecessarily. In general, we recommend that you use them only to identify or to clarify a segment of code. In the GET macro definition in figure 11-18, you can see that internal comments have been coded to indicate the latest changes made to the macro definition.

How to use character selection   When the GET macro is executed for a file other than a VSAM file, an *inner macro* named IHBINNRA is executed. An inner macro is another name for a macro coded within a macro definition. This macro is listed in figure 11-19.

Statement 600002 in this macro illustrates the selection of characters from a character string:

```
AIF   ('&A' EQ '(1)' OR '&A'(1,1) EQ '(').LDREG
```

Here, the second part of the logical expression

```
'&A'(1,1)
```

means: Select a character string beginning in position 1 of &A and continue for a length of 1. In this case, the first character of the filename operand is compared to a left parenthesis (&CB in the GET macro definition becomes &A in the IHBINNRA definition). Although the presentation of the GET macro in chapter 5 didn't mention it, the filename operand of GET can be the number of a register enclosed in parentheses. If used, the register is expected to contain the address of the DCB. This AIF statement, then, is checking to see if the register notation is used.

When to check for operand omissions   When you code a macro definition that checks the validity of the operands in the macro instruction, most of the routine is likely to be involved with the checking. Nevertheless, most macro definitions should at least check for operand omissions that will lead to program errors. If an omitted operand just means that a default value will be used, your macro definition doesn't have to check to make sure that the operand is present. But operand omissions

```
MEMBER NAME  GET
             MACRO                                                       00050C00
&NAME   GET     &CB,&AREA,&RPL=,&TYPE=                        XL03123     00100000
.*           CHANGE LEVEL = 07                                           00150000
.*           DATE OF LAST CHANGE = 21 JULY 83 (OZ       )               00187500
.*           &TYPE PARAMETER DROPPED, ADDED WITH OZ                     00225000
             AIF    ('&CB' NE '').NJES        NON JES EXPANSION   XL03123 00262500
             AIF    ('&RPL' NE '').JES        JES MACRO EXPANSION        00300000
             IHBERMAC 02                                        XL03123  00350000
             MEXIT                                                       00400000
.NJES   ANOP                                                            00450000
&NAME   IHBINNRA &CB,&AREA                                      XL03123  00475C00
             AIF    ('&TYPE' EQ '').GET40                      XL03123  00500000
             AIF    ('&TYPE' NE 'P').E2                        XL03123  00525000
             L      15,4(0,1)                 LOAD PARALLEL GET RTN ADDR 00550000
             AGO    .GET45                                     XL03123  00575000
.GET40  L      15,48(0,1)                     LOAD GET ROUTINE ADDR      00600000
.GET45  BALR   14,15                          LINK TO GET ROUTINE        00625000
             MEXIT                                                       00650000
.JES    ANOP                                                            00700000
&NAME   DS      0H                                                      00750000
             AIF    ('&RPL'(1,1) EQ '(').RPLR                           00800000
             LA     1,&RPL                    LOAD RPL ADDR              00850000
             AGO    .AREG                                                00900000
.RPLR   LR      1,&RPL(1)                     LOAD RPL ADDR VIA REG      00950000
.AREG   LA      0,X'00'                       INDICATE GET IN REG        01000000
             L      15,24(1)                  LOAD ACB ADDR FROM RPL     01050000
             L      15,8(15)                  LOAD JES INTERFACE MOD ADDR 01300000
             BALR   14,15                     LINK TO INTERFACE ROUTINE  01400000
             MEXIT                                            XL03123  01433300
.E2     IHBERMAC 48,,&TYPE                    INVALID TYPE OPND  XL03123 01466600
             MEND                                                        01500000
```

Figure 11-18   The GET macro definition

often mean that the macro cannot be generated properly. As a result, omission checking is done in the IBM-supplied standard macros. And you should code routines for omission checking in your macros if they are of any consequence.

Three macro definitions for text manipulation

The GET and IHBINNRA macros   Figures 11-18 and 11-19 present the source listings for the IBM GET and IHBINNRA macros. As you have already seen, they illustrate extensive use of conditional assembly statements. By studying them, you can get a better appreciation for what writing a complex macro definition involves. If you relate the definitions to the code generated by the macros in your assembly listings, you should be able to figure you how your code was expanded. But it's not easy.

A move-long macro   To give you a chance to study a text manipulation macro that isn't quite so complex, figure 11-20 presents a move-long macro. You don't need a macro like this on a System/370 because the MVCL statement does the same function. But I wrote a macro like this

```
MEMBER NAME  IHBINNRA
           MACRO                                                              0005C002
&NAME      IHBINNRA   &A,&B,&C,&D,&E                              LC0A  0C100002
.*0000000360                                                     LC0A  00150002
           LCLA   &ASUM                                          19015 00200002
           LCLB   &BIT(2)                                        19015 00250002
           LCLC   &GVALU                                         LC0A  00300002
&GVALU     SETC   'IHB'.'&SYSNDX'                                LC0A  00350002
           AIF    ('&E' EQ '').NOPT                              19015 00400002
&BIT(1)    SETB   ('&E' EQ 'REWIND')                             19015 00450002
&BIT(2)    SETB   ('&E' EQ 'LEAVE')                              19015 00500002
&ASUM      SETA   &BIT(1)*32+&BIT(2)*48                          19015 00550002
           AIF    ('&A' EQ '(1)' OR '&A'(1,1) EQ '(').LDREG      19015 00600002
           CNOP   0,4                                            19015 00650002
&NAME      BAL    1,*+8                    BR AROUND LIST         19015 00700002
           DC     AL1(&ASUM)              OPTION BYTE            19015 00750002
           DC     AL3(&A(1))                                     19015 00800002
           L      1,0(1,0)                LOAD REG 1           YM1995 00850002
           AGO    .END                                           19015 00900002
.LDREG     ANOP                                                  19015 00950002
           AIF    ('&A' EQ '(1)').ORIT                           19015 01000002
           CNOP   0,4                                            19015 01050002
&NAME      BAL    1,*+8                    BR AROUND LIST         19015 01100002
           DC     AL1(&ASUM)              OPTION BYTE            19015 01150002
           DC     AL3(0)                                         19015 01200002
           L      1,0(1,0)                LOAD R 1 WITH OPTION BYTEYM1995 01250002
           OR     1,&A(1)                 OR IN DCB ADDRESS      19015 01300002
           AGO    .END                                           19015 01350002
.ORIT      ANOP                                                  19015 01400002
           CNOP   0,4                                            19015 01450002
&NAME      O      1,*+8                    SET OPTION BYTE IN REG 1 19015 01500002
           B      *+8                                            19015 01550002
           DC     AL1(&ASUM)              OPTION BYTE            19015 01600002
           DC     AL3(0)                                         19015 01650002
           AGO    .END                                           19015 01700002
.NOPT      AIF    ('&A' EQ '' OR '&A' EQ '(1)').NAMEIT           19015 01750002
           AIF    ('&A'(1,1) EQ '(').REGA                              01800002
           AIF    ('&C' NE '').HOH1                              LC0A  01850002
&NAME      LA     1,&A                     LOAD PARAMETER REG 1        01900002
           AGO    .CHKB                                               01950002
.REGA      ANOP                                                       02000002
&NAME      LR     1,&A(1)                  LOAD PARAMETER REG 1        02050002
           AGO    .CHKB                                               02100002
.NAMEIT    AIF    ('&NAME' EQ '').CHKB                                02150002
&NAME      DS     0H                                                  02200002
.CHKB      AIF    ('&B' EQ '' OR '&B' EQ '(0)').END                   02250002
           AIF    ('&B'(1,1) EQ '(').REGB                             02300002
           AIF    ('&A' EQ '').GEN                               LC0A  02350002
           AIF    ('&D' EQ '1').END                              LC0A  02400002
.GEN       ANOP                                                  LC0A  02450002
           LA     0,&B                     LOAD PARAMETER REG 0        02500002
           AGO    .END                                                02550002
.HOH1      ANOP                                                  LC0A  02600002
           AIF    ('&C' EQ '1').H1                               LC0A  02650002
&NAME      L      0,&GVALU  LOAD FOR HIARCHY ZERO                LC0A  02700002
           AGO    .HCHK                                          LC0A  02750002
.H1        ANOP                                                  LC0A  02800002
```

Figure 11-19   The IHBINNRA macro definition (part 1 of 2)

```
&NAME    L      0,&GVALU.A     LOAD FOR HIARCHY ONE              LC0A 02850002
.HCHK    ANOP                                                    LC0A 02900002
         CNOP   2,4                                              LC0A 02950002
         LA     1,&A                                             LC0A 03000002
         OR     1,0                                              LC0A 03050002
         AIF    ('&D' NE '1').TTT                                LC0A 03100002
         LA     0,*+8                                            LC0A 03150002
         B      *+16                                             LC0A 03200002
         DC     CL8'&B'                                          LC0A 03250002
         AGO    .SSS                                             LC0A 03300002
.TTT     ANOP                                                    LC0A 03350002
         B      *+8                                              LC0A 03400002
.SSS     AIF    ('&C' EQ '1').L1                                 LC0A 03450002
&GVALU   EQU    *                                                LC0A 03500002
         DC     X'01000000'                                      LC0A 03550002
         AGO    .CHKB                                            LC0A 03600002
.L1      ANOP                                                    LC0A 03650002
&GVALU.A EQU    *                                                LC0A 03700002
         DC     X'02000000'                                      LC0A 03750002
         AGO    .CHKB                                            LC0A 03800002
.REGB    LR     0,&B(1)              LOAD PARAMETER REG 0        03850002
.END     MEND                                                    03900002
```

Figure 11-19   The IHBINNRA macro definition (part 2 of 2)

many years ago for the System/360 to get around the 256-byte limitation of the MVC instruction.

The move-long macro allows a move of any number of bytes to be coded in a single macro instruction. The first two operands name the receiving and sending fields; the third operand specifies the number of bytes to be moved. During macro expansion, the macro will generate one or more MVC instructions that move the data in 256-byte chunks plus one last MVC instruction that moves 256 bytes or fewer.

To show how this macro definition is expanded, assume that

```
MOVERCD    MOVEL OUTA,RCD,600
```

has been coded in a program. This means the following assignments are made at the start of the macro expansion: &LABEL=MOVERCD, &RFLD=OUTA, &SFLD=RCD, and &LGTH=600. Then, the symbols &DISP, &ALGTH, and &FIRST are declared so the first two are given initial values of zero and &FIRST is given an initial value of null. At this point the assembler reaches these SET statements:

```
&ALGTH    SETA    &LGTH
&FIRST    SETC    '&LABEL'
```

The first statement assigns the value 600 to &ALGTH; the second assigns the string MOVERCD to &FIRST.

Next, the assembler encounters this AIF statement:

```
.LOOP     AIF    (&ALGTH LE 256).LAST
```

Since &ALGTH has a value of 600, the statement is false, no branch takes place, and this statement is reached by the assembler:

```
&FIRST    MVC    &RFLD+&DISP.(256),&SFLD+&DISP
```

When the current variable values are substituted in this statement, the following source instruction is expanded into the source program:

```
MOVERCD   MVC    OUTA+0(256),RCD+0
```

Then, the assembler reaches these statements:

```
&DISP     SETA   &DISP+256
&ALGTH    SETA   &ALGTH-256
&FIRST    SETC   ''
          AGO    .LOOP
```

As a result, the value of &DISP is increased by 256, the value of &ALGTH is decreased by 256, and the value of &FIRST is set to a null string. The AGO statement then branches the assembler back to the first statement in the loop.

The second time through the loop, the value of &ALGTH is 344 so the AIF still doesn't branch. Then, the following source instruction is generated:

```
          MVC    OUTA+256(256),RCD+256
```

Note here that no label is given to the instruction since &FIRST has a null value at this time.

The third time through the loop, &ALGTH has a value of 88 so the branch to .LAST takes place. Since the operation code of this statement is ANOP, the assembler goes on to the MVC model statement so this final source instruction is generated:

```
          MVC    OUTA+512(88),RCD+512
```

When the assembler reaches the MEND statement, it returns to the source instructions following the MOVEL macro.

Discussion

Although this topic is intended to familiarize you with advanced macro writing techniques, it is only a start. Before you can write macros such as the GET or IHBINNRA , you'll probably have to put many hours of study into macro writing. If you want to learn some of the additional macro writing facilities, you can find them in *OS/VS—DOS/VSE—VM/370 Assembler Language*(GC33-4010). At this time, however, you should be able to write simple text-manipulation macros like the move-long macro without too much difficulty.

Macro definition

```
           MACRO
&LABEL     MOVEL   &RFLD,&SFLD,&LGTH
           LCLA    &DISP,&ALGTH
           LCLC    &FIRST
&ALGTH     SETA    &LGTH
&FIRST     SETC    '&LABEL'
.LOOP      AIF     (&ALGTH LE 256).LAST
&FIRST     MVC     &RFLD+&DISP.(256),&SFLD+&DISP
&DISP      SETA    &DISP+256
&ALGTH     SETA    &ALGTH-256
&FIRST     SETC    ''
           AGO     .LOOP
.LAST      ANOP
&FIRST     MVC     &RFLD+&DISP.(&ALGTH),&SFLD+&DISP
           MEND
```

Macro instruction

```
MOVERCD   MOVEL   OUTA,RCD,600
```

Macro expansion

```
MOVERCD   MVC    OUTA+0(256),RCD+0
          MVC    OUTA+256(256),RCD+256
          MVC    OUTA+512(88),RCD+512
```

Figure 11-20   A move-long macro definition for the System/360

Terminology

text insertion
text insertion with modification
text manipulation
SET symbol
conditional assembly statement
local SET symbol
global SET symbol
symbol declaration
length attribute
type attribute
number attribute
sublist

subscript
count attribute
arithmetic expression
self-defining term
arithmetic operator
logical expression
logical operator
sequence symbol
severity code
internal comment
inner macro

Objective

Given specifications for a text-manipulation macro, code its macro definition. Your definition will require the use of SET symbols and conditional assembly statements.

Chapter   12

Floating-point arithmetic

Floating-point is the most powerful form of System/370 arithmetic for several reasons. First, it's faster than fixed-point binary or decimal arithmetic. Second, the floating-point data format can store a wider range of values than the other formats. Third, the floating-point format can store fractional values and, when the floating-point instructions are executed, they automatically align the decimal positions.

In business data processing, however, there is little need for this power. In fact, due to the problem of converting data to and from floating-point format, floating-point instructions are rarely used for business arithmetic. So, as you study this chapter, we think you should have one major objective: to develop a better understanding of high-level languages that use floating-point instructions in the resulting object code.

Data formats   Floating-point data is stored in a fullword (*short form*) or a doubleword (*long form*) as illustrated in figure 12-1. The difference between short and long form is the number of digits that can be carried in the fraction. This is referred to as the *precision* of a number. In short form, which is often called *single precision*, the equivalent of about 7 decimal digits can be stored in the fraction; in long form, which is often called *double precision*, the equivalent of about 16 decimal digits can be stored.

In either form, the leftmost bit represents the sign of the field: "off" represents plus, and "on" represents minus. The next seven bits represent the *exponent* of the number; the remaining bits (bits 8-31 in the short form, 8-63 in the long form) represent the *fraction*. This is something like the exponential notation that you may have used in chemistry or physics classes in which a value like 1,563,487 can be written as $0.1563487E+7$ meaning 0.1563487×10^7 (10^7 means 10 to the seventh power). The exponent (in this case, $+7$) is sometimes called the *characteristic*; the fraction (in this case, 0.1563487) is sometimes called the *mantissa*.

The format of a floating-point exponent   The exponent in the floating-point format is expressed as a power of 16 (instead of 10). This exponent value is stored as a binary number in bits 1-7. To allow both plus and minus exponents, the exponent is stored in *excess-64 format*. This means that the value stored as the exponent is 64 more than the actual exponent. If, for example, the value stored is 65, it really means 65 minus 64, or 1. Thus, the fraction is multiplied by 16 to the first power. If the exponent value is less than 64, it indicates a negative exponent; for instance, a value of 62 means 62 minus 64, or an exponent of -2. (Negative exponents allow storage of very small fractional values as in 0.18×10^{-12} which equals .00000000000018.) Because the seven exponent bits can represent a number from 0 through 127, the exponent can range from -64 to $+63$. Thus, the range of a floating-point number in either form is approximately from 10^{-78} to 10^{+75}.

The format of a floating-point fraction   The fraction portion of a floating-point number assumes a decimal point before bit number 8. Thus, the place values of bits 8 through 31 in the short form, or bits 8 through 63 in the long form, are 2^{-1}, 2^{-2}, 2^{-3}, 2^{-4}, and so on. The fractional values of these place values are 1/2, 1/4, 1/8, 1/16, and so on. Figure 12-2 illustrates some short-form floating-point numbers in binary along with their decimal equivalents. Unlike fixed-point format, negative fractions are not in complement form.

How to normalize a floating-point number   A floating-point value is *normalized* if the fraction bits have been shifted left as much as possible so that the exponent is at the minimum possible value. In contrast, the last example in figure 12-2 is *unnormalized*. In this case, the fraction can be shifted left four bits and the exponent reduced by one without changing the value stored. Since normalization allows a maximum number of fraction bits to be carried, thereby offering the highest level of precision,

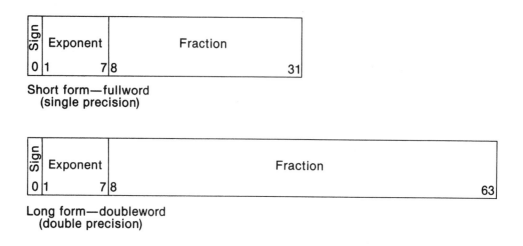

Short form—fullword
(single precision)

Long form—doubleword
(double precision)

Figure 12-1 Floating-point data formats

floating-point fields are usually normalized. Although there are eight
instructions for manipulating unnormalized fields and there are cases
when these instructions have value, they are rarely used. As a result, they
aren't covered in this book.

How to define a floating-point field To define a floating-point field,
you use the type codes E and D. Type code E indicates short form and type
code D indicates long form as illustrated in figure 12-3. As you can see,
you can write the nominal value in an E or D type definition in regular
decimal form or in exponential notation. If you use exponential notation,
the exponent in decimal must be preceded by E and a plus or minus sign.
The E type reserves a fullword of storage; the D type reserves a
doubleword.

Figure 12-4 illustrates some additional constant definitions with the
hex constant shown as it will appear both on an assembly listing and in a
storage dump. Notice that hex 40 in the exponent portion of a field is
equivalent to a zero exponent (64 minus 64). Note also that a value like 0.1
can't be expressed exactly in floating-point. In the single precision format,
for example, the hex representation is 4019999A where 40 is the exponent
and 19999A is the fraction. This is an approximate value of .09999999.

Instructions

As in fixed-point binary arithmetic, all arithmetic operations for floating-
point are performed in registers. For this purpose, a System/370 provides
four *floating-point registers*. These are doubleword registers that are used
only for floating-point operations. The registers are numbered 0, 2, 4, and
6, and they accommodate both short- and long-form data. For short-form
instructions, only the first of the two words in each register are used; for
the long-form instructions, both words are used.

Sign	Exponent	Fraction			Determining value
0	1000000	10100000	00000000	00000000	Exponent $= (64 - 64) = 0; 16^0 = 2^0$ Fraction $= (2^{-1} + 2^{-3})$ Value $= 2^0(2^{-1} + 2^{-3}) = (2^{-1} + 2^{-3}) = (.500 + .125) = 0.625$
1	1000001	01100000	00000000	00000000	Exponent $= (65 - 64) = 1; 16^1 = 2^4$ Fraction $= (2^{-2} + 2^{-3})$ Value $= -2^4(2^{-2} + 2^{-3}) = -(2^2 + 2^1) = -(4 + 2) = -6$
0	0111110	01000000	00000000	00000000	Exponent $= (62 - 64) = -2; 16^{-2} = 2^{-8}$ Fraction $= (2^{-2})$ Value $= 2^{-8}(2^{-2}) = (2^{-10}) = \dfrac{1}{1024} = .009765625$
0	1000100	00001001	00000000	01000000	Exponent $= (68 - 64) = 4; 16^4 = 2^{16}$ Fraction $= (2^{-5} + 2^{-8} + 2^{-18})$ Value $= 2^{+16}(2^{-5} + 2^{-8} + 2^{-18}) = (2^{11} + 2^8 + 2^{-2})$ $= (2048 + 256 + 0.25) = 2304.25$

Figure 12-2   Some floating-point numbers and their equivalents

There are 44 floating-point instructions on the System/370. They cover operations for loading, storing, addition, subtraction, multiplication, division, and comparison. The 32 instructions that are summarized in figure 12-5 are presented in this topic.

Store   There are two forms of the floating-point store instruction as indicated in figure 12-5. In these instructions, as in all floating-point instructions, the character E in the operation code means short form and the character D means long form. The operands of all the floating-point instructions also have identical requirements: the first operand must always be one of the floating-point register numbers; the second operand must be either a fullword (short form), a doubleword (long form), or another floating-point register.

Load   In addition to the basic forms of the load instruction, several special forms are available. These special instructions load a value while forcing the sign of the value to be positive, negative, or the opposite of its original value. Because negative floating-point numbers aren't stored in complement form, the load complement instructions change the sign of a field by reversing only the sign bit.

```
SINGLE    DS    E
DOUBLE    DS    D
FPVAL1    DC    E'3.141596'
FPVAL2    DC    D'1.86E+5'
FPVAL3    DC    E'-1.0E-6'
```

Figure 12-3   Some floating-point field definitions

Hex code on assembly listing	Source code		Object code in storage dump
+00.000000	DC	E'0'	00000000
+41.100000	DC	E'1'	41100000
+43.FFF000	DC	E'4095'	43FFF000
+44.100000	DC	E'4096'	44100000
-41.100000	DC	E'-1'	C1100000
-43.FFF000	DC	E'-4095'	C3FFF000
-44.100000	DC	E'-4096'	C4100000
+40.800000	DC	E'0.5'	40800000
+41.180000	DC	E'1.5'	41180000
+40.19999A	DC	E'0.1'	4019999A
+3F.28F5C3	DC	E'0.01'	3F28F5C3
+3E.418937	DC	E'0.001'	3E418937
+48.4C2CBC	DC	E'12.78E+8'	484C2CBC
+51.56BC76	DC	E'1E+20'	5156BC76
-6A.BF9572	DC	E'-2.8E+50'	EABF9572
+00.00000000000000	DC	D'0'	0000000000000000
+41.10000000000000	DC	D'1'	4110000000000000
+40.80000000000000	DC	D'0.5'	4080000000000000
+40.1999999999999A	DC	D'0.1'	401999999999999A
+17.3BD0F495A9703E	DC	D'0.1E-49'	173BD0F495A9703E
+40.1F9ADD3739635F	DC	D'12345.6789E-5'	401F9ADD3739635F

Figure 12-4   Some representations of floating-point numbers as they would appear in an assembly listing and a storage dump

Add and subtract   The add and subtract instructions follow a similar pattern. When these instructions are executed, the value in the second operand is added to or subtracted from the first operand with the result replacing the first operand. Any alignment of decimal points is performed automatically, and the result is normalized before it is placed in the first operand register.

Operation code	Instruction name	Example	
STE	Store short	STE	2,FPSAVE
STD	Store long	STD	4,FPDBLE
LE	Load short	LE	4,FWORD
LD	Load long	LD	6,DWORD
LER	Load short RR	LER	0,4
LDR	Load long RR	LDR	2,0
LPER	Load positive short	LPER	2,NEGF
LPDR	Load positive long	LPDR	4,NEGD
LNER	Load negative short	LNER	2,POSF
LNDR	Load negative long	LNDR	4,POSD
LCER	Load complement short	LCER	6,COMPF
LCDR	Load complement long	LCDR	6,COMPD
AE	Add short	AE	0,FACT1
AD	Add long	AD	4,DFACT
AER	Add short RR	AER	0,6
ADR	Add long RR	ADR	4,6
SE	Subtract short	SE	2,SUBWORD
SD	Subtract long	SD	6,DBLESUB
SER	Subtract short RR	SER	4,2
SDR	Subtract long RR	SDR	6,0
ME	Multiply short	ME	0,FACT
MD	Multiply long	MD	4,FACT
MER	Multiply short RR	MER	2,4
MDR	Multiply long RR	MDR	2,6
DE	Divide short	DE	2,DIV
DD	Divide long	DD	4,DDIVS
DER	Divide short RR	DER	2,0
DDR	Divide long RR	DDR	2,6
CE	Compare short	CE	2,VAL1
CD	Compare long	CD	6,VAL2
CER	Compare short RR	CER	0,2
CDR	Compare long RR	CDR	2,4

Figure 12-5   The floating-point instructions

Multiply   The floating-point multiply instruction can have either a storage field or another floating-point register as the second operand. When the instruction is executed, the first operand is multiplied by the second with the product replacing the first operand. Like signs result in a positive result, unlike signs in a negative result. An *exponent overflow* exception occurs if the resulting exponent value is greater than 127 and *exponent underflow* occurs if it's less than 0.

Divide   The floating-point divide instruction is similar. When executed, the quotient replaces the dividend in the first operand register and no remainder is saved. Exponent overflow and underflow can occur as in a multiply instruction, and an attempt to divide by zero leads to a floating-point divide exception.

Compare   The floating-point compare instructions provide an arithmetic comparison of floating-point values. After a compare instruction, you normally use a conditional branch instruction to test the condition code and branch accordingly.

Imprecision in floating-point arithmetic

One thing you should understand about floating-point arithmetic is that it doesn't always give exact results. For example, you have already seen how some decimal values (like 0.1) can't be expressed exactly in hexadecimal floating-point format. Another problem is that hex digits on the right of a fraction may be lost during an arithmetic operation.

To illustrate, suppose the add-long instruction adds two values, one with a hex exponent of 40, another with a hex exponent of 43. Prior to addition, the fraction with the smaller exponent is shifted right three hex digits to align the fractions. This means the rightmost 12 bits of the smaller number are moved out of the register, which can mean lost hex digits. After addition, the result is normalized (if necessary), so the result is shifted left.

To reduce the number of lost digits in floating-point arithmetic operations, the electronic circuitry that actually does the shifting has four extra bit positions to the right of the fraction that is shifted. These four bit positions are called a *guard digit*. Then, if a fraction is shifted right three hex digits, only two of the digits are lost when the result is normalized. Nevertheless, the result of a floating-point operation is likely to be less precise than that of a fixed-point binary or decimal operation.

This imprecision is an important notion to grasp because it can affect the coding of branching operations. To illustrate, suppose a program compares a floating-point constant of 0.1 with a field in which a decreasing value eventually should reach 0.1. When they are equal, the program should branch. Since the constant 0.1 can't be represented exactly and since the manipulated value may lose digits as it approaches 0.1, the two fields may never be exactly equal. Because of this, a branch code of BNL or BNH should be used so the program will branch when the manipulated value equals or passes the constant value. If BE is used, the program may never branch.

Data conversion

The main reason floating-point arithmetic isn't used in business programming is that data conversion is a problem. Since there is no instruction that converts other data formats to floating-point format, you must code a

```
               .
               .
               .
CONV      PACK     DWORD,RINT
          CVB      7,DWORK
          L        6,EXPONENT
          STM      6,7,DWORK
          LD       0,DWORK
          AD       0,FPZERO
          PACK     DWORK,RFRAC
          CVB      7,DWORK
          L        6,EXPONENT
          STM      6,7,DWORK
          LD       2,DWORK
          DD       2,FRACADJ
          ADR      0,2
          STD      0,FPVAL
          CLI      RSIGN,C'-'
          BNE      CONT
          OI       FPVAL,X'80'
CONT      .
          .
          .
DWORK     DS       D
FPVAL     DS       D
FPZERO    DC       D'0'
FRACADJ   DC       D'1.0E+4'
EXPONENT  DC       X'4E000000'
               .
               .
               .
RECVAL    DS       0CL10      (SXXXX.XXXX)
RSIGN     DS       C
RINT      DS       CL4
RPOINT    DS       C
RFRAC     DS       CL4
```

Figure 12-6   A floating-point conversion routine

conversion routine. Figure 12-6, for example, illustrates a simple routine that converts an EBCDIC input field to floating point. It is relatively simple because the input format is rigid: the leftmost column of the ten-column field contains the sign, followed by a four-column integer, followed by a decimal point, followed by a four-column decimal fraction. Imagine how much more complex a FORTRAN conversion routine must be since the decimal point can be anywhere in a field and E notation is optional.

In figure 12-6, the integer and fraction portions are converted to floating point separately and then added together. First, the digits are converted to binary in register 7. Then, a valid floating-point exponent value followed by binary zeros is placed into register 6 using the load instruction. In this case, an exponent of hex 4E (the equivalent of +14) is placed in the register. Since there are 14 hex digits in the fraction portion of a double precision field, this means the decimal point is assumed to be to the right of all the hex digits in the fraction. In other words, the value stored in registers 6 and 7 is a valid, unnormalized whole number.

At this point, the value in register 6 and 7 is loaded into floating-point register 0 and a value of zero is added to it. After the addition takes place, the result is automatically normalized so the original integer value is shifted left as many hex digits as appropriate and the exponent is reduced accordingly. That means floating-point register 0 contains the proper normalized floating-point number for the integer portion of the input field.

The conversion of the fraction takes place in the same manner as the integer conversion until after the decimal fraction is loaded as an integer into floating-point register 2. Then, the value is divided by 10,000 so it takes on its true fractional value.

Next, the routine adds the fractional value of the input field in floating-point register 2 to the integer value in floating-point register 0. After the addition takes place, the floating point value is stored in the field named FPVAL.

To make sure the sign of the field is correct, the routine then tests the first byte of the input field for a minus sign. If a minus sign is present, a one bit is ORed into the first bit position of FPVAL using the OI instruction (described in detail in chapter 10). This makes FPVAL negative.

Discussion

As I mentioned earlier, floating-point instructions are rarely used for business arithmetic. Instead, the floating-point facilities are used for solving scientific problems—ones in which very large or very small values may be involved or ones in which decimal alignment may be extremely difficult to keep track of when using fixed-point arithmetic.

The vast majority of scientific programming, however, isn't done in assembler language. Instead, a mathematical language such as FORTRAN is used. As a result, it is unlikely that you will ever actually use floating-point instructions in an assembler language program.

Terminology

short form	mantissa
long form	excess-64 format
precision	normalized
single precision	unnormalized
double precision	floating-point register
exponent	exponent overflow
fraction	exponent underflow
characteristic	guard digit

Objective

Give two reasons why a numeric result that is derived by floating-point instructions may not be exactly equal to a result that is derived by fixed-point instructions.

Section 4

Assembler language for DASD access methods

This section shows you how to use the DASD access methods in assembler language. That includes the native access methods (SAM, ISAM, and DAM) as well as the VSAM access methods. You can study this section any time after you complete section 2.

This section is designed so you have to read chapter 13 on SAM files before you read the other chapters in the section. However, once you read chapter 13, you can read any one of the other chapters in this section. For instance, you may find that you only need information on SAM and VSAM files, so you will only read chapter 13 and chapter 16 in this section.

If you use assembler language today, you will most likely use SAM and VSAM files at one time or another. However, you may never need to use ISAM and DAM files. On the other hand, if you are asked to modify an old program that uses ISAM or DAM, the material in chapters 14 and 15 will come in handy.

Chapter 13

The Queued Sequential Access Method (QSAM)

In section 2 of this book, you were introduced to the coding for sequential input files. Since they are relatively simple in concept, I hope you haven't had any problem understanding how they are used.

In this chapter, I'm going to give you more information about using sequential files. In topic 1, you'll learn about variable-length records and blocks. In topic 2, you'll learn assembler language for sequential input, output, and update files in both fixed-length and variable-length format. Finally, in topic 3, you'll learn more about the MVS JCL you use for sequential files. You can read this chapter any time after you complete section 2.

TOPIC 1   QSAM concepts

The *Queued Sequential Access Method (QSAM)* is used to store records on a DASD and to retrieve them from a DASD in sequential order. When a QSAM file is created on a DASD, the records are written on the device one after the other starting with the first record position in the area for the file and continuing until all of the records have been written in the area or there's no more room for the next record. When a sequential file is read, the records are read starting with the record in the first record position and continuing until an end-of-file record is read. An *end-of-file record* on a CKD device is simply a count area that indicates a data area with a length of zero.

Because QSAM files are relatively simple conceptually, there's no point in dwelling on them. In this topic, then, I'll simply review blocked records, introduce you to variable-length records, and give you some ideas about how to determine block sizes.

Blocked records

In chapter 1, I introduced you to *blocked records*. This simply means that more than one record in a file is stored in a *block* of records on a DASD. For example, in a file with a *blocking factor* of ten, ten records are stored in each block. Blocking records makes efficient use of disk space because less space is used up in the gaps between records or blocks. It can also speed up I/O operations because only one I/O execution is required to read or write an entire block of records.

To read blocked records, a program must deblock the records. To illustrate, suppose a program reads a block of ten records. This means that one I/O instruction reads a block of ten records into storage. Then, the program must process one of the ten records at a time, just as if the records were presented to it in unblocked format. The routine that does this is called a *deblocking routine*. Similarly, a program that writes a block of records requires a *blocking routine* to assemble the records in a block before they are written to a DASD.

You have already learned how to deblock sequential input records in two ways. First, in chapter 5, you learned how to use move mode for deblocking. In this case, the next record in the file is moved from the buffer area into your work area each time a GET instruction is executed. Then, in chapter 7, you learned how to use locate mode for deblocking. In this case, the records in the block stay in the buffer area. However, the address in register 1 is adjusted each time a GET instruction is executed so it always points to the start of the next record to be processed. In both of these cases, if the records are blocked ten to a block, the GET instruction only reads a block into the buffer area once for every ten times the instruction is executed. As you will see in the next topic, you can provide for blocking records in much the same way that you provide for deblocking records.

Variable-length
records

When the records in a file vary in length, they are referred to as *variable-length records*. Sometimes, for example, a file will consist of more than one type of record. Then, if these record types have different lengths, the file consists of variable-length records. For instance, a set of records representing one transaction may consist of a header record that is 250-bytes long, detail records that are 50-bytes long, and a trailer record that is 150-bytes long. In this case, the maximum record length in the file is 250 bytes.

Another type of variable-length record consists of a *root segment* plus a variable number of other segments. For example, inventory records that give warehouse locations may be in variable-length format. In this case, the root segment of each record contains the basic inventory data like item number, item description, total quantity on hand, and so on. Then, a variable number of additional segments follow the root segment. These segments (one for each warehouse location in which some of the item is stored) specify the warehouse location (typically, warehouse number and bin number), the quantity stored there, and maybe even the date it was stored. As a result, an item stored in only one location has only one of these location segments attached to the root segment; an item stored in 10 locations has 10 location segments.

Like fixed-length records, variable-length records are stored one after another in consecutive order. If the records are blocked, each block contains as many records as will fit in the maximum block size. So the system knows how long the blocks and the records are, each block and each record is preceded by a four-byte length field as illustrated in figure 13-1. For each record, the number of bytes contained in the record, including the four-byte record-length field, is recorded as a binary value in the first two bytes of the record-length field. The second two bytes are reserved for use by MVS and usually contain EBCDIC blanks. For each block, the number of bytes contained in the block, including the four-byte block-length field, is recorded in the block-length field. This field is in the same format as the record-length field.

When one of your programs creates a variable-length record, it must calculate the record length and store it in the record-length field before the record can be written. Since the length is stored in binary format, the length is usually accumulated in a register and stored using the store-halfword instruction. The block length, however, is calculated automatically and stored in the block-length field.

Determining
block size

When you write a program that reads a sequential file, you normally are given the block size as part of the program specifications. For fixed-length records, the block size is a multiple of the record size. For variable-length records, the block size must provide for at least one record of maximum length.

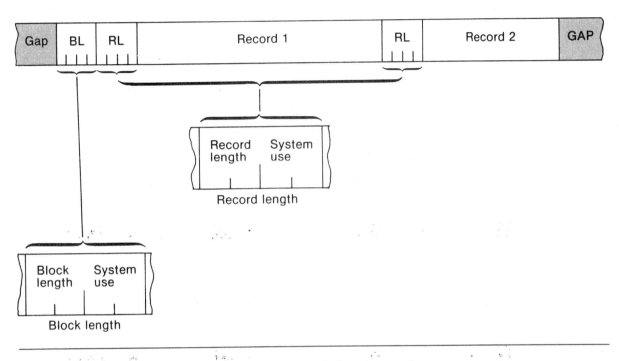

Figure 13-1   The format of blocked variable-length records

However, when you write a program that creates a sequential file, you may not be given the block size. If you know that your operations group is going to determine the block size for your program after you test it, this presents no problem. In this case, you simply assume that the records will be blocked and select a block size that is consistent with your test data. You understand that your program will be changed later on so it uses a block size that maximizes program and storage efficiency.

On the other hand, if you are asked to select an efficient block size, you should know that block sizes of around 4000 bytes tend to maximize program and storage efficiency. This means that blocks of this size minimize the number of I/O operations required to read or write a file while they maximize the amount of data that can be stored on a track of a DASD. Although larger block sizes can improve these two factors even more, they continue to increase the size of your program which can decrease its efficiency. As a result, it becomes a case of diminishing returns.

As a rule of thumb, then, you should select a block size that is close to 4000 bytes long. In addition, if the file will always be stored on the same type of DASD, you should select a block size that is consistent with the device type. To do this, you use the tables in the manual for the device.

Terminology   Queued Sequential Access Method
                  QSAM
                  end-of-file record
                  blocked records
                  block
                  blocking factor
                  deblocking routine
                  blocking routine
                  variable-length records
                  root segment

Objective   1. Explain how blocking records can reduce the time required to read or
                      write a file.

                  2. Describe the format for blocked, variable-length records.

TOPIC 2   Assembler language for QSAM files

In chapter 5, you were introduced to sequential disk file processing in the reorder-listing program. However, that chapter only showed you how to process input files with blocked or unblocked fixed-length records. In this topic, I'll show you how to use sequential update and output files as well as input files in both fixed- and variable-length formats. First, I'll present some new information for coding the operands of the DCB macro for variable-length files. Then, I'll present two programs that illustrate sequential file processing.

DCB operands

The operands of the DCB macro for files being used for update and output are the same as those used for input files. These operands are summarized in figure 13-2, similar to the way I summarized them in chapter 5. However, there is a difference in two of the operands when they are coded for variable-length files.

When you code the BLKSIZE and LRECL operands for a variable-length file, you specify the maximum block and record lengths for the file. The maximum block length must include the four bytes for block length at the start of each block, and the maximum record length must include the four bytes for record length at the start of each record. I described these extra bytes in the last topic.

Later on, when you define the work area for a variable-length file in move mode, the first four bytes of the record description must be the record length field. For an output file, this record length field must be set to the appropriate value each time a record is written to the file. For an input file, this field will receive the record length bytes from the input record. Note, however, that you don't have to worry about setting the block length field for a variable-length file. That's done automatically by MVS.

Two illustrative programs

Because sequential files are relatively simple in concept, you shouldn't have much trouble coding the assembler language for processing them. As a result, I'll only present two short programs in this topic to illustrate the use of the assembler language macros for QSAM files.

An update program that uses fixed-length records   Figure 13-3 gives a program overview for a simple update program. Briefly, a shipment file is used to update an order master file representing unfilled customer orders. Both files are in sequence by product number within order number. After

Keyword	Programmer code	Remarks
DSORG	PS	Specifies the data set organization. PS for Physical Sequential is used for sequential disk files and for printer files.
RECFM	F, FA FB, FBA V, VBA	F is for fixed-length records; V is for variable-length records. B indicates blocked records. A indicates that ASA control characters will be used for a print file. As a result, the most common code for a disk file is FB. The most common code for a print file is FA or FBA.
MACRF	GM, GL PM, PL	Specifies whether GET (G) or PUT (P) macros will be used for the file and whether the records will be processed in move (M) or locate (L) mode.
BLKSIZE	Block length	The maximum block length for a file. For variable-length records, you should include four bytes for block length.
LRECL	Record length	The maximum record length for a file. If fixed-length records aren't blocked, the record length will equal the block size. For variable length records, you should include four bytes for record length.
DDNAME	DD name	This name must be the same as the ddname in the DD job control statement for the file.
EODAD	Instruction label	The label or address of the first instruction of the end-of-file (or end-of-data-set) routine.

Figure 13-2   DCB operands for QSAM

an order record has been updated, it is written in its original location on the order file and a report record is written on a report file. This report file is used later as input to a disk-to-printer program. But if a shipment record doesn't have a matching order record, the unmatched transaction is printed on the error listing. This program, of course, is unrealistic because it has been simplified for illustrative purposes.

Figure 13-4 presents a traditional flowchart for this program, and figure 13-5 presents its assembler language code. As you might guess, the decision block on the flowchart is the critical point in the program. Here, the control number (order number plus product number) in the shipment record (the transaction) is compared with the control number in the order record (the master). A *control number*, or *control field*, is a field or combination of fields within a record or set of records that determines the pro-

Program: ORDUPD Update order file	Page: 1
Designer: Anne Prince	Date: 11-06-85

Input/output specifications

File	Description	Use
SHIPTR	Shipment transaction file	Input
ORDERS	Order master file	Update
RPTTR	Report transaction file	Output
ERRLIST	Printer file: Error transaction listing	Output

Process specifications

The order master file contains records of items that have been ordered but not shipped with one record for each item on order. The shipment transaction file is used to update this file in place with one record for each item that has just been shipped. Both files are in sequence by product code within order number, and there can only be one shipment transaction for a matching order record. To update a master record, the program moves the product code, quantity shipped, and shipment date from the shipment record into the corresponding fields of the master record.

If a transaction is processed correctly, a copy of the updated order record should be written in the report transaction file for use by a report-preparation program later on. If the program can't find a matching master record for a transaction, a line should be printed on the error listing. This listing is simplified for illustrative purposes, so the format of a record line is simply the 24 bytes of the transaction record followed by the message, UNMATCHED SHIPMENT TRANSACTION. Also, the program doesn't have to provide for page overflow or headings on this error listing.

Shipment record format

Bytes	Field name
1-2	Transaction code
3-6	Order number
7-12	Product code
13-16	Quantity shipped
17-24	Shipment date (MM/DD/YY)

Order record format

Bytes	Field name
1-4	Customer number
5-24	Customer name
25-28	Order number
29-34	Product code ordered
35-38	Quantity ordered
39-46	Date ordered (MM/DD/YY)
47-52	Product code shipped
53-56	Quantity shipped
57-64	Date shipped (MM/DD/YY)
65-80	Not used

All data is in character (C) format.

Figure 13-3   A program overview for a sequential update program

cessing of a program. As you study the logic in the flowchart, remember that both transaction and master file are in sequence by product number within order number. Otherwise, this control-number comparison wouldn't work correctly.

If the control numbers are equal (T=M), the order record is updated and written back onto the file and a report record is written on the report file. If the control number in the transaction record is greater than the one in the master record (T>M), another master record is read and the loop repeats. If the control number in the transaction is less than the one in the master (T<M), it indicates an *unmatched transaction*. In this case, an error line is printed, another transaction is read, and processing continues.

The only other point of interest in the flowchart is the end-of-file processing for the master file. If this end-of-file condition is reached before the end of the shipment file, it indicates one or more unmatched shipment records. Then, the program prints an error line on the error listing, reads another shipment record, and repeats the loop. When the shipment end-of-file is reached within this loop, the program ends.

There are several things you should notice in the code in figure 13-5. First, the MACRF operand of the DCB for the order master file, ORDERS, is coded like this:

```
MACRF=(GL,PM)
```

This means that both GET and PUT macros will be issued for the file. As long as you use the automatic I/O buffering of QSAM, this is the only way to code the MACRF operand for update-in-place processing. In this example, locate mode is used for GET functions, while move mode is used for PUT functions. When you have to code two parameters in the MACRF operand, as in the above example, you enclose the parameters in parentheses and separate them with a comma.

Because locate mode is used in the GET function for the order file, a USING statement is coded to relate register 4 to the DSECT named ORDMASK. Then, after each GET macro for the order file is executed, register 4 is loaded with the contents of register 1. (Remember that a GET function in locate mode puts the address of the next record to be processed in register 1.)

Another point of interest in figure 13-5 is the option parameter that's coded for the ORDERS file on the OPEN macro. This parameter, UPDAT, means that blocks in the file will be read and rewritten in place.

To rewrite the updated records to the order file, the program uses a PUTX macro. This form of PUT is only used for the update-in-place function. Its only operand is the label of the DCB for the file to be updated. When PUTX is executed, MVS turns on an internal switch indicating that the current block of records must be written back on the file. Then, when all the records in the block have been processed and a GET is issued for the first record of the next block, the current block is rewritten on the disk. The current block is also rewritten when the file is closed.

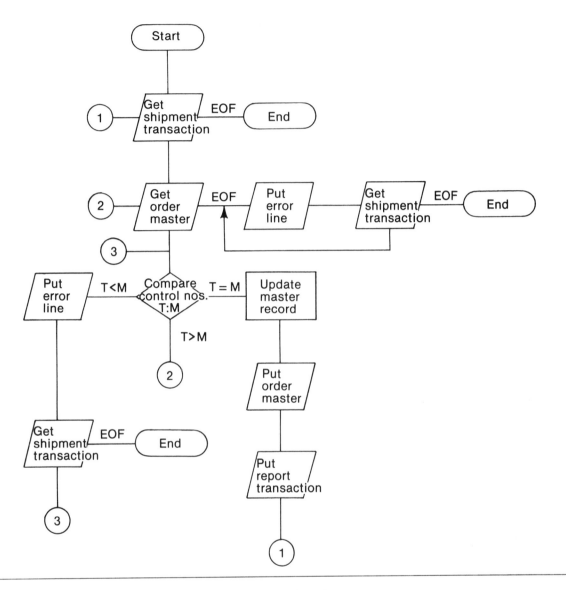

Figure 13-4   A flowchart for the sequential update program

Finally, you should notice how the PUT macro works in locate mode for the report transaction file. As you can see in figure 13-5, the PUT macro is actually issued before the record to be written is constructed. When the PUT macro is issued, the address of the next output area is passed to the program in register 1. Then, the program moves the data at the address in register 4 (the last order record) to the address in register 1. Although locate mode works well for this report transaction file, you should realize that it is more difficult to use when the individual fields of the output record have to be addressed. For that reason, it's more common to use move mode for output records.

```
ORDUPD     START 0
BEGIN      SAVE  (14,12)
           BALR  3,0
           USING *,3
           USING ORDMASK,4
           ST    13,SAVE+4
           LA    13,SAVE
           OPEN  (SHIPTR,INPUT,ORDERS,UPDAT,RPTTR,OUTPUT,ERRLIST,OUTPUT)
READSHIP   GET   SHIPTR,SHIPWRK
READORD    GET   ORDERS
           LR    4,1
TEST       CLC   ORDCTL,SHCTL
           BL    READORD
           BE    MATCH
           MVC   ERRTR,SHIPWRK
           PUT   ERRLIST,ERRLINE
           GET   SHIPTR,SHIPWRK
           B     TEST
MATCH      MVC   ORPRODSH,SHPROD
           MVC   ORQTYSH,SHQTY
           MVC   ORDATESH,SHDATE
           PUTX  ORDERS
           PUT   RPTTR
           MVC   0(80,1),0(4)
           B     READSHIP
EOFSHIP    CLOSE (SHIPTR,,ORDERS,,RPTTR,,ERRLIST)
           L     13,SAVE+4
           RETURN (14,12)
EOFORD     MVC   ERRTR,SHIPWRK
           PUT   ERRLIST,ERRLINE
           GET   SHIPTR,SHIPWRK
           B     EOFORD
SHIPTR     DCB   DSORG=PS,                                                 X
                 RECFM=FB,                                                 X
                 MACRF=GM,                                                 X
                 BLKSIZE=240,                                              X
                 LRECL=24,                                                 X
                 DDNAME=SHIPTR,                                            X
                 EODAD=EOFSHIP
ORDERS     DCB   DSORG=PS,                                                 X
                 RECFM=FB,                                                 X
                 MACRF=(GL,PM),                                            X
                 BLKSIZE=400,                                              X
                 LRECL=80,                                                 X
                 DDNAME=ORDERS,                                            X
                 EODAD=EOFORD
RPTTR      DCB   DSORG=PS,                                                 X
                 RECFM=FB,                                                 X
                 MACRF=PL,                                                 X
                 BLKSIZE=400,                                              X
                 LRECL=80,                                                 X
                 DDNAME=RPTTR
ERRLIST    DCB   DSORG=PS,                                                 X
                 RECFM=F,                                                  X
                 MACRF=PM,                                                 X
```

Figure 13-5   A sequential update program (part 1 of 2)

```
                      BLKSIZE=132,                                         X
                      LRECL=132,                                          X
                      DDNAME=ERRLIST
SAVE       DS    18F
SHIPWRK    DS    0CL24
SHTRCODE   DS    CL2
SHCTL      DS    0CL10
SHORDNBR   DS    CL4
SHPROD     DS    CL6
SHQTY      DS    CL4
SHDATE     DS    CL8
ORDMASK    DSECT
           DS    CL24
ORDCTL     DS    0CL10
ORDNBR     DS    CL4
ORPRODOR   DS    CL6
ORQTYOR    DS    CL4
ORDATEOR   DS    CL8
ORPRODSH   DS    CL6
ORQTYSH    DS    CL4
ORDATESH   DS    CL8
           DS    CL16
ORDUPD     CSECT
ERRLINE    DS    0CL132
           DC    20C' '
ERRTR      DS    CL24
           DC    CL88'        UNMATCHED SHIPMENT TRANSACTION'
           END   BEGIN
```

Figure 13-5   A sequential update program (part 2 of 2)

A disk-to-printer program that uses variable-length records   Figure 13-6 presents the program overview for a variable-length, disk-to-printer program. This program prepares a listing of students and courses as indicated by the print chart in figure 13-7. As you can see in figure 13-6, the student master file consists of a root segment plus course segments with one course segment for each course a student is taking. In this school, a student may take up to ten courses in a semester, so the maximum number of course segments in a record is ten. Again, this program is unrealistic because it has been simplified for illustrative purposes.

The logic of the program is simple. For each course segment of each student record, a line is printed on the student course listing. For the first course for each student, the information in the root segment is printed along with the course information. Otherwise, only the course information is printed in a line.

Figure 13-8 is the assembler language listing for this program. Although there is little in this program that is new to you, other than the characteristics of the file, there are a few things I would like to point out.

Program: DSKTOPRT Prepare course listing	Page: 1
Designer: Anne Prince	Date: 11-06-85

Input/output specifications

File	Description	Use
STUDENT	Student master file (variable length records)	Input
CRSELST	Printer file: Student course listing	Output

Process specifications

This program prepares a student course listing from a student master file. This file consists of variable-length records. The root segment gives information about the student. Each course segment gives information about one course that the student is taking with a maximum of ten course segments per student.

The format of the listing, which is shown on the next page, is simplified for illustrative purposes. To further simplify, the program doesn't have to provide for page overflow or headings on this listing. To prepare the listing, the program prints one line for each course segment in a record. For the first course segment line, the program also prints the information in the root segment.

Student master record format

Segment	Bytes	Field name	Format
Root	1-6	Student ID number	CL6
	7-31	Student name	CL25
	32-33	Total credit hours	PL2
Course	1-4	Course code	CL4
	5-29	Course title	CL25
	30-31	Course credit hours	PL2

Figure 13-6 A program overview for a variable-length, disk-to-printer program

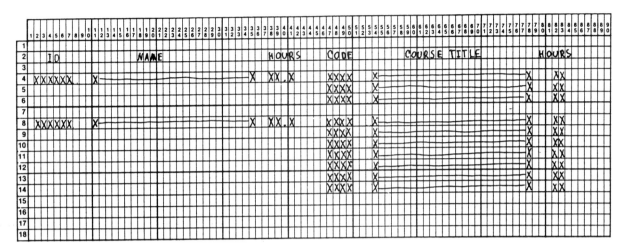

Figure 13-7   A print chart for the variable-length, disk-to-printer program

First, notice that the DCB for the student master file specifies blocked, variable-length records with a block size of 704 bytes. Since the minimum block length is ten course segments (310 bytes) plus one root segment (33 bytes) plus the block and record length fields (8 bytes), this block size is satisfactory for testing the program. Later on, the block size can be increased by the operations department to improve execution and storage efficiency. When the program is executed, the actual sizes of the blocks will vary depending on the number of courses taken by each student. But since the deblocking routine is handled automatically by assembler language, you don't have to worry about the actual size of each block.

Second, take a look at the procedure I used to determine if there are additional course segments to be processed for each student record read. First, register 5 is loaded with the actual record length. Next, the length of the root segment including the four bytes for record length is subtracted from register 5. As a result, the length remaining in register 5 is the length of the course segments. Then, after each course segment is processed, the length of a single course segment is subtracted from register 5 and the resulting length is compared to zero. If the length is equal to zero, it means that all course segments have been processed and the next student record is read. Otherwise, the next course segment is processed.

Third, look at the definition of the work area for the variable-length record. As I explained in the last topic, the first two bytes of a variable-length record contain the record length. Since the length is stored in binary format, it is defined as a halfword in the first field before the root segment. Then, the next two bytes are reserved for use by the operating system.

Finally, note that I coded a DSECT for the course segments. After each new student record is read, the base register for the DSECT is loaded with the address of the course segment area in the student record. Then, after each course segment is processed, if another segment is present, the register is increased by 31 bytes so it addresses the next segment.

```
DSKTOPRT START  0
BEGIN     SAVE   (14,12)
          BALR   3,0
          USING  *,3
          USING  SCOURSE,4              ASSIGN R4 AS BASE FOR DSECT
          ST     13,SAVE+4
          LA     13,SAVE
          OPEN   (STUDENT,INPUT,CRSELST,OUTPUT)
READSTUD  GET    STUDENT,STUDREC
          MVC    LSID,SID
          MVC    LSNAME,SNAME
          MVC    LSHOURS,HRSEDIT
          ED     LSHOURS,SHOURS
          LA     4,SSEGAREA             LOAD FIRST SEGMENT ADDRESS
          LH     5,SLGTH                LOAD R5 WITH RECORD LENGTH
          S      5,=F'37'               SUBTRACT ROOT SEGMENT LENGTH
NXTCRSE   MVC    LCNBR,SCNBR
          MVC    LCNAME,SCNAME
          MVC    LCHRS,HRSEDIT
          ED     LCHRS,SCHRS
          PUT    CRSELST,LLINE
          MVI    LLINE,X'40'
          MVC    LLINE+1(131),LLINE
          S      5,=F'31'               SUBTRACT SEGMENT LENGTH
          C      5,=F'0'
          BNH    READSTUD
          LA     4,31(4)                ADJUST ADDRESS IN R4 TO NEXT SEGMENT
          B      NXTCRSE
EOFDISK   CLOSE  (STUDENT,,CRSELST)
          L      13,SAVE+4
          RETURN (14,12)
STUDENT   DCB    DSORG=PS,                                                        X
                 RECFM=VB,                                                        X
                 MACRF=GM,                                                        X
                 BLKSIZE=704,                                                     X
                 LRECL=347,                                                       X
                 DDNAME=STUDENT,                                                  X
                 EODAD=EOFDISK                                                    X
CRSELST   DCB    DSORG=PS,                                                        X
                 RECFM=F,                                                         X
                 MACRF=PM,                                                        X
                 BLKSIZE=132,                                                     X
                 LRECL=132,                                                       X
                 DDNAME=CRSELST
SAVE      DS     18F
STUDREC   DS     0CL347
SLGTH     DS     H
          DS     CL2
SID       DS     CL6
SNAME     DS     CL25
SHOURS    DS     PL2
SSEGAREA  DS     CL310
SCOURSE   DSECT
SCNBR     DS     CL4
SCNAME    DS     CL25
SCHRS     DS     PL2
DSKTOPRT  CSECT
```

Figure 13-8   A variable-length disk-to-printer program (part 1 of 2)

```
LLINE     DS    0CL132
          DS    C' '
LSID      DS    CL6
          DC    3C' '
LSNAME    DS    CL25
          DC    C' '
LSHOURS   DS    CL5
          DC    3C' '
LCNBR     DS    CL4
          DC    3C' '
LCNAME    DS    CL25
LCHRS     DS    CL5
          DC    51C' '
HRSEDIT   DC    X'4020214B21'
          END   BEGIN
```

Figure 13-8   A variable-length disk-to-printer program (part 2 of 2)

Discussion

If you understand the programs presented in this topic, you shouldn't have any problem with sequential files. In contrast, it's considerably more difficult to use ISAM, BDAM, and VSAM files. You'll learn about these files in the next three chapters.

Terminology

control number
control field
unmatched transaction

Objective

Given program specifications that require the use of one or more QSAM files, code an assembler language program that satisfies the specifications.

TOPIC 3   MVS JCL for QSAM files

In chapter 3, I introduced you to the JCL required to compile and test disk-to-printer programs that read sequential files. Now, in this topic, I am going to expand upon that presentation. I'll start by telling you more about the DD statement. Then, I'll present a job that assembles and tests a a sequential update program.

The DD statement

Figure 13-9 presents an expanded format for the DD statement. You're already familiar with the first four operands, but the last two are probably new to you. After I give you more information about the DSNAME and DISP operands, I'll describe the new operands in detail.

The DSNAME operand   The DSNAME operand specifies the data set name of an existing data set or the name that's to be assigned to a data set that's being created. It can be coded in any of three forms: (1) as a permanent name, (2) as a temporary name, or (3) as a backward reference. In this book, however, I'll only present the first form.

A *permanent data set* is a data set that exists from one job to another. The data set may last only a short time, like a few minutes, or it may last a long time, like months or years. In contrast, a *temporary data set* is one that exists only within the boundaries of a single job. When the job ends, the data set is no longer available to the system.

A permanent data set must be assigned a *permanent data set name*. If the data set is cataloged, the data set name must be qualified. A *qualified data set name* is formed by concatenating two or more simple names, each consisting of from 1 to 8 characters. The total length of a data set name can't exceed 44 characters.

When a qualified data set name is used to catalog a data set, the leftmost name must indicate the user catalog in which the data set is to reside. This name is called the *high-level qualifier*. For example, in the data set name

```
MMA2.ACCT.GLMAST
```

the high-level qualifier is MMA2, which means that the data set will reside in the catalog identified by MMA2.

The names that follow the high-level qualifier are used to distinguish the file from other files in the catalog. In the above example, I used the names ACCT and GLMAST to indicate that this file is used by the accounting subsystem and that it contains the general ledger records. Most shops have standards for forming qualified data set names for cataloged files so you should be sure to find out what they are in your shop.

```
//ddname   DD  [DSNAME=data-set-name]
               [,DISP=(status,normal-disposition,abnormal-disposition)]
               [,UNIT=group-name
               [,VOLUME=SER=serial-number]
               [,SPACE=(units,(primary-allocation,secondary-allocation),
                       RLSE,CONTIG)]
               [,DCB=(...)]
```

Figure 13-9   The format of the DD statement

Files that aren't cataloged can also be given qualified names, although that isn't required. In this case, however, the high-level qualifier doesn't indicate a catalog. It simply specifies the highest level of qualification. If no qualification is necessary to identify a data set, the data set name can consist of one simple name of eight characters or less. However, it's more common for data set names to be qualified.

A special form of DSNAME is used to refer to a member of a partitioned data set. You saw an example of this in figure 3-16. In the second part of this figure, the source program was stored in a source library, so I coded the DSNAME operand for the ASM.SYSIN DD statement as follows:

```
//ASM.SYSIN    DD     DSN=MMA.USER1.SOURCE(INV3520)
```

Here, the name in parentheses is the member name.

The DISP operand   The DISP operand tells MVS the current status of the file, what to do with the file upon successful completion of the job step, and what action to take in case of abnormal termination of the job step. The codes that can be specified for status are NEW, OLD, SHR, and MOD. Some codes that can be specified for the normal and abnormal disposition of permanent data sets are KEEP, CATLG, DELETE, and UN-CATLG. You should be familiar with most of these codes.

When you create a permanent data set, you often catalog it if the step proceeds normally, but delete it if the step fails. To do that, you code:

```
DISP=(NEW,CATLG,DELETE)
```

In this case, DELETE must be specified for abnormal termination. Otherwise, the data set will be cataloged.

MOD indicates that a data set is to be modified. It can be used either to add records to the end of an existing data set or to create a sequential data set. For example, suppose you're writing a program that writes records to a transaction file and you want to accumulate the transactions throughout a given time period. Then, if you specify MOD for the file, the file will be created the first time the program is run. Every other time the program is run, the file will be extended.

UNCATLG is probably the least used of the DISP codes. Its purpose is to uncatalog a data set that has been previously cataloged. If, for example, a data set is created and cataloged in one job step and records are added to it in another step, you might want to uncatalog the data set if the second job step terminates abnormally. That way, the job can be rerun without any changes after the problem that caused the termination is corrected.

The SPACE operand   The SPACE operand is used to request disk space for a new file. The units entry can request disk space in terms of cylinders (CYL) or tracks (TRK), or the block length can be specified as a number. The *primary allocation* then specifies how many of these units are to be reserved as the initial disk space for the file.

If you're not sure that the primary allocation will be enough to hold all the records or if you want to allow more space for additions to the file at some later time, you can also code a *secondary allocation*. It indicates the number of units of disk space that will be added to the file each time the file area is filled up. Up to 15 secondary allocations can be added. The size of the secondary allocation is usually coded as a number that is from 5 to 20 percent of the primary allocation.

Suppose, for example, that you have to code the SPACE parameter for a new file. One way to code it is like this:

```
SPACE=(240,(100,10))
```

Here, the blocks are 240 bytes long; the data set will contain 100 blocks initially; and 10 blocks will be added to the data set each time more space is needed.

Similarly, if want to create a sequential file of 700-byte blocks on a 3350 DASD and expect about 4000 blocks, the SPACE operand for the file can be coded in several ways:

```
SPACE=(CYL,5)
SPACE=(TRK,150)
SPACE=(700,4000)
```

Each of these operands reserves about the same amount of space. If you want to include secondary allocations, the SPACE operands can be coded like this:

```
SPACE=(CYL,(5,1))
SPACE=(TRK,(150,30))
SPACE=(400,(5000,1000))
```

About one cylinder is specified by each of these secondary allocations.

After the space allocations, you can code one or both of the optional entries: RLSE and CONTIG. RLSE causes any unused portion of the initial allocation of a new file to be released. It means, for example, that if the primary allocation for a file was 10 cylinders but the loaded records only filled 8 cylinders, the extra 2 cylinders are released so they are available for some other file. Unless you'll be adding records to a test file, you should use the RLSE option when you create it.

The CONTIG entry requests that the space allocated for a new file be a contiguous disk area. For a three cylinder file, that means that three adjacent cylinders should be used. For test files, you normally don't code CONTIG because it doesn't matter whether the disk space is contiguous.

The DCB operand   You can code some of the operands of the DCB macro in the DD statement for the file rather than in the DCB macro in the source program. This makes it possible for one program to process a file in more than one form.

One DCB operand that is often supplied by the DD statement for a sequential file is the BLKSIZE operand. This allows the block size of the file to be changed without reassembling all the programs that use it. If, for example, the assembler language DCB doesn't specify the BLKSIZE operand, it can be specified in the DD statement like this:

```
DCB=BLKSIZE=800
```

If more than one DCB entry is coded in the DCB operand, the entries should be separated by commas and enclosed in parentheses as in this example:

```
DCB=(LRECL=200,BLKSIZE=1600)
```

Here, the DCB operand specifies a record length of 200 and a block length of 1600.

In this book, the programs always specify all of the DCB operands for a file because it is a book on assembler language. In practice, though, the DCB operand of the DD statement is frequently used to supply DCB information. If you're interested, you can get a complete list of the DCB operands that can be coded in a DD statement by referring to the JCL reference manual for your system.

A job stream for testing a sequential update program

Figure 13-10 presents the job stream that I used for testing the sequential update program of figure 13-5. It illustrates how you use DD statements as you test your programs. You should be able to follow this job stream without too much trouble, so let's just focus on the DD statements for the update and output files.

If you look at the DD statement for the ORDERS file, you can see it is coded just as if it were an input file only. However, the DISP operand is coded as OLD, not as SHR. That way, the update program can update the data in the file and write the updated records back on the disk in their original locations without any interference from another program that is sharing the file. In this example, the file is not cataloged so the UNIT and VOLUME operands are coded.

Now, look at the DD statement for the RPTTR file that is to be created by the program. Its SPACE operand requests a file with an initial allocation of 100 240-byte blocks of data. If that isn't enough space for the file, it requests additional allocations of 10 blocks each. The DISP operand for this file specifies that it's a new file, that it should be kept if the program terminates normally, and that it should be deleted if the program terminates abnormally.

To make sure that the program has updated the ORDERS file and created the RPTTR file correctly, the contents of these files should be printed after the program finishes its execution. You can print these files by using an MVS utility, but I'm not going to present utilities in this book. My only point is that you can delete the RPTTR file when you print it by coding the DISP operand of the file as

```
DISP=(OLD,DELETE)
```

That way you won't keep the file on the disk when it is no longer needed.

Discussion Whenever I've presented JCL in this book, I've mentioned that this book only begins to introduce MVS JCL. So if you want more information about JCL, let me once again recommend our *MVS JCL* book by Doug Lowe. It will show you how to use temporary names, backward references, many of the other operands and codes in DD statements, and much more.

Terminology

permanent data set
temporary data set
permanent dat set name
qualified data set name
high-level qualifier
primary allocation
secondary allocation

Objectives Given the file specifications for a program that processes one or more sequential files, code the JCL for running the program.

```
//PRINCE          JOB  (MMA,PRINCE),'ANNE PRINCE'
//                EXEC ASMFCG
//ASM.SYSIN       DD   *
                  .
                  .  SOURCE PROGRAM
                  .
//GO.SYSUDUMP     DD   SYSOUT=A
//GO.ERRS         DD   SYSOUT=A
//GO.SHIPTR       DD   DSN=MMA.TEST.SHIPTR,DISP=(OLD,KEEP),
//                UNIT=SYSDA,VOLUME=SER=MMA800
//GO.ORDERS       DD   DSN=MMA.TEST.ORDERS,DISP=(OLD,KEEP),
//                UNIT=SYSDA,VOLUME=SER=MMA800
//GO.RPTTR        DD   DSN=MMA.TEST.RPTTR,DISP=(NEW,KEEP,DELETE),
//                UNIT=SYSDA,VOLUME=SER=MMA800,
//                SPACE=(240,(100,10))
//
```

Figure 13-10   The MVS JCL for assembling and testing the sequential update program in figure 13-5

Chapter 14

The Indexed
Sequential Access Method (ISAM)

Although sequential file organization has its advantages, it also has limitations. For example, although a blocked sequential file makes maximum use of the storage capacity of a DASD, it has many of the limitations of a tape file. To update a sequential file, all of the records in the file must be read rather than just those affected by transactions, and the entire file has to be rewritten in order to add a record to the file. Using indexed sequential organization, the records in a file are stored so they can be read sequentially or randomly, and records can be added to a file without having to rewrite the entire file.

Under MVS, you can use either the ISAM access methods (QISAM and BISAM) or VSAM for creating and processing indexed sequential files. Although the ISAM access methods were widely used during the 1970's, they have been superseded by the VSAM methods. As a result, ISAM files are rarely used today in new programs, but most shops still use many old programs that process them. That's why you may never need to use QISAM and BISAM for new program development, but you may use them when you modify old programs.

In case you do need to use the ISAM access methods someday, this chapter shows you how. Topic 1 presents the ISAM concepts you need to be familiar with. Topic 2 presents assembler language for ISAM files. Topic 3 presents the JCL you need to know for processing ISAM files.

TOPIC 1   ISAM concepts

Before you can write assembler language programs that process ISAM files, you need to understand how they are organized. As a result, this topic introduces you to the ISAM concepts you need to know.

ISAM file organization

The Indexed Sequential Access Methods are designed to allow both sequential and random processing of DASD files. As a result, the structure of an ISAM file is more complicated than that of a QSAM file. It contains not only a sequential grouping of data records, but also index elements and, usually, overflow areas.

The prime data area   The *prime data area* of an ISAM file is just what its name implies: it contains the bulk of the file's data records. Within the prime data area, records are ordered sequentially based on their key values.

The *key* field in each record in an ISAM file contains a value that uniquely identifies it. For instance, customer number or code is usually the key field in a customer file, and the customer numbers are assigned so each customer has its own number. Similarly, inventory number or code is usually the key field in an inventory file.

Indexes   To retrieve records at random, ISAM requires an index structure. Every ISAM file uses two kinds of indexes to locate specific records: a cylinder index and track indexes. In addition, large ISAM files may use a third index type: a master index. After I describe cylinder and track indexes, I'll describe the master index.

The *cylinder index* contains one entry for each cylinder in the prime data area. Each entry contains two elements: (1) the highest key value of the records stored in the cylinder and (2) the address of a lower level index for that cylinder, the track index. The *track index*, located at the beginning of each cylinder in the prime data area, contains one entry for each track within that cylinder. Like the entries in the cylinder index, each entry in the track index contains two elements: (1) the highest key value of the records stored on the track and (2) the track number itself.

Figure 14-1 shows how the records in an ISAM file are located using the cylinder and track indexes. Here, the record with the key value 428 is to be retrieved. First, the cylinder index is searched to determine that the record is on cylinder 11. Then, the track index is searched to determine that the record is on track 7 of that cylinder. Finally, track 7 is searched to find the record with key value 428.

If an ISAM file is large, the cylinder index may require several tracks. When that's the case, locating an entry in it may be unacceptably time-consuming. If so, the file may be created with an optional master index. The *master index* points directly to each track of the cylinder index. As a result, the time required to search the cylinder index is reduced.

Overflow areas   An ISAM file can include *overflow areas* that are used when records are added to a file. As a result, the entire file doesn't have to be rewritten to add new records in their proper positions within the key sequence, as is the case with a QSAM file. When records are added to an overflow area, the index structure is updated so records can still be retrieved in key sequence.

There are two kinds of overflow areas you should be familiar with: cylinder overflow areas and the independent overflow area. When you use *cylinder overflow areas*, one or more tracks in each cylinder in the prime data area are reserved for inserted records. When you use an *independent overflow area*, one or more cylinders, usually located at the end of a file area, are reserved for additions to the file.

When records are added to an overflow area, the index structure is adjusted to point to them. As more and more records are added to the file, it becomes necessary at some point to *reorganize* it. When a file is reorganized, the records in the overflow areas are rewritten in key sequence in the prime data area and the index structure is rebuilt. If ISAM files that have many insertions aren't periodically reorganized, serious performance degradation can result.

ISAM file handling logic

When an ISAM file is created, the records are written in key sequence in the prime data area. As the records are written, the indexes are created to allow the records in the file to be accessed directly. When all of the records have been stored in the file, an end-of-file record is written just as if the file had sequential organization.

After the file has been loaded, track 1 of each cylinder contains the track index records. Any area left on track 1 and all of the remaining tracks, excluding those reserved for cylinder overflow, contain the records of the file in sequence. The tracks that make up the cylinder overflow area contain no data at all, and the independent overflow area contains no data either.

Before new records are added to a file, the file handling logic is fairly simple. For sequential retrieval, the records in the prime data area are read one after the other. For random retrieval, after the proper cylinder is located, the track index is checked to locate the track the record is on. Then, the prime data area on that track is searched to find the record with the appropriate key.

After new records have been added to the file, this logic becomes more complicated. Index entries for the overflow areas have to be used

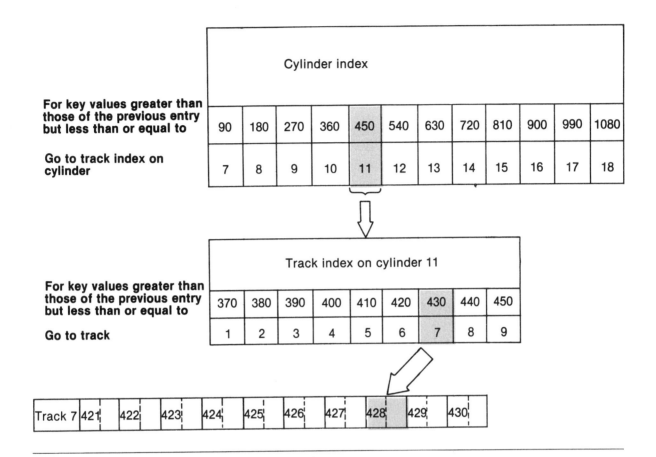

Figure 14-1   How ISAM searches cylinder and track indexes to locate a record

and existing records have to be moved to the overflow areas to make room for new records. From a programmer's point of view, though, you don't need to know how records are added to the overflow areas or how they are retrieved from them since the ISAM access methods handle this logic for you. You should realize, though, that ISAM file processing becomes more and more inefficient as the number of records in the overflow areas increases. That's why these files need to be reorganized frequently.

Discussion

Although ISAM file organization offered the benefits of both sequential and random processing, it was relatively inefficient. That's why it has been superseded by VSAM. In comparision, VSAM for indexed sequential files is more efficient no matter what type of file processing is being done: creating a file, adding records to a file, retrieving records sequentially, or retrieving records randomly.

Terminology

prime data area
key
cylinder index
track index
master index
overflow area
cylinder overflow area
independent overflow area
file reorganization

Objective

Explain the significance of the following as they relate to ISAM file organization:

master index
cylinder index
track index
prime data area
key
cylinder overflow area
independent overflow area
file reorganization

TOPIC 2   Assembler language for ISAM files

Because the organization of ISAM files is complex, the assembler language for processing them is complex too. To make matters worse, two different access methods are used to access ISAM files. For all the sequential modes of ISAM processing (file loading, sequential retrieval, update, and file reorganization), you can use the *Queued Indexed Sequential Access Method (QISAM)*. This provides for automatic buffer handling, I/O overlap control, and error handling. For all of the random functions, however, you must use the *Basic Indexed Sequential Access Method (BISAM)*. As you'll see later in this topic, BISAM forces you to be more aware of buffer handling, overlap control, and error handling.

Each ISAM file to be used by a program must, of course, be described by a DCB macro. Since the selection of operands for the ISAM DCB depends primarily on whether the file will be processed using QISAM or BISAM, I've separated this topic into two parts. First, I'll show you how to process ISAM files using QISAM. Then I'll show you how to process them using BISAM.

**QISAM
PROCESSING**

In addition to the operands coded on the DCB macro, you may also need to know how to use a couple of new macros. As a result, after I present the operands of the DCB macro, I'll present these new macros. Then, I'll introduce you to the QISAM error status bytes. Finally, I'll present two programs that illustrate QISAM processing.

DCB operands

Figure 14-2 summarizes the most widely used operands for ISAM file processing using QISAM. This summary should be self-explanatory for those operands you are already familiar with, so I won't explain them further. However, I will describe the new operands.

Before I describe the new operands, though, note that most of the operands that describe physical aspects of the file (BLKSIZE, KEYLEN, LRECL, RECFM and RKP) are coded only when the file is created (or *loaded*). At that time, all of these factors are stored in the data set label in the VTOC. Then, in programs that process the file sequentially, these operands are extracted from the label when the file is opened.

KEYLEN   The KEYLEN operand specifies the number of bytes in the key for a file. It only needs to be specified when the file is being loaded.

RKP   When ISAM records are blocked, only the highest control field number in the block is stored in the key area for the block. That means *embedded keys* (keys within the actual records) must be used for finding individual records. In this case, the RKP operand gives the relative position of the key field within each record. If, for example, the control field is found beginning in byte 11, you code this operand as RKP=10. If the control field is found beginning in the first byte, you code RKP=0. By combining this operand with the KEYLEN operand, the assembler can tell where a key field is located within a record. Again, this operand only needs to be coded when a file is being loaded.

OPTCD   When processing an ISAM file, several optional services can be requested. This is done by coding special options on the OPTCD operand. The options that can be coded are presented in figure 14-3. For example, if you code OPTCD=MY, a master index is created and overflow records are placed in the cylinder overflow area. Although the OPTCD operand can be coded for all ISAM functions, it's usually coded only for the load function. Then, when the file is accessed later on, the options are extracted from the data set label. In other words, you only need to code OPTCD if you want to change the options that were specified when the file was created.

NTM   If M is coded as one of the options on the OPTCD operand, it means that a master index is to be created. Then, the NTM operand must be coded when the file is loaded to specify when the master index should be created. The number specified for this operand indicates the maximum number of tracks that the cylinder index can contain before a master index is created. For example, if you code NTM=3, a master index is created when more than three tracks are required by the cylinder index.

CYLOFL   If Y is coded as one of the options on the OPTCD operand, it means that overflow records are to be placed in the cylinder overflow areas. Then, the CYLOFL operand must be coded when the file is loaded to indicate how many tracks per cylinder are to be used for overflow records. For example, if you code CYLOFL=3, three tracks on each cylinder are reserved as an overflow area.

SYNAD   For some types of ISAM processing, you'll want to perform specific error checking, even though the access method performs most of it. The SYNAD operand specifies the label of the error-checking routine that you code as part of your program. This error routine will then be given control if the I/O module detects any errors. Normally, an error routine tests for certain allowable errors, like a sequence error during a file load, and decides whether to continue processing or to abort the execution of the program. If no SYNAD operand is coded in the DCB and an error occurs, the job is abnormally terminated.

Keyword	Programmer code	Remarks
DSORG	IS	The data set organization.
RECFM	F,FB V,VB	F for fixed length; V for variable length; B for blocked. Specified only for a load function.
MACRF	GM,GL PM,PL (GM,SK),(GL,SK) (GL,PU) (GL,SK,PU)	SK is used if sequential processing is to begin other than at the first record of the file. PU is used if records are to be rewritten on the file.
BLKSIZE	Block length	Must be the same as the record length or an even multiple of it. Specified only for a load function.
LRECL	Record length	For variable-length records, use the maximum record length plus the four prefix bytes. Specified only for a load function.
KEYLEN	Key length	Length of the key for a file. Specified only for a load function.
RKP	Relative position of the key field in blocked records	For blocked records, the key is embedded in the data of each record so this operand locates the start of the key. The default is 0. Specified only for a load function.
OPTCD	Access method options	See figure 14-3.
NTM	Number of tracks of of cylinder index allowed before a master index is created	Required when OPTCD = M. Specified only for a load function.
CYLOFL	Number of tracks per cylinder for overflow records	The number depends on addition activity. Specified only for a load function.
SYNAD	Label of the error checking routine	The label of the routine that is given control if the I/O module detects an error.
DDNAME	DD name	The ddname in the DD job control statement for the file.
EODAD	Label of the first instruction of the EOF routine	

Figure 14-2   DCB operands for QISAM

One thing you should be aware of when you use the SYNAD operand is that control must be returned to the I/O module after the error-checking routine has completed its processing. To do this, the error routine has to issue the RETURN macro. You'll see how this is done in the programs at the end of this section.

The SETL and ESETL macros

You use the SETL and ESETL macros when you want to start processing at some point in a file other than the beginning. You use the SETL (set limits) macro to specify where processing should begin. You use the ESETL (end set limit) macro to end the current sequence of processing. Although you probably won't need to use these macros in most of the programs you write, you should understand how and when they are used.

The SETL macro has several forms. The three most common are:

```
SETL  dcb-address,K,keyfield-address
SETL  dcb-address,KC,keyfield-address
SETL  dcb-address,B
```

Here, the first operand gives the address of the DCB for the file being accessed. The second operand specifies how the file is to be accessed. And the third operand, if required, gives the address of a key field. Usually, the first and third operands are coded as the labels of the DCB and the key field.

If you want to start processing with a specific key in the file, you can specify K as the second operand. Then, the starting key value must be placed in the field identified by the third operand. This field must be defined somewhere in the program and must be the same length as specified in the KEYLEN operand of the DCB for the file. Usually, this field will be the key field defined in the work area for the file. If you want to use this starting method, you must specify SK in the MACRF operand in the DCB for the file.

When the SETL macro is executed, it doesn't read a record. It only positions the file. Using the first form of the macro, if the file doesn't contain a record with the key specified in the key field, no positioning takes place. Instead, the no-record found error condition is turned on. Since this usually isn't what you want, the second form of the SETL macro is more commonly used than the first.

When you use the second form (with KC as the second operand), the SETL macro specifies a *generic key*. Then, the SETL macro positions the file at the first record with a key equal to or greater than the key field specified in the macro. If, for example, a file contains account master records keyed by account number, you can specify that processing is to start with the first account in the 1000 series without knowing if the first key is 1000, 1002, or 1009. In this case, a value of 1000 must be placed in the field named as the third operand. Here again, to use this starting

Code	Meaning
I	Requests that the independent overflow area be used for overflow records.
L	Requests that the delete option be exercised by the I/O module. This means that records that have a delete code of hex FF in the first byte are not returned to your program in sequential processing or in random retrieval, and they can be written over if a record to be added to the file logically falls in that record space. However, the delete option cannot be requested if the first byte of the record is part of the key.
M	Requests that a master index be created according to the specification in the NTM operand.
R	Requests that reorganization information be placed in the DCB by the I/O module.
U	Requests that track indexes be accumulated in storage and be written as a group for each track of the track index.
W	Requests that write-verification be performed after each write operation. Since write-verification operations are time consuming, this option is rarely specified.
Y	Requests that overflow records be placed in the cylinder-overflow areas.

Figure 14-3   Summary of OPTCD options for QISAM

method, you must specify SK in the MACRF operand in the DCB for the file.

The third form of the SETL macro lets you begin processing at the first record in a file. Although you don't need to code this macro if you want to start processing at the beginning of the file immediately after the file is opened, you do need to code it if you process records in another part of the file and then want to go back to the beginning of the file. With this form, a third operand isn't required.

To end sequential processing, you use the ESETL macro. Its only operand is the address of the DCB for the file. You must issue this macro after every SETL macro if you intend to issue another SETL macro. However, you don't have to issue the ESETL macro before you close a file, because the CLOSE macro does the same thing. Nevertheless, for consistency, we recommend that you pair all SETL macros with ESETL macros.

In some programs, SETL and ESETL are coded several times in order to start and end processing at several different points in a file. First, one section of the file is processed, then another section, and so on. This type of processing is called *skip-sequential processing*. Using the account master record as an example, the program could process the records from keys 1000-1500, followed by the records from keys 500-750, followed by the records from keys 2800-2850.

QISAM error status bytes

As I told you earlier in this topic, the SYNAD operand of the DCB macro is used to override the normal error handling for QISAM processing. When an error occurs, control is given to the instruction named in the SYNAD operand. Before the branch is made, however, the I/O module posts the error conditions in two special bytes of the DCB area for the file; specifically, the 81st and 82nd bytes. These bytes can then be used to determine the cause of the error.

The meaning for each bit of the error bytes is shown in figure 14-4. If a bit is on, it means the indicated error condition has occurred. Notice that the types of errors that can occur depend on the type of macro that was used. In the load program that follows, you'll see how these error bytes can be used.

Two illustrative programs

Now that you have some idea of what the DCB for an ISAM file should look like for sequential access, I will present two program examples. The first program will show you how to load an ISAM file. The second program will show you how to retrieve records from an ISAM file.

A file creation program   Loading an ISAM file is much like creating a sequential file. Usually, a sequential input file provides the data that goes into each ISAM record. Since the ISAM records must be loaded in key sequence, the records in the input file must also be in key sequence.

Figure 14-5 presents a program that loads an ISAM file of inventory records from a sequential disk file. The new records are to be 70 bytes long. The basic processing loop of the program reads a record from the sequential file, moves and packs its data into the ISAM record, and writes an output record.

You normally have to make several decisions about an ISAM file before you can code a load program for it. You must decide what blocking factor to use, whether a master index is necessary, how much overflow area should be reserved, and what types of overflow areas should be used. In the program in figure 14-5, I assumed that the file would be a maximum of 4500 records with nine records per block. I also assumed that a single track per cylinder would be enough overflow area for the file. Because this file is small, a master index isn't needed.

In figure 14-5, the DCB for the inventory master file reflects these decisions. The BLKSIZE and LRECL operands reflect the record length and blocking factor I've chosen. KEYLEN is 6 bytes, and, because this is a blocked file, RKP must be included. Since the key (item number) begins in the second byte of the record, its relative position is 1, so RKP=1. Also, because I want overflow records to be written to the cylinder overflow areas, I coded OPTCD=Y and CYLOFL=1 so that one track on each cylinder is used for overflow records.

Byte	Bit	CLOSE	GET	PUT	PUTX	SETL	Cause	Remarks
DCB address +80	0					X	Record not found	Can't find record with key given in SETL macro (type SK).
	1					X	Invalid disk address	Can't find record at disk address given in SETL macro (type S, which isn't covered in this book).
	2			X			No space for new record	Overflow area is filled.
	3					X	Invalid request	Either of two causes: (1) SETL type isn't specified in the DCB MACRF operand, or (2) a previous SETL macro hasn't been terminated by an ESETL macro.
	4		X				Uncorrectable input error	
	5	X		X	X		Uncorrectable output error	
	6		X			X	Block couldn't be reached during retrieval	Indicates an error in the indexes or the chain of records in the overflow area.
	7	X	X				Block couldn't be reached during update	Indicates an error in the indexes or the chain of records in the overflow area.
DCB address +81	0			X			Sequence check	An out-of-sequence record was detected during loading.
	1			X			Duplicate record	A duplicate record was detected during loading.
	2	X					Error encountered during CLOSE	Program must return to the address in register 14 to allow continuation in the I/O module so the file will be closed.
	3		X				Record retrieved from overflow area	This doesn't cause an entry to the SYNAD routine unless another error bit is on too.
	4-7						Reserved	

Figure 14-4   DCB error bits for QISAM processing

```
INVLOAD    START  0
BEGIN      SAVE   (14,12)
           BALR   3,0
           USING  *,3
           ST     13,SAVE+4
           LA     13,SAVE
           OPEN   (INPUT,INPUT,INVMSTR,OUTPUT,AUDIT,OUTPUT)
READREC    GET    INPUT,INPTWRKA
           MVI    MDELCODE,X'00'
           MVC    MSTRRCD+1(32),INPTWRKA
           PACK   MORDQTY,IORDQTY
           PACK   MORDPT,IORDPT
           PACK   MSAFSTK,ISAFSTK
           PACK   MONHAND,IONHAND
           PACK   MONORD,IONORD
           PACK   MALLOC,IALLOC
           MVI    AUDITWRK,C' '
           MVC    AUDITWRK+1(131),AUDITWRK
           MVC    AUDITRCD,INPTWRKA
           PUT    INVMSTR,MSTRRCD        WRITE ISAM OUTPUT RECORD
PUTAUDIT   PUT    AUDIT,AUDITWRK
           B      READREC
ERRCHK     TM     INVMSTR+80,X'FF'       TEST ERROR BYTE 1
           BZ     ERRCHK2
           B      DUMP
ERRCHK2    TM     INVMSTR+81,X'80'       TEST FOR SEQUENCE ERROR
           BO     SEQERR
           TM     INVMSTR+81,X'40'       TEST FOR DUPLICATE RECORD
           BO     DUPERR
DUMP       ABEND  500,DUMP
SEQERR     MVC    AUDITMSG,=C'SEQUENCE ERROR'
           RETURN (14,12)                RETURN TO I/O MODULE
DUPERR     MVC    AUDITMSG,=C'DUPLICATE KEY '
           RETURN (14,12)                RETURN TO I/O MODULE
EOFDSK     CLOSE  (INPUT,,INVMSTR,,AUDIT)
           L      13,SAVE+4
           RETURN (14,12)
INPUT      DCB    DSORG=PS,                                          X
                  RECFM=FB,                                          X
                  MACRF=GM,                                          X
                  BLKSIZE=248,                                       X
                  LRECL=62,                                          X
                  DDNAME=INPUT,                                      X
                  EODAD=EOFDSK
INVMSTR    DCB    DSORG=IS,                                          X
                  RECFM=FB,                                          X
                  MACRF=PM,                                          X
                  BLKSIZE=630,                                       X
                  LRECL=70,                                          X
                  KEYLEN=6,                                          X
                  RKP=1,                                             X
                  OPTCD=LY,                                          X
                  CYLOFL=1,                                          X
                  SYNAD=ERRCHK,                                      X
                  DDNAME=INVMSTR
```

Figure 14-5   An ISAM file-creation program (part 1 of 2)

```
AUDIT      DCB    DSORG=PS,                                                X
                  RECFM=F,                                                 X
                  MACRF=PM,                                                X
                  BLKSIZE=132,                                             X
                  LRECL=132,                                               X
                  DDNAME=AUDIT
SAVE       DS     18F
INPTWRKA   DS     0CL62
IITEM      DS     CL6
IDESC      DS     CL20
IUM        DS     CL4
IORDPOL    DS     CL2
IORDQTY    DS     CL5
IORDPT     DS     CL5
ISAFSTK    DS     CL5
IONHAND    DS     CL5
IONORD     DS     CL5
IALLOC     DS     CL5
MSTRRCD    DS     0CL70
MDELCODE   DS     CL1
MITEM      DS     CL6
MDESC      DS     CL20
MUM        DS     CL4
MORDPOL    DS     CL2
MORDQTY    DS     PL4
MORDPT     DS     PL4
MSAFSTK    DS     PL4
MONHAND    DS     PL4
MONORD     DS     PL4
MALLOC     DS     PL4
           DC     13X'00'
AUDITWRK   DS     0CL132
           DS     CL6
AUDITRCD   DS     CL62
           DS     CL10
AUDITMSG   DS     CL14
           DS     CL40
           END    BEGIN
```

Figure 14-5   An ISAM file-creation program (part 2 of 2)

I coded L on the OPTCD operand for the inventory master file. That indicates that records in the file may be marked for deletion. A record is marked for deletion if it contains hex FF in the first byte of the record. Then, when the file is processed sequentially, records marked for deletion aren't returned to your program.

So I could do my own error processing, I coded the SYNAD operand on the DCB for the inventory master file. This operand overrides the normal error handling of QISAM. In figure 14-5, the SYNAD operand specifies an error routine named ERRCHK. As a result, if QISAM detects an error, it will branch to the instruction labelled ERRCHK instead of terminating the program abnormally.

I coded the SYNAD operand so the program wouldn't be cancelled when two types of errors occur. These errors are (1) an out-of-sequence record and (2) a duplicate record (one that has the same key as a record already loaded on the file). Instead of cancelling the program if these errors occur, the program should bypass the input record and continue with the next input record. You'll see how this routine works in a minute.

Other than the error processing, you should be able to understand this load program without any trouble. In the main processing loop, an input record is read, the master record and audit record are assembled in their work areas, and the inventory record is written to the master file. If the new record is written to the file without any errors, the program continues by printing a line on the audit file and the processing loop is repeated.

If the I/O module does detect an error, however, control is given to the ERRCHK routine. This routine checks the error bytes associated with the file to determine what caused the error. For the load program in figure 14-5, I'm interested only in the errors that can result from a PUT macro. If you check figure 14-4, you can see that there are four possible error conditions. For the load program, I want to cancel the program if there's no more space available for writing new records or if an uncorrectable output error occurs. However, I want to bypass the record causing the error if it is out of sequence or a duplicate.

To test the actual bits in the error bytes, I used the test-under-mask (TM) instruction. This instruction, which is covered in detail in chapter 10, lets you test the condition of one or more bits within a byte. The branch instruction that follows it can then branch based on the resulting condition code.

To illustrate, consider the first three instructions of the ERRCHK routine:

```
ERRCHK    TM    INVMSTR+80,X'FF'
          BZ    ERRCHK2
          B     DUMP
```

The TM instruction tests the status bits indicated by the immediate operand, X'FF', to see whether they are ones or zeros. Since hex FF is binary 11111111, all bits of the first byte are tested. Then, if they are all 0's (meaning the record has been written with no errors indicated in the first error byte), the program will branch to ERRCHK2, a routine that tests the bits of the second error byte. If at least one of the bits is on, however, the branch won't take place. Then, the next instruction will cause a branch to DUMP, which will terminate the program and print a storage dump.

If no error bit in byte one is on, the load program reaches these instructions:

```
ERRCHK2    TM    INVMSTR+81,X'80'
           BO    SEQERR
           TM    INVMSTR+81,X'40'
           BO    DUPERR
DUMP       ABEND 500,DUMP
```

Since hex 80 is binary 10000000, the first bit of the second error byte is tested by the first TM instruction. If it's one, a branch to SEQERR occurs. Similarly, since hex 40 is binary 01000000, the second TM instruction tests the second bit. If it is one, a branch to DUPERR takes place. Since these are the only error bits that can be on for a PUT operation, all possible error conditions have now been tested.

In the SEQERR and DUPERR routines, an error message is moved into the record that will be written on the audit file. Then, the RETURN macro is used to pass control back to the I/O module so it can complete its processing. When the I/O module finishes, it branches to the statement after the PUT for the disk file; that is, the PUT for the audit file.

A function similar to loading an ISAM file is extending a file. When you *extend* an ISAM file, you add records to the file that have keys greater than the highest key in the file, and these records are stored in the prime data area. There are two ways you can extend an ISAM file using QISAM. First, you can use the same code as for a load program and specify DISP=MOD on the DD statement for the file in the JCL. Second, you can specify the EXTEND option on the OPEN instruction for the file. Since the first method allows you to both load and extend a file using the same program, it's generally the preferred method.

A sequential retrieval program   Figure 14-6 presents a program that illustrates sequential record retrieval. It reads the inventory master file created by the program in figure 14-5 and prepares an inventory report from it. Since the logic of the program is straightforward, you should have no difficulty following it. However, there are several things I'd like to point out.

If you review the DCB for the ISAM file, you'll notice that only a few of the operands had to be coded. That's because most of the file attributes were placed in the data set label when it was created. The only thing special about the way the operands are coded is that the MACRF operand specifies locate mode. Also, note that no SYNAD operand is included. If you check figure 14-4, you'll see that the only errors that can result from a GET macro are serious ones. So, I elected to let the I/O module terminate the execution of the program if any of these errors occurred. (Although bit 3 of the second error byte isn't a serious error, it also doesn't cause the program to be cancelled.) One more thing to remember is that the delete option was specified when the file was loaded. So, if any of the records have been marked for deletion, they won't be processed by this program.

As presented in chapter 7, I've included a dummy section to describe the master record and a USING statement to assign register 4 as the dummy section's base register. The locate mode GET macro is then coded without a second operand and is followed by a load-register instruction that transfers the record address returned in register 1 to register 4.

The rest of the program should be clear to you. One point of interest is the editing of the six output fields starting with RORDQTY before a line is printed. Since the edit pattern uses field separators (hex 22s) and since all six packed fields are adjacent in storage, only one edit instruction is needed. This use of field separators is described in detail in chapter 10.

```
          PRINT NOGEN
INVSTAT   START 0
BEGIN     SAVE  (14,12)
          BALR  3,0
          USING *,3
          ST    13,SAVE+4
          LA    13,SAVE
          USING MSTRRCD,4
          OPEN  (INVMSTR,INPUT,STATUS,OUTPUT)
NXTRCD    GET   INVMSTR
          LR    4,1                   LOAD R4 WITH RECORD ADDRESS
          MVI   RLINE,X'40'
          MVC   RLINE+1(132),RLINE
          MVC   RITEM,MITEM
          MVC   RDESC,MDESC
          MVC   RUM,MUM
          MVC   RORDPOL,MORDPOL
          MVC   RORDQTY(61),PATTERN
          ED    RORDQTY(61),MORDQTY   EDIT SIX FIELDS
          ZAP   AVAILWK,MONHAND
          AP    AVAILWK,MONORD
          SP    AVAILWK,MALLOC
          MVC   RAVAIL,PATTERN
          ED    RAVAIL,AVAILWK
          CP    LCOUNT,=P'50'
          BL    PRTDET
          PUT   STATUS,RHEAD
          ZAP   LCOUNT,=P'0'
          MVI   RCTL,C'0'
PRTDET    PUT   STATUS,RLINE
          AP    LCOUNT,=P'1'
          B     NXTRCD
EOFMSTR   CLOSE (INVMSTR,,STATUS)
          L     13,SAVE+4
          RETURN (14,12)
INVMSTR   DCB   DSORG=IS,                                              X
                MACRF=GL,                                              X
                DDNAME=INVMSTR,                                        X
                EODAD=EOFMSTR
STATUS    DCB   DSORG=PS,                                              X
                RECFM=FA,                                              X
                MACRF=PM,                                              X
                BLKSIZE=133,                                           X
                LRECL=133,                                             X
                DDNAME=STATUS
SAVE      DS    18F
AVAILWK   DS    PL4
LCOUNT    DC    P'50'
PATTERN   DS    0CL61
          DC    X'40'
          DC    6X'20202020202021222222'
RHEAD     DS    0CL133
          DC    CL105'1        ITEM   DESCRIPTION           U/M X
                OP      ORDQTY   ORDPNT    SAFSTK      ONHAND    ONORDR'
          DC    CL28'   ALLOC    AVAIL      '
```

Figure 14-6 An ISAM sequential retrieval program (part 1 of 2)

```
RLINE       DS      0CL133
RCTL        DS      CL1
            DS      CL12
RITEM       DS      CL6
            DS      CL2
RDESC       DS      CL20
            DS      CL4
RUM         DS      CL4
            DS      CL2
RORDPOL     DS      CL2
            DS      CL4
RORDQTY     DS      CL8
            DS      CL2
RORDPT      DS      CL8
            DS      CL2
RSAFSTK     DS      CL8
            DS      CL2
RONHAND     DS      CL8
            DS      CL2
RONORD      DS      CL8
            DS      CL2
RALLOC      DS      CL8
            DS      CL2
RAVAIL      DS      CL8
            DS      CL8
MSTRRCD     DSECT
MDELCODE    DS      CL1
MITEM       DS      CL6
MDESC       DS      CL20
MUM         DS      CL4
MORDPOL     DS      CL2
MORDQTY     DS      PL4
MORDPT      DS      PL4
MSAFSTX     DS      PL4
MONHAND     DS      PL4
MONORD      DS      PL4
MALLOC      DS      PL4
            DS      CL13
            END     BEGIN
```

Figure 14-6   An ISAM sequential retrieval program (part 2 of 2)

This program illustrates the simplest form of processing ISAM records sequentially. It begins by reading the first record in the file and proceeds all the way through to the end of the file. If you want to start processing at some other point in the file, you use the SETL macro to indicate what starting point you want.

During the sequential processing of an ISAM file, you can also update records in place just as you can in a sequential disk file. In fact, the coding to do so is exactly the same: a PUTX macro with the DCB name as its only operand performs a rewrite of the disk record previously retrieved by a GET macro.

BISAM PROCESSING

For any of the random ISAM functions (random retrieval, random update, and maintenance), you must use the Basic Indexed Sequential Access Method. In this access method, the records are always referred to by key. To execute an I/O operation when using a basic access method, your program must provide three items to the I/O module. First, the file must be described in a DCB. Second, a data management parameter list called a *Data Event Control Block (DECB)* must be defined and filled with data to be passed to the I/O module (the type of operation to be performed, the address of the DCB, the address of the key field, etc). Third, a link must be made to the I/O module at the proper point in your program.

Obviously, the DCB is provided by coding a DCB macro. The DECB and the link to the I/O module, however, are provided by coding READ and WRITE macros. In the remainder of this topic, then, I'll present the BISAM DCB macro, the BISAM READ and WRITE macros, and three other macros you need to know about for BISAM file handling. I'll finish by presenting a random update program that illustrates the use of these macros.

DCB operands

The DCB operands used to randomly access a file using BISAM are listed in figure 14-7. Since you are already familiar with the DDNAME and DSORG operands, I won't cover them here. The rest, however, are either new operands or require some additional explanation.

MACRF   As you can see, the MACRF operand must supply more information for BISAM than for QSAM or QISAM. First, it not only indicates whether a READ (R) or WRITE (W) macro will be issued, but also whether update-in-place (U) is to be performed. It indicates whether a WAIT (no code) or CHECK macro (C) will be used. (I'll discuss them in a minute.) And it indicates whether records are going to be added to the file (A) and whether dynamic buffering (S) is to be used. The programmer code in figure 14-7 presents the most commonly used forms of this operand, and figure 14-8 presents all of the possible combinations.

OPTCD   Like QISAM, BISAM provides several optional services that can be requested by coding the OPTCD operand. The three options available are L for the delete option, R for the reorganization option, and W for the write-verification option. All of these options have the same meaning as for QISAM so you can refer to figure 14-3 for a more detailed description. In most cases, these options are specified when the file is loaded under QISAM so you should rarely code this operand in programs that use BISAM processing.

MSHI and SMSI   It is possible to have the highest level index for a file read into storage at the start of a program. Then, the searches through the index are done at CPU speeds rather than at the slower DASD speeds. This can improve processing speeds dramatically.

If this feature is used, the MSHI operand gives the name of the index area in storage, and the SMSI operand gives the number of bytes in the area. Figure 14-9 shows the formula for calculating the size required to hold the entire index. As you can see, this formula requires that you know

Keyword	Programmer code	Remarks
DSORG	IS	The data set organization.
MACRF	RS	Read only, dynamic buffering, WAIT.
	RSC	Read only, dynamic buffering, CHECK.
	(RUS,WU)	Read and update, dynamic buffering, WAIT.
	(RUSC,WUC)	Read and update, dynamic buffering, CHECK.
	(RUSC,WUAC)	Read and update, additions, dynamic buffering, CHECK.
	WA	Write additions, WAIT.
	WAC	Write additions, CHECK.
OPTCD	L,R,W	Access method options. See figure 14-3 for an explanation of these options.
MSHI	Label of index area in storage	Label of area to be used for the highest level index in storage.
SMSI	nnnn	Size of the index in storage.
SYNAD	Label of the error checking routine	Label of the routine that is given control if the I/O module detects an error.
DDNAME	DD name	The ddname in the DD job control statement for the file.

Figure 14-7   DCB operands for BISAM

Formats

```
READ only          R [S] [C]
```

```
                     ⎛U ⎞
WRITE only         W ⎨A ⎬ [C]
                     ⎝UA⎠
```

```
                     ⎛S ⎞       ⎛U ⎞
READ and WRITE    (R⎨U ⎬ [C],W ⎨A ⎬ [C])
                     ⎝US⎠       ⎝UA⎠
```

Explanation

A = Records are to be added to the file.
C = The CHECK macro will be used.
R = The READ macro will be used.
U = Records are to be updated.
     If U is coded with R, it must also be coded with W.
W = The WRITE macro will be used.

Figure 14-8   MACRF entries for BISAM DCBs

SMSI = (tracks in master index)
    X (index entries per track)
    X (key length + 10)

Tracks in master index = tracks in cylinder index
    ÷ index entries per track

Tracks in cylinder index = (track indexes + 1)
    ÷ index entries per track

Figure 14-9   Calculating the SMSI operand

quite a bit about the indexes of the file. To avoid these calculations, you can specify a number that's less than this maximum amount. If you do, only a portion of the index will be read into storage at one time with a resulting decrease in efficiency.

SYNAD   Since the BISAM I/O modules do little error checking, an error handling routine should always be included in BISAM programs. Then, the SYNAD operand specifies the label of the first instruction of this routine.

Creating and using the DECB

As I've already mentioned, the READ and WRITE macros are used to create the DECB and the instructions that link to the I/O module. So, first, I'll show you how to code these macros. Then, I'll give you some ideas on when to use the different forms of these macros. Finally, I'll show you how you can use the DECB values in your programs.

The READ and WRITE macros

The READ and WRITE macros have three forms. The *standard form* of each macro creates both a DECB and the instructions that link to the I/O module. The *list form* of each macro creates only a DECB. And the *execute form* creates only the instructions that link to the I/O module. Figure 14-10 presents the READ and WRITE macros for BISAM processing. Since it's important that you understand how these macros work, I'll discuss each of the operands in detail.

DECB name   As part of the expansion of a standard or list form READ or WRITE macro, a DECB is created and filled with proper values. The name that you code for the DECB-name operand becomes the label of the DECB. Then, you can refer to the DECB by that name in your program.

Format

$$\begin{Bmatrix} \texttt{READ} \\ \texttt{WRITE} \end{Bmatrix} \texttt{DECB-name,type,DCB-address,} \begin{Bmatrix} \texttt{area-address} \\ \texttt{'S'} \end{Bmatrix},$$

$$\begin{Bmatrix} \texttt{length} \\ \texttt{'S'} \end{Bmatrix} \texttt{,key-address,[MF=} \begin{Bmatrix} \texttt{L} \\ \texttt{E} \end{Bmatrix} \texttt{]}$$

Explanation

DECB address — The label assigned to the DECB as part of the macro expansion.

type — For READ, K indicates retrieval by key, KU indicates the record is to be updated and rewritten. For WRITE, K indicates an updated record is to be written back on the file, KN indicates that a new record is to be added to the file.

DCB address — The address, usually in label form, of the DCB that describes the file.

area address — The address, usually in label form, of the area into which the block is to be read (READ) or the storage area that contains the record to be written (WRITE). The first 16 bytes are reserved for use by the control program. Code 'S' to indicate dynamic buffering. If 'S' is coded for a READ, the address of the buffer is placed in the DECB when the READ is issued. For a WRITE, 'S' can only be coded for an update function.

length — The number of bytes to be read or written. For READ, 'S' must be coded with blocked records and is usually coded for unblocked records. For WRITE, 'S' is almost always used.

key address — The address, usually in label form, of the field that contains the key of the record to be retrieved (READ), or the key of the new or updated record to be written (WRITE).

MF — This operand indicates the form of the macro. If it's omitted, standard is assumed. L indicates list form. E indicates execute form.

Figure 14-10 The READ and WRITE macros for BISAM

Type   The type operand indicates what type of operation is to be performed. For READ, it can be K for random retrieval by key, or KU to indicate that the randomly retrieved record is to be updated and rewritten. For WRITE, it can be K for a record already present in the file, or KN for a new record.

DCB address   This operand specifies the address of the DCB for the file. It's usually coded as the label of the DCB. It can, however, specify the number of a register, in parentheses, that has been loaded with the address of the DCB.

Area address   This operand must indicate, in one of two ways, where the I/O area for the block to be read or written is located. One way of doing this is to define an area in your program equal to the length of a block plus a 16-byte prefix (the 16-byte prefix will be used by the I/O module). You then code the label of this area as the area-address operand.

In most cases, however, you will want to take advantage of dynamic buffering by coding 'S' for this operand. Then, when a record is read, the control program will dynamically acquire a storage area for the block and place its address in the DECB for your use. Once the record has been read, it can be rewritten using this address.

For a WRITE macro, the 'S' form of this operand can only be used for an update. It cannot be used to write a new record to a file. It also cannot be used if a variable-length record is being rewritten with a different length.

Length   The length operand specifies the number of bytes to be read from or written to a file. For a READ macro, although the length can be specified for unblocked ISAM files, it's usually coded 'S' to allow the I/O module to get the proper length from the DCB. And it must be coded 'S' for blocked files. For the WRITE macro, 'S' should always be coded unless a variable-length record is being rewritten with a different length.

Key address   The key address operand specifies the label of the field containing the key of the record to be retrieved.

MF   The MF operand specifies the form of the macro to be generated. If you omit the operand, standard form is assumed. If you code MF=L, the list form is generated. If you code MF=E, the execute form is generated.

Using the different forms of the READ and WRITE macros

Now that you are familiar with the different forms of the READ and WRITE macros, you should know when to use them. In general, if a program only reads or only writes records from a file, the standard forms of the macros should be used. However, if a program both reads and writes records from the same file, the list and execute forms should be used. In this case, the list form of the READ macro is used to create the DECB for the file. Then, the execute forms of the READ and WRITE macros are used to read records from and write records to the file, using the DECB created by the list form of the READ macro. You'll see an example of how this works in the illustrative program later in this topic.

Displacement	Length	Field
0	4	ECB (Event Control Block)
4	2	Type indicator
6	2	Length value
8	4	DCB address
12	4	Buffer area address
16	4	Record address
20	4	Key field address
24	2	Error bytes (see figure 14-12)
26	2	Unused for BISAM

Figure 14-11   DECB fields for BISAM

Using the values in the DECB

The format of the DECB for BISAM is presented in figure 14-11. Some of its fields are supplied either directly or indirectly by the operands coded on the READ or WRITE macro used to create it. Some of the fields, however, are not determined until the related I/O module is executed. The fields you will most often use in your programs are the record-address and error-bytes fields, which are set by the I/O module.

The record-address field contains the buffer address of the record being processed. When the I/O module is executed, the record address is placed in the DECB in a four-byte field beginning at byte 17 (displacement 16). Then, the program can use this address to refer to the fields in the record. You'll see how this works in a moment.

If an I/O error occurs, the I/O module also sets the error byte fields. They're in bytes 25 and 26 of the DECB (displacement 24 and 25), and they can be used to determine the cause of the error. The meaning of each of the bit positions in these two error bytes is given in figure 14-12.

For a READ macro, those errors indicated by bits 1, 3, 4, and 5 are serious. If any of these bits are on, the program should probably be aborted. Bits 0 and 6, however, indicate less serious conditions. If bit 6 is on, no error has actually occurred. In fact, if this is the only error bit on, the I/O module doesn't pass control to the SYNAD routine. If bit 0 is the

Byte	Bit	READ	WRITE	Error condition
1	0	X	X (type K)	No record found.
	1	X	X	Record length check.
	2		X (type KN)	Not enough space to add record.
	3	X	X (type K)	Invalid request. Usually, this occurs because dynamic buffering is specified in the READ or WRITE macro that created the DECB, but it is not coded in the MACRF operand of the DCB for the file.
	4	X	X	Uncorrectable disk I/O error.
	5	X	X	Unreachable block. Usually, this indicates an index error.
	6	X		Record was read from an overflow area.
	7		X (type KN)	Duplicate record. Record to be added has a key that is a duplicate of one already on the file.
2	0-7			Reserved.

Figure 14-12   DECB error bytes for BISAM

only one on, it indicates that the requested key is not in the file. If this error occurs, the key value should be noted and the program should continue with the next input record.

For a WRITE macro, those errors indicated by bits 0 through 5 are serious. Usually, a program should be aborted when one of these errors occurs. In contrast, bit 7 indicates a less serious error. It just means that the file already has a record with a key equal to the one for the record that the program is trying to add to the file. In most cases, then, the program should note the problem and continue with the next record to be processed.

Other macros for BISAM file handling

In addition to the DCB, READ, and WRITE macros, three other macros are commonly used for BISAM processing. These are the CHECK, WAIT, and FREEDBUF macros. Their formats are given in figure 14-13.

The CHECK and WAIT Macros   The CHECK or WAIT macro must be coded following any BISAM READ or WRITE macro in standard or execute form. They both cause the program to wait until the I/O operation is completed before continuing the program. These macros are necessary because MVS doesn't wait to make sure a BISAM I/O operation is completed before it returns control to a program. If, for example, you

The CHECK macro

$$\text{CHECK} \qquad \text{DECB-address,DSORG=} \begin{Bmatrix} \text{IS} \\ \text{ALL} \end{Bmatrix}$$

The WAIT macro

```
WAIT      ECB=DECB-address
```

The FREEDBUF macro

```
FREEDBUF  DECB-name,K,DCB-address
```

Figure 14-13   The CHECK, WAIT, and FREEDBUF macros for BISAM

issue a standard or execute form READ macro and follow it with instructions that are to process the data just read, the execution of the processing instructions may begin before the data from the record has been read into storage. However, if you code the CHECK or WAIT macro after the READ macro, you can be sure that the data has been read into storage before your program starts to process it.

As you can see in figure 14-13, the first operand of both macros must be the label of the DECB for the file. For the CHECK macro, you just code the DECB label. For the WAIT macro, you code the label preceded by ECB=. For the CHECK macro only, a second operand is required that indicates the type of file you're processing. For a BISAM file, you can code either IS (for BISAM only) or ALL (for all the basic access methods), but you cannot omit the operand.

Although both the CHECK and WAIT macros cause your program to wait until an I/O operation is completed, there is one significant difference between the two. The WAIT macro will always cause an abnormal program termination if an I/O error has been detected. If no error has been detected, the program continues with the first instruction after the WAIT macro.

The CHECK macro, on the other hand, includes a basic error checking function. If no error results from an I/O operation, control falls through to the next instruction. If an error does occur, control is passed to the routine named in the SYNAD operand in the DCB for the file. However, if no SYNAD operand is included in the DCB, the program is abnormally terminated, so the CHECK macro functions like the WAIT macro. As a general rule, you will find it best to use a CHECK macro with a SYNAD routine whenever you use BISAM processing.

The FREEDBUF macro   When dynamic buffering is used to process the records in a file, a buffer area is allocated to each block in the file when it's read. Then, when the block is rewritten, the area allocated to that block is released. The area is also released when the next READ macro is issued for the file. And the area is released when the file is closed.

Occasionally, you will write a program or subprogram that doesn't release a buffer area in one of the ways I've just mentioned. Then, you may want to explicitly release a buffer area. To do this, you use the FREEDBUF macro with the format given in figure 14-13. For instance, this macro

```
FREEDBUF IMDECB,K,INVMAST
```

releases the buffer for a block of records read from a file with a DCB named INVMAST and a DECB named IMDECB. The K indicates that BISAM is being used.

A random update program

Figure 14-14 is a program that updates an ISAM file on a random basis. The input file is a sequential shipment transaction file; the updated file is the ISAM inventory master file that was created by the program in figure 14-5. The basic logic of this program is to read a shipment transaction, read the master record with the same key on a random basis, update the data in the master record, and rewrite the updated master record in its original location on the DASD.

The first thing you should notice is the DCB for the ISAM file (INVMSTR). For the MACRF operand, I've coded RUSC,WUC which indicates that the file will be read and updated and that dynamic buffering and the CHECK macro will be used. Also, I've included the SYNAD operand to indicate that an error routine will be executed if an I/O error occurs and the CHECK macro is coded. You'll see how this error routine works in a minute. Finally, although I didn't code the OPTCD operand, you should remember that the delete option was specified when the file was loaded. Therefore, any records that have been marked for deletion won't be processed by this program.

Because records are being read from and written to the same file, I used the list and execute forms of the READ and WRITE macros. That way, after the READ macro in list form is assembled and the DECB is created, I can retrieve and update records in the file by using the READ and WRITE macros in execute form.

Notice that the READ macro that creates the DECB is coded after the DCB macros. There are two reasons for this. First, the list form of the macro doesn't create any executable code so there's no reason for it to be with the instructions. Second, when this form is used, the DECB is actually assembled into your program. So, if you code it within the instructions, your program has to branch around the DECB it creates. It makes more sense, then, to code it with the DCBs and data definitions.

Now let's take a look at the operands coded on the list form of the READ macro. First, the DECB is assigned the name INVDECB. Then, KU indicates that the records will be retrieved by key and that they'll be updated. INVMSTR is the label of the DCB for the file, and the two S's indicate that dynamic buffering will be used. As a result, dynamic buffering must also be specified in the MACRF operand of the DCB for the file for this to work properly. Next, ITEMKEY is specified as the field in which the key of the record to be retrieved will be placed. Finally, L is coded for the MF operand, which indicates list form.

The processing of the program should be easy for you to follow. After an input record has been read, the item number in the transaction is moved to a field named ITEMKEY, which is the key field specified in the READ and WRITE macros. The execute form of the READ macro then tries to read the master record randomly by key. Its format is identical to the list form of the macro except for the MF operand.

Following the READ macro is the CHECK macro. If an error is encountered by the I/O module, the CHECK macro causes the program to branch to the error routine, ERRCHK. In this routine, the first test-under-mask instruction checks to see if bit 1, 3, 4, or 5 is on since hex 5C is binary 01011100. If any of these bits are on, the program branches to ABORT. Then, the ABEND macro ends the program and prints a storage dump.

If bits 1, 3, 4, and 5 are off, the program continues with the second TM instruction. Because hex 80 is binary 10000000, this instruction tests bit 0. If it's on, the program branches to NOTFOUND, a no-record-found message is printed on the error log, and processing continues with the next input record. If bit 0 is off, the ABEND macro is executed. (Remember, if bit 6 is on, indicating that the record was read from an overflow area, control is not given to the SYNAD error routine. For that reason, it's not necessary to check this bit.)

Unlike QISAM processing, a BISAM program does not need to return to the I/O module after an error-checking routine. Instead, the program continues as normal. Therefore, it's not appropriate to code a RETURN macro following a BISAM error routine as you did after a QISAM routine.

If no errors occur during the execution of the READ macro, the CHECK macro causes the program to wait for the input record to be available; then, processing continues. In this case, the next instruction loads the address of the record just retrieved into register 4. As you can see, this address is extracted from the DECB where it was placed by the I/O module. Since I have associated register 4 in a USING instruction with a DSECT that defines the inventory master record, I can now refer to the fields in the record by name.

After the quantity on hand is updated in the master record, the record is rewritten on the file. This is done using a WRITE macro in execute form. Notice that this macro refers to the same DECB as the READ macro. Then, since the DECB already has the address of the last record read, the record can be rewritten in the same place on the file. Also notice that K has

```
//DLOWE2X7      JOB   USER=DLOWE2,PASSWORD=MMAPW3,MSGLEVEL=1
//DELETE     EXEC PGM=IEFBR14
//SHIPTR     DD   DSN=DLOWE2.SHIPTR,DISP=(OLD,DELETE),UNIT=SYSDA,
//           VOL=SER=MPS800
//EXCS154A  EXEC ASMFCG
//ASM.SYSIN DD    *
          PRINT NOGEN
LDSHIP    START 0
BEGIN     SAVE  (14,12)
RDMUPD    START 0
BEGIN     SAVE  (14,12)
          BALR  3,0
          USING *,3
          USING MSTRRCD,4
          ST    13,SAVE+4
          LA    13,SAVE
          OPEN  (SHIPTR,INPUT,ERRMSG,OUTPUT,INVMSTR)
READSHP   GET   SHIPTR,SHPWRKA
          MVC   ITEMKEY,SHPITEM
          READ  INVDECB,KU,INVMSTR,'S','S',ITEMKEY,MF=E
          CHECK INVDECB,DSORG=IS      CHECK FOR I/O ERRORS
          L     4,INVDECB+16          LOAD R4 WITH ADDRESS OF BUFFER AREA
          PACK  PACKQTY,SHPQTY
          SP    MONHAND,PACKQTY
          WRITE INVDECB,K,INVMSTR,'S','S',ITEMKEY,MF=E
          WAIT  ECB=INVDECB           WAIT FOR BLOCK TO BE WRITTEN
          B     READSHP
ERRCHK    TM    INVDECB+24,X'5C'      TEST FOR SERIOUS I/O ERRORS
          BM    ABORT
          TM    INVDECB+24,X'80'      TEST FOR NOT FOUND CONDITION
          BO    NOTFOUND
ABORT     ABEND 600,DUMP
NOTFOUND  MVC   LITEM,SHPITEM
          MVC   LERR,=C'NO RECORD FOUND'
          PUT   ERRMSG,ERRLINE
          B     READSHP
EOFINPT   CLOSE (SHIPTR,,ERRMSG,,INVMSTR)
          L     13,SAVE+4
          RETURN (14,12)
SHIPTR    DCB   DSORG=PS,                                            X
                RECFM=FB,                                            X
                MACRF=GM,                                            X
                BLKSIZE=240,                                         X
                LRECL=24,                                            X
                DDNAME=SHIPTR,                                       X
                EODAD=EOFINPT
ERRMSG    DCB   DSORG=PS,                                            X
                RECFM=F,                                             X
                MACRF=PM,                                            X
                BLKSIZE=132,                                         X
                LRECL=132,                                           X
                DDNAME=ERRMSG
```

Figure 14-14   An ISAM random update program (part 1 of 2)

```
INVMSTR   DCB    DSORG=IS,                                              X
                 MACRF=(RUSC,WUC),                                      X
                 SYNAD=ERRCHK,                                          X
                 DDNAME=INVMSTR
          READ   INVDEC3,KU,INVMSTR,'S','S',ITEMKEY,MF=L
SAVE      DS     18F
PACKQTY   DS     PL4
ITEMKEY   DS     CL6
SHPWRKA   DS     0CL24
          DS     CL6
SHPITEM   DS     CL6
SHPQTY    DS     CL4
          DS     CL8
ERRLINE   DS     0CL132
          DC     5C' '
LITEM     DS     CL6
          DC     52C' '
LERR      DS     CL15
          DC     54C' '
MSTRRCD   DSECT
MDELCODE  DS     CL1
MSTITEM   DS     CL6
MDESC     DS     CL20
          DS     CL18
MONHAND   DS     PL4
          DS     CL21
          END    BEGIN
```

Figure 14-14   An ISAM random update program (part 2 of 2)

been specified for the type operand of the WRITE macro, indicating that the record is to be written by key.

Following the WRITE macro is the WAIT macro. I've coded the WAIT macro here instead of the CHECK macro because I don't want the SYNAD error routine to be given control if an error occurs. Instead, because all of the errors are serious, I want the program to end.

One more thing you should notice in the random update program is that no option is specified for the ISAM file in the OPEN statement. It is not required by BISAM and is ignored if coded. That's because BISAM gets the type of operation from the DCB for the file.

Other file-handling functions

The random update program I've just presented should provide you with enough background for most of the BISAM programming you'll ever do. However, you should be aware that there are two other functions that I haven't illustrated. These are adding records to a file and deleting records from a file. So let me briefly describe programs that perform these functions.

File additions   A program that adds records to an ISAM file is much like a program that updates records. However, there are several differences you should be aware of.

First, because the records aren't read before they're written to the file, the standard form of the WRITE macro should be used to define the DECB for the file. That also means that the MACRF operand of the DCB for the file must be coded differently. In this case, it's usually coded MACRF=WAC to indicate that the WRITE macro will be used to add records to the file and the CHECK macro will be used to check for errors.

The type operand of the WRITE macro must be coded to indicate that records will be added to the file (KN). Also, because a buffer area isn't provided for the records being written to the file, a work area must be specified for the area address operand. That's why dynamic buffering isn't specified in the MACRF operand. When you code the work area, remember that it must be preceded by a 16-byte area to be used by the I/O module.

In addition to these differences, the error-checking routine in a file-addition program is likely to be more complicated than it is in an update program. If a record to be added to a file has a key that is a duplicate of one already on the file, an error message is usually printed and the program goes on to the next input record. If a record can't be added to a file because there is no room for it, a message is usually printed and the program ends.

File deletions   The BISAM access method doesn't directly provide for deleting records from an ISAM file. However, as discussed earlier in this topic, the delete option of BISAM can be used to simulate deletion. When you use this option, the first byte of the record is reserved for a deletion code. To delete a record, then, a program moves hex FF to this byte, which indicates that the record has been deleted, and the record is rewritten on the file.

Note, however, that the deleted records actually remain on the file until it is reorganized. As a result, the delete option must ignore the records that have the deletion code turned on in all of the programs that process the file. To reorganize the file, a reload program reads the old file, ignoring records that have been deleted, and loads a new file. Thus, deleted records are dropped from the file.

DISCUSSION   As you should realize by now, the trick to processing ISAM files in assembler language is coding the DCB and the other I/O macros properly. To make sure you use the correct macros for each ISAM function, you can use the summary in figure 14-15. Although it doesn't present all of the possible combinations, it does present the most common ones.

Loading or extending

```
PUT
```

Sequential retrieval and updating

```
SETL
GET
ESETL
PUTX
```

Random additions

```
WRITE (standard)
CHECK
```

Random retrieval

```
READ (standard)
CHECK
```

Random updating

```
READ (list)
READ (execute)
CHECK
WRITE (execute)
WAIT
```

Figure 14-15   ISAM I/O macro summary

Terminology

Queued Indexed Sequential
    Access Method
QISAM
Basic Indexed Sequential
    Access Method
BISAM
loading a file
embedded key

generic key
skip-sequential processing
extending a file
Data Event Control Block
DECB
standard macro form
list macro form
execute macro form

Objective

Given program specifications that require the use of ISAM files, code an assembler language program that satisies the specifications. The specifications may require any of the following functions: loading a file, adding records to a file, deleting records from a file, sequentially or randomly updating a file, and sequentially or randomly retrieving records from a file. They may also require that cylinder overflow, independent overflow, or an index in storage be used.

TOPIC 3 MVS JCL for ISAM files

In topic 3 of the last chapter, I presented the basic JCL for processing sequential disk files. However, to process ISAM files, you need to code the DD statement differently. This topic will present the required formats and show you how they are used in some ISAM job streams.

The DD statement

Because an ISAM file can consist of three different areas, three separate DD statements can be coded: one for the prime data area, one for the index area, and one for the overflow area. However, an ISAM file can also be defined with only one or two DD statements. The number of statements you code depends on the particular file and whether it's being loaded or retrieved.

When you're loading an ISAM file, if you define it with only one area, the file will have *embedded index* and *overflow areas*. That means the cylinder index area (and optional master index area) and the independent overflow area will be contained in the disk space allocated to the prime data area. If you code two DD statements for a file, you code one for the prime data area and one for either the index or overflow area. Then, the area that's not defined by a DD statement is embedded in the prime data area.

The number of DD statements you need to code when you retrieve an ISAM file depends on whether all three of the areas (prime data, index, and overflow) reside on the same volume and whether the file is cataloged. If the areas are all on the same volume or if the file was cataloged, only one DD statement is required. Obviously, if the file was created with only one DD statement, all three areas reside on the same volume. If multiple DD statements were coded when the file was created, however, the areas may have been allocated to different volumes. If so, the same number of DD statements must be coded, unless the file was cataloged.

For testing your assembler language programs, you'll probably only need to use one disk area. That's because most test files are relatively small and will have few records added to them. However, most of your permanent ISAM files will require that at least two of the areas be defined. Therefore, I'll present the DD statement operands for both kinds of files. The operands not presented here are coded the same as for sequential files.

The DSN operand   When only one DD statement is used to define an ISAM file, the DSN operand is coded the same as for a sequential file. However, a special form of the DSN operand is used for ISAM files when areas of the file are defined separately. In this case, a qualifier name in parentheses is appended to the permanent name of the file like this:

```
//ISAMFILE      DD      DSN=MSTRFLE(INDEX),...
//              DD      DSN=MSTRFLE(PRIME),...
//              DD      DSN=MSTRFLE(OVFLOW),...
```

Note that the ddname is coded only for the first DD statement and that the permanent name portion must be exactly the same for all three areas. In addition, the qualifier names must be spelled exactly as shown and the areas must be defined in the order presented above: the index area followed by the prime data area followed by the overflow area.

The SPACE operand   The SPACE operand must be coded on each of the DD statements for an ISAM file. When requesting space, the unit of measure must be CYL. Also, only the primary allocation can be specified; you cannot request a secondary allocation for an ISAM file.

If the DD statement for the index area is omitted (if the index area is embedded in the prime data area), the index parameter can be used to specify how many cylinders of the prime area are to be allocated to the index. For example, if you wanted to allocate ten cylinders to an ISAM file and you wanted the index to be embedded in the prime data area and to occupy one cylinder, you can code the SPACE operand like this:

```
SPACE=(CYL,(10,,1))
```

Notice in this example that, although the secondary allocation must be omitted, two commas must be included to indicate its omission.

You can also code the CONTIG parameter just as you can for sequential files, and you'll probably want to do this for most of your test files. However, you can't code the RLSE parameter for an ISAM file.

The DCB operand   As I mentioned in the last chapter, the DCB operand can be used to specify some of the operands normally coded in the DCB macro for a file. For an ISAM file, those operands include LRECL, BLKSIZE, RECFM, DSORG, KEYLEN, CYLOFL, NTM, OPTCD, and RKP. All of these parameters are optional for an ISAM file except when the file is being loaded. Then, the DSORG operand must be coded in the DD statement for the file even if it's coded in the DCB macro in the program. This operand is coded as

```
DCB=DSORG=IS
```

Two illustrative job streams

Figures 14-16 and 14-17 show two job streams that include DD statements for ISAM files. Figure 14-16 shows the JCL that I used to test the file creation program in figure 14-5. As you can see, I decided to code only one

```
//PRINCE        JOB    (MMA,PRINCE),'ANNE PRINCE'
//              EXEC   ASMFCG
//ASM.SYSIN     DD     *
                .
                .  SOURCE PROGRAM
                .
//GO.SYSUDUMP   DD     SYSOUT=A
//GO.AUDIT      DD     SYSOUT=A
//GO.INVLOAD    DD     DSN=MMA.TEST.INVLOAD,DISP=(OLD,KEEP),
//              UNIT=SYSDA,VOLUME=SER=MMA800
//GO.INVMSTR    DD     DSN=MMA.TEST.INVMSTR,DISP=(NEW,KEEP,DELETE),
//              UNIT=SYSDA,VOLUME=SER=MMA800,
//              SPACE=(CYL,3,,CONTIG),
//              DCB=DSORG=IS
//
```

Figure 14-16   The MVS JCL for the ISAM file creation program in figure 14-5

```
//PRINCE        JOB    (MMA,PRINCE),'ANNE PRINCE'
//              EXEC   ASMFCG
//ASM.SYSIN     DD     *
                .
                .  SOURCE PROGRAM
                .
//GO.SYSUDUMP   DD     SYSOUT=A
//GO.ERRMSG     DD     SYSOUT=A
//GO.SHIPTR     DD     DSN=MMA.TEST.SHIPTR,DISP=(OLD,KEEP),
//              UNIT=SYSDA,VOLUME=SER=MMA800
//GO.INVMSTR    DD     DSN=MMA.TEST.INVMSTR,DISP=(OLD,KEEP),
//              UNIT=SYSDA,VOLUME=SER=MMA800
//
```

Figure 14-17   The MVS JCL for the random update program in figure 14-14

DD statement for the ISAM file and let the index and overflow areas be embedded in the space allocated to the prime data area. In this case, the entire file will be contained in three cylinders, as indicated by the SPACE operand. In addition, I've requested that the three cylinders be contiguous by specifying the CONTIG parameter of the SPACE operand. The only other thing to notice in this DD statement is that the DCB operand has been coded to indicate the organization of the file.

Figure 14-17 shows the JCL I used to test the random update program in figure 14-14. As you can see, the operands coded for the ISAM file are the same as the operands for the sequential file. Because the ISAM file already exists, the DCB and SPACE parameters aren't required. And, because all three areas of the file reside on the same volume, only one DD statement is required.

Discussion

The most difficult part of writing the JCL statements for ISAM files is determining how large the index, prime data, and overflow areas should be. For test files, that difficulty can usually be eliminated by allocating enough space for all three areas and letting MVS determine how much of that space is to be used for each. For permanent files, however, you have to analyze the file to determine the space necessary for each area. Once you have this information, it is relatively simple to write the DD statements for an ISAM file. If you want more information about MVS JCL for ISAM files, we recommend our *MVS JCL* by Doug Lowe.

Terminology

embedded index area
embedded overflow area

Objective

Given the file specifications for a program that processes one or more ISAM files, code the JCL for running the program.

Chapter 15

The Basic Direct Access Method (BDAM)

 Because of the complexities of direct file processing, the Basic Direct Access Method (BDAM) is used infrequently. As a result, you may never be called upon to code routines for BDAM files in assembler language. On the other hand, some programmers prefer BDAM files for some purposes because they have more control over them than they have over the files of other access methods. As a result, if you know what you're doing, you can write file-handling routines for BDAM files that are extremely efficient.

In case you ever use them, this chapter presents what you need to know in order to use BDAM files. Topic 1 presents the BDAM concepts. Topic 2 presents assembler language for BDAM files. Topic 3 presents the JCL you need to know for processing BDAM files.

TOPIC 1   BDAM concepts

The main concern when creating BDAM files is determining where to store each record. The main concern when accessing the records in BDAM files is finding each record. To understand these concerns, you first need to know how you can address the records in a file when using BDAM. Then, you need to become familiar with the techniques you can use to store and locate records. In this topic, I'll first present the BDAM disk address formats. Then, I'll introduce you to file-handling techniques for BDAM files.

BDAM disk address formats

To access records in a BDAM file, you must supply the proper disk address each time a record is read or written. In other words, as far as BDAM is concerned, the records in a direct file have no sequence or organization. Only the disk addresses matter.

Figure 15-1 summarizes the three types of disk addresses you can use with BDAM. As you will see, the second and third formats have a distinct advantage over the first, so you probably won't use the first format in new programs. However, you might come in contact with the first format when you work with old programs.

Physical disk address format   The first format is cylinder number, head number, and record number. These values are supplied as hex (binary) values in an eight-byte format. For most devices, bytes 0-2 aren't used so they are set to hex zeros. In particular, bytes 1-2 apply to a data cell device that is all but obsolete. Bytes 3-4 must specify the cylinder number. If, for example, a device has 200 cylinders, the cylinder number can range from zero through 199. Bytes 5-6 must contain the head number, which is the same as the track number within the cylinder. If, for example, a device has 20 disk surfaces, the head numbers can range from 0 through 19. Finally, byte 8 is for record number. If the records are referred to by keys, the record number must be set to zero. But if the records are referred to by record number, it must be a value from 1 to the number of records stored on the track.

Relative track address format   The second disk address format is relative track number plus record number. A *relative track number* is the number of the track that a record is supposed to be on relative to the first track in the area for the file. Since the first track in a file is always relative track number zero, the relative track number can range from zero to the total number of tracks allocated to the file minus one.

Format 1:
An 8-byte physical disk address in hex (MBBCCHHR)

Bytes	Format	Contents	Remarks
0	M	Module number	Usually X'00' for disk.
1-2	BB	Bin number	Always X'0000' for disk.
3-4	CC	Cylinder number	Range is from zero to the number of cylinders per device minus 1.
5-6	HH	Head (or track) number	Range is from zero to the number of tracks per cylinder minus 1.
7	R	Record number	Zero if records are accessed by key. Otherwise, the number of the record on the track ranging from 1 to the number of records on the track.

Format 2:
A 3-byte relative track address in hex (TTR)

Bytes	Format	Contents	Remarks
0-1	TT	Relative track number	Range is from zero to the number of tracks allocated to the file.
2	R	Record number	Zero if records are accessed by key. Otherwise, the number of the record on the track ranging from 1 to the number of records on the track.

Format 3:
A 3-byte relative bolck address in hex (BBB)

Bytes	Format	Contents	Remarks
0-2	BBB	Relative track number	Range is from zero to the number of blocks allocated to the file.

Figure 15-1   Disk address formats for the DAM access method

The first two bytes of this addressing format specify the relative track number in hex. If, for example, you want to read a record located on track zero of cylinder 62 within a file that begins on track zero of cylinder 60 on a model 3330 DASD, the value in the relative track number field should be hex 26 (decimal 38) since there are 19 usable tracks in each cylinder of a 3330. For a record on track 15 of cylinder 63, the relative track number should be hex 48 (decimal 72).

The last byte of this format must contain the record number as a hex value. Again, if the records are referred to by key, the record number should be zero. Otherwise, the record number can range from one to the number of records per track.

When you use this address format, you don't have to be concerned with the actual location of a file as you do when you use the physical address format. A reference to relative track 38, for instance, will search the proper track whether the file begins on cylinder 60 or cylinder 128. That means that a file can be moved from one area of a disk to another without modifying the program. As a result, you'll probably use this address format or the one that follows whenever you use BDAM files.

Relative block address format   The third address format is relative block number. A *relative block number* is the number of the block that a record is supposed to be in relative to the first block in the file. Since direct files are always unblocked as far as BDAM is concerned, the block number is the same as the record number. In this format, the block number must be specified as a 3-byte hex value.

An introduction to file-handling techniques for BDAM files

Before you can create a direct file, you usually develop a routine that will determine the placement of each record in the file. A routine like this can be called a *randomizing routine* because it assigns disk locations to the records of a file on a random basis. A randomizing routine for a BDAM file converts the value of a field within a record (usually, the key field) to a disk address in one of the three forms that is acceptable to BDAM.

Because the purpose of this book is to teach you assembler language, not how to develop randomizing routines, I'm not going to try to present different techniques that can be used in randomizing routines. If you ever use BDAM, you'll probably be able to develop your own routines without any special training. Otherwise, you can do some research on your own to learn more about randomizing routines. At this time, then, I will present only one example of a randomizing routine so you have the general idea of what one entails.

Figure 15-2 presents a simple example of a randomizing routine for loading and accessing the records in a BDAM file. In this case, 3000 inventory master records are supposed to be stored in a disk area consisting of 200 tracks with a maximum of 20 records per track. These records are supposed to be in count-key-data format so they can be accessed by relative track number plus key. As you would guess, the key area for each record will contain the part number of the inventory item. Since the part numbers are seven digits long in character format, the key areas are seven bytes long.

Since 3000 records can be stored in only 150 tracks with 20 records per track, you can see that 1000 of the record positions won't be used for this file. These positions can be used for records that are added to the file

Characteristics of the file

A file of 3000 inventory master records is to be stored in a BDAM file of 200 tracks with a maximum of 20 records per track. The records will be stored in count-key-data format, and they will be accessed by relative track number plus key.

Problem of the randomizing routine

To convert the seven-digit key (part number) of each master record to a relative track number.

The division/remainder method for calculating relative track number

Divide the key in each master record by 200. Then, the remainder is a number between 0 and 199 that can be used as the relative track number for the record.

The routine for loading the records in the file

1. Convert the part number to relative track number using the division/remainder method.

2. Write the record in the next available record position on the relative track. If the track is full, write the record in the next available record position on any of the nine tracks that follow. If relative track 199 is reached, continue the search for an open position with relative track zero. If an open position can't be found in the relative track or the nine tracks that follow, print an error message and skip the record.

The routine for accessing the records in the file

1. Convert the part number of the desired record to relative track number using the division/remainder method.

2. Search the relative track for a key equal to the key of the desired record. If an equal key can't be found, search the next track in sequence and continue the search until a total of ten tracks have been searched. If the relative track number reaches 199 during the search, continue with relative track zero. If a record can't be found in the relative track or the nine tracks that follow, stop searching and assume the record can't be found.

3. When an equal key is found, read the record that follows the key area.

Figure 15-2   One method of loading and accessing the records in a direct file using BDAM

later on. Also, as you will see in a moment, they make it easier for the file loading routine to find available record positions for the records of the file. In general, then, you allocate more space to a direct file than is actually needed for the number of records in the file.

The problem of the randomizing routine is to convert a record's part number, which may range from 0000000 through 9999999 to a relative track number between 0 and 199. This data will be used to move the access mechanism to the selected cylinder and to turn the selected head on. Then, the appropriate record can be located by searching for a key equal to the record's part number.

One common method for calculating relative track number is called the *division/remainder method*. In figure 15-2, this method is used to calculate the relative track number for a record by dividing the part number by the number of tracks allocated to the file. Since 200 tracks are allocated to the file, each part number is divided by 200. Then, the remainder is a number between zero and 199, so it can be used as the relative track number for the record.

The problem with this method is that the calculation may generate the same track number for more than 20 records, but each track can hold a maximum of 20 records. This means that *track overflow* will occur for the 21st record that is assigned to each track and all subsequent records that are assigned to that track. As a result, the routines for loading and accessing the records in the file must provide for track overflow.

If you check the routines for loading and accessing records in figure 15-2, you can see that they provide for track overflow in a straightforward manner. If a track is full when a loading routine tries to write a record on it, the routine writes the record on the next available record location in the tracks that follow it. If the routine can't find an open location after looking for one in ten successive tracks, it prints an error message, skips the record, and continues the loading process with the next record in the input file.

The accessing routine in figure 15-2 is consistent with the loading routine. If an accessing routine can't find a record on a track, it searches for the record in the tracks that follow. After ten tracks have been searched, the accessing routine assumes the record can't be found. Since 1000 extra record positions are assigned to the file, the loading routine should be able to find open positions for each record without too much searching. Similarly, the accessing routine shouldn't have to do too much searching to find a record either.

Although this example is quite simple, I hope you get the general idea of what the file-handling routines for a BDAM file must provide for. Sometimes, if the keys of the file are planned with direct file processing in mind, the routine can be quite simple with no provision for track overflow because it won't ever be necessary. Sometimes, it can be extremely difficult to develop a routine that provides for track overflow and that still runs with satisfactory efficiency.

When records in a BDAM file are blocked, additional programming is required because BDAM doesn't provide for blocked records. As a result, you must provide your own blocking and deblocking routines. To load a blocked file, the records have to be randomized to a block of records rather than to a relative track. Then, overflow records for each block can be stored in the next available block or in separate overflow areas. To access the records, the randomizing routine must search the selected block and the related overflow areas until the desired record is found.

Discussion	As you will see in the next topic, the assembler language macros for BDAM files are relatively difficult to use. In addition, the routines for loading and accessing BDAM files are likely to be relatively difficult to design and code. Because of these difficulties, BDAM files are used infrequently.
Terminology	relative track number relative block number randomizing routine division/remainder method track overflow
Objective	Describe the disk address formats that BDAM offers for accessing a record by relative track number plus key or record number and by relative block number.

TOPIC 2   Assembler language for BDAM files

In the last chapter, I discussed the three items that a program using a basic access method must pass to the I/O module in order to perform an I/O operation. In case you didn't read the last chapter yet, let me review these items. First, the program must pass a DCB, which is done by coding a DCB macro. Second, the program must pass a DECB, which is done by coding READ or WRITE macros in standard or list form. Third, the program must provide a link to and from the I/O module, which is done by coding a READ or WRITE macro in standard or execute form.

In this topic, I'll first describe the operands of the DCB macro for BDAM files. Second, I'll show you how to use DECBs by coding READ and WRITE macros. Third, I'll present three other macros used for processing BDAM files. Finally, I'll present two programs that illustrate BDAM processing.

Because direct files can be processed in many different ways, I make no attempt in this chapter to illustrate the most common ways that BDAM files are used. Nevertheless, when you complete this chapter, you should be able to apply the BDAM macros to a wide range of programming problems.

DCB OPERANDS

The most widely used operands of the DCB macro for BDAM files are summarized in figure 15-3. Although this summary is largely self-explanatory, here is some additional information about some of the operands.

DSORG   The DSORG operand is coded DA for all direct file operations except file creation. Creation is a unique function because the direct file is actually generated as a sequential file processed through the *Basic Sequential Access Method (BSAM)*. Therefore, the DSORG operand is coded PS for file creation. However, when the file-creation program is executed, the DD statement in the JCL for the file must specify direct organization. The result is that the file is created as a sequential file, but it can be processed as a direct file later on.

RECFM   Although you can provide blocking and deblocking routines of your own, BDAM regards all records as unblocked. The records can be fixed-length, variable-length, or undefined. In most cases, you will use F for unblocked, fixed-length records. If V is specified, the programmer is responsible for calculating the block length and for placing it in the

Keyword	Programmer code	Remarks
DSORG	PS DA	To create a direct file, use PS. Otherwise, use DA.
RECFM	F,V,U	Use F for fixed-length unblocked records; V for variable-length unblocked records; U for undefined records.
MACRF	See figure 15-4	
BLKSIZE	Block length	The maximum length of the data area for a record in the file. This does **not** include the count or key area.
KEYLEN	Key length	The length of the key area for the file. Specified only for load functions.
BUFNO	Number of buffers	This must be coded when the file is created, unless it's specified in the DD statement for the file. It's usually coded as 2.
BUFL	Buffer length	Same as block size unless dynamic buffering is used for the key area as well as the data area. Then, the buffer length must include the key length.
OPTCD	Access method options	One or more of the following codes can be used: A = Physical disk address format E = Extended search F = Feedback should be in the format passed to the I/O module; if omitted, feedback should be in physical disk address format R = Relative block address format W = Write verification If neither A nor R is coded, relative track address format is assumed.
LIMCT	Number of tracks or blocks to be searched	Required if OPTCD = E. If relative block format is used, the number is in blocks. If relative track format is used, the number is in tracks.
SYNAD	Label	Label of error checking routine.
DDNAME	DD name	

Figure 15-3   DCB operands for BDAM

appropriate format in the first four bytes of the block area. The format of these four bytes is the same as it is for the bytes in variable-length QSAM files, as described in chapter 13. However, the variable-length format for BDAM files is rarely used. When U is specified, the records can be fixed- or variable-length.

MACRF   Figure 15-4 presents the most frequently coded forms of the MACRF operand for BDAM files. The first form (WL) is a special form that's used only for loading BDAM files. It indicates that the WRITE macro is to be used and that BSAM will be used to create a BDAM file. It's only valid if DSORG=PS is specified.

For all other types of operations, MACRF indicates whether a READ (R) or WRITE (W) macro, or both, will be issued. It also indicates whether the records will be retrieved by address including the record number on the track (I), by key (K), or both. If READ operations are specified, dynamic buffering may be requested (S), but dynamic buffering is invalid for WRITE operations. If you omit this code, any READ macro must name a work area defined in the program. For a WRITE operation, the MACRF operand indicates whether records are going to be added to the file (A). Finally, the MACRF operand indicates whether the WAIT (no code) or CHECK (C) macro will be used.

BLKSIZE   The BLKSIZE operand specifies the maximum length of the data area for a block. This does not include the count or key area for a block. After a file has been created, you don't have to code this operand because MVS can get it from the label for the file.

KEYLEN   If a BDAM file is in count-key-data format, the KEYLEN operand must be coded in a program that creates the file. It specifies the length of the key field. However, you don't have to code this operand once a file has been created because MVS can get it from the label for the file.

BUFNO   When you create a direct file using BSAM, you have to specify the number of buffers to be used. You can do this either by coding the BUFNO operand of the DCB macro or by including the BUFNO parameter in the DCB operand of the DD statement for the file. In either case, it's common to specify two buffers unless the execution time of the program is critical, in which case more buffers may improve performance.

BUFL   If dynamic buffering is specified in the MACRF operand, you must code the BUFL operand. It specifies the buffer length. This length is normally equal to the block size. If, however, the file is in count-key-data format and the READ or WRITE macros that process the file specify dynamic buffering for the key area as well as the data area, the buffer length must include the length of the key.

OPTCD   You use the OPTCD operand to specify several unrelated BDAM options. First, it indicates the type of disk address format to be used: A indicates physical address format and R indicates relative block format. If neither A nor R is coded, relative track format is assumed.

Next, you can request the *extended search option* by coding E. When you code this option, the program searches multiple tracks or blocks (depending on the disk address format used) to locate a specified record or to find available space for a record to be added to the file. The number of

Formats

Create only	WL
READ only	$R\left\{\begin{matrix}K\\ I\\ KI\end{matrix}\right\}[S][C]$
WRITE only	$W\left\{\begin{matrix}A\\ K\\ I\\ AK\\ AI\\ KI\\ AKI\end{matrix}\right\}[C]$
READ and WRITE	$(R\left\{\begin{matrix}K\\ I\\ KI\end{matrix}\right\}[S][C],W\left\{\begin{matrix}A\\ K\\ I\\ AK\\ AI\\ KI\\ AKI\end{matrix}\right\}[C])$

Explanation

A = New blocks are to be added to the file.

C = The CHECK macro will be used.

I = The search is to be made by block number.

K = The search is to be made by key.

R = The READ macro will be used.

S = Dynamic buffering will be requested.

W = The WRITE macro will be used.

Figure 15-4 MACRF entries for BDAM DCBs

tracks or blocks searched is specified by the LIMCT operand, which I'll discuss in a moment.

When you issue a READ or WRITE macro, you can request *feedback*. This means that the I/O module should return the address of the record being processed to the program. When feedback is requested, the F option of the OPTCD operand specifies that the returned address be in the format passed to the I/O module. If F is not coded and a READ or WRITE macro requests feedback, the returned disk address is in physical address format.

Finally, you can use option code W to request a validity check on write operations. Because this is a time consuming operation, it is rarely used.

LIMCT   If the extended search option is requested, the LIMCT operand must be specified. If relative track address format is used, LIMCT specifies the number of tracks to be searched, including the starting track. If relative block address format is used, LIMCT specifies the number of blocks to be searched, including the starting block. Both the request for extended search and LIMCT are ignored if physical disk address format is used.

SYNAD   Little error analysis is done by the BDAM I/O modules themselves. As a result, you should include the SYNAD operand in most programs that process BDAM files. This operand specifies the label of the instruction that's given control when an I/O error occurs.

CREATING AND USING A DECB

The READ and WRITE macros are used to create the DECB for a file and the instructions that link to the I/O modules for the access method. In this section, I'll show you how to use these macros and the DECB they create. If you've read the last chapter, this material will be mostly review for you. However, there are a few differences in the coding of the macros and in the DECB itself that you need to be aware of when you use BDAM files.

The READ and WRITE macros

The READ and WRITE macros have three forms, just as they do for a BISAM file. The standard form of each macro creates both a DECB and the instructions that link to an I/O module. The list form of each macro creates only a DECB, while the execute form creates only the instructions that link to the I/O module. Figure 15-5 presents the format of the READ and WRITE macros for BDAM processing.

DECB name   The first operand, DECB name, gives the label that's assigned to the DECB that's generated as part of the macro expansion. This label can be used to refer to the DECB in your program.

Type   The type operand specifies the type of operation to be performed. For a READ macro, the type code can be DI for a search by address or DK for a search by key. For a WRITE macro, the type code can be DA, DI, or DK. DA is used to add a new block to a file wherever space is available with the search starting at the address in the block-address field. DI is used to write a block at the address specified in the block-address field. And DK is used to write a block identified by the key in the key-address field.
   For both the READ and WRITE macros, F can be specified (DAF, DIF, DKF) to request feedback. When feedback is requested, the block address is returned in the area specified by the block-address operand. If

Format

$$\begin{Bmatrix} READ \\ WRITE \end{Bmatrix} \text{DECB-name,type,DCB-address,} \begin{Bmatrix} area-address \\ 'S' \end{Bmatrix},$$

$$\begin{Bmatrix} length \\ 'S' \end{Bmatrix}, \begin{Bmatrix} key-address \\ 'S' \\ 0 \end{Bmatrix}, \text{ block-address,[MF=} \begin{Bmatrix} L \\ E \end{Bmatrix}]$$

Explanation

DECB address — The label assigned to the DECB as part of the macro expansion.

type — DK indicates search by key; DI indicates search by address; and DA (WRITE only) indicates new records will be added to the file. F requests feedback.

DCB address — The address, usually in label form, of the DCB that describes the file.

area address — The address, usually in label form, of the area into which the block is to be read (READ) or of the area from which the record is to be written (WRITE). 'S' can be coded to indicate dynamic buffering. If 'S' is coded for a READ operation, the address of the buffer is placed in the DECB when the READ is issued. For a WRITE operation, 'S' can only be coded for an update function.

length — The number of bytes to be read or written. Code 'S' to have the length extracted from the DCB.

key address — The label of the key area in the program. This field must contain the record key for a READ or WRITE operation by key. Otherwise, the key is read into or written from this area. Code 'S' if you want to include the key in the buffer area. Code 0 if the key isn't used.

block address — The address, as a label or register number, of the program area that contains the disk address. It must be large enough to provide for an address in the format specified in the OPTCD operand of the DCB. If feedback is requested, the returned address will be placed in this field.

MF — This operand indicates the form of the macro. If omitted, standard is assumed. If specified, L indicates list form; E indicates execute form.

Figure 15-5 The READ and WRITE macros for BDAM

OPTCD=F has been specified in the DCB for the file, the address is returned in the format that was originally passed to the I/O module. Otherwise, the address is returned in physical disk format.

DCB address The DCB-address operand specifies the address of the DCB macro for the file. It's usually coded as the label of the DCB, but it may also specify a register that's been loaded with the address of the DCB.

Area address The area-address operand specifies where the area for the block to be read or written is located. This area can be defined in your program, or 'S' can be specified to indicate dynamic buffering. For a WRITE operation, 'S' can only be coded for an update operation and only if 'S' was coded for the area-address operand in the associated READ macro.

Length   The length operand specifies the number of bytes to be read or written. Although a specific length can be specified, 'S' is usually coded to allow the length to be extracted from the DCB.

Key address   The key-address operand can be coded in three forms depending on the type of READ or WRITE macro being issued. If the file is to be searched by key, you should code the label of the field that contains the key of the record to be read or written. Otherwise, if 'S' was specified for the area-address operand, 'S' can be specified for the key-address operand so the key will be read into or written from the buffer area. In this case, the buffer area must be large enough to contain both the key and data areas, and this length must be specified in the BUFL operand of the DCB for the file. If the key isn't going to be used at all, you should code 0.

Block address   The block-address operand identifies the field that contains the disk address. The length of this field depends on the address format used and whether feedback is requested. If feedback is requested, the address is returned to the field addressed by this operand.

MF   The MF operand specifies the form of the macro to be generated. If you omit this operand, standard form is assumed. If you code MF=L, the list form is generated. If you code MF=E, the execute form is generated.

Using the different forms of the READ and WRITE macros

If you code a program that reads or writes a BDAM file, you normally code the standard forms of the READ and WRITE macros. However, if you code a program that reads records from and writes records to the same file, the list and execute forms must be used. Then, the same DECB can be used by both macros.

In addition to the forms of the READ and WRITE macros presented in figure 15-5, a special form of the WRITE macro is used when a direct file is created. (Remember, it's really BSAM that's being invoked when a BDAM file is created.) The format of this WRITE macro is given in figure 15-6. As you can see, it's like the standard WRITE macro for BDAM, but 'S' can't be specified for the area-address operand and the key-address and block-address operands are omitted.

For the type code, SF is usually coded, which indicates that a new data block is to be written in the next available disk location. In this case, the block to be written must be in the area addressed by the area-address operand. Also, if the records in the file contain keys, the key must precede the data in this area.

Format

```
WRITE DECB-name,type,DCB-name,area-address,{length}
                                            {'S'   }
```

Explanation

DECB name	The label assigned to the DECB as part of the macro expansion.
type	Code SF to add new blocks of data; SD to add dummy blocks of data with keys.
DCB name	The address of the DCB that describes the file.
area address	The address of the storage area that contains the block to be written. If key format is used, the key must precede the data in this area. For an SD type WRITE, the area need only be large enough to contain the key plus one byte.
length	Coded only for blocks with undefined lengths. It specifies the number of data bytes to be written. Code 'S' if you want the length extracted from the DCB.

Figure 15-6   The standard WRITE macro for BDAM file creation

Sometimes, a direct file is created as a file of dummy records. In this case, a program creates a file of records with the proper lengths, but no meaningful data is placed in the records. They're usually just filled with hex 00 or hex FF. To create a file of dummy records without keys, you just write them as if they contained meaningful data.

To create a file of dummy records with keys, you use the WRITE macro with type code SD. Then, the I/O module generates a dummy key for each record on a track. The key has hex FF in the leftmost byte and the rest of the key is filled with hex zeros. In addition, the I/O module fills the first byte of each data record with a binary number whose value is equal to the number of the record on the track. For example, in a file with four-byte keys, the dummy key generated for the thirteenth record on each track will be hex FF000000, and the first byte of the data area will contain hex 0D. When type code SD is used, the length of the buffer area is the key length plus one byte for the data area. The rest of the data area on disk is filled with hex zeros.

Using the values in the DECB

The values in the DECB for a BDAM file are used in much the same way that they are for a BISAM file. However, the format of the DECB, which is presented in figure 15-7, is slightly different. The two fields you need to be familiar with are the error-bytes field and the buffer-area-address field. Both of these fields are placed in the DECB when the link to the I/O module is executed.

Displacement	Length	Field
0	4	ECB (Event Control Block)
1	2	Error bytes (actually, bytes 2 and 3 of the ECB)
4	2	Type indicator
6	2	Length value
8	4	DCB address
12	4	Buffer area address
16	4	IOB address
20	4	Key field address
24	4	Block address

Figure 15-7   DECB fields for BDAM files

If you're using dynamic buffering for a file and you want to refer to specific fields in a record, you'll need to use the buffer-area-address field of the DECB. This address is in bytes 13 through 16 (displacement 12 through 15) of the DECB. If the records are in count-key-data format and you specify that dynamic buffering is to be used for the key area as well as for the data area, this field addresses the first byte of the key for the record. If dynamic buffering isn't used for the key or if the records are in count-data format, it addresses the first byte of the data area. You'll see how this address is used in the random update program later in this topic.

The other field that's of use is the error-bytes field. It's located in bytes 2 and 3 (displacements 1 and 2) of the DECB. These are actually the middle bytes of the Event Control Block. Figure 15-8 gives the meanings of each of the bit positions in these two error bytes. The bit you'll probably need to check most often is bit 0, which indicates a not-found condition. In most cases, the program should be terminated if any of the other errors occur.

OTHER MACROS FOR BDAM FILE HANDLING

In addition to the DCB, READ, and WRITE macros, there are three other macros that are commonly used for BDAM processing. These are the CHECK, WAIT, and FREEDBUF macros. Their formats are given in figure 15-9, and they work just as they do for ISAM files.

Byte	Bit position	READ	WRITE	Error condition
1	0	X	X	No record found.
	1	X	X	Record length check.
	2		X	Not enough space to write the record.
	3	X	X	Invalid request (one of the bits in error byte 2 will be on also).
	4	X	X	Uncorrectable I/O error.
	5	X	X	End-of-data record has been read.
	6	X	X	Uncorrectable error.
	7		X	Exclusive control requested for a record that wasn't read with exclusive control (not covered in this book).
2	0			Not used.
	1		X	File opened as input, but the WRITE macro requests output.
	2	X	X	LIMCT = 0 when extended search was requested.
	3	X	X	Block requested is outside file limits.
	4	X	X	Attempt made to write a record on a track in record position 0.
	5	X	X	Key search requested when key length was zero or no key address was supplied.
	6	X	X	Options not coded in DCB were requested.
	7		X	Attempt made to add a record with a key beginning with hex FF (a dummy record).

Figure 15-8   DECB error bytes for BDAM files

The CHECK and WAIT macros   Either a CHECK or WAIT macro must follow each READ or WRITE macro that you use. One of these macros is necessary because MVS doesn't wait for an I/O operation to finish before returning control to a program. As a result, you must code the CHECK or WAIT macro to stop the execution of your program until the preceding I/O operation has been completed. If an I/O error occurs, the CHECK macro causes the SYNAD error routine to be invoked; the WAIT macro causes the program to terminate abnormally. If the SYNAD operand isn't coded on the DCB for a file and an error occurs, the CHECK macro also causes the program to terminate abnormally.

The CHECK macro

```
CHECK        DECB-address
             [,DSORG=ALL]
```

The WAIT macro

```
WAIT         ECB=DECB-address
```

The FREEDBUF macro

```
FREEDBUF     DECB-name,D,DCB-address
```

Figure 15-9   The CHECK, WAIT, and FREEDBUF macros for BDAM

When you code the CHECK macro, you can either omit the DSORG operand or code it as ALL. If you omit it, the macro can't be used for BISAM files. If you code it as ALL, the macro can be used for all files. You can use this macro for more than one access method by coding a register number instead of a label for the DECB address.

The FREEDBUF macro   When a WRITE macro is issued, any buffers allocated dynamically to a file are released so they can be used for subsequent records read by the program. However, when a WRITE macro isn't issued after a block has been read, the block stays in the buffer area until the file is closed. To avoid this, you can use the FREEDBUF macro to explicitly release a block in the buffer area. For instance, this macro would release the buffer for a file named INVMAST that has a DECB named IMDECB:

```
FREEDBUF IMDECB,D,INVMAST
```

Here, the D indicates that BDAM is being used.

TWO ILLUSTRATIVE PROGRAMS

Normally, when a direct file is created, some type of randomizing routine is used to determine the address of each record in the file. However, the illustrative programs in figures 15-10 and 15-11 don't use randomizing routines. Instead, a BDAM file is created by writing the records in sequence on the tracks of the file. Then, to access the records, the update program simply searches for the desired records in sequence by key, one track after another.

For most jobs, of course, this method of loading and accessing records would be so inefficient that it wouldn't be practical. However, if a file is small, this loading and accessing method could be practical. So, as you study these programs, assume that the file will require a maximum of only four tracks. This will make the programs somewhat more realistic. In any event, keep in mind that the purpose of these programs is to show you the assembler language code for BDAM files, not the routines that determine disk addresses.

A file creation program   The program in figure 15-10 creates a BDAM file of inventory master records from a sequential disk file with records that have a similar format. The key for each output record is the item number (6 bytes) and the rest of the output record is 50 bytes. If you assume that the entire file will fit on just four tracks of one cylinder, all of the tracks in the file can be searched by just one READ macro using the extended search option.

In the DCB for the BDAM file in figure 15-10, the operands must be coded in the special form required for direct file creation. DSORG must be coded PS, and MACRF must be coded WL. In addition, the BLKSIZE operand must specify the length of the data area (50), and the KEYLEN operand must specify the length of the key area (6).

For this program, the work area for the BDAM record must be large enough to contain both the data area and the key area. As a result, the work area is 56 bytes long. It is named DAWRKA.

The program logic is quite simple. First, a GET macro is executed to read a sequential input record into a work area defined in the program. Then, the fields in the record are moved or packed, one at a time, into the fields in the output record. Next, a WRITE macro is issued using the special form required for direct file creation. The CHECK macro that follows the WRITE macro refers to the DECB that was created by the WRITE macro. Since no SYNAD operand was coded in the DCB for the direct file, however, an error will cause the I/O module to terminate the execution of the program. If the record is processed without errors, the program branches back to get the next input record and the processing loop is repeated.

To load these records on a random basis, instead of a sequential basis, you would need two programs. The first program would fill the space reserved for the file with dummy records as discussed earlier. The second program would perform an update operation to load the actual data into the records. In other words, a randomizing routine would develop a disk address for each record in the file so the program could read the dummy record at that address. Then, the key and data for that record would be updated and the record would be rewritten at the same address.

A random update program   Figure 15-11 presents a program that updates the BDAM file created by the program in figure 15-10. In this program, a QSAM file of shipment transactions is used to update the inventory master records.

Let's start by looking at the operands of the DCB that describes the BDAM inventory master file. First, for the MACRF operand, I've coded

```
LOADDA     START  0
BEGIN      SAVE   (14,12)
           BALR   3,0
           USING  *,3
           ST     13,SAVE+4
           LA     13,SAVE
           OPEN   (SEQFILE,INPUT,DAFILE,OUTPUT)
NXTREC     GET    SEQFILE,INPTWRKA
           MVC    DITEM,IITEM
           MVC    DDESC,IDESC
           MVC    DUM,IUM
           MVC    DORDPOL,IORDPOL
           PACK   DORDQTY,IORDQTY
           PACK   DORDPT,IORDPT
           PACK   DSAFSTK,ISAFSTK
           PACK   DONHAND,IONHAND
           PACK   DONORD,IONORD
           PACK   DALLOC,IALLOC
WRITE      WRITE  DADECB,SF,DAFILE,DAWRKA       WRITE RECORD IN SEQUENCE
           CHECK  DADECB                        CHECK FOR I/O ERRORS
           B      NXTREC
EOFDISK    CLOSE  (SEQFILE,,DAFILE)
           L      13,SAVE+4
           RETURN (14,12)
SEQFILE    DCB    DSORG=PS,                                              X
                  RECFM=FB,                                              X
                  MACRF=GM,                                              X
                  BLKSIZE=248,                                           X
                  LRECL=62,                                              X
                  DDNAME=INPTREC,                                        X
                  EODAD=EOFDISK
DAFILE     DCB    DSORG=PS,                                              X
                  RECFM=F,                                               X
                  MACRF=WL,                                              X
                  BLKSIZE=50,                                            X
                  KEYLEN=6,                                              X
                  BUFNO=2,                                               X
                  DDNAME=DAFILE
SAVE       DS     18F
INPTWRKA   DS     0CL62
IITEM      DS     CL6
IDESC      DS     CL20
IUM        DS     CL4
IORDPOL    DS     CL2
IORDQTY    DS     CL5
IORDPT     DS     CL5
ISAFSTK    DS     CL5
IONHAND    DS     CL5
IONORD     DS     CL5
IALLOC     DS     CL5
DAWRKA     DS     0CL56
DITEM      DS     CL6
DDESC      DS     CL20
DUM        DS     CL4
```

Figure 15-10   A BDAM file creation program (part 1 of 2)

```
DORDPOL   DS    CL2
DORDQTY   DS    PL4
DORDPT    DS    PL4
DSAFSTK   DS    PL4
DONHAND   DS    PL4
DONORD    DS    PL4
DALLOC    DS    PL4
          END   BEGIN
```

Figure 15-10   A BDAM file creation program (part 2 of 2)

(RKSC,WK), which indicates that both the READ and WRITE macros will be used and that both will access records by key. With the READ macro, dynamic buffering and the CHECK macro will be used; with the WRITE macro, the WAIT macro will be used since code C isn't specified.

The OPTCD operand in the DCB macro specifies E, which means that the extended search option is to be used. Also, because neither A nor R is specified in the OPTCD operand, relative track addressing is assumed. In conjunction with the extended search option, the LIMCT operand specifies 4, which means that the search will continue by key for three tracks after the addressed track. Finally, because dynamic buffering is used only for the data area of each record and not for the key area, the buffer area only needs to be long enough for the data area of each block (50 bytes).

Now, take a look at the READ and WRITE macros for the file. After the DCBs for the files, you will find a READ macro for the BDAM file in list mode. Then, in the main body of the program, you will find READ and WRITE macros for the file in execute mode. The list mode macro creates the DECB for the file; each execute mode macro links to the I/O module for the required function. In this program, the operands for all three macros are identical, except for the MF operand, which indicates the mode of the macro.

All of the macros for the BDAM file indicate that the records are to be retrieved by key (DK), that dynamic buffering is to be used for the data areas of the records, that the record key will be placed in a field named ITEMKEY, and that the search should start at the address in the field named BLKADDR. Because the value of BLKADDR has been initialized as zero, this will cause the search to start at the first track of the file. In this case, the block address field is three bytes long because the OPTCD operand in the DCB for the file indicates (by omission) relative track address format.

Now, look at the instructions to see how the program works. First, a transaction record is read and the item number is moved into the key field of the inventory master record (ITEMKEY). Then, the execute form of the READ macro is issued followed by a CHECK macro. This causes a search of the four-track file starting with the first track. When the I/O operation finishes, the CHECK macro causes the SYNAD routine to be executed if an error has occurred.

```
RDMUPD    START 0
BEGIN     SAVE  (14,12)
          BALR  3,0
          USING *,3
          USING MSTRRCD,4
          ST    13,SAVE+4
          LA    13,SAVE
          OPEN  (SHIPTR,INPUT,ERRMSG,OUTPUT,INVMSTR,UPDAT)
READSHP   GET   SHIPTR,SHPWRKA
          MVC   ITEMKEY,SHPITEM
          READ  INVDECB,DK,INVMSTR,'S','S',ITEMKEY,BLKADDR,MF=E
          CHECK INVDECB                CHECK FOR I/O ERRORS
          L     4,INVDECB+12           LOAD R4 WITH ADDRESS OF BUFFER AREA
          PACK  PACKQTY,SHPQTY
          SP    MONHAND,PACKQTY
          WRITE INVDECB,DK,INVMSTR,'S','S',ITEMKEY,BLKADDR,MF=E
          WAIT  ECB=INVDECB            WAIT FOR RECORD TO BE WRITTEN
          B     READSHP
ERRCHK    TM    INVDECB+1,X'80'        TEST FOR NOT FOUND CONDITION
          BNO   ABORT
          MVC   LITEM,SHPITEM
          MVC   LERR,=C'NO RECORD FOUND'
          PUT   ERRMSG,ERRLINE
          B     READSHP
ABORT     ABEND 700,DUMP
EOFINPT   CLOSE (SHIPTR,,ERRMSG,,INVMSTR)
          L     13,SAVE+4
          RETURN (14,12)
SHIPTR    DCB   DSORG=PS,                                        X
                RECFM=FB,                                        X
                MACRF=GM,                                        X
                BLKSIZE=240,                                     X
                LRECL=24,                                        X
                DDNAME=SHIPTR,                                   X
                EODAD=EOFINPT
ERRMSG    DCB   DSORG=PS,                                        X
                RECFM=F,                                         X
                MACRF=PM,                                        X
                BLKSIZE=132,                                     X
                LRECL=132,                                       X
                DDNAME=ERRMSG
INVMSTR   DCB   DSORG=DA,                                        X
                RECFM=F,                                         X
                MACRF=(RKSC,WK),                                 X
                BUFL=50,                                         X
                OPTCD=E,                                         X
                LIMCT=3,                                         X
                SYNAD=ERRCHK,                                    X
                DDNAME=INVMSTR
          READ  INVDECB,DK,INVMSTR,'S','S',ITEMKEY,BLKADDR,MF=L
SAVE      DS    18F
PACKQTY   DS    PL4
ITEMKEY   DS    CL6
BLKADDR   DC    X'000000'
```

Figure 15-11   A BDAM random update program (part 1 of 2)

```
SHPWRKA   DS    OCL24
          DS    CL6
SHPITEM   DS    CL6
SHPQTY    DS    CL4
          DS    CL8
ERRLINE   DS    OCL132
          DC    5C' '
LITEM     DS    CL6
          DC    52C' '
LERR      DS    CL15
          DC    54C' '
MSTRRCD   DSECT
MDESC     DS    CL20
MUM       DS    CL4
MORDPOL   DS    CL2
MORDQTY   DS    PL4
MORDPT    DS    PL4
MSAFSTK   DS    PL4
MONHAND   DS    PL4
MONORD    DS    PL4
MALLOC    DS    PL4
          END   BEGIN
```

Figure 15-11   A BDAM random update program (part 2 of 2)

If the key is found and the record is successfully read, the address of the buffer area is loaded into register 4. This address is loaded from the DECB for the file (INVDECB+12). Because register 4 is associated with a DSECT that defines the master record, the fields in the buffer can be referred to by the names in the DSECT. Then, the program updates the master record and writes it back on the file in its original location using the execute form of the WRITE macro. The WAIT macro, which follows the WRITE macro, causes an abnormal program termination if the WRITE operation didn't execute successfully. Finally, the program branches back to read the next input record.

If an I/O error occurs during the execution of the READ macro, the program tests the error bytes in the DECB to see what caused the error. If no record is found with the key specified, the first bit of the first error byte will be on. This bit is tested by the TM instruction, which is the first instruction of the ERRHCK routine. If this bit is on, an error line is printed on the error report and the program branches to read the next input record. If this bit is off, it means that some other error has occurred, so the program branches to ABORT, where the ABEND macro is issued to terminate the program.

DISCUSSION

Although it may seem like BDAM files are relatively easy to use, they're much more difficult when they're accessed by address rather than by key and when randomizing routines are used. Because of these difficulties, BDAM files aren't popular. In some cases, though, a BDAM file can offer a good solution to a particular programming need.

Terminology

Basic Sequential Access Method
BSAM
extended search option
feedback

Objective

Given program specifications that require the use of BDAM files, code a program that satisfies the specifications.

TOPIC 3   MVS JCL for BDAM files

The JCL required for BDAM files is almost identical to that for QSAM files. For that reason, I won't cover the required JCL statements in detail here. Instead, I will simply present an example of the JCL required for processing a BDAM file.

A job stream for creating a BDAM file

Figure 15-12 is the job stream I used for assembling and testing the file creation program in figure 15-10. The only new thing here is the DSORG operand. This operand must always be coded as DA, even when the DSORG operand in the DCB is coded PS for file creation. That way, even though the file is created as a sequential file, it can be accessed later as a direct file. The DSORG operand is only required when the file is created.

You should already be familiar with the rest of the code in figure 15-12. The UNIT and VOLUME operands specify that the file is to reside on a direct access device with serial number MMA800. The SPACE operand specifies that it's to be placed on four contiguous tracks.

It's also common for some additional DCB operands to be coded in the DD statement for a direct file. For example, when a direct file is created using BSAM, the BUFNO parameter must be coded if it isn't coded in the DCB macro for the file. Also, when an existing direct file is processed, it's common for the LIMCT and OPTCD operands to be coded in the DD statement. That way, you can use JCL to request the extended search option and to specify the number of tracks or blocks to be searched; you don't have to request it in the program.

Discussion   If you have already read the topic on JCL for sequential disk files, you shouldn't have any problem coding JCL for direct files. The only differences are in the coding of the DCB operand of the DD statement. For a description of all of the parameters that can be coded on the DCB operand, you can refer to the *Macro Instruction Reference* manual for your system.

Terminology   None

Objective   Given the file specifications for a program that processes a BDAM file, write the JCL for running the program.

```
//PRINCE          JOB    (MMA,PRINCE),'ANNE PRINCE'
//                EXEC   ASMFCG
//ASM.SYSIN       DD     *
                   .
                   .   SOURCE PROGRAM
                   .
//GO.SYSUDUMP     DD     SYSOUT=A
//GO.SEQFILE      DD     DSN=MMA.TEST.SEQFILE,DISP=(OLD,KEEP),
//                UNIT=SYSDA,VOLUME=SER=MMA800,
//GO.DAFILE       DD     DSN=MMA.TEST.DAFILE,DISP=(NEW,KEEP,DELETE),
//                UNIT=SYSDA,VOLUME=SER=MMA800,
//                SPACE=(TRK,4,CONTIG),
//                DCB=DSORG=DA
//
```

Figure 15-12   The MVS JCL for the BDAM file creation program in figure 15-10

Chapter 16

The Virtual Storage Access Method (VSAM)

VSAM (*Virtual Storage Access Method*) is the predominant DASD access method on MVS systems. But VSAM does more than just replace QSAM, ISAM, and BDAM with its entry-sequenced, key-sequenced, and relative-record data sets. It also provides efficiency improvements and better space management facilities than the non-VSAM access methods. In addition, it includes a multifunction utility program called *Access Method Services* (*AMS*) that lets you perform a variety of file-related functions.

Because VSAM is such a comprehensive access method, I couldn't begin to present everything there is to know about it in one chapter. Instead, I will present only the minimum that you need to know to write simple assembler programs that process VSAM files. Topic 1 introduces you to VSAM concepts and terminology. Topic 2 presents the assembler language for VSAM files. Topic 3 presents the JCL for VSAM files.

TOPIC 1   VSAM concepts

This topic introduces you to the terms and concepts you need to understand for processing VSAM files. First, it describes VSAM catalogs and areas. Then, it shows you how the three kinds of VSAM files are organized. By the way, the facilities this topic describes are for MVS/XA VSAM release 1.2, so if you're using a different release, some details may differ. Nevertheless, the basic concepts are the same.

VSAM CATALOGS

DASD files that use MVS's non-VSAM access methods are identified with labels stored in the VTOC of the volume on which they reside. In contrast, individual VSAM files don't have VTOC labels. They're identified by information stored in VSAM *catalogs*.

VSAM uses two kinds of catalogs: a *master catalog* and *user catalogs*. There's only one master catalog on a system. It stores label information for all user catalogs. In addition, it may store information for some VSAM data files. More often, though, information for a VSAM file is stored in a user catalog. The file is then said to be "cataloged" in and "owned" by the user catalog.

Figure 16-1 shows the relationships among the master catalog, user catalogs, and files. The shaded areas in the figure represent areas under the control of VSAM. Notice that there's no more than one catalog on each volume; that's a VSAM rule.

A catalog can own items on more than just the volume where it resides. For instance, user catalog 3 owns VSAM files on volumes 3, 4, and 5. Notice also that a catalog can own VSAM files that are on volumes that have other catalogs. For instance, user catalog 3 owns VSAM files on volume 3, but volume 3 contains user catalog 2. It's even possible for non-VSAM files to be cataloged in a VSAM catalog.

VSAM AREAS

Data spaces   The areas labelled "VSAM files" in figure 16-1 represent VSAM *data spaces*. As far as MVS is concerned, those areas are just that: VSAM space. The VSAM files that reside within a VSAM space (there may be many) aren't recorded in the VTOC. What's in the VSAM spaces is transparent to standard MVS facilities.

In the simplest case, an entire DASD volume can be defined as one VSAM space. But it's possible for only a part of a volume to be defined as a VSAM space. In figure 16-1, all of volume 4 is defined as VSAM space, but only part of volume 5 is. It's also possible for several VSAM data spaces to be defined on the same volume, as with volumes 1, 2, and 3 in the figure.

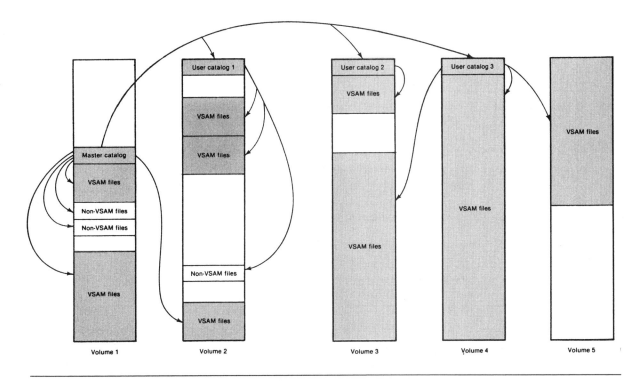

Figure 16-1   Possible VSAM catalog and file relationships

Clusters   In VSAM terms, a file, or *data set*, is a *cluster*. A cluster consists of a *data component* plus an optional *index component*. Before any records can be written to a VSAM file, you have to use AMS to define its cluster. This is in contrast to files managed by the non-VSAM access methods. With them, all you have to do is open the file and it's ready for use.

Control intervals and control areas   The unit of data that VSAM transfers between DASD and virtual storage is the *control interval*. A control interval may contain one or more fixed or variable length records, but the control interval itself is always fixed length. VSAM determines the optimum control interval size for a file based on the characteristics of the file and the DASDs that store it.

The VSAM control interval concept is much like blocking used with non-VSAM files. However, a control interval contains control information that isn't in a block. In addition, part of a control interval may be left empty so additions to the file can be made easily. That's not true, of course, for blocks in files that are managed by the non-VSAM access methods.

A group of adjacent control intervals forms a *control area* within a data space. When you define a cluster, VSAM formats control areas so

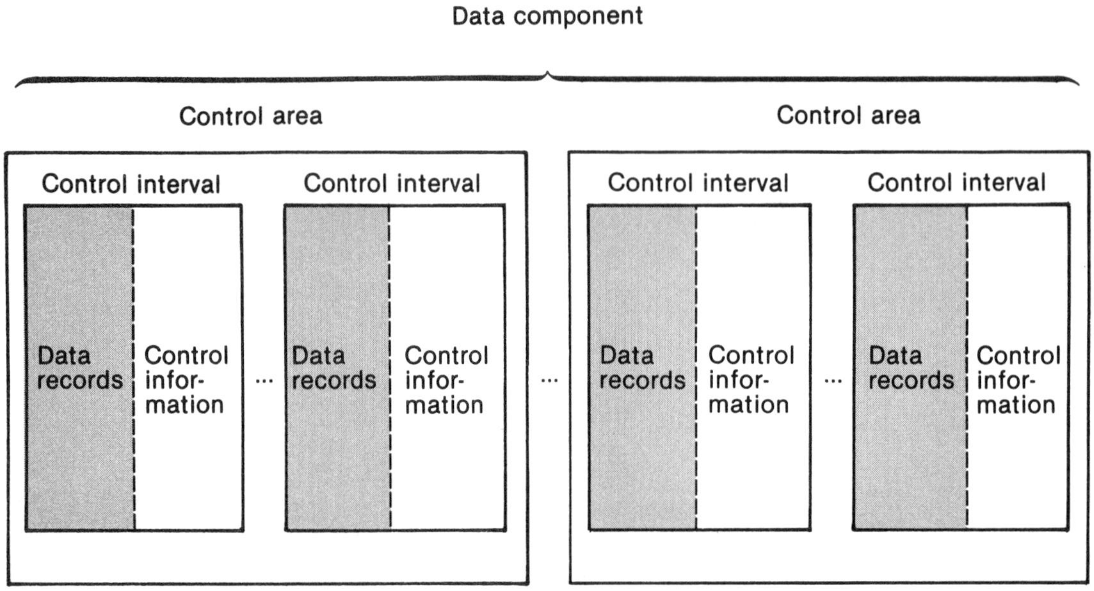

Data component

Figure 16-2   Structure of a VSAM file's data component

they can be processed more efficiently. Just as sections within control intervals may be left empty to make additions easier, entire control intervals within control areas may be left empty.

Figure 16-2 illustrates the structure of a VSAM file's data component. Several control areas make up the data component of a cluster. Within each control area are several control intervals, each containing data records and control information. Of course, figure 16-2 is simplified. A typical VSAM file's data component consists of many control areas, each with perhaps hundreds of control intervals.

VSAM FILE ORGANIZATIONS

The three VSAM file organizations parallel the non-VSAM access methods. An *entry-sequenced data set (ESDS)* is a VSAM file with sequential organization; a *key-sequenced data set (KSDS)* is a VSAM file with indexed sequential organization; and a *relative-record data set (RRDS)* is a VSAM file with direct organization. But don't confuse these VSAM organizations with the non-VSAM access methods. For example, even though a VSAM ESDS has sequential organization, QSAM can't process it.

Entry-sequenced
data sets

An ESDS simply consists of a data component. All additions to it are made at the end of the file. Within an ESDS, records are identified by *relative byte addresses*, or *RBAs*. The RBA is an indication of how far, in bytes, each record is displaced from the beginning of the file. In an ESDS of 256-byte records, for example, the first record has RBA 0, the second has RBA 256, the third has RBA 512, and so on.

Key-sequenced
data sets

A KSDS is similar in many ways to an ISAM file. In fact, one of the reasons IBM developed VSAM was to replace ISAM. However, VSAM uses an improved index structure and handles overflow processing more efficiently than ISAM.

Like an ISAM file, you can process a KSDS sequentially or randomly. When you use sequential processing, records are processed one at a time in the order of the key values stored in the file's index. When you use random processing, you supply the value of the key in the record you want to access.

A KSDS consists of two components: a data component and an index component. The data component contains the records and the index component contains the indexes necessary to access them. Figure 16-3 illustrates these two components of a KSDS.

The index component   As you can see in figure 16-3, the index component of a KSDS has two parts: a *sequence set* and an *index set*. The sequence set is the lowest level of the index. It is searched to determine the control interval in the data component that contains a particular record. The index set is a higher level index to the sequence set.

To understand how this works, consider the KSDS in figure 16-4. Here, the key value is a four-digit item number in a file of inventory records. The index set contains four entries, each with a pointer to a record in the sequence set as well as the highest key value referenced in that sequence set record. Each record in the sequence set in turn contains pointers to control intervals in the data component and the highest key value in each of them. In the data component, records are stored sequentially by key value.

To find a record, VSAM searches the index set sequentially for a key value greater than or equal to that of the desired record. When it's found, VSAM searches the indicated record in the sequence set sequentially to find the control interval that contains the record. Then, VSAM reads that control interval and searches it sequentially until it finds the data record.

For example, to retrieve the record with the key value 1239, VSAM first searches the index set in the index component to determine the record in the sequence set to access (record 3). Then, the entries in the sequence set record are searched to find the control interval in the data component that contains the record (control interval 11). Finally, VSAM reads control interval 11 and retrieves record 1239.

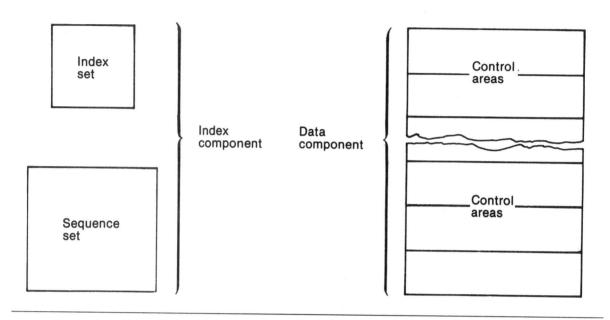

Figure 16-3   Elements of a KSDS

Index component					Data component						
Index set (level 1)		Sequence set									
Key	Pointer	Record	Key	Pointer	Control interval	Keys in control interval					
397	S1	1	187	C1	1	012	041	049	094	101	187
			284	C2	2	188	210	218	247	250	284
940	S2		322	C3	3	287	291	294	301	307	322
			397	C4	4	341	348	354	363	370	397
1391	S3	2	513	C5	5	410	415	420	434	470	513
			641	C6	6	585	592	601	615	621	641
1833	S4		787	C7	7	660	680	685	710	740	787
			940	C8	8	812	819	901	914	927	940
		3	991	C9	9	951	957	967	984	985	991
			1205	C10	10	1032	1105	1117	1121	1187	1205
			1297	C11	11	1207	1208	1231	1239	1250	1297
			1391	C12	12	1330	1337	1341	1355	1366	1391
		4	1522	C13	13	1410	1415	1423	1480	1481	1522
			1639	C14	14	1523	1530	1537	1539	1599	1639
			1740	C15	15	1641	1645	1691	1701	1703	1740
			1833	C16	16	1748	1780	1788	1790	1805	1833

Figure 16-4   Accessing a record in a KSDS

Control area

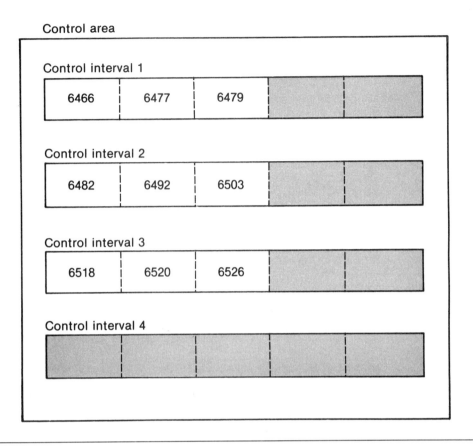

Figure 16-5   Free space distribution in the data component of a KSDS

Free space in a KSDS   When a KSDS is defined, free space is reserved to accommodate new records. This space can be reserved in two ways: (1) space within each control interval may be left empty, and (2) entire control intervals may be left empty. When you define a KSDS with AMS, you can specify both types of free space.

Figure 16-5 shows a control area that consists of four control intervals. Three of the four each contain three records and enough free space for two more so 40 percent of the free space is available in each of these control intervals. The numbers in each record area indicate key values (notice that they're in sequence). The fourth control interval contains no records. So 25 percent of the control intervals in the control area are free.

When a record is added to a KSDS, it's inserted in its correct sequential location in the data component and the records that follow it in the control interval are moved down one position. That's what figure 16-6 shows. It indicates what the control area in figure 16-5 would look like after record 6494 is added to the file.

This is like what happens when a record is added to a track in an ISAM file that has free space in its cylinder overflow area. VSAM differs,

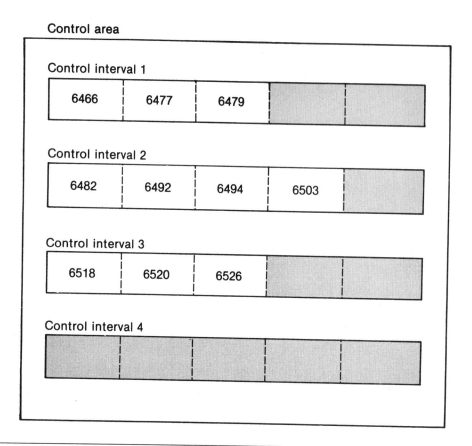

Figure 16-6 Free space distribution in the data component of a KSDS after adding a record to it

however, because it moves records within the control interval in a virtual storage buffer. It doesn't actually rewrite the records on a DASD until the space in the buffer is needed by another control interval. As a result, insertions in a KSDS are processed more efficiently than insertions in an ISAM file.

If an insertion is to be made into a control interval that's already full, the records that would otherwise follow it are written to a free control interval. (That would be the fourth control interval in figure 16-5 or 16-6.) This is called a *control interval split*. Then, the free space in both the original control interval and the one used for overflow is available for insertions. Compare this to the relatively clumsy way ISAM handles insertions.

When a record is deleted from a VSAM KSDS, it's actually removed from its control interval and the space it occupied is available for a new record. Under ISAM, deletions are logical rather than physical; logically deleted records still remain in an ISAM file, using valuable storage space. Because deletions don't waste space in the VSAM file and because insertions are handled more sensibly, a KSDS doesn't have to be reorganized as often as an equivalent ISAM file.

Relative-record data sets

You can implement a VSAM file with direct organization as a relative-record data set (RRDS). Frankly, as with BDAM files, there are relatively few applications in which an RRDS is a substantially better choice than a KSDS. Even so, I want to give you a brief description of an RRDS.

Figure 16-7 shows a VSAM RRDS. The file consists of *record slots* that contain either data or free space. Each record slot is numbered, and it's those numbers, called *relative record numbers*, or *RRNs*, that identify records. If, for example, a file consists of one thousand slots, the slots are identified by relative record numbers from 1 through 1000.

When an RRDS is processed sequentially, the record slots are accessed in sequential order. If a slot doesn't contain any data, it's skipped over. When a program processes an RRDS randomly, it accesses slots, not records, so it's possible for a program to access a slot that doesn't have a record in it. For example, in figure 16-7, that would happen if you accessed slot 6, 9, 15, 16, 18, or 20.

Additions to an RRDS can be handled in two ways. First, records can be added to the end of the file. Alternatively, records can be inserted in empty slots wherever they exist in the file. To do so, however, the application program has to be able to identify the slots that are empty.

When records in an RRDS are processed randomly, they are accessed by RRNs. As a result, an RRDS doesn't need an index component and doesn't have one. That explains why an RRDS can often be processed more efficiently than a KSDS. As a result, if an application lends itself to an RRN addressing scheme, an RRDS can be a practical alternative to a KSDS.

DISCUSSION

If this is your first introduction to VSAM, it may seem complex to you. Although VSAM is complicated, it's a significant improvement over the non-VSAM access methods. In particular, as you will see in the next topic, VSAM offers dramatic improvements in efficiency.

Terminology

VSAM	entry-sequenced data set
Virtual Storage Access Method	ESDS
Access Method Services	key-sequenced data set
AMS	KSDS
catalog	relative-record data set
master catalog	RRDS
user catalog	relative byte address
data space	RBA
data set	sequence set
cluster	index set
data component	control interval split
index component	record slot
control interval	relative record number
control area	RRN

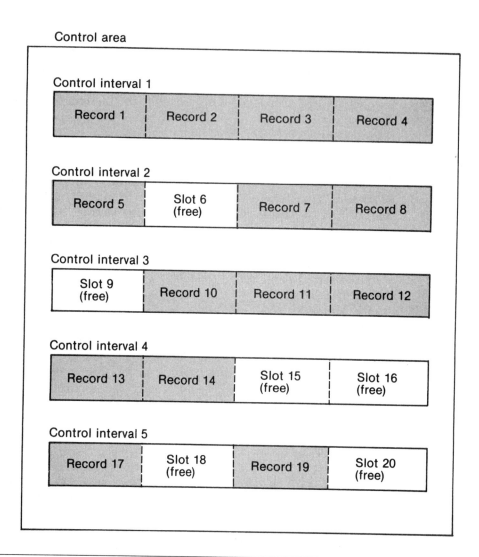

Figure 16-7 Record organization in an RRDS

Objectives

1. Describe the relationships among the VSAM master catalog, user catalogs, data spaces, and clusters.

2. Name and describe the three VSAM file organizations.

TOPIC 2   Assembler language for VSAM files

As you might guess, the assembler language for processing VSAM files is complex. In particular, you need to learn several new macros for VSAM file handling, some with extensive lists of operands. In this topic, though, I won't try to present all the VSAM macros and all the operands. Instead, I will present a subset that you will find useful for application programming. Then, if you need to code VSAM functions that aren't presented in this topic, you will have the background you need to research the VSAM manuals on your own.

In this topic, I will first present the macros that you need to define and access VSAM files. Then, I will present some other macros that you may find useful when processing VSAM files. Last, I will present three illustrative programs that use VSAM files.

MACROS FOR DEFINING VSAM FILES AND THEIR ACCESSES

To access a file using one of the non-VSAM access methods, you must define the characteristics of the file by coding a DCB macro. However, this macro isn't used for VSAM files. Instead, you code three different macros: the ACB, EXLST, and RPL macros. These macros define a file, provide for error-handling routines, and define access requests to the file.

The ACB macro   The *ACB* (*access method control block*) macro provides some basic information about a VSAM file. So you must code one ACB macro for each VSAM file that your program uses. Figure 16-8 summarizes the most commonly used operands of the ACB macro. I will cover each of them in detail.

The AM operand   The AM (access method) operand specifies whether you're defining a VSAM or VTAM control block. Unless your shop uses VTAM as well as VSAM, there is no particular reason for coding this operand. This operand is used only for documentation.

The BUFND, BUFNI, and BUFSP operands   The BUFND, BUFNI, and BUFSP operands specify the number and size of the I/O buffers needed for data and index control intervals. Although these operands are important for program efficiency, their use is beyond the scope of this book. As a result, the illustrative programs use the default values for these operands.

The DDNAME operand   The DDNAME operand is used to specify the name of the file. It must be the same as the name specified in the DD statement for the file. If this operand is omitted, the label of the ACB macro must be the same as the filename used in the DD statement.

The EXLST operand   The EXLST operand specifies the address of the EXLST macro. This address is usually supplied in the form of a label, so this operand usually gives the label of the EXLST macro. Since the EXLST macro generates a list of addresses for exit routines, this operand actually gives the address of a list of addresses.

The MACRF operand   The MACRF operand specifies the type of processing to be performed on the file. Figure 16-9 gives the format of the MACRF operand along with its most commonly-used options. Notice that the options are in groups and that the underlined word in each group is the default value. The brackets before and after each word in each group indicate that the enclosed word is optional.

The first group of options specifies the type or types of accesses to be used for a file: address, control interval, or key. Accessing by address is used for ESDS files in which the records are accessed by relative byte addresses. Accessing by key is used for either KSDS or RRDS files in which the records are accessed by keys or relative record numbers.

Although you'll probably never use *control interval access*, let me describe it briefly. When you use control interval access, data is retrieved and stored by control intervals rather than by single records. A control interval is identified by specifying its relative byte address. When you use this access method, the programmer is responsible for determining the relative byte addresses for the control intervals.

The second group of options of the MACRF operand specifies the type of processing to be performed: direct, sequential, or skip sequential. *Skip sequential processing* means processing a portion of a file in sequence, then skipping to another portion of the file and processing it, and so on. Normally, an ESDS is processed using sequential processing, while a KSDS or RRDS can be processed using any of the three processing methods.

The third group of options specifies whether a file is to be used as input only or output. If OUT is specified, the file can be used for output only or for both input and output.

Although I won't illustrate it in this book, it is acceptable to code more than one of the options from each group. If, for example, you will be processing records both directly and sequentially, you code your MACRF operand like this:

```
MACRF=(KEY,DIR,SEQ,IN)
```

Then, before you issue a GET macro, you must specify which processing method you want to use. You will see how this works when I discuss the RPL macro. Note in the coding for the macro above that the operands are enclosed within parentheses with no intervening blanks.

Priority	Keyword	Programmer code	Remarks
Optional	AM	VSAM	Used for documentation only.
Optional	BUFND	Number of I/O buffers used for data control intervals	If you specify less than the minimum, VSAM overrides your specification. The default is 2.
Optional	BUFNI	Number of I/O buffers used for index control intervals	If you specify less than the minimum, VSAM overrides your specification. The default is 1.
Optional	BUFSP	Size of an area for data and index I/O buffers	Must be at least as large as the buffer space size recorded in the catalog entry for the file. The default is the size recorded in the catalog.
Optional	DDNAME	Filename to be used in the DD statement for the file	If you omit this operand, the DD filename must be the same as the name of the ACB macro.
Optional	EXLST	Address of the EXLST macro	The EXLST macro generates a list of addresses for user routines. As a result, the address of the EXLST macro is the address of an address list. This operand is usually coded with the label of the EXLST macro.
Optional	MACRF	Types of processing that the file will do	See figure 16-9 for the format of this operand.

Figure 16-8   The operands of the ACB macro

The EXLST macro

The *EXLST (exit list)* macro is optional. It produces a list of addresses for routines that VSAM may branch to. Then, when the related VSAM condition occurs, VSAM exits its routine and passes control to the programmer's routine for handling that condition.

Figure 16-10 lists the possible operands of the EXLST macro. Again, the AM operand is used only for documentation. The rest of the operands give the addresses of routines that are to be executed when specific VSAM conditions occur. Normally, an address is given as the label of the first instruction of the programmer's routine.

The operand that you will probably use most frequently is EODAD. This means that VSAM should exit to the addressed routine when an end-of-data-set (end-of-file) condition occurs. You'll see this operand used in one of the illustrative programs.

The other operands are used for specialized processing functions that are beyond the scope of this book. The EXCPAD operand can be used to provide an exit for a routine that provides for overlapped VSAM I/O operations and processing. The JRNAD operand can be used to provide an

Operand format

```
MACRF=([ADR][,CNV][,KEY]

       [,DIR][,SEQ][,SKP]

       [,IN][,OUT])
```

Code	Meaning
ADR	Access by relative byte address
CNV	Access by control interval
KEY	Access by key
DIR	Direct processing
SEQ	Sequential processing
SKP	Skip sequential processing
IN	Used for input only
OUT	Used for output or both input and output

Figure 16-9   The format of the MACRF operand of the ACB macro

exit for a routine that records VSAM transactions. And the LERAD and SYNAD operands can be used to provide exits for routines that handle logical errors (LERAD) and physical errors (SYNAD). This is similar to the SYNAD operation that can be specified on the DCB macro for a non-VSAM file, but the errors that cause the routine to be executed are not the same.

After the address (or label) of each exit routine, you can code two options. The first indicates whether the exit is active or inactive. Since A is underlined, the default is active, so the VSAM exit will take place if this option isn't specified. In contrast, if an option is specified as inactive (N), the exit won't take place even though the operand is coded. Then, to change this option to active, the program must issue the MODCB macro, which will be presented in a moment.

The second option indicates that the programmer's routine is a load module stored in a load library. Then, the address given in this operand must be the address of a field that contains the name of the phase in the load library.

The RPL macro

The *RPL (request parameter list)* macro generates the information needed to access a record in a file. Then, when you use a GET, PUT, ERASE, or POINT macro, you usually code the label of the RPL macro as the only operand. Figure 16-11 presents a list of the most commonly used operands of the RPL macro.

Macro format

```
EXLST   [AM=VSAM]
        [,EODAD=(address[, |A| ][,L])]
                           |N|

        [,EXCPAD=(address[, |A| ][,L])]
                            |N|

        [,JRNAD=(address[, |A| ][,L])]
                           |N|

        [,LERAD=(address[, |A| ][,L])]
                           |N|

        [,SYNAD=(address[, |A| ][,L])]
                           |N|
```

Code	Meaning
EODAD	End of data set
EXCPAD	Execute channel program
JRNAD	Journal
LERAD	Logical error
SYNAD	Physical error
A	Active
N	Inactive
L	The exit routine is a load module that is stored in the load library.

Figure 16-10   The format of the EXLST macro

The ACB operand   The ACB operand specifies the address of the ACB macro generated for the file. The address is usually coded as the label of the ACB macro.

The AREA operand   The AREA operand specifies the address of the work area to be used for the file being defined. What this work area contains depends on whether the OPTCD parameter specifies locate mode or move mode. In move mode, each record is processed in this work area just as it is with the non-VSAM access methods. In locate mode, VSAM puts the address of the record in this work area. This is different from the non-VSAM access methods which return the address in register 1.

The AREALEN operand   The AREALEN operand specifies the length of the work area identified by the AREA operand. If the records are being processed in move mode, the work area must be large enough to hold the largest record that will be processed. If the records are being processed in

Priority	Keyword	Programmer code	Remarks
Required	ACB	Address of the ACB macro	Usually, the label of the ACB macro.
Optional	AM	VSAM	Used for documentation only.
Required	AREA	Address of the work area for the file	For move mode, VSAM uses this area as a work area for records that are read or written. For locate mode, VSAM puts the address of the record being processed into this work area.
Required	AREALEN	Length of the work area	For move mode, the work area must be large enough to store the largest record retrieved or written. For locate mode, it must be at least 4 bytes long so it can hold the address of the record in the VSAM buffer.
Optional	RECLEN	Length of data record	For a PUT request, the program must store the length of the output record in this field. For a GET request, VSAM puts the length of the record in this field.
Optional	ARG	Address of the field that contains the search argument	Used with the GET, POINT, and PUT macros.
Optional	OPTCD	Types of access	See figure 16-12 for the format of this operand.

Figure 16-11   The operands of the RPL macro

locate mode, the work area must be at least four bytes long to hold the address of the record in the VSAM buffer.

The RECLEN operand   The RECLEN operand specifies the length of the records in the file. You only need to specify this operand for a PUT request. If the records are variable-length, you need to use the MODCB macro to modify this value each time a record with a different length is to be written on the file. For a GET request, VSAM puts the length of each record read into this field.

The ARG operand   The ARG operand specifies the address of the field containing the search argument for the record to be retrieved from or written on a file. It is normally coded with the label of the field that contains the search argument. When direct processing is used, the search argument is the key value for a KSDS, the relative record number for an RRDS, or the RBA for an ESDS. (Generic keys can also be used, but I'm not going to cover them in this book.)

Operand format

$$OPTCD = (\quad \begin{bmatrix} ADR \\ CNV \\ \underline{KEY} \end{bmatrix} \quad , \quad \begin{bmatrix} DIR \\ \underline{SEQ} \\ SKP \end{bmatrix} \quad , \quad \begin{bmatrix} \underline{FWD} \\ BWD \end{bmatrix} \quad ,$$

$$\begin{bmatrix} \underline{ARD} \\ LRD \end{bmatrix} \quad , \quad \begin{bmatrix} NSP \\ \underline{NUP} \\ UPD \end{bmatrix} \quad , \quad \begin{bmatrix} LOC \\ \underline{MVE} \end{bmatrix} \quad)$$

Code	Meaning
ADR	Access by relative byte address
CNV	Access by control interval
KEY	Access by key
DIR	Direct processing
SEQ	Sequential processing
SKP	Skip sequential processing
FWD	Forward sequential processing
BWD	Backward sequential processing
ARD	Start sequential processing (forward or backward) with the record identified by the ARG field.
LRD	For backward processing, start with the last record in the file.
NSP	No updating (for direct processing only; VSAM is positioned at the next record for subsequent processing)
NUP	No updating (VSAM is not positioned for subsequent processing)
UPD	Record updating
LOC	Locate mode (records will be processed in the VSAM buffer area)
MVE	Move mode (records will be processed in a work area)

Figure 16-12   The format of the OPTCD operand of the RPL macro

The OPTCD operand   The OPTCD operand specifies how the records in a file are to be accessed. Its format and options are given in figure 16-12. As you can see, the options are in groups, with one default value in each group. The stacking of the items in the groups means that you can only code one option from each group. These options must be consistent with one another, and they must also be consistent with the options coded in the MACRF operand of the ACB macro.

The first two groups of options correspond to the options of the MACRF operand in the ACB macro. The third group specifies whether a file is to be processed in a forward or backward direction. The fourth group specifies whether processing is to start with the last record in the file or with the record identified by the data in the ARG field. The fifth group specifies whether each record is to be updated and, if not, which record should be read next. The last group specifies whether the records will be processed in locate mode or move mode.

When I presented the MACRF operand of the ACB macro, I pointed out that you could specify more than one type of accessing and processing for a single VSAM file. In the OPTCD operand of the RPL macro, though, you can only specify one option in each group. Then, when you want to change to another set of the options that were specified in the MACRF operand, you must use the MODCB macro to change the RPL options. (Although you can code more than one RPL for a file, you only do this if you are processing a file by two different sets of options simultaneously, which is beyond the scope of this book).

MACROS FOR REQUESTING ACCESS TO VSAM FILES

In order to access VSAM files, you use the OPEN, CLOSE, GET and PUT macros. In addition, you can use the ERASE macro to delete a record and the POINT macro to position VSAM for a record access.

The OPEN and CLOSE macros

The formats of the OPEN and CLOSE macros for VSAM files are the same as for non-VSAM files. The first operand is the address of the ACB for the file. This address is normally coded as the label given to the ACB macro, but it can also be coded as a register number in parentheses. Then, the register must contain the appropriate address when the macro is executed. For VSAM, the second operand for each file isn't coded. However, because the operands are positional, a comma must be coded to indicate the placement of the second operand.

If both VSAM and non-VSAM files are coded as operands in the same OPEN or CLOSE macros, the VSAM files should always be coded together. I will explain this in a moment when I discuss the use of the LTR instruction.

The GET and PUT macros

The GET and PUT macros have the format illustrated in figure 16-13. As you can see, the only operand required is the address of the associated RPL. This address is usually the label given to the RPL macro, but it can also be the number of the register that contains the address of the related RPL macro.

The ERASE macro

The ERASE macro deletes a record from a file. It has the same format as the GET and PUT macros, as illustrated in figure 16-13. Again, the only operand is the address of the related RPL macro. Before issuing the ERASE macro, the record to be deleted must be retrieved for update.

This macro illustrates one advantage that VSAM has over ISAM. If you've read chapter 14, you should remember that ISAM doesn't provide for record deletion. The only way to physically delete records from a file is to ignore records that are marked for deletion during the reorganization of

$$\begin{Bmatrix}GET\\PUT\\ERASE\\POINT\end{Bmatrix}\quad RPL=\begin{Bmatrix}label\ of\ RPL\ macro\\(register)\end{Bmatrix}$$

Macro	Request
GET	Retrieve a record
PUT	Store a record
ERASE	Delete a record
POINT	Position for access

Figure 16-13   The format of the GET, PUT, ERASE, and POINT macros

the file. In contrast, the ERASE macro causes a record to be physically deleted from a file so the space can be used for another record.

The POINT macro

You use the POINT macro to position VSAM at a specific record within a file. The position is determined by the value given in the ARG field that is defined by the RPL macro. The POINT macro is generally used to set a starting point for sequential or skip sequential processing. Its format is the same as the format of the GET and PUT macros, as illustrated in figure 16-13.

MACROS FOR CONTROL BLOCK MANIPULATION

When you use assembler language, you can examine, test, and modify the information that is stored in the control block for a VSAM file. You do this by using the SHOWCB, TESTCB, and MODCB macros. In addition, you can generate the control block for a file without using the ACB, EXLST, and RPL macros. You do this by using the GENCB macro. All of these macros are called *control block manipulation macros*.

Although you don't have to use these macros much in simple application programs, they are useful when you want to perform systems programming functions. As a result, you should be familiar with them. Then, you can do more research on them later on when you see the need for them in your assembler language programs.

The SHOWCB macro

Figure 16-14 presents the operands of the SHOWCB macro. This macro lets you examine the fields generated by an ACB, EXLST, or RPL macro. It does this by putting the contents of the specified fields into the work area specified.

Priority	Keyword	Programmer code	Remarks
Required	{ ACB EXLST RPL }	Address of ACB, EXLST, or RPL macro	Usually coded with the label of the selected macro.
Optional	AM	VSAM	Used for documentation only.
Required	AREA	Area in which VSAM will put the contents of the specified fields	The contents of the fields are placed in the area in the order in which they are specified.
Required	FIELDS	List of fields to be examined in this format: (keyword[,keyword...])	A field in the list can be most any keyword of the ACB, EXLST, RPL, or GENCB macros; the length of any ACB, EXLST, or RPL macro using the keyword ACBLEN, EXLLEN, or RPLLEN; or any attribute of an open file or index.
Required	LENGTH	Length of the area specified as the AREA operand	Each field of an ACB, EXLST, or RPL macro is a fullword except for DDNAME, which is two fullwords.
Optional	OBJECT	DATA or INDEX	Specifies whether the attributes of a file's data or its index are to be examined.

Figure 16-14   The operands of the SHOWCB macro

To use this macro effectively, you must know the keywords for the fields that you want to capture. To start, a keyword in the SHOWCB macro can be most any keyword of the ACB, EXLST, RPL, or GENCB macros. If, for example, you want to examine the address of the EXLST macro, you code the SHOWCB macro like this:

```
SHOWCB ACB=INVMSTR,AREA=SHOWADDR,
       FIELDS=EXLST,LENGTH=4
```

Then, the address of the EXLST is put into the four-byte field named SHOWADDR. If two or more keywords are coded, you must separate them with commas and enclose them in parentheses.

You can also use the SHOWCB macro to examine the length of any ACB, EXLST, or RPL macro. To do this, the keywords are ACBLEN, EXLLEN, and RPLLEN.

Finally, you can use this macro to examine any attribute of an open file. To do this, you use the keywords in figure 16-15. Although this isn't a complete list, it includes most of the commonly used attributes for an open file. If, for example, you want to know the percent of free control intervals

Keyword	Meaning
AVSPAC	Number of bytes of available space
BUFNO	Number of buffers being used
CINV	Size of a control interval
FS	Percent of free control intervals
KEYLEN	Length of the key field
LRECL	Maximum record length
NCIS	Number of control-interval splits
NDELR	Number of records deleted from the file
NEXT	Number of extents allocated to the file
NINSR	Number of records inserted into the file
NLOGR	Number of records in the file
NRETR	Number of records retrieved from the file
NUPDR	Number of data records updated in the file
RKP	Position of the record key relative to the beginning of the file

Figure 16-15   Some common attributes of an open file that can be examined by the SHOWCB macro

in the control areas of a frequently used file, you can code the SHOWCB macro like this:

```
SHOWCB ACB=INVMSTR,AREA=FREECI,FIELDS=FS,LENGTH=4
```

This statement puts the percentage of free control intervals in the file labeled INVMSTR into the four-byte work area named FREECI. If this macro is executed each time a file is opened, you can keep track of the free space available in the file. When an attribute can apply to either the data or index component of a file, you use the DATA or INDEX operand to specify which attribute the SHOWCB macro should capture.

The TESTCB macro

Figure 16-16 gives the operands of the TESTCB macro. It is similar to the SHOWCB macro except that it tests rather than captures the one specified field. It can test one of the fields of an ACB, EXLST, or RPL macro or one of the attributes of an open file such as those listed in figure 16-15. It compares the values of the specified field with the value specified in the macro.

In addition to the attributes given in figure 16-15, the TESTCB macro can test if a file is open as in this instruction:

```
TESTCB ACB=INVMSTR,OFLAGS=OPEN
```

Here, the keyword is OFLAGS and the value is OPEN. Then, your program can branch depending on the results of the test using the mnemonic operation codes for branching such as BE and BNE.

Priority	Keyword	Programmer code	Remarks
Required	$\begin{Bmatrix} \text{ACB} \\ \text{EXLST} \\ \text{RPL} \end{Bmatrix}$	Address of ACB, EXLST, or RPL macro	Usually coded with the label of the selected macro.
Optional	AM	VSAM	Used for documentation only.
Optional	ERET	Address of error routine	If the condition specified can't be tested, VSAM branches to the address specified in this operand. The routine at this address can inspect the return code in register 15 to determine the problem.
Required	keyword	Field to be tested	The field specified can be any keyword of the ACB, EXLST, RPL, or GENCB macros; the length of any ACB, EXLST, or RPL macro using the keyword ACBLEN, EXLLEN, or RPLLEN; or any attribute of an open file or index.
Optional	OBJECT	DATA or INDEX	Specifies whether the attributes of a file's data or its index are to be examined.

Figure 16-16   The operands of the TESTCB macro

You can also use the TESTCB macro to test the results of an I/O operation. You do this by coding the keyword FDBK (feedback) and the error code you want to compare it with. Figure 16-17 gives some of the common error codes you are likely to test for when using the FDBK keyword. If, for example, you want to test whether a record couldn't be added to a KSDS because it had a duplicate key, you could code the TESTCB macro this way:

```
TESTCB RPL=INVMSTR,FDBK=8
BE     DUPKEY
```

Here, the program branches to DUPKEY when a record can't be written because it has a duplicate key.

The MODCB macro

The MODCB macro is used to modify the control blocks generated by the ACB, EXLST, RPL, and GENCB macros. Its standard format is given in figure 16-18.

Although you probably won't use it often, let me give you two examples of situations in which you might need to use it. First, if you need to access a file using two different types of processing in the same program (not simultaneously), you have to change the access request specified in

Code	Explanation
8	Duplicate key
12	Record out of sequence
16	No record found
68	Access requested doesn't match access specified
92	A PUT for update or an ERASE is issued without a preceding GET for update
104	Invalid or conflicting RPL options or parameters

Figure 16-17   Some common VSAM error codes for the FDBK keyword of the TESTCB macro

Priority	Keyword	Programmer code	Remarks
Required	ACB EXLST RPL	Address of ACB, EXLST, or RPL macro	Type of control block to be modified.
Optional	AM	VSAM	Used for documentation only.
Required	Operand keyword	New value for operand	The operand keywords are those used in the ACB, EXLST, and RPL macros.

Figure 16-18   The operands of the MODCB macro

the RPL for that file. The only way to do that is to code a MODCB macro. Second, if you're processing a file of variable-length records, you need to change the record length field of the RPL each time the record length changes.

To illustrate, consider this MODCB macro:

```
MODCB RPL=INVRPL,OPTCD=(DIR)
```

This changes the processing option in the OPTCD operand of the RPL macro from sequential to direct. Then, if the program needs to change back to sequential processing, it must issue this macro:

```
MODCB RPL=INVRPL,OPTCD=(SEQ)
```

As you can see, then, the MODCB macro lets you change the starting values of the ACB, EXLST, or RPL macros whenever you need to.

The GENCB macro	The GENCB macro is used to generate VSAM control blocks at program execution time instead of at assembly time. As a result, this macro can take the place of a set of ACB, EXLST, and RPL macros for a file. Its operands are shown in figure 16-19.

The benefit of using GENCB is that your programs don't have to be reassembled each time the specifications for a control block change (due to a new release of VSAM, for example). Instead, the GENCB macro generates the control blocks in the current format each time the program is executed. The drawback, of course, is that it takes additional processing time and storage to generate these macros each time a program is executed.

THREE ILLUSTRATIVE PROGRAMS

To show how the VSAM macros are used within programs, I'm now going to present three simple programs that use VSAM files. If you read the chapter on ISAM, you'll see that these programs are like the ones that were used to illustrate ISAM coding. In the first program, a KSDS master file is created from a QSAM file. In the second program, the KSDS master file is updated based on the transactions in an ESDS transaction file. In the third program, a report is prepared by reading the KSDS master file sequentially.

A file creation program	Figure 16-20 presents a program that loads a KSDS file of inventory records from a QSAM disk file. The new records are to be 70 bytes long. The basic processing loop of the program reads a record from the sequential file, moves and packs its data into the KSDS record, and writes an output record.

To start, look at the ACB and RPL macros for the inventory master file. If these macros look brief, remember that the cluster (file) must be defined by the AMS program. As a result, MVS already knows that the file is going to be key sequenced, that its keys are in the first six bytes of each record, and so on. Then, the ACB macro only has to specify that the file will be an output file. And the RPL macro only has to give the name and size of the work area for the file and the size of each output record. Because the defaults in both the ACB and RPL macros are for sequential processing by key, they don't have to be specified in these macros.

If you look at the instruction after each VSAM access request macro in the program, you'll see that it's an LTR instruction. You can find this instruction after the OPEN, PUT, and CLOSE macro for the KSDS file. As you will learn in a moment, each LTR instruction tests the contents of register 15. Why? Because VSAM places a return code in register 15 after each I/O request to tell what the result of the request was. Furthermore, VSAM doesn't automatically cancel a program when an I/O error occurs. Instead, the program must check the contents of register 15 and provide appropriate error-handling routines.

Priority	Keyword	Programmer code	Remarks
Required	BLK	ACB, EXLST, or RPL	Type of control block to be generated.
Optional	AM	VSAM	Used for documentation only.
Optional	COPIES	Number of control blocks to be generated	If multiple control blocks are generated they are identical and MODCB must be used to modify them. The default is 1.
Optional	keyword	Characteristics of the control block in this form: keyword = value	The keywords and values that can be coded are the same as those used in the ACB, EXLST, and RPL macros. If a keyword is omitted, VSAM provides default values.
Optional	WAREA	The address of the area in which VSAM is to put the control block	If this operand isn't coded, VSAM will obtain an area in which to put the control block.
Optional	LENGTH	Length of the area specified as the WAREA operand	The length required for a control block can be determined by coding a SHOWCB macro. This area is required if the WAREA operand is coded.

Figure 16-19   The operands of the GENCB macro

When the LTR instruction is executed, it moves the contents of the register specified as operand 2 into the register specified as operand 1 and sets the condition code according to the value of operand 2 (plus, minus, or zero). In figure 16-20, though, both operand 1 and operand 2 specify the same register:

```
LTR    15,15
```

As a result, the effect is to set the condition code based on the value in register 15. Then, the condition code can be tested using a branch instruction. If it doesn't indicate a zero value, an error has occurred. If an error is indicated in the program in figure 16-20, the program issues the ABEND macro and terminates.

When you use the LTR instruction to test the return code following an OPEN or CLOSE macro, you must be careful about the sequence in which you code the operands of the OPEN or CLOSE macro if they are for both VSAM and non-VSAM files. If all the VSAM files are listed consecutively, the return code generated will apply to all of the VSAM files. However, if the VSAM and non-VSAM files are interspersed, the return code will only apply to the VSAM files that follow the last non-VSAM file listed. For this reason, when you code your OPEN and CLOSE macros, we recommend that you list all non-VSAM files first, followed by all VSAM files.

```
INVLOAD   START  0
BEGIN     SAVE   (14,12)
          BALR   3,0
          USING  *,3
          ST     13,SAVE+4
          LA     13,SAVE
          OPEN   (INPUT,INPUT,INVMSTR)
          LTR    15,15                    TEST FOR VSAM I/O ERROR
          BNZ    DUMP
READREC   GET    INPUT,INPTWRKA
          MVC    MSTRRCD(32),INPTWRKA     MOVE 32 BYTES TO OUTPUT AREA
          PACK   MORDQTY,IORDQTY          PACK INPUT FIELDS
          PACK   MORDPT,IORDPT
          PACK   MSAFSTK,ISAFSTK
          PACK   MONHAND,IONHAND
          PACK   MONORD,IONORD
          PACK   MALLOC,IALLOC
          PUT    RPL=RPL1                 WRITE OUTPUT RECORD
          LTR    15,15                    TEST FOR VSAM I/O ERROR
          BZ     READREC
DUMP      ABEND  800,DUMP
EOFDSK    CLOSE  (INPUT,,INVMSTR)
          LTR    15,15                    TEST FOR VSAM I/O ERROR
          BNZ    DUMP
          L      13,SAVE+4
          RETURN (14,12)
INPUT     DCB    DSORG=PS,                                              X
                 RECFM=FB,                                              X
                 MACRF=GM,                                              X
                 BLKSIZE=248,                                           X
                 LRECL=62,                                              X
                 DDNAME=INPUT,                                          X
                 EODAD=EOFDSK
INVMSTR   ACB    MACRF=OUT
RPL1      RPL    ACB=INVMSTR,                                           X
                 AREA=MSTRRCD,                                          X
                 AREALEN=70,                                            X
                 RECLEN=70
SAVE      DS     18F
INPTWRKA  DS     0CL62
IITEM     DS     CL6
IDESC     DS     CL20
IUM       DS     CL4
IORDPOL   DS     CL2
IORDQTY   DS     CL5
IORDPT    DS     CL5
ISAFSTK   DS     CL5
IONHAND   DS     CL5
IONORD    DS     CL5
IALLOC    DS     CL5
MSTRRCD   DS     0CL70
MITEM     DS     CL6
MDESC     DS     CL20
MUM       DS     CL4
```

Figure 16-20 A VSAM KSDS file creation program (part 1 of 2)

```
MORDPOL   DS    CL2
MORDQTY   DS    PL4
MORDPT    DS    PL4
MSAFSTK   DS    PL4
MONHAND   DS    PL4
MONORD    DS    PL4
MALLOC    DS    PL4
          DC    14X'00'
          END   BEGIN
```

Figure 16-20   A VSAM KSDS file creation program (part 2 of 2)

A random update program

Figure 16-21 is a program that updates a KSDS file on a random basis. The input file is an ESDS shipment transaction file. The updated file is the KSDS inventory master file that was created by the program in figure 16-20. The basic logic of this program is to read a shipment transaction, to read the master record with the same key on a random basis, and to rewrite the updated master record in its original location on the file. This program also prints a report listing any records that aren't found in the master file.

To define the ESDS transaction file, both the ACB and RPL macros specify access by address (ADR). This is required because access by key is the default. In addition, the EXLST macro is used for this file. It specifies an exit routine for an end-of-data-set condition. That means that VSAM will automatically branch to the address specified (EOFINPT) when the end-of-file condition is detected.

To define the KSDS master file, the ACB macro specifies direct processing (DIR) of an output (OUT) file. Similarly, the OPTCD operand of the RPL macro specifies direct processing (DIR) and record updating (UPD). In addition, the ARG operand is coded in the RPL macro to specify the field (ITEMKEY) that will contain the key of the master record to be processed.

If you read through the program, you can see that the logic is straightforward. Again, the LTR instruction is used after each VSAM access request macro to see whether an I/O error has occurred. If an error has occurred during any I/O operation other than the GET for the KSDS master file, the program branches to DUMP and the program terminates. However, if an error is detected after the GET macro for the KSDS master file, the program branches to ERROR so the program can test for the not-found condition by using the TESTCB macro.

The test for the not-found condition is coded this way:

```
ERROR     TESTCB RPL=RPL2,FDBK=16
          BNE    DUMP
```

```
UPDTINV   START  0
BEGIN     SAVE   (14,12)
          BALR   3,0
          USING  *,3
          ST     13,SAVE+4
          LA     13,SAVE
          OPEN   (ERRMSG,OUTPUT,SHIPTR,,INVMSTR)
          LTR    15,15                    TEST FOR VSAM I/O ERROR
          BNZ    DUMP
READSHP   GET    RPL=RPL1                 READ VSAM RECORD FOR FILE 1
          LTR    15,15                    TEST FOR VSAM I/O ERROR
          BNZ    DUMP
          MVC    ITEMKEY,SHPITEM
          GET    RPL=RPL2                 READ VSAM RECORD FOR FILE 2
          LTR    15,15                    TEST FOR VSAM I/O ERROR
          BNZ    ERROR
          PACK   QTYONHND,SHPQTY
          SP     MONHAND,QTYONHND
          PUT    RPL=RPL2                 UPDATE VSAM RECORD IN FILE 2
          LTR    15,15                    TEST FOR VSAM I/O ERROR
          BNZ    DUMP
          B      READSHP
ERROR     TESTCB RPL=RPL2,FDBK=16         TEST FOR NO RECORD FOUND
          BNE    DUMP
          MVC    LITEM,SHPITEM
          PUT    ERRMSG,ERRLINE
          B      READSHP
DUMP      ABEND  1000,DUMP
EOFINPT   CLOSE  (ERRMSG,,SHIPTR,,INVMSTR)
          LTR    15,15                    TEST FOR VSAM I/O ERROR
          BNZ    DUMP
          L      13,SAVE+4
          RETURN (14,12)
SHIPTR    ACB    EXLST=EXIT,                                              X
                 MACRF=ADR
EXIT      EXLST  EODAD=EOFINPT
RPL1      RPL    ACB=SHIPTR,                                              X
                 AREA=SHPWRKA,                                            X
                 AREALEN=24,                                              X
                 OPTCD=ADR
INVMSTR   ACB    MACRF=(DIR,OUT)
RPL2      RPL    ACB=INVMSTR,                                             X
                 AREA=MSTRRCD,                                            X
                 AREALEN=70,                                              X
                 RECLEN=70,                                               X
                 ARG=ITEMKEY,                                             X
                 OPTCD=(DIR,UPD)
ERRMSG    DCB    DSORG=PS,                                                X
                 RECFM=F,                                                 X
                 MACRF=PM,                                                X
                 BLKSIZE=132,                                             X
                 LRECL=132,                                               X
                 DDNAME=ERRMSG
SAVE      DS     18F
```

Figure 16-21   A VSAM KSDS random update program (part 1 of 2)

```
ERRLINE   DS    0CL132
          DC    5C' '
LITEM     DS    CL6
          DC    52C' '
LERR      DC    CL15'NO RECORD FOUND'
          DC    54C' '
ITEMKEY   DS    CL6
QTYONHND  DS    PL4
SHPWRKA   DS    0CL24
          DS    CL6
SHPITEM   DS    CL6
SHPQTY    DS    CL4
          DS    CL8
MSTRRCD   DS    0CL70
MSTITEM   DS    CL6
MDESC     DS    CL20
          DS    CL18
MONHAND   DS    PL4
          DS    CL22
          END   BEGIN
```

Figure 16-21   A VSAM KSDS random update program (part 2 of 2)

The feedback field specified in the TESTCB macro (FDBK) contains more information about a VSAM I/O area. Figure 16-17 lists some of the most common codes you may need to test for, and you can find a complete list of these codes in IBM's *VSAM Administration: Macro Instruction Reference (GC26-4016)*. In the instruction above, the TESTCB macro tests to see if FDBK is equal to 16, which is the error code that indicates a not-found condition. If the error is a not-found condition, the program continues by printing a line on the error listing. Otherwise, the program branches to DUMP where the ABEND macro is issued.

A sequential retrieval program

Figure 16-22 presents a program that illustrates sequential retrieval of a KSDS file. It reads the inventory master file created by the program in figure 16-20 and prepares an inventory report from it. Since the logic of the program is straightforward, you should have little difficulty understanding it.

If you review the macros that define the master file, you can see that the RPL specifies locate mode for the file. As a result, the AREALEN is only four, because it will only contain the address of the record that is being processed. The record will reside in the VSAM buffer area. Note also that the EXLST macro specifies an exit routine for the end-of-file condition on the master file. This will cause an automatic branch to EOFMSTR when there are no more records in the master file.

```
INVSTAT    START  0
BEGIN      SAVE   (14,12)
           BALR   3,0
           USING  *,3
           USING  MSTRAREA,4
           ST     13,SAVE+4
           LA     13,SAVE
           OPEN   (REPORT,OUTPUT,INVMSTR)        OPEN FILES
           LTR    15,15                          TEST FOR VSAM I/O ERROR
           BNZ    DUMP
PROCESS    GET    RPL=RPL1                       READ VSAM RECORD
           LTR    15,15                          TEST FOR VSAM I/O ERROR
           BNZ    DUMP
           L      4,MSTRADR
           MVI    RLINE,X'40'
           MVC    RLINE+1(132),RLINE
           MVC    RITEM,MITEM
           MVC    RDESC,MDESC
           MVC    RUM,MUM
           MVC    RORDPCL,MORDPOL
           MVC    RORDQTY(61),PATTERN
           ED     RORDQTY(61),MORDQTY            EDIT SIX FIELDS
           ZAP    AVAILWK,MONHAND
           AP     AVAILWK,MONORD
           SP     AVAILWK,MALLOC
           MVC    RAVAIL,PATTERN
           ED     RAVAIL,AVAILWK
           CP     LCOUNT,=P'50'
           BL     PRTDET
           PUT    REPORT,RHEAD
           ZAP    LCOUNT,=P'0'
           MVI    RCTL,C'0'
PRTDET     PUT    REPORT,RLINE
           AP     LCOUNT,=P'1'
           B      PROCESS
DUMP       ABEND  900,DUMP
EOFMSTR    CLOSE  (INVMSTR,,REPORT)              CLOSE FILES
           LTR    15,15                          TEST FOR VSAM I/O ERROR
           BNZ    DUMP
           L      13,SAVE+4
           RETURN (14,12)
REPORT     DCB    DSORG=PS,                                               X
                  RECFM=FA,                                               X
                  MACRF=PM,                                               X
                  BLKSIZE=133,                                            X
                  LRECL=133,                                              X
                  DDNAME=REPORT
INVMSTR    ACB    EXLST=EXITS
EXITS      EXLST  EODAD=EOFMSTR
RPL1       RPL    ACB=INVMSTR,                                            X
                  AREA=MSTRADR,                                           X
                  AREALEN=4,                                              X
                  OPTCD=(LOC)
```

Figure 16-22   A VSAM KSDS disk-to-printer program (part 1 of 2)

```
SAVE       DS     18F
AVAILWK    DS     PL4
LCOUNT     DC     P'50'
PATTERN    DS     0CL61
           DC     X'40'
           DC     6X'202020202020021222222'
MSTRADR    DS     F
MSTRAREA   DSECT
MSTRRCD    DS     0CL70
MITEM      DS     CL6
MDESC      DS     CL20
MUM        DS     CL4
MORDPOL    DS     CL2
MORDQTY    DS     PL4
MORDPT     DS     PL4
MSAFSTX    DS     PL4
MONHAND    DS     PL4
MONORD     DS     PL4
MALLOC     DS     PL4
           DS     CL14
INVSTAT    CSECT
RHEAD      DS     0CL133
           DC     CL105'1              ITEM    DESCRIPTION            U/M  X
                  OP       ORDQTY      ORDPNT    SAFSTK    ONHAND   ONORDR'
           DC     CL28'    ALLOC       AVAIL         '
RLINE      DS     0CL133
RCTL       DS     CL1
           DS     CL12
RITEM      DS     CL6
           DS     CL2
RDESC      DS     CL20
           DS     CL4
RUM        DS     CL4
           DS     CL2
RORDPOL    DS     CL2
           DS     CL4
RORDQTY    DS     CL8
           DS     CL2
RORDPT     DS     CL8
           DS     CL2
RSAFSTK    DS     CL8
           DS     CL2
RONHAND    DS     CL8
           DS     CL2
RONORD     DS     CL8
           DS     CL2
RALLOC     DS     CL8
           DS     CL2
RAVAIL     DS     CL8
           DS     CL8
           END    BEGIN
```

Figure 16-22   A VSAM KSDS disk-to-printer program (part 2 of 2)

Again, LTR instructions are used to test register 15 after each VSAM access request macro. If an error is detected, the program branches to DUMP and terminates.

To provide for locate mode processing, the program uses a DSECT in combination with register 4. Then, after each GET macro for the master file, VSAM moves the address of the record into MSTRADR, and the program loads the contents of MSTRADR into register 4. As a result, the instructions of the program will address the fields of MSTRRCD properly.

DISCUSSION

You may have noticed that I didn't present a programming example using a relative-record file. However, the coding of the macros for an RRDS is similar to the coding for a KSDS since the relative-record numbers are treated as keys. With this in mind, you should be able to develop assembler language programs that use simple ESDS, KSDS, and RRDS files at this time.

On the other hand, you should realize that this topic is at best an introduction to VSAM processing in assembler language. As such, it doesn't begin to present all of the VSAM functions that you code when you use assembler language. For example, files can be set up with more than one key. Also, it's okay for the secondary keys to have duplicates. And on and on. If you want to do some research on your own, be sure to get the IBM manuals called *VSAM Administration Guide (GC26-4015)* and *VSAM Administration: Macro Instruction Reference (GC26-4016)*.

Terminology

ACB
access method control block
control-interval access
skip sequential processing
EXLST
exit list
RPL
request parameter list
control block manipulation macro

Objective

Given specifications for an application program that processes simple VSAM files (ESDS, KSDS, or RRDS), develop a program that satisifies the specifications.

TOPIC 3   MVS JCL for VSAM files

Before you can store data in a VSAM file, you must define it using a VSAM utility program called AMS (or IDCAMS). Once you do this, the information that defines and locates the file is in the file's VSAM catalog. As a result, it's easy to code the DD statement for a VSAM file.

Figure 16-23 presents the MVS JCL that I used for testing the file-creation program in figure 16-20. As you can see, the DD statement for the VSAM file is simpler than one for an ISAM file. That's because the characteristics of the file have already been defined using AMS. The only required operands are DSN and DISP. Both of these operands are coded just as they are for non-VSAM files.

The only thing to note in the JCL is the status parameter in the DISP operand for the VSAM file; it's coded OLD. That's because the file already exists, even though this is a file-creation program. The file just doesn't have any records in it yet. As a result, this same DD statement can be used for any program that accesses the file.

Discussion

At this point, I think you can see that it's relatively easy to code the JCL for VSAM files. In particular, you don't have to worry about coding the device or volume for a VSAM file. VSAM keeps track of that information for you in its catalogs.

I want you to realize, though, that this topic is just a brief introduction to the JCL required for using VSAM files. It doesn't show you how to define a VSAM space or cluster using IDCAMS, and it doesn't present all the DD operands that can be used with VSAM files. If you want more information about VSE JCL for VSAM files, we recommend our *MVS JCL* by Doug Lowe.

Terminology

None

Objective

Given specifications for a job that uses one or more VSAM files, code the JCL for running the program.

```
//PRINCE          JOB    (MMA,PRINCE),'ANNE PRINCE'
//               EXEC   ASMFCG
//ASM.SYSIN      DD     *
                 .
                 .  SOURCE PROGRAM
                 .
//GO.SYSUDUMP    DD     SYSOUT=A
//GO.AUDIT       DD     SYSOUT=A
//GO.INVLOAD     DD     DSN=MMA.TEST.INVLOAD,DISP=(OLD,KEEP),
//               UNIT=SYSDA,VOLUME=SER=MMA800
//GO.INVMSTR     DD     DSN=MMA.VSAM.INVMSTR,DISP=(OLD,KEEP)
//
```

Figure 16-23   The MVS JCL for the VSAM file creation program in figure 16-20

Section 5

Program development techniques

This section contains three chapters. Chapter 17 shows you how to assemble a source program and correct any diagnostic errors it contains. You can read this chapter any time after you complete chapter 5. But we recommend that you read it just before you assemble your first program or right after you get your first diagnostics.

Chapter 18 shows you how to test and debug a program. Again, you can read this chapter any time after you complete chapter 5. But we recommend that you read it just before you test your first program or right after you get your first test run output.

Chapter 19 is an optional chapter, but one that we believe will help you become a more effective programmer. You can think of it as an idea chapter that you can read any time after you complete chapter 8. We recommend, though, that you read it sooner rather than later, because it's likely to give you ideas that will help you do your case study problems more efficiently.

Chapter 17

How to assemble a source program and correct its diagnostics

After you code a source program and enter it into the system, you must assemble it using a procedure like the one presented in chapter 3. Then, if the assembly produces any diagnostic messages, you must correct them and reassemble the program until it assembles without diagnostics. At that time, you can test and debug the program as described in the next chapter.

This chapter starts by presenting the assembly output you are likely to get when you assemble a source program. Then, it shows you how to go about correcting diagnostics. You can read this chapter any time after you complete chapter 5 of this book. But the best time is probably just before you assemble your first program or right after you assemble it.

ASSEMBLY OUTPUT

When a program is assembled, several different types of output are printed. These are illustrated in figures 17-1 through 17-6. This assembly output is for the refined reorder-listing program presented in topic 2 of chapter 5. However, we've put a few coding errors into the program so the assembly produces some diagnostics.

Each type of assembly output starts on a new page and continues for as many pages as needed. In sequence, the normal assembly output consists of (1) the external symbol dictionary, (2) the assembly listing, (3) the relocation dictionary, (4) the cross-reference listing, (5) the literal cross-reference listing, and (6) the diagnostics and statistics listing.

The external symbol dictionary

Figure 17-1 presents the *external symbol dictionary* for the reorder-listing program. Because you can get this information in other ways, you won't need to use external symbol dictionaries in this course. As a result, we won't show them in the assembly output for any of the other programs in this book.

The assembly listing

Sometimes, all of the assembly output is referred to as the assembly listing. More precisely, though, the *assembly listing* for the reorder-listing program is just the listing shown in figure 17-2. From left to right, there are six columns of information on the assembly listing. Since it contains considerable information, I will go over each column in detail.

The source statement column   The rightmost column of the assembly listing, headed SOURCE STATEMENT, is a listing of the source program. In addition, though, instructions generated from macro instructions are shown. These are preceded by a plus sign. For example, the GET macro has generated 4 statements. Similarly, the DCB macro for the printer file has generated 45 lines of source code.

After the END statement in the source listing are data definitions representing the literals used by the program. The three statements here represent the literals used for packed values 50, 1, and 0.

The statement number column   To the left of the source statements is a column headed STMT, short for statement number. This column gives a number to each of the source statements of the program. The statement numbers are then used in the cross-reference and diagnostic listings to refer to the source statements.

The location counter column   The leftmost column of information is headed LOC, which stands for *location counter*. The location counter is a field that is used during assembly to keep track of the starting location of each machine instruction or data field of the program. For the first machine instruction, the STM instruction generated by the SAVE macro, the location is the value given in the START instruction (in this case, zero). For each subsequent instruction or data definition, the location is determined by adding the length of the instruction or field to the previous location counter value. Since STM is a four-byte instruction, the second machine instruction has a location of 000004.

Notice that the location values are given in hex. If you scan the LOC column, you can see that the increments from instruction to instruction are two, four or six bytes. These, of course, are the lengths of the System/370 instructions. If a source line doesn't generate any object code, the location counter value is not increased.

```
                                    EXTERNAL SYMBOL DICTIONARY                PAGE   1

                                                                   ASM 0201 15.05 11/05/86

SYMBOL   TYPE  ID   ADDR   LENGTH  LDID
REORDLST  SD  0001 000000 0004CC
```

Figure 17-1 The external symbol dictionary for the reorder-listing program

ASM 0201 15.05 11/05/86   PAGE 2

LOC	OBJECT CODE	ADDR1	ADDR2	STMT	SOURCE STATEMENT	
000000				1	REORDLST START 0	00C400
				2	BEGIN SAVE (14,12) SAVE REGISTERS	00C500
000000				3+BEGIN	DS 0H	0165C000
000000	90EC D00C		0000C	4+	STM 14,12,12(13)	0295C000
000004	0530			5	BALR 3,0	00C600
				6	USING *,3	00C700
000006	5000 345A		00460	7	ST 13,SAVE+4	00C800
00000A	41D0 3456		0045C	8	LA 13,SAVE	00C900
				9	OPEN (INVMAST,INPUT,PRTOUT,OUTPUT)	001000
00000E	0700			10+	CNOP 0,4 ALIGN LIST TO FULLWORD	0174C000
000010	4510 3016		0001C	11+	BAL 1,*+12 LOAD REG1 W/LIST ADDR.	C178C000
000014	00			12+	DC AL1(0) OPTION BYTE	C190C000
000015	000000			13+	DC AL3(INVMAST) DCB ADDRESS	C192C000
	*** ERROR ***					
000018	8F			14+	DC AL1(143) OPTION BYTE	0190C000
000019	000110			15+	DC AL3(PRTOUT) DCB ADDRESS	C192C000
00001C	0A13			16+	SVC 19 ISSUE OPEN SVC	C400C000
00001E	0000 0000			17	READINV GET INVMAST,INVWRKA READ RECORD INTO WORK AREA	001100
00001E		00000		18+READINV	LA 1,INVMAST LOAD PARAMETER REG 1	0190C002
	*** ERROR ***					
000022	4100 316A		00170	19+	LA 0,INVWRKA LOAD PARAMETER REG 0	0250C002
000026	58F0 1030		00030	20+	L 15,48(0,1) LOAD GET ROUTINE ADDR	CC60C000
00002A	05EF			21+	BALR 14,15 LINK TO GET ROUTINE	0625C000
00002C	F420 3437 34C4	004BD	004CA	22	AP COUNT,=P'1' ADD ONE TO COUNT	001200
000032	F224 34AB 3192	004B1	00198	23	PACK WRKAVAIL,INVONHND	001300
000038	F224 34AE 3197	004B4	0019D	24	PACK WRKONORD,INVONORD	001400
				25	ADD WRKAVAIL,WRKONORD ADD ON HAND AND ON ORDER	001500
	*** ERROR ***					
00003E	F224 34B1 318D	004B1	0018D	26	PACK WRKORDPT,INVORDPT	001600
000044	F922 34AB 34B1	004AB	004B1	27	CP WRKAVAIL,WRKORDPT COMPARE AVAILABLE, REORDER POINT	001700
00004A	4780 3018		0001E	28	BNL READINV	001800
00004E	F224 3434 316A	00434	00170	29	PACK PACKAREA,INVITNBR	001900
				30	MVL PRTITNBR,PATTERN1	002000
	*** ERROR ***					
000054	DE05 34A4 3434	004A4	00434	31	ED PRTITNBR,PACKAREA EDIT ITEM NUMBER FIELD	002100
00005A	D213 3355 316F	00355	0016F	32	MVC PRTITDES,INVITDES MOVE ITEM DESCRIPTION	002200
000060	F224 3434 3188	00434	00188	33	PACK PACKAREA,INVPRICE	002300
000066	D206 336D 34A4	0036D	004A4	34	MVC PRTPRICE,PATTERN2	002400
00006C	DE06 336D 34A4	0036D	004A4	35	ED PRTPRICE,PACKAREA EDIT UNIT PRICE	002500
000072	D205 3378 349E	00378	0049E	36	MVC PRTAVAIL,PATTERN1	002600
000078	DE05 3378 34AB	00378	004AB	37	ED PRTAVAIL,WRKAVAIL EDIT AVAILABLE	002700
00007E	D205 3382 349E	00382	0049E	38	MVC PRTORDPT,PATTERN1	002800
000084	DE05 3382 34B1	00382	004B1	39	ED PRTORDPT,WRKORDPT EDIT ORDER POINT	002900
00008A	F911 34BA 34C2	004BA	004C2	40	CP LINECNT,=P'50' COMPARE LINE COUNT TO 50	003000
000090	4740 30C2		000C8	41	BL PRTDET BRANCH ON LOW TO PRTDET	003100
				42	PUT PRTOUT,HDGLINE1 PRINT FIRST HEADING LINE	003200
	*** ERROR ***					
000094	4110 310A		00110	43+	LA 1,PRTOUT LOAD PARAMETER REG 1	0190C002
000098	4100 313A		001C0	44+	LA 0,HDGLINE1 LOAD PARAMETER REG 0	0250C002
00009C	58F0 1030		00030	45+	L 15,48(0,1) LOAD PUT ROUTINE ADDR	0055C000
0000A0	05EF			46+	BALR 14,15 LINK TO PUT ROUTINE	0060C000
				47	PUT PRTOUT,HDGLINE2 PRINT SECOND HEADING LINE	003300
0000A2	4110 310A		00110	48+	LA 1,PRTOUT LOAD PARAMETER REG 1	C190C002
0000A6	4100 323F		00245	49+	LA 0,HDGLINE2 LOAD PARAMETER REG 0	0250C002
0000AA	58F0 1030		00030	50+	L 15,48(0,1) LOAD PUT ROUTINE ADDR	0055C000
0000AE	05EF			51+	BALR 14,15 LINK TO PUT ROUTINE	0060C000

Figure 17-2   The assembly listing for the reorder-listing program (part 1 of 5)

PAGE 3

```
                                                          ASM C2C1 15.05 11/05/86

LOC    OBJECT CODE      ADDR1 ADDR2  STMT   SOURCE STATEMENT

0000B0 4110 310A        00110          52          PUT   PRTOUT,HDGLINE3   PRINT THIRD HEADING LINE        003400
0000B4 4100 32C4        002C4          53+         LA    1,PRTOUT          LOAD PARAMETER REG 1            C190C002
0000B8 58F0 1030        00030          54+         LA    0,HDGLINE3        LOAD PARAMETER REG 0            0250C002
0000BC 05EF                            55+         L     15,48(0,1)        LOAD PUT ROUTINE ADDR           0060C000
0000BE F810 349A 34C5   004C0 004C8    56+         BALR  14,15             LINK TO PUT ROUTINE             003500
0000C4 92F0 3349        0034F          57          ZAP   LINECNT,=P'0'     RESET LINE COUNT TO ZERO        003600
                                       58          MVI   PRTDCTL,C'0'      MOVE ZERO TC ASA CONTROL BYTE   003700
0000C8 4110 310A        00110          59 PRTDET   PUT   PRTOUT,PRTDETL    PRINT DETAIL LINE               0190C002
0000CC 4100 3349        0034F          60+PRTDET   LA    1,PRTOUT          LOAD PARAMETER REG 1            0250C002
0000D0 58F0 1030        00030          61+         LA    0,PRTDETL         LOAD PARAMETER REG 0            0055C000
0000D4 05EF                            62+         L     15,48(0,1)        LOAD PUT ROUTINE ADDR           C060C000
0000D6 FA10 349A 34C4   004C0 004CA    63+         BALR  14,15             LINK TO PUT ROUTINE             003800
0000DC 9240 3349        0034F          64          AP    LINECNT,=P'1'     ADD ONE TO LINE COUNT           003900
0000E0 47F0 3013        0001E          65          MVI   PRTDCTL,C' '      MOVE BLANK TO ASA CONTROL BYTE  004000
0000E4 DE06 33CF 34B7   003D5 004BD    66          B     READINV                                           004100
0000EA 4110 310A        00110          67 INVEOF   ED    CNTPATRN,COUNT    EDIT COUNT                      004200
0000EE 4100 33CE        003CE          68          PUT   PRTOUT,CNTLINE    PRINT COUNT LINE                0190C002
0000F2 58F0 1030        00030          69+         LA    1,PRTOUT          LOAD PARAMETER REG 1            0250C002
0000F6 05EF                            70+         LA    0,CNTLINE         LOAD PARAMETER REG 0            0055C000
                                       71+         L     15,48(0,1)        LOAD PUT ROUTINE ADDR           0060C000
                                       72+         BALR  14,15             LINK TO PUT ROUTINE             004300
0000F8 4510 30FE        00104          73          CLOSE (INVMAST,,PRTOUT)                                 0242C000
0000FC 00                              74+         CNOP  0,4               ALIGN LIST TC FULLWORD          0246C000
0000FD 000000                          75+         BAL   1,*+12            LOAD REG1 W/LIST ADDR           0258C000
       *** ERROR ***                   76+         DC    AL1(0)            OPTION BYTE                     C260C000
000100 80                              77+         DC    AL3(INVMAST)      DCB ADDRESS                     0258C000
000101 000110                          78+         DC    AL1(128)          OPTION BYTE                     0260C000
000106 0A14                            79+         DC    AL3(PRTOUT)       DCB ADDRESS                     0164C000
                                       80+         SVC   20                ISSUE CLOSE SVC                 004400
                       00460           81          L     13,SAVE+4                                         004500
00010A 98EC D00C       0000C           82          RETURN (14,12)                                          0065C000
00010E 07FE                            83+         LM    14,12,12(13)      RESTORE THE REGISTERS           C200C000
                                       84+         BR    14                RETURN                          004600
       *** ERROR ***                   85 *  THE INVENTORY FILE DEFINITION                                004700
                                       86 INVMAST  DCB   DSORG=PS,                                      X  004800
                                                         RECFM=F3,                                     X  004900
                                                         MACRF=GM,                                     X  005100
                                                         BLKSIZE=500,                                  X  005200
                                                         LRECL=50,                                     X  005300
                                                         DDNAME=INVMST,                                X  005400
                                                         EODAD=INVEOF                                     005500
                                       87 *  THE PRINTER FILE DEFINITION                                  005600
                                       88 PRTOUT   DCB   DSORG=PS,                                      X  005700
                                                         RECFM=FA,                                     X  005800
                                                         MACRF=PM,                                     X  005900
                                                         BLKSIZE=133,                                  X  006000
                                                         LRECL=133,                                   
                                                         DDNAME=REPORT

                                       90+                    DATA CONTROL BLOCK                           2277C000
                                       91+                                                                2286C000
000110 0000            00110           92+PRTOUT   DC    0F'0'   ORIGIN ON WORD BOUNDARY                  22914C00
```

Figure 17-2 The assembly listing for the reorder-listing program (part 2 of 5)

```
LOC    OBJECT CODE       ADDR1 ADDR2 STMT  SOURCE STATEMENT                               ASM 0201 15.05  11/05/86   PAGE  4

                                     94**          DIRECT ACCESS DEVICE INTERFACE                                    2736C000
000110 0000000000000000            96+      DC  BL16'0'                    FDAD,DVTBL                                2754C000
000120 00000000                    97+      DC  A(0)                       KEYLE,DEVT,TRBAL                          2772C000

                                     99**          COMMON ACCESS METHOD INTERFACE                                    4869C000

000124 00                         101+      DC  AL1(0)                     BUFNO                                     4995C000
000125 000001                     102+      DC  AL3(1)                     BUFCB                                     5472C000
000128 0000                       103+      DC  AL2(0)                     BUFL                                      5517C000
00012A 4000                       104+      DC  BL2'01C000C000000000'                                               *5590C000
                                                                                                                     5589C000
00012C 00000001                   105+      DC  A(1)                       ICGE/ICBAD   DSORG                         5634C000

                                    107**          FOUNDATION EXTENSION                                              5661C000

00013C 00                         109+      DC  BL1'0C000000'              BFTEK,BFLN,HIARCHY                        5935C000
000131 000001                     110+      DC  AL3(1)                     EODAD                                     6597C000
000134 84                         111+      DC  BL1'10000100'                                                       *6615C000
                                                                                                                     6624C000
000135 000000                     112+      DC  AL3(0)                     RECFM  EXLST                              6633C000

                                    114**          FOUNDATION BLOCK                                                  6669C000

000138 D9C5D7D6D9E34040           116+      DC  CL8'REPORT'                DDNAME                                    6687C000
000140 02                         117+      DC  BL1'00000010'              OFLGS                                     6322C000
000141 00                         118+      DC  BL1'00000000'                                                        6831C000
000142 0050                       119+      DC  BL2'000000000001010000'                IFLG                         *6840C000
                                                                                                                     6849C000
                                          +                                MACR                                      6858C000

                                    121**          BSAM-BPAM-QSAM INTERFACE                                          7443C000

000144 00                         123+      DC  BL1'00000000'                                               RER1    *7461C000
                                          +                                                                          7470C000
000145 000001                     124+      DC  AL3(1)                     CHECK, GERR, PERR                         7488C000
00C 48 00000001                   125+      DC  A(1)                       SYNAD                                     7497C000
00014C 0000                       126+      DC  H'0'                       CIND1, CIND2                              7524C000
00014E 0085                       127+      DC  AL2(133)                   BLKSIZE                                   7587C000
000150 00000000                   128+      DC  F'0'                       WCPO, WCPL, OFFSR, OFFSW                  7596C000
000154 00000001                   129+      DC  A(1)                       ICBA                                      7605C000
000158 00                         130+      DC  AL1(0)                     NCP                                       7614C000
000159 0C0001                     131+      DC  AL3(1)                     ECBR, EOBAD

                                    133**          QSAM INTERFACE                                                    8145C000

00015C 00000001                   135+      DC  A(1)                       RECAD                                     8163C000
000160 0000                       136+      DC  H'0'                       QSWS                                      8181C000
000162 0085                       137+      DC  AL2(133)                   LRECL                                     8073C000
000164 00                         138+      DC  BL1'00000000'              EROPT                                     8253C000
000165 000001                     139+      DC  AL3(1)                     CNTRL                                     8262C000
000168 00000000                   140+      DC  F'0'                       PRECL                                     8271C000
00016C 00000001                   141+      DC  A(1)                       ECB                                       8280C000
                                    142 *         THE DATA DEFINITIONS FOR THE INVENTORY FILE WORK AREA              006100
000170                              143 INVWRKA  DS  0CL50                                                           006200
```

Figure 17-2   The assembly listing for the reorder-listing program (part 3 of 5)

```
LOC      OBJECT CODE         ADDR1 ADDR2  STMT  SOURCE STATEMENT

000170                                    144   INVITNBR DS   CL5
000175                                    145   INVITDES DS   CL20
000189                                    146   INVPRICE DS   CL5
00018E                                    147   INVORDPT DS   CL5
000193                                    148   INVONHND DS   CL5
000198                                    149   INVONORD DS   CL5
00019D                                    150            DS   CL30
                                          151   *
                                          152   *  THE DATA DEFINITIONS FOR THE PRINTER HEADING LINES
0001C0                                    153   HDGLINE1 DS   OCL133
0001C0   F1                               154            DC   C'1'
0001C1   4040404040404040                 155            DC   24C' '
0001D9   D9C5D6D9C4C5D940                 156            DC   C'REORDER LISTING'
0001E8   4040404040404040                 157            DC   93C' '
000245                                    158   HDGLINE2 DS   OCL133
000245   F0                               159            DC   C'0'
000246   40C9E3C5D4404040                 160            DC   C'   ITEM       ITEM           UNIT          X
00024E   4040404040404040                                     REORDER'
000285   4040404040404040                 161            DC   69C' '
0002CA                                    162   HDGLINE3 DS   OCL133
0002CA   40                               163            DC   C' '
0002CB   40D5D64B4040C4C5                 164            DC   C'   NO.      DESCRIPTION        PRICE    AVAILABLEX
0002D3   4040404040404040                                     POINT'
000309   4040404040404040                 165            DC   70C' '
                                          166   *  THE DATA DEFINITIONS FOR THE PRINTER DETAIL LINE
00034F                                    167   PRTDETL  DS   OCL133
00034F                                    168   PRTDCTL  DC   C'-'
000350                                    169   PRTITNBR DS   CL6
000356   404040404040                     170            DC   5C' '
00035B                                    171   PRTITDES DS   CL20
00036F   40404040                         172            DC   4C' '
000373                                    173   PRTPRICE DS   CL7
00037A   40404040                         174            DC   4C' '
00037E                                    175   PRTAVAIL DS   CL6
000384   40404040                         176            DC   4C' '
000388                                    177   PRTORDPT DS   CL6
00038E   404040404040404040               178            DC   70C' '
                                          179   *  THE DATA DEFINITIONS FOR THE COUNT LINE
0003D4                                    180   CNTLINE  DS   OCL133
0003D4   60                               181            DC   C'-'
0003D5   40202063202020                   182   CNTPATRN DC   X'40202063202020'
0003DC   40D9C5C5D6D9C4E2                 183            DC   C' RECORDS IN THE INPUT FILE'
0003F6   4040404040404040                 184            DC   99C' '
                                          185   *  THE DATA DEFINITIONS FOR OTHER REQUIRED WORK AREAS
00045C                                    186   SAVE     DS   18F
0004A4   40202020202020                   187   PATTERN1 DC   X'40202020202020'
0004AA   402020214B2020                   188   PATTERN2 DC   X'402020214B2020'
0004B1                                    189   WRKAVAIL DS   PL3
0004B4                                    190   WRKONORD DS   PL3
0004B7                                    191   WRKORDPT DS   PL3
0004BA                                    192   PACKAREA DS   PL3
0004BD   00000C                           193   COUNT    DC   PL3'0'
0004C0   050C                             194   LINECNT  DC   P'50'
000000                                    195            END  BEGIN
0004C8   050C                             196            =P'50'
```

Figure 17-2   The assembly listing for the reorder-listing program (part 4 of 5)

```
                                                      PAGE    6

                                         ASM 0201 15.05 11/05/86

LOC    OBJECT CODE   ADDR1 ADDR2  STMT  SOURCE STATEMENT

0004CA 1C                          197         =P'1'
0004CB OC                          198         =P'0'
```

Figure 17-2   The assembly listing for the reorder-listing program (part 5 of 5)

```
                                                      PAGE    7

                         RELOCATION DICTIONARY

                                         ASM 0201 15.05 11/05/86

POS.ID  REL.ID  FLAGS  ADDRESS

0001    0001     08    000019
0001    0001     08    000101
```

Figure 17-3   The relocation dictionary for the reorder-listing program

CROSS-REFERENCE

SYMBOL	LEN	VALUE	DEFN	REFERENCES						
BEGIN	00002	00000000	00003	00195						
CNTLINE	00133	000003D4	00180	00070						
CNTPATRN	00007	000003D5	00182	00067						
COUNT	00003	0000048D	00193	00022	00067					
HDGLINE1	00133	000001C0	00153	00044						
HDGLINE2	00133	00000245	00158	00049						
HDGLINE3	00133	000002CA	00162	00054						
INVITDES	00020	00000175	00145	00032						
INVITNBR	00005	00000170	00144	00029						
INVMAST	****UNDEFINED****		00013	00018	00077					
INVONHND	00005	00000198	00149	00023						
INVONORD	00005	0000019D	00150	00024						
INVORDPT	00005	00000193	00148	00026						
INVPRICE	00005	0000018E	00147	00033						
INVWRKA	00050	00000170	00143	00019						
LINECNT	00002	000004C0	00194	00040	00057	00064				
PACKAREA	00003	0000048A	00192	00029	00031	00033	00035			
PATTERN1	00006	000004A4	00187	00036	00038					
PATTERN2	00007	000004AA	00188	00034						
PRTAVAIL	00006	0000037E	00175	00036	00058	00065				
PRTDCTL	00001	0000034F	00060	00037						
PRTDET	00004	000000C8	00167	00041						
PRTDETL	00133	0000034F	00171	00061						
PRTITDES	00020	00000359	00169	00032						
PRTITNBR	00006	00000350	00169	00031						
PRTORDPT	00006	00000388	00177	00038	00039					
PRTOUT	00004	00000110	00092	00015	00043	00048	00053	00060	00069	00379
PRTPRICE	00007	00000373	00173	00034	00035					
READINV	00004	0000001E	00018	00028	00066					
SAVE	00004	0000045C	00186	00007	00008	00081				
WRKAVAIL	00003	00000481	00189	00023	00027	00037				
WRKONORD	00003	00000484	00190	00024						
WRKORDPT	00003	00000487	00191	00026	00027	00039				

Figure 17-4   The cross-reference listing for the reorder-listing program

LITERAL CROSS-REFERENCE

SYMBOL	LEN	VALUE	DEFN	REFERENCES	
=P'50'	00002	000004C8	00196	00040	
=P'1'	00001	000004CA	00197	00022	00064
=P'0'	00001	000004CB	00198	00057	

Figure 17-5   The literal cross-reference listing for the reorder-listing program

ASSEMBLER DIAGNOSTICS AND STATISTICS

STMT	ERROR CODE	MESSAGE
13	IF0188	INVMAST IS AN UNDEFINED SYMBOL
18	IF0188	INVMAST IS AN UNDEFINED SYMBOL
25	IF0078	UNDEFINED OP CODE
30	IF0078	UNDEFINED OP CODE
77	IF0188	INVMAST IS AN UNDEFINED SYMBOL
86	IF0078	UNDEFINED OP CODE

NUMBER OF STATEMENTS FLAGGED IN THIS ASSEMBLY =   6
HIGHEST SEVERITY WAS   8
OPTIONS FOR THIS ASSEMBLY
ALIGN, ALOGIC, BUFSIZE(STD), DECK, ESD, FLAG(0), LINECOUNT(55), LIST, NOMCALL, YFLAG, WORKSIZE(2097152)
NOMLOGIC, NONUMBER, NOOBJECT, NORENT, RLD, NOSTMT, NOLIBMAC, NOTERMINAL, NOTEST, XREF(SHORT)
SYSPARM()
WORK FILE BUFFER SIZE/NUMBER =32758/ 1
TOTAL RECORDS READ FROM SYSTEM INPUT   113
TOTAL RECORDS READ FROM SYSTEM LIBRARY   3495
TOTAL RECORDS PUNCHED   29
TOTAL RECORDS PRINTED   298

Figure 17-6   The diagnostics and statistics listing for the reorder-listing program

For data definitions, the location counter is increased by the total number of bytes reserved (that is, the duplication factor times the length modifier). To illustrate, look at statements 143 and 144. Because the duplication factor is zero in statement 143, both INVWRKA and INVITNBR have the same location counter value, hex 170. However, INVWRKA has a length attribute of 50 and INVITNBR has a length attribute of 5.

The object code column   The second column from the left is headed OBJECT CODE. This column shows the actual machine language assembled for a statement just as it will be stored in the computer. It is in hex notation with two hex digits representing one byte of storage. If a statement causes no object code to be generated, this column is blank.

For instructions, there are two, four, or six bytes represented in the object code column. The format of this data corresponds to the instruction formats presented in chapter 4. The BALR statement, for instance, is translated into two bytes of object code, hex 0530. The first byte is the operation code, hex 05; the second byte holds two register numbers, 3 and 0. Similarly, the MVC instruction in statement 32 is translated into hex D2133355316F. By referring to the MVC instruction format, you can determine that D2 is the operation code, hex 13 is the length, address 1 consists of a base address in register 3 plus a displacement of hex 355, and so on.

For DC statements, the object code column usually shows only the first eight bytes of the field. If you want all of the defined data to print, you can use a PRINT assembler command as described in chapter 6. Remember that DS statements do not cause object code to be created even if they are given nominal values.

You might notice that ***ERROR*** is printed in the object code column when the assembler cannot create object code due to a diagnostic error. As you will see, the diagnostics refer to these statements so the errors can be corrected.

The operand address columns   The ADDR1 and ADDR2 columns give the location counter values for operands 1 and 2 of each instruction. If an operand is a register or if no operand is present, the corresponding column is left blank. As you will see in the next chapter, the location values are helpful when you are debugging.

The relocation dictionary

Figure 17-3 is the relocation dictionary for the reorder-listing program. However, you won't need to use these dictionaries in this course. As a result, these dictionaries won't be shown in the assembly output for any other programs in this book.

The cross-reference listing

Figure 17-4 is the *cross-reference listing* for the reorder-listing program. In the SYMBOL column of this listing, you can see the labels of all instructions or fields used in the program. For instance, BEGIN is the name of the first machine instruction in the program, and INVORDPT is the name of one of the fields in the input work area. Because this is a *sorted* cross-reference listing, the symbol names are listed in alphabetic order.

The four columns to the right of each symbol name give information that is useful when you are correcting diagnostics or debugging. First, the LEN column gives the length attribute of each label. For instance, BEGIN, which is the label of the SAVE macro, has a length attribute of 2; INVITDES has a length attribute of 20. Second, the VALUE column gives the location counter value assigned to the label. Third, the DEFN column gives the number of the statement that defines the label. And fourth, the REFERENCES column gives the numbers of all statements that use the label as an operand. If necessary, more than one line is used for these reference numbers.

The literal cross-reference listing

The *literal cross-reference listing* in figure 17-5 is a cross reference of any literals coded as instruction operands in the program. While you will rarely need to refer to this list, it's occasionally useful when debugging a program.

The diagnostics and statistics listing

Figure 17-6 shows the *assembler diagnostics and statistics listing* for the reorder-listing program. In practice, this name is shortened to the *diagnostic listing*. For each diagnostic message on the listing, you can see the statement number of the instruction in error (STMT) followed by an error code (ERROR CODE) followed by an error message (MESSAGE).

An error number, like IF0078, for the OS/VS assembler refers to an expanded explanation of the error message that can be found in IBM's *OS/VS—VM/370 Assembler Programmer's Guide* (GC33-4021). In general, though, the message on the diagnostic listing tells you all you need to know so you should rarely need this manual.

In addition to the diagnostics, this listing also gives some program information that includes the options used for the assembly and some statistical information related to the execution of the assembler. Of the two, the option list will probably be the most interesting to you. As you can see in figure 17-6, this assembly of the reorder-listing program was done with the XREF and RLD options on. If you don't want the cross-reference listing or relocation dictionary to print, you can turn these options off by coding the appropriate operands on the PARM parameter of the EXEC statement as described in topic 2 of chapter 3. For most assemblies, though, you will want a cross-reference listing.

HOW TO CORRECT DIAGNOSTICS

When it comes to correcting diagnostics, you should realize from the start that the assembler's ability to find errors is limited. It can find coding errors like invalid operation codes, invalid formats for operands, undefined labels, and missing commas, but it cannot detect errors in the logic of a program. As a result, it's possible to write a series of statements that assemble without error but that make no sense at all as far as the function of a program is concerned.

You should also know that the assembler does not require strict alignment of statement parts even though the programs in this book are all coded with the operation codes starting in column 10 and the operands starting in column 16. Although the label must start in column 1, the operation code can start anywhere as long as one or more blanks separate it from the label. Similarly, the operands can start anywhere as long as one or more blanks separate them from the operation code. If a statement doesn't have a label, the operation code can start anywhere after column 1. Of course, the sequence from left to right in the statement is critical; it must be label followed by operation code followed by operands.

Although the assembler can produce many different diagnostic messages, the majority of errors are covered by just a few messages. To illustrate, the diagnostic listings in figures 17-6 and 17-7 present some of the common messages. Both of these listings are for the same reorder-listing program, but with different coding errors. As you will see, it's relatively easy to figure out how to correct the coding errors, even though the messages aren't always clear.

The first diagnostic listing

In figure 17-6, there are six diagnostic messages. All of these relate to invalid operation codes. The third diagnostic message, for example, is UNDEFINED OP CODE. It refers to statement 25. Since ADD is an invalid operation code, the assembler was unable to create the object code for this statement so it printed the diagnostic message. In this case, of course, the operation code should be AP.

The fourth diagnostic has the same message. This time the message was caused by the invalid operation code MVL instead of the intended MVC. An error like this is often just a typographical error made during the entry of the source program.

The sixth diagnostic is for an undefined operation code in statement 86. In this case, the source program has DCP for the operation code when DCB is correct. Because of this error, the label of the DCB, INVMAST, is not considered to be defined. This is shown in the cross-reference listing.

The error in the operation code for the DCB also accounts for the other three diagnostic messages in figure 17-6. All of these refer to an undefined symbol, INVMAST, which is the label of the DCB for the master file. These diagnostics refer to the instructions in statements 13, 18, and 77, which are generated by the OPEN, CLOSE, and GET macros.

When a diagnostic is caused by an undefined operation code, it's usually easy to correct the coding error. At first, it might be confusing when the diagnostic refers to an instruction generated by a macro. However, if you study the macro rather than the generated instructions, you should be able to find a coding error in it.

The second diagnostic listing

Figure 17-7 illustrates the assembly output for another version of the reorder-listing program. This output includes the assembly listing, the sorted cross-reference listing, and the diagnostic listing. This diagnostic listing illustrates some common coding errors that weren't shown in the first listing.

The diagnostic for statement 36 indicates PREMATURE END OF OPERAND. Can you see, in statement 36, that this diagnostic is caused by the blank that precedes the second operand? You can correct this error by removing the blank so the second operand immediately follows the comma. NEAR OPERAND COLUMN 9 in the diagnostic message indicates the approximate location of the error in the operand area of the source statement.

All three of the messages that declare LINECNT as an UNDEFINED SYMBOL (statements 40, 57, and 64) are caused by the error identified in the last diagnostic. This message indicates that statement 249, the definition of the work field LINECNT, is a DC or DS instruction that contains an INVALID TYPE code. If you look at statement 249, you can see that the type code P for packed decimal was omitted.

A second diagnostic, ILLEGAL CHARACTER IN EXPRESSION, was generated for statement 57. In this case the actual problem is that the second operand of the zero-and-add instruction was supposed to be a literal constant but the equals sign that should precede it was omitted. The assembler then tried to interpret P'0' as a valid label and flagged the apostrophes as invalid characters.

The diagnostic for statement 141 demonstrates how misleading a diagnostic message can sometimes be. It says that statement 141 has an IN-VALID OPERATION CODE. But statement 141 was not intended to have an operation code. It's the continuation of the DCB statement for the input file. Obviously, this continuation line was not connected to the first part of the DCB as intended. If you look at the DCB, you can see that a continuation character wasn't coded following the LRECL operand. Another clue, if we needed it, is presented by statement 87. It's a special comment generated during the expansion of the DCB macro. It says that the ddname wasn't specified in the DCB statement.

A similar type of error occurs when the continuation character is present, but the comma following the first operand of the line is missing. This causes the next line of the DCB to be regarded as a remark, not as an additional operand. If that had been the error in this program, the only clue would be the message in statement 87 since the diagnostic for the continuation statement would not exist.

```
LOC    OBJECT CODE   ADDR1 ADDR2  STMT   SOURCE STATEMENT

000000                             1 REORDLST START 0                                                 00C400
000000 90EC D00C                   2 BEGIN    SAVE  (14,12)              SAVE REGISTERS              00C500
                                   3+BEGIN    DS    0H                                               C165C000
000000 90EC D00C                   4+         STM   14,12,12(13)                                     0295C000
000004 0530                        5          BALR  3,0                                              00C600
                      00006        6          USING *,3                                              00C700
000006 50D0 34C6      004CC        7          ST    13,SAVE+4                                        00C800
00000A 41D0 34C2      004C8        8          LA    13,SAVE                                          00C900
00000E 0700                        9          OPEN  (INVMAST,INPUT,PRTOUT,OUTPUT)                    001000
00000E 0700                       10+         CNOP  0,4                                              0174C000
000010 4510 3016      0001C       11+         BAL   1,*+12               ALIGN LIST TO FULLWORD      0178C000
000014 00                         12+         DC    AL1(0)               LOAD REG1 W/LIST ADDR.      0190C000
000015 00001C                     13+         DC    AL3(INVMAST)            OPTION BYTE              C192C000
000018 8F                         14+         DC    AL1(143)             DCB ADDRESS                 0190C000
000019 00017C                     15+         DC    AL3(PRTOUT)             OPTION BYTE              C192C000
00001C 0A13                       16+         SVC   19                   DCB ADDRESS                 C400C000
                                             ISSUE OPEN SVC
00001E 4110 3116      0011C       17 READINV  GET   INVMAST,INVWRKA      READ RECORD INTO WORK AREA  001100
00001E 4110 3116      0011C       18+READINV  LA    1,INVMAST            LOAD PARAMETER REG 1        0190C002
000022 4100 31D6      001DC       19+         LA    0,INVWRKA            LOAD PARAMETER REG 0        0250C002
000026 58F0 1030      00030       20+         L     15,48(C,1)           LOAD GET ROUTINE ADDR       C060C0C0
00002A 05EF                       21+         BALR  14,15                LINK TO GET ROUTINE         00625000
00002C FA20 3520 352C 00526 00532 22          AP    COUNT,=P'1'          ADD ONE TO COUNT            001300
000032 F224 3517 31FE 00520 00204 23          PACK  WRKAVAIL,INVONHND                                001400
000038 F224 351A 3203 00520 00209 24          PACK  WRKCNORD,INVONORD                                001500
00003E FA22 3517 351A 00520 0051D 25          AP    WRKAVAIL,WRKONORD    ADD ON HAND AND ON ORDER    001600
000044 F922 3517 351D 00523 00520 26          PACK  WRKORDPT,INVORDPT                                001700
00004A F922 3517 351D 001FF 00523 27          CP    WRKAVAIL,WRKORDPT    COMPARE AVAILABLE, REORDER POINT  001900
000050 4760 3018      0001E       28          BNL   READINV                                          002000
000054 F224 351D 31D6 00523 001DC 29          PACK  PACKAREA,INVITNBR                                002100
00005A D205 351D 350A 00523 0051C 30          MVC   PRTITNBR,PATTERN1                                002200
000060 DE05 3386 351D 003BC 00523 31          ED    PRTITNBR,PACKAREA    EDIT ITEM NUMBER FIELD      002300
000066 D213 33C1 31DB 003C7 001E1 32          MVC   PRTITDES,INVITDES    MOVE ITEM DESCRIPTION       002400
00006C F206 351D 31F4 00523 001FA 33          PACK  PACKAREA,INVPRICE                                002500
000072 D206 3309 3510 003DF 00516 34          MVC   PRTPRICE,PATTERN2                                002600
000078 DE06 3309 351D 003DF 00523 35          ED    PRTPRICE,PACKAREA    EDIT UNIT PRICE             002700
00007E 0000 0000 0000 003EA 00000 36          MVC   PRTAVAIL,PATTERN1                                002800
   *** ERROR ***
000084 DE05 33E4 3517 003EA 0051D 37          ED    PRTAVAIL,WRKAVAIL    EDIT AVAILABLE              002900
00008A D205 33EE 350A 003F4 00510 38          MVC   PRTORDPT,PATTERN1                                003000
000090 DE05 33EE 351D 003F4 00523 39          ED    PRTORDPT,WRKORDPT    EDIT ORDER POINT            003100
000096 F940 0000 0000 00000 00530 40          CP    LINECNT,=P'50'       COMPARE LINE COUNT TO 50    003200
   *** ERROR ***
00009C 4740 30CE      000D4        41          BL    PRTDET               BRANCH ON LOW TO PRTDET     0190C002
0000A0 4110 3176      0017C        42          PUT   PRTOUT,HDGLINE1      PRINT FIRST HEADING LINE    0250C002
0000A4 4100 3226      0022C        43+         LA    1,PRTOUT             LOAD PARAMETER REG 1        0055C000
0000A8 58F0 1030      00030        44+         LA    0,HDGLINE1           LOAD PARAMETER REG 0        0060C000
0000AC 05EF                        45+         L     15,48(0,1)           LOAD PUT ROUTINE ADDR       003300
                                   46+         BALR  14,15                LINK TO PUT ROUTINE
0000AE 4110 3176      0017C        47          PUT   PRTOUT,HDGLINE2      PRINT SECOND HEADING LINE   0190C002
0000B2 4100 32A8      02B1         48+         LA    1,PRTOUT             LOAD PARAMETER REG 1        0250C002
0000B6 58F0 1030      00030        49+         LA    0,HDGLINE2           LOAD PARAMETER REG 0        0055C000
0000BA 05EF                        50+         L     15,48(0,1)           LOAD PUT ROUTINE ADDR       0060C000
                                   51+         BALR  14,15                LINK TO PUT ROUTINE         003400
0000BC 4110 3176      0017C        52          PUT   PRTOUT,HDGLINE3      PRINT THIRD HEADING LINE    C190C002
                                   53+         LA    1,PRTOUT             LOAD PARAMETER REG 1
```

Figure 17-7   Assembly output for another version of the reorder-listing program (part 1 of 8)

```
                                                        ASM C201 15.06  11/05/86                              PAGE   3

LOC     OBJECT CODE       ADDR1 ADDR2  STMT   SOURCE STATEMENT

0000C0  4100 3330         00336         54+         LA    0,HDGLINE3          LOAD PARAMETER REG 0     C250C002
0000C4  58F0 1030         00030         55+         L     15,48(0,1)          LOAD ROUTINE ADDR        0055C000
0000C8  05EF                             56+        BALR  14,15               LINK TO PUT ROUTINE      0060C000
0000CA  0000 0000 0000    00000 00000    57         ZAP   LINECNT,P'0'        RESET LINE COUNT TO ZERO 003500
        *** ERROR ***
0000D0  92F0 3385         003BB         58         MVI   PRTDCTL,C'0'        MOVE ZERO TO ASA CONTROL BYTE  003600
                                        59  PRTDET PUT   PRTOUT,PRTDETL      PRINT DETAIL LINE        003700
0000D4  4110 3176         0017C         60+PRTDET  LA    1,PRTOUT            LOAD PARAMETER REG 1     0190C002
0000D8  4100 3385         003BB         61+        LA    0,PRTDETL           LOAD PARAMETER REG 0     C250C002
0000DC  58F0 1030         00030         62+        L     15,48(0,1)          LOAD ROUTINE ADDR        0055C000
0000E0  05EF                             63+       BALR  14,15               LINK TO PUT ROUTINE      0060C000
0000E2  0000 0000 0000    00000 00532    64        AP    LINECNT,=P'1'       ADD ONE TO LINE COUNT    003800
        *** ERROR ***
0000E8  9240 3385         003BB         65         MVI   PRTDCTL,C' '        MOVE BLANK TO ASA CONTROL BYTE  003900
0000EC  47F0 3018         0001E         66         READINV B  READINV                                 004000
0000F0  DE06 343S 3520    00441 00526   67  INVEOF ED    CNTPATRN,COUNT      EDIT COUNT               004100
                                        68         PUT   PRTOUT,CNTLINE      PRINT COUNT LINE         004200
0000F6  4110 3176         0017C         69+        LA    1,PRTOUT            LOAD PARAMETER REG 1     0190C002
0000FA  4100 343A         00440         70+        LA    0,CNTLINE           LOAD PARAMETER REG 0     C250C002
0000FE  58F0 1030         00030         71+        L     15,48(0,1)          LOAD PUT ROUTINE ADDR    0055C000
000102  05EF                             72+       BALR  14,15               LINK TO PUT ROUTINE      0060C000
                                        73         CLOSE (INVMAST,,PRTOUT)                            004300
                                        74+        CNOP  0,4                 ALIGN LIST TO FULLWORD   C242C000
000104  4510 310A         00110         75+        BAL   1,*+12              LOAD REG1 W/LIST ADDR    0246C000
000108  00                               76+       DC    AL1(0)              OPTION BYTE              0258C000
000109  000011C                          77+       DC    AL3(INVMAST)        DCB ADDRESS              0260C000
00010C  80                               78+       DC    AL1(128)            OPTION BYTE              0258C000
00010D  00017C                           79+       DC    AL3(PRTOUT)         DCB ADDRESS              0260C000
000110  0A14                             80+       SVC   20                  ISSUE CLOSE SVC          C164C000
000112  58D0 34C6         004CC         81         L     13,SAVE+4                                    004400
                                        82         RETURN (14,12)                                     004500
000116  98EC D00C         0000C         83+        LM    14,12,12(13)        RESTORE THE REGISTERS    0065C000
00011A  07FE                             84+       BR    14                  RETURN                   0200C000
                                        85  *    THE INVENTORY FILE DEFINITION                        004600
                                        86  INVMAST DC3  DSORG=PS,                               X    004700
                                                        RECFM=FB,                               X    004800
                                                        MACRF=GM,                               X    004900
                                                        BLKSIZE=500,                            X    005000
                                                        LRECL=50,                               X    005100
                                        87+**,*** IHB061 DDNAME NOT SPECIFIED

                                                                      DATA CONTROL BLOCK                 2277C000
                                        89+**                                                            2286C000
                                        90+**                   ORIGIN ON WORD BOUNDARY                  22914000
00011C                                  91+INVMAST DC   0F'0'                                            2736C000

                                        93+**                   DIRECT ACCESS DEVICE INTERFACE

00011C  00C000000000000000              95+        DC    BL16'0'             FDAD,DVTBL                  2754C000
00012C  00C00000                        96+        DC    A(0)                KEYLE,DEVT,TRBAL            2772C000

                                        98+**                   COMMON ACCESS METHOD INTERFACE           4869C000

000130  00                              100+       DC    AL1(0)              BUFNO                        4905C000
000131  0C0001                          101+       DC    AL3(1)              BUFC3                        5472C000
```

Figure 17-7   Assembly output for another version of the reorder-listing program (part 2 of 8)

```
LOC     OBJECT CODE    ADDR1 ADDR2  STMT   SOURCE STATEMENT

000134  0C00                        1C2+        DC    AL2(0)                   BUFL                        5517C000
000136  4000                        1C3+        DC    BL2'0100000000000000'                              *5580C000
                                                                                                          5589C000
                                                                                                          5634C000
000138  00000001                    104+        DC    A(1)                     ICQE/IOBAD                 5661C000

                                    106+*                   FOUNDATION EXTENSION

00013C  00                          108+        DC    BL1'00000000'            BFTEK,BFLN,HIARCHY         5985C000
00013D  000001                      109+        DC    AL3(1)                   EODAD                      6597C000
000140  90                          110+        DC    BL1'10010000'                                      *6615C000
                                       +                                                                  6624C000
000141  000000                      111+        DC    AL3(0)                   RECFM                      6633C000
                                                                               EXLST

                                    113+*                   FOUNDATION BLOCK

000144  F040404040404040            115+        DC    CL8' '                   DDNAME                     6669C000
00014C  02                          116+        DC    BL1'00000010'            OFLGS                      6687C000
00014D  00                          117+        DC    BL1'00000000'            IFLG                       6822C000
00014E  5000                        118+        DC    BL2'0101000000000000'                               6831C000
                                       +                                                                 *6840C000
                                       +                                                                  6849C000
                                                                                                          6858C000

                                    120+*                   BSAM-BPAM-GSAM INTERFACE

000150  00                          122+        DC    BL1'00000000'            MACR                       7443C000
                                       +                                                                 *7461C000  RER1
000151  000001                      123+        DC    AL3(1)                   CHECK, GERR, PERR          7470C000
000154  00000001                    124+        DC    A(1)                     SYNAD                      7479C000
000158  0000                        125+        DC    H'0'                     CIND1, CIND2               7488C000
00015A  01F4                        126+        DC    AL2(500)                 BLKSIZE                    7497C000
00015C  00000000                    127+        DC    F'0'                     WCPO, WCPL, OFFSR, OFFSW   7524C000
000160  00000001                    128+        DC    A(1)                     ICBA                       7587C000
000164  00                          129+        DC    AL1(0)                   NCP                        7596C000
000165  000001                      130+        DC    AL3(1)                   ECBR, EOBAD                7605C000
                                                                                                          7614C000

                                    132+*                   QSAM INTERFACE

000168  00000001                    134+        DC    A(1)                     RECAD                      8163C000
00016C  0000                        135+        DC    H'0'                     QSWS                       8181C000
00016E  0032                        136+        DC    AL2(50)                  LRECL                      8073C000
000170  00                          137+        DC    BL1'00000000'            EROPT                      8253C000
000171  000001                      138+        DC    AL3(1)                   CNTRL                      8262C000
000174  00000000                    139+        DC    F'0'                     PRECL                      8271C000
000178  00000001                    140+        DC    A(1)                     ECB                        8280C000
                                    141+                                       DDNAME=INVMST,          X  005200

                            *** ERROR ***

                                    142 *    THE PRINTER FILE DEFINITION                                 005300
                                    143 PRTOUT  DCB   EODAD=INVEOF                                        005400
                                                      DSORG=PS,                                        X 005500
                                                      RECFM=FA,                                        X 005600
                                                      MACRF=PM,                                        X 005700
                                                      BLKSIZE=133,                                     X 005800
                                                      LRECL=133,                                       X 005900
                                                      DDNAME=REPORT                                       036000
```

Figure 17-7   Assembly output for another version of the reorder-listing program (part 3 of 8)

ASM 0201 15.06 11/05/86   PAGE 5

```
LOC    OBJECT CODE        ADDR1  ADDR2  STMT  SOURCE STATEMENT

00017C                                  145++              DATA CONTROL BLOCK
                                        146++
                                        147+PRTOUT  DC  0F'0'   ORIGIN ON WORD BOUNDARY

                                        149++              DIRECT ACCESS DEVICE INTERFACE

00017C 0000000000000000000              151+    DC  BL16'0'     FDAD,DVTBL
00018C 00000000                         152+    DC  A(0)        KEYLE,DEVT,TRBAL

                                        154++              COMMON ACCESS METHOD INTERFACE

000190 00                               156+    DC  AL1(0)          BUFNO
000191 000001                           157+    DC  AL3(1)          BUFC3
000194 0000                             158+    DC  AL2(0)
000196 4000                             159+    DC  BL2'0100000000000000'  BUFL

000198 00000001                         160+    DC  A(1)        ICQE/ICBAD  DSORG

                                        162++              FOUNDATION EXTENSION

00019C 00                               164+    DC  BL1'00000000'   BFTEK,BFLN,HIARCHY
00019D 000001                           165+    DC  AL3(1)          ECDAD
0001A0 84                               166+    DC  BL1'10000100'    RECFM
                                             +                      EXLST
0001A1 000000                           167+    DC  AL3(0)

                                        169++              FOUNDATION BLOCK

0001A4 D9C5D7D6D9E34040                 171+    DC  CL8'REPORT'      DDNAME
0001AC 02                               172+    DC  BL1'00000010'    OFLGS
0001AD 00                               173+    DC  BL1'00000000'
0001AE 0050                             174+    DC  BL2'0000000001010000'  IFLG
                                             +                      MACR

                                        176++              BSAM-BPAM-QSAM INTERFACE

0001B0 00                               178+    DC  BL1'00000000'
                                             +
0001B1 000001                           179+    DC  AL3(1)          CHECK, GERR, PERR
0001B4 00000001                         180+    DC  A(1)            SYNAD
000198 0000                             181+    DC  H'0'            CIND1, CIND2
0001BA 0085                             182+    DC  AL2(133)        BLKSIZE
0001BC 00000000                         183+    DC  F'0'            WCPO, WCPL, OFFSR, OFFSW
0001C0 00000001                         184+    DC  A(1)            IOBA
0001C4 00                               185+    DC  AL1(0)          NCP
0001C5 000001                           186+    DC  AL3(1)          ECBR, EOBAD

                                        188++              QSAM INTERFACE

0001C8 00000001                         190+    DC  A(1)            RECAD
0001CC 0000                             191+    DC  H'0'            QSWS
0001CE 0085                             192+    DC  AL2(133)        LRECL
0001D0 00                               193+    DC  BL1'00000000'   EROPT
0001D1 000001                           194+    DC  AL3(1)          CNTRL
```

```
22770000
22860000
22914000
27360000
27540000
27720000
48690000
49050000
54720000
55170000
*55800000
55890000
56340000
5661C000
59850000
6597C000
*6615C000
66240000
66330000
66690000
66870000
68220000
68310000
*68400000
68490000
68580000
74430000
*74610000  RER1
74700000
74790000
74880000
74970000
75240000
75870000
75960000
76050000
76140000
81450000
81630000
81810000
80730000
82530000
82620000
```

Figure 17-7   Assembly output for another version of the reorder-listing program (part 4 of 8)

```
                                                              ASM 0201 15.06  11/05/86            PAGE    6

LOC      OBJECT CODE        ADDR1 ADDR2  STMT   SOURCE STATEMENT

0001D4   00000000                        195+        DC    F'0'                          PRECL
0001D8   00000001                        196+        DC    A(1)                          ECB
                                         197   *     THE DATA DEFINITIONS FOR THE INVENTORY FILE WORK AREA
0001DC                                   198   INVWRKA  DS    0CL50
0001DC                                   199   INVITNBR DS    CL5
0001E1                                   200   INVITDES DS    CL20
0001F5                                   201   INVPRICE DS    CL5
0001FA                                   202   INVORDPT DS    CL5
0001FF                                   203   INVONHND DS    CL5
000204                                   204   INVONORD DS    CL5
000209                                   205   INVONORD DS    CL5
00020E                                   206            DS    CL30
                                         207   *     THE DATA DEFINITIONS FOR THE PRINTER HEADING LINES
00022C                                   208   HDGLINE1 DS    0CL133
00022C   F1                              209            DC    C'1'
00022D   40404040404040                  210            DC    24C' '
000245   D9C5D6D9C4C5D940                211            DC    C'REORDER LISTING'
000254   4040404040404040                212            DC    93C' '
000281                                   213   HDGLINE2 DS    0CL133
000281   F0                              214            DC    C'0'
000292   40C9E3C5D440404040              215            DC    C' ITEM          ITEM                UNIT          X
0002A8   4040404040404040                                     REORDER'
0002F1   4040404040404040
000336                                   216   HDGLINE3 DS    0CL133
000336   40                              217            DC    69C' '
000337   4040D5D64B404040C5              218            DC    C' NO.       DESCRIPTION          PRICE    AVAILABLEX
00033F   4040404040404C5                                      POINT'
000375   404040404040404040
                                         220   *     THE DATA DEFINITIONS FOR THE PRINTER DETAIL LINE
0003B3                                   221   PRTDETL  DS    0CL133
0003B8                                   222   PRTDCTL  DS    CL1
0003BC                                   223   PRTITNBR DS    CL6
0003C2   404040404040                    224            DC    5C' '
0003C7                                   225   PRTITDES DS    CL20
0003DB   40404040                        226            DC    4C' '
0003DF                                   227
0003E6   40404040                        228   PRTPRICE DS    CL7
0003EA                                   229            DC    4C' '
0003F0   40404040                        230   PRTAVAIL DS    CL6
0003F4                                   231            DC    4C' '
0003FA   404040404040404040              232   PRTORDPT DS    CL6
                                         233            DC    70C' '
                                         234   *     THE DATA DEFINITIONS FOR THE COUNT LINE
000440                                   235   CNTLINE  DS    0CL133
000440   60                              236            DC    CL1
000441   4020206B202020                  237   CNTPATRN DC    X'4020206B202020'
000448   40D9C5C3D6D9C4E2                238            DC    C' RECORDS IN THE INPUT FILE'
000462   404040404040404040              239            DC    99C' '
                                         240   *     THE DATA DEFINITIONS FOR OTHER REQUIRED WORK AREAS
0004C8                                   241   SAVE     DS    18F
000510   402020202020                    242   PATTERN1 DC    X'402020202020'
000516   4020202148B2020                 243   PATTERN2 DC    X'402020214B2020'
00051D                                   244   WRKAVAIL DS    PL3
000520                                   245   WRKONORD DS    PL3
000523                                   246   WRKORDPT DC    PL3

                                         *** ERROR ***
```

Figure 17-7   Assembly output for another version of the reorder-listing program (part 5 of 8)

ASM 0201 15.06 11/05/86   PAGE   7

LOC	OBJECT CODE	ADDR1	ADDR2	STMT	SOURCE STATEMENT			
000523				247	PACKAREA	DS	PL3	011300
000526	00000C			248	COUNT	DC	PL3'0'	011400
000529				249	LINECNT	DC	'50'	011500
	*** ERROR ***							
000000				250		END	BEGIN	011600
000530	050C			251			=P'50'	
000532	1C			252			=P'1'	

Figure 17-7   Assembly output for another version of the reorder-listing program (part 6 of 8)

CROSS-REFERENCE

ASM 0201 15.06 11/05/86   PAGE   9

SYMBOL	LEN	VALUE	DEFN	REFERENCES						
BEGIN	00002	00000000	00003	00250						
CNTLINE	00133	0000044C	00235	00070						
CNTPATRN	00007	00000441	00237	00067	00067					
COUNT	00003	00000526	00248	00044						
HDGLINE1	00133	0000022C	00208	00044						
HDGLINE2	00133	00000281	00213	00049						
HDGLINE3	00133	00000336	00217	00054						
INVITDES	00020	000001E1	00200	00032						
INVITNBR	00005	000001DC	00199	00029						
INVMAST	00004	0000011C	00091	00013	00077					
INVONHND	00005	00000204	00204	00023						
INVONORD	00005	00000209	00205	00024						
INVORDPT	00005	000001FF	00203	00026						
INVPRICE	00005	000001FA	00202	00033						
INVWRKA	00050	000001DC	00198	00019						
LINECNT	00001	00000529	00249	0004C	00057	00064				
PACKAREA	00003	00000523	00247	00029	0C031	0C053	00035			
PATTERN1	00006	00000526	00242	00030	0C038					
PATTERN2	00007	00000516	00243	00034						
PRTAVAIL	00006	000003EA	00230	00036	00037					
PRTDCTL	0C001	000003BB	00223	00058	0C065					
PRTDET	00004	000000D4	00060	00041						
PRTDETL	00133	000003B3	00222	00061						
PRTITDES	00020	000003C7	00226	00032						
PRTITNBR	00005	000003BC	00224	00030	00031					
PRTORDPT	00006	000003F4	00232	00038	00039					
PRTOUT	00004	0000017C	00147	00015	00043	00048	00053	00060	00069	00079
PRTPRICE	00007	000003DF	00228	00034	00035					
READINV	00004	0000001E	00018	00028	00066					
SAVE	00004	000004C8	00241	00007	00008	00081				
WRKAVAIL	00003	0000051D	00244	00023	00025	0C025	0C027	00037		
WRKONORD	00003	00000520	00245	00024	00025	00027	00039			
WRKORDPT	00001	00000523	00246	00026	00027					

Figure 17-7   Assembly output for another version of the reorder-listing program (part 7 of 8)

```
ASSEMBLER DIAGNOSTICS AND STATISTICS                    ASM 0201 15.06 11/05/86        PAGE   11

STMT   ERROR CODE   MESSAGE
  36   IFO212       PREMATURE END OF OPERAND NEAR OPERAND COLUMN 9
  40   IFO188       LINECNT IS AN UNDEFINED SYMBOL
  57   IFO188       LINECNT IS AN UNDEFINED SYMBOL
  57   IFO236       ILLEGAL CHARACTER IN EXPRESSION NEAR OPERAND COLUMN 9
  64   IFO188       LINECNT IS AN UNDEFINED SYMBOL
 141   IFO054       INVALID OPERATION CODE
 246   IFO178       SYNTAX ERROR NEAR OPERAND COLUMN 4
 249   IFO198       INVALID TYPE DECLARED ON DC/DS/DXD CONSTANT NEAR OPERAND COLUMN 1

NUMBER OF STATEMENTS FLAGGED IN THIS ASSEMBLY =   7
HIGHEST SEVERITY WAS   8
OPTIONS FOR THIS ASSEMBLY
 ALIGN, ALOGIC, BUFSIZE(STD), DECK, ESD, FLAG(0), LINECOUNT(55), LIST, NOMCALL, YFLAG, WORKSIZE(2097152)
 NOMLOGIC, NONUMBER, NOOBJECT, NORENT, RLD, NOSTMT, NCLIBMAC, NOTERMINAL, NOTEST, XREF(SHORT)
 SYSPARM()
WORK FILE BUFFER SIZE/NUMBER =32758/ 1
TOTAL RECORDS READ FROM SYSTEM INPUT      113
TOTAL RECORDS READ FROM SYSTEM LIBRARY    3495
TOTAL RECORDS PUNCHED      31
TOTAL RECORDS PRINTED      362
```

Figure 17-7   Assembly output for another version of the reorder-listing program (part 8 of 8)

The diagnostic for statement 246 indicates SYNTAX ERROR. Actually, however, it's the operation code that's wrong. It should be DS instead of DC. Because the operand was coded without a nominal value, the assembler assumed the operand was incorrect.

The reverse of this mistake (coding DS for DC) is also common. When you do this, though, the error won't be caught by the assembler because it is acceptable to have a nominal value in a DS operand. This is a more serious error than coding DC for DS because the program is assembled but the intended value isn't put into the field. As a result, an error will normally result when the program is executed.

DISCUSSION

When you correct diagnostics, you normally take the diagnostics in sequence and correct operation codes and operands as necessary. But if you come to a message that you can't figure out, you can skip it at first since one of the later diagnostics may indicate its cause. If after going through all diagnostics, there are still a few you can't figure out, you might try reassembling the program with all other errors corrected. On some occasions, this will solve your problem because the problem diagnostics were caused by errors you have already corrected.

Terminology

external symbol dictionary
assembly listing
location counter
cross-reference listing
literal cross-reference listing
assembler diagnostics and statistics listing
diagnostic listing

Objective

Given the assembly output for a program including diagnostics, correct the source code so it will assemble without errors.

Chapter 18

How to test and debug an assembler language program

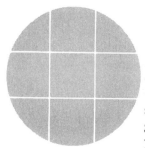

When you *test* a program, you try to find all the errors the program contains. When you *debug* a program, you try to correct the errors that you found when you tested it. In topic 1 of this chapter, you'll learn a general procedure for testing a program. Then, in topic 2, you'll learn some specific techniques for debugging a program. You can read this chapter any time after you complete chapter 5. But the best time is probably right before you test your first assembler language program or right after you discover your first bugs.

TOPIC 1   How to test a program

In general, programs are tested in three phases: unit test, systems test, and acceptance test. The *unit test* is the programmer's test of his or her own program. In this phase of testing, you should do your best to make sure that all the modules in your program function properly. Since you know your program better than anyone else, you are the person most qualified to test it.

The *system test* is designed to test the interfaces between the programs within a system. For instance, if you're writing an update program, the system test will determine whether or not the edit programs create transaction files that are acceptable to your program. But if the test data used for the edit programs is incomplete, the output from the edit programs will be an inadequate test of your update program. So you can't rely on the system test to test all aspects of your program.

The *acceptance test* is designed to determine whether the programs in a system perform the way that the user intended them to. Although the data for this test should be developed by a creative person with plenty of testing experience, this isn't always the case. So you can't count on this phase of testing to test all aspects of your program either. To a large extent, then, the burden of proof is on the programmer in the unit test.

Although this book isn't designed to teach you precise procedures for unit testing a production program, I would like to give you a few ideas that will help you test your programs more effectively. Most important, we recommend that you take the time to plan your test runs. All too often, it seems, programmers test their programs without any planning. As a result, their programs are *not* tested by all the possible combinations of data, and they are put into production with dozens of bugs.

It's relatively easy, though, to create a test plan for a program. Once you have one, you are more likely to create test data that adequately tests your program. Then, you will have a solid basis for believing that your program is free of bugs after you test it on the data you have created. In general, if your test plan is good, you are likely to do an adequate job of testing. If it isn't, you most likely won't do an adequate job of testing.

How to create a test plan

Before you start your *test plan*, you should review your program and list all the conditions that you must test for. To do this, you should review your program specifications, your design document, and even your assembler language code, writing down any conditions that come to mind as you review these items. Then, if you create test data that tests for all of these conditions, you increase the likelihood that your program will be adequately tested.

Figure 18-1 is a *condition list* that I developed for the refined reorder-listing program of chapter 5. Although making a list like this can be a laborious job if the program is large, you really have no other choice. If your job as programmer is to prove that your program works for all possible conditions, you must know what those conditions are. As you will see, however, your test data usually won't have to be extensive just because your list of conditions is long.

After you have made your list of conditions, you are ready to create the test plan. Specifically, you want to decide in what sequence the conditions should be tested. The intent here is to discover the major problems first. So, you should start by testing the main functions and conditions of the program. Then, once you are satisfied that they are working properly, you can go on to test the less critical conditions.

Figure 18-2 shows a test plan for the refined reorder-listing program. Although this program is extremely limited, I think it will give you an idea of what a test plan should look like. As you can see, I've decided that I will only need to have two test runs. The first one will test the main function of the program. It will also test the main condition: whether available is equal to, is less than, or is greater than the reorder point. Then, the second test run can test all of the remaining functions and conditions, including page overflow.

You should notice in figure 18-2 that I didn't provide for every condition that is listed in figure 18-1. When I reflected upon them, I decided that I didn't need to test the program using an empty master file since this condition shouldn't occur in the first place and since it shouldn't cause any problems if it does occur no matter how the program handles it. When you create a test plan, you should consider every condition on your condition list even though you may decide that you don't have to test for some of them. If you decide *not* to test a condition, you should have a good reason for your decision.

As you create your test plan, you should also decide where the test data will come from. Will you code the data yourself and create the proper input files using utilities? Will you use a test data generator? Can you copy some "live" data for your test files? Does another program create test data that you can use? Here again, you should make these decisions in a thoughtful, controlled manner.

How to create test data

As a general rule, the *test data* you use in your first test runs for a program should be low in volume, often just a couple of records for each input file. That way, it's relatively easy to figure out what output your program should produce. For instance, the three records listed in figure 18-3 are enough for the first phase of testing shown in the test plan in figure 18-2. Record 1 will cause a greater-than comparison of available and reorder point, record 2 will cause a less-than comparison, and record 3 will cause an equal comparison.

Program: REORDLST	Page: 1
Designer: Anne Prince	Date: 07-31-85

Test conditions

1. Are all records in the inventory master file processed?

2. What happens if the master file is empty?

3. Does the program branch properly depending on the relationship between available stock and reorder point?

4. Are all the fields on the report edited properly?

5. Does page overflow work properly?

6. Do heading lines print properly?

7. Are the correct number of lines printed on each page?

8. Is the spacing between lines on the reorder listing okay?

9. Is the total count correct?

Figure 18-1   A list of test conditions for the reorder-listing program

Program: REORDLST	Prepare Reorder Listing	Page: 1
Designer: Anne Prince		Date: 07-31-85

Test phase	Data	Data source
1. Main branching logic	Three inventory master records; one with available = reorder point, one with available > reorder point, and one with available < reorder point	Self
2. Page overflow	Enough inventory master records to cause page overflow	Test data generator

Figure 18-2   A test plan for the reorder-listing program

	Item number	Description	Unit price	On hand quantity	On order quantity	Reorder point
Record 1	00101	GENERATOR	12345	00070	00050	00100
Record 2	00103	HEATER SOLENOID	98765	00034	00000	00050
Record 3	95432	AAAAAAAAAAAAAAAAAAAA	00005	15000	05000	20000

Figure 18-3   Test data for the first test run for the reorder-listing program

After a program has been tested on small volumes of data, the program can be tested on a volume of data that is large enough to test all the conditions that may occur. In the case of the reorder-listing program, for example, the input file must contain enough records to force page overflow. If a program is large, the test plan may require several low-volume tests and several high-volume tests.

If you don't know what the output of a test run should be, you can't tell if your program worked properly. So, after you create the test data for a test run, you should figure out what the output should be. In some cases, doing this will also help you uncover problems in your specifications and program design.

How to document a test run

After you have created the necessary test data for each test phase, you are ready to perform the test run. Then, after each execution of a test run, you compare the actual output of the test run with the expected output. If the program involves tape or disk input or output, appropriate listings of the input and output files must be made before and after the test run. In a disk-update run, for example, the contents of the disk file must be printed before testing and after testing to see what changes were made in the file. In a disk-to-printer program, though, only the printed output usually needs to be checked because you already know what data the disk file contains. In any event, if the actual output disagrees with the expected output, you must find the cause of the error, change the source code, and test again.

After a test run, you should document it so you can review your test runs if that should become necessary. In some shops, in fact, you may be required to document each of your test runs. In general, your documentation for a test run should consist of the items listed in figure 18-4. Because a typical programmer works on more than one program at a time, this documentation can save a considerable amount of backtracking and confusion.

The documentation for a test run

1. The assembly listing for the test run marked with changes that should be made for the next test run

2. A listing of each input file used for the test run

3. The printed output for the test run

4. A listing of each file that is created or updated by the test run

---

Figure 18-4 The documentation for a test run

Discussion

Normally, in a programming course, you don't have to develop your own test data. Instead, it is provided for you. That way, everyone in the class should get the same test results if they write the program correctly. This makes it easy for your instructor to check your work. Nevertheless, you should know how to create test data for an assembler language program so you can do production work later on.

The point of this topic, of course, is to get you to test your production programs in an orderly fashion. If you take the time to develop condition lists and test plans before you start to test your programs, we're confident that you'll test your programs more effectively.

Terminology

unit test
system test
acceptance test
test plan
condition list
test data

Objective

Given a program's specifications and its design document, create a test plan and test data for it.

TOPIC 2   How to debug a program

When you test a program, there are two possible outcomes. First, the program can run to completion. This is often referred to as a *normal termination*, a *normal end-of-job*, or a *normal EOJ*. Second, the program can be cancelled. This is referred to as an *abnormal termination*, or an *abend*. In the remainder of this chapter, I'll show you how to debug programs that end normally or abnormally.

HOW TO DEBUG A PROGRAM
THAT ENDS IN A NORMAL TERMINATION

If the program runs to a normal EOJ, you start by comparing the actual output with expected output. To illustrate, suppose the reorder-listing program runs to completion using the test data in figure 18-3. Suppose also that figure 18-5 gives the actual output of the test run along with the expected output. If you compare the two, you can see that the program has some bugs. In fact, I've shaded them. Specifically, the unit price isn't edited correctly in the second detail line; the second detail line shouldn't have printed at all since available equals reorder point; and the count of the number of records in the file hasn't printed.

To correct these bugs, you analyze the code that has produced the output, because something must be wrong with it. Since the unit price in figure 18-5 prints correctly in the first detail line, there's probably some minor problem with its edit pattern such as a misplaced or missing significance starter. Since the second detail line prints when it shouldn't, there must be something wrong with the compare and branch instructions that determine when a line is to be printed. And, since the count doesn't print at all, there must be something wrong with the way it's accumulated or the way it is printed.

Since you can encounter so many different kinds of bugs when you test a program, I can't give you a precise procedure for correcting them. As I see it, this is an analytical part of the programmer's job that can't easily be taught. Although certain types of bugs seem to repeat themselves from one program to the next, some bugs are so abstruse that they baffle the most experienced programmers.

How to use debugging instructions and the SNAP macro   If a program is long or its calculations are complex, it can be extremely difficult to figure out why the actual output isn't what you expected. Then, you may want to add *debugging instructions* to your program.

A debugging instruction is an instruction that you put into your program temporarily to help you figure out why the program isn't

Expected printer output for the test run

REORDER LISTING

ITEM NO.	DESCRIPTION	UNIT PRICE	AVAILABLE	REORDER POINT
103	HEATER SOLENOID	123.45	34	50

1 RECORDS IN THE FILE

Actual printer output for the test run

REORDER LISTING

ITEM NO.	DESCRIPTION	UNIT PRICE	AVAILABLE	REORDER POINT
103	HEATER SOLENOID	123.45	34	50
95432	AAAAAAAAAAAAAAAAAAAA	5	65000	65000

RECORDS IN THE FILE

Figure 18-5   The expected output and the actual output for a test run that ends in a normal program termination

working correctly. For instance, you can add debugging instructions that print messages as a program executes. These messages can show the contents of selected storage fields or indicate what routine is being executed. This data in turn can help you find the source instructions that have caused the bugs. After the errors have been corrected, you remove the extra statements from the source code, reassemble it, and test again.

One of the instructions that you may want to add to your program as a debugging aid is the SNAP macro as described in chapter 6. This macro lets you print the contents of a portion of your program in storage dump format. After you read the rest of this chapter and topic 2 of chapter 6, you will be able to use this macro in your debugging efforts. I'm sure you will find it useful.

HOW TO DEBUG A PROGRAM THAT ENDS IN AN ABNORMAL TERMINATION

An abnormal program termination can also be referred to as a *program check*. A program check indicates that the program tried to do something invalid like trying to execute the add decimal (AP) instruction on EBCDIC data. When a program check occurs, you must (1) find the instruction that led to the program check, (2) find the cause of the error, and (3) correct it.

To illustrate the analysis of a program check, I will use the reorder-listing program. In the source code of this program, I have included a minor error that will cause an abend during a test run that uses the test data in figure 18-3. Although the expected printer output is shown in figure 18-5, the program prints nothing during this test run.

Figure 18-6 shows the output of the test run. Part 1 consists of the *job log* and the *statistics log*. These logs give some general information about the execution of the job.

Part 2 of the listing contains the *JCL log*. It consists of the JCL supplied by the programmer and the JCL supplied by the procedure. In this case, the procedure ASMFCG is being executed. This procedure assembles the source program, then loads and executes the resulting object module. This is the procedure you'll probably use most often when testing your student programs.

In some cases, your program won't assemble or test due to a faulty job control statement that you have supplied. For example, you might have spelled the procedure name wrong or have used the wrong DD names for the input or output files. If an error is detected in your job control statements, an appropriate error message is printed on the JCL log.

Parts 3 and 4 of the figure are the *message log*. This log contains JES and system messages pertaining to the execution of the job. What's included in this log depends on the option coded on the MSGLEVEL operand of the JOB statement (not covered in this book) and the way your system is set up. If you don't code the MSGLEVEL operand, you'll get a message log that conforms to the default values for your system.

If you wonder how messages about the execution of a job can be printed before the data for the job, you must remember that none of the data for an MVS job is printed until the entire job is completed. In the meantime, all output intended for the printer is stored on disk files. At the end of the job, then, a summary of the job execution can be printed before the actual job output.

Parts 5 through 12 of figure 18-6 are the assembly listing, the cross-reference listings, and the diagnostics listing. Then, part 13 is the *load map* which is created by the loader program when the object module is loaded into storage. This map gives the starting addresses of all object modules loaded into storage. Finally, parts 14 through 16 are the *storage dump*. The storage dump, also known as a *storage printout* or *core dump*, lists the contents of storage at the time of the program check.

How to find the instruction that caused a program check

To find the instruction that has caused a program check, you use the completion code message in the storage dump, the load map, and the assembly listing.

The completion code message   The basic cause of an abnormal termination is indicated by the *completion code message* near the top of the

```
J E S 2   J O B   L O G   --   S Y S T E M   M V S E   --   N O D E   M V S P S 1

12.37.09 JOB 7042  ICH70001I DLOWE2   LAST ACCESS AT 17:52:48 ON WEDNESDAY, NOVEMBER 5, 1986
12.37.09 JOB 7042  $HASP373 DLOWE214 STARTED - INIT  1 - CLASS A - SYS MVSE
12.37.33 JOB 7042                              --TIMINGS (MINS.)--          ----PAGING COUNTS---
12.37.33 JOB 7042  JOBNAME  STEPNAME PROCSTEP   RC   EXCP   CPU   SRB  CLOCK    SERV   PG  PAGE  SWAP  VIO  SWAPS
12.37.33 JOB 7042  DLOWE214 ASM                 00    545   .02   .00   .3    11636    1    0   103   325    1
12.37.35 JOB 7042  IEA995I SYMPTOM DUMP OUTPUT
                   ABEND CODE SYSTEM=0C7  TIME=12.37.35  SEQ=00946  CPU=0000  ASID=002A
                   PSW AT TIME OF ERROR   078D2000   0000D0AC  ILC 6  INTC 07
                   ACTIVE LOAD MODULE=**GO    ADDRESS=0000D000  OFFSET=00000AC
                   DATA AT PSW  0000D0A6 - F9113526  352A4740  30CE4110
                   GPR  0-3   0000D1EC  0000D1EC  80005F7C  4000D016
                   GPR  4-7   0000FFA   FFFFFFFF  00005F98  00000FF
                   GPR  8-11  0000000   00005EC0  00005FE0  0000D000
                   GPR 12-15  00006D6C  6000D4D8  6000D03C  12B899A6
                   END OF SYMPTOM DUMP
12.37.39 JOB 7042  +IEW1991 ERROR - USER PROGRAM HAS ABNORMALLY TERMINATED
12.37.39 JOB 7042  DLOWE214 GO                 *SOC7    169    .01   .00   .1    4626    1    0         0    0
12.37.39 JOB 7042  DLOWE214 ENDED.  NAME-                    TOTAL CPU TIME=    .03  TOTAL ELAPSED TIME=   .4
12.37.39 JOB 7042  $HASP395 DLOWE214 ENDED

------ JES2 JOB STATISTICS ------

06 NOV 86 JOB EXECUTION DATE

    116 CARDS READ

  2,644 SYSOUT PRINT RECORDS

      0 SYSOUT PUNCH RECORDS

    264 SYSOUT SPOOL KBYTES

   0.51 MINUTES EXECUTION TIME
```

Figure 18-6   Test run output for the reorder-listing program: the job log and the statistics log (part 1 of 16)

```
1    //DLOWE214   JOB USER=DLOWE2,PASSWORD=,MSGLEVEL=1                          JOB 7042
2    //           EXEC ASMFCG                                                    000200
3    XXASMFCG     PROC MAC='SYS1.MACLIB',MAC1='SYS1.MACLIB'                    00010000
     *** REFER    SYS1.PROCLIB(ASMFCG)                                         00020000
     *** COMPID   SYSTEM                                                       00030000
     *** DOC      THIS PROCEDURE IS FOR ASSEMBLE AND GO. IT EXECUTES IFOX00    00040000
     ***          AND THE LOADER.                                             00050000
                                                                              00060000
4    XXASM        EXEC PGM=IFOX00,PARM=OBJ                                     00070070
5    XXSYSLIB     DD   DSN=&MAC,DISP=SHR                                       00080070
     IEF653I SUBSTITUTION JCL - DSN=SYS1.MACLIB,DISP=SHR
6    XX           DD   DSN=&MAC1,DISP=SHR                                      00090070
     IEF653I SUBSTITUTION JCL - DSN=SYS1.MACLIB,DISP=SHR
7    XXSYSUT1     DD   DSN=&&SYSUT1,UNIT=VIO,SPACE=(1700,(600,100))            00100070
8    XXSYSUT2     DD   DSN=&&SYSUT2,UNIT=VIO,SPACE=(1700,(300,50))             00110070
9    XXSYSUT3     DD   DSN=&&SYSUT3,UNIT=VIO,SPACE=(1700,(300,50))             00120070
10   XXSYSPRINT   DD   SYSOUT=*,DCB=BLKSIZE=1089                              00130070
11   XXSYSPUNCH   DD   DUMMY                                                  00140070
12   XXSYSGO      DD   DSN=&&OBJSET,UNIT=SYSDA,SPACE=(80,(200,50)),           00150070
     XX           DISP=(MOD,PASS)                                             00160000
                                                                                000300
13   //ASM.SYSIN DD   *                                                       00170070
14   XXGO         EXEC PGM=LOADER,PARM='MAP,PRINT,NOCALL,LET',                00180000
     XX           COND=(8,LT,ASM)                                             00190070
15   XXSYSLIN     DD   DSN=&&OBJSET,DISP=(OLD,DELETE)                         00200070
16   XXSYSLOUT    DD   SYSOUT=*                                                 011000
17   //GO.SYSUDUMP DD  SYSOUT=A                                                 011100
18   //GO.REPORT  DD   SYSOUT=A                                                 011200
19   //GO.INVMST  DD   *                                                        011600
     //
```

Figure 18-6   Test run output for the reorder-listing program: the JCL log (part 2 of 16)

```
ICH70001I DLOWE2    LAST ACCESS AT 17:52:48 ON WEDNESDAY, NOVEMBER 5, 1986
IEF236I ALLOC. FOR DLOWE214 ASM
IEF237I D22 ALLOCATED TO SYSLIB
IEF237I D22 ALLOCATED TO
IEF237I VIO ALLOCATED TO SYSUT1
IEF237I VIO ALLOCATED TO SYSUT2
IEF237I VIO ALLOCATED TO SYSUT3
IEF237I JES2 ALLOCATED TO SYSPRINT
IEF237I DMY ALLOCATED TO SYSPUNCH
IEF237I 269 ALLOCATED TO SYSGO
IEF237I JES2 ALLOCATED TO SYSIN
IEF142I DLOWE214 ASM - STEP WAS EXECUTED - COND CODE 0000
IEF285I    SYS1.MACLIB                                  KEPT
IEF285I       VOL SER NOS= MVSE11.
IEF285I    SYS1.MACLIB                                  KEPT
IEF285I       VOL SER NOS= MVSE11.
IEF285I    SYS86310.T123709.RA000.DLOWE214.SYSUT1       DELETED
IEF285I    SYS86310.T123709.RA000.DLOWE214.SYSUT2       DELETED
IEF285I    SYS86310.T123709.RA000.DLOWE214.SYSUT3       DELETED
IEF285I    JES2.JOB07042.SO0103                         SYSOUT
IEF285I    SYS86310.T123709.RA000.DLOWE214.OBJSET       PASSED
IEF285I       VOL SER NOS= MPS800.
IEF285I    JES2.JOB07042.SIO101                         SYSIN
```

```
EXCPS:  *SYSIN*(CRDR)=105      SYSLIB(D22)=41      SYSUT1(VIO)=125      SYSUT2(VIO)=9
        SYSUT3(VIO)=8          SYSGO(269)=31

PAGING:       PRIVATE       COMMON       LPA       VIO       SWAPS(1)
        IN    0             5            1         183       50
        OUT   0             0            0         142       53
        RECLAIMS 0          0            0         690

SERVICE UNITS:CPU=5,616   SRB=210    I/O=2,690    MSO=3,120    TOTAL=11,636

PERFORMANCE GROUP=1    DISPATCHING PRIORITY=9    ELAPSED TIME=00:00:23.28

IEF373I STEP /ASM    / START 86310.1237
IEF374I STEP /ASM    / STOP  86310.1237 CPU    0MIN 01.34SEC SRB   0MIN 00.05SEC VIRT   756K SYS   448K EXT   CK SYS   8820K
IEF236I ALLOC. FOR DLOWE214 GC
IEF237I 269 ALLOCATED TO SYSLIN
IEF237I JES2 ALLOCATED TO SYSLOUT
IEF237I JES2 ALLOCATED TO SYSUDUMP
IEF237I JES2 ALLOCATED TO REPORT
IEF237I JES2 ALLOCATED TO INVMST
IEA995I SYMPTOM DUMP OUTPUT
ABEND CODE SYSTEM=0C7  TIME=12.37.35  SEQ=00946 CPU=0000 ASID=002A
PSW AT TIME OF ERROR  078D2000  0000D0AC  ILC 6  INTC 07
ACTIVE LOAD MODULE=**GO  ADDRESS=0000D000  OFFSET=0000000AC
DATA AT PSW  0000D0A6 - F9113526  352A4740  30CE4110
GPR  0-3   0000D1EC  8000SF7C  4000D016
GPR  4-7   0000SFFA  FFFFFFFF  0000SF98  00000OFF
GPR  8-11  00000000  0000SEC0  0000SFED  0000D000
GPR 12-15  00000DDC  0000D4D8  6000D03C  12B899A6
END OF SYMPTOM DUMP
```

Figure 18-6   Test run output for the reorder-listing program: the message log (part 3 of 16)

```
IEW1991 ERROR - USER PROGRAM HAS ABNORMALLY TERMINATED
IEF472I DLOWE214 GO - COMPLETION CODE - SYSTEM=0C7 USER=0000 REASON=00000000
IEF285I   SYS86310.T123709.RA000.DLOWE214.OBJSET        DELETED
IEF285I   VOL SER NOS= MPS800.
IEF285I   JES2.JOB07042.SO0104                          SYSOUT
IEF285I   JES2.JOB07042.SO0105                          SYSOUT
IEF285I   JES2.JOB07042.SO0106                          SYSOUT
IEF285I   JES2.JOB07042.SI0102                          SYSIN

EXCPS:  *SYSIN*(RDR)=2            SYSLIN(269)=32

PAGING:          PRIVATE      COMMON       LPA        VIC         SWAPS(C)
        IN  0                   47          47          0            0
        OUT 0                    0           0          0            0
        RECLAIMS 0               0                      0

SERVICE UNITS:CPU=2,677      SRB=143        I/O=700      MSO=1,106     TOTAL=4,626

PERFORMANCE GROUP=1          DISPATCHING PRIORITY=9                  ELAPSED TIME=00:00:06.20

IEF373I STEP /GO      / START 86310.1237
IEF374I STEP /GO      / STOP  86310.1237 CPU    0MIN 00.64SEC SRB    0MIN 00.04SEC VIRT  332K SYS  364K EXT    4K SYS   8856K

SERVICE UNITS:CPU=8,293      SRB=353        I/O=3,390    MSO=4,226     TOTAL=16,262

SYSTEM ID=TK3J    CPU ID=223148     MODEL=3083      MVS RELEASE=SP2.1.2     ELAPSED TIME=00:00:29.59

IEF375I JOB /DLOWE214/ START 86310.1237
IEF376I JOB /DLOWE214/ STOP  86310.1237 CPU    0MIN 01.98SEC SRB    0MIN 00.09SEC
```

Figure 18-6   Test run output for the reorder-listing program: the message log (part 4 of 16)

```
LOC     OBJECT CODE      ADDR1 ADDR2   STMT   SOURCE STATEMENT

000000                                  1   REORDLST START 0                                      00C400
000000                                  2   BEGIN    SAVE  (14,12)      SAVE REGISTERS            00C500
000000                                  3+BEGIN      DS    0H                                     C165C000
000000  90EC D00C        0000C          4+          STM   14,12,12(13)                            C295C000
000004  0530                            5           BALR  3,0                                      00C600
000006                   00006          6           USING *,3                                      00C700
000006  50D0 34C6        004CC          7           ST    13,SAVE+4                                00C800
00000A  41D0 34C2        004C8          8           LA    13,SAVE                                  00C900
                                        9           OPEN  (INVMAST,INPUT,PRTOUT,OUTPUT)            001000
00000E  0700                           10+          CNOP  0,4           ALIGN LIST TO FULLWORD     0174C000
000010  4510 3016        0001C         11+          BAL   1,*+12        LOAD REG1 W/LIST ADDR.     0178C000
000014  00                             12+          DC    AL1(0)        OPTION BYTE                0190C000
000015  00001C                         13+          DC    AL3(INVMAST)  DCB ADDRESS                0192C000
000018  8F                             14+          DC    AL1(143)      OPTION BYTE                0190C000
000019  00017C                         15+          DC    AL3(PRTOUT)   DCB ADDRESS                0192C000
00001C  0A13                           16+          SVC   19            ISSUE OPEN SVC             0400C000
                                       17   READINV  GET   INVMAST,INVWRKA    READ RECORD          000100
00001E  4110 3116        0011C         18+READINV    LA    1,INVMAST    LOAD PARAMETER REG 1       0190C002
000022  4100 31D6        001DC         19+          LA    0,INVWRKA     LOAD PARAMETER REG 0       0250C002
000026  58F0 1030        00030         20+          L     15,48(0,1)    LOAD GET ROUTINE ADDR      0060C000
00002A  05EF                           21+          BALR  14,15         LINK TO GET ROUTINE        00625000
00002C  FA20 3523 352C   00529 00532   22           AP    COUNT,=P'1'   ADD ONE TO COUNT           001200
000032  F224 3517 31FE   0051D 00204   23           PACK  WRKAVAIL,INVONHND                        001300
000038  F224 351A 3203   00520 00209   24           PACK  WRKONORD,INVONORD                        0014C0
00003E  FA22 3517 351A   0051D 00520   25           AP    WRKAVAIL,WRKONORD   ADD ON HAND AND ON ORDER  001500
000044  F224 351D 31F9   00523 001FF   26           PACK  WRKORDPT,INVORDPT                        001600
00004A  F922 3517 3518   0051D 0051E   27           CP    WRKAVAIL,WRKORDPT   COMPARE AVAILABLE, REORDER POINT  001700
000050  4780 3018              0001E   28           BNL   READINV                                  001800
000054  F224 3520 31D6   00526 001DC   29           PACK  PACKAREA,INVITNBR                        001900
00005A  D205 3386 350A   0038C 00510   30           MVC   PRTITNBR,PATTERN1   EDIT ITEM NUMBER FIELD   002000
000060  DE05 3396 3520   0039C 00526   31           ED    PRTITNBR,PACKAREA                        002100
000066  D213 33C1 31DB   003C7 001E1   32           MVC   PRTITDES,INVITDES   MOVE ITEM DESCRIPTION    002200
00006C  F224 3520 31F4   00526 001FA   33           PACK  PACKAREA,INVPRICE                        002300
000072  D206 33D9 3520   003DF 00526   34           MVC   PRTPRICE,PATTERN2   EDIT UNIT PRICE          002400
000078  DE06 33D9 3520   003DF 00526   35           ED    PRTPRICE,PACKAREA                        002500
00007E  D205 33E4 350A   003EA 00510   36           MVC   PRTAVAIL,PATTERN1                        002600
000084  DE05 33E4 3517   003EA 0051D   37           ED    PRTAVAIL,WRKAVAIL   EDIT AVAILABLE           002700
00008A  D205 33EE 350A   003F4 00510   38           MVC   PRTORDPT,PATTERN1                        002800
000090  DE05 33EE 3520   003F4 00526   39           ED    PRTORDPT,WRKORDPT   EDIT ORDER POINT         002900
000096  F911 3526 352A   0052C 00530   40           CP    LINECNT,=P'50'      COMPARE LINE COUNT TO 50 003000
00009C  4740 30CE              000D4   41           BL    PRTDET        BRANCH ON LOW TO PRTDET    003100
                                       42           PUT   PRTOUT,HDGLINE1     PRINT FIRST HEADING LINE 003200
0000A0  4110 3176        0017C         43+          LA    1,PRTOUT      LOAD PARAMETER REG 1       0190C002
0000A4  4100 3226        0022C         44+          LA    0,HDGLINE1    LOAD PARAMETER REG 0       C250C002
0000A8  58F0 1030        00030         45+          L     15,48(0,1)    LOAD PUT ROUTINE ADDR      0055C000
0000AC  05EF                           46+          BALR  14,15         LINK TO PUT ROUTINE        0060C000
                                       47           PUT   PRTOUT,HDGLINE2     PRINT SECOND HEADING LINE 003300
0000AE  4110 3176        0017C         48+          LA    1,PRTOUT      LOAD PARAMETER REG 1       0190C002
0000B2  4100 32AB        002B1         49+          LA    0,HDGLINE2    LOAD PARAMETER REG 0       0250C002
0000B6  58F0 1030        00030         50+          L     15,48(0,1)    LOAD PUT ROUTINE ADDR      0060C000
0000BA  05EF                           51+          BALR  14,15         LINK TO PUT ROUTINE        0055C000
                                       52           PUT   PRTOUT,HDGLINE3     PRINT THIRD HEADING LINE 003400
0000BC  4110 3176        0017C         53+          LA    1,PRTOUT      LOAD PARAMETER REG 1       0190C002
0000C0  4100 3350        00356         54+          LA    0,HDGLINE3    LOAD PARAMETER REG 0       0250C002
0000C4  58F0 1030        00030         55+          L     15,48(0,1)    LOAD PUT ROUTINE ADDR      0055C000
```

Figure 18-6   Test run output for the reorder-listing program: the assembly listing (part 5 of 16)

ASM 0201 12.37 11/06/86   PAGE   3

```
LOC     OBJECT CODE       ADDR1  ADDR2  STMT  SOURCE STATEMENT

0000C8  05EF                             56+        BALR  14,15                  LINK TO PUT ROUTINE               0060C000
0000CA  F810 3526 352D    0052C  00533   57         ZAP   LINCNT,=P'0'           RESET LINE COUNT TO ZERO          003500
0000D0  92F0 33B5         003BB           58         MVI   PRTDCTL,C'0'           MOVE ZERO TO DETAIL CONTROL BYTE  003600
                                          59  PRTDET PUT   PRTOUT,PRTDETL         PRINT DETAIL LINE                 003700
0000D4  4110 3176         0017C           60+ PRTDET LA    1,PRTOUT               LOAD PARAMETER REG 1              0190C002
0000D8  4100 33B5         003BB           61+        LA    0,PRTDETL              LOAD PARAMETER REG 0              0250C002
0000DC  58F0 1030         00030           62+        L     15,48(0,1)             LOAD PUT ROUTINE ADDR            0055C000
0000E0  05EF                              63+        BALR  14,15                  LINK TO PUT ROUTINE               0060C000
0000E2  FA10 3526 352C    0052C  00532    64         AP    LINCNT,=P'1'           ADD ONE TO LINE COUNT            003800
0000E8  9240 33B5         003BB           65         MVI   PRTDCTL,C' '           MOVE BLANK TO DETAIL CONTROL BYTE 003900
0000EC  47F0 3018         0001E           66         B     READINV                BRANCH TO READINV                004000
0000F0  DE06 343B 0441    0044B  00529    67  INVEOF ED    CNTPATRN,COUNT         EDIT COUNT                        004100
                                          68         PUT   PRTOUT,CNTLINE         PRINT COUNT LINE                  004200
0000F6  4110 3176         0017C           69+        LA    1,PRTOUT               LOAD PARAMETER REG 1              0190C002
0000FA  4100 343A         0044A           70+        LA    0,CNTLINE              LOAD PARAMETER REG 0              0250C002
0000FE  58F0 1030         00030           71+        L     15,48(0,1)             LOAD PUT ROUTINE ADDR            0055C000
000102  05EF                              72+        BALR  14,15                  LINK TO PUT ROUTINE               0060C000
                                          73         CLOSE (INVMAST,,PRTOUT)                                        004300
000104                                    74+        CNOP  0,4                    ALIGN LIST TO FULLWORD           0242C000
000104  4510 310A         00110           75+        BAL   1,*+12                 LOAD REG1 W/LIST ADDR            0246C000
000108  00                                76+        DC    AL1(O)                 OPTION BYTE                      0258C000
000109  00011C                            77+        DC    AL3(INVMAST)           DCB ADDRESS                      0260C000
00010C  80                                78+        DC    AL1(128)               OPTION BYTE                      0258C000
00010D  00017C                            79+        DC    AL3(PRTOUT)            DCB ADDRESS                      0260C000
000110  0A14                              80+        SVC   20                     ISSUE CLOSE SVC                  0164C000
                                          81         RETURN (14,12)                                                004400
000112  58D0 34C6         004CC           82         L     13,SAVE+4                                               004500
000116  98EC D00C         0000C           83+        LM    14,12,12(13)           RESTORE THE REGISTERS           0065C000
00011A  07FE                              84+        BR    14                     RETURN                           0200C000
                                          85  *  THE INVENTORY FILE DEFINITION FOLLOWS                             004600
                                          86  INVMAST DCB  DSORG=PS,RECFM=F,MACRF=GM,BLKSIZE=80,LRECL=80,       X  004700
                                                          DDNAME=INVMST,EODAD=INVEOF                               004800

                                          86++                  DATA CONTROL BLOCK                                 2277C000
                                          89++                                                                     2286C000
00011C                                    90+ INVMAST DC  0F'0'                   ORIGIN ON WORD BOUNDARY          2291400
                                          92++                  DIRECT ACCESS DEVICE INTERFACE                     2736C000
00011C  0000000000000000                  94+        DC    BL16'0'                FDAD,DVTBL                        2754C000
00012C  00000000                          95+        DC    A(0)                   KEYLE,DEVT,TRBAL                  2772C000
                                          97++                  COMMON ACCESS METHOD INTERFACE                     4869C000
000130  00                                99+        DC    AL1(O)                 BUFNO                             4905C000
000131  000001                            100+       DC    AL3(1)                 BUFCB                             5472C000
000134  0000                              101+       DC    AL2(O)                 BUFL                              5517C000
000136  4000                              102+       DC    BL2'01000000000000000'                                *5580C000
                                          +                                                                        5589C000
000138  00000001                          103+       DC    A(1)                   ICQE/IOBAD   DSORG                5634C000
                                          105++                 FOUNDATION EXTENSION                               5651C000
00013C  00                                107+       DC    BL1'00000000'          BFTEK,BFLN,HIAPCHY                5985C000
```

Figure 18-6   Test run output for the reorder-listing program: the assembly listing (part 6 of 16)

```
                                                              ASM C201  12.37  11/06/86        PAGE   4

 LOC    OBJECT CODE      ADDR1 ADDR2  STMT  SOURCE STATEMENT

000013D 0000F0                        108+      DC    AL3(INVEOF)              EODAD         6597C000
000140  80                            109+      DC    BL1'10000000'                         *6615C000
                                        +                                      RECFM         6624C000
000141  000000                        110+      DC    AL3(0)                   EXLST         6633C000
                                        +
                                      112**                FOUNDATION BLOCK                  6669C000

000144  C9D5E5D4E2E34040              114+      DC    CL8'INVMST'              DDNAME        6687C000
00014C  02                            115+      DC    BL1'00000010'            OFLGS         6822C000
00014D  00                            116+      DC    BL1'00000000'     IFLG                 6831C000
00014E  5000                          117+      DC    BL2'0101000000000000'                 *6840C000
                                        +                                                    *6849C000
                                        +                                      MACR          6858C000

                                      119**            BSAM-BPAM-QSAM INTERFACE              7443C000

000150  00                            121+      DC    BL1'00000000'                     RER1*7461C000
                                        +                                                    7470C000
000151  000001                        122+      DC    AL3(1)          CHECK, GERR, PERR      7479C000
000154  30000001                      123+      DC    A(1)                     SYNAD         7488C000
000158  0000                          124+      DC    H'0'             CIND1, CIND2          7497C000
00015A  0050                          125+      DC    AL2(80)                  BLKSIZE       7524C000
00015C  00000000                      126+      DC    F'0'        WCPO, WCPL, OFFSR, OFFSW   7587C000
000160  00000001                      127+      DC    A(1)                     ICBA          7596C000
000164  00                            128+      DC    AL1(0)                   NCP           7605C000
000165  000001                        129+      DC    AL3(1)                   EOBR, EOBAD   7614C000

                                      131**                  QSAM INTERFACE                  8145C000

000168  00000001                      133+      DC    A(1)                     RECAD         8163C000
00016C  0000                          134+      DC    H'0'                     QSWS          8181C000
00016E  0050                          135+      DC    AL2(80)          LRECL                 8073C000
000170  00000000                      136+      DC    BL1'00000000'            EROPT         8253C000
000171  000001                        137+      DC    AL3(1)                   CNTRL         8262C000
000174  00000000                      138+      DC    F'0'                     PRECL         8271C000
000178  00000001                      139+      DC    A(1)                     EOB           8280C000
                                      140 * THE PRINTER FILE DEFINITION FOLLOWS              004900
                                      141 PRTOUT DC8 DSORG=PS,RECFM=FA,MACRF=PM,BLKSIZE=133,LRECL=133, X 005000
                                              DDNAME=REPORT                                  005100

                                      143**              DATA CONTROL BLOCK                  2277C000
                                      144**                                                 2286C000
00017C                                145+PRTOUT DC    OF'0'        ORIGIN ON WORD BOUNDARY  2291C000

                                      147**          DIRECT ACCESS DEVICE INTERFACE          2736C000

00017C  000000000000000000            149+      DC    BL16'0'                  FDAD,DVTBL    2754C000
00018C  00000000                      150+      DC    A(0)                     KEYLE,DEVT,TRBAL 2772C000

                                      152**         COMMON ACCESS METHOD INTERFACE           4869C000

000190  00                            154+      DC    AL1(0)                   BUFNO         4905C000
000191  000001                        155+      DC    AL3(1)                   BUFCB         5472C000
000194  0000                          156+      DC    AL2(0)            BUFL                 5517C000
```

Figure 18-6   Test run output for the reorder-listing program: the assembly listing (part 7 of 16)

ASM 0201   12.37   11/06/86   PAGE   5

LOC	OBJECT CODE	ADDR1	ADDR2	STMT	SOURCE STATEMENT	
000196	4000			157+	DC BL2'0100000000000000'	*5580C000
						5589C000
000198	00000001			158+	DC A(1) ICGE/IOBAD DSORG	5634C000
				160++	FOUNDATION EXTENSION	5661C000
00019C	00			162+	DC BL1'00000000' BFTEK,BFLN,HIARCHY	5995C000
00019D	000001			163+	DC AL3(1) ECDAD	6597C000
0001A0	84			164+	DC BL1'10000100' RECFM	*6615C000
						6624C000
0001A1	000000			165+	DC AL3(0) EXLST	6633C000
				167++	FOUNDATION BLOCK	6669C000
0001A4	D9C5D7D6D9E34040			169+	DC CL8'REPORT' DDNAME	6687C000
0001AC	02			170+	DC BL1'00000010' OFLGS	6822C000
0001AD	00			171+	DC BL1'00000000'	6831C000
0001AE	0050			172+	DC BL2'0000000001010000' IFLG	*6840C000
						6849C000
						6858C000
				174++	BSAM-BPAM-QSAM INTERFACE	7443C000
0001B0	00			176+	DC BL1'00000000'	RER1 7461C000
						7470C000
0001B1	000001			177+	DC AL3(1) CHECK, GERR, PERR	7479C000
0001B4	00000001			178+	DC A(1) SYNAD	7488C000
0001B8	0000			179+	DC H'0' CIND1, CIND2	7497C000
0001BA	0085			180+	DC AL2(133) BLKSIZE	7524C000
0001BC	00000000			181+	DC F'0' WCPO, WCPL, OFFSR, OFFSW	7587C000
0001C0	00000001			182+	DC A(1) ICBA	7596C000
0001C4	00			183+	DC AL1(0) NCP	7605C000
0001C5	000001			184+	DC AL3(1) ECBR, EOBAD	7614C000
				186++	QSAM INTERFACE	8145C000
0001C8	00000001			188+	DC A(1) RECAD	8163C000
0001CC	0000			189+	DC H'0' QSWS	8181C000
0001CE	0085			190+	DC AL2(133) LRECL	8073C000
0001D0	00			191+	DC BL1'00000000' EROPT	8253C000
0001D1	000001			192+	DC AL3(1) CNTRL	8262C000
0001D4	00000000			193+	DC F'0' PRECL	8271C000
0001D8	00000001			194+	DC A(1) ECB	8280C000
				195	* THE DATA DEFINITIONS FOR THE INVENTORY FILE WORK AREA FOLLOW	005200
0001DC				196	INVWRKA DS OCL80	005300
0001DC				197	INVITNBR DS CL5	005400
0001E1				198	INVITDES DS CL20	005500
0001F5				199	INVPRICE DS CL5	005600
0001FA				200	INVORDPT DS CL5	005700
0001FF				201	INVONHND DS CL5	005800
000204				2C2	INVONORD DS CL5	005900
000209				203	DS CL5	006000
00020E				2C4	DS CL30	006100
				205	* THE DATA DEFINITIONS FOR THE PRINTER HEADING LINES FOLLOW	006200
00022C				206	HDGLINE1 DS OCL133	006300

Figure 18-6   Test run output for the reorder-listing program: the assembly listing (part 8 of 16)

ASM 0201 12.37 11/06/86

LOC	OBJECT CODE	ADDR1	ADDR2	STMT	SOURCE STATEMENT		
00022C	F1			207		DC	C'1'
00022D	4040404040404040			208		DC	24C' '
000245	D9C5D6D9C4C5D943			209		DC	C'REORDER LISTING'
000254	4040404040404040			210		DC	93C' '
000281				211	HDGLINE2	DS	0CL133
000281	F0			212		DC	C'0'
000282	4CC9E3C5D4404040			213		DC	C' ITEM REOPDER' ITEM UNIT X
00028A	40404040404040						
0002F1	4040404040C4C040			214		DC	69C' '
000336				215	HDGLINE3	DS	0CL133
000336	40			216		DC	C' NO.'
000337	40D5D6484C04040			217		DC	C' POINT' DESCRIPTION PRICE AVAILABLEX
00033F	4040404040404CC5						
000375	4040404040404040						
				218	* THE DATA DEFINITIONS FOR THE PRINTER DETAIL LINE FOLLOW		
				219	*		
000388				220	PRTDETL	DS	0CL133
00038B				221	PRTDCTL	DS	CL1
00038C				222	PRTITNBR	DS	CL6
0003C2	4040404040			223		DC	5C' '
0003C7				224	PRTITDES	DS	CL20
0003D3	40404040			225		DC	4C' '
0003DF				226	PRTPRICE	DS	CL7
0003E6	40404040			227		DC	4C' '
0003EA				228	PRTAVAIL	DS	CL5
0003F0	40404040			229		DC	4C' '
0003F4				230	PRTORDPT	DS	CL6
0003FA	4040404040404040			231		DC	70C' '
				232	* THE DATA DEFINITIONS FOR THE FINAL TOTAL LINE FOLLOW		
00044C				233	CNTLINE	DS	0CL133
000440	60			234		DC	C'-'
000441	402020 6B202020			235	CNTPATRN	DC	X'402020 6B202020'
000448	40D9C5C3D6D9C4E2			236		DC	C' RECORDS IN THE INPUT FILE'
000462	4040404040404040			237		DC	99C' '
				238	* THE DATA DEFINITIONS THAT FOLLOW DEFINE OTHER WORK AREAS NEEDED		
				239	* BY THE PROGRAM		
0004C8				240	SAVE	DS	18F
000510	402020202020			241	PATTERN1	DC	X'402020202020'
000516	402020214B2020			242	PATTERN2	DC	X'402020214B2020'
00051D				243	WRKAVAIL	DS	PL3
000520				244	WRKONORD	DS	PL3
000523				245	WRKORDPT	DS	PL3
000526				246	PACKAREA	DS	PL3
000529	00000C			247	COUNT	DC	PL3'0'
00052C				248	LINECNT	DS	P'50'
000000				249		END	BEGIN
000530	050C			250			=P'50'
000532	1C			251			=P'1'
000533	0C			252			=P'0'

Figure 18-6   Test run output for the reorder-listing program: the assembly listing (part 9 of 16)

CROSS-REFERENCE

SYMBOL	LEN	VALUE	DEFN	REFERENCES				
BEGIN	00002	00000000	00003	00249				
CNTLINE	00133	00000440	00233	00070				
CNTPATRN	00007	00000441	00235	00067				
COUNT	00003	00000529	00247	00022	00067			
HDGLINE1	00133	0000022C	00206	00044				
HDGLINE2	00133	000002B1	00211	00049				
HDGLINE3	00133	00C00336	00215	00054				
INVEOF	00006	000000F0	00067	00108				
INVITDES	00020	000001E1	00198	00032				
INVITNBR	00005	000001DC	00197	00029				
INVMAST	00005	0000011C	00090	00013	00018	00077		
INVONHND	00005	0C000204	00202	00023				
INVONORD	00005	000001FF	00201	00026				
INVORDPT	00005	000001FA	00200	00033				
INVPRICE	00005	000001DC	00200	00019				
INVWRKA	00080	000001DC	00196	00040	00057	00064		
LINECNT	00002	0000052C	00248	00029	00031	00033	00035	
PACKAREA	00003	00000526	00246	00030	00030	00038		
PATTERN1	00006	00000510	00241	00034				
PATTERN2	00007	00000516	00242	00036	00037			
PRTAVAIL	00005	000003EA	00228	00058	00065			
PRTDCTL	00001	000003B3	00221	00041				
PRTDET	00004	000000D4	00060	00061				
PRTDETL	00133	000003B9	00220	00032				
PRTITDES	00020	000003C7	00224	00030				
PRTITNBR	00006	000003BC	00222	00038	00039			
PRTORDPT	00006	000003F4	0023C	00015	00043	00048	00053	00060	00069	00079
PRTOUT	00004	0000017C	00145	00034	00035			
PRTPRICE	00007	000003DF	00226	00028	00066			
READINV	00004	0000001E	00018	00007	00008	00081	00037	
SAVE	00004	000004C8	00240	00023	00025	00027	00037	
WRKAVAIL	00003	0000051D	00243	00024	00025			
WRKONORD	00003	00000520	00244	00026				
WRKORDPT	00003	00000523	00245	00027	00039			

Figure 18-6   Test run output for the reorder-listing program: the cross-reference listing (part 10 of 16)

```
                                      LITERAL CROSS-REFERENCE                                      PAGE    9

                                                                          ASM C201 12.37 11/06/86

SYMBOL     LEN  VALUE      DEFN   REFERENCES

=P'50'     00002 00000530 00250  00C40
=P'1'      00001 00000532 00251  00022 00064
=P'0'      00001 00000533 00252  00057
```

Figure 18-6   Test run output for the reorder-listing program: the literal cross-reference listing (part 11 of 16)

```
                               ASSEMBLER DIAGNOSTICS AND STATISTICS                           PAGE   10

                                                                          ASM C201 12.37 11/06/86

NO STATEMENTS FLAGGED IN THIS ASSEMBLY
HIGHEST SEVERITY WAS     0
OPTIONS FOR THIS ASSEMBLY
 ALIGN, ALOGIC, BUFSIZE(STD), DECK, ESD, FLAG(0), LINECOUNT(55), LIST, NOMCALL, YFLAG, WORKSIZE(2097152)
 NOMLOGIC, NCNUMBER, OBJECT, NORENT, RLD, NOSTMT, NOLIBMAC, NOTERMINAL, NOTEST, XREF(SHORT)
 SYSPARM()
WORK FILE BUFFER SIZE/NUMBER =32758/ 1
TOTAL RECORDS READ FROM SYSTEM INPUT       105
TOTAL RECORDS READ FROM SYSTEM LIBRARY    3495
TOTAL RECORDS PUNCHED                        31
TOTAL RECORDS PRINTED                       341
```

Figure 18-6   Test run output for the reorder-listing program: the diagnostics listing (part 12 of 16)

```
                                           DFP LOADER

OPTIONS USED - PRINT,MAP,LET,NOCALL,NORES,NOTERM,SIZE=307200,NAME=**GO

NAME     TYPE   ADDR     NAME     TYPE   ADDR     NAME     TYPE   ADDR     NAME     TYPE   ADDR

REORDLST  SD    DC10

TOTAL LENGTH     538
ENTRY ADDRESS    D010
```

Figure 18-6   Test run output for the reorder-listing program: the load map (part 13 of 16)

JOB DLOWE214   STEP GO   TIME 123736   DATE 86310   ID = 00C   CPUID = A12231483083   PAGE 0000001

COMPLETION CODE   SYSTEM = 0C7

PSW AT ENTRY TO ABEND   078D2000 0000DCAC   ILC 6   INTC 0007

PSW LOAD MODULE = **GO   ADDRESS = 0000D0AC   OFFSET = 0000C0AC

Figure 18-6   Test run output for the reorder-listing program: the storage dump (part 14 of 16)

JOB DLOWE214   STEP GO   TIME 123736   DATE 86310   ID = 000   PAGE 0000009

SAVE AREA TRACE

INTERRUPT AT 0000D0AC

PROCEEDING BACK VIA REG 13

UNKNOWN WAS ENTERED VIA CALL   AT EP 05..05..01..05..05..05.........K..............

SA 0000D4D8 WD1 00000000 HSA 0005E78 LSA 8005E78 RET 6000D03C EPA 12B899A6 R0 0000D1EC
              R1 0000D1EC   R2 8005F7C   R3 4000D016 R4 0005FFA   R5 FFFFFFF   R6 0005F98
              R7 000000FF   R8 0000000   R9 0005EC0   R10 0005FE0   R11 0000000   R12 00006D6C

VSAM TCBVAT 7BEFA4 000004

7BEFA0   00000000   *   ....   *

NO VSAM VGTT CHAIN PRESENT FOR THIS ASCB

NO VSAM VSI CHAIN PRESENT

END OF VSAM DATA

REGS AT ENTRY TO ABEND

FLTR 0-6   0000000000000000   0000000000000000   0000000000000000   0000000000000000

REGS 0-7   0000D1EC   80005F7C   4000D016   0000D1EC   FFFFFFF   0005F98   000000FF

REGS 8-15   00005EC0   00005FE0   0000D000   00006D6C   0005FFA   0000D4D8   6000D03C   12B899A6

ACTIVE LOAD MODULES

Figure 18-6   Test run output for the reorder-listing program: the storage dump (part 15 of 16)

```
LPA/JPA MODULE     **GO
0000D000 5C5CC7D6 40404040 00000000 00000000   90ECD00C 053050D0 34C641D0 34C20700   *..GO    ................F...B..*
0000D020 45103016 0000D12C 8F00D18C 0A134110   31164100 31D658F0 103005EF FA203523   *......J...J...........0.0........*
0000D040 352CF224 351731FE F224351A 3203FA22   3517351A F224351D 31F9F922 3517351D   *..2.....2...........2....99.....*
0000D060 47B03018 F2243520 31D6D205 33B6350A   DE0533B6 3520D213 33C131DB F2243520   *....2....CK...........K..A..2...*
0000D080 31F4D206 33D93510 DE0633D9 3520D205   33E4350A DE0533E4 3517D205 33EE350A   *.4K..R.....R..K..U.....U..K.....*
0000D0A0 DE0533EE 351DF911 3526352A 474030CE   41103176 41003226 58F01030 05EF4110   *......9......  ...........0......*
0000D0C0 31764100 32AB58F0 103005EF 41103176   41003330 58F01030 05EFF810 3526352D   *........0.............0....8.....*
0000D0E0 92F033B5 41103176 410033B5 58F01030   05EFFA10 3526352C 924033B5 47F03018   *.0...........0..........  ...C..*
0000D100 DE06343B 35234110 31764100 343A58F0   103005EF 4510310A 0000D12C 8000D18C   *................0..........J...J.*
0000D120 0A1458D0 34C698EC D000C07FE 00000000  00000000 0000C000 00000000 00000C00   *.....F...........................*
0000D140 05007E68 00504000 00005E60 0600D100   80000000 00685000 007C4F8C 12B899A6   *......  .......J..................*
0000D160 00B5B048 00000001 08090050 00000000   00005D10 00007EC0 00007E70 00000C50   *.................................*
0000D180 00000001 00000000 00000001 00000000   00000000 00000000 00000000 00000C00   *.................................*
0000D1A0 01007DD8 00854000 00005CF8 06000001   84000000 00540050 007C4EF8 92B899B2   *...Q..  ....8...............8....*
0000D1C0 00000001 00000001 08090085 0C000000   00005BA8 00007E65 00007E65 00000085   *.................................*
0000D1E0 00000001 00000000 00000001 F0F0F1F0   F3C8C5C1 E3C5D940 E2D6D3C5 D5D6C9C4   *............0C103HEATER SOLENOID*
0000D200 40404040 40404040 4040F3F4 F5F0F0F0   F0F0F5F0 F0F0F0F3 F4F0F0F0 F0F04040   *              34500000500003400000C  *
0000D220 40404040 40404040 40404040 40404040   40404040 4040F0F1 F1F4F0F0 F1404040   *                        0114001    *
0000D240 40404040 40404040 40404040 40404040   40404040 40D9C5D6 D9C4C5D9 40D3C9E2   *                       REORDER LIS*
0000D260 E3C9D5C7 40404040 40404040 40404040   40404040 40404040 40404040 40404040   *TING                             *
0000D280 40404040 40404040 40404040 40404040   40404040 40404040 40404040 40404040   *                                 *
      LINE 0000D2A0    SAME AS ABOVE
0000D2C0 40F040C9 E3C5D440 40404040 40404040   404040C9 E3C5D440 40404040 40404040   * 0 ITEM              ITEM          *
0000D2E0 40404040 40404040 E4D5C9E3 40404040   40404040 40404040 4040D9C5 D6D9C4C5   *        UNIT                 REORDE*
0000D300 D9404040 40404040 40404040 40404040   40404040 40404040 40404040 40404040   *R                                *
0000D320 40404040 40404040 40404040 40404040   40404040 40404040 40404040 40404040   *                                 *
0000D340 40404040 40404040 40D5D64B 40404040   40404040 40C4C5E2 C3D9C9D7 E3C9D6D5   *           NO.        DESCRIPTION*
0000D360 40404040 40404040 40404040 D7D9C9C3   C5404040 C1E5C1C9 D3C1C2D3 C5404040   *              PRICE    AVAILABLE  *
0000D380 D7D6C9D5 E3404040 40404040 40404040   40404040 40404040 40404040 40404040   *POINT                            *
0000D3A0 40404040 40404040 40404040 40404040   40404040 40404040 40404040 40404040   *                                 *
0000D3C0 40404040 40404040 40404040 404040F1   F0F34040 404040C8 C5C1E3C5 D940E2D6   *                 103     HEATER SO*
0000D3E0 D3C5D5D6 C9C44040 40404040 40404040   F3F4F54B F0F04040 40404040 4040F3F4   *LENOID             345.00       34*
0000D400 40404040 40404040 F5F04040 40404040   40404040 40404040 40404040 40404040   *        50                       *
0000D420 40404040 40404040 40404040 40404040   40404040 40404040 40404040 40404040   *                                 *
0000D440 40404040 40404040 40404040 40404040   60402020 6B202020 40D9C5C3 D6D9C4E2   *                    . ......  RECORDS*
0000D460 40C9D540 E3C8C540 C9D5D7E4 E340C6C9   D3C54040 40404040 40404040 40404040   * IN THE INPUT FILE                *
0000D480 40404040 40404040 40404040 40404040   40404040 40404040 40404040 40404040   *                                 *
      LINE 0000D4A0    SAME AS ABOVE
0000D4C0 40404040 40404040 40404040 40404040   40404040 40000000 00000000 00005E78   *                       ..........*
0000D4E0 00000000 6000D03C 123899A6 0000D1EC   0000D1EC 80005F7C 4000D016 00005FFA   *..............J...J.....  .......*
0000D500 FFFFFFFF 00005F98 000000FF 00000000   00005EC0 00005FE0 0000D000 00006D6C   *.................................*
0000D520 40202020 20204020 20214B20 2C00034C   00000F00 050F3450 0F00002C 00000C00   * .....  ..........................*
0000D540 050C1C0C 00000000                                                          *........                         *
```

Figure 18-6 Test run output for the reorder-listing program: the storage dump (part 16 of 16)

Code	Exception type	Explanation
0C1	Operation	The machine has encountered an invalid operation code. This is often caused by a branch to a data name or the failure to branch around file or data definitions.
0C5	Addressing	An instruction has tried to use an address that is beyond the highest valid storage address. This is often caused by loading an incorrect value into a register that is used for addressing.
0C7	Data	An instruction has tried to operate on data that is invalid for it. Most often, the instruction is trying to do decimal arithmetic on a field that isn't in packed decimal form.
0CA	Decimal overflow	A decimal add, subtract, or multiply instruction develops a result that is too large for the receiving field. This is often caused by bad input data.
0CB	Decimal divide	A decimal divide instruction develops a quotient that is too large for the receiving field. This is usually caused by a divisor with a zero value.

Figure 18-7   Some common program checks

first page of the dump. There are two types of completion codes. A *user completion code* indicates that the termination was caused by the program itself, usually with an ABEND macro. When this type of termination occurs, the completion code is a four-digit decimal number as described in chapter 6. A *system completion code* indicates that the supervisor terminated the program. When this type of termination occurs, the completion code is a three-digit hex code. For program checks, this code is in the form 0CX, where X ranges from 1 through F.

Some of the most common causes of program checks are listed in figure 18-7. These should be adequate for most of the program checks you'll experience as part of this course. Later on, if you need to refer to the complete list, you'll find it in the *Principles of Operation* manual for your system.

As figure 18-7 explains, *data exception* indicates that an operand has invalid data like EBCDIC data for a packed decimal instruction. In contrast, an *operation exception* indicates that the operation code of an instruction is invalid. This can happen, for example, if a branch instruction specifies a data name instead of an instruction label. An *addressing exception* occurs when an instruction tries to address an area in storage outside of the program area. A *decimal overflow exception* occurs when a decimal arithmetic instruction leads to a result larger than the receiving field can hold. And a *decimal divide exception* occurs when the quotient of a decimal divide instruction is larger than the receiving field can hold. By far the most common of the exceptions, though, is the data exception.

After the completion code message is a message that gives the location of the instruction that caused the abnormal termination. The message is in this format:

```
PSW AT ENTRY TO ABEND   XXXXXXXX YYYYYYYY
```

The *interrupt address* (or *abend address*) given in this message (YYYYYYYY) is the address of the next instruction to be executed at the time of the program check. In figure 18-6, the interrupt address is 0000D0AC so you know the instruction just before this address is the one that caused the program check.

The load map   Once you've determined the type of error that occurred in your program, you must find the *load address* (or starting address) of the program. You do this by referring to the load map (part 13 of figure 8-6), which tells you where your program has been loaded into storage. In this case, the entry address is D010, which means that's the first byte used by your program. Notice that the load map also gives the total length in bytes of your program. In addition, it gives the name, type, and address of each of the object modules that the load module contains. In this case, the load module consists of only one object module, REORDLST.

How to calculate the location counter value of the instruction after the one that caused the program check   To find out which instruction caused the program check in figure 18-6, you subtract the load address of REORDLST (D010) from the interrupt address (D0AC). The result is the location counter value of the instruction after the one that caused the program check. You can then use the location counter value to look up the instruction in the assembly listing.

When you do your subtraction, remember that you're working with hex values. The easiest way to do the subtraction, of course, is to use a hex calculator. But if you don't have one with you, you can subtract in much the same way you do decimal subtraction:

```
 D0AC
 D010
 ────
   9C
```

Starting from the right in this example, 0 from C is obviously C. Then, if you realize that hex A is decimal 10, you can figure that hex 1 from hex A is hex 9.

The calculation is a little more complicated when borrowing is involved. Consider this computation, for example:

```
 D100
 D010
 ────
   F0
```

Here, in order to subtract 1 from 0 in the tens decimal position, you must first carry a 1 over from the hundreds decimal position, so you're actually subtracting hex 1 from hex 10. Then, since hex 10 is decimal 16, hex 10 minus hex 1 is decimal 15, or hex F.

How to locate an instruction in the assembly listing   Once you have the location counter value for an instruction, you can find it in the assembly listing. If you scan down the location counter values to a value of hex 9C in the assembly listing in figure 18-6, you can see that statement 40 caused the program check:

```
CP      LINECNT,=P'50'
```

(Remember, the instruction that caused the program check is the one before the calculated location counter value.) Then, if the cause of the program check isn't obvious, you can examine the data fields involved by looking them up in the storage dump.

How to analyze storage dump data

After the completion messages at the beginning of the storage dump (part 14 of figure 18-6), you'll find some information related to the control blocks used by the program. After these areas are the contents of the register save area, the contents of the eight floating-point registers, the contents of the 16 general-purpose registers, and the contents of the modules used by the program. The contents of the problem program area are found under the heading LPA/JPA **GO.

In figure 18-6, I have omitted the areas after the completion messages and before the register save area, and I have omitted the contents of storage before and after the problem program area because you will rarely, if ever, need to use the data in these areas. And you certainly won't need to use them in this course. However, you will want to analyze the data in the register save area, in the registers, and in the fields in your program area.

The contents of the register save area   You should recall from chapter 5 that all MVS programs and subprograms use a standard register save technique. When MVS transfers control to your program, for example, it loads the address of its save area into register 13. Your program then issues a SAVE macro to store the contents of the registers in the MVS save area. Next, your program loads register 13 with the address of its own save area so an I/O module or any other subprogram can save the register contents in that save area. Sometimes in a debugging problem, it's necessary to look at these save areas to find out what the contents of one or more registers were before a link to a subprogram occurred.

The register save areas are printed in the dump under the heading PROCEEDING BACK VIA REG 13. In figure 18-6, for example, one save area was dumped since the program consisted of only one module. This is the save area defined in the reorder-listing program. As you can see, each of the 18 words of the save area is labelled for easy identification. R0 through R12 refer to general registers zero through 12. RET identifies register 14, which usually contains the return address when returning from a subprogram. And EPA identifies register 15, which usually contains the entry point address when branching to a subprogram. (Register save areas, return addresses, and entry point addresses are presented in detail in chapter 8, in case you haven't read that chapter yet.)

Since a link to the disk I/O module had been made before the program check occurred, the registers were saved at that time. As a result, they contain some addresses that are meaningful to the reorder-listing program. For example, register 3 contains the base address of the reorder-listing program that was loaded by the BALR instruction (the leftmost byte is ignored). Similarly, register zero (R0) contains meaningful data. When the link to the I/O module was made, R0 was used to pass the address of the record work area to the I/O module. If you subtract the load address of the program from the address shown in the R0 register, you will find that it is the location counter value of the record work area as shown on the assembly listing. Register 14 (the return register) is also used when the link to the I/O module is made by the GET macro. It is loaded with the address of the instruction that immediately follows the GET macro, the AP instruction.

In your early test runs, you may have little need to examine register save areas. In more complex programs, however, these areas may be essential to your debugging. In particular, the save area dumps may be necessary to trace the flow of control between subprograms.

The contents of the registers   The contents of the general-purpose and floating-point registers are printed under the heading REGS AT ENTRY TO ABEND. It's in part 15 of figure 18-6. If you use floating-point operations as described in chapter 12, you may need to analyze the data in the floating-point registers. The contents of these registers are printed in the line headed FLTR 0-6. There are four of these registers (numbered 0, 2, 4, and 6), but they all contained hex zeros at the time the storage dump in figure 18-6 was created.

The general-purpose registers are printed right after those of the floating-point registers in the two lines headed REGS 0-7 and REGS 8-15. For example, register 3, which is the base register for this program, contained a value of hex 4000D016 at the time of the storage dump in figure 18-6. Since only the rightmost three bytes are involved in base addressing, the base address is hex 00D016. This is the address of the first instruction following the BALR. Because the general-purpose registers are used in many assembler language operations, you will frequently need to analyze the data in these registers.

The contents of the fields in the user's program area   In the storage portion of the storage dump (part 16 of figure 18-6), 32 bytes of storage are printed in groups of four bytes with the address of the first byte of the

Address	Storage contents
D060-D063	47B03018
D064-D067	F2243520
D068-D06B	31D6D205
D06C-D06F	33B6350A
D070-D073	DE0533B6
D074-D077	3520D213
D078-D07B	33C131DB
D07C-D07F	F2243520

Figure 18-8   The contents of storage positions D060 through D07F in the storage dump in figure 18-6

line in the left margin. The line next to address D060, for example, displays the 32 bytes from D060-D07F with all data in hex. In figure 18-8, I have presented the code from this line of the storage dump in a modified form so it's clear what the addresses are and what the storage contents are. If you compare the object code in the assembly listing with the object code starting at address D010, you will find them identical.

To the right of the eight columns that give the contents of 32 bytes of storage in hex notation is a column of data that represents the same 32 bytes in character notation. If a period is printed for a storage position, it means the byte either contains a period or it doesn't contain an EBCDIC code that can be printed. Otherwise, the character representing the code is printed. If, for example, you look at the storage dump in figure 18-6, you can see the constant word DESCRIPTION in the character portion of the dump. Then, if you relate this to the address at the far left of that line of print, you can determine that DESCRIPTION is stored in bytes D355-D35F. And if you analyze the hex portion of the dump for the same bytes of storage, you can see the hex codes for the letters in this word: C4 for D, C5 for E, and so on.

How to calculate the address of a field or an instruction in the storage dump   To locate a field or an instruction in your program area, you must first calculate its starting address. You do this by adding its location counter value to the relocation factor given in the load map. You can find the location counter value for a field in the ADDR1 or ADDR2 columns of the assembly listing or in the cross-reference listing. For instance, the ADDR1 column in statement 40 in figure 18-6 gives 52C as the location counter value for LINECNT and so does the cross-reference listing. As a result, the address of the field in storage is hex D53C (hex 52C plus hex D010).

Here, the problem is simple addition. However, when carrying is involved, the calculation is a little more difficult. For example, consider the computation

```
D010
 5FA
────
D60A
```

Starting from the right, 0 plus A is A. Next, 1 plus F (decimal 15) is decimal 16, which is hex 10. As a result, 1 is carried over to the hundreds decimal position. Then, 1 (the carried digit) plus 0 plus 5 is 6.

How to locate a field or an instruction in the storage dump   To find a field or an instruction in the storage dump once you know its address, you scan down the column of addresses on the left side of the storage dump until you come to the nearest address below it. Then, you count over until you locate the start of the field.

In the case of LINECNT in figure 18-6, for example, you scan the column of addresses until you come to address D520. That is, the nearest address below D53C, the address of LINECNT. Then, you count over to the hex digits representing address D53C. Since the first byte of the line starts at address D520, you count D520 for the first byte, D521 for the second byte, and so on.

When you reach byte D53C, you know that this is the start of the LINECNT field. Then, since the LINECNT field is two bytes long, you examine two bytes of data. If you do this, you'll see that the field contains 0000, which isn't valid packed decimal data. So that's the cause of the data exception.

How to debug a program check at an address within your program

After you've located the instruction in your program that caused the program check and after you've analyzed the related fields in storage, you must still figure out what's wrong with your source code. In some cases, you may be surprised to discover that the bug won't be in the instruction that caused the program check or in the data definitions of the fields that the instruction operates upon. Instead, the bug will be elsewhere in the program.

In the case of the program in figure 18-6, though, the bug is fairly obvious. Since we know that LINECNT contained invalid packed decimal data at the time of the program check, we must find out why it did. Since LINECNT isn't an input field, you have to assume that the error is in the source code, not in the input data. Then, if you check the definition of LINECNT, you can see the error:

```
LINECNT   DS      P'50'
```

Because this definition uses DS instead of DC, the program assembled cleanly but no starting value was given to the field. As a result, LINECNT took on whatever value was left in its storage positions by the previous program. By changing the DS to DC, the bug should be corrected.

Using debugging instructions and the SNAP macro   If a bug is difficult to isolate, you may not be able to debug it using just the storage dump at the time of the program check. In this case, you may want to add debugging instructions to your program and rerun the test. As I've mentioned, the SNAP macro is particularly useful as a debugging instruction. By using SNAP, you can dump portions of your storage area whenever you want to during the execution of your program. For instance, you can dump the contents of selected storage fields before a series of calculations is made and after the calculations are made. Then, you can compare the before and after values to see what went wrong.

How to debug a program check at an address within a subprogram

The program check in figure 18-6 was caused by an instruction within the user's program. But that isn't always the case. Sometimes, the address of the offending instruction is in another module of the program.

To illustrate, figure 18-9 presents part of the output from a job that assembles a program, links it with a subprogram module named GETIME, and loads and executes the resulting module. Because the two modules have to be link edited, I used the ASMFCLG procedure, presented in chapter 8. When you use this procedure, instead of getting a load map, you get a *link edit map*. This is illustrated in part 1 of the output given in figure 18-9.

As you can see in figure 18-9, both the REORDLST and GETIME modules are listed on the link edit map. However, since the linkage editor program doesn't actually load the program into storage, no load address appears on the link edit map. Instead, the load address must be calculated from information on the first page of the dump. This is illustrated in part 2 of figure 18-9.

If you compare part 2 of figure 18-9 with the first page of the dump in figure 18-6, you'll see an additional line:

```
PSW LOAD MODULE = GO
```

This is followed by an address and an offset. The address is the same as the abend address in the previous line. The offset is the address of the abend

```
H96-LEVEL LINKAGE EDITOR OPTIONS SPECIFIED XREF,LET,LIST,NCAL
      DEFAULT OPTION(S) USED - SIZE=(262144,65536)
      SYSPRINT DEFAULT BLOCKING USED  1 - 1

                          CROSS REFERENCE TABLE

CONTROL SECTION                ENTRY
   NAME    ORIGIN  LENGTH    NAME  LOCATION   NAME  LOCATION   NAME  LOCATION   NAME  LOCATION
 REORDLST    00     554
 GETIME     558      88

LOCATION  REFERS TO SYMBOL   IN CONTROL SECTION        LOCATION  REFERS TO SYMBOL   IN CONTROL SECTION
   A4             GETIME            GETIME
ENTRY ADDRESS         00

TOTAL LENGTH      5E0
****GO   DOES NOT EXIST BUT HAS BEEN ADDED TO DATA SET      AMODE 24
RMODE IS 24
AUTHORIZATION CODE IS      0.
```

Figure 18-9 Test run output with a program check in the GETIME subprogram: the link edit map (part 1 of 2)

```
JOB DLOWE214        STEP GO        TIME 123804        DATE 86310        ID = 000        CPUID = A12231483083        PAGE 00000001

COMPLETION CODE        SYSTEM = 0C4

PSW AT ENTRY TO ABEND    078D1300 00006F9C        ILC 6        INTC C004

PSW LOAD MODULE = GO        ADDRESS = 00006F9C        OFFSET = 0000057C

ASCB
00F62780
+0000  ASCB 00000000   FWDP 00F47A00              BWDP 00F1F200   CMSF 00000000   SVRB 007FD540
+0014  SYNC 00005012   IOSP 00000000              TNEW 007BDE88   CPUS 00000001   ASID 001C
+0026  SEQN 0020       LL5  00                    RV01 00         HLHI 01          DP   34
+002C  RV00 00000000   LDA  7FF144E8              RSMF 00         RV81 00          CSCB 00F72680
+003C  TSB  00000000   EJST 00000000   034F3400   EWST 98CA04E4                    2D4C3A00
+0050  JSTL 00D141A4   ECB  807FDAD8              UBET 93C9FF35   TLCH 00           DUMP 007FD080
+0064  AFFN FFFF       RCTF 00                    FLG1 00         TMCH 0000         ASXB 007FDC20
+0070  SWCT 2068       DSP1 000F                  FLG2 00         RSV  00           SRBS 0000
+0078  VSC  0000       NVSC 0000                  RCTP 007FDE40                     LSQH 00000000
+0088  QECB 00000000   MECB 40000000              OUCB 01A092E0   LOCK 01ACFF18     FMCT 003A
+009A  LEVL 01         RV02 00                    XMPQ 00000000   IQEA 00000000     RTMC 00000000
+00A8  MCC  00000000   JBNI 00F240D0              JBNS 00F72690   SRQ1 00           SRQ2 00
+00B6  SRQ3 00         SRQ4 00                    VGTT 00000000   PCTT 00000000     SSRB 0000
+00C2  SMCT 00         SPB* 07                    SWTL 00141DD    SRBT 00000001     0112FC00
+00D0  LSMQ 00000000   LSPL 00000000              TCBS 00000000   TCBL 30           WPRB 007FE800
+00E4  NDP  34         TNDP FF                    NTSG FF         IODP 00           LOCI 00000000
+00EC  CMLH 00000000   CMLC 00000000              SSO1 00000000   SS04 00           ASTE 00F711C0
+00FC  LTOV 7FFDC000   ATOV 7FFE7750              ETC  0000CC00   ETCN 0000         LXR  0000
+010A  AXR  0000       STKH 0000                  GGEL 00000000   LQEL 0000CC00     GSYN 00257390
+011C  XTCB 0079DE88   CS1  93CA04CD              RV58 00         GXL  000000       EATT 00000002
+012C       20E09C00   INTS A44D600                               LL1  00           LL2  000
+013A  LL3  01F4       LL4  00000000              RCMS 00         IOSC 00000016     PKML 0000
+0146  XCNT 00000000   NSQA 00000000              ASM  00000000   RV3C 011510F0     TCME 00000000
+0158  RV70 00000000                                              CREG 00000003     RV82 00000000
+0170             ARC  00000000              RSMA 00000000   DCTI 01151048   00002245

*** ADDRESS SPACE SWITCH EVENT MASK OFF (CASTESSEM = 0) ***

TCB
007BDE88
+0000  RBP      007FD450   PIE  00000000   DEB  00000000   TIO 007D7600   CMP 007C5000
+0014  TRN      00000000   MSS  7FFFD3B8   PKF  7FFFD388   FLGS 80        00  01000000
+0022  LMP      FF         DSP  FF         LLS  FF         JLB  007D4CD0   JPQ 007D4CF0
+0030  GPR0-3   00000000   007C3908   007C37F0   80C64386   940C4C00
+0040  GPR4-7   007BDE88   007FD45C   00000044   80C6488C
+0050  GPR8-11  007FD338   00000000   007FD2F8   80C646E6
+0060  GPR12-15 007D42A8   0079A830   007C3904   00000000   00000000
+0070  FSA      00005FB0   TCB  00000000   TME  00000000   NTC 007BDE88
+0084  OTC      007FF140   LTC  00000000   IQE  00000000   ECB 007D4D74   TSFLG 20
+0095  STPCT    00         TSLP 00         TSDP 03                         RD  7FF1451C   AE 7FF13FD0
+00A0  STAB     007F2270   TCT  807FF7D8   USER 807FF7D8   NDSP 00000000   MDIDS 00000000
+00B4  JSCB     007D4E84   SSAT 00F9E3B0   IOBRC 00F9E3B0   EXCPD 00000000   EXT1 00000000
+00C8  BITS     0000000C0  DAR  0000000C0  RSV37 00         SYSCT 00        STMCT 00
+00D0  EXT2     0075DFE0   AECB 0075DFE0   XSB  00000000   BACK 007FD520   RTWA 007FF140
+00E4  NSSP     00000000   XLAS 00000000   ABCUR 00000000                  TID 00          007D42B0
```

Figure 18-9   Test run output with a program check in the GETIME subprogram: the first page of the storage dump (part 2 of 2)

relative to the beginning of the program. Then, to figure out the load address, you simply subtract the offset from the abend address. In this case, the load address is 6A20 (6F9C - 57C).

To calculate the address of the subprogram, you have to use the address listed in the ORIGIN column for GETIME in the link edit map. This address is the offset of the subprogram from the beginning of the load module. By adding this offset to the load address, you'll get the address of the subprogram. In this case, the subprogram is located at the address 6F78 (6A20 + 558).

Now, look at the program check message in part 2 of figure 8-9. Notice that the program abended at address 6F9C. But the subprogram was loaded at 6F78. This means that the program abended within the subprogram.

If you haven't read chapter 8, you'll learn about subprograms and subprogram linkage when you do. For now, though, you should know that you debug a subprogram the same way that you debug a main program. By subtracting the load address for the module from the program check address, you get the location counter value of the instruction after the instruction that caused the program check in the subprogram. Then, you can find this instruction in the assembly listing of the subprogram, analyze related fields in the storage dump, etc.

What if the subprogram has been in use for years and you have to assume that it works correctly? You must then assume that your program didn't call the subprogram correctly. In most cases, this will mean that your program didn't pass its data to the subprogram in the sequence or format that the subprogram expected it to be in. You can correct this type of bug by making sure that your fields are in the right order and the right format. This should be clear to you after you read chapter 8.

A procedure for debugging abnormal terminations

Because debugging an abnormal termination takes several steps, figure 18-10 summarizes the debugging procedure. If this seems like a lengthy process to go through to find one trivial error, take heart. Once you have found the cause of a program check a few times, you will be able to locate instructions and fields in the storage dump with considerable speed.

DISCUSSION   Debugging is one of the most challenging jobs you will have as a programmer. In a large, complex program, debugging an error can be like solving a mystery. From the output clues, you trace backwards to figure out what happened until you find the culprit: a coding or an input error.

Unfortunately, debugging can also be a frustrating task. Sometimes, a trivial coding error will cause a bug that takes hours or days to correct. That's why it's important that you use an orderly procedure like the one in figure 18-10 when you debug your programs.

A debugging procedure for abnormal terminations

1. Find the completion-code message and determine the cause of the termination.

2. Get the load address of your program and the load addresses of any subprograms that your program calls. If you have a load map, it will give you these load addresses. If you have a link edit map, you must calculate these addresses. After you have these addresses, determine if the program check occurred in the program or a subprogram by comparing the load addresses of the modules to the abend address. If the abend address isn't in one of the modules of your load module, get help.

3. Derive the location counter value of the abend address by subtracting the load address of your program or subprogram from the abend address.

4. Use the location counter value to find the instruction in the assembly listing of your program or subprogram. Then, find the instruction before the one indicated by the location counter address. That's the instruction that caused the program check.

5. At this point, you may want to analyze registers, register save areas, fields, or instructions in the storage dump depending on the type of exception you're dealing with. To find the starting byte of any field or instruction, add its location counter value to the load address. Your analysis may be simple, as in the case of a data exception, or it may by complicated.

6. If you can't debug the problem by analyzing the data in the storage dump, you may want to add debugging statements to the source program, reassemble it, and do the test run again. For instance, you may want to add SNAP macros to your source program so you can get the before and after values of the fields or registers used by your program. The SNAP macro is presented in chapter 6.

7. When you find the bug in the source code, correct it, reassemble the source program or subprogram, and rerun the test.

Figure 18-10   A debugging procedure for abnormal terminations

Terminology		
	normal termination	core dump
	normal end-of-job	completion code message
	normal EOJ	user completion code
	abnormal termination	system completion code
	abend	data exception
	debugging instruction	operation exception
	program check	addressing exception
	job log	decimal overflow exception
	statistics log	decimal divide exception
	JCL log	interrupt address
	message log	abend address
	load map	load address
	storage dump	link edit map
	storage printout	

Objective   Given test run output for a program, debug it. The test run output will include the assembly listing, load or link edit map, program check message, and storage printout.

Chapter 19

An introduction
to structured program development

When I presented the program flowchart in chapter 3, I told you that we believe there are better techniques for designing assembler language programs. Then, in chapter 8, I presented modular flowcharting, which we believe is a significant improvement over traditional program flowcharting. Now, in this chapter, I'm going to introduce you to structured program development.

The term *structured programming* includes a collection of techniques that are designed to help you improve both your productivity and the quality of your programs. The techniques include structured program design, structured module planning via pseudocode, structured coding, and top-down testing. When you finish this chapter, I hope you'll agree that structured design techniques are major improvements over both flowcharting and modular flowcharting. And I hope you'll understand that these design techniques make structured coding and top-down testing possible.

You can read this chapter any time after you complete chapter 8. In fact, we recommend that you read it right after you complete chapter 8. Then, you can use the structured techniques in your work on the case study for this course.

I'll start this chapter by presenting the theory of structured programming. Next, I'll show you the design and coding for the reorder-listing program in structured style. Then, I'll show you how to design a program using a structure chart, how to plan the modules of a program using pseudocode, how to code a program in structured style, and how to test a program from the top down.

THE THEORY OF STRUCTURED PROGRAMMING

The basic theory of structured programming is that any program can be written using three logical structures: sequence, selection, and iteration. These structures, illustrated in figure 19-1, have only one entry point and one exit point.

The first structure, the *sequence structure*, is simply a set of imperative statements executed in sequence, one after another. The entry point is at the start of the sequence; the exit point is after the last function in the sequence. A sequence structure may consist of a single function or of many functions.

The second structure, the *selection structure*, is a choice between two, and only two, functions based on a condition. This structure is often referred to as the IF-THEN-ELSE structure, and most programming languages have code that approximates it. Note that one of the functions may be null. In other words, if the condition is not met, the flow of control may pass directly to the structure's exit point with no intervening statements or structures.

The third structure, the *iteration structure*, is often called the DO-WHILE structure. It provides for doing a function as long as a condition is true. As you can see in variation 1 of the iteration structure, the condition is tested before the function is performed. When the condition is no longer true, the program continues with the next structure.

Related to the DO-WHILE structure are the DO-UNTIL and the COBOL PERFORM-UNTIL structures. As you can see in the DO-UNTIL structure in figure 19-1, the condition is tested after the function is performed and the function is performed until a condition is true. In the PERFORM-UNTIL structure, the function is also performed until the condition is true, but it is tested before the function is performed.

Again, let me stress that all of the structures in figure 19-1 have only one entry point and one exit point. As a result, a program made up of these structures will have only one entry point and one exit point. This means the program will be executed in a controlled manner from the first statement to the last. These characteristics make up a *proper program*.

To create a proper program, any of the three structures can be substituted for a function box in any of the other structures. The result will still be a proper program. Conversely, two or more of the basic structures in sequence can be treated as a single function box. This means that structures of great complexity can be created with the assurance that they will have only one entry point and one exit point.

This theory is an important contribution to the art of programming because it places necessary restrictions on program structure. For instance, branch statements or GOTO statements are unacceptable in structured programming. As a result, uncontrolled branching is impossible. This reduces the likelikood of bugs and makes bugs that do occur easier to find and correct. This also makes a structured program easier to read and understand than an unstructured one.

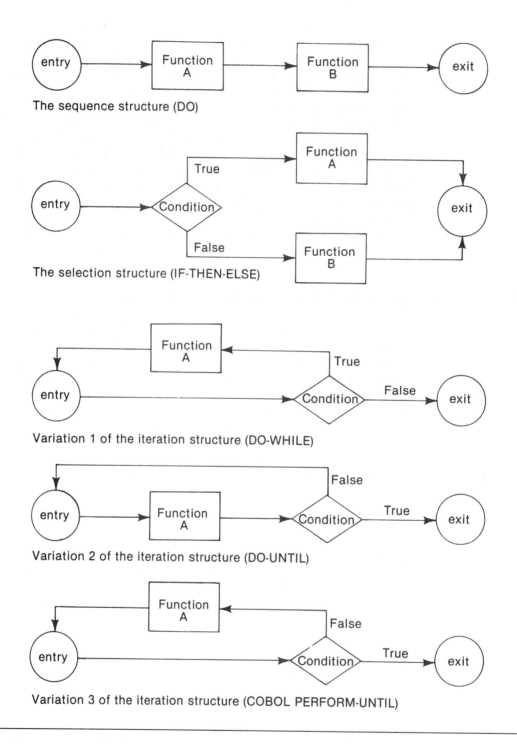

The sequence structure (DO)

The selection structure (IF-THEN-ELSE)

Variation 1 of the iteration structure (DO-WHILE)

Variation 2 of the iteration structure (DO-UNTIL)

Variation 3 of the iteration structure (COBOL PERFORM-UNTIL)

Figure 19-1   The basic structures of structured programming

Unfortunately, assembler language doesn't provide for the selection and iteration structures. And you can't code assembler language programs without using branch instructions in one form or another. So, it's impossible to comply with the principles of structured programming when you develop assembler language programs. That's one reason why assembler language is rarely used today for developing application programs.

On the other hand, you can design an assembler language program using structured design techniques. And you can plan the modules of the program so each one has only one entry and exit point. Then, you can code the modules in a structured style so the progression from one module to another is orderly. And, if you want to, you can test the program using top-down testing. If you do these things, you will get many of the benefits of structured programming, even though your program won't technically comply with the principles of structured programming.

A STRUCTURED VERSION OF THE REORDER-LISTING PROGRAM

Figures 19-2, 19-3, and 19-4 present the documentation for a structured version of the reorder-listing program. This program works like the reorder-listing program presented in topic 2 of chapter 5, except that the current date and time are printed in the first heading line of the reorder listing. Figure 19-2 presents the structure chart for this program. Figure 19-3 presents the pseudocode for the modules of this program. And figure 19-4 presents the assembler language code for this program.

The structure chart

The *structure chart* in figure 19-2 is an index to the subroutines and subprograms used in the assembler language program in figure 19-4. Any box in the structure chart with a number above it becomes a subroutine in the assembler language code. Any box with a stripe in it represents a subprogram called by the program. For instance, box 300 is a subroutine that is named REORD300 in the assembler language code. And the box with the GETIME stripe in it represents a subprogram that is called by module 100 in the reorder-listing program.

When you create a structure chart like the one in figure 19-2, you design from the top down until each box represents a function or subfunction that can be coded in 30 lines or fewer. That way the program consists of modules that are relatively easy to code. In contrast, studies have shown that modules of more than 30 lines become increasingly more difficult to code and understand as their size increases.

One of the benefits of structured design is that it lets you design modules for a program until each module is small enough to be manageable. In addition, a structure chart shows all the modules of a program as well as the relationships between the modules so it becomes an index to the resulting code. In contrast, traditional flowcharting techniques don't help you divide a program into modules. And modular flowcharts don't become an effective index to the resulting code.

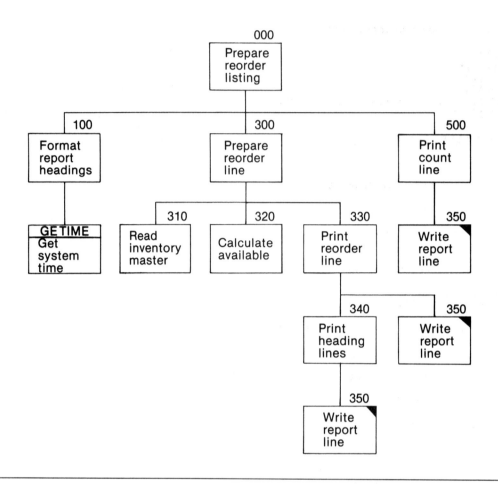

Figure 19-2   A structure chart for a version of the reorder-listing program

The pseudocode

Figure 19-3 presents the *pseudocode* for the modules of the structure chart in figure 19-2. The pseudocode is the plan for the coding of the assembler language modules. In this sense, pseudocode is a replacement for flowcharts. However, you only use the sequence, iteration, and selection structures when you use pseudocode so your modules only have one entry and exit point. In addition, you can create and modify pseudocode much more easily than you can create and modify flowcharts.

The source listing

Figure 19-4 presents the source listing for the program that is planned by the pseudocode in figure 19-3. Here, you can see that one subroutine is coded for each of the subroutine boxes in the structure chart. For instance, the program consists of subroutines named REORD000, REORD100, REORD300, REORD310, and so on. In this program, module 330 is the longest module, but it consists of only 22 lines. As a result, the entire program is relatively easy to read and understand.

REORD000:   Prepare reorder listing

```
DO REORD100.
SAVE registers.
OPEN files.
DO REORD300
    UNTIL all records processed.
DO REORD500.
CLOSE files.
RESTORE registers.
EOJ.
```

REORD100:   Format report heading

```
Get system date.
CALL GETIME.
Format heading.
```

REORD300:   Prepare reorder line

```
DO REORD310.
IF NOT end-of-file
    DO REORD320
    IF available less than reorder-point
        DO REORD330.
```

REORD310:   Read inventory master

```
Read inventory master.
IF end-of-file
    set EOFSWTCH to X'FF'
ELSE
    add 1 to record count.
```

REORD320:   Calculate available

```
Calculate available.
```

REORD330:   Print reorder line

```
Set ASA control character for detailed line to single spacing.
IF line count = 54
    DO REORD340.
Format reorder line.
Move reorder line to printer work area.
DO REORD350.
```

Figure 19-3   Pseudocode for the modules of the reorder-listing program that is charted in figure 19-2 (part 1 of 2)

If you review the code, you can see that comment lines have been used to identify the modules in the program. They are also used to identify groups of data definitions. This helps make the program easy to read. Otherwise, the coding is much like the coding presented in chapter 8.

REORD340:   Print heading lines

```
Move heading line 1 to printer work area.
DO REORD350.
Move heading line 2 to printer work area.
DO REORD350.
Move heading line 3 to printer work area.
DO REORD350.
Reset line count to zero.
Set ASA control character for detail line to double spacing.
```

REORD350:   Write report line

```
Write line on printer.
Add 1 to line count.
```

REORD500:   Print count line

```
Format count line.
Move count line to printer work area.
DO REORD350.
```

Figure 19-3   Pseudocode for the modules of the reorder-listing program that is charted in figure 19-2 (part 2 of 2)

HOW TO DESIGN A PROGRAM USING A STRUCTURE CHART

To develop a structure chart, you start at the top with one box that represents the entire program. At the next level, you draw a box for the one primary function that the top-level box requires. You also add boxes at this level for any functions that must be done before or after the primary function. Then, you expand each of the functions at the second level into subfunctions. You continue in this way until each box on the chart represents a function or subfunction that can be coded with limited difficulty.

To name the functions and subfunctions represented by the boxes of a chart, you use a verb, one or two adjectives, and a noun. Thus, the name of the top-level box in figure 19-2 is "prepare reorder listing." And the name of box 310 is "read inventory master."

I'm now going to present a five-step procedure for developing structure charts. This introductory procedure should help you design the programs required by the case study in appendix B. And it should help you design production programs of limited length and complexity.

```
*
*   MODULE 000:   PREPARE REORDER LISTING
*
REORDLST START 0
BEGIN     SAVE  (14,12)
          BALR  3,0
          USING *,3
          ST    13,SAVE+4
          LA    13,SAVE
          BAL   11,REORD100
          OPEN  (INVMAST,INPUT,PRTOUT,OUTPUT)
DU000N1   BAL   11,REORD300
          CLI   EOFSWTCH,X'FF'
          BNE   DU000N1
ENDOJOB   BAL   11,REORD500
          CLOSE (INVMAST,,PRTOUT)
          L     13,SAVE+4
          RETURN (14,12)
*
*   MODULE 100:   FORMAT REPORT HEADINGS
*
REORD100 TIME  DEC
          ST    1,DATE
          ED    HDG1DATE,DATE+1
          ST    0,TIME
          MVN   TIME+3(1),=X'0F'
          ED    HDG1TIME,TIME
          BR    11
*
*   MODULE 300:   PREPARE REORDER LINE
*
REORD300 ST    11,REOSAV11
          BAL   11,REORD310
IF300N1   CLI   EOFSWTCH,X'FF'
          BE    R300EXIT
IF300N1A BAL   11,REORD320
IF300N2   CP    WRKAVAIL,WRKORDPT
          BNL   R300EXIT
IF300N2A BAL   11,REORD330
R300EXIT L     11,REOSAV11
          BR    11
REOSAV11 DS    F
*
*   MODULE 310:   READ INVENTORY MASTER
*
REORD310 GET   INVMAST,INVWRKA
          AP    COUNT,=P'1'
          B     R310EXIT
INVEOF    MVI   EOFSWTCH,X'FF'
R310EXIT BR    11
*
*   MODULE 320:   CALCULATE AVAILABLE
*
REORD320 PACK  WRKAVAIL,INVONHND
```

Figure 19-4   The source listing for the structured reorder-listing program that is planned by the pseudocode in figure 19-3 (part 1 of 4)

```
            PACK    WRKONORD,INVONORD
            AP      WRKAVAIL,WRKONORD
            PACK    WRKORDPT,INVORDPT
            BR      11
*
*   MODULE 330:   PRINT REORDER LINE
*
REORD330 ST      11,PRTSAV11
            MVI     PRTDETL,X'40'
            MVC     PRTDETL+1(132),PRTDETL
IF330N1  CP      LINECNT,=P'54'
            BL      IF330N1B
IF330N1A BAL     11,REORD340
IF330N1B PACK    PACKAREA,INVITNBR
            MVC     PRTITNBR,PATTERN1
            ED      PRTITNBR,PACKAREA
            MVC     PRTITDES,INVITDES
            PACK    PACKAREA,INVPRICE
            MVC     PRTPRICE,PATTERN2
            ED      PRTPRICE,PACKAREA
            MVC     PRTAVAIL,PATTERN1
            ED      PRTAVAIL,WRKAVAIL
            MVC     PRTORDPT,PATTERN1
            ED      PRTORDPT,WRKORDPT
            MVC     PRTAREA,PRTDETL
            BAL     11,REORD350
            L       11,PRTSAV11
            BR      11
PRTSAV11 DS      F
*
*   MODULE 340:   PRINT HEADING LINES
*
REORD340 ST      11,HDSAV11
            MVC     PRTAREA,HDGLINE1
            BAL     11,REORD350
            MVC     PRTAREA,HDGLINE2
            BAL     11,REORD350
            MVC     PRTAREA,HDGLINE3
            BAL     11,REORD350
            ZAP     LINECNT,=P'0'
            MVI     PRTDCTL,C'0'
            L       11,HDSAV11
            BR      11
HDSAV11  DS      F
*
*   MODULE 350:   WRITE REPORT LINE
*
REORD350 PUT     PRTOUT,PRTAREA
            AP      LINECNT,=P'1'
            BR      11
*
*   MODULE 500:   PRINT COUNT LINE
*
REORD500 ST      11,CNTSAV11
```

Figure 19-4   The source listing for the structured reorder-listing program that is planned by the pseudocode in figure 19-3 (part 2 of 4)

```
          ED        CNTPATRN,COUNT
          MVC       PRTAREA,CNTLINE
          BAL       11,REORD350
          L         11,CNTSAV11
          BR        11
CNTSAV11  DS        F
*
*  FILE DEFINITIONS
*
INVMAST   DCB       DSORG=PS,                                          X
                    RECFM=FB,                                          X
                    MACRF=GM,                                          X
                    BLKSIZE=500,                                       X
                    LRECL=50,                                          X
                    DDNAME=INVMST,                                     X
                    EODAD=INVEOF
PRTOUT    DCB       DSORG=PS,                                          X
                    RECFM=FA,                                          X
                    MACRF=PM,                                          X
                    BLKSIZE=133,                                       X
                    LRECL=133,                                         X
                    DDNAME=REPORT
*
*   WORK AREAS
*
INVWRKA   DS        0CL50
INVITNBR  DS        CL5
INVITDES  DS        CL20
          DS        CL5
INVPRICE  DS        CL5
INVORDPT  DS        CL5
INVONHND  DS        CL5
INVONORD  DS        CL5
          DS        CL30
*
HDGLINE1  DS        0CL133
          DC        C'1'
          DC        C'DATE: '
HDG1DATE  DC        X'40212061202020'
          DC        11C' '
          DC        C'REORDER LISTING'
          DC        12C' '
          DC        C'TIME: '
HDG1TIME  DC        X'4021207A2020'
          DC        69C' '
*
HDGLINE2  DS        0CL133
          DC        C'0'
          DC        C' ITEM            ITEM              UNIT         X
                    REORDER'
          DC        69C' '
*
HDGLINE3  DS        0CL133
          DC        C' '
```

Figure 19-4   The source listing for the structured reorder-listing program that is planned by the pseudocode in figure 19-3 (part 3 of 4)

```
          DC    C'  NO.              DESCRIPTION          PRICE     AVAILABLEX
                POINT'
          DC    70C' '
*
PRTDETL   DS    OCL133
PRTDCTL   DS    CL1
PRTITNBR  DS    CL6
          DC    5C' '
PRTITDES  DS    CL20
          DC    4C' '
PRTPRICE  DS    CL7
          DC    4C' '
PRTAVAIL  DS    CL6
          DC    4C' '
PRTORDPT  DS    CL6
          DC    70C' '
*
CNTLINE   DS    OCL133
          DC    C'-'
CNTPATRN  DC    X'4020206B202020'
          DC    C' RECORDS IN THE INPUT FILE'
          DC    99C' '
*
* PROGRAM SAVE AREA
*
SAVE      DS    18F
*
* SWITCHES
*
EOFSWTCH  DS    X'00'
*
* WORK FIELDS
*
TIME      DS    F
DATE      DS    F
WRKAVAIL  DS    PL3
WRKONORD  DS    PL3
WRKORDPT  DS    PL3
PACKAREA  DS    PL3
*
* COUNT FIELDS
*
COUNT     DC    PL3'0'
*
* PRINT FIELDS
*
PRTAREA   DS    CL133
LINECNT   DC    P'54'
*
* PATTERNS
*
PATTERN1  DC    X'402020202020'
PATTERN2  DC    X'4020202014B2020'
*
          END   BEGIN
```

Figure 19-4 The source listing for the structured reorder-listing program that is planned by the pseudocode in figure 19-3 (part 4 of 4)

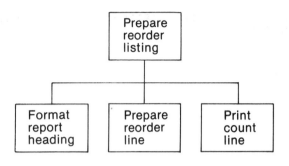

Figure 19-5   A structure chart showing the first two levels of the reorder-listing program

Step 1:   Draw the function boxes for the first two levels

To design a structure chart, you start with a top-level module that represents the entire program. Next, you decide on the one primary functional module that will be performed repeatedly during the execution of the program, and you draw this module at the second level of the chart. Next, decide whether your program requires any functional modules that need to be performed before and after this primary module. If so, you draw boxes for these functions to the left or the right of the primary module at the second level.

To illustrate, figure 19-5 represents the first two levels of the chart for the reorder-listing program. The top-level box is named "prepare reorder listing," and the primary module at the second level is named "prepare reorder line." The prepare-reorder-line module is the primary module because it will be executed repeatedly during the execution of the program. It will be executed one time for each master record until all records in the master file have been read and processed. In other words, the primary module represents the processing for one input record or one set of input records.

Because the reorder-listing program must get the date and time for the first heading line of the reorder listing, the module to the left of the prepare-reorder-line module is named "format report heading." This module will get the date and time and edit them into the appropriate fields in the first heading line. If other functions must be performed before the primary module is executed, they can also be drawn to the left of the primary module. For instance, a program that uses a table might require a module to load the table from a file into storage at the start of the program.

Because the reorder-listing program must print a count line after all reorder lines have been printed, the module to the right of the prepare-reorder-line module is named "print count line." If other functions must be performed after the function of the primary module has been completed, they can also be drawn to the right of the primary module.

As you get more experience with structured program development, you'll realize that all programs can be charted at the first two levels with a structure similar to the one in figure 19-5. Every program has one primary function, although it may not be related to a set of input records. And most programs require functions that must be performed before or after the primary function.

Step 2: Design the subordinate function boxes until each module of the program can be coded in 30 lines or fewer

Step 2 is to divide the modules at the second level into their subordinate functions and subfunctions until each module of the program can be coded in 30 lines or fewer. To illustrate, figure 19-6 shows the functions and subfunctions that I designed for the modules in figure 19-5.

To start, I asked what subordinate modules (if any) the format-report-heading module required. Since I knew a subprogram named GETIME was available for formatting the system's time, I drew the GETIME box as a subordinate function. At that point, I knew that I could code the format-report-heading line box in 30 lines or fewer so it didn't require other subordinates.

Next, I designed the subordinate functions for the prepare-reorder-line module. As you can see in figure 19-6, I designed three functions subordinate to this module in the third level of the chart. Each time the prepare-reorder-line module is executed, it must (1) read an inventory record, (2) calculate available, and (3) print a reorder line if available is less than reorder point. I then asked if any of these modules required subordinates, and I decided that only the print-reorder-line module needed one. Whenever page overflow is required, the report headings must be printed on the new page. As a result, the print-heading-lines module is subordinate to the print-reorder-line module.

If the read or calculate modules required subordinates, of course, I would have drawn them at the next level of the chart. And I would have continued this process until I had designed down to the lowest level. For this simple program, though, figure 19-6 represents all the functional modules that are required by the prepare-reorder-line module.

Last, I asked whether the print-count-line module required any subordinates. I decided that it didn't. As a result, figure 19-6 represents all the functional modules required by the reorder-listing program. And I'm confident that I can code any one of them in 30 lines or fewer.

Of course, the number 30 is arbitrary. I chose it because modules of this size can be coded and tested with relative ease by the average programmer. In contrast, modules become increasingly more difficult to code as their size increases. So a 60 line module may be four times as difficult to code as a 30 line module. Nevertheless, as you get more experience with assembler language, you may want to change this arbitrary number to suit your style or your shop. From a practical point of view, though, I don't think you should use a number that is less than 20 or greater than 50.

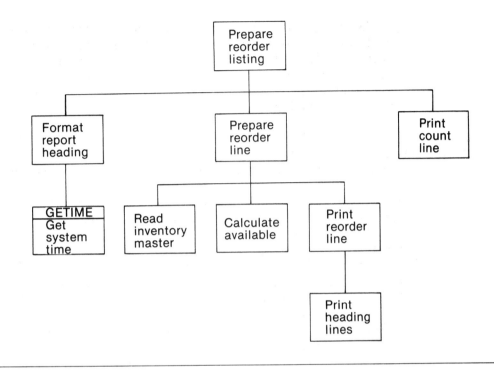

Figure 19-6   The expanded structure chart for the reorder-listing program

When you draw modules on a structure chart, keep in mind that a left-to-right sequence of execution is expected at each level of subordination. At the third level in figure 19-6, for example, you would expect the subordinates for the prepare-reorder-line module to be executed in the sequence of read, calculate, and print. However, when you actually code the program, that may not be the case. So the expected sequence can be varied as required by the program specifications. In other words, you can't always tell what the sequence will be at the time that you design a program's modules.

Step 3:   Add one function box for each I/O operation

In step 3, you add one function box for each I/O operation required by a program. This makes it possible to code a program with only one GET or PUT instruction for each I/O operation. If you look at the chart in figure 19-2, for example, you can see that I added three write modules for the printer file in step 3 of the design procedure. I didn't add a read module for the inventory master file, because the chart already had one.

When you isolate the I/O instructions in their own modules like this, you end up with a more efficient program. For instance, the program in figure 19-4 has only one PUT instruction for the printer file in contrast to the five PUT instructions used in the reorder-listing program in chapter 5.

This also makes it easier to provide for functions like counting the number of records read or written by a program, because you can code functions like this in the related I/O module. The alternative in a large program is to have several GET or PUT statements for each file dispersed throughout the program, a practice that can make the logic of the program difficult to follow.

Step 4:   Shade the common modules

In step 4, you shade the upper righthand corners of the modules that are used in more than once place in the program. These modules are called *common modules*. In figure 19-2, for example, the write-report-line modules are common modules, so their corners are shaded. Although this program doesn't illustrate it, modules that aren't I/O modules can also be common modules in which case they should be shaded too.

Step 5:   Number the subroutine modules

In step 5, you number all of the modules that represent subroutines. That includes all of the modules except the subprogram modules. For most programs, a simple numbering system like the one used in figure 19-2 is adequate. That means you give the top-level module number 000. Next, you number the modules in the second level by 100s, but you leave enough space between the hundreds so it will provide for the modules at the lower levels of the chart. Finally, you number the modules at the next levels by 10s.

Note that the numbers do *not* indicate at what level a module can be found. This means that you can add modules to the chart at any level without changing the numbers of any of the other modules. For instance, you could add a module 150 as a subordinate to module 000. You could add a module 325 as a subordinate to module 300. Or, you could add a module 335 as a subordinate to module 330. As a result, a structure chart like this is easy to enhance or modify.

HOW TO PLAN THE MODULES OF A PROGRAM USING PSEUDOCODE

Once you have completed the structure chart for a program, you can use pseudocode to plan the code for the modules of the program before you actually code them. For instance, figure 19-3 gives the pseudocode for all of the modules charted in figure 19-2. Pseudocode is a language that you can use as a replacement for flowcharting. It lets you plan the operations and logic of a module using only the legal structures of structured programming. And it lets you plan the modules quickly and easily.

When you use pseudocode, you should remember that it is a personal language. As a result, you don't have to follow rigid coding rules. In general, you should capitalize all of the structure words like DO, UNTIL, IF, and ELSE. And you probably should capitalize assembler language names like REORD000 and EOFSWTCH. Beyond this, you simply try to state what each module must do in a style that you feel comfortable with.

When you use pseudocode, you should use indentation to make the code as readable as possible. This is illustrated by the code in figure 19-3. In the DO-UNTIL statement in module 000, for example, the UNTIL portion is indented four spaces. Similarly, in the IF statement in module 310, the IF and ELSE portions are indented to show their relationships.

In module 300, you can see *nested IF statements*. This refers to the fact that one IF statement is coded within another one. In this case, I used indentation to show the nesting of the statements. If these statements had ELSE portions, I would have used indentation to highlight the IF and ELSE portions of each statement as well as the nesting.

When you use pseudocode, you should realize that you don't have to plan every aspect of a module. You'll note in figure 19-3, for example, that none of the modules show the code that is required for subroutine linkage. I didn't show this code because it obviously is required and because the linkage is going to be coded in a standard way. Similarly, you may decide that the "format" statements in modules 330 and 500 are obvious so you don't have to show them in your pseudocode.

If you look closely at the pseudocode in figure 19-3, you can see that I/O modules can be used for more than just the I/O function. For instance, the read module is used to count the number of records read by the program and the write module is used to count the number of lines printed on a page. Since the write module counts both heading and detail lines, the IF statement in module 330 compares the line count with 54 rather than with 50 as used in the earlier versions of the reorder-listing program. When there is a separate I/O module for each I/O operation, it is easy to place the code for counting occurrences that are related to I/O operations.

When you use pseudocode for module planning, you don't necessarily have to plan every module in a program. For instance, modules 100, 320, 330, 340, 350, and 500 in figure 19-3 are relatively trivial. As a result, you may only want to plan modules 000, 300, and 310 for this program. When you design a structured program, you'll usually find that just a few modules are complicated enough to require planning, because all of the modules will be relatively short. On the other hand, if you're not sure how a module should be coded, it's worth taking the time to plan it with pseudocode.

HOW TO CODE A STRUCTURED PROGRAM IN ASSEMBLER LANGUAGE

When it comes to coding, structured programming implies three things. First, it implies that you have a structured design for the program. Second, it implies that the program will be coded using only the accepted structures of structured programming. And third, it implies a style of coding that is designed to increase the readability of a program.

Since you should already have some idea of how to design a structured program and how to plan the modules using only the valid structures, I will now show you how to code a structured program in assembler language. First, I will show you how to code the basic structures in assembler language. Then, I will give you some guidelines for using assembler language in a readable manner.

The basic structures in assembler language

To review, the basic structures of structured programming are the sequence, iteration, and selection structures. In addition, structured programming requires a facility for calling subordinate modules; this can be referred to as a *DO structure*. As you will see, the sequence structure presents no special problems in assembler language, but the best you can do with the other structures is to simulate them.

Figure 19-7 shows you how to code each of the basic structures in assembler language. Of course, you can code these structures in other ways. But the coding in figure 19-7 is relatively easy to use and understand, and it will get you started writing structured assembler language. Once you get used to this coding, you can modify it to suit your style. Later on, if you want to work at a more sophisticated level, you can write macro definitions for the iteration and selection structures using the techniques presented in chapter 11.

The sequence structure   In assembler language, any non-conditional, non-branching statement is a sequence structure. Similarly, a succession of two or more of these statements is a sequence structure. Thus, a series of move instructions is a sequence structure, and a series of arithmetic statements is a sequence structure. As a result, coding a sequence structure in assembler language doesn't require any special effort.

The DO structure   A DO structure in assembler language is a call to a subroutine and a return from the subroutine to the next instruction in the calling module. In chapter 8, you learned how to provide this linkage with a branch-and-link instruction like this:

```
BAL    11,REORD100
```

Before the branch takes place, the address of the next instruction to be executed is saved in the specified register (in this case, register 11). Then, when the subroutine completes its processing, it branches back to the

The sequence structure

```
        PACK   WRKAVAIL,INVONORD
        PACK   WRKONORD,INVONORD
        AP     WRKAVAIL,WRKONORD
```

The DO structure

```
        BAL    11,REORD100            DO REORD100
        .
        .
REORD100 .
        .
        BR     11                     RETURN TO CALLING MODULE
```

The DO UNTIL structure

```
DU000N1 BAL    11,REORD300            DO REORD300
        CLI    EOFSWTCH,X'FF'             UNTIL EOFSWTCH=X'FF'
        BNE    DU000N1
        .
        .
REORD300 .
        .
        BR     11                     RETURN TO CALLING MODULE
```

The IF structure

```
IF300N1 CLC    FIELDA,FIELDB          IF FIELDA NOT = FIELDB
        BE     IF300N1B
IF300N1A .                                THEN DO STATEMENT GROUP A
        .
        B      IF300N1E
IF300N1B .                                ELSE DO STATEMENT GROUP B
        .
IF300N1E .                            END IF
        .
        .
```

Figure 19-7   One way to code the basic structures in assembler language

saved address using a branch instruction like this:

```
        BR     11
```

When you use a DO structure, there are a couple things to keep in mind. First, to comply with the principles of structured programming, each module (subroutine) can only have one entry and one exit point. Second, the last instruction of a subroutine *must* be an unconditional branch instruction. Although the theory of structured programming prohibits branching like this, you have no other choice in assembler language. Just be sure that the final branch instruction in the subroutine returns control to the instruction after the calling instruction.

The iteration structure   When you use the iteration structure in assembler language, you can use any one of the three variations in figure 19-1. One of these variations, the DO UNTIL, is shown in figure 19-7. When you use it, a module is performed *until* a condition is satisfied.

Since there's no statement like the DO UNTIL in assembler language, you have to simulate it using code like the code shown in figure 19-7. Here, the branch-and-link instruction is used to branch to the module that is to be executed until the condition is met. Then, when the called module branches back to the calling routine, the calling routine tests to see if the condition has been met. If it has, processing continues with the next instruction in sequence. If it hasn't, the calling routine branches back to the start of the DO-UNTIL structure so the called module can be called again.

In figure 19-7, you can see that I used the name DU000N1 as the label for the start of the DO-UNTIL structure. This is DU (for DO UNTIL) followed by the number of the module that contains the structure (000) followed by the number of the DO-UNTIL structure in that module (N1 for number 1). If the module required a second DO-UNTIL structure, I would have named it DU000N2. And so on. Although you can modify this naming convention to suit your style, it is a simple one that easily identifies the DO-UNTIL structures that you use.

The selection structure   Since there's no statement like the IF statement in assembler language, you have to simulate it using code like the code shown in figure 19-7. Here, the structure starts with a comparison of two fields. Then, based on this comparison, the program either branches to a group of instructions that starts with the label IF300N1B or it falls through to a group of instructions that starts with the label IF300N1A. To make sure the structure has only one entry and one exit point, a branch instruction at the end of statement group A branches to the end of the selection structure, which is named IF300N1E.

I hope that the naming conventions used in this IF structure are obvious. Each IF structure starts with a label like IF300N1; that is, IF followed by the module number that contains the structure followed by the number of the IF statement in that module. Then, the label at the start of statement group A is the same label followed by the letter A; the label at the start of statement group B is the same label followed by the letter B; and the label of the exit point (or the label of the first instruction following the IF structure) is the same label followed by the letter E.

You can see how this labelling convention works in module 300 of the reorder-listing program in figure 19-4. Here, two IF structures are coded in the same module. However, neither IF statement has an ELSE portion (both are null) so there is no statement group B for either structure. In addition, the exit points for both IF statements are the same because the IF statements are nested. Finally, since the exit points of the IF statements are the same as the exit point for the entire module, I used the name of the subroutine exit (R300EXIT) as the label for the exit points of the IF statements.

When selection structures are nested, you code one selection structure within either statement group A or B of another selection structure. Although this can become quite complicated, you can keep it manageable if you use strict naming conventions. If your selection structures are nested several levels deep, however, the coding can get out of control. In this case, you can often cut down the number of levels of nesting by modifying the structure chart.

Guidelines for readability

A primary goal of structured programming is to create code that is easy to read because a program that is readable is easier to develop, test, debug, and maintain than one that isn't. Here, then, are some guidelines that will help you create more readable code.

Use module names that refer back to the structure chart   When you code a module, the name you give it should relate it to a box on your structure chart. In the reorder-listing program in figure 19-4, you can see that all of the modules consist of the prefix REORD followed by the module number taken from the structure chart in figure 19-2. That way the structure chart becomes a directory to the modules that are coded in the assembly listing. Then, if you have to maintain a program, the structure chart will point you to the code that needs to be modified.

Put the source code modules in sequence by module number
Theoretically, it doesn't matter in what sequence the subroutines of a program are placed in the source code as long as the system starts executing the first instruction of the top-level module. If the sequence is arbitrary, though, both the original programmer and subsequent maintenance programmers will have a difficult time locating modules in the assembly listing. That's why we recommend that the modules be in sequence by module number as shown in the program in figure 19-4.

Group related data items   If you group data items by type, the data portion of your program will have a structure of its own. That way, it will be easier for you to locate data items in the program when you need to do so. Data items that you can group include switches, save areas, print control fields, editing patterns, and so on. In figure 19-4, you can see how I grouped these items in the reorder-listing program.

　　If you do a lot of assembler language programming, you may also want to adopt a standard sequence for data groups in your programs. For example, you may want to code your data groups in this sequence: save areas, input areas, output areas, input work areas, output work areas, printer work areas, switches, edit patterns, and other work areas. That way it will be easier for you to find a group of data items as you move from one program to the next.

Code local data names in the modules that use them   If a data name is only used in one module, you can call it a *local data name* (or a *local* *variable*). Then, if you code local data names in the modules that use them, you simplify the data descriptions that apply to more than one module. In the program in figure 19-4, for example, the one word save areas used by modules 300, 330, 340, and 500 are all described in these modules. Otherwise, they would be described along with all the other data names at the end of the program.

Although the reorder-listing program only uses save areas as local data names, some programs will use other types of fields and areas as local data names. Then, there is more benefit to describing these names within the modules that use them.

Use meaningful data names   When you create data names, you should make them as descriptive as you can. Of course, that isn't always easy in assembler language because of its restrictions. Nevertheless, the clearer you make your data names, the more readable your programs will be.

At the least, when data items are part of the same group or structure, you should add a prefix or a suffix to each name to identify the item as part of the group. For example, each data name in the description for the inventory master record in figure 19-4 starts with the letters INV. Using prefixes and suffixes for related fields helps you cut down on coding errors.

Use comment lines to highlight modules and data groups   If you look at the reorder-listing program in figure 19-4, you can see that three comment lines have been used before each module of the program and before each data group. In each case, the first and third comment lines are blank, while the second comment line identifies the module or data group. This makes these blocks of code easy to find.

Don't use comments unless they are necessary   Comments are the notes you can put in assembler language instructions to the right of the operands. Because unstructured assembler language can be extremely difficult to follow, comments have traditionally been used to clarify code. However, it takes time to put them into a program, and, if they are coded incorrectly, they can make a program even more difficult to follow. To illustrate, imagine a comment that says BRANCH WHEN EQUAL in an instruction with an operation code of BNE. This type of contradiction can originate during debugging when you change an operation code, but not the related comment.

In contrast to traditional practices, then, we recommend that you avoid using comments unless they are necessary. In fact, we don't even recommend comments like those in figure 19-7. If you use structured design, your modules should consist of 30 lines or fewer so they should be relatively easy to read in the first place. Then, if you code your basic structures using a style like that shown in figure 19-7, your code should be largely self-documenting.

HOW TO TEST A PROGRAM USING TOP-DOWN TESTING

When you design a program on a top-down basis using structured design, you can develop it using *top-down coding and testing*. In fact, we recommend that you use top-down coding and testing on any program that takes more than a day to develop.

When you use top-down coding and testing, you don't code the entire program and then test it. Instead, you code and test in phases. You normally start by coding the top-level module and one or more of the modules in the second level. Then, after correcting any bugs, you add one or more modules to this coding and test again. When this much of the program runs correctly, you code a few more modules, add them to what you have, and test again. You continue in this way until all the modules have been coded and you are testing the entire program. Because top-down coding and testing always go together, the phrase *top-down testing* implies top-down coding.

The primary benefit of top-down testing is improved testing efficiency (or improved productivity). To illustrate, imagine an assembler language program of 1000 lines or more. If you test the entire program at once with all of its bugs, it's likely that your testing will proceed very inefficiently. For example, it may take several days of testing just to debug a couple of minor clerical errors. But if you test on a top-down basis, testing proceeds in increments of a few modules, perhaps 50 instructions or fewer at a time. Then, it is relatively easy to find any bugs that are discovered during a test phase because they almost have to be in the modules just added or in the interfaces between the old modules and the new.

How to create a top-down test plan

When you use top-down testing, you start by developing a top-down test plan like the one in figure 19-8. In this plan for the reorder-listing program that is charted in figure 19-2, five modules are tested in phase 1, two more are added in phase 2, the last two are added in phase 3, and phase 4 is a volume test. Since the read module isn't tested until phase 3, no test data is needed for the first two phases.

When you create a test plan, you have considerable choice as to what modules you test in each phase. As long as you proceed from the top down and add one or more modules in each phase, you are adhering to the principles of top-down testing. Whether you add one, two, or more modules at a time depends on your experience and on the length and complexity of the modules. In a short program like the reorder-listing program, it doesn't matter too much what sequence you use, but in a larger, more realistic program you must carefully plan the development sequence.

In general, your goal should be to use the sequence of testing that will be most efficient in terms of coding and testing. When you develop your test plan, then, you should ask questions like: Where are the major module interfaces in the program? Where, if anywhere, in the structure chart do I have doubts about the design? In what modules do I have doubts about how the coding should be done? In most cases, you should try to code and resolve the major problems first.

After you test the first two or three levels of a program, it often becomes a case of mop-up. Eventually, you have to code and test all of the modules, so you may as well take them one group at a time, introducing data that applies to each group as you go along.

Incidentally, you don't have to code the file or data definitions required by a module until you add the module to the program. For instance, since the read module in figure 19-8 isn't added to the program until phase 3, you don't have to code the DCB for the inventory master file until phase 3. On the other hand, since module 330 requires the data in the work area for the inventory master file, you have to code the data definitions for this area as part of your coding for phase 2.

How to code program stubs

To use top-down testing, you must code *program stubs*, or *dummy modules*, for the modules in a phase that are called, but not tested. Using the test plan in figure 19-8, for example, modules 310, 320, and 330 are dummy modules in phase 1 so you must code program stubs for them. Similarly, modules 310 and 320 are dummy modules in phase 2.

In phase 1 of figure 19-8, the program stubs for modules 310, 320, and 330 don't have to do anything other than provide the subroutine linkage because the modules that are being tested don't require any data that is developed by them. As a result, you can code the program stub for module 310 like this:

```
REORD310 BR      11
```

Similarly, you can code the stubs for modules 320 and 330 in the same way. This code simply passes control back to the calling module.

If you want to make sure that the linkage works correctly during your test run, you can code program stubs that print messages showing that the subroutines were called properly. For instance, you can code this stub for module 310:

```
REORD310 PUT     PRTOUT,R310MSG
         BR      11
R310MSG  DC      CL133' 310   READ INVENTORY RECORD'
```

When executed, this stub will print the number and name of the module to show that it has been executed. Then, if you code modules 320 and 330 in the same way, the printed output will indicate whether the dummy modules have been called properly.

Program: REORDLST Prepare Reorder Listing		Page: 1
Designer: Anne Prince		Date: 10-31-85
Test phase	**Data**	**Data source**
1. Modules 000, 100, 300, 500 and 350	None	Not applicable
2. Add modules 330 and 340	None	Not applicable
3. Add modules 310 and 320	Three inventory master records; one with available = reorder point, one with available > reorder point, and one with available < reorder point	Self
4. Volume test	Enough inventory master records to cause page overflow	Test data generator

Figure 19-8   A top-down test plan for the program that is charted in figure 19-2

Module 310: Read inventory master

```
REORD310 CP     COUNT,=P'1'                              STUB
         BE     INVEOF                                   STUB
         MVC    INVITNBR,=C'00123'                       STUB
         MVC    INVITDES,=C'DUMMY RECORD 1'              STUB
         MVC    INVPRICE,=C'00005'                       STUB
         MVC    INVORDPT,=C'01000'                       STUB
         MVC    INVONHND,=C'00500'                       STUB
         MVC    INVONORD,=C'00250'                       STUB
         AP     COUNT,=P'1'
         B      R310EXIT
INVEOF   MVI    EOFSWTCH,X'FF'
R310EXIT BR     11
```

Module 320: Calculate available

```
REORD320 MVC    WRKAVAIL,=P'00750'                       STUB
         BR     11
```

Figure 19-9   Program stubs for phase 2 of the test plan in figure 19-8

In phase 2 of figure 19-8, the program stubs should develop some data in order to test module 330. To do this, the program stubs can be coded as in figure 19-9. Here, module 310 simulates the reading of one input record the first time it is executed. The second time it is executed, it moves hex FF to EOFSWTCH indicating that all records in the file have been read. Similarly, module 320 simulates the calculation of available by moving a value into WRKAVAIL. If the stubs are coded like this, module 330 can print the data for one reorder line so all of the modules except the stubs will get tested.

When you code program stubs, you must try to be practical. At some point, it becomes more practical to code the actual module than it is to simulate the function of the module. If, for example, you look at the stub for the read module in figure 19-9, you can see that the code for the stub is longer than the code for the actual module will be. So is it worth coding this stub? Similarly, the actual code for the calculate module is only four lines while the stub is two lines, so is it worth coding the stub? That, of course, depends on the program, the module, and your experience. In the case of the stubs in figure 19-9, I think it's worth coding the read stub that way, because you simulate a one record file before you even have to create a test file. On the other hand, I don't think it's worth coding the calculate stub that way because the coding for the actual module will work just as well.

DISCUSSION   Although this chapter is just an introduction to the techniques of structured programming, I hope you can see how they can help you improve your productivity as well as the quality of your programs. You should realize, though, that this chapter has presented but one set of techniques for structured program development. If you read the literature on structured programming, you will learn that there are several different approaches to structured programming in assembler language. In these development systems, several different types of charts are used for structured design. The numbering and naming conventions used for the modules of a program vary. And even the approaches to determining the modules of a program vary. Similarly, there are other ways to go about structured module planning, structured coding, and top-down testing.

Nevertheless, we believe that the methods presented in this chapter are at least as good as any of the other methods. We believe that the methods presented in this chapter will help you reach a professional level of productivity. And, we believe that these methods will help you write programs that meet professional standards for reliability and maintainability.

Terminology

structured programming
sequence structure
selection structure
iteration structure
proper program
structure chart
pseudocode
common module
nested IF statements
DO structure
local data name
local variable
top-down coding and testing
top-down testing
program stub
dummy module

Objectives

1. Explain the theory of structured programming.

2. Given program specifications, use structured development techniques to design the program, plan the coding of its modules, code it in structured style, and test it using top-down testing.

Appendix A

Assembler language reference summary

This appendix presents a summary of the instructions and commands presented in this text. In sequence, you will find the following:

DCB operand summary for sequential files
Common EBCDIC codes in binary and hexadecimal
DS and DC type codes
Common editing characters
ASA printer control characters
Instruction formats for a general subset
Instruction formats for decimal arithmetic
Instruction formats for bit manipulation and
    translation
Instruction formats for register operations and
    fixed-point arithmetic
Instruction formats for floating-point arithmetic
Mnemonic operation codes for branching
Standard macros
Assembler commands for controlling an assembly listing
Assembler commands for controlling an assembly
Assembler commands for macro definition and
    conditional assembly

Of course, assembler language consists of many more instructions, macros, and commands than those presented in this book.

Although this appendix presents operand summaries for the DCB macro for sequential files , it does not present any reference materials for the ISAM, BDAM, or VSAM access methods. Instead, we recommend that you use the figures in chapters 14 through 16 as reference materials for these access methods.

Keyword	Programmer code	Remarks
DSORG	PS	Specifies the data set organization. PS for Physical Sequential is used for sequential disk files and for printer files.
RECFM	F, FA FB, FBA V, VBA	F is for fixed-length records; V for variable-length records. B indicates blocked records. A indicates that ASA control characters will be used for a print file. As a result, the most common code for a disk file is FB. The most common code for a print file is FA or FBA.
MACRF	GM, GL PM, PL	Specifies whether GET (G) or PUT (P) macros will be used for the file and whether the records will be processed in move (M) or locate (L) mode.
BLKSIZE	Block length	The maximum block length for a file. For variable-length records, you should include four bytes for block length.
LRECL	Record length	The maximum record length for a file. If fixed-length records aren't blocked, the record length will equal the block size. For variable length records, you should include four bytes for record length.
DDNAME	DD name	This name must be the same as the ddname in the DD job control statement for the file.
EODAD	Instruction label	The label or address of the first instruction of the end-of-file (or end-of-data-set) routine.

DCB operand summary for sequential files

Character	Zone bits	Digit bits	Hexadecimal code
blank	0100	0000	40
.	0100	1011	4B
(	0100	1101	4D
+	0100	1110	4E
&	0101	0000	50
$	0101	1011	5B
*	0101	1100	5C
)	0101	1101	5D
;	0101	1110	5E
-	0110	0000	60
/	0110	0001	61
,	0110	1011	6B
%	0110	1100	6C
?	0110	1111	6F
:	0111	1010	7A
#	0111	1011	7B
'	0111	1101	7D
=	0111	1110	7E
"	0111	1111	7F
A	1100	0001	C1
B	1100	0010	C2
C	1100	0011	C3
D	1100	0100	C4
E	1100	0101	C5
F	1100	0110	C6
G	1100	0111	C7
H	1100	1000	C8
I	1100	1001	C9
J	1101	0001	D1
K	1101	0010	D2
L	1101	0011	D3
M	1101	0100	D4
N	1101	0101	D5
O	1101	0110	D6
P	1101	0111	D7
Q	1101	1000	D8
R	1101	1001	D9

Common EBCDIC codes in binary and hexadecimal (part 1 of 2)

Character	Zone bits	Digit bits	Hexadecimal code
S	1110	0010	E2
T	1110	0011	E3
U	1110	0100	E4
V	1110	0101	E5
W	1110	0110	E6
X	1110	0111	E7
Y	1110	1000	E8
Z	1110	1001	E9
0	1111	0000	F0
1	1111	0001	F1
2	1111	0010	F2
3	1111	0011	F3
4	1111	0100	F4
5	1111	0101	F5
6	1111	0110	F6
7	1111	0111	F7
8	1111	1000	F8
9	1111	1001	F9

Common EBCDIC codes in binary and hexadecimal (part 2 of 2)

Code	Type	Implied length	Truncation/ padding	Alignment if ALIGN is on
C	Characters	None	Right	None
X	Hexadecimal	None	Left	None
B	Binary	None	Left	None
F	Fullword (fixed-point)	4 bytes	Left	Fullword
H	Halfword (fixed-point)	2 bytes	Left	Halfword
E	Short floating-point	4 bytes	Right	Fullword
D	Long floating-point	8 bytes	Right	Doubleword
P	Packed decimal	None	Left	None
Z	Zoned decimal	None	Left	None
A	Address constant (adcon)	4 bytes	Left	Fullword
V	Externally defined adcon	4 bytes	Left	Fullword

DS and DC type codes

Hex code	Meaning
20	Digit selector
21	Significance starter
22	Field separator
40	Blank
4B	Period
5B	Dollar sign
5C	Asterisk
6B	Comma
60	—
C3D9	CR
C4C2	DB

Common editing characters

Code	Action before printing
blank	Space 1 line
0	Space 2 lines
–	Space 3 lines
+	Suppress spacing
1	Skip to first line on new page

ASA printer control characters

Instruction	Mnemonic operation	Type	Explicit operand format
Branch and link	BAL	RX	R1,D2(X2,B2)
Branch and link register	BALR	RR	R1,R2
Branch on condition	BC	RX	M1,D2(X2,B2)
Compare logical characters	CLC	SS	D1(L,B1),D2(B2)
Compare logical immediate	CLI	SI	D1(B1),I2
Edit	ED	SS	D1(L,B1),D2(B2)
Edit and mark	EDMK	SS	D1(L,B1),D2(B2)
Move characters	MVC	SS	D1(L,B1),D2(B2)
Move immediate	MVI	SI	D1(B1),I2
Move numerics	MVN	SS	D1(L,B1),D2(B2)
Move with offset	MVO	SS	D1(L1,B1),D2(L2,B2)
Move zones	MVZ	SS	D1(L,B1),D2(B2)

Instruction formats for a general subset

Instruction	Mnemonic operation	Type	Explicit operand format
Add decimal	AP	SS	D1(L1,B1),D2(L2,B2)
Compare decimal	CP	SS	D1(L1,B1),D2(L2,B2)
Divide decimal	DP	SS	D1(L1,B1),D2(L2,B2)
Multiply decimal	MP	SS	D1(L1,B1),D2(L2,B2)
Subtract decimal	SP	SS	D1(L1,B1),D2(L2,B2)
Zero and add decimal	ZAP	SS	D1(L1,B1),D2(L2,B2)
Pack	PACK	SS	D1(L1,B1),D2(L2,B2)
Unpack	UNPK	SS	D1(L1,B1),D2(L2,B2)
Shift and round decimal	SRP	SS	D1(L1,B1),D2(B2),I3

Instruction formats for decimal arithmetic

Instruction	Mnemonic operation	Type	Explicit operand format
AND logical	N	RX	R1,D2(X2,B2)
AND logical	NC	SS	D1(L,B1),D2(B2)
AND logical immediate	NI	SI	D1(B1),I2
AND logical	NR	RR	R1,R2
Execute	EX	RX	R1,D2(X2,B2)
OR logical	O	RX	R1,D2(X2,B2)
OR logical	OC	SS	D1(L,B1),D2(B2)
OR logical immediate	OI	SI	D1(B1),I2
OR logical	OR	RR	R1,R2
Test under mask	TM	SI	D1(B1),I2
Translate	TR	SS	D1(L,B1),D2(B2)
Translate and test	TRT	SS	D1(L,B1),D2(B2)

Instruction formats for bit manipulation and translation

Instruction	Mnemonic operation	Type	Explicit operand format
Add	A	RX	R1,D2(X2,B2)
Add halfword	AH	RX	R1,D2(X2,B2)
Add register	AR	RR	R1,R2
Branch on count	BCT	RX	R1,D2(X2,B2)
Branch on count register	BCTR	RR	R1,R2
Compare	C	RX	R1,D2(X2,B2)
Compare halfword	CH	RX	R1,D2(X2,B2)
Compare logical long	CLCL	RR	R1,R2
Compare register	CR	RR	R1,R2
Convert to binary	CVB	RX	R1,D2(X2,B2)
Convert to decimal	CVD	RX	R1,D2(X2,B2)
Divide	D	RX	R1,D2(X2,B2)
Divide register	DR	RR	R1,R2
Insert characters under mask	ICM	RS	R1,M3,D2(B2)
Load	L	RX	R1,D2(X2,B2)
Load address	LA	RX	R1,D2(X2,B2)
Load halfword	LH	RX	R1,D2(X2,B2)
Load multiple	LM	RS	R1,R3,D2(B2)
Load register	LR	RR	R1,R2
Load and test register	LTR	RR	R1,R2
Move characters long	MVCL	RR	R1,R2
Multiply	M	RX	R1,D2(X2,B2)
Multiply halfword	MH	RX	R1,D2(X2,B2)
Multiply register	MR	RR	R1,R2
Store	ST	RX	R1,D2(X2,B2)
Store characters under mask	STCM	RS	R1,M3,D2(B2)
Store halfword	STH	RX	R1,D2(X2,B2)
Store multiple	STM	RS	R1,R3,D2(B2)
Subtract	S	RX	R1,D2(X2,B2)
Subtract halfword	SH	RX	R1,D2(X2,B2)
Subtract register	SR	RR	R1,R2

Instruction formats for register operations and fixed-point arithmetic

Instruction	Mnemonic operation	Type	Explicit operand format
Add normalized short	AE	RX	R1,D2(X2,B2)
Add normalized long	AD	RX	R1,D2(X2,B2)
Add normalized short	AER	RR	R1,R2
Add normalized long	ADR	RR	R1,R2
Compare short	CE	RX	R1,D2(X2,B2)
Compare long	CD	RX	R1,D2(X2,B2)
Compare short	CER	RR	R1,R2
Compare long	CDR	RR	R1,R2
Divide short	DE	RX	R1,D2(X2,B2)
Divide long	DD	RX	R1,D2(X2,B2)
Divide short	DER	RR	R1,R2
Divide long	DDR	RR	R1,R2
Load short	LE	RX	R1,D2(X2,B2)
Load long	LD	RX	R1,D2(X2,B2)
Load short	LER	RR	R1,R2
Load long	LDR	RR	R1,R2
Load positive short	LPER	RR	R1,R2
Load positive long	LPDR	RR	R1,R2
Load negative short	LNER	RR	R1,R2
Load negative long	LNDR	RR	R1,R2
Load complement short	LCER	RR	R1,R2
Load complement long	LCDR	RR	R1,R2
Multiply short	ME	RX	R1,D2(X2,B2)
Multiply long	MD	RX	R1,D2(X2,B2)
Multiply short	MER	RR	R1,R2
Multiply long	MDR	RR	R1,R2
Store short	STE	RX	R1,D2(X2,B2)
Store long	STD	RX	R1,D2(X2,B2)
Subtract normalized short	SE	RX	R1,D2(X2,B2)
Subtract normalized long	SD	RX	R1,D2(X2,B2)
Subtract normalized short	SER	RR	R1,R2
Subtract normalized long	SDR	RR	R1,R2

Instruction formats for floating-point arithmetic

Use	Code	Meaning
General	B or BR	Unconditional branch
After Compare Instructions (A:B)	BH or BHR	Branch on A high
	BL or BLR	Branch on A low
	BE or BER	Branch on A equal B
	BNH or BNHR	Branch on A not high
	BNL or BNLR	Branch on A not low
	BNE or BNER	Branch on A not equal B
After Arithmetic Instructions	BO or BOR	Branch on overflow
	BP or BPR	Branch on plus
	BM or BMR	Branch on minus
	BZ or BZR	Branch on zero
	BNP or BNPR	Branch on not plus
	BNM or BNMR	Branch on not minus
	BNZ or BNZR	Branch on not zero
After the Test under Mask Instruction	BO or BOR	Branch if ones
	BM or BMR	Branch if mixed
	BZ or BZR	Branch if zeros
	BNO or BNOR	Branch if not ones

Mnemonic operation codes for branching

Code	Operands	Meaning
TIME	DEC BIN TU	Store the date in register 1 in the format YYDDD and store the time in register 0 in one of three formats. The default is DEC. DEC format is HHMMSSTH in modified packed decimal; BIN is the number of 1/100 of a second since midnight in binary; and TU is the number of timer units (26.04 microseconds) since midnight in binary.
ABEND	completion-code, REASON = reason-code [,DUMP][,STEP]	Cancel the program and print a dump of the registers and all storage.
SNAP	DCB = dcb-address, ID = nnn, PDATE = (codes), STORAGE = (starting-address, ending-address,...)	Print a dump of the area between the starting and ending addresses and include those areas specified in the PDATE operand.
WTO	'message', ROUTCODE = route-code, DESC = description-code	Send the specified message to the operator consoles specified by the route-code using the disposition specified by the disposition code.
SAVE	(register-1,register-2)	Store the contents of the registers from register-1 through reigster-2 in an 18-word standard save area. The address of the save area must be in register 13. The wrap-around concept applies.
CALL	subprogram,(label-1,...)	Construct an address list for the labels given in the second operand. Store the address of this list in register 1. Store the address of the subprogram in register 15. Store the return address in register 14. Branch to the address in register 15.
RETURN	(register-1,register-2)	Load the contents of the registers from register-1 through register-2 from an 18-word standard save area. The address of the save area must be in register 13. The wrap-around concept applies. Then, branch to the address in register 14.

Standard macros

Code	Operands	Meaning
EJECT	none	Skip to the first line of a new page of the assembly listing.
PRINT	ON OFF	Print the assembly listing. Don't print the assembly listing.
	GEN NOGEN	Print the instructions generated by macros. Don't print the instructions generated by macros.
	DATA NODATA	Print all DC and literal data. Print only the first eight bytes of the data defined by each DC or literal.
SPACE	number	Space the assembly listing the specified number of lines. If the number is more than the number of lines remaining on the page, skip to the first line of a new page.
TITLE	'title'	Print the specified title on each page of the assembly listing.

Assembler commands for controlling an assembly listing

Code	Operands	Meaning
COPY	bookname	Insert the code from the specified book in the source statement library into the source program.
CSECT	none	Restore the location counter after a DSECT. The label should be the same as the program name given in the label of the START instruction.
DSECT	none	Signal the start of a dummy section. The label must be assigned to a base register by a USING command.
END	entry-point	Signal the end of a source program. The operand names the entry point of the program.
ENTRY	entry-point	Identify the entry point of a subprogram.
EQU	label or expression	Assign the address and length of the operand to the label of the macro.
EXTRN	external-name	The specified name is defined outside the program so it should be resolved by the linkage editor.
LTORG	none	Define all literals used to this point in the program at this point in the program.
ORG	label or expression	Change the location counter value to the address of the label or to the value of the expression given as the operand.
START	self-defining term	Start the assembly of the program using the value of the operand as the starting location counter value.
USING	*,register-1,register-2	Use the registers from register-1 through register-2 as the base registers for this program.
USING	dsect-name,register	Use the register number given in the second operand as the base register for the DSECT named.

Assembler commands for controlling an assembly

Code	Operands	Meaning
AGO	sequence symbol	Branch to the specified sequence symbol.
AIF	(logical expression) sequence symbol	Branch to the specified sequence symbol if the logical expression is true.
GBLA	symbol-1,...	Declare arithmetic global SET symbols.
GBLB	symbol-1,...	Declare binary global SET symbols.
GBLC	symbol-1,...	Declare character global SET symbols.
LCLA	symbol-1,...	Declare arithmetic local SET symbols.
LCLB	symbol-1,...	Declare binary local SET symbols.
LCLC	symbol-1,...	Declare character local SET symbols.
MACRO	none	Start a macro definition.
MEND	none	End a macro definition.
MEXIT	none	Terminate macro expansion.
MNOTE	severity-code,'message'	Print a message during macro expansion. If a severity code is present, print the message in the diagnostic listing too.
SETA	arithmetic expression	Assign the operand value to the arithmetic SET symbol coded as the label of the command.
SETB	0 or 1	Assign the value of 0 or 1 to the binary SET symbol coded as the label of the command.
SETB	logical expression	If the expression is true, assign a value of 1 to the binary SET symbol coded as the label of the command. If the expression is false, assign a value of 0 to the symbol.
SETC	'character expression'	Assign the operand value to the character SET symbol coded as the label of the command.

Assembler commands for macro definition and conditional assembly

Appendix B

A comprehensive case study

The case study that follows asks you to develop one program after you finish chapter 5 in the text. Then, for chapters 6 through 16, you will be asked to enhance this program in many different ways. By the time you code and test all the enhancements, you will have coded over 600 lines of code. And you will have used most of the functions provided for by assembler language.

If you don't have time to complete all of the tasks in the case study, you should at least do the tasks for chapters 5 through 8. Since these chapters present a professional subset of assembler language, you will have a useful background in assembler language once you complete the tasks for these chapters.

Instead of doing one program enhancement at a time, you may prefer to do the tasks for several chapters as a single work unit. This should reduce the number of assemblies and test runs you will have to make for the case study. But whether or not you combine tasks will depend on your working style, how much access you have to a computer terminal, and the instructions given you by your instructor.

Even if you don't have access to an MVS computer system, we still recommend that you code the phases of this case study because that's a critical test of your learning progress. If you can code all phases of this case study with confidence that your coding will work correctly, we're confident that you will have met the objectives of this book.

Input/output specifications

File	Description	Use
CUSTMST	Customer master file	Input
SLSRPT	Print file: Sales report	Output
CUSTEXT	Customer extension file (used only for the tasks in section 4)	Input

Process specifications

This program prepares a year-to-date (YTD) sales report from a file of customer records. The records are in sequence by customer key and the report should be printed in the same sequence. The program should print headings at the top of each page of the report and skip to a new page after 50 detail lines have been printed on a page.

The customer key is not a numeric field, so a key like NOR101 is valid. Since net sales equals gross sales minus returns, any of the net sales fields can be negative. As a result, a minus sign should be printed after a number to show that it is negative, as indicated by the minus signs on the print chart in positions 77, 92, and 109. If a number is positive, nothing should be printed in these positions.

This program is designed so you can add code to it as you proceed through the book. When you complete chapter 5, for example, you aren't expected to be able to write a program that produces the shaded portions of the print chart. As a result, your program should only produce the unshaded data. Then, when you complete chapter 6, you'll be able to enhance your program so it produces the shaded data in the first two heading lines and all of total line 2. When you complete chapter 7, you'll be able to enhance your program so it produces the shaded data in print positions 79-92. And so on.

Disk file specifications

If the customer master file is cataloged, you only need to know the data set name in order to create the JCL for testing this program. If the file isn't cataloged, you need to know the following specifications:

Data set name:
Block size:
Unit:
Volume serial number:

In either case, your instructor should supply the information you need for the disk file's DD statement.

Record Layout for the Customer Master Record (CUSTMST)

Field name	Field description	Characteristics
CMKEY	Customer key	CL6
CMNAME	Customer name	CL31
CMADDR	Customer address	CL31
CMCITY	Customer city	CL18
CMSTATE	State code	CL2
CMZIP5	Zip code (5 digits)	CL5
CMZIPX	Zip code extension (4 digits)	CL4
CMYSLSD	YTD $ gross sales	CL8 (two decimal positions)
CMYSLSQ	YTD quantity gross sales	CL5
CMYRTNSD	YTD $ returns	CL7 (two decimal positions)
CMYRTNSQ	YTD quantity returns	CL4
CMMONSLS	12 monthly sales segments	CL252
	Monthly $ gross sales	ZL7 (two decimal positions)
	Monthly $ returns	ZL7 (two decimal positions)
	Monthly $ net sales	ZL7 (two decimal positions)
	Unused	CL27

Record Layout for the Customer Extension Record (CUSTEXT)

Field name	Field description	Characteristics
CESTATUS	Record status	CL1
CEKEY	Customer key	CL6
CELYSLS	12 monthly YTD sales segments	CL168
	Last YTD $ gross sales	PL5 (two decimal positions)
	Last YTD $ returns	PL4 (two decimal positions)
	Last YTD $ net sales	PL5 (two decimal positions)
	Unused	CL25

Document name: Sales by customer   Date: 11-13-85
Program name: CUST5230   Designer: AMP

Record Name

Heading line 1 (6)	1	DATE: MM/DD/YY ... PAGE: XXX
Heading line 2 (6)	2	TIME: HH:MM ... CUST5230
Heading line 3	3	YTD SALES BY CUSTOMER IN DOLLARS ... FILE MAINTENANCE
	4	KEY CUSTOMER NAME YTD SALES YTD RETURNS YTD NET SLS NET SLS 3 MOS NET LAST YTD
	5	
Detail lines	6	XXXXXX XXXXXXXXXXXXXXXXXX XXX,XXX.XX XX,XXX.XX XXX,XXX.XX XXX,XXX XXX,XXX INVALID STATE CODE
	7	XXXXXX XXXXXXXXXXXXXXXXXX XXX,XXX.XX XX,XXX.XX XXX,XXX.XX XXX,XXX XXX,XXX INVALID ZIP CODE
	8	XXXXXX XXXXXXXXXXXXXXXXXX XXX,XXX.XX XX,XXX.XX XXX,XXX.XX XXX,XXX XXX,XXX ZIP CODE NOT NUMERIC
	9	XXXXXX XXXXXXXXXXXXXXXXXX XXX,XXX.XX XX,XXX.XX XXX,XXX.XX XXX,XXX XXX,XXX NO EXTENSION RECORD
	10	
Total line 1	11	RECORDS IN CUSTOMER FILE = XX,XXX
Total line 2 (6)	12	AVG. NET SALES/CUSTOMER = XXX,XXX X,XXX,XXX.XX X,XXX,XXX.XX X,XXX,XXX.XX X,XXX,XXX.XX XX,XXX,XXX.XX

(C7)   Section #   (C9, C11 and Section #)

Development tasks by chapter

Section 2   A professional subset of assembler language

Chapter 5   An introductory subset of assembler language

When you finish chapter 5 in the text, develop a program that produces the report represented by the unshaded portion of the print chart. When you get your first assembly listing, you will want to read chapter 17 to learn how to read the output and correct the diagnostics. When you test your program, you will want to read chapter 18 to learn how to solve your debugging problems.

If you want to start this case study before you finish chapter 5, you can write a program to produce just the detail lines of the report after you finish topic 1 of chapter 5. If the input file you'll be using is blocked, you'll have to look ahead to topic 2 to see how the DCB is coded for blocked records.

Chapter 6   Completing a basic subset of assembler language

Topic 1   Enhance your program to produce total line 2. Average net sales is YTD net sales divided by the number of records in the customer file. But note that average sales is rounded to the nearest whole dollar.

Also, use relative addressing and explicit lengths to set the detail line to blanks. Modify the detail line definition appropriately.

Topic 2   Enhance your program to produce the date and time data in the first two heading lines of the report. Then, use the appropriate macro to print a snapshot dump of your data definitions after all records have been processed but before your program ends. After you've produced this dump output once, remove the dump macro from your program so you won't produce this unnecessary output when you test subsequent enhancements of your program.

Topic 3   Replace your data definitions for the customer master record's work area with a COPY instruction. This instruction should insert the copy book named CUSTMST into your program. Find out what library this book is going to be in and use the MAC1 operand of the EXEC statement in your JCL if it is necessary.

Also, use the assembler commands (1) to skip to the top of a new page in the assembly listing between the instructions of the program and the DCBs and data definitions, and (2) to suppress the printing of instructions generated by macros. If your program requires more than one base register, code the USING command and adcons to provide for the additional registers.

Chapter 7   Register operations, binary arithmetic, and storage definition techniques

Enhance your program to produce the data in print positions 79-92 on the print chart. This column of data is the sales total for the last 3-month period. To derive this total, you use the net sales fields in the monthly sales segments in the master records. There are 12 of these segments, one for each of the last 12 months. In your program, then, you want to accumulate the data for the last three segments, segments 10, 11, and 12.

Use a DSECT to provide for the processing of the fields in the segments. Also, use binary arithmetic to accumulate the 3-month total for each customer. This will give you experience with the conversion requirements for binary arithmetic.

Chapter 8   Using subroutines and subprograms

Topic 1   At this point, redesign your program using modular program design. Then, modify the code so the program uses one subroutine for each of the modules of the program. Your program should consist of a mainline module and at least these three other modules: a read module, a process module, and a print module. The more thoughtful your design is, the easier it will be to make the program enhancements required for the remaining chapters of the book.

Alternative for topic 1   Instead of redesigning your program using modular program design, redesign it using structured design as described in chapter 19. This will make it easier for you to modify your program and to add modules to it as you do the tasks for chapters 9 through 16. If you choose this option or your instructor requires it, skip to the task for chapter 19 at this time.

Topic 2   Modify your program so it calls a subprogram called GETIME to put the time in the form of HH:MM into a field described as CL5. In other words, your program passes a five-character field to the subprogram and the subprogram puts the time into this field. After you modify your program, write the subprogram to perform this function. You can test your subprogram and your linkage by assembling both calling program and subprogram in a single job as described in the text.

After you test your subprogram, you can use the subprogram called GETIME that's already available in one of the object libraries. Then, you can remove your own subprogram from the assemble-and-test job as you proceed with the development tasks that follow. To use the system's GETIME subprogram, be sure you have identified the correct object library in your JCL for the linkage editor. So find out what the name of this library is.

Section 3   Assembler language capabilities by function

Chapter 9   Table handling

A copy book named STATABLE is available in one of the source libraries. It contains 51 DCs, one for each of the 50 states and one containing hex Fs to indicate the last entry. For instance, the first three DCs are these:

```
DC      CL12'AL3500036999'
DC      CL12'AK9950099999'
DC      CL12'AZ8500086599'
```

This table can be used to check the validity of the state codes and the five-digit zip codes used in an address. For a state code to be valid, it must match one of the 50 state code entries (bytes 1-2 in each DC). For a zip code to be valid, it must be equal to or greater than the first zip code given for a state (bytes 3-7 in each DC) and it must be equal to or less than the second zip code (bytes 8-12).

Using this table, enhance your program to produce the shaded data in print positions 112-129 of the print chart. To produce this data, the program first checks each record's state code for validity. If it is invalid, the program prints INVALID STATE CODE in the FILE MAINTENANCE area; in this case, the program doesn't do the validity checking for the zip code. But if the state code is valid, the program checks the zip code. If it is invalid, it prints INVALID ZIP CODE in the FILE MAINTENANCE area of the report; if it isn't, the program prints nothing in this area.

Chapter 10   Editing, bit manipulation, and translation

Editing   Modify your program so the net sales per customer amount in total line 2 is printed with a floating dollar sign to its left. Also, change the edit patterns used for the net sales fields so a negative amount is indicated by CR instead of a minus sign.

Bit manipulation   To give you some practice with bit manipulation, modify your program so it tests the bits of the rightmost half-byte of the customer key field. Then, if all of the bits in this digit half of the byte are off, the program should *not* print the customer record on the listing. However, if the bits in this half-byte are mixed or if they're all on, the customer line should print as usual. You can check to see whether your program worked right by comparing the customer listing prepared by this program with earlier versions of the customer listing.

Translation   To give you some practice with character manipulation, modify your program so it prints the words in a customer's name with one word per line after the YTD sales line as in this example:

```
KEY        CUSTOMER NAME                          YTD SALES

MMAINC     MIKE MURACH & ASSOCIATES, INC.   12,345.67
           MIKE
           MURACH
           &
           ASSOCIATES
           INC
```

To identify words, your program must search for blanks within the name field. For this to work properly, it must determine the actual length of each name before it performs the translation so that trailing blanks aren't processed. Your program should also ignore commas and periods as in the above example. So the listing will be easy to read, your program should double space after the last word in a name.

Chapter 11   Writing macro definitions

A GETIME macro   Write a macro definition that will generate instructions to get the time and store it in a five-byte field in the form HH:MM. The macro code should be GETIME and its operand should be the name of the five-byte field as in this macro instruction:

```
GETIME HTIME
```

After you've written this macro, modify your program so it gets the time with the GETIME macro rather than with the GETIME subprogram.

An EDIT macro   Write a macro definition that will generate instructions to check a field to make sure that it contains valid zoned decimal data. Specifically, the macro should check to make sure that each byte has hex F in its zone portion and a hex digit from 0 through 9 in its digit portion. If the field is valid, the macro should move hex 40 into a switch field specified in the macro instruction. If the field is invalid, the macro should move hex FF into the switch field.

In the first version of this macro, assume that the field to be edited is five-bytes long. Then, the macro will have two operands as in this example:

```
ZDTEST FIELDA,SWITCHA
```

After you write this macro definition, modify your program so it uses this macro to test the zip code field before the zip code is tested by using the zip code table described in the task for chapter 9. If the macro finds the zip code to be valid, continue with the table lookup. Otherwise, this message should be printed in the FILE MAINTENANCE area:

```
ZIP CODE NOT NUMERIC
```

After you get this first version of the macro working, modify the macro so it will test a field of any length. In this case, the macro instruction has three operands as in this example:

```
ZDTEST FIELDA,SWITCHA,7
```

In this case, the third operand is a number that gives the length of the field to be tested. Assume that the maximum field length is 16.

Once you have this version of the macro working, enhance your macro definition so it checks to make sure the operands are valid. Specifically, the first two operands should be labels and the third one should be a number between 1 and 16 that is equal to the length of the first operand. If the operands aren't valid, generate appropriate error messages.

Section 4   Assembler language for the DASD access methods

For all of the tasks required in this section, assume that a customer extension file (CUSTEXT) is available. This file is defined on the record layout page in the program specifications. For each record in the master file, there should be a record with matching key in the extension file.

If you review its record layout, you can see that the customer extension file contains the year-to-date data from the previous year. The first year-to-date segment contains the YTD data through January of the previous year; the second segment contains the data through February; and so on. This data is in a separate file because it is only needed for occasional reports.

The extension file is used to produce the data in print positions 97-109 of the print chart. To produce this data, your program must read the extension record that matches a customer master record. Then, your program should get the net YTD data from the appropriate segment of the extension record and print it in the NET LAST YTD column of the report. The appropriate segment is the one for the month before the current month.

Unfortunately, your program doesn't have the current month available to it in its present form. Instead, it has the day of the year as a number between 1 and 366. As a result, the program enhancements must provide a routine to convert the day of the year to a month before the correct segments in the extension records can be accessed. Because writing a routine like this can be quite time-consuming, we suggest that you simplify the routine in this way: Just divide the day of the year by 30 to get the appropriate month number. Thus, day 250 becomes month 8; the remainder is dropped. This simplified routine produces a reasonable approximation of the desired month number and shouldn't take long to develop. That way you can concentrate on the file handling aspects of the problems in this section.

All of the program enhancements that follow use the extension file. However, each one uses a different MVS access method to get the file. In other words, the extension file is available in four different forms: as a sequential file, as an ISAM file, as a BDAM file, and as a key-sequenced VSAM file.

No matter what access method your program is using, if it can't find a matching extension record for a customer master record, it should print this message in positions 112-130 of the report:

```
NO EXTENSION RECORD
```

In this case, print positions 97-109 in the detail line should be blank.

Chapter 13 The Queued Sequential Access Method (QSAM)

Modify your program so it reads one extension record for each master record and prints the last YTD data in print positions 97-109 of the report. For this task, the extension file is a sequential file. Before you can code and test this program, you must get the required specifications for the extension file from your instructor:

Data set name:
Block size:
Unit:
Volume serial number:

If the file is cataloged, you only need to know the data set name.

Chapter 14 The Indexed Sequential Access Method (ISAM)

Modify your program so it reads one extension record for each master record and prints the last YTD data in print positions 97-109 of the report. For this problem, the extension file is an indexed sequential file. The keys are embedded in the record as shown in the record layout in the program specifications. When applicable, the keys are also in the key areas.

You should do this problem in two parts: one using sequential access, the other using random access. Before you can code and test the program modifications either way, though, you must get the required specifications for the extension file:

Data set name:
Block size:
Unit:
Volume serial number:
Location of index area (if separate from prime data area):
Location of independent overflow area (if separate from prime data area):

If the file is cataloged, you only need to know the data set name.

Sequential access   Code the program so the ISAM extension file is accessed on a sequential basis. In other words, your program logic will be the same as it was in the program enhancement for chapter 13.

Random access   Code the program so the ISAM extension file is accessed on a random basis. The program logic for random access should be quite a bit different than that used for sequential access. In fact, it should be quite a bit simpler.

Chapter 15   The Basic Direct Access Method (BDAM)

Modify your program so it reads one extension record for each master record and prints the last YTD data in print positions 97-109 of the report. For this problem, the extension file is a direct file with unblocked records.
    The steps used in the randomizing algorithm for this file follow:

1.   Convert the zone halfs of the bytes in the customer key in the customer master record to hex Fs. This converts the alphanumeric field to a zoned decimal field.

2.   Divide the zoned-decimal key field by 15 and save the remainder. This remainder identifies the relative track for the matching extension record.

3.   Search the relative track for a record with a key that matches the original key in the customer master record. If your program doesn't find the matching record on this track, it should search the next track. If your program can't find the matching record on either track, assume that there is no matching extension record.

    Before you can code and test the program modifications for this task, you must get the required specifications for the extension file:

    Data set name:
    Unit:
    Volume serial number:

If the file is cataloged, you only need to know the data set name.

Chapter 16   The Virtual Storage Access Method (VSAM)

Modify your program so it reads one extension record for each master record and prints the last YTD data in print positions 97-109 of the report. For this problem, the extension file is a key-sequenced VSAM file (a KSDS).

You should do this problem in two parts: one using sequential access, the other using random access. Before you can code and test the program modifications either way, though, you must get the data set name for the extension file.

Sequential access   Code the program so the KSDS extension file is accessed on a sequential basis. In other words, your program logic will be the same as it was for the program enhancement for chapter 13.

Random access   Code the program so the KSDS extension file is accessed on a random basis. The program logic for random access should be quite a bit different than that used for sequential access. In fact, it should be quite a bit simpler.

Section 5   Program development techniques

Chapter 19   An introduction to structured program development

You can do the task for this chapter any time after you read chapter 8 in the text. No matter what stage your program is at, though, the task is to redesign the program using structured design. The result should be a structure chart that consists of at least three levels and at least seven modules. If you design your program in this way before you do the tasks for chapters 8 through 16, it should be easier for you to make the required program enhancements.

After you've redesigned your program using structured design, you should code it so the program uses one subroutine for each of the modules of the structure chart. Be sure to code each subroutine module so it has only one entry and one exit point. As you reorganize your code into modules, you should also modify it so it becomes more readable.

Index

MVS JCL

MVS/ESA • MVS/XA • MVS/370   **Doug Lowe**

Anyone who's worked in an MVS shop knows that JCL is tough to master. You learn enough to get by...but then you stick to that. It's just too frustrating to try to put together a job using the IBM manuals. And too time-consuming to keep asking your co-workers for help...especially since they're often limping along with the JCL they know, too.

That's why you need a copy of *MVS JCL*. It zeroes in on the JCL you need for everyday jobs...so you can learn to code significant job streams in a hurry.

You'll learn how to compile, link-edit, load, and execute programs. Process all types of data sets. Code JES2/JES3 control statements to manage job and program execution, data set allocation, and SYSOUT processing. Create and use JCL procedures. Execute general-purpose utility programs. And much more.

But that's not all this book does. Beyond teaching you JCL, it explains the basics of how MVS works so you can apply that understanding as you code JCL.

MVS JCL, 17 chapters, 496 pages, **$42.50**
ISBN 0-911625-85-2

MVS TSO

Part 1: Concepts and ISPF   **Doug Lowe**

Now you can quickly master ISPF with this practical book.

Chapter 1 introduces you to MVS (both MVS/XA and MVS/ESA)...good background no matter how much MVS experience you've had. It also shows you how TSO/ISPF relates to MVS, so you'll understand how to use ISPF to control the operating system functions.

The remaining 7 chapters teach you all the specifics of using ISPF for everyday programming tasks. You'll learn how to: edit and browse data sets...use the ISPF utilities to manage your data sets and libraries...compile,

link, and execute programs interactively...use the VS COBOL II or OS COBOL interactive debugger... process batch jobs in a background region...manage your background jobs more easily using the Spool Display & Search Facility (SDSF)...use member parts lists to track the use of subprograms and COPY members within program libraries...use two library management systems that support hierarchical libraries—the Library Management Facility (LMF) and the Software Configuration and Library Manager (SCLM)...and more!

MVS TSO, Part 1, 8 chapters, 467 pages, **$36.50**
ISBN 0-911625-56-9

MVS TSO

Part 2: Commands and Procedures (CLIST and REXX)   **Doug Lowe**

If you're ready to expand your skills beyond ISPF and become a TSO user who can write complex CLIST and REXX procedures with ease, this is the book for you. It starts by teaching you how to use TSO commands for common programming tasks like managing data sets and libraries, running programs in foreground mode, and submitting jobs for background execution. Then, it

shows you how to combine those commands into CLIST or REXX procedures for the jobs you do most often...including procedures that you can use as edit macros under the ISPF editor and procedures that use ISPF dialog functions to display full-screen panels.

MVS TSO, Part 2, 10 chapters, 450 pages, **$36.50**
ISBN 0-911625-57-7

VSAM

Access Method Services and Application Programming   **Doug Lowe**

As its title suggests, *VSAM: Access Method Services and Application Programming* has two main purposes: (1) to teach you how to use the Access Method Services (AMS) utility to define and manipulate VSAM files; and (2) to teach you how to process VSAM files using various programming languages. To be specific, you'll learn:

- how VSAM data sets and catalogs are organized and used

- how to use AMS commands to define VSAM catalogs, space, clusters, alternate indexes, and paths

- how to set AMS performance options so you make the best possible use of your system's resources

- what recovery and security considerations are important when you use AMS

- how to code MVS and DOS/VSE JCL for VSAM files, and how to allocate VSAM files under TSO and VM/CMS

- how to process VSAM files in COBOL, CICS, and assembler language

You'll find the answers to questions like these

- How much primary and secondary space should I allocate to my VSAM files?

- What's an appropriate free space allocation for a KSDS?

- What's the best control interval size for VSAM files that are accessed both sequentially and directly?

- Do I always need to use VERIFY to check the integrity of my files?

- What's the difference between regular VSAM catalogs and the ICF catalog structure?

- When should I...and shouldn't I...use the IMBED and REPLICATE options to improve performance?

- It's easy to find out how many records are in a file's index component. But how do I find out how many of those records are in the sequence set?

- How do I determine the best buffer allocation for my files?

- What's the best way to back up my VSAM files— REPRO, EXPORT, or something else?

So why wait any longer to sharpen your VSAM skills? Get your copy of *VSAM: AMS and Application Programming* TODAY!

VSAM: AMS & Application Programming,
12 chapters, 260 pages, **$27.50**
ISBN 0-911625-33-X

VSAM for the COBOL Programmer

Second Edition   **Doug Lowe**

If you're looking for a no-frills approach to VSAM that teaches you only what you need to know to code COBOL programs, this is the book for you. You'll learn: the meanings of the critical terms and concepts that apply to VSAM files; the COBOL elements for handling VSAM files; how to handle alternate indexes and dynamic access; why error processing is a must; how to use the Access Method Services utility (AMS)

to create, print, copy, and rename VSAM files; how to code the MVS and VSE JCL to run programs that use VSAM files; and how your COBOL code is affected if you're working under VS COBOL II.

VSAM for COBOL, 6 chapters, 187 pages, **$22.50**
ISBN 0-911625-45-3

CICS for the COBOL Programmer

Second Edition   **Doug Lowe**

This 2-part course is designed to help COBOL programmers become outstanding CICS programmers.

Part 1: An Introductory Course covers the basic CICS elements you'll use in just about every program you write. So you'll learn about basic mapping support (BMS), pseudo-conversational programming, basic CICS commands, sensible program design using event-driven design techniques, testing and debugging using IBM-supplied transactions (like CEMT, CECI, and CEDF) or a transaction dump, and efficiency considerations.

Part 2: An Advanced Course covers CICS features you'll use regularly, though you won't need all of them for every program. That means you'll learn about browse commands, temporary storage, transient data, data tables (including the shared data table feature of CICS 3.3), DB2 and DL/I processing considerations,

distributed processing features, interval control commands, BMS page building, and more! In addition, *Part 2* teaches you which features do similar things and when to use each one. So you won't just learn how to code new functions...you'll also learn how to choose the best CICS solution for each programming problem you face.

Both books cover all versions of CICS up through 3.3. Both cover OS/VS COBOL, VS COBOL II, and COBOL/370, so it doesn't matter which COBOL compiler you're using. And all the program examples in both books conform to CUA's Entry Model for screen design.

CICS, Part 1, 12 chapters, 409 pages, **$36.50**
ISBN 0-911625-60-7

CICS, Part 2, 12 chapters, 352 pages, **$36.50**
ISBN 0-911625-67-4

The CICS Programmer's Desk Reference

Second Edition   **Doug Lowe**

Ever feel buried by IBM manuals?

It seems like you need stacks of them, close at hand, if you want to be an effective CICS programmer. Because frankly, there's just too much you have to know to do your job well; you can't keep it all in your head.

That's why Doug Lowe decided to write *The CICS Programmer's Desk Reference*. In it, he's collected all the information you need to have at your fingertips, and organized it into 12 sections that make it easy for you to find what you're looking for. So there are sections on:

- BMS macro instructions—their formats (with an explanation of each parameter) and coding examples

- CICS commands—their syntax (with an explanation of each parameter), coding examples, and suggestions on how and when to use each one most effectively

- MVS and DOS/VSE JCL for CICS applications

- AMS commands for handling VSAM files

- details for MVS users on how to use ISPF

- complete model programs, including specs, design, and code

- a summary of CICS program design techniques that lead to simple, maintainable, and efficient programs

- guidelines for testing and debugging CICS applications

- and more!

So clear the IBM manuals off your terminal table. Let the *Desk Reference* be your everyday guide to CICS instead.

CICS Desk Reference, 12 sections, 507 pages, **$42.50**
ISBN 0-911625-68-2

Call toll-free 1-800-221-5528 (Weekdays, 8-5 Pacific Time) • Fax 1-559-440-0963 • www.murach.com

DL/I and IMS books from Mike Murach & Associates

IMS for the COBOL Programmer

Part 1: DL/I Data Base Processing   **Steve Eckols**

This how-to book will have you writing batch DL/I programs in a minimum of time—whether you're working on a VSE or an MVS system. But it doesn't neglect the conceptual background you must have to create programs that work. So you'll learn:

- what a DL/I data base is and how its data elements are organized into a hierarchical structure
- the COBOL elements for creating, accessing, and updating DL/I data bases...including logical data bases and data bases with secondary indexing
- how to use DL/I recovery and restart features
- the basic DL/I considerations for coding interactive programs using IMS/DC or CICS

- how data bases with the 4 common types of DL/I data base organizations are stored (this material will help you program more logically and efficiently for the type of data base you're using)
- and more!

7 complete COBOL programs show you how to process DL/I data bases in various ways. Use them as models for production work in your shop, and you'll save hours of development time.

IMS, Part 1, 16 chapters, 333 pages, **$36.50**
ISBN 0-911625-29-1

IMS for the COBOL Programmer

Part 2: Data Communications and Message Format Service   **Steve Eckols**

The second part of *IMS for the COBOL Programmer* is for MVS programmers only. It teaches how to develop online programs that access IMS data bases and run under the data communications (DC) component of IMS. So you'll learn:

- why you code message processing programs (MPPs) the way you do (DC programs are called MPPs because they process messages sent from and to user terminals)
- what COBOL elements you use for MPPs
- how to use Message Format Service (MFS), a facility for formatting complex terminal displays so you can enhance the look and operation of your DC programs
- how to develop applications that use more than one screen format or that use physical and logical paging

- how to develop batch message processing (BMP) programs to update IMS data bases in batch even while they're being used by other programs
- how to use Batch Terminal Simulator (BTS) to test DC applications using IMS resources, but without disrupting the everyday IMS processing that's going on
- and more!

8 complete programs—including MFS format sets, program design, and COBOL code—show you how to handle various DC and MFS applications. Use them as models to save yourself hours of coding and debugging.

IMS, Part 2, 16 chapters, 398 pages, **$36.50**
ISBN 0-911625-30-5

 Call toll-free 1-800-221-5528 (Weekdays, 8-5 Pacific Time) • Fax 1-559-440-0963 • www.murach.com

DB2 for the COBOL Programmer

Part 1 / Second Edition (Covers Version 4.1)   **Curtis Garvin and Steve Eckols**

If you're looking for a practical DB2 book that focuses on application programming, this is the book for you. Written from the programmer's point of view, it will quickly teach you what you need to know to access and process DB2 data in your COBOL programs using embedded SQL. You'll learn:

* what DB2 is and how it works, so you'll have the background you need to program more easily and logically

* how to design and code application programs that retrieve and update DB2 data

* how to use joins and unions to combine data from two or more tables into a single table (that includes Version 4 enhancements like outer joins and the explicit syntax for inner joins that simplify your coding)

* how to work with column functions, scalar functions, and subqueries to manipulate DB2 data

* how to handle the complications caused by variable-length data and null values in DB2 tables

* how to use error handling techniques and ROLL-BACK to protect DB2 data

* why program efficiency is vital under DB2...and how to use the locking features right so you don't tie up the whole system

* how to use SPUFI and QMF to create the test tables you need to debug your programs

* how to develop DB2 programs interactively (using DB2I, a TSO facility) or in batch

So if you want to learn how to write DB2 application programs, get a copy of this book today!

DB2, Part 1, 15 chapters, 431 pages, **$45.00**
ISBN 1-890774-02-2

DB2 for the COBOL Programmer

Part 2 / Second Edition (Covers Version 4.1)   **Curtis Garvin and Steve Eckols**

Once you've mastered the basics of DB2 programming, there's still plenty to learn. So this book teaches you all the advanced DB2 features that a senior programmer or programmer/analyst needs to know...and shows you when to use each one. You'll learn:

* how to use dynamic SQL

* how to work with distributed DB2 data

* how to execute stored procedures

* how to work with advanced locking and concurrency features

* how to use DB2 from CICS programs

* what you need to know about database administration to set up a quality assurance environment

* and more!

So don't wait to expand your DB2 skills. Get a copy of this book TODAY.

DB2, Part 2, 15 chapters, approx. 400 pages, **$45.00**
ISBN 1-890774-03-0

Scheduled for June 1999; check our web site for availability (until then, the First Edition, covering up through DB2 Version 2.2, is available)

VS COBOL II: A Guide for Programmers and Managers

Second Edition

Anne Prince

This book builds on your COBOL knowledge to quickly teach you everything you need to know about VS COBOL II, the IBM 1985 COBOL compiler for MVS shops: how to code the language elements that are new in the compiler (and what language elements you can't use any more)...CICS considerations...how to use the debugger...how the compiler's features can make your programs compile and run more efficiently...plus, guidelines for converting to VS COBOL II (that includes coverage of the conversion aids IBM supplies).

So if you're in a shop that's already converted to VS COBOL II, you'll learn how to benefit from the language elements and features the compiler has to offer. If you aren't yet working in VS COBOL II, you'll learn how to write programs now that will be easy to convert later on. And if you're a manager, you'll get some practical ideas on when to convert and how to do it as painlessly as possible.

VS COBOL II, 7 chapters, 271 pages, **$27.50**
ISBN 0-911625-54-2

Structured ANS COBOL

A 2-part course in 1974 and 1985 ANS COBOL

Mike Murach and Paul Noll

This 2-part course teaches you how to use standard COBOL the way the top professionals do.

Part 1: A Course for Novices teaches people with no programming experience how to design and code COBOL programs that prepare reports. Because report programs often call subprograms, use COPY members, handle one-level tables, and read indexed files, it covers these subjects too. But the real emphasis in this book is on the structure and logic of report programs, because most beginning programmers have more trouble with structure and logic than they do with COBOL itself.

Part 2: An Advanced Course also emphasizes program structure and logic, focusing on edit, update, and maintenance programs. But beyond that, it's a

complete guide to the language elements that all COBOL programmers should know how to use (though many don't). So it covers: sequential, indexed, and relative file handling...alternate indexing and dynamic processing...internal sorts and merges...the COPY library...subprograms...multi-level table handling... character manipulation...and more! In fact, no matter how much COBOL experience you've had, you'll value *Part 2* as a handy reference to all the COBOL elements you'll ever want to use.

COBOL, Part 1, 13 chapters, 438 pages, **$32.50**
ISBN 0-911625-37-2

COBOL, Part 2, 12 chapters, 498 pages, **$32.50**
ISBN 0-911625-38-0

Structured COBOL Methods

Practical guidelines and model programs

Paul Noll

Unlike other books with "structured" in the title, this little book presents ideas on COBOL program development that are simple, cost-effective, time-tested, and yet revolutionary in many shops. It doesn't teach the COBOL language itself; instead, it teaches you how to design, code, and test your COBOL programs so they're easier to debug, document, and maintain.

Just open up to any page, take a look at the concepts or the sample design and code, and picture what a difference these methods can make in the program you're working on right now. Then, go to work and start experimenting. You'll be delighted at the results!

Structured COBOL Methods, 6 chapters +
5 model programs, 208 pages, **$25.00**
ISBN 0-911625-94-1

Comment Form

Your opinions count

If you have any comments, criticisms, or suggestions for us, I'm eager to hear from you. Your opinions today will affect our products of tomorrow. And if you find any errors in this book, typographical or otherwise, please point them out so we can correct them in the next printing.

Thanks for your help.

Mike Murach

Book title: MVS Assembler Language

Dear Mike: _____

_____

_____

_____

_____

_____

_____

_____

_____

_____

_____

_____

_____

_____

_____

_____

_____

Name _____

Company (if company address) _____

Address _____

City, State, Zip _____

Fold where indicated and tape closed.

No postage needed if mailed in the U.S.

NO POSTAGE
NECESSARY
IF MAILED
IN THE
UNITED STATES

BUSINESS REPLY MAIL
FIRST-CLASS MAIL   PERMIT NO. 3063   FRESNO, CA

POSTAGE WILL BE PAID BY ADDRESSEE

Mike Murach & Associates, Inc.
2560 W SHAW LN STE 101
FRESNO, CA 93711-9866

Order Form

Our Unlimited Guarantee

To our customers who order directly from us: You must be satisfied. Our books must work for you, or you can send them back for a full refund...no questions asked.

Name & Title _____

Company (if company address) _____

Street Address _____

City, State, Zip _____

Phone number (including area code) _____

Fax number (if you fax your order to us) _____

Qty	Product code and title	*Price
MVS		
___ MBAL	MVS Assembler Language	$36.50
___ MJLR	MVS JCL (Second Edition)	42.50
___ TSO1	MVS TSO, Part 1: Concepts and ISPF	36.50
___ TSO2	MVS TSO, Part 2: Commands and Procedures (CLIST and REXX)	36.50
___ OSUT	OS Utilities	17.50
CICS		
___ CC1R	CICS for the COBOL Programmer Part 1 (Second Edition)	$36.50
___ CC2R	CICS for the COBOL Programmer Part 2 (Second Edition)	36.50
___ CRFR	The CICS Programmer's Desk Reference (Second Edition)	42.50
COBOL		
___ VC2R	VS COBOL II (Second Edition)	$27.50
___ SC1R	Structured ANS COBOL, Part 1	32.50
___ SC2R	Structured ANS COBOL, Part 2	32.50
___ SCMD	Structured COBOL Methods	25.00

Qty	Product code and title	*Price
Database		
___ DB1R	DB2 for the COBOL Programmer Part 1 (Second Edition)	$45.00
___ DB2R	DB2 for the COBOL Programmer Part 2 (Second Edition)	**Available June 1999**
___ DB22	DB2 for the COBOL Programmer Part 2 (First Edition—DB2 Version 2.2)	36.50
___ IMS1	IMS for the COBOL Programmer Part 1: DL/I Data Base Processing	36.50
___ IMS2	IMS for the COBOL Programmer Part 2: Data Communications and MFS	36.50
VSAM		
___ VSMX	VSAM: Access Method Services and Application Programming	$27.50
___ VSMR	VSAM for the COBOL Programmer (Second Edition)	22.50
Client/Server		
___ VB50	Client/Server Programming: Visual Basic 5	$40.00
___ AC97	Client/Server Programming: Access 97	40.00

❑ Charge the books plus UPS shipping and handling (and sales tax within California) to my

   ___Visa ___MasterCard ___American Express:

   Card number _____

   Valid thru (mo/yr) _____

   Cardowner's signature _____

❑ Bill my company.
   P.O.# _____

❑ I want to **SAVE** shipping and handling charges. Here's my check or money order for the books ($_____). California residents, please add sales tax to your total. (Offer valid in U.S.)

*Prices are subject to change. Please call for current prices.

To order now,

Call toll-free 1-800-221-5528
(Weekdays, 8 am to 5 pm Pacific Time)

Fax: 1-559-440-0963

Web: www.murach.com

Mike Murach & Associates, Inc.
2560 West Shaw Lane, Suite 101
Fresno, California 93711-2765
(559) 440-9071 • murachbooks@murach.com